NCERT
SOLUTIONS

BIOLOGY

CLASS 11th

NCERT
SOLUTIONS

BIOLOGY

CLASS 11th

by
Dr. Poonam Sharma

ARIHANT PRAKASHAN, MEERUT

ARIHANT PRAKASHAN, MEERUT

卐 Administrative & Production Offices

Corporate Office: 'Ramchhaya' 4577/15, Agarwal Road, Darya Ganj, New Delhi -110002
Tele: 011- 47630600, 43518550; Fax: 011- 23280316

Head Office: Kalindi, TP Nagar, Meerut (UP) - 250002
Tele: 0121-2401479, 2512970, 4004199; Fax: 0121-2401648

All disputes subject to Meerut (UP) jurisdiction only.

卐 Sales & Support Offices

Agra, Ahmedabad, Bengaluru, Bhubaneswar, Bareilly, Chennai, Delhi, Guwahati, Haldwani Hyderabad, Jaipur, Jalandhar, Jhansi, Kolkata, Kota, Lucknow, Meerut, Nagpur & Pune

卐 ISBN 978-93-5141-626-5

卐 Price : ₹ 210

PO No. : TXT-59-T045502-2-22

Typeset by Arihant DTP Unit at Meerut

PRINTED & BOUND BY
ARIHANT PUBLICATIONS (I) LTD. (PRESS UNIT)

For further information about the products from Arihant log on to **www.arihantbooks.com** or email to **info@arihantbooks.com**

Preface

Feeling the immense importance and value of NCERT books, we are presenting this book, having the **NCERT Exercises Solutions.** For the overall benefit of the students we have made this book unique in such a way that it presents not only solutions but also detailed explanations. Through these detailed and through explanations, students can learn the concepts which will enhance their thinking and learning abilities.

We have introduced some Additional Features with the solutions which are given below :

- **Explanatory Solutions** Along with the solutions to questions we have given all the points that tell how to approach to solve a problem. Here we have tried to cover all those loopholes which may lead to confusion. All formulae and hints are discussed in full detail.
- **Note** We have provided notes also to solutions in which special points are mentioned which are of great value for the students.
- This book also covers solutions to selected problems of **NCERT Exemplar Problems.**

Apart from all those who helped in the compilation of this book a special note of thanks to Ms Rakhi Rasniya, Ms Chavi Gupta and Dr Kanchan Upreti. With the hope that this book will be of great help to the students, we wish great success to our readers.

Dr Poonam Sharma

Contents

1

The Living World

Important Points

1. Biology is the science, which deals with the study of living organisms and their life processes. The term **biology** was first introduced by **GR Treviranus** and **Jean Baptiste de Lamarck** (1802).
2. All living beings share certain key characteristics such as cellular organisation, sensitivity, growth, development, reproduction, regulation, homeostatis and metabolism, etc.
3. Systematics is the branch of biology concerned with reconstructing phylogenies and with naming and classifying species. The term 'systematics' was coined by **Linnaeus.**
4. Life is an expression of energy changes and the exchange of matter. It is due to the relationship of molecules.
5. The art of identifying distinctions among organisms and placing them into groups to determine their relationship is called **classification.**
6. Taxonomy is the branch of biology concerned with the study of classification of organisms according to their resemblances and differences.
7. Taxonomic journals provide information on the results of ongoing research.
8. **de Jussieu** of France was the first to gave a system of classification based on natural characters.
9. The study of systematics was started in the beginning of **Vedic period** (2500 BC to 650 BC) during, which about **740 plants** and **250 animals** were recorded. In earlier times, plants were classified on the basis of their medicinal value.

10. Species is the basic unit of classification, which consists of natural populations of individuals that resemble one another in all essential morphological, anatomical, cytological, biochemical characters and reproduction.
11. Term 'species' was coined by **John Ray** 1693.
12. Sibling species are morphologically looking similar but are reproductively isolated, *i.e.*, cannot breed among themselves.
13. A monograph is a comprehensive taxonomic treatment of a taxonomic graph, generally a genus or a family, providing all the taxonomic data relating to that group.
14. A manual is a more exhaustive treatment than flora, always having keys for identification, description and glossary but generally covering specialised groups of plants.
15. Zoological Parks are protected areas/enclosed space where live wide animals are kept in conditions as close as possible to natural habitats for public exhibition for understanding wild life, recration, education as well as *in situ* conservation.
16. In India, the first was set up in **Madras**. Largest zoo of the world is in Kruger (S. Africa).
17. National Zoological Park, Delhi, established in 1959. It is one of the finest zoo of Asia, which covers an area of 214 acres and displays about 22000 animals.
18. There are more than 1200 well organised herbaria in the world.
19. The biggest herbarium of India is at the Indian Botanic Garden, Kolkata.
20. A standard herbarium sheet is 29×41.5 cm $(11\frac{1}{2} \times 16\frac{1}{2}'')$ and made up of thick hand made paper or a card sheet.
21. **ICVN** stands for International Code for Viral Nomenclature.
22. **de Candolle** (1813) coined the term **taxonomy**.
23. **Carolus Linnaeus**, father of taxonomy, introduced binomial nomenclature, wrote **Philosophica Botanica** (ref. 1751), **Species Plantarum** (ref. 1753) and **Systema Naturae** (ref. 1758, 10th edition).
24. Term 'Taxon' was introduced by **Adolf Meyer** in 1926 (for animal groups).
25. Kingdom is the highest taxonomic category, *e.g.*, kingdom–Plantae and Animalia.
26. A species that plays a central role in the ecology of a place is known as **keystone species**.

27. **Lamarck** firstly proposed that species are not fixed but liable to change with time.
28. **ICBN** stands for International Code for Botanical Nomenclature.
29. **Sir William Hooker** (Father of JD Hooker) was the first official director of Royal Botanical Garden.
30. The great banyan tree (*Ficus benghalensis*) of Indian Botanical Garden is one of the largest living creatures in the world, which is two centuries old and possess about one thousand trunks. It is about 100 feet high and its canopy covers 4 acre of ground.
31. Continental flora covers the entire continent.
32. The Indian Botanical Garden has gardens of succulent plants especially belong to the family–Euphorbiaceae and Cactaceae. It also has big propagation nursery, which is one of the best in **Asia**.
33. **William Roxburgh** is known as the father of Indian botany and Indian herbaria.

Exercises

Question 1. Why are living organisms classified?

Answer It is estimated that about 5-30 million species of living organisms exist today. With so many organisms in the world, it is important to classify them in groups to understand their origin, diversity, distribution and inter relationship. Classification is the grouping and ranking of organisms in the hierarchy of taxonomy on the basis of similarities and dissimilarities. It's purpose is to organise the vast number of known plants and animals into categories that could be named, remembered and studied systematically. The process of placing living organisms into groups to study them precisely and to determine the relationship is called classification.

Question 2. Why are the classification systems changing every now and then?

Answer Evolution is the major factor responsible for the change in classification systems. Since, evolution still continues, so many different species of plants and animals are added in the already existed biodiversity. These newly discovered plant and animal specimens are then identified, classified and named according to the already existing classification systems. Due to evolution, animal and plant species keep on changing, so necessary changes in the already existed classification systems are necessary to place every newly discovered plant and animal in their respective ranks.

Question 3. What different criteria would you choose to classify people that you meet often?

Answer The different scientific criteria to classify people that we often would be

(i) Nomenclature

(ii) Classification

(iii) Identification

(i) **Nomenclature** is the science of providing distinct and proper names to the organisms. It is the determination of correct name as per established universal practices and rules.

(ii) **Classification** is the arrangement of organisms into categories based on systematic planning. In classification various categories used are class, order, family, genus and species.

(iii) **Identification** is the determination of correct name and place of an organism. Identification is used to tell that a particular species is similar to other organism of known identify. This includes assigning an organism to a particular taxonomic group.

The same criteria can be applied to the people we meet daily. We can identify them will their names classify them according to their living areas, profession, etc.

Question 4. What do we learn from identification of individual and populations?

Answer Identification of individuals and population categorized it into a species. Each species has unique characteristic features. On the basis of these features, it can be distinguished from other closely related species. *e.g.*,

Genus	Species	
Solanum	*tuberosum*	Both are different species of potato
Solanum	*nigrum*	

Question 5. Given below is the scientific name of mango. Identify the correctly written name.

Mangifera Indica
Mangifera indica

Answer The correctly written scientific name of mango is *Mangifera indica*. Where, *Mangifera* is a genera name and *indica* is a species name.

Question 6. Define a taxon. Give some examples of taxa at different hierarchical levels.

Answer Taxon is a grouping of organisms of any level in hierarchical classification, which is based on some common characteristics, *e.g.*, insects represent a class of phylum–Arthropoda. All the insects possess common characters of three pairs of jointed legs. The term 'taxon' was introduced by ICBN in 1956. Examples of taxa are kingdom, phylum or division, class, order, family, genus and species. These taxa form taxonomic hierarchy.

e.g., taxa for human:

Phylum	—	Chordata
Class	—	Mammalia
Order	—	Primata
Family	—	Hominidae
Genus	—	*Homo*
Species	—	*sapiens*

Question 7. Can you identify the correct sequence of taxonomical categories?

(a) Species ⟶ Order ⟶ Phylum ⟶ Kingdom
(b) Genus ⟶ Species ⟶ Order ⟶ Kingdom
(c) Species ⟶ Genus ⟶ Order ⟶ Phylum

Answer The correct sequence of taxonomical categories is as follows :

Species ⟶ Genus ⟶ Order ⟶ Phylum.

Question 8. Try to collect all the currently accepted meanings for the word 'species'. Discuss with your teacher the meaning of species in case of higher plants and animals on one hand and bacteria on the hand.

Answer A group of individual organisms with fundamental similarities is called species. It can be distinguished from other closely related species on the basis of distinct morphological differences.

In case of higher plants and animals, one genus may have one or more than one species, *e.g.*, *Panthera leo* (lion) and *Panthera tigris* (tiger).

In this example, *Panthera* is genus, which includes *leo* (lion) and *tigris* (tiger) as species.

In case of bacteria, different categories are present on the basis of shape. These are spherical, coccus, rod-shaped, comma and spiral-shaped. Thus, meaning of species in case of higher organisms and bacteria are different.

Question 9. Define and understand the following terms
(i) Phylum (ii) Class (iii) Family
(iv) Order (v) Genus

Answer

(i) **Phylum** A category, which is higher than class and consisting of one or more related classes with certain common features. Botanists use the term division for phylum.

(ii) **Class** A taxonomic category higher in rank than order and consisting of one or more related orders with some common features.

(iii) **Family** A category having one or more related genera with some similar common features.

(iv) **Order** (Cohort) A category consisting of one or more related families having some common or correlated characters.

(v) **Genus** A taxonomic category higher in rank than species having one or more assemblage of related species, having a common ancestory and similar correlated characters.

Question 10. How is a key helpful in the identification and classification of an organism?

Answer Key is a device (scheme) of diagnostic alternate (contrasting) characters, which provide an easy means for the identification of unknown organism. The keys are taxonomic literature based on the contrasting characters generally a pair called couplet. Each statement in the key is called a lead. Separate taxonomic keys are required for each taxonomic category such as family, genus and species for identification purposes. Being analytical in nature, two types of keys are commonly used—indented key and bracketed key.

(i) **Indented key** provides sequence of choice between two or more statements of characters of species. The user has to make correct choice for identification.

(ii) **Bracketed key** (1) are used for contrasting characters like indented key but they are not repeated by intervening sub-dividing character and each character is given a number in brackets.

	Indented Key		**Bracketed Key**
1	External ears present	(1)	External ears present ...... (2)
2	Wings present ...... Bat	(1)	External ears absent ...... (3)
2	Wings absent ...... Cat	(2)	Wings present ......Bat
1	External ears absent	(2)	Wings absent ...... Cat
2	Wings present ...... Bird	(3)	Wings present ...... Bird
2	Wings absent	(3)	Wings absent ...... (4)
3	Limbs present ...... Frog	(4)	Limbs present ...... Frog

	Indented Key		Bracketed Key
3	Limbs absent	(4)	Limbs absent ...... (5)
4	Gills present ...... Fish	(5)	Gills present ...... Fish
5	Gills absent ...... Snake	(5)	Gills absent ...... Snake

Question 11. Illustrate the taxonomical hierarchy with suitable examples of a plant and an animal.

Answer Taxonomic hierarchy is the system of arrangement of taxonomic categories in a descending order depending upon their relative dimensions. It was introduced by Linnaeus (1751) and is therefore, also called Linnaeus hierarchy. Each category, referred to as a unit of classification, commonly called as taxon (pl. taxa), *e.g.,* taxonomic categories and hierarchy can be illustrated by a group of organisms, *i.e.,* insects. The common features of insects is 'three pair of jointed legs'. It means insects are recognisable objects which can be classified, so given a rank or category.

Category further denotes a rank. Each rank or taxon, represents a unit of classification taxonomic studies of all plants and animals led to the development of common categories such as kingdom, phylum or division (for plants) class, order, family, genus and species. All organisms, including tose in the plant and animal kingdoms have 'species' as the lowest category.

To place an organism in various categories is to have the knowledge of characters of an individual or group of organism. This help to identity similarities and dissimilarities among the individual of the same kind of organisms as well as of other kinds of organism. Some organisms with their taxonomical categories are given in following table.

Kingdom
↑
Phylum/Division
↑
Sub-phylum
↑
Class
↑
Order
↑
Family
↑
Genus
↑
Species

Taxonomic hierarchial arrangement

Organisms with their Taxonomic Categories

Common Name	Biological Name	Genus	Family	Order	Class	Phylum/ Division
Man	*Homo sapiens*	*Homo*	Hominidae	Primata	Mammalia	Chordata
Housefly	*Musca domestica*	*Musca*	Muscidae	Diptera	Insecta	Arthropoda
Mango	*Mangifera indica*	*Mangifera*	Anacardia-ceae	Sapin-dales	Dicotyle-donae	Angiospermae
Wheat	*Triticum aestivum*	*Triticum*	Poaceae	Poales	Monocotyle-donae	Angiospermae

Selected NCERT Exemplar Problems

Very Short Answer Type Questions

Question 1. Linnaeus is considered as Father of Taxonomy. Name two other botanists known for their contribution to the field of plant taxonomy?

Answer George Bentham and JD Hooker gave the most important system of classification of angiosperms. Eichler is the pioneer of phylogenetic system.

Question 2. What does ICZN stand for?

Answer International Code of Zoological Nomenclature.

Question 3. Couplet in taxonomic key means.

Answer Contrasting characters.

Question 4. What is a monograph?

Answer A monograph contains descriptive information on any one taxon.

Question 5. *Amoeba* multiplies by mitotic cell division. Is this phenomena growth or reproduction? Explain.

Answer *Amoeba* is an unicellular organism. In this animal, reproduction is synonymous with growth, *i.e.*, increase in number of cells.

Question 6. Define metabolism.

Answer Metabolism is the sum total of all chemical reactions that occurs in an organised and controlled fashion in living organisms. Metabolism has two types of reactions, *i.e.*, catabolism and anabolism.

Question 7. Which is the largest botanical garden in the world? Name a few well known botanical gardens in India.

Answer The largest botanical garden in the world is Royal Botanic Garden (RBG), Kew (London). The well known Botanic Gardens in India are

(i) Indian Botanic Garden, Sibpur (Howrah), Kolkata (WB)
(ii) Lloyd Botanic Garden, Darjeeling
(iii) Botanic Garden of FRI, Dehradun (UA)
(iv) National Botanic Garden (NBG), Lucknow (UP).

Short Answer Type Questions

Question 1. A ball of snow when rolled over snow increases in mass, volume and size. Is this comparable to growth as seen in living organisms? Why?

Answer In case of living organisms, the growth is due to internal addition of protoplasmic materials by which cells enlarge and divide. Non-living organisms may also grow but in them growth occurs due to deposition of similar material over the surface. We can say that non-living things also grow, if we take increase in biomass as a criterian for growth. Thus, a ball of snow when increase in mass, volume and size due to rolling over of snow on its surface, exhibits growth.

Question 2. In a given habitat we have 20 plant species and 20 animal species. Should we call this as 'diversity' or 'biodiversity'? Justify your answer.

Answer Different plants and animal species in an area constitute biodiversity. Plants have many diverse forms such as aquatic plants, herbs, shrubs, trees, seed plants, non-seed plants, vascular plants and non-vascular plants. Similarly, animals are of different kinds such as invertebrates, vertebrates, aquatic and terrestrial. Plants and animals with so many diverse forms constitute the biodiversity. So, if a habitat with 20 different plant and animal species constitute the biodiversity.

Question 3. A plant species shows several morphological variations in response to altitudinal gradient. When grown under similar conditions of growth, the morphological variations disappear and all the variants have common morphology. What are these variants called?

Answer A plant species in response to altitudinal gradient shows morphological variations such as number and arrangement of leaves, flower colour, flower number, etc. But when under similar environmental conditions, the morphological variations in number and arrangement of leaves and floral parts disappear and all the variants exhibit common morphological traits. These variations are known as morphological variations and the variants are called as **biotypes.**

Question 4. How do you prepare your own herbarium sheets? What are the different tools you carry with you while collecting plants for the preparation of a herbarium? What information should a preserved plant material on the herbarium sheet provide for taxonomical studies?

Answer One can prepare herbarium sheets by cutting papers of size 29×41.5 cm ($11\frac{1}{2} \times 16\frac{1}{2}$"). The preparation of a herbarium specimen required following steps, *i.e.*,

(i) **Collection** of plant or plant parts.

(ii) **Pressing** It involves the spreading and pressing of collected specimen over a newspaper so as to preserve its all parts.

(iii) **Drying** It involves the drying of the specimen between the folds of newspaper.

(iv) **Poisoning** Antifungal (dipping in 2% $HgCl_2$) and pesticidal (DDT) treatment of the dried specimen.

(v) **Mounting** It involves mounting of the specimen over a herbarium sheet.

(vi) **Labelling** and identification of the dried specimen are the last steps, while preparing a herbarium sheet.

Tools/equipments required for the collection of herbarium specimens are as follows

(a) A tin or aluminium container of $50 \times 30 \times 15$ cm size.

(b) Collection bags/plastic/polythene bags.

(c) Digger for digging roots.

(d) Magnifying lens of atleast 10X magnification.

(e) Field note book.

A preserved plant material on the herbarium sheet may provide information about the family, genus, species, date of collection, area of collection, etc., for taxonomic studies.

Question 5. What is the differences between flora, fauna and vegetation? *Eichhornia crassipes* is called as an exotic species, while *Rauwolfia serpentina* is an endemic species in India. What do these terms exotic and endemic refer to?

Answer Differences between flora, fauna and vegetation.

(i) **Flora** It is the plant life that occur in a particular region or time.

(ii) **Fauna** It is the animal life that occur in a particular region or time.

(iii) **Vegetation** It is a general term used for the plant species of a region.

Eichhornia crassipes is an exotic species, whereas *Rauwolfia serpentina* is an endemic species in India.

(i) **Endemic species** These are indigenous species and are native to the environment where they are found, *e.g.*, *Rauwolfia serpentina*.

(ii) **Exotic species** These species are introduced in an area from outside, *e.g.*, *Eichhornia crassipes*.

Question 6. **A plant may have different names in different regions of the country or world. How do botanists solve this problem?**

Answer A plant may have different name in different parts of the country. Sometimes, even a single popular name is assigned to many plants in different areas. Due to this, it is not possible to identify the organisms universally, based on their vernacular names. The first step to solve this problem was made by **Karl Von Linne** who introduced a binomial nomenclature system.

According to the binomial system of nomenclature of an organism name consists of two parts first generic name (genus) and second specific name (species). The names are in Latin language which is a universally known language. The first letter of generic name is written in capital letter, while specific name is written in small letter, *e.g., Mangifera indica* (mango). Other botanists all other the country, followed the binomial nomenclature system to slove the problems of different names of plants.

Question 7. **Brinjal and potato belong to the same genus *Solanum*, but two different species. What defines them as separate species?**

Answer The scientific name of brinjal is *Solanum melongena* and that of potato is *Solanum tuberosum*. Both these plants belong to the family–Solanaceae and resemble one another in most of their vegetative characters. The difference lies here is that brinjal – the fruit, which is considered as vegetable is produced above the ground but in case of potato – the tubers (fruits) are produced below the ground.

Further, both members of this genus cannot breed with each other as they are reproductively isolated. So, inspite of having many common characters both these species, *i.e.*, *Solanum tuberosum* and *Solanum melongena* are belong to different species.

Question 8. **Properties of cell organelles are not always found in the molecular constituents of cell organelles. Justify.**

Answer A cell contains many organelles such as endoplasmic reticulum, Golgi apparatus, ribosomes, mitochondria and plastids, etc. Each cell organelle is made up of several constituent molecules such as protein, lipids, a variety of enzymes and certain metallic ions like Mg^{2+}, Ca^{2+} and Mn^{2+}, etc., *e.g.*, the molecular constituents of mitochondria are proteins (60-70%), lipids (25-30%), RNA (5-7%), enzymes, Mn^{2+}, etc. All these molecules work together and perform a common function of respiration and make mitochondria the power house of the cell.

Question 9. **The number and kinds of organisms is not constant. How do you explain this statement?**

Answer Scientists believe that the total number of species of living beings may be anywhere between 5-30 million because every year, 15000 new species are discovered. Reproduction which is one of the characteristics of living beings is the reason behind the increase in the number of living beings.

Environment brings about changes in the genetic constitution of organisms by introducing the variations. Variations form the raw material for evolution of new species. Thus, we can say that the number and kind of organisms in this universe are not constant. Reproduction and evolution bring about changes in the number and kind of organisms.

Long Answer Type Questions

Question 1. What is meant by living? Give any four defining features of life forms.

Answer The organism, which shows characteristics of life, such as growth, development, responsiveness, adaptation and reproduction is known as living.

Four definite features of life forms are

(i) **Growth** All living organisms shows growth either by multiplication or by increase in size. Growth is living things is internal.

(ii) **Reproduction** All living beings reproduce, passing on traits from one generation to the next. The process of reproduction is essential for the continuity of life on the Earth.

(iii) **Metabolism** It is the process by which all living things assimilate energy and use it to grow. It is the characteristic feature of living beings.

(iv) **Cellular organisation** All organisms consist of one or more cells.

Cells work together in hierarchical fashion, form tissues, organs and organ systems and lastly the organism.

Question 2. A scientist has come across a plant which he feels is a new species. How will he go about its identification, classification and nomenclature?

Answer A scientist identifies a new plant species by studying its morphological and anatomical characters. Herbarium and botanical gardens, which are repositories of plants/plant parts also help in the identification, nomenclature and classification of newly discovered plant species.

Similarly, taxonomic keys provide necessary information for the identification of unknown organisms. So, a scientist can identify, classify and name a newly discovered plant species by consulting herbaria, botanical gardens and taxonomic keys.

Question 3. *Brassica compestris* Linn.

(a) Give the common name of the plant.

(b) What do the first two parts of the name denote?

(c) Why are they written in italics?

(d) What is the meaning of Linn. written at the end of the name?

Answer

(a) Mustard

(b) The first two parts of the name denote the generic and specific names. The first letter is the name of genus and, the second letter is the name of the species.

(c) *Brassica compestris* Linn. name is written in italics because according to the rules of nomenclature the scientific names of plants and animals should be printed in italics.

(d) Linn. word at the end of the name *Brassica compestris* stands for Linnaeus, the name of the author discovered this plant for the first time.

Question 4. What are taxonomical aids? Give the importance of herbaria and museums. How are Botanical gardens and Zoological parks useful in conserving biodiversity?

Answer **Taxonomic Aids** The aids, which help in the identification, classification and nomenclature of plants and animals are known as taxonomic aids, *i.e.,* herbaria, botanical gardens, museums, zoological parks, monographs, manuals and publications, etc.

Importance of Herbaria Herbarium is a great filling system for information about plants. It provides scientific information on plants to the people through exhibitions and training courses.

The museums help in acquisition, recording, preservation, research, education reference and exhibition of materials.

Botanical gardens serve as the repository for living plants of the century and selected exotic species to provide information on local flora for the taxonomic and botanical studies. They hold unique germplasm of native and exotic species.

Similarly, zoological parks are protected areas, where wild animals are kept in conditions as close as possible to natural habitats. They help in *in situ* conservation of rare fauna. These parks also prove facility for breeding of rare fauna.

Question 5. A student of taxonomy was puzzled when told by his professor to look for a key to identify a plant. He went to his friend to clarify, what 'key' the professor was referring to? What would the friend explain to him?

Answer In this question, the word 'key' stands for taxonomic keys. In systematics, a taxonomic key is a device of diagnostic alternate characters which provide an easy means for identification of unknown organisms. The concept of key was introduced by Ray. The taxonomic keys help an individual in the identification, nomenclature and classification of a newly discovered plant or animal specimen. Separate taxonomic keys are required for each taxonomic category. Keys are analytical in nature.

Question 6. Metabolism is a defining feature of all living organisms without exception. Isolated metabolic reactions *in vitro* are not living things but surely living reactions. Comment.

Answer Metabolism is the set of chemical reactions that occur in the cells of living organisms to sustain life. These processes allow organisms to grow and reproduce, maintain their structures and respond to their environment. The word metabolism can also refers to all chemical reactions that occur in living organisms, including digestion and the transport of substances into and between different cells.

In the laboratory, the reactions usually occur in organic solvents and there is no need to isolate the products of these reactions. Inside the body, there is no need for separation of biochemical products of the metabolism in the cell. The enzyme mediated biochemical reactions are highly selective and specific in their progression. This is rarely observed in the laboratory with normal non-biological reactions. The chemical reactions usually involve multiple products of the reaction that posses difficulties of separating them. In this respect, enzyme catalysed reactions are superior to chemical reactions that take place in the laboratory.

Question 7. Do you consider a person in coma-living or dead?

Answer A coma is a profound or deep state of unconsciousness. The affected person is alive but is not able to react or respond to life around him/her. Coma may occur due to either prolong illness or head trauma. In persistent vegetative state, the individual loses the higher cerebral power of the brain, but the functions of the brainstem such as respiration (breathing) and circulation, remain relatively intact.

Spontaneous movements may occur and the eyes may open in response to external stimuli but the patient does not speak or obey commands. Patients in a vegetative state may appear somewhat normal. They may occasionally grimace, cry or laugh. Thus, keeping these points in mind, we can consider a coma person as a living dead.

Question 8. What is the similarity and dissimilarity between 'Whole moong daal' and 'broken moong daal' in terms of respiration and growth? Based on these parameters classify them into living or non-living?

Answer Embryo is the living entity of a moong dal seed. If whole moong dal soaks in water, then after 6-7 hours the embryo, which is in live form resumes normal life activities such as respiration and growth. It start respiring, resumes normal metabolic activities and starts growing into a seedling. But in case of 'broken moong dal' where embryo is dead, no normal life activities such as respiration and growth are seen.

Even if the broken moong dal soaks in water, no respiration and growth take place. The 'broken moong dal' shows no breakdown reactions, *i.e.*, catabolism. No energy in the form of ATP is produced in these broken seeds. Similarly, no anabolic reactions as characteristics of growth processes takes place in 'broken moong dal'. From this, we can conclude that 'whole moong dal' is a living entity, whereas a broken moong dal is a non-living one.

2

Biological Classification

Important Points

1. The first attempt to classify organisms on scientific basis was done by **Aristotle.** He classify the plants on the basis of their morphological characters and categorise them into tree, shrubs and herbs.
2. Two kingdom classification was given by **Linnaeus**. Plantae and Animalia kingdom were developed including plants and animals.
3. **RH Whittaker** (1969) proposed five kingdom classification **Monera, Protista, Fungi, Plantae** and **Animalia.**

   Classification was done on the basis of following characters

   (i) **Cell type** Prokaryotic and eukaryotic

   (ii) **Cell wall** Non-cellulosic/ cellulosic/ chitinaceous

   (iii) **Nuclear membrane** Present or absent

   (iv) **Body organisation** Unicellular/ multicellular

   (v) **Mode of nutrition** Autotrophic/heterotrophic/ saprophytic.
4. **Kingdom–Monera** includes prokaryotic microorganism like bacteria.
5. Bacteria are prokaryotes. They do not have well defined nucleus. Membrane bound cell organelles are absent. They live in extreme habitats like springs, snow, deep oceans as free living or parasites.

6. On the basis of their shape they are divided into

   Coccus (cocci) – Spherical

   Bacillus (bacilli) – Rod-shaped

   Vibrium (vibrio) – Comma-shaped

   Spirillum (spirilla) – Spiral-shaped.
7. Bacteria shows wide range of mode of nutrition. They may be autotrophic, chemotrophic, saprophytic or heterotrophic.
8. Bacteria are further divided into **Archaebacteria** and **Eubacteria.**
9. **Archaebacteria** lives in extreme environmental conditions. These include
   - (i) **Halophiles** Bacteria residing in salty areas.
   - (ii) **Thermoacidophiles** Bacteria residing in hot springs.
   - (iii) **Methanogens** Bacteria which survive in marshy areas (these are present in gut of many ruminant animals like cows and buffaloes.
   - (vi) **Basophiles** Bacteria which survive in alkaline medium.
10. Archaebacteria differs from other bacteria in having different cell wall structure. Their cell wall is made up of **murein** and contain high amount of unsaturated fafty acids, which is responsible for their survival in extreme conditions.
11. Another class–Eubacteria is also known as 'true bacteria'.
12. These have rigid cell wall made up of peptidoglycan.
13. They could be photosynthetic autotrophs, chemosynthetic, autotrophs and heterotrophic bacteria.
14. **Photosynthetic autotrophs** include blue-green algae, which have chlorophyll-*a* similar to green plants. Also known as **cyanobacteria.**
15. They could be unicellular, colonial or filamentous, fresh water/marine or terrestrial algae.
16. Some bacteria can fix atmospheric nitrogen in a specialised cells known as **heterocyst**, *e.g.*, in *Nostoc* and *Anabaena*.
17. Some bacteria utilises inorganic substances like nitrate, nitrite, ammonia, etc., for oxidation and release of energy for ATP production. These are known as **chemosynthetic autotrophic bacteria.**
18. **Heterotrophic bacteria** are dependent on other organism for nutrition. These include N_2-fixing bacteria pathogens, etc.
19. They reproduce asexually by **binary fission.**

20. During unfavourable conditions these form spores.
21. They also show conjugation. Sort of sexual reproduction in which DNA is transferred from one bacteria to another through conjugal tube.
22. Pleumorphic bacteria, which lacks cell wall is known as mycoplasma. They are pathogenic and smallest microorganism known.
23. **Kingdom–Protista** includes unicellular eukaryotes.
24. These include chrysophytes, dinoflagellates, euglenoid, slime mould, protozoans.
25. They shows well defined nucleus and membrane bound organelles.
26. They reproduce sexually and asexually.
27. **Chrysophytes** includes **diatoms** and **golden** algae known as **desmids.**
28. They resides in marine water and photosynthetic.
29. The cell wall of diatoms is embedded with silica and form two thin overlapping sheat as in soap box.
30. **Diatomoceous earth** is the large amount of cell wall deposits of diatoms in their habitat. These are used in polishing, filtration of oils and syrups.
31. Dinoflagellates are marine and photosynthetic microorganisms.
32. As the name suggest they have two flagella one lies longitudinally and other transversely in furrow between wall plates.
33. Due to presence of different pigments they appear yellow, green, brown and red.
34. *Gonyaulax* is a red dinoflagellate, which undergoes rapid multiplication and forms red tides.
35. Euglenoids are freshwater organism found in standing water.
36. Cell wall is absent, a protein rich layer called pellicle is present over the surface.
37. In presence of sunlight, they behave as autotrophs, while in its absence they behave as heterotrophs, *e.g.*, *Euglena*.
38. **Slime moulds** are saprophyte, which are dependent on dead and decaying organic matter.
39. They form an aggregation called **plasmodium.**

40. During unfavourable conditions they forms spores, which are highly resistant.
41. **Protozoans** are heterotrophs. They are predators or live as parasites. These include
    (i) **Amoeboid protozoans** They live in fresh and marine H_2O. They have irregular body. They can change their shape due to the formation of broad finger-like pseudopodia.
    (ii) **Flagellated protozoans** They are free-living parasitic microorganisms. They have flagella, *e.g.*, *Trypanosoma.*
    (iii) **Ciliated protozoans** They have cilia all over their body. They have cavity, which opens outside the cell surface, *e.g., Paramecium.*
    (iv) **Sporozoans** These include spore forming infectious agents, *e.g.*, *Plasmodium,* which causes malaria.
42. **Kingdom–Fungi** include heterotrophic organism. They rely on extracellular digestion.
43. These resides in air, water, soil or animals.
44. Yeast are unicellular fungi.
45. Usually fungi are filamentous in nature and forms long, slender, thread-like structure called **hyphae**. A network of hyphae is known as mycelium.
46. **Hyphae could be coenocytic** Continuous tube filled with multinucleated cytoplasm or septate or cross walls in the hyphae.
47. Cell wall is made up of **chitin**.
48. They may be saprophytic or parasitic in nature.
49. They exist in symbiotic relationship with algae known as **lichens** and with roots of higher plants called **mycorrhiza**.
50. Algal component in lichen is known as **phycobiont** and fungal component as mycobiont. Algae prepare food for fungi and fungi provide shelter to algae.
51. Fungi reproduce asexually by vegetative means like fragmentation, fission, buddy or by forming spores called conidia/sporangia spores/zoospores.
52. Sexual reproduction occurs with the help of oospores, ascospores and basidiospores.
53. Sexual cycle includes three steps
    (i) **Plasmogamy** Fusion of protoplasm between two motile or non-motile gametes.
    (ii) **Karyogamy** Fusion of two nuclei.
    (iii) Meiosis in zygote resulting in haploid spores.

54. In some fungi two haploid cells, results in diploid cells. In some cases dikaryon stage occurs in which two nuclei are present within a cell. This phase is known as dikaryophase of fungus.
55. Fungi is divided into various classes on the basic of mycelium mode of spore formation and fruiting bodies.
56. Phycomycetes are obligate parasite on plants. The mycelium is aseptate and coenocytic.
57. Asexual reproduction take place through zoospores, which are motile or through non-motile aplanospores.

    Gametes formed by these spores could be

    (i) **Isogamous** (similar in morphology)

    (ii) **Oogamous** (dissimilar in morphology female gamete is bigger than male gamete).

    (iii) **Anisogamous**, *e.g.*, in case of *Mucor, Rhizopus* and *Albugo.*

    (iv) **Ascomycetes** are known as sac fungi usually multicellular like *Penicillium.*
58. They are saprophytic, decomposers, parasitic or ceprophilous. Mycelium is branched and septate.
59. Asexual spores are formed in special mycelium called **conidiophores.**
60. Sexual spores are produced in fruiting body called ascospores *e.g.*, *Aspergillus claviceps* and *Neurospora crassa.*
61. Basidiomycetes include mushrooms/bracket fungi/ puffballs.
62. Their mycelium is branched and septate.
63. Mode of reproduction is fragmentation sex organs are absent.
64. Vegetative or somatic cells fuses known as plasmogamy and give rise to dikaryon.
65. Dikaryon give rise to basidium which produces four basidiospores.
66. Basidiospores are produced on basidium.
67. The basidia are arranged in fruiting body called basidiocarp, *e.g.*, *Agaricus* (mushroom), *Ustilago* (smut) and *Puccinia.*
68. Deuteromycetes are known as imperfect fungi, since sexual reproduction is not reported in them.
69. They reproduce only by asexual spores known as **conidia.**
70. Mycelium is septate and branched, *e.g.*, *Alternaria, Colletotrichum* and *Trichoderma.*
71. **Kingdom–Plantae** includes eukaryotic autotrophic chlorophyll containing organisms.

72. These may be partially heterotrophic as in case of insectivorous plants like *Cuscuta*.
73. They have distinct nucleus, chloroplast and cellulosic cell wall.
74. It includes **algae, bryophytes, pteridophyte**, **gymnosperms** and **angiosperms**.
75. They show **alteration of generation,** diploid sporophytic phase and haploid gametophytic phase.
76. Kingdom–Animalia includes heterotrophic eukaryotic, multicellular organisms.
77. Their cells do not have cell walls.
78. Mode of nutrition is **holozoic**, *i.e.*, ingestion of food.
79. They reserve food material as glycogen or fat.
80. Capable of locomotion and have specialised sensory and neuromotor system.
81. They show definate growth pattern.
82. They show sexual mode of reproduction.
83. **Viruses** and **viroids** are the non-cellular organised, which are not characterised in the classification of **Whittaker**.
84. They have both living and non-living characteristics.
85. They form inert crystalline structure outside the living cell, but inside the host cell they can multiply.
86. They take over the host machinery and replicate themselves.
87. **Pasteur DJ Ivanowsky** give the name virus, which means venom or poisonous fluid.
88. **MW Bejerinck in 1898,** called fluid obtained from infected tobacco plant as *contagium vivum fluidum* (infectious living fluid).
89. Viruses are obligate parasite. They are inert outside specific host cell and exist in crystallise form as demonstrated by **WM Stanley**.
90. Genetic material of viruses could be DNA or RNA.
91. Nucleic acid is protein by protein coat called capsid, which is made up of capsomeres. Capsomeres are arranged in a helical or polyhedral geometric form.
92. Viruses which infect plants are *ss*RNA, while which infect animals are either *ss*DNA/RNA or *ds*DNA/RNA.
93. Viruses which infect bacteria are known as **bacteriophage**. They are usually *ds*DNA viruses.

94. In humans, virus causes various diseases like AIDS, mumps, small pox, herpes and influenza.
95. In plants, it causes leaf rolling and curling, yellowing and vein clearing dwarfing and stunted growth.
96. **Viroids** are the infectious agent, which have naked nucleic acid (mainly RNA). It was discovered by **TO Diener** in year **1971**.
97. It causes **potato spindle tuber disease.**

Exercises

Question 1. Discuss how classification systems have undergone several changes over a period of time?

Answer

(i) Linnaeus proposed a two kingdom system of classification with Plantae and Animalia kingdoms was developed that included all plants and animals respectively. But as this system did not distinguish between the eukaryotes and prokaryotes, unicellular and multicellular organisms and photosynthetic (green algae) and non-photosynthetic (fungi) organisms, so scientists found it an inadequate system of classification. Classification systems for the living organisms have hence, undergone several changes over time.

(ii) The two kingdom system of classification was replaced by three kingdom system, then by four and finally by five kingdom system of classification of RH Whittaker (1969).

(iii) The five kingdoms included Monera, Protista, Fungi, Plantae and Animalia. This is the most accepted system of classification of living organisms.

(iv) But, Whittaker has not described viruses lichens. Then, Stanley described viruses, viroids, etc.

Thus, over a period of time, classification system have undergone several changes.

Question 2. State two economically important uses of

(a) Heterotrophic bacteria (b) Archaebacteria

Answer

(a) **Heterotrophic bacteria**

- Maintain soil fertility by nitrogen fixation, ammonification and nitrification, *e.g., Rhizobium* bacteria (in the root nodules of legumes).

- The milk products such as butter, cheese, curd, etc., are obtained by the action of bacteria. The milk contains bacterial forms like *Streptococcus lacti, Escherichia coli, Lactobacillus lactis* and *Clostridium* sp., etc.

(b) **Archaebacteria**

- Metanogens are responsible for the production of methane (biogas) from the dung of these animals.
- Archaebacteria help in the degradation of waste materials.

Question 3. What is the nature of cell wall in diatoms?

Answer In case of diatoms, the cell wall forms two thin overlapping cells, which fit together as in a soap box. The cell wall is made up of silica. Due to siliceous nature of cell wall, it is known as diatomite or diatomaceous Earth. Diatomaceous Earth is a whitish, highly porous, chemically inert, highly absorbant and fire proof substance.

Question 4. Find out what do the term 'algal bloom' and 'red tides' signify?

Answer Sometimes, green algae such as *Chlorella, Scenedesmus* and *Spirogyra*, etc., grow in excess in water bodies and impart green colour to the water. These are called **algal blooms.** Red dinoflagellates (*Gonyaulax*) grow in abundance in sea and impart red colour to the ocean. This looks like red tides. Both due to algal blooms and 'red tide' the animal life declines due to toxins and deficiency of oxygen inside water.

Question 5. How are viroids different from viruses?

Answer Viroids different from viruses

S.N.	Virus	Viroids
1.	These are smaller than bacteria.	Smaller than viruses.
2.	Both RNA and DNA present.	Only RNA is present.
3.	Protein coat present.	Protein coat absent.
4.	Causes diseases like mumps and AIDS.	Causes plant diseases like spindle tuber diseases-potato.

Question 6. Describe briefly the four major groups of Protozoa?

Answer Protozoans are divided into four phyla on the basis of locomotory organelles—Zooflagellata, Sarcodina, Sporozoa and Cilliates.

(i) **Zooflagellates** These protozoans possess one to several flagella for locomotion. Zooflagellates are generally uninucleate, occasionally multinucleate.

The body is covered by a firm pellicle. There is also present cyst formation.

Examples *Giardia, Trypanosoma, Leishmania* and *Trichonympha*, etc.

(ii) **Sarcodines** These protozoans possess pseudopodia for locomotion. Pseudopodia are of four types, *i.e.*, lobopodia, filopodia, axopodia and reticulopodia. Pseudopodia are also used for engulfing food particles. Sarcodines are mostly free living, found in freshwater, sea water and on damp soil only a few are parasitic. Nutrition is commonly holozoic. Sarcodines are generally uninucleates.

Sarcodines are of four types—Amoebids (*i.e., Amoeba,* etc.), radiolarians (*i.e., Acanthometra*, etc.), foraminiferans (*i.e., Elphidium*, etc.) and heliozoans (*i.e., Actinophrys*, etc.).

(iii) **Sporozoans** All of them are endoparasites. Locomotory organelles (cilia, flagella, pseudopodia, etc.) are absent. Nutrition is parasitic (absorptive). Phagotrophy is rare. The body is covered with an elastic pellicle or cuticle. Nucleus is single. Contractile vacuoles are absent. Life cycle consists of two distinct asexual and sexual phases. They may be passed in one (monogenetic) or two different hosts (digenetic), *e.g., Plasmodium, Monocystis*, etc.

(iv) **Ciliates** These are aquatic, actively moving organisms because of the presence of thousands of cilia. They have a cavity (gullet) that opens to the outside of the cell surface. The coordinated movements of rows of cilia causes the water laden with food to enter into the gullet, *e.g., Paramecium*.

Question 7. Plants and autotrophic can you think of some plants that are partially heterotrophic?

Answer Plants are autotrophs, *i.e.*, they prepare their own food through the process of photosynthesis. But, in nature there are also some other plants which are partially heterotrophic, *i.e.*, they partially depend upon another organisms for food requirements, *e.g.*,

(i) *Loranthus* and *Viscum* are partial stem parasites which have leathery leaves. They attack several fruit and forest trees and with the help of their haustoria draw sap from the xylem tissue of the host.

(ii) Insectivorous plants have special leaves to trap insects. The trapped insects are killed and digested by proteolytic enzymes secreted by the epidermis of the leaves, *e.g.*, pitcher plant.

(iii) Parasitic plant, *e.g., Cuscutta* develops haustoria, which penetrate, the vascular bundles of the host plant to absorb water and solutes.

Question 8. What do the terms phycobiont and mycobiont signify?

Answer In case of lichens (*i.e.*, an association of algae and fungi), the algal partner which is capable of carrying out photosynthesis is known as phycobiont, whereas the fungal partner which is heterotrophic in nature is known as **mycobiont**.

Question 9. Give a comparative account of the classes of kingdom fungi under the following

(i) Mode of nutrition (ii) Mode of reproduction

Answer

Fungal Class	Mode of Nutrition	Mode of Reproduction
Myxomycetes	Heterotrophic and mostly saprophytic	Asexual and sexual reproduction
Phycomycetes	Mostly parasites	Asexual and sexual methods
Zygomycetes	Mostly saprophytic	Asexual and sexual reproduction
Ascomycetes	Saprophytes or parasites	Asexual and sexual reproduction
Basidiomycetes	Saprophytes or parasites	Asexual and sexual method
Deuteromycetes	Saprophytes or parasites	Only asexual reproduction

Question 10. What are the characteristic features of euglenoids?

Answer

The characteristic features of euglenoids are as follows:

(i) They occur in freshwater habitats and damp soils.

(ii) A single long flagella present at the anterior end.

(iii) Creeping movements occur by expansion and expansion of their body known as euglenoid movements.

(iv) Mode of nutrition is holophytic, saprobic or holozoic.

(v) Reserve food material is paramylum.

(vi) Euglenoids are known as plant and animal.

Plant characters of them are

(a) Presence of chloroplasts with chlorophyll.

(b) Holophytic nutrition.

Animal characters of them are

(a) Presence of pellicle, which is made up of proteins and not a cellulose.

(b) Presence of stigma.

(c) Presence of contractile vacuole.

(d) Presene of longitudinal binary fission.

(vii) Under favourable conditions euglenoids multiply by longitudinal binary fission, *e.g.*, *Euglena*, *Phacus*, *Paranema*, etc.

Question 11. Give a brief account of viruses with respect to their structure and nature of genetic material. Also name four common viral diseases.

Answer Viruses are non-cellular, ultramicroscopic, infectious particles. They are made up of envelope, capsid, nucleoid and occasionally one or two enzymes. Viruses possess an outer thin loose covering called envelope. The central portion of nucleoid is surrounded by capsid that is made up of smaller sub-units known as capsomeres.

The nucleic acid present in the viruses is known as nucleoid. It is the infective part of the virus which utilises the host cell machinery. The genetic material of viruses is of four types— (i) Double stranded DNA (*ds*DNA) as found in pox virus, hepatitis-B virus and herpes virus, etc. (ii) Single stranded DNA (*ss*DNA) occur in coliphage fd, coliphage fx174. (iii) Double stranded RNA (*ds*RNA) occur in Reo virus, (iv) Single stranded RNA : (*ss*RNA) occur in TMV virus, polio virus, etc.

Four common viral diseases are (i) Polio, (ii) AIDS, (iii) Hepatitis-B, (iv) Rabies.

Question 12. Organise a discussion in your class on the topic are viruses living or non-living?

Answer Viruses are non-living features intermediate between non-living and living organisms. On the basis of characters, such as non-cellular organisation, inactivity outside the host organism, lack of respiration and cellular metabolism, these are caused non-living. Moreover, similar to non-living objects viruses can be crystallised and precipitated.

Living Feature Similar to living beings, they possess genetic material (DNA or RNA), property of mutation, irritability, can grow and multiply inside the host cell. They are intracellular obligate parasites and attack specific hosts. Thus, keeping these points in mind, it is quite difficult to ascertain whether viruses are living or non-living.

Selected NCERT Exemplar Problems

Very Short Answer Type Questions

Question 1. What is the principle underlying the use of cyanobacteria in agricultural fields for crop improvement?

Answer Cyanobacteria such as *Anabaena, Nostoc, Aulosira, Stigonema* and *Cylindrospermum*, etc., can perform nitrogen fixation due to the presence of heterocysts while performing oxygenic photosynthesis. Nitrogenase a nitrogen fixing enzyme is present in heterocysts. These organisms fix the soil nitrogen and make it available to the plants. Thus, they increase the fertility of agricultural fields. *Anabaena oryzae* is an important nitrogen fixer in rice fields.

Question 2. Suppose you accidentally find an old preserved permanent slide without a label. In your effort to identify it, you place the slide under microscope and observe the following features

(a) Unicellular, (b) Well defined nucleus, (c) Biflagellate-one flagellum lying longitudinally and the other transversely.

What would you identify it as? Can you name the kingdom it belong to?

Answer It is a dinoflagellate. It belongs to the kingdom–Protista.

Question 3. How is the five kingdom classification advantageous over the two kingdom classification?

Answer As the five kingdom classification is based upon cell structure, (whether complex eukaryote or simple prokaryote), body structure (unicellular or multicellular, nutrition (autotrophic or heterotrophic) and life style, so it is more useful as compared to two kingdom system of classificaton.

Question 4. Polluted water bodies have usually very high abundance of plants like *Nostoc* and *Oscillatoria*. Give reasons.

Answer Sewage which contains phosphate containing detergents when added to water bodies, stimulate the algal growth due to nutrient enrichment. The increased nutrient content of polluted water bodies increase the rapid growth of water plants, *i.e.*, algae especially *Nostoc* and *Oscillatoria, etc.*

Question 5. Are chemosynthetic bacteria-autotrophic or heterotrophic?

Answer Chemosynthetic bacteria are autotrophs. These bacteria oxidise various inorganic substances such as nitrates, nitrites and ammonia and use the released energy for their ATP production.

Question 6. The common name of pea is simpler than its botanical (scientific) name *Pisum sativum*. Why then is simpler common name not used instead of the complex scientific/botanical name in biology?

Answer The common or vernacular names change with the change in place, so they cause confusion regarding specimen identification. In spite of this, the botanical names being in Latin are universally same as understood. Thus, botanical names are commonly.

Question 7. A virus is considered as a living organism and an obligate parasite when inside a host cell. But virus is not classified along with bacteria or fungi. What are the characters of virus that are similar to non-living objects?

Answer Viruses are considered living organisms and cause diseases inside a host cell but outside the living host, they are inert, cannot reproduct on their own. Morever, they can be crystallised in crystalline form and lack cellular organisation, incapable of growth and division. These characters make them identical to non-living objects.

Question 8. In the five kingdom system of Whittaker, how many kingdoms are eukaryotes?

Answer In the five kingdom classification of Whittaker the four kingdoms, *i.e.*, Protista, Fungi, Plantae and Animalia are eukaryotes.

Short Answer Type Questions

Question 1. Diatoms are also called as 'pearls of ocean.' Why? What is diatomaceous Earth?

Answer Diatoms are the main producers in the ocean. Being siliceous in nature, after death they add silica in the ocean. They prepare food not only for themselves, but for other plants also in the ocean. So, they are also called as 'Pearls of Ocean'.

Diatomaceous Earth is the deposits of highly siliceous cell walls (frustules) of unicellular diatoms (algae). It is a whitish, highly porous, insoluble, chemically inert, highly absorbent and fire proof substance. It is used in making sound proof buildings, living furnaces and boiless, as insulating material and also as a filter for oils.

Question 2. There is a myth that immediately after heavy rains in forest, mushrooms appear in large number and make a very large ring or circle, which may be several metres in diameter. These are called as 'fairy rings'. Can you explain this myth of fairy rings in biological terms?

Answer The fruiting bodies also known as basidiocarps of *Agaricus* arise in concentric rings from the mycelium present in the soil. As these basidiocarps resemble button in shape and develop in rings, they are known as fairy rings or fungal flowers. In fact, these are the fruiting bodies of this fungus. These rings of underground mycelium spreads centrifugally, the diameter of fairy ring also increase every year.

Question 3. *Neurospora* an Ascomycetes fungus has been used as a biological tool to understand the mechanism of plant genetics much in the same way as *Drosophila* has been used to study animal genetics. What makes *Neurospora* so important as a genetic tool?

Answer *Neurospora* fungus was selected and proved to be a very good genetic tool because this fungus can very easily be grown under laboratory conditions by providing a 'minimal medium' (*i.e.*, certain inorganic salts, a carbohydrate source and the vitamin biotin). By X-rays treatment, a number of mutations can be induced. The products of all four meiotic divisions can be observed directly and finally, the individual ascospores can be separated from an ascus and can be grown on a separate culture.

Question 4. Cyanobacteria and heterotrophic bacteria have been clubbed together in eubacteria of kingdom–Monera as per the 'Five Kingdom Classification' even though the two are vastly different from each other. In this grouping of the two types of taxa in the same kingdom justified? If so, why?

Answer Both these groups are prokaryotic in nature, *i.e.*, they do not have well defined nucleus. Their nucleus lacks nucleolus and nuclear membrane. Their genetic material, *i.e.*, DNA lies freely in the cytoplasm. They have 70 S type of ribosomes. That is why these are placed together in eubacteria group.

Question 5. Fungi are cosmopolitan, write the role of fungi in your daily life.

Answer

Role of Fungi

(i) Some fungi are used as nutritious and delicious foods, *e.g.*, *Agaricus bisporus* and *A. compestris* (mushrooms). *Morchella* is an important source of our food. Similarly, some yeasts are used as an important source of vitamin-B. A food called 'sufu' is produced from *Mucor* and *anti Mucor.*

(ii) Saprophytic fungi live upon dead organic matter and thus breakdown complex subtances into simple ones, which are again absorbed by the plants.

(iii) *Absidia*, *Aspergillus*, *Mucor*, *Penicillium* and *Rhizopus* have soil binding properties and they make the soil good.

(iv) Yeast (*Saccharomyces*) has the property of fermentation, thus it is used for the preparation of alcohol and dough.

(v) Many fungi such as *Empusa, Ferinosa,* etc., can be used to control insect pests.

(vi) Soil inhabiting fungus *Trichoderma* kills root rot fungus, *i.e., Pythium.*

Question 6. What observable features in *Trypanosoma* would make you classify it under kingdom-Protista?

Answer *Trypanosoma* is classified under kingdom Protista because like protists it is unicellular, having flagella as the organ of locomotion. It is uninucleate with centrally located nucleus and contains prominent nucleolus or endosome. It resembles protistians in mode of asexual reproduction, *i.e.,* by binary fission and the reserve food material is in the form of granules.

Long Answer Type Questions

Question 1. Algae are known to reproduce asexually by a variety of spores under different environmental conditions. Name these spores and the conditions under which they are produced.

Answer In algae, usually spores are reproductive units specialized for asexual reproduction.These are of following types:

(i) **Zoospores** It Chlorophyceae and Phaeophyceae, motile and flagellated zoospores are produced from zoosporangia during favourable conditions. Zoospores may be biflagellate as in *Chlamydomonas* and *Ulothrix*. In *Vaucheria*, the zoospores are multi-flagellate and called as synzoospores.

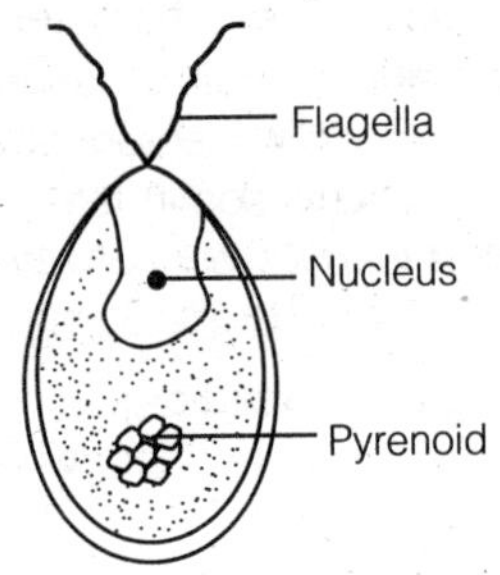

Zoospore of *Chlamydomonas*

(ii) **Aplanospores** These are unicellular, uninucleate, non-motile and thin-walled spors, produced under unfavourable conditions, *e.g., Spirogyra.*

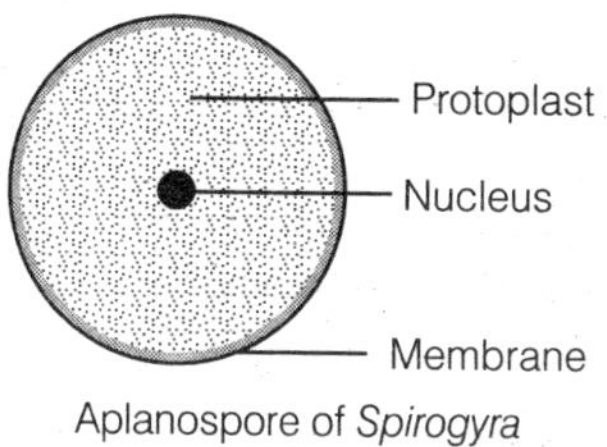

Aplanospore of *Spirogyra*

(iii) **Hypnospores** These are thick-walled spores produced under unfavourable conditions, *e.g., Vaucheria, Ulothrix.*

(iv) **Akinetes** These are special thick-walled vegetative cells in the filaments, which germinate on return of favourable conditions and can withstand unfavourable conditions as in *Spirogyra.*

(v) **Statospores** These are thick-walled spores produced in diatoms.

(vi) **Neutral spores** In certain algae, the protoplast of vegetative cells directly function as spores. These are called neutral spores, *e.g., Ectocarpus.*

Question 2. Apart from chlorophyll, algae have several other pigments in their chloroplast. What pigments are found in blue-green, red and brown algae that are responsible for their characteristic colours?

Answer Apart from chlorophyll, algae have pigments such as β-carotene, xanthophyll and fucoxanthin. The characteristic pigments of class Rhodophyceae are phycocyanin and phycoerythrin which give red colour, the class–Phaeophyceae, *i.e.*, brown algae have characteristic pigment fucoxanthin. Similarly, the pigments which impart blue-green colour to the members of class–Cyanophyceae are phycobilins, *i.e.*, phycocyanin, allophycocyanin an phycoerythrin. These pigments play an important role in the classification of algae.

Question 3. Make a list of algae and fungi that have commercial value as source of food, chemicals, medicines and fodder.

Answer **Some Important Algae and Fungi used as Food , Chemical and Medicines**

S.N.	Organism	Food Source	Chemical	Medicine
1.	Algae	*Porphyra*, *Laminaria*, *Alaria*, *Monostroma*, *Undaria*, *Ulva*, *Chlorella*, *Nostoc*, *Durvillea*, *Codium*, *Spirulina* and *Scenedesmus*	*Macrocystis*, *Laminaria*, *Ascophyllum*, *Lessonia*, *Ecklonia* and *Eisenia*	*Chlorella*, *Cladophora*, *Lyngbya*, *Digenea*, *Codium*, *Alsidium* and *Durvillea*
2.	Fungi	*Agaricus compestris*, *Variela volvacea*, *Armillaria mellea*, *Agaricus bisporus*, *Lentinus edodes*, *Lycoperdon*, *Morchella*, *Pleurotus*, *Saccharomyces*, *Rhizopogon and Mucor*	*Aspergillus niger*, *A. wentil* and *Mucor* (Citric acid), *Aspergillus niger* and *P. purpurogenum* (gluconic acid), *P. glacum and A. gallomyces* (gallic acid), *A. oryzae* (kojic acid), *Rhizopus stolonifer* (fumaric acid), *Fusarium moniliforme* (gibberellic acid), *Saccharomyces* sp. (Vitamin-B and D)	Penicillin (*Penicillium notatum* and *P. chrysogenum*), Glyotoxin (*Trichoderma sp.*), Chitrinine (*Penicillium citrinine*), Baccatin-A (*Gibberella baccata*), Ergotine (*Claviceps purpurea*), Clavicin (*Aspergillus clavatus*), Flavicin (*A. flavus and A. fumigatus*), Fumigallin (*A. fumigatus*), Jawaharine (*A. niger*), Chaetomin (*Chaetomium cochloides*), Proliferin (*Aspergillus proliferans*), Griseofulvinium (*Penicillium griseofulvum*)

Question 4. Peat is an important source of domestic fuel in several countries. How is 'peat' formed in nature?

Answer 'Peat' is produced by *Sphagnum* moss. This moss occurs in acidic bogs. It is usually formed after the deposition of plants of *Sphagnum* in the acidic soils of the bogs. In due course of time, these preserved *Sphagnum* plants get hardened and change into peat. Peat find its applications in the preparation of ethyl alcohol, peat tar, ammonia, paraffin, etc. It is also used to tie gifs and in seed beds because of its high water retention capacity. Peat is also used to cover the roots during transportation. This shows enormous values of peat for human kind. *Sphagnum* is the chief constituent of peat.

3

Plant Kingdom

Important Points

1. Kingdom–Plantae includes **algae**, **bryophytes**, **pteridophytes**, **gymnosperms** and **angiosperms**.
2. Plants were classified on the basis of different characters. There are three main types of classification **Artificial**, **Natural** and **Phylogeneticystem**.
3. **Artificial system** of classification was given by **Linnaeus** and based on **morphological characters**.
4. **Natural system** of classification was developed by **Bentham and Hooker** based on natural affinities among the organism. It was based on both external and internal features like anatomy, structure embryology. It is the most common system of classification followed.
5. **Phylogenetic system of classification** was given by **Engler** and **Prantl** based on evolutionary relationship of organism. It is also known as **Hutchinson's system.**
6. Classification done on the basis of cytological information, chromosome structure, behaviour, etc., is known as cytotaxonomy.
7. Classification on the basis of chemical constituents of plant is known as **chemotaxonomy**.
8. **Numerical taxonomy** includes classification on the basis of observed characters. Number and codes are given to all characters and data is processed.
9. The first phylum, which comes under kingdom–Plantae is **algae**.

10. Algae are autotrophic chlorophyll bearing thalloid mostly aquatic organisms.
11. These include unicellular forms like *Chlamydomonas*, filamentous like *Ulothrix, Spirogyra.* They reproduce vegetatively, asexually and sexually.
12. Vegetative reproduction includes fragmentation, each fragment develops into thallus.
13. Algae produce different type of spores called zoospores, asexually, these are motile flagellated and give rise to new plant on germination.
14. Sexual reproduction occurs through fusion of two gametes.

    These gametes could be
    (i) **Isogamous** Both gametes are similar in size and non-motile, *e.g., Chlamydomonas.*
    (ii) **Anisogamous** Both gametes dissimilar in size.
    (iii) **Oogamous** Fusion between one large female gamete and a smaller motile male gamete, *e.g., Volvox* and *Fucus.*
15. Algae plays an important role in carbondioxide fixation on Earth through photosynthesis and increase the level of O_2.
16. They are chief primary producers.
17. 70 species of marine algae like *Porphyra, Laminaria* and *Sargassum* are used as food.
18. They are used commercially for various products like.
    (i) **Algin** from brown algae.
    (ii) **Carrageen** from red algae.
    (iii) **Agar** from *Gelidium* and *Gracilaria.*
19. *Spirullina* and *Chlorella* are used by space travellers.
20. Algae is divided into three main classes–**Chlorophyceae, Phaeophyceae** and **Rhodophyceae**.
21. Members of Chlorophyceae are unicellular, colonial or filamentous have definite chloroplast commonly known as **green algae**.
22. They are green due to the presence of chlorophyll-*a* and *b* pigments localised in chloroplast.
23. Shape of the chloroplast varies like discoid, plate like, reticulate, cup-shaped, spiral or ribbon-shape.
24. Algae store food in form of starch in a specialised structures called **pyrenoids** located in chloroplast food may be stored in form of oil droplets.

25. Inner layer of cell wall is made up of cellulose, while outer layer is made up of pectose.
26. Vegetative reproduction occurs through fragmentation.
27. Asexual reproduction is done by zoospores by zoosporangia.
28. Sexual reproduction occurs through different modes like isogamous, anisogamous or oogamous, *e.g.*, *Volvox, Ulothrix, Spirogyra, Chlamydomonas* and *Chara.*
29. Members of **Phaeophyceae** are known as **brown algae**. They have characteristic pigments like chlorophyll-*a*, *c*, carotenoids and xanthophyll. Brown colour is due to presence of **fucoxanthin**.
30. These range from simple branched. filamentous forms to profusely branched, forms like kelps. Which reach to the height of 100 meters.
31. Food is stored in form of **mannitol** or **laminarian**.
32. They have gelatinous coating outside the, cellulosic cell wall called **algin**.
33. Cell contain chloroplast (plastid), centrally located vacuole and nucleus.
34. Plant body is differentiated into **holdfast** (substratum), **stripe** (stalk) and **frond** (photosynthetic organ).
35. Asexual reproduction occurs through biflagellate zoospores (have unequal laterally attached flagella).
36. Sexual reproduction may be, oogamous, isogamous or anisogamous. Union of gametes take place in H_2O within oogonium in case of oogamous species, *e.g.*, *Sargassum*, *Fucus*, *Ectocarpus*, *Dictyota and Laminaria.*
37. Members of **Rhodophyceae** are known as **red algae** due to the presence of red pigment *r*-phycoerythrin usually marine occurs close to the surface of H_2O.
38. Food is stored in form of **floridian starch**.
39. They reproduce vegetatively through fragmentation.
40. They reproduce sexually and asexually through non-motile spores/gametes. Sexual reproduction is oogamous.
41. **Bryophytes** are known as **amphibians of plant kingdom**. These include **mosses** and **liverworts.** They grow in soil but are dependent on water for fusion of gametes or sexual reproduction.
42. They occur in humid, damp and shaded localities.

43. They are thallus like, prostrate or erect and attached to substratum by unicellular or multicellular rhizoids.
44. Bryophyte main plant body is haploid which forms gametophyte.
45. Sex organs are multicellular, male sex organ is **anthredium,** while female sex organ is **archegonium**.
46. Anthredium produces biflagellate **antherozoids**.
47. Female sex organ produces one egg.
48. Antherozoids are released in water where it come in contact of archegonium and egg cell. It fuses with egg cell to produce the zygote.
49. Zygote undergoes mitotic division and give rise to sporophyte $(2n)$.
50. Sporophyte remain attached to the gametophyte and take nourishment.
51. Sporophyte undergoes reductional division or meiosis to produce haploid spores. These spores later germinate and give rise to haploid gametophyte.
52. Bryophytes shows considerable economic importance.
53. *Sphagnum* a moss is used as fuel it provides peat.
54. They play can important ecological role. They colonise on barren rocks along with lichens and decompose rocks.
55. Bryophytes are divided into **liverworts** and **mosses.**
56. **Liver worts** are thallus like structures closely attached to substrate. Leafy members have tiny appendages usually grow in moist, damp, shady habitats. *e.g.*, *Marchantia.*
57. They reproduce asexually by the formation of specialised structure called **gemmae** or through fragmentation of thalli.
58. Gemmae are asexual buds, which originate from small receptacles called **gemma cups**.
59. Sexual reproduction occurs by the fusion of antherozoids and egg, which are produced in antheridium and archegonium respectively.
60. Both male and female sex organ may be present on same thalli or different thalli.
61. Zygote give rise to sporophyte, which is differentiated into **foot, seta** and **capsule**. Some cells of capsule undergoes meiosis and give rise to haploid spores. These spores give rise to gametophyte (n).

62. **Mosses** are green, leafy, upright and radial in symmetry. They are highly developed of all the bryophytes.
63. Juvenile stage of moss is **Protonema**. It consist of slender, green, branching system of filaments.
64. Leafy stage develops from the secondary protonema as later bud. It bears the sex organs.
65. Asexual reproduction occurs through fragmentation or through bud in secondary protonema.
66. Sexual reproduction occurs in a similar way as in case of liverworts. Sporophyte is differentiated into **foot, seta** and **capsule**. Capsule bears spores, which give rise to gametophyte after meiosis, *e.g., Funaria, Polytrichum* and *Sphagnum.*
67. **Pteridophytes** are called **vascular cryptogams**, also known as **seedless vascular plants**. They produce spores rather than seeds. These include **horsetails** and **ferns.**
68. These are found near the marshy cool and damp places.
69. Dominant phase in pteridophytes is sporophyte, which is differentiated into root ($2n$) stem and leaf.
70. Pteridophytes are divided into four sub-division
    (i) **Psilophytopsida** (Psilopsida)
    (ii) **Lycophyta** (Lepidophyta)
    (iii) **Arthrophyta** (Sphenophyta)
    (iv) **Pterophyta** (Filicophyta).
71. Vascular tissue consist of xylem (without true vessels) and phloem (without companion cells).
72. Sporophyte consist of leaf like appendages called **sporophylls.** Sporophyll in cluster form distinct compact structure called **strobili** cones, *e.g.*, *Selaginella* and *Equisetum.*
73. Some cells of sporangium undergoes meiosis and produces haploid spores. These could be **homosporous** (spores of similar kind) or **heterosporous** (*i.e.*, macro and micro spores). These haploid spores germinate to give rise male and female gametophyte also known as **prothallus**.
74. Male gametophyte bears anthredia, while female gametophyte bears archegonium, which produces antherozoids and egg cell respectively, antherozoids and egg cell fuses to give rise zygote. Zygote develops into young embryo. This event is called **seed habit** and is considered an important stop in evolution.
75. Embryo give rise to sporophyte.
76. These are used for medicinal purposes and act as soil binders. They are also grown as ornamental plants.

77. **Gymnosperms** are **naked seeded plants**, which were evolved earlier than the flowering plants.
78. Dominant phase is sporophyte. They are heterosporous produce haploid megaspore and microspores, which are produced within sporangia borne on sporophyll, which are arranged spirally along an axis to form compact cones.
79. Cone containing microspores is called **microsporangia** or **microsporophyll**. Microspores develop into male gametophyte called pollen grain. Its development occurs in microsporophyll.
80. Cones bearing megaspores are called **megasporangia** or **macrosporangiate** or **female strobili**. Both megasporophyll and microsporophyll may be present on same plant (*e.g.*, *Pinus*) or may be present separately (*e.g.*, *Cycas*).
81. Megaspore differentiate to give rise to composite structure called ovule. Megaspore mother cell divides meiotically to give rise four haploid megaspores.
82. Megaspores enclosed in megasporangium give rise to archegonia.
83. Pollen grain is released from microsporangium and carried with the help of air current. It comes in contact with opening of **ovules.**
84. Pollen tube carries the male gamete towards archegonia and discharge contents in the mouth of archegonium.
85. Male gamete fuses with egg to give rise zygote. Zygote develops into embryo and embryo into seeds. Seeds are naked.
86. **Angiosperms** are distinct group of seed plants. They are also called **flowering plants**. Seeds are enclosed by fruit.
87. They are divided into two classes **dicotyledons** and **monocotyledons**.
88. Dicotyledon have two cotyledon in their seed and monocotyledon have one.
89. Flower bears male and female sex organs.
90. Male sex organ is **stamen** also known as **androecium**. It consist of an anther lobe and a filament. Anther produces pollen grains.
91. Female sex organ is **carpel** also known as **pistil/gynoecium**. It consist of three parts **style, stigma** and **ovary**.
92. Ovary encloses ovules which give rise to female gametophyte called **embryo sac**.

93. Megaspore mother cell of ovule undergoes meiotic cell division and give rise to embryo sac.
94. Embryo sac consist of one egg cell two **synergids**, three **antipedal** and **two polar nuclei**.
95. Pollen grain from anther after dispersal reaches to the stigma of ovary with the help of various agents like wind, air insects. This process is known as **pollination**.
96. Pollen grain reaches to embryo **sac** after its germination on stigma and through pollen tube. Pollen tube carries two male gamete and discharge it into embryo sac.
97. One male gamete fuses with egg to form zygote, this event is called **syngamy**.
98. Other male gamete (n) fuses with polar nuclei to give rise **triploid endosperm** ($3n$) or **PEN** (Primary Endosperm Nucleus). This event in called **triple fusion**.
99. The above two fusions together known as **double fertilisation**, which is a unique characteristic of angiosperms.
100. Zygote develops into embryo and PEN develops into endosperm, which provide nourishment to embryo.
101. Embryo finally give rise to seeds and ovaries develop into fruit.
102. Plant life cycle shows alteration of generation, *i.e.*, haploid and diploid phases. There are three types of life cycle patterns.
    (i) **Haplontic**
    (ii) **Diplontic**
    (iii) **Haplo-diplontic**
103. **Haplontic** life cycle is followed by algae such as *Spirogyra*. In this cycle gametophyte is dominant and sporophyte is single celled **zygote**. Zygote undergoes meiosis to form haploid spores. These spores give rise to haploid gametophyte after mitotic cell division.
104. **Haplo-diplontic life cycle** is followed by bryophytes and pteridophytes. In this case sporophytic as well as gametophytic phase is multicellular. In bryophytes gametophytic phase is dominant, while in pteridophytes sporophytic phase is dominant.
105. **Diplontic life cycle** is followed by seed bearing plants, *i.e.,* gymnosperms and angiosperms. Dominant phase is sporophyte gametophytic phase is represented by few celled **gametophyte**.

Exercises

Question 1. What is the basis of classification of algae?

Answer Algae are classified on the basis of type of pigments they possess, chemical nature of reserve food material, kinds, number and points of insertion of flagella of motile cells and the presence or absence of organised nucleus in the cell.

Divisions of Algae and their Main Characteristics

Classes	Common Name	Major Pigment	Stored Food	Cell Wall	Habitat
Chloro-phyceae	Green algae	Chlorophyll-*a*, *b*	Starch	Cellulose	Freshwater, brackish water and saltwater
Phaeo-phyceae	Brown algae	Chlorophyll-*a*, *c* Fucoxanthin	Mannitol laminarin	Cellulose and algin	Freshwater, brackish water and salt water
Rhodo-phyceae	Red algae	Chlorophyll-*a*, *d* and phycoerythrin	Floridean starch	Cellulose, pectin and poly sulphate esters	Freshwater, brackish water and salt water
Cyano-phyceae	Blue-green algae	Chlorophyll-*a*, Phycocyanin and Phycoerythrin	Volutin granules and lipid droplets	Peptidoglycan	Marine or terrestrial

Question 2. When and where does reduction division take place in the life cycle of a liverwort, a moss, a fern, a gymnosperm and an angiosperm?

Answer Reduction divisions in the life cycle of a liverwort, a moss, a fern and a gymnosperm take place during the production of spores from spore mother cells. In case of an angiosperm, the reduction division occurs during pollen grain formation from anthers and during production of embryo sac from ovule.

Question 3. Name three groups of plants that bear archegonia. Briefly describe the life cycle of any one of them.

Answer Three groups of plants that bear archegonia are bryophytes, pteridophytes and gymnosperms.

Life cycle of a pteridophyte The life cycle of a pteridophyte consists of two morphologically distinct phases:

(i) The gametophytic phase

(ii) The sporophytic phase.

These two phases come one after another in the life cycle of a pteridophyte. This phenomenon is called **alternation of generation**. The gametophyte is haploid with single set of chromosomes. It produces male sex organs antheridia and female sex organs archegonia.

(i) The antheridia may be embedded or projecting type. Each antheridium has single layered sterile jacket enclosing a mass of androcytes.

(ii) The androcytes are flask-shaped, sessile or shortly stalked and differentiated into globular venter and tubular neck.

(iii) The archegonium contains large egg, which is non-motile.

(iv) The antherozoids after liberation from antheridium, reaches up to the archegonium fuses with the egg and forms a diploid structure known as zygotes.

(v) The diploid zygote is the first cell of sporophytic generation. It is retained inside the archegonium and forms the embryo.

(vi) The embryo grows and develop to form sporophyte which is differentiated into roots, stem and leaves.

(vii) At maturity the plant bears sporangia, which encloses spore mother cells.

(viii) Each spore mother cell gives rise to four haploid spores which are usually arranged in tetrads.

(ix) The sporophytic generation ends with the production of spores.

(x) Each spore is the first cell of gametophytic generation. It germinates to produce gametophyte and completes its life cycle.

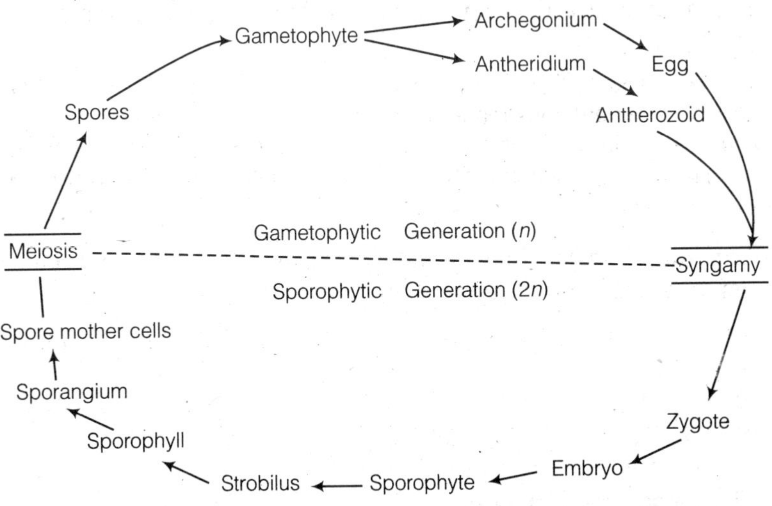

Diagrammatic representation of the life cycle of homosporous pteridophyte (*e.g., Lycopodium*)

Question 4. Mention the ploidy of the following protonemal cell of a moss; primary endosperm nucleus in dicot, leaf cell of a moss; prothallus cell of a fern; gemma cell in *Marchantia;* meristem cell of monocot, ovum of a liverwort and zygote of a fern.

Answer

(i) Protonemal cell of moss-haploid.
(ii) Primary endosperm nucleus of a dicot triploid.
(iii) Leaf cell of a moss diploid.
(iv) Prothallus cell of a fern haploid.
(v) Gemma cell in *Marchantia*-haploid.
(vi) Ovum of a liverwort-haploid.
(vii) Zygote of a fern-diploid.

Question 5. Write a note on economic importance of algae and gymnosperms.

Answer **Economic Importance of Algae**

(i) Red algae provides food, fodder and commercial products. *Porphyra tenera* (laver) is rich in protein, carbohydrates and vitamin-A, B, E and C.

(ii) Corallina has vermifuge properties.

(iii) Agar-agar a gelatin substance used as soldifying agent in culture media is obtained from *Gelidium* and *Gracilaria* algae. *Funori* is a glue used as adhesive and in sizing textiles, papers, etc. *Chondrus* is most widely used in sea weed in Europe.

(iv) Mucilage extracted from *Chondrus* is used in sampoos, shoe polish and creams.

(v) Carrageenin is a sulphated polysaccharide obtained from cell wall of *Chondrus crispus* and *Gigartina* and is used in confectionary, bakery, jelly, creams, etc.

Economic Importance of Gymnosperms

(i) Gymnosperms hold soil particles and thus check soil erosion.

(ii) Many gymnosperms are grown in gardens as ornamental plants, *i.e., Cycas, Thiya, Araucaria, Taxus, Agathis,* Maiden hair tree, etc.

(iii) Sago is a kind of starch obtained from cortex and pith of stem and seeds of *Cycas.* Roasted seeds of *Pinus gerardiana* (chilgoza) are used as dry fruit.

(iv) Paper pulp is obtained from wood of *Picea* (spruce), *Gnetum, Pinus* (pine) and *Larix* (larck).

(v) The wood of *Juniperus virginiana* (red cedar) is used to make pencils, holders and cigar boxes. Wood of *Taxus* is heaviest amongest soft woods and is used for making bows for archery.

(vi) Dry leaves of *Cycas* are used to make baskets and brooms. Needles of *Pinus* in making fibre board. Electric and telephone pones are made of stem of conifers.

(vii) Essential oils are obtained from *Juniperus, Tsugo, Picea, Abies, Cedrus*, etc. Resins are obtained from many species of *Pinus*.

Question 6. Both gymnosperms and angiosperms bear seeds, then why are they classified separately?

Answer Both gymnosperms and angiosperms bear seeds, but they are yet classified separately. Because, in case of gymnosperms the seeds are naked, *i.e.*, the seeds are not produced inside the fruit but in case of angiosperms the seeds are enclosed inside the fruit.

Question 7. What is heterospory? Briefly comment on its significance. Give two examples.

Answer Heterospory is the phenomenon of formation of two types of spores, *i.e.*, smaller microspore and larger megaspore. This phenomenon was firstly reported in *Selaginella*, a pteridophyte.

The phenomenon of heterospory lead to the reduction of gametophyte, *in situ* germination of spores, retention of megagametophyte in the megasporangia and finally to the seed development. Examples of heterospory are *Selaginella, Salvinia* and *Marsilea*, etc.

Question 8. Explain briefly the following terms with suitable examples. (i) Protonema (ii) Antheridium (iii) Archegonium (iv) Diplontic (v) Sporophyll (vi) Isogamy.

Answer

(i) **Protonema** It is the juvenile stage of a moss. It results from the germinating meiospore. When fully grown, it consists of a slender, green, branching system of filaments called the protonema.

(ii) **Antheridium** The male sex organ of bryophyte and pteridophyte is known as antheridium. It has a single-layered sterile jacket enclosing a large number of androcytes. The androcytes metamorphose into flagellated motile antherozoids.

(iii) **Archegonium** The female sex organ of bryophytes, which is multicellular and differentiated into neck and venter. The neck consists of neck canal cells and venter contains the venter canal cells and egg.

(iv) **Diplontic** A kind of life cycle in which the sporophyte is the dominant, photosynthetic, independent phase of the plant and alternate with haploid gametophytic phase is known as diplontic life cycle.

(v) **Sporophyll** The sporangium bearing structure in case of *Selaginella* is known as sporophyll.

(vi) **Isogamy** It is the process of fusion between two similar gametes, *i.e., Chlamydomonas.*

Question 9. Differentiate between the following

(i) red algae and brown algae.
(ii) liverworts and moss.
(iii) homosporous and heterosporous pteridophyte.
(iv) syngamy and triple fusion.

Answer (i) **Differences between Red Algae and Brown Algae**

S.N.	Red Algae	Brown Algae
1.	It belongs to the class–Rhodophyceae.	It belongs to the class–Phaeophyceae.
2.	It is red in colour due to the presence of pigments chlorophyll-*a*, *c* and phycoerythrin.	It is brown in colour due to the presence of pigments phycocyanin and phycophaecin.
	Example *Stylolema*, *Rhodela*.	**Example** *Sargassum*, *Microcystis*

(ii) **Differences between Liverworts and Moss**

S.N.	Liverwort	Moss
1.	These are the member of class–Hepaticopsida of bryophytes.	These belongs to class–Bryopsida of Bryophyta.
2.	Thallus is dorsoventrally flattened and lobed liver like.	Thallus is leafy and radially symmetrical.
3.	Rhizoids unicellular	Rhizoids are multicellular.
4.	Elaters are present in capsule to assist dispersal of spores.	Elaters are absent, but peristome teeth are present in the capsule assist dispersal of spores.

(iii) **Differences between Homosporous and Heterosporous Pteridophytes**

Homosporous Pteridophyte	Heterosporous Pteridophyte
Pteridophyters, which produce only one kind of spores.	These produce two kinds of spores, *i.e.,* large megaspore and smallar microspore.
Example *Lycopodium*	**Example** *Selaginella*

(iv) **Differences between Syngamy and Triple Fusion**

Syngamy	Triple Fusion
It is the act of fusion of one male gamete with the egg cell to form zygote.	The act of fusion of second male gamete with secondary nucleus to form triploid endosperm is called triple endosperm is called triple fusion.

Question 10. How would you distinguish monocots from dicots?

Answer **Differences between Monocots and Dicots**

S.N.	Monocot	Dicot
1.	Parallel venation present in leaves	Reticulate venation present.
2.	Adventitious root system present.	Tap root, adventitious root both present.
3.	Single cotyledon is present	Double cotyledons are present.
4.	Seeds are endospermic	Seeds are non-endospermic.

Question 11. Match the following column I and Column II.

Column I	Column II
A. *Chlamydomonas*	1. Moss
B. *Cycas*	2. Pteridophyte
C. *Selaginella*	3. Algae
D. *Sphagnum*	4. Gymnosperm

Answer

Column I		Column II
A. *Chlamydomonas*	3.	Aglae
B. *Cycas*	4.	Gymnosperm
C. *Selaginella*	2.	Pteridophyte
D. *Sphagnum*	1.	Moss

Question 12. Describe the important characteristics of gymnosperms.

Answer Gymnosperms are vascular plants with naked seeds. The important characters of gymnosperms are as follows:

(i) The plants are perennial forming a dominant flora in colder areas.

(ii) Leaves are generally dimorphic, foliage and scale leaves.

(iii) The foliage leaves do not have lateral veins, instead transfusion tissue occurs internally for lateral transport.

(iv) Sporophylls produce strobili or cones. Flowers are absent.

(v) Microsporophylls do not show distinction of filament and anther. Megasporophylls are also not rolled-like carpels.

(vi) Ovules are unitegmic (sometimes bitegmic in gnetales). Each ovule has a mass of tissue called **nucleus**. It is equivalent to megasporangium. A megaspore mother cell develops in it.

(vii) Female gametophyte develops archegonia.

(viii) Pollination brings pollen grains over the micropylar end of ovules (direct pollination), siphonogamy occurs.

(ix) Endosperm is gametophytic.

(x) Secondary growth is present in some gymnosperms. Vascular tissues are otherwise similar to those of pteridophytes with vessels present in gnetales.

Selected NCERT Exemplar Problems

Very Short Answer Type Questions

Question 1. Food is stored as floridean starch in Rhodophyceae. Mannitol is the reserve food material of which group of algae?

Answer Mannitol is the reserve food material present in group-Phaeophyceae to algae.

Question 2. Give an example of plants with

(i) haplontic life cycle
(ii) diplontic life cycle
(iii) haplo-diplontic life cycle

Answer

(i) **Haplontic life cycle** *Spirogyra* and *Chlamydomonas*, etc.

(ii) **Diplontic life cycle** Gymnosperms (*Pinus*) and Angiosperms (*Solanum tuberosum*).

(iii) **Haplo-diplontic life cycle** *Funaria* (bryophyte) and *Selaginella* (pteridophyte).

Question 3. The plant body in higher plants is well-differentiated and well-developed. Roots are the organs used for the absorption. What is the equivalent of roots in the less developed lower plants?

Answer In algae, in place of roots, **hold fast** and **haptern** are present. In case of fungi, **haustorium** as absorbing organ in place of roots are present, whereas bryophytes possess the **rhizoids** as absorbing organs.

Question 4. Most algal genera show haplontic life style. Name an alga which is

(i) haplo-diplontic
(ii) diplontic

Answer

(i) Haplo-diplontic alga is *Ectocarpus*.
(ii) Diplontic algae is *Fucus*.

Question 5. In bryophytes male and female sex organs are called .... and ....

Answer Male sex organ of bryophytes is antheridium and female sex organ of bryophytes is archegonium.

Short Answer Type Questions

Question 1. Why are bryophytes called the amphibians of plant kingdom?

Answer Bryophytes are basically terrestrial plants and adapted to grow under land conditions but they require water to complete their life cycle. Water is necessary for dehiscence of antheridia, liberation and swimming of motile sperms (antherozoids) for fertilizing the egg, opening of archegonial neck and entery of sperm into the archegonium. Thus, bryophytes are called the amphibians of the plant kingdom.

Question 2. The male and female reproductive organs of several pteridophytes and gymnosperms comparable to floral structures of angiosperms. Make an attempt to compare the various reproductive parts of pteridophytes and gymnosperms with reproductive structures of angiosperms.

Answer **Reproductive Structures of Pteridophytes, Gymnosperms and Angiosperms**

Angiosperm	Pteridophyte	Gymnosperm
Flower	Cone or strobili, sporophyll	Cone or strobili
Stamens	Microsporophyll	Microsporophyll
Carpel	Megasporophyll	Megaspholophyll
Ovule	Megasporangium	Megasporangium
Anther	Microsporangium	Microsporangium
Pollen grains	Microspore	Microspore
Embryo sac	Megaspore	Megaspore

Question 3. Heterospory, *i.e.*, formation of two types of spores-microspores and megaspores is a characteristic feature in the life cycle of a few members of pteridophytes and all spermatophytes. Do you think heterospory has some evolutionary significance in plant kingdom?

Answer Heterospory leads to the reduction of gametophyte, *in situ* germination of spores, retention of megagametophyte in the megasporangia and finally to the seed development. Seeds are highly developed in gymnosperms and angiosperms. The gymnospermic seeds are naked, whereas in case of angiosperms, the seeds are present inside the fruit. Thus, heterospory a pioneer point towards seed development suggest that gymnosperms have evolved from pteridophytes and which in turn give rise to angiosperms.

Question 4. Each plant of group of plants has some phylogenetic significance in relation to evolution. *Cycas* one of the few living members of gymnosperms is called as the 'relic of past' can you establish a phylogenetic relationship of *Cycas* with any other group of plants that justifies the above statement?

Answer *Cycas* one of the few living members of gymnosperms is called as the 'relic of past'. It exhibit phylogenetic relationship with pteridophytes. Its evolutionary characters are

(i) Slow growth
(ii) Shedding of seed when the embryo is still immature
(iii) Little secondary growth and manoxylic wood
(iv) Leaf like megasporophyllus
(v) Flagellate sperms even when pollen tube is present
(vi) Persistent leaf bases
(vii) Circinat ptyasix
(viii) Arrangement of microsporangia in well defined archegonia.

Question 5. The heterosporous pteridophytes show certain characteristics. Which are precursor to the seed habit in gymnosperms. Explain.

Answer Heterospory, *i.e.*, production of two types of spores smaller microspores and larger megaspore was first reported in *Selaginella* a pteridophyte. In *Selaginella*, the smaller microspores are destined to produce male gametophytes and the larger megaspores to female gametophyte. The male gametophyte produces male gametes, whereas the female gametophyte produces archegonia and also provides nourishment to the developing embryo.

The phenomenon of heterospory, thus lead to the reduction of gametophyte, *in situ* germination of spores, retention of megagametophyte in the megasporangia and finally to the seed development. Thus, the heterospory in *Selaginella* forms the base for seed habit development in gymnosperms.

Question 6. How are male and female gametophytes of pteridophytes and gymnosperms different from each other?

Answer **Male and Female Gametophytes of Pteridophytes** In case of *Selaginella*, the male gametophyte produced from haploid microspores is highly reduced, usually endoscopic and unisexual. It bear only antheridia. The female gametophyte bear only archegonia.

Male and Female Gametophyte of Gymnosperms In case of gymnosperms the male gametophyte is highly reduced and is confined to only a limited number of cells. This reduced gametophyte is called a pollen grain. The female gametophyte of a gymnosperm of multicellular and bears two or more archegonia or female sex organs. The multicellular female gametophyte is also retained within megasporangium.

Question 7. In which plant will you look for mycorrhiza and coralloid roots? Also explain what these terms mean.

Answer Mycorrhiza is a symbiotic association between fungi and roots of higher plants. These help in absorption of nutrients from the soil and make it available to the host plant. Mycorrhizal associations are present in conifers, *i.e., Pinus, Cedrus, Abies* and *Picea*, etc.

Coralloid roots are dichotomously branched and exhibit the presence of N_2 fixing blue-green algae, *i.e., Nostoc*. These roots are present in case of gymnosperm, *i.e., Cycas*.

Long Answer Type Questions

Question 1. Gametophyte is a dominant phase in the life cycle of a bryophyte. Explain.

Answer The main plant body of a bryophyte is a gametophyte which is the dominant phase in the life cycle. It is thallus-like and prostrate or erect, attached to the substratum by unicellular or multicellular rhizoids. They may possess root like, leaf like or stem like structures. The gametophytic plant body is haploid. It produces gametes. The sex organs in bryophytes are multicellular. The male sex organ is called antheridium and the female sex organ is called archegonium. Antheridium produces the antherozoids whereas, the archegonium give rise to egg. Antherozoids and egg fuse to form the zygote (a diploid structure) zygote is the first cell of sporophytic generation.

Question 2. With the help of a schematic diagram discribe the haplo-diplontic life cycle pattern of a plant group.

Answer The haplo-diplontic type of life cycle is present in case of pteridophytes. It is described as the life cycle of a pteridophyte consists of two distinct phases, *i.e.,* gametophytic phase and sporophytic phase. These two phase come one after another in the life cycle of an individual. This phenomenon is known as **alternation of generation**.

The gametophyte produces male sex organs antheridia and female sex organ archegonia. Antheridia produces the male gametes, *i.e.,* antherozoids and archegonia produces the egg, which fuses with the antherozoid and forms the diploid zygote. The gametophytic phase ends with the production of zygote, which divide and redivide and forms the main plant body, *i.e.,* sporophyte, which bears roots, leaves and stem. The sporophyte is a diploid phase. It bears the sporangia which after meiosis forms spores. Spore germinates to produce gametophyte.

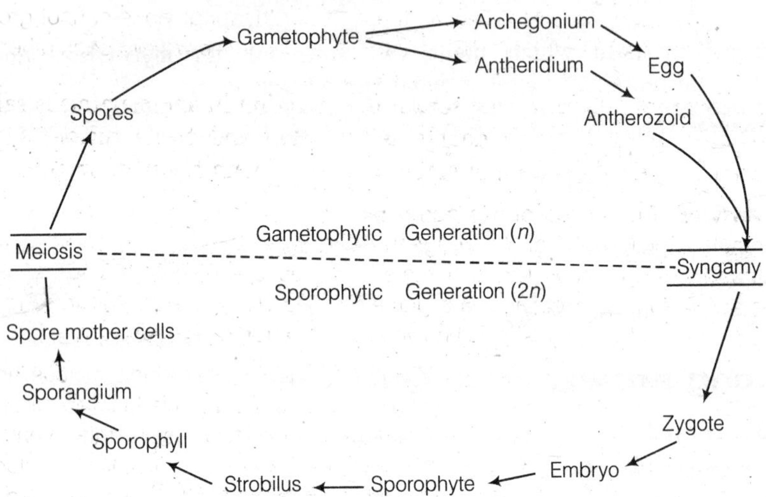

Schematic diagram represent the life cycle of a pteridophyte (homosporous one, haplo-diplontic type of life cycle.

Question 3. Lichen is usually cited as an example of 'symbiosis' in plants, where an algal and a fungal species live together for their mutual benefit. Which of the following will happen if algal and fungal partners are separated from each other?

(i) Both will survive and grow normally and indepenent from each other.

(ii) Both will die

(iii) Algal component will survive while the fungal component will die.

(iv) Fungal component will survive while algal partner will die.

Based on your answer how do you justify this association as symbiosis.

Answer (ii) is correct. Lichen is a symbiotic association between an alga and a fungi, which live together for their mutual benefit. If both are separated from each other then they will die. The fungus holds water, provides protection and ideal housing to the alga. The alga in turn supplies carbohydrate food for the fungus. If the alga is capable of fixing nitrogen (*e.g., Nostoc*), it supplies fixed nitrogen to the fungus. The kind of mutual interdependence helps lichens to grow on dry, barren rocks, where the other plants fail to exist. Morever, the algae or the fungi alone cannot grow in such places. Thus, both the partners cannot survive without each other.

Question 4. Explain why sexual reproduction in angiosperms is said to take place through double fertilization and triple fusion. Also draw a labelled diagram of embryo sac to explain the phenomena.

Answer The pollen grains germinate on the stigma of a flower and the resulting pollen tube grow through the tissues of stigma and style and reach the egg apparatus. The two male gametes are discharged within the embryo sac. One of the male gamete fuses with the egg cell to form a diploid zygote. This fusion is known as **fertilization** or **syngamy**.

The second male gamete fuses with the diploid secondary nucleus and forms the triploid Primary Endosperm Nucleus (PEN). This fusion is known as triple fusion. Because of the involvement of two fusion, this event in angiosperms is termed as **double fertilization.** The zygote then develops into embryo and PEN develops into endosperm which provides nourishment to the developing embryo.

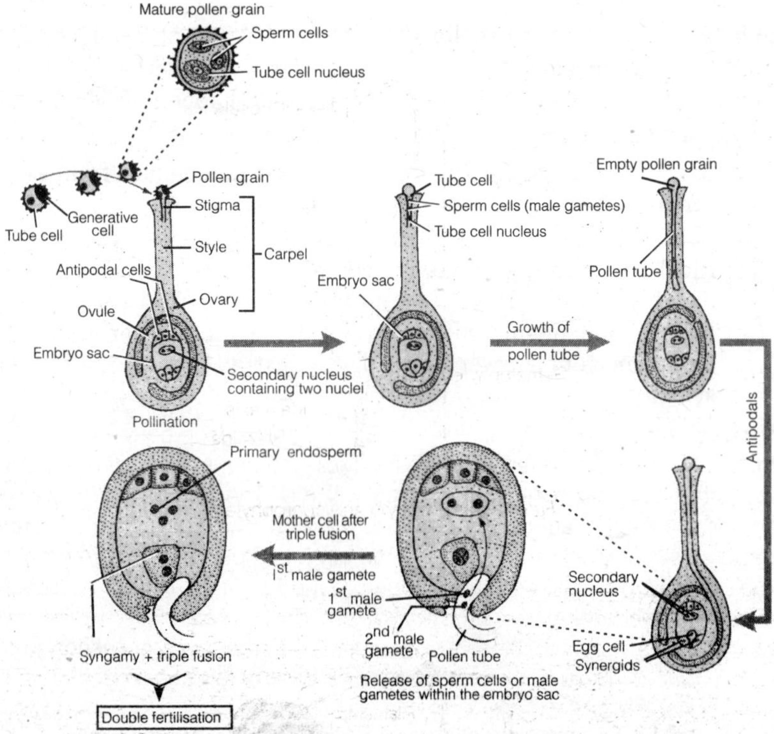

The process of fertilisation and double fertilisation

Question 5. Draw labelled diagrams of

(i) Female and male thallus of a liverwort.
(ii) Gametophyte and sporophyte of *Funaria*.
(iii) Alternation of generation of angiosperms.

Answer (i)

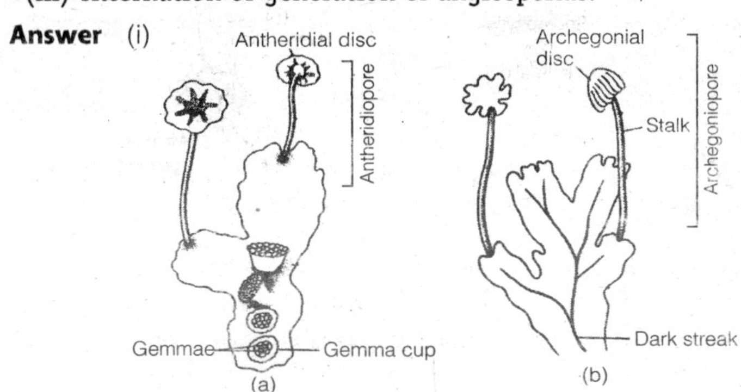

Liverworts (a) Male thallus of *M. polymorpha*

(ii)

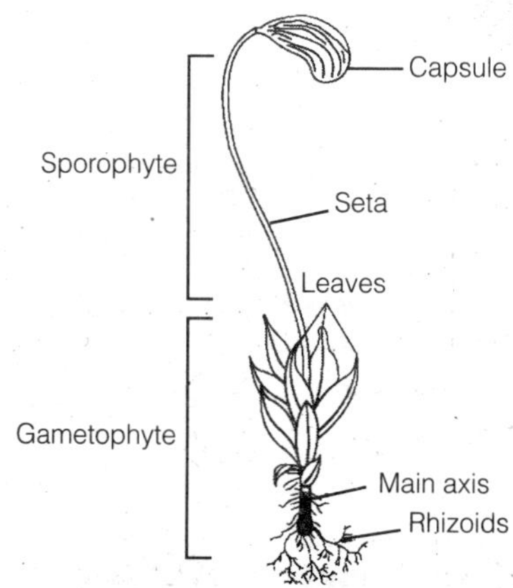

Funaria gametophyte and sporophyte

(iii)

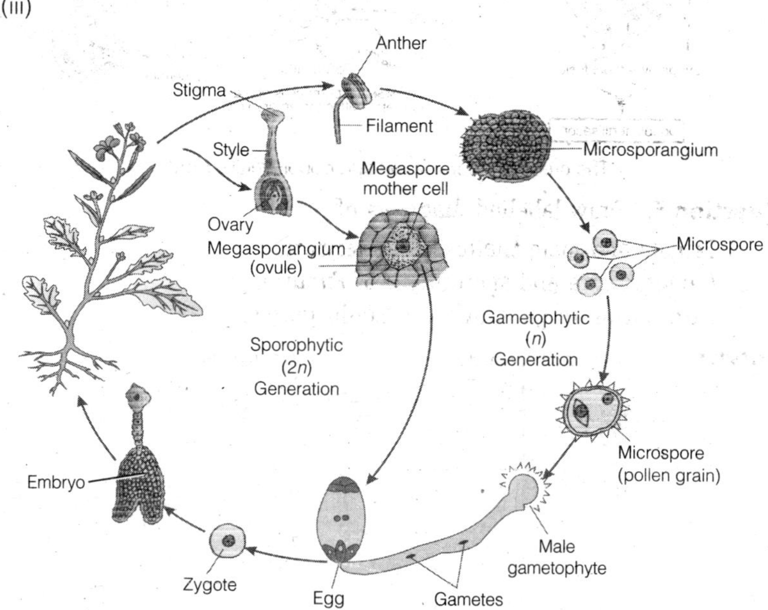

Life cycle of an angiosperm showing alteration of generation

4

Animal Kingdom

Important Points

1. Animals are classified on the basis of level of organisation, symmetry. Body cavity or coelom, pattern of arrangement of cells.
2. Animals exhibit different level of organisation, like tissue level, cellular level and organ level of organisation.
3. Cellular level of organisation is shown by sponges where cells are arranged as loose cell aggregates.
4. In **coelenterates**, cells are arranged into tissue and perform specific function.
5. Member of **phylum–Platyhelminthes** and higher members exhibit organ level of organisation, where tissues are grouped together to form organs.
6. Animals are also categorised on the basis of symmetry. There are three types of symmetry
   (i) Asymmetrical
   (ii) Radial symmetry
   (iii) Bilateral symmetry.
7. Sponges are asymmetrical. When divided through any plane passing through centre, they are not divided into equal halves.
8. Radial symmetry is shown by members of coelenterates, ctenophores and echinoderms when divided through central axis they give rise to equal identical halves.
9. Arthropods, annelids, etc., shows bilateral symmetry where body can be divided into identical left and right halves.

10. Embryonic cells in animals are arranged into different embryonic layers. On the basis of it animals are classified as
    (i) **Diploblastic** Cells are arranged into two embryonic layers ectoderm and endoderm.
    (ii) **Triploblastic** Cells are arranged into three embryonic layers ectoderm, mesoderm and endoderm.
11. **Coelom** is the body cavity, which is lined by mesoderm. Classification is also based on presence and absence of coelom.
12. Animals which possesses coelom are known as **coelomates**, *e.g.*, annelids, molluscs, arthropods and echinoderms.
13. In some animal mesoderm does not line the body cavity and present in between ectoderm and endoderm. Such body cavity is called **pseudocoelomates** like **Aschelminthes**.
14. Some animals do not possess body cavity and known as **acoelomates**, *e.g.*, Platyhelminthes, etc.
15. In some animals there is repetition of some organs and body is divided into segments, *e.g.*, in case of earthworm. This phenomenon of segmentation is known as **metamerism.**
16. During embryonic development, mesodermal cells forms a red-like structure on the dorsal surface called **notochord**. Animals with notochord are known as **chordates** and animals without notochord are known as **non-chordates.**
17. On the basis of above mentioned characteristics animals are divided into **11 broad phylum**
    (i) Porifera (ii) Coelenterata (Cnidaria)
    (iii) Ctenophora (iv) Platyhelminthes
    (v) Aschelminthes (vi) Annelida
    (vii) Arthropoda (viii) Mollusca
    (ix) Echinodermata (x) Hemichordata
    (xi) Chordata.
    (i) **Phylum–Porifera** includes **sponges** which are usually marine and asymmetrical animals.
        (a) They show cellular level of organisation and water transport system.
        (b) Central cavity present in sponges is known as **spongocoel** it is lined by collar cells or **choanocytes.**
        (c) H_2O enters the spongocoel through minute pores called **ostia** and moves out through **osculum.**
        (d) They are supported by **spicules or spongin** and proteins fibres, which forms skeletal system.

(e) They are hermaphrodite both male and female gametes are produced within same individual fertilisation is internal.

(f) Larval stage is distinct from adult phase. *e.g., Sycon, Spongilla, Euspongia.*

(ii) **Phylum–Cnidaria** (Coelenterata) consist of aquatic, marine, sessile, radially symmetrical animals.

(a) They exhibit tissue level of organisation.

(b) **Tentacles** are present over the body which contain cnidoblasts or cnidocytes (it contain stinging capsule nematocytes.

(c) **Cnidoblast** are used for anchorage, defense and capture of prey.

(d) **Hypostome** is the single opening at mouth with gastro vascular cavity.

(e) They show basic two body plans **medusa** and **polyps**.

(f) **Polyp** are fixed, sessile, cylindrical found near low water attached to rocks/weeds. Tentacles faces upwards and helpful in catching food, *e.g., Hydra, Adamsia,* etc.

(g) **Medusa** are umbrella-shaped and free swimming. Tentacles face downward and present all over the margin, *e.g., Aurelia* or jelly fish.

(h) Some cnidarians exhibit both forms and show alternation generation known as **metagenesis**. Polyp produce medusa asexually, while medusa produce polyps sexually (*e.g., Obelia*).

(i) In some cnidarians skeleton is made up of calcium carbonate, *e.g.,* coral.

e.g., Physalia (Portugese man of war), *Adamsia* (sea anemone), *Pannatula* (sea-pen) and *Gergonia* (sea-fan).

(iii) **Phylum-Ctenophora** are known as **sea walnuts** or **comb jellies**.

(a) They are exclusively marine, radially symmetrical, diplo-blastic organism.

(b) They show tissue level of organisation.

(c) They show property of **bioluminescence**.

(d) Their body bears 8 external rows of ciliated comb plates which helps in locomotion.

(e) Digestion is extracellular and intracellular.

(f) Reproduction occurs sexually.

e.g., Pleurobrachia and *Ctenoplana.*

(iv) **Phylum–Platyhelminthes** are called **flatworms**.

(a) Flatworms are bilaterally symmetrical. Triploblastic and acoelomate animals shows organ level of organisation. They are mostly endoparasites.

(b) They have specialised cells called **flame cell**. Which play an important role in osmoregulation and excretion.

(c) They possess high regeneration capacity like planaria.

e.g., Taenia (tapeworm) and *Fasciola* (liverfluke).

(v) **Phylum–Aschelminthes** is known as **round worms.**

(a) They show organ level of organisation.

(b) They are freeliving, aquatic, terrestial or parasitic in plants.

(c) Shows bilateral symmetry, triploblastic pseudocoelomate animal.

(d) They show developed muscular pharynx and alimentary canal is complete.

(e) They are dioecious, *i.e.,* male and females are different.

(f) Fertilisation is internal.

(g) Excretion is done through excretory pore.

e.g., Ascaris (roundworm), *Wauchereria* (filariaworm) and *Ancylostoma* (hookworm).

(vi) **Phylum–Annelides** are also known as (segmented worms).

(a) They show organ level of organisation triploblastic shows bilateral symmetry.

(b) They show metameric segmentation.

(c) Body is covered by transparent moist non-chitinous cuticle secreted by endoderm.

(d) Locomotion is done by appendages called **parapodia**.

(e) Digestion is extracellular, Circulatory system is closed.

(f) Excretion is done through **nephridia**.

(g) Neural system consist of dorsal. Cerebral ganglia or brain nerve ring and double ventral nerve cord with nerves ganglia in each segment, *e.g., Nereis, Pheretima* (earthworm), *Hirudinaria* (leech).

(vii) **Phylum–Arthropoda** is the largest phylum of Animalia, which includes **insects**.

(a) They are triploblastic, segmented, bilaterally, symmetrical coelomate animals. Body is covered by chitinous exoskeleton.

(b) They show organ system level of organisation.

(c) Their body consist of **head, thorax** and **abdomen**.

(d) *Arthos* means joint and poda-appendages. They show **jointed appendages**.

(e) Circulatory system is open type forming a haemocoel.

(f) Respiratory system show diverse range, *e.g.*, gills, tracheal, tubes, book lungs, general body surface in some cases.

(g) They show sexual mode of reproduction and are dioeceous.

(h) Eyes, antennae are present as sensory organs.

(i) Excretion occurs through **Malpighian tubules**.

(j) Some examples of arthropods are economically important insects.

e.g., *Apis* (honey bee), *Bombyx* (sikworm) and *Laccifer* (lac insect).

Vectors *Anopheles*, *Culex* and *Aedes* (mosquitoes).

Gregarious pest *Locusta*.

Living fossil *Limulus* (king crab).

(viii) **Phylum–Mollusca** is the second largest phylum.

(a) These are marine or freshwater.

(b) They are bilateral, symmetrical, triploblastic and coelomate animals.

(c) Body is covered by a calcareous shell.

(d) Body is unsegmented but consist of distinct **head, muscular foot** and **visceral hump**.

(e) Over a visceral hump soft spongy layer of skin forms a mantle. Space between hump and mantle is known as **mantle cavity.** It shows both respiratory and excretory functions.

(f) Sensory tentacles are present at the anterior portion.

(g) Feeding is done through radula.

(h) They are dioecious and oviparous in development.

e.g., *Pila,Octopus, Pinctada* and *Sepia*.

(ix) **Phylum–Echinodermata** have an endoskeleton of **calcareous ossicles** and named as Echinodermata.

(a) They show organ system level of organisation.

(b) They are radially symmetrical at adult stage and bilateral symmetrical at larval stage triploblastic and coelomate animals.

(c) Water vascular system is present, which helps in locomotion, capture and transport of food and respiration.

(d) They exhibit sexual mode of reproduction fertilisation is external.

(e) Complete digestive system is present with mouth on ventral side and anus at dorsal side.

(f) Excretory system is absent.

e.g., Asterias (star fish), *Echinus* (sea urchin), *Cucumaria* (sea cucumber) and *Ophiura* (brittle star).

(x) **Phylum–Hemichordata** is considered as a sub-phylum–Chordata.

(a) It consist of worm-like marine animals.

(b) They are triploblastic, coelomic and bilaterally symmetrical animals.

(c) Their body is cylindrical and composed of anterior proboscis a collar and a trunk.

(d) Excretion occurs through **proboscis gland**.

(e) Respiration occurs through gills.

(f) Fertilisation is external.

e.g., Balanoglossus and *Saccoglossus.*

(xi) **Phylum–Chordata** shows some chief characteristics like

(a) Presence of notochord.

(b) Presence of post-anal tail.

(c) Pharynx is perforated by gill slits.

(d) Central nervous system is dorsal, hollow and single.

(e) Heart is ventral.

(f) They are bilaterally symmetrical, triploblastic coelomic organisms.

(g) They show organ system level of organisation.

(h) Phylum–Chordata is divided into three sub-phylum—

- Urochordata or Tunicata
- Cephalochordata
- Vertebrata

} Protochordata

(i) In case of vertebrates notochord is replaced by **vertebral column.**

(j) Some key features shown by vertebrates

- Two, three, four-chambered ventral muscular heart.
- Paired appendages like fins or limbs.
- Kidneys for excretion and osmoregulation.

(k) Vertebrates are divided into two divisions—
- Agnatha (lacks jaw)
- Gnathostomata (bears jaw).

(l) Agnatha have one class **Cyclostomata**.

(m) Gnathostomata is divided into two super-class—
- Pisces (bear fins)
- Tetrapoda (bear limbs).

(n) Pisces are divided into two sub-class—
- Chondrichthyes
- Osteichthyes.

(o) Tetrapoda divided into four sub-class—
- Amphibia
- Reptilia
- Aves
- Mammals.

18. Members of **class–Cyclostomata** are ectoparasites and some fishes.
    (i) Possess 6-15 pair of gill slits for respiration.
    (ii) Body is devoid of scales and haved paired fins. Vertebral column and cranium is cartilaginous.
    (iii) Closed type of circulation system is present.
    e.g., *Petromyzon* (lamprey) and *Myxine* (hagfish).

19. Member of **class–Chondrichthyes** are the **cartilaginous fishes,** always marine streamlined body. Skin is covered with placoid scales/dermal dentine.
    (i) Notochord is well developed and persistant for whole life.
    (ii) Mouth is on ventral side.
    (iii) Show sexual dimorphism and fertilisation is internal.
    (iv) Heart is two chambered and are cold–blooded (poikilothermous) animals. They connot regulate their body temperature.
    (v) They have uncovered gills (operculum is absent gill cover).
    (vi) They are predaceous. Some of them have electric organs (*e.g., Torpedo*) and some possess poison sting (*e.g., Trygon*).

20. Member of **class–Osteichthyes** are marine as well as fresh water bony fishes.
    (i) Body is spindle–shaped.
    (ii) Mouth is terminal and skin is covered by ganoid, cycloid or ctenoid scales.
    (iii) Four pairs of filamentous gills covered by an operculum.
    (iv) Presence of air bladder which regulate buoyancy.

(v) Fertilisation is external sexes are separate.

(vi) They are mostly oviparous.

(vii) Heart is two-chambered, *e.g.*, Marine *Exocoetus* (flying fish) and *Hippocampus* (sea horse).

Freshwater *Labeo* (rohu), *Catla* (catla) *Clarias* (magur).

Aquarium *Belta* (fighting fish) and *Pterophyllum* (angel fish).

21. Members of **class–Amphibia** can be found in freshwater or moist land. They are the first terrestrial organism observed.

(i) They are **poikilothermic, ectothermal** or **cold-blooded animal**.

(ii) Body is divided into **head** and **trunk**. Trunk may be extended to tail region.

(iii) They respire through moist skin, gills and lungs.

(iv) Heart is three-chambered (two auricles and one ventricle).

(v) Exoskeleton is absent and endoskeleton is cartilaginous.

(vi) RBCs are oval, biconvex and nucleated.

(vii) Pronephros kidney in larval form and mesonephros kidney in adult.

(viii) **Tympinanum** represents the ear.

(ix) Sexes are separate and fertilisation is external.

(x) Alimentary canal, urinary and reproductive tract opens into common chamber called **cloaca**.

e.g., *Bufo* (toad), *Rana* (frog), *Hyla* (tree frog), *Salamandra* (salamander) and *Ichthyeophis* (limbless amphibia).

22. Members of **class–Reptilia** are the first true terrestrial vertebrates.

(i) They show creeping or crawling made of locomotion.

(ii) They are **poikilothermic exothermal** or **cold-blooded animals**.

(iii) Body is covered with dry, conified and non-glandular.

(iv) Alimentary canal terminates into cloaca.

(v) Heart is three-chambered (two auricles and one-ventricle partially divided). In crocodiles heart is four-chambered.

(vi) Tympanum represents ear.

(vii) Kidney is metanephric.

(viii) Fertilisation is internal. They are oviparous.

e.g., Chelone (turtle), *Testudo* (tortoise), *Chameleon* (tree lizard), Calotes (garden lizard), *Crocodilus* (crocodiles), *Alligators* (alligators) and *Hemidactylus* (wall lizard).

Poisonous snakes *Naja* (cobra), *Bangerous* (krait) and *Vipera* (viper).

23. Members of **class–Aves** of characterised by the presence of **feathers**. Most of them can fly except flightless bird, (*e.g.*, ostrich).
    (i) They possess beak. Forelimbs are modified into wings.
    (ii) They are **Homeothermal, endothermal or warm–blooded animals**. Their body temperature is generally 42°C and may reach to 45°C.
    (iii) Their skin is dry except oil glands present at the tail.
    (iv) Exoskeleton is in the form of feathers scales and claws.
    (v) Endoskeleton is bony (ossified) and bones are hollow with air cavities (pneumatic).
    (vi) Respiration is pulmonary (through lungs).
    (vii) Heart is completely four-chambered (two auricles, two ventricles).
    (viii) Hepatic portal system is well developed and renal portal system is vestigial.
    (ix) Sexes are separate with well marked sexaul dimorphism.
    (x) Fertilisation is internal and they are oviparous, *e.g., Corvus* (crow), *Psittacula* (parrot), *Columba* (pigeon), *Struthio* (ostrich), *Pavo* (peacock), *Aptenodytes* (penguin) and *Neophron* (vulture).

24. Members of **class–Mammalia** are characterised by the presence of milk producing glands called **mammary glands** and give birth to young ones.
    (i) They have two pairs of limbs, adapted for walking, running, climbing, burrowing, swimming or flying.
    (ii) They are adapted to fly or live in water and found in a variety of habitats, *i.e.,* polar ice caps, deserts, mountains, forests, grasslands and dark caves.
    (iii) They are homeothermal, endothermal or warm blooded animals.
    (iv) Body is divisible into head, neck, trunk and tail.
    (v) Shows presence of muscular diaphragm.
    (vi) Skin is glandular with sweat gland and is unique in possessing hair.
    (vii) Respiration is pulmonary.
    (viii) Sexes are separate and fertilisation is internal.

(ix) They are viviparous with some exceptions.

(x) External ear or **pinna** is present.

(xi) Heart is four-chambered. Showing double circulation.

(xii) They have metanephrc kidneys and excretion is ureotelic (urea).

e.g., **oviparous** *Ornithrohynchus* (platypus). **Viviparous** *Marcopus* (kangaroo), *Pteropus* (flying fox), *Camelus* (camel), *Macaca* (monkey), *Rattus* (rat), *Canis* (dog), *Felis* (cat), *Elephas* (elephant), *Equus* (horse), *Panthera tigris* (tiger), *Pathera leo* (lion) and *Homo sapiens* (human being).

Exercises

Question 1. What are the difficulties that you would face in classification of animals, if common fundamental features are not taken into account?

Answer The major difficulties in the classification of animals are on the followings lines

(i) Some show cellular level of organisation, some have tissue level and even some have organ system level of organisation.

(ii) Regarding symmetry, some are radially symmetrical, while some have bilateral symmetry.

(iii) Some have open circulatory system, while others have closed type.

(iv) Regarding digestion, some animals have extracellular digestion, while others have intracellular digestion.

(v) In case of body cavity, some have true coelom, while others are pseudocoelomates.

(vi) Regarding reproduction, some have only asexual reproduction, while others reproduce both by sexual and asexual means.

So, these are difficulties that zoologists face in the classification of animals.

Question 2. If you are given a specimen, what are the steps that you would follow to classify it?

Answer If I am given an animal specimen, then I will classify it on the basis of fundamental features which are common to all animal types inspite of the presence of some major differences in the structure and form of animals. The features taken into consideration during classification of animal are as follows :

(i) The type of arrangement of cells.
(ii) Body symmetry.
(iii) Nature of coelom.
(iv) Pattern of digestive system.
(v) Type of circulatory system.
(vi) Type of methods of reproduction.

Question 3. How useful is the study of the nature of body cavity and coelom in the classification of animals?

Answer Presence or absence of a cavity between the body wall and the gut wall is very important in classification. The body cavity which is lined by mesoderm is called coelom.

(i) Animals possessing coelom are called coelomata, *e.g.*, annelids, molluscs, arthropods, echinoderms, hemichordates and chordates.
(ii) In some animals, the body cavity is not mesoderm, instead the mesoderm is present as scattered pouches in between the ectoderm and endoderm. Such a body cavity is called pseudocoelom and the animals possessing them are called pseudocoelomates, *e.g.*, Aschelminthes.
(iii) The animals in which the body cavity is absent are known as Acoelomates, *e.g.*, Platyhelminthes.

Question 4. Distinguish between intracellular and extracellular digestion?

Answer Differences between intracellular and extracellular digestion

(i) **Intracellular digestion** It occurs inside the living cells with the help of lysosomal enzymes. Food particle is taken in through endocytosis. It forms a phagosome which fuses with a lysosome. The digested material pass into the cytoplasm. The undigested matter is throwh out by exocytosis. It occurs in *Amoeba, Paramecium*, etc.,
(ii) **Extracellular digestion** In case of coelentrates digestion occurs in gastrovascular cavity. This cavity has gland cells which secrete digestive enzymes over the food. The partially digested fragmented food particles are ingested by nutritive cells. It occurs in *Hydra, Aurelia,* etc.

Question 5. What is the differences between direct and indirect development?

Answer Differences between direct and indirect development

(i) **Direct development** In case of direct development, the life cycle of an adult individual lacks any larval stage in its life cycle. The adults give rise to young ones which directly develop into the adult, *e.g.*, mammals.

(ii) **Indirect development** It is present mostly in case of lower animals the adult individual gives rise to eggs mostly which develop into the adult after being passing through several larval stages *e.g.*, echinoderms, *Ascaris*, cockroach have prolonged larval stages in their life cycle.

Question 6. What are the peculiar features that you find in parasitic Platyhelminthes?

Answer The characteristic features of parasitic Platyhelminthes

(i) These are free living, parasitic forms. Tissue organ grade of body organisation is seen.

(ii) Body wall is three-layered. Outermost covering is epidermis which is often cilliated and covered by cuticle.

(iii) Digestive tract is incomplete or absent.

(iv) Respiration is anaerobic. No special organs for respiration are present.

(v) The anterior part of body contains specialised organs for attachment to the host. These are hooks, suckers, eyes as eye spots and auricles, etc.

(vi) Sensory organs are not well-developed.

(vii) Reproductive system of parasitic forms is highly developed with enormous power to reproduce.

(viii) Well defined excretory organs such as flame cells are present.

Question 7. What are the reasons that you can think of for the arthropods to constitute the largest group of the animal kingdom?

Answer Arthropods constitute the largest group of the animal kingdom. It is estimated that the Arthropoda population of the world is approximately a billion (10^{18}) individuals, in terms of species diversity, number of individuals and geographical distribution. It is the most successful phylum on the Earth that have ever existed. Arthropods are equipped with jointed appendages, which are variously adapted for walking, swimming, feeding, sensory reception and defence. The appendages of abdomen are associated with locomotion, reproduction and in some cases with defence as well.

The appendages of head are related to defence, whereas those of thorax are mainly associated with locomotion. These features are responsible for its large diversity.

Question 8. Water vascular system is the characteristic of which group of the following?

(i) Porifera (ii) Ctenophora
(iii) Echinodermata (iv) Chordata

Answer Echinodermata have the water vascular system.

Question 9. 'All vertebrates are chordates but all chordates are not vertebrates'. Justify the statement.

Answer Notochord is a characteristic feature of all chordates. The members of sub-phylum—Vertebrata possess notochord during the embryonic stage. But in adults the notochord is replaced by a cartilaginous or bony vertebral column. Whereas in member of other Sub-phyla of Chordata the notochord remain as such. The urochordate and cephalochordates retain the notochord during their entire life cycle. Thus, the absence of notochord in adult vertebrates suggest that all vertebrates are chordates but all chordates are not vertebrates.

Question 10. How important is the presence of air bladder is Pisces?

Answer In case of fishes, of class–Osteichthyes, *i.e.*, *Exocoetus* (flying fish), *Hippocampus* (sea horse), *Labeo* (rohu) and *Clarias* (magur), etc., air bladders are present which regulate the buoyancy and help these animals in swimming in deeper layers of water.

Question 11. What are the modifications that are observed in birds that help them fly?

Answer Flight adaptations in birds

(i) Boat-shaped body helps to propel through the air easily.
(ii) Feathery covering of body to reduce the friction of air.
(iii) Holding the twigs automatically by hindlimbs.
(iv) Extremely powerful muscles that enables the wings to work during flight.
(v) Bones are light, hollow and provide more space for muscle attachment. Presence of pneumatic bones which reduce the weight of body and help in flight.
(vi) The first four thoracic vertebrae are fused to form a furculum for walking of the wings.
(vii) Lungs are solid and elastic and have associated air sacs.

(viii) The power of accomodation of eyes is well developed due to the presence of comb-like structure pecten.

(ix) A single left ovary and oviduct to reduce the body weight.

Question 12. Could the number of eggs or young ones produced by an oviparous and viviparous mother be equal? Why?

Answer The number of eggs or young ones produced by an oviparous or viviparous mother cannot be equal. An oviparous mother gives rise to more number of eggs as some of them die during hatching and as they have to pass through a large number of developmental stages before becoming an adult. On the other hand, a viviparous mother gives rise to fewer number of young ones because there are less chances of their death. Moreover, they did not have to pass through any larval stage.

Question 13. Segmentation in the body is first observed in which of the following

(i) Platyhelminthes (ii) Annelida
(iii) Aschelminthes (iv) Arthropoda

Answer Segmentation in the body is first observed in Annelida. This phenomenon is known as metamerism.

Question 14. Match the following

A. Operculum	1. Ctenophora
B. Parapodia	2. Mollusca
C. Scales	3. Porifera
D. Comb plates	4. Reptilia
E. Radula	5. Annelida
F. Hairs	6. Cyclostomata and Chondrichthyes
G. Choanocytes	7. Mammalia
H. Gill slits	8. Osteichthyes

Answer

A. Operculum	8. Osteichthyes
B. Parapodia	5. Annelida
C. Scales	4. Reptilia
D. Comb plates	1. Ctenophora
E. Radula	2. Mollusca
F. Hairs	7. Mammalia
G. Choanocytes	3. Porifera
H. Gill slits	6. Cyclostomata and Chondrichthyes

Question 15. Prepare a list of some animals that are found parasitic on human beings.

Answer A list of parasitic animals on human beings

Parasite	In Part of Human Body
Leishmania donovani	Blood
Trichomonas vaginalis	Vagina of human female
Plasmodium vivax	Blood
Taenia solium	Intestine
Ascaris lumbricoides	Small intestine
Wuchereria bancrofti	Lymphatic and muscular system
Loa loa	Eyes
Fasciola hepatica	Liver and bile ducts
Entamoeba histolytica	Intestine
Trypanosoma gambiense	Blood

Selected NCERT Exemplar Problems

Very Short Answer Type Questions

Question 1. Identify the phylum in which adults exhibit radial symmetry and larva exhibit bilateral symmetry.

Answer Echinodermata.

Question 2. What is the importance of pneumatic bones and air sacs in Aves?

Answer Pneumatic bones in birds help in flight as they have air cavities to reduce weight. Air sacs are present in connection with lungs. They aid in the process of respiration.

Question 3. What is metagenesis? Mention an example, which exhibits this phenomenon.

Answer **Metagenesis** It is the phenomenon of alternation of generation, *i.e.*, one diploid generation alternates with the other haploid generation, *e.g.*, in *Obelia* two forms, *i.e.*, polyp and medusae are present. Polyp form asexually gives rise to medusae and medusae in turn sexually gives rise to polyps.

Question 4. What is the role of feathers?

Answer **The role of feathers** Feathers constitute very smooth covering over the body of birds to reduce the friction of the air. Due to non-conducting nature of these, body temperature is maintained. Feathers of wings, which are known as remiges form a continuous sheet for striking kwith the air in propulsion. Feathers of tail rectrices form fan-like structure and steer the body during flight.

Question 5. Which group of chordates possess sucking and circular mouth without jaws?

Answer Cyclostomates.

Question 6. Give one example each for an animal possessing placoid scales and that with cycloid scales.

Answer *Scolidon* (dog fish) have placoid scales, whereas cycloid scales are present in *Exocoetus* (flying fish).

Question 7. Mention two modifications in reptiles required for terrestrial mode of life.

Answer In order to lead terrestrial mode of life, the reptiles have their body covered by dry and cornified skin and epidermal layer is covered by scales or scutes, *e.g.*, *Testudo* (tortoise) and *Crocodilus* (crocodile), etc.

Question 8. Mention one example each for animals with chitinous exoskeleton and those covered by a calcareous shell.

Answer Animals with chitinous exoskeleton are *Anopheles*, *Cul*ex and *Aedes* mosquitoes. All these belong to phylum–Arthropoda. The animals of phylum–Mollusca have body covered by calcareous shell these are *Pila*, *Unio*, *Loligo*, etc.

Question 9. What is the role of radula in molluscs?

Answer Radula is a file-like rasping organ present in mollusca. Radula helps in feeding.

Question 10. Name the animal, which exhibits the phenomenon of bioluminescence. Mention the phylum to which it belongs.

Answer *Ctenoplana* exhibit the phenomenon of bioluminescence. It belongs to phylum–Ctenophora.

Question 11. Write one example each of the following in the space provided.

(a) Cold blooded animal …… .
(b) Warm blooded animal …… .
(c) Animal possessing dry and cornified skin …… .
(d) Dioecious animal …… .

Answer (a) *Scolidon* (dog fish)
(b) *Columba* (pigeon) and a bird
(c) *Testudo* (tortoise)
(d) *Ascaris* (round worm).

Question 12. Differentiate between a diploblastic and a triploblastic animal.

Answer Diploblastic animal are those in which body have two germ layers, *i.e.,* an external ectoderm and an internal endoderm, *e.g.,* coelenterates, triploblastic animals are those in which in addition to ectoderm and endoderm, a third germ layer, i.e., mesoglea is present in between, *e.g.,* chordates.

Question 13. Give an example of the following
(a) Roundworm
(b) Fish possessing poison sting
(c) A limbless reptile/amphibian
(d) An oviparous mammal

Answer (a) *Ascaris* (b) *Trygon* fish have poison sting (c) *Ichthyophis* Amphibia (d) *Bufo* (toad) is oviparous.

Question 14. Provide appropriate technical term in the space provided.
(a) Blood-filled cavity in arthropods ....
(b) Free-floating form of cnidaria ....
(c) Stinging organ of jelly fishes ....
(d) Lateral appendages in aquatic annelids ....

Answer (a) coelom
(b) medusa
(c) nematocytes
(d) parapodia.

Question 15. Match the following

Animals	Locomotory Organ
A. *Octopus*	1. Limbs
B. Crocodile	2. Comb plates
C. *Catla*	3. Tentacles
D. *Ctenophana*	4. Fins

Answer

	Animals	Locomotory Organ
A.	*Octopus*	3. Tentacles
B.	Crocodile	1. Limbs
C.	*Catla*	4. Fins
D.	*Ctenophana*	2. Comb plates

Short Answer Type Questions

Question 1. Differentiate between

(a) Open circulatory system and closed circulatory system.
(b) Oviparous and viviparous characteristic.
(c) Direct development and indirect development.

Answer

(a) **Differences between Open and Closed Circulatory System**

Open circulatory system The blood is pumped out from the heart and the cells and tissues directly bath in it.

Closed circulatory system The blood is circulated through a series of varying diameter vessels (arteries, veins and capillaries).

(b) **Differences between Oviparous and Viviparous Characters**

Oviparous These animals give birth to offsprings by egg production, *e.g.*, arthropods.

Viviparous These animals give birth to young ones, *e.g.*, mammals.

(c) Refer to Ans. 5 in Exercises of this chapter.

Question 2. Sort out the animals on the basis of their symmetry (radial or bilateral) coelenterates, ctenophores, annelids, arthropods and echinoderms.

Answer

S.N.	Animal	Type of Symmetry they Possess
1.	Coelenterates	Radial symmetry
2.	Ctenophores	Radial symmetry
3.	Annelids	Bilateral symmetry
4.	Arthropods	Bilateral symmetry
5.	Echinoderms	Radial symmetry

Question 3. There has been an increase in the number of chambers in heart during evolution of vertebrates. Give the names of the class of vertebrates having two, three or four chambered heart.

Answer

Vertebrate Class	Chambers in Heart
Chondrichthyes	Two
Amphibia	Three
Aves	Four

Question 4. Fill in the blank spaces appropriately

Phylum/Class	Excretory Organ	Circulatory Organ	Respiratory Organ
Arthropoda	—	—	Lungs/gills/tracheal system
—	Nephridia	Closed	Skin/parapodia
—	Metanephridia	Open	—
Amphibia	—	Closed	Lung

Answer

Phylum/Class	Excretory Organ	Circulatory Organ	Respiratory Organ
Arthropoda	Malpighian tubules	Open	Lungs/gills/tracheal System
Annelida	Nephridia	Closed	Skin/parapodia
Mollusca	Metanephridia	Open	Gills
Mammalia	Kidneys	Closed	Lung

Question 5. Match the following

A. Amphibia	1. Air bladder
B. Mammals	2. Cartilaginous notochord
C. Chondrichthyes	3. Mammary glands
D. Osteichthyes	4. Pneumatic bones
E. Cyclostomata	5. Dual habitat
F. Aves	6. Sucking and circular mouth without jaws

Answer

A. Amphibia	5. Dual habitat
B. Mammas	3. Mammary glands
C. Chondrichthyes	2. Cartilaginous notochord
D. Osteichthyes	1. Air bladder
E. Cyclostomata	6. Sucking and circular mouth without jaws
F. Aves	4. Pneumatic bones

Question 6. Endoparasites are found inside the host body. Mention the special structure, possessed by these and which enables them to survive in those conditions.

Answer The endoparasites such as *Taenia solium* and *Fasciola hepatica*, etc., are found inside the host body.

Special Features

(i) These have anaerobic respiration and gaseous exchange takes place through the general body surface.

(ii) These possess additional organs for attachment to the host. *Fasciola hepatica* possess acetabulum or posterior sucker for the attachment. *Taenia solium* possess hooks and suckers for attachment to host.

(iii) These organisms in order to survive inside host have shifted from aerobic mode respiration to anaerobic one.

Question 7. Match the following

Animal	Characteristic
A. *Pila*	1. Jointed appendages
B. Cockroach	2. Perching
C. *Asterias*	3. Water vascular system
D. *Torpedo*	4. Electric organ
E. Parrot	5. Presence of shell
F. Dog fish	6. Placoid scales

Answer

Animal	Characteristic
A. *Pila*	5. Presence of shell
B. Cockroach	1. Jointed appendages
C. *Asterias*	3. Water vascular system
D. *Torpedo*	6. Electric organ
E. Parrot	2. Perching
F. Dog fish	4. Placoid scales

Question 8. Differentiate between

(a) Open and closed circulatory system.
(b) Oviparity and viviparity.
(c) Direct and indirect development.
(d) Acoelomate and pseudocoelomate.
(e) Notochord and nerve cord.
(f) Polyp and medusa.

Answer

(a) **Open circulatory system** The blood is pumped out of heart and the cells and tissues directly bath in it.

Closed circulatory system The blood is pumped through a series of vessels of varying diameter (arteries veins and capillaries).

(b) **Oviparity and viviparity** The act of giving birth to young ones is known as viviparity as in mammals, whereas the process of formation of eggs by the adult is known as oviparity such as in arthropods.

(c) **Direct and indirect development** The development of an individual from adult without passing through any larval stage is known as direct development as in birds. In case of indirect development juvenile changes into adult one after passing through several larval stages as in insects.

(d) **Acoelomates** These animals lack the body cavity, *i.e.,* coelom, *e.g.,* Platyhelminthes.

Pseudocoelomates These animals have body cavity, which is not lined by the mesoderm, *e.g.,* Aschelminthes.

(e) **Notochord and nerve cord** Notochord is a mesodermally derived rod-like structure formed on the dorsal side during embryonic development in some animals. Nerve cord is a sensory tissue made up of nerve cells.

(f) **Polyp and medusa** The coelenterates exist in two forms, *i.e.,* polyp and medusa. Polyp is a sessile and cylindrical form, whereas medusa is umbrella-shaped and free swimming. Polyps produce medusae asexually and medusae forms the polyps sexually.

Question 9. Give the characteristic features of the following citing one example of each

(a) Chondrichthyes and Osteichthyes

(b) Urochordata and Cephalochordata

Answer (a) **Characteristic features of Chondrichthyes**

(i) These are marine animals with streamlined body and have cartilaginous endoskeleton.

(ii) Mouth is located ventrally. Gill slits are separate and without operculum.

(iii) In males, pelvic fins bear claspers, *e.g., Scoliodon* (dog fish).

Characteristic features of Osteichthyes

(i) It includes both marine and freshwater fishes with body endoskeleton.

(ii) The body is streamlined with terminal mouth.

(iii) Skin is covered with cycloid/ctenoid scales.

(iv) Air bladder is present which regulates buoyancy.

e.g., *Exocoetus* (flying fish), *Labeo* (rohu).

(b) **Characteristic features of Urochordata** Notochord is present only in larval tail. These are marine animals, *e.g.*, *Ascidia*, *Salpa*, etc.

Characteristic features of Cephalochordata The notochord extends from head to tail region and is persistent throughout their life, *e.g.*, *Branchiostoma* or Lancelet.

Question 10. Mention two similarities between

(a) Aves and mammals (b) A frog and crocodile

(c) A turtle and *Pila*

Answer

(a) **Similarities between aves and mammals**

(i) The members of both these groups are homeotherms, *i.e.*, warm blooded. They are able to maintain constant body temperature.

(ii) Heart is completely four-chambered.

(b) **Similarities between frog and crocodile**

(i) The members of both these groups are poikilothermous, *i.e.*, they lack the capacity to regulate their body temperature. They are cold-blooded animals.

(ii) Frog and crocodile are oviparous animals.

(c) **Similarities between turtle and *Pila***

(i) In both these animals, the body is covered with dry and cornified skin. In turtle the epidermal covering is known as scales, whereas in case of *Pila* it is known as calcerous shell.

(ii) Both these animals are oviparous.

Question 11. Name

(a) A limbless animal.

(b) A cold-blooded animal.

(c) A warm-blooded animal.

(d) An animal possessing dry and cornified skin

(e) An animal having canal system and spicules.

(f) An animal with cnidoblasts.

Answer (a) *Ichthyophis* (b) *Scoliodon* (dog fish)
(c) *Columba* (pigeon) (d) *Sycon* (sponge)
(e) *Obelia*.

Question 12. Give an example for each of the following
(a) A viviparous animal.
(b) A fish possessing a poison sting.
(c) A fish possessing an electric organ.
(d) An organ, which regulates buoyancy.
(e) Animal, which exhibits alternation of generation.
(f) Oviparous animal with mammary gland.

Answer (a) Human beings
(b) *Trygon*
(c) *Torpedo*
(d) Air bladder
(e) *Obelia*
(f) Platypus

Question 13. Excretory organs of different animals are given below.

Animal	Excretory Organ/Unit
A. *Balanoglossus*	1. Metanephridia
B. Leech	2. Nephridia
C. Locust	3. Flame cells
D. Liver fluke	4. Absent
E. Sea urchin	5. Malpighian tubules
F. *Pila*	6. Proboscis gland

Answer

Animal	Excretory Organ/Unit
A. *Balanoglossus*	c. Proboscis gland
B. Leech	2. Nephridia
C. Locust	5. Malpighian tubules
D. Liver fluke	3. Flame cells
E. Sea urchin	4. Absent
F. *Pila*	1. Metanephridia

Long Answer Type Questions

Question 1. Give three major differences between chordates and non-chordates and draw a schematic sketch of a Chordata showing those features.

Answer Differences between Chordates and Non-chordates

S.N.	Chordata	Non-chordata
1.	Notochord present.	Notochord absent.
2.	Central nervous system is dorsal, hollow and single.	Central nervous system is ventral, solid and double.
3.	Pharynx perforated by gill slits.	Gill slits are absent.
4.	Heart is ventral.	Heart is dorsal (if present).
5.	A post anal part (tail) is present.	Post anal tail is absent.

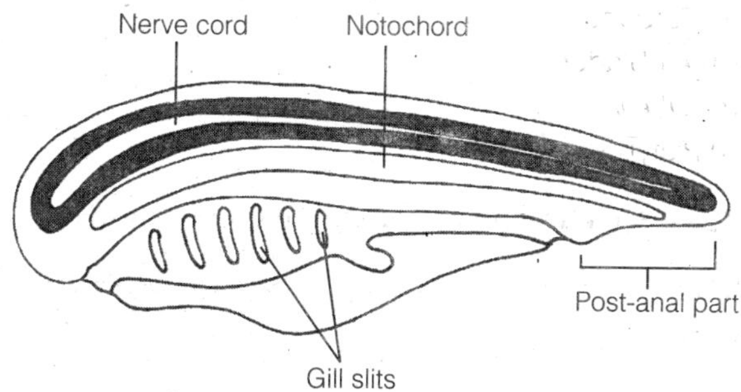

Schematic sketch to showing characteristics of Chordata

Question 2. What is the relationship between germinal layers and the formation of body cavity in case of coelomate, acoelomates and pseudocoelomates.

Answer There is a close relationship between germinal layers, *i.e.*, ectoderm, mesoderm, endoderm and the formation of body cavity.

(i) The body cavity, which is lined by mesoderm is known as **coelom**. Animals possessing coelom are called **coelomates**, *e.g.*, annelids, molluscs, arthropods, echinoderms, hemichordates and chordates.

(ii) In some animals instead of mesoderm, there are present scattered pouches in between the ectoderm and endoderm. Such type of body cavity is called pseudocoelom and the animals possessing them are called pseudocoelomates, *e.g.*, Aschelminthes.

(iii) There are some animals in which the body cavity is totally absent. These are known as acoelomates, *i.e.*, Platyhelminthes.

Question 3. Mammals are most adapted among the vertebrates. Elaborate.

Answer Mammals are the most adapted among the vertebrates. The following features explain this statements

(i) They have occur in all sorts of habitats including polar ice, deserts, oceans, mountains, forests of grasslands and dark caves.

(ii) They have better developed brain. Their brain has large cerebrum and cerebellum.

(iii) Mammals are homeothermous (warm-blooded), *i.e.*, they are capable is regulating their body temperature according to surrounding environment.

(iv) They have body covered with hairs and have mammary or milk producing glands.

(v) They are the only animals which nourish their young ones with milk.

(vi) They possess oil glands (sebaceous glands) and sweat glands (sudoriferous glands) in the skin.

(vii) They possess stwo pairs of limbs, which are adapted for walking, running, climbing, swimming, burrowing or flying.

(viii) Fertilisation is internal. They exhibit viviparity, *i.e.*, they give rise to young ones similar to them.

5

Morphology of Flowering Plants

Important Points

1. Morphology is the study of external structures on the basis of morphology plants are classified. Plants adapts various morphological adaptation according to the surrounding environment. Main two plants part are
   (i) root system (ii) shoot system
2. Root system includes the underground part of the flowering plant.
   (i) From seeds, radicle elongates and grows inside the soil to form primary root. In case of dicotyledonous plant, primary root elongates and bears lateral root of several orders referred as secondary and tertiary roots. This system is known as tap root system. These cell are rapidly dividing cell.
   (ii) Next to the meristematic zone. Zone of elongation is present. It gradually differentiates and mature.
   (iii) Next to zone of the elongation, zone of maturation is present. Those are fully matured cell which has lost the ability of cell division. The epidermal cells forms a very delicate thread-like structures called root hairs.
3. Roots are modified to perform different functions apart from mineral ion absorption some modification of root are:

(i) For storage
 (a) Tuberous — *Mirabilis jalapa*
 (b) Napiform tap root — *Beta vulgaris*
 (c) Conical tap root — Carrot
 (d) Fusiform tap root — Radish
 (e) Fasciculated root — Dahlia

(ii) For mechanical support.

(iii) In monocot plants like wheat primary root is short and large number of roots arises from base of the stem known as **fibrous root system**.

(iv) Adventitious root system is present in some plants, root arises from parts of the plants other than the radicle.

(v) Main functions of the root system are
 (a) absorption of water and mineral from soil.
 (b) provides proper anchorage support to the plant parts.
 (c) stores reserve food material and synthesise plant growth regulators.

4. Various parts of roots are

(i) **Root cap** Thimble-like structure present at apex of the root.

(ii) **Meristematic zone** Above the root there is region of meristematic activity. This region is very small, thin-walled and have dense cytoplasm.
 (a) **Stilt or brace root** These root develop obliquely from the basal nodes of the stem near the soil and grows downward into the soil known as stilt roots *e.g., Saccharum officinarum* (sugarcane), *Zea mays* (maize) and *Sorghum*.
 (b) **Prop or pillar roots** These are the adventitious roots, which develop from the large horizontal branches in trees like banyan (*Ficus benghalensis*).
 (c) **Climbing or clinging roots** Helps the plants in climbing by penetrating the cracks of the support, *e.g., Pothos* the money plant.

(iii) Physiological functions
 (a) **Assimilatory or photosynthetic roots** These are green and carryout photosynthesis *Trapa* and *Podostemon*.
 (b) **Parasitic or haustoria roots** Roots developed from parasitic plants for absorbing nourishment from their host.

(c) **Respiratory roots** In swampy areas many roots comes out of the ground and grows vertically upwards and as pneumatophores, *e.g.*, in **mangroves plant**.

5. Stem is an ascending part of the main axis of plant. It forms shoot system of the plant body.

   Characteristic features of stem are

   (i) It develops from the plumule of embryo.

   (ii) Clearly differentiated into nodes and internodes.

   (iii) Nodes bear leaves having axillary bud.

   (iv) Usually green when young, late it become woody and dark brown.

   (v) Stem spread out branches, which bears leaves, flower and fruit.

   (vi) Main functions of stem are

   (a) storage of food

   (b) support

   (c) protection

   (d) vegetative propagation.

6. Stems are also modified to perform various functions like

   (i) **Tendrils** Axillary buds are modified to form slender and spirally coiled tendril and help the plants to climb, *e.g.*, cucumber, pumpkin, watermelon and grape vines.

   (ii) **Thorns** Axillary buds are also modified into woody and Straight pointed thorns. These are found in many plants like (*Citrus* and *Bougainvillea*). These thorns protects the plant from browsing animals.

   (iii) Stems are also modified as underground stem like sucker, rhizome, corm, tuber and bulb.

   (iv) Lateral branch with short internodes and each node bears a rosette of leaves and a tuft of root found in aquatic plants like *Pistia* and *Eichhornia*.

7. Leaves are the most important vegetative organ of plant. Characteristic features of leaves are

   (i) It develops at node and bears a bud in its axil. Axillary bud later develop into branch.

   (ii) Leaves originate from shoot apical meristem and arranged in an acropetal order.

   (iii) It performs photosynthesis.

   (iv) Leaves consist of mainly three parts

   (a) Leaf base (b) Petiole (c) Lamina.

(v) Leaves are attached to the base of the stem through petiole. Lateral small leaf-like structures are present called **stipules**.

(vi) Sometimes leaf base is swollen and known as **pulvinus**.

(vii) Lamina or leaf blade is the green expanded part of the leaf with veins and veinlets.

8. Venation is the arrangement of veins and veinlets in the lamina of the leaf. Two type of venation is present
   (i) **Reticulate venation** Veinlets forms a network egg in dicotyledonous plant.
   (ii) **Parallel venation** Venis are parallel to each other within a vein, *e.g.*, in monocotyledonous plant.

9. Leaves are of two types

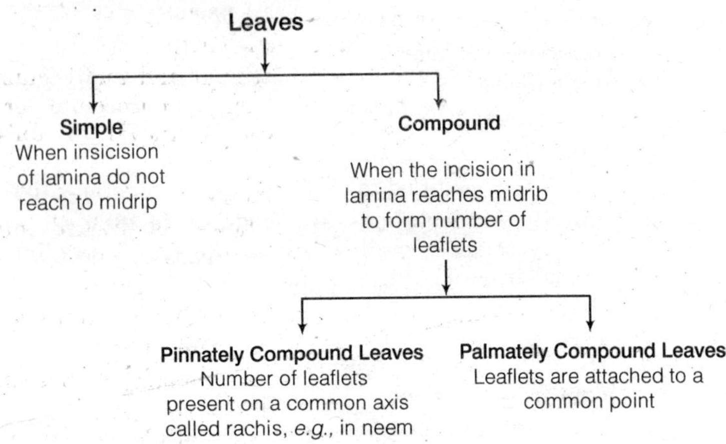
Leaves
Simple
When insicision of lamina do not reach to midrip
Compound
When the incision in lamina reaches midrib to form number of leaflets
Pinnately Compound Leaves
Number of leaflets present on a common axis called rachis, e.g., in neem
Palmately Compound Leaves
Leaflets are attached to a common point

10. Pattern of arrangement of leaves on the stem or branch. It is of three types
    (i) **Alternate type** Single leaf arises at each node in an alternate manner, *e.g.*, China rose, mustard, etc.
    (ii) **Opposite type** A pair of leaves arises at each node and opposite to each other, *e.g.*, in *Calotropis* and guava plants.

11. (i) Leaves may be converted into spines, *e.g.*, in cacti.
    (ii) Petioles may turn green to perform photosynthesis.
    (iii) Leaves of certain insectivorous plant are modified such as pitcher plant venus fly trap.

12. Flower is a condensed modified shoot in which internodes do not elongate shoot apical meristem changes to the floral meristem.

(i) Inflorescence is the arrangement of flowers on the floral axis two major type of inflorescence are
   (a) racemose (b) cymose type
(ii) In racemose type of inflorescence, flowers are borne on the lateral side of the main axis.
(iii) In cymose type of inflorescence main axis terminates in a flower and flowers are arranged in a basipetal manners.

13. Reproductive unit of plants is the flower meant for sexual reproduction
   (i) Swollen stalk or pedicle of the flower is known as **thalamus** or **receptacle**.
   (ii) These are two essential and two non-essential whorls.
   (iii) Two non-essential whorls are
      (a) calyx (b) corolla
   (iv) Two essential whorls are
      (a) **Gynoecium** (carpel—female parts)
      (b) **Androecium** (anther —male part)
   (v) When flower bears both gynoecium and androecium it is called bisexual flowers. If only androecium or only gynoecium are present flower is known as unisexual flower.
   (vi) Flower shows two type of symmetry
      (a) **Actinomorphic** When flower is divided into two similar halves in any plane passing through center, *e.g.*, mustard, datura.
      (b) **Zygomorphic** When flower is divided into two equal halves when cut in a one particular plane.
   (vii) Depending upon number of floral appendages these may be trimerous, tetramerous or pentamerous.
   (viii) At the base of the flower reduced leaf-like structure called bracts is present.
   (ix) On the basis of position of gynoecium flowers are described as
      (a) **Hypogynous flower** (superior ovary) Gynoecium is present above also other floral parts, *e.g.*, China rose, brinjal.
      (b) **Perigynous** Gynoecium is situated at the centre and other floral parts are present on the rim of thalamus, *e.g.*, plum, rose, peach. Ovary is half inferior.
      (c) **Epigynous** Ovary is fused with thalamus and other floral parts are present above the ovary.

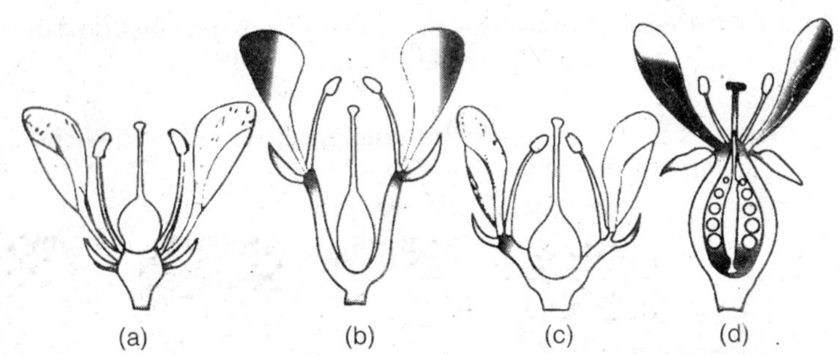

Position of floral parts on thalamus : (a) Hypogynous (b) and (c) Perigynous (d) Epigynous

14. Various parts of the flower are
    (i) **Calyx**
        (a) Outermost whorl called sepals.
        (b) These are green leaf like.
        (c) May be [Gamosepalous (sepals united) / Polysepalous (sepals free).
    (ii) **Corolla**
        (a) It is coloured component of flower called petals. Those are bright in colour and attract insects for pollination.
        (b) Corolla may be [Gamopetalous (petals united) / Polypetalous (petals free)
    (iii) Arrangement pattern sepals and petals in flower with respect to each other is called aestivation. Main type of aestivation are
        (a) **Valvate** sepals and petals just touch each other at the margin without overlapping.
        (b) **Twisted** One appendage overlaps the other appendage.
        (c) **Imbricate** margins of sepals and petals overlap. One another not in one direction, *e.g.*, margins of sepals and petals.
        (d) **Vexillary** In vexillary or papilionaceous type of aestivation there are five petals largest overlaps the two lateral petals (wings).

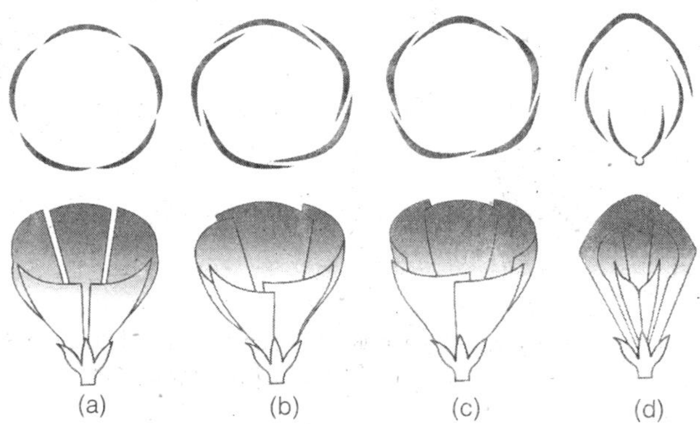

Types of aestivation in corolla : (a) Valvate (b) Twisted (c) Imbricate (d) Vexillary

15. Androecium is composed of stamens which represents male reproductive organ consist of a stalk/ filament anther.
    (i) **Anther** is bilobed having two chambers in one lobe called pollen sacs. Pollen grains are produced in pollen sac.
    (ii) If pollen grain are non-durable then stamen is called **staminode**.
    (iii) Stamens may be attached to petals called epipetalous condition, *e.g.*, in brinjal.
    (iv) When stamens are attached to perianth in the flower condition is epiphyllous condition.
    (v) Stamens may be united into one bundle called
        (a) monadelphous condition (stamens form one bundle)
        (b) diadelphous condition (stamens fuses to form two bundles).
16. Female reproductive part of flower is carpel which consist of three part namely (a) Ovary (b) Style and (c) Stigma.
    (i) Uppermost part is stigma to which pollen grain attaches.
    (ii) Ovary has enlarged basal part.
    (iii) Style connects the ovary to the stigma.
    (iv) Ovules are present inside ovary attached to placenta.
    (v) One or more carpels may be free (apocarpous) or may be fused. Syncarpous, *e.g.*, mustard and tomato plant.
    (vi) Ovules are arranged in ovary in a particular pattern known as placentation. It may be
        (a) **Marginal** ovules are born on ridge since placenta forms a ridge.

(b) **Axile** placenta is axial and ovules are attached to multilocular ovary, *e.g.*, in China rose, tomato, lemon.
(c) **Parietal placentation** ovules develop on the inner wall of ovary. It is one chambered or two chambered due to formation of false septum, *e.g.*, mustard and argemone.
(d) **Free central placentation** Ovules are brone of central axis and septa are absent, *e.g.*, in dianthus and primrose.
(e) **Basal placentation** It develops at the base of the ovary and single ovule is attached to it, *e.g.*, in sunflower and marigold.

17. After fertilisation, ovary matures and ripens to form fruit.
    (i) If fruit is formed without fertilisation, it is known as parthenocarpic fruit.
    (ii) It consists of three walls
        (a) pericarp outer covering of fruit
        (b) mesocarp
        (d) endocarp
    (iii) Mango and coconut are drupe they develop from monocarpellary superior ovaries and are one seeded. It is differentiated into thin epicarp middle fleshy mesocarp inner stony endocarp.

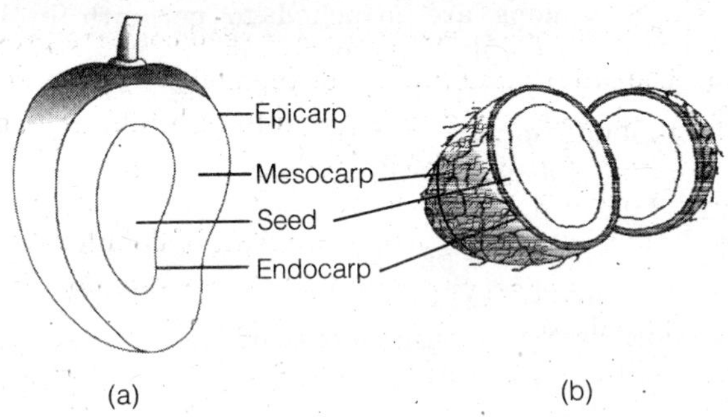

Parts of a fruit : (a) Mango (b) Coconut

18. After fertilisation ovules develops into seed made up of seed coat and an embryo.

    On the basis of number of cotyledons present. These are divided into
    (i) monocotyledonous plant.
    (ii) dicotyledonous plant.

(i) Monocotyledonous seeds are
   (a) endospermic (except orchids).
   (b) seed coat is membranous and fused with cell wall.
   (c) outer covering of endosperm called aluerone layer is present, which separates the embryo from endosperm.
   (d) embryo is small and shield shaped. Cotyledon is present called scutellum. Has short axis with a plumule and radicle.
   (e) cleoptile covers plumule, while radicle is enclosed by coleorhiza.

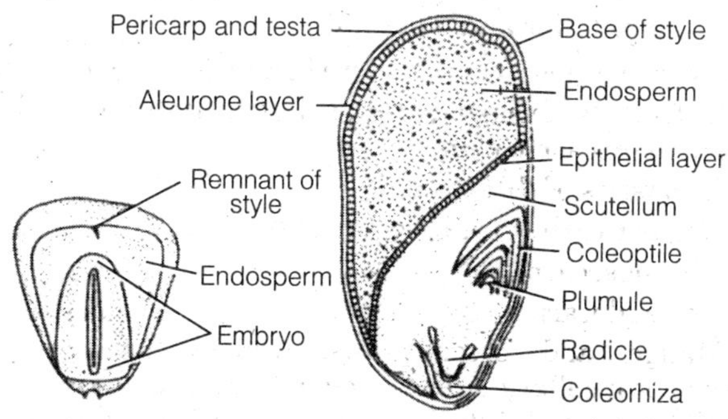

Structure of a monocotyledonous seed

(ii) In dicotyledonous seed two outer seed coat are present
   (a) The outer testa and inner tegmen.
   (b) Seed is attached to fruit through hilum. It has a small pore called micropyle.
   (c) Cotyledons are fleshy.
   (d) Endosperm is formed as a result of dobule fertilisation.
   (e) Seeds of bean, gram and pea are non-endospermic.

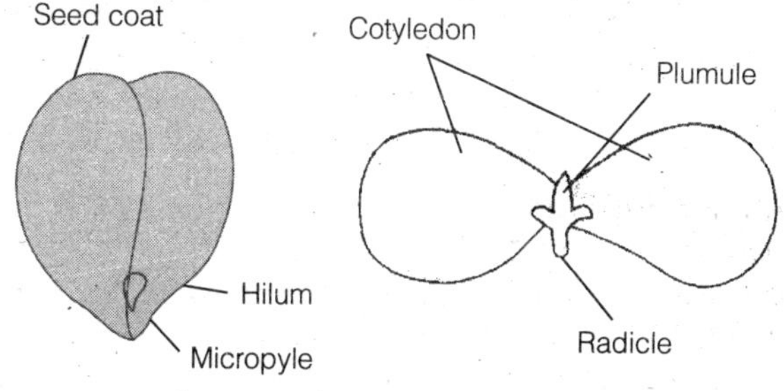

Structure of a dicotyledonous seed

19. Technical description of flowering plant.
20. Floral formula and floral diagram represent the floral characters inflorescence and flower parts various symbols in floral formula is represented by

    (a) Br — Bracteate
    (b) K — Calyx
    (c) C — Corolla
    (d) P — Perianth
    (e) A — Androecium
    (f) G — Gynoecium
    (g) $\underline{G}$ — Superior ovary
    (h) $\overline{\quad}$ — Inferior ovary
    (i) ♂ — Male
    (j) ♀ — Female
    (k) ⚥ — Bisexual
    (l) ϕ — Actinomorphic
    (m) % — Zygomorphic

21. Floral formula of some families

    (i) **Fabaceae/Leguminaceae/Papillonoidae** vegetative characters – Trees, shrubs, herbs, root with root nodules.

    Stem Erect or climber
    Leaves Alternate, pinately compound
    Floral characters Bisexual zygomorphic
    Inflorescence 5 sepals
    Flower Bisexual zygomorphic
    Calyx 5 gamosepalous

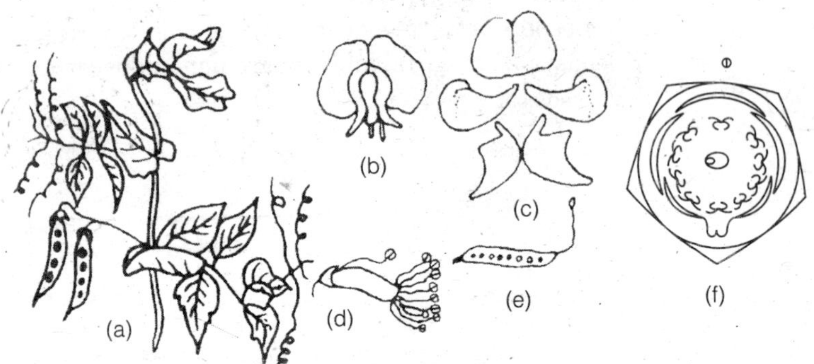

Pisum sativum (pea) plant : (a) Flowering twig (b) Flower (c) Petals (d) Reproductive parts (e) L.S. carpel (f) Floral diagram

Corolla 5 polypetalous

Androecium Ten, diadelphous, anther dithecous

Gynoecium Ovary superior

Fruit

Floral formula $\%, ⚥\ K_{(5)}\ C_{1+2+(2)}\ A_{(9)+1}\ G_{\underline{1}}$

(ii) **Solanaceae** (potato family)

Distributed in tropics and sub-tropics. Mostly herbs, shrubs and tress.

Stem Herbaceous rarely woody, erect and cylindrical

Leaves Alternate simple

Floral characters Solitary, axillary and cymose

Flower Bisexual and actinomorphic

Calyx 5 and united valvate aestivation

Corolla 5 and valvate aestivation

Androecium 5 and epipetalous.

Gynoecium Bicarpellary and syncarpous

Fruit Berry or capsule

Seeds Endospermous

Floral formula $\oplus, ⚥\ K_{(5)}\ \overset{\frown}{C_{(5)}\ A_5}\ G_{(\underline{2})}$

Economically

Important cultivers Tomato , brinjal, chilli, potato, etc.

Medicine Ashwgandha.

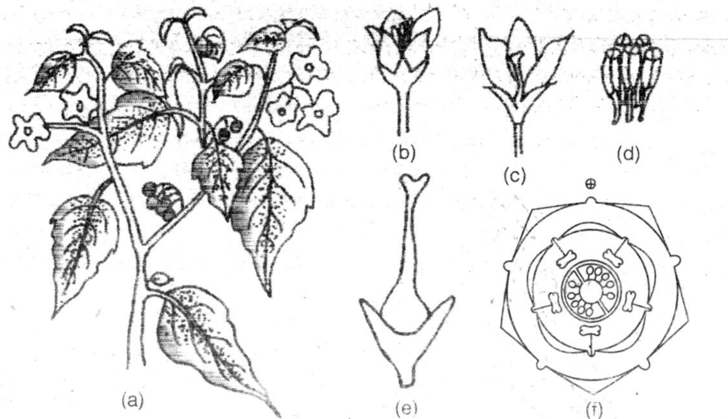

Solanum nigrum (makoi) plant : (a) Flowering twig (b) Flower (c) L.S. of flower (d) Stamens (e) Carpel (f) Floral diagram

(iii) **Liliaceae**

Vegetative character Representative of monocotyledonous plant.

Perennial herbs with underground bulbs/ corms/ rhizomes.

Leaves Basal, alternate, parallel venation

Inflorescence Solitary / cymose

Flower Bisexual, actinomorphic

Perianth Tepal six (3 + 3) valvate aestivation

Androecium Stamen six (3 + 3)

Gynoecium Tricarpellary, syncarpous and ovary superior

Fruit Capsule

Seed Endospermous

Floral formula Br ⊕ ⚥ P_{3+3} A_{3+3} $G_{(\underline{3})}$

Economic important plants

Ornamental Tulip, *Gloriosa*

Medicinal *Aloe*

Vegetable *Asparagus*

Colchicine *Colchicum autumnale*

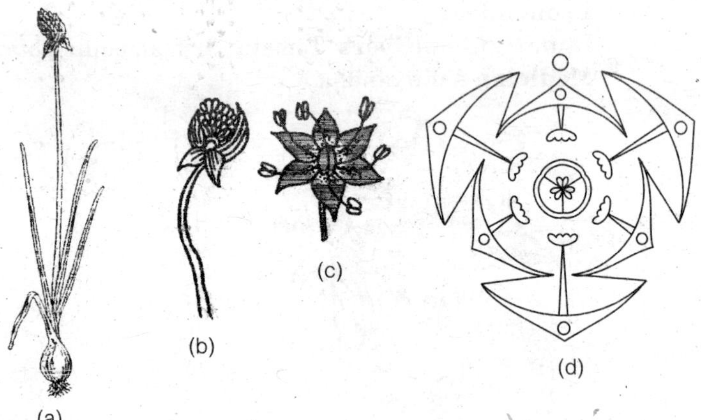

Allium cepa (onion) plant : (a) Plant (b) Inflorescence (c) Flower (d) Floral diagram

Exercises

Question 1. What is meant by modification of root? What type of modification of root is found in the

(a) Banyan tree (b) Turnip
(c) Mangrove trees

Answer **Modification of root** Roots in some plants change their shape and structure and become modified to perform functions, other than absorption and conduction of water and minerals. The roots are modified for water, absorption, support, storage of food and respiration.

(a) A banyan tree have hanging roots known as prop roots.
(b) The roots of turnip get modified to become swollen and store food.
(c) The roots of mangrove trees get modified to grow vertically upwards and help to get oxygen for respiration. These are known as pneumatophores.

Question 2. Justify the following statements on the basis of external features

(a) Underground parts of a plant are not always roots.
(b) Flower is a modified shoot.

Answer

(a) Underground parts of a plant are not always roots, they are subterranean stems which do not have root hairs and root cap.

Have terminal bud, nodes and internodes.

Have leaves on the nodes.

Most of the underground stems such as sucker, rhizome, corm, tubers, bulb, etc., store food, form aerial shoots.

(b) Flower is a modified shoot because
 (i) It possess nodes and internodes.
 (ii) It may develop in the axil of small leaf-like structure called bract.
 (iii) Flowers get modified into bulbils or fleshy buds in some plants.
 (iv) Anatomically the pedicel and thalamus of a flower resemble that of stem.
 (v) The vascular supply of different organs of flower resemble that of normal leaves.
 (vi) In the flower of *Degeneria*, the stamens are expanded like leaves and the carpels appear like folded leaves.

Question 3. How is a pinnately compound leaf different from a palmately compound leaf?

Answer In pinnately compound leaf, the number of leaflets are present on a common axis, the rachis, which represents the midrib of the leaf as in neem. In case of a palmately compound leaf, the leaflets are attached at a common point, *i.e.*, at the tip of petiole as in silk cotton.

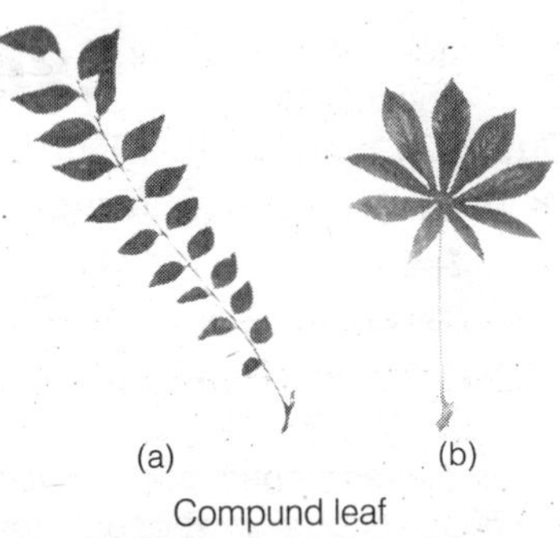

Compund leaf
(a) Pinnately (b) Palmately

Question 4. Explain with suitable examples the different types of phyllotaxy.

Answer Phyllotaxy is the pattern of arrangement of leaves on the stem or branch. This is usually of three types – alternate, opposite and whorled.

(i) In **alternate** phyllotaxy, a single leaf arises at each node in alternate manner, as in China rose, mustard and sunflower plants.

(ii) In **opposite** type of phyllotaxy, a pair of leaves arise at each node and lie opposite to each other as in *Calotropis* and guava plants.

(iii) If more than two leaves arise at each node and form a whorl, it is called as **whorled**, as in *Alstonia*.

Different types of phyllotaxy (a) Alternate (b) Opposite (c) Whorled

Question 5. Define the following terms

(a) Aestivation (b) Placentation (c) Actinomorphic
(d) Zygomorphic (e) Superior Ovary (f) Perigynous Flower
(g) Epipetalous

Answer

(a) **Aestivation** The mode of arrangement of sepals or petals in floral bud with respect to the other members of the same whorl is known as aestivation. The main types of aestivations are twisted, valvate, imbricate, etc.

(b) **Placentation** The arrangement of ovules within the ovary is known as placentation. The main types of placentations are marginal, parietal, basal, free central and axile.

(c) **Actinomorphic** When a flower can be cut into two equal radial halves in any radial plane passing through the centre, it is said to be actinomorphic, *e.g.,* mustard.

(d) **Zygomorphic** When a flower cannot be cut into two equal radial halves in any radial plane passing through the centre, it is said to be zygomorphic, *e.g.*, pea.

(e) **Superior ovary** In hypogymous flower, the gynoecium occupies the highest position while the other parts are situated below it. The ovary in such flower is said to be superior, *e.g.,* mustard.

(f) **Perigynous flower** If gynoecium is situated in the centre and other parts of the flower are located on the rim of the thalamus almost at the same level. Then this is known as a perigynous flower, *e.g.,* plum, etc.

(g) **Epipetalous flower** A flower in which the stamens are attached to the petals as in brinjal.

Question 6. Differentiate between

(a) Racemose and cymose inflorescence
(b) Fibrous root and adventitious root
(c) Apocarpous and syncarpous ovary

Answer

(a) **Racemose and cymose inflorescence** Racemose inflorescence is indeterminate or indefinite inflorescence in which penduncle can produce indefinite number of flowers due to continued activity of growing point. For example, Raceme, spike, spadix inflorescences, etc. In cymose inflorescence, the growing point of the peduncle is used in the formation of a flower.

(b) **Fibrous root and adventitious root** Fibrous roots are underground roots which are thin, branched and thread like. They develop from the base of erect stem, *e.g.,* wheat, barley. The adventitous roots arise from part of the flower other than radicle. Such as in sweet potato, etc.

(c) **Apocarpous and syncarpous ovary** If the carpels are two or more, and are fused. The fused condition of the carpels is known as syncarpous, *e.g.,* pentacarpellary condition in China rose. It there are two or more carpels and they are free, then this condition is called apocarpous, *e.g.,* polycarpellary apocarpous as in *Ranunculus*.

Question 7. Draw the labelled diagrams of the following

(a) Gram seed

(b) V.S. of maize

Answer

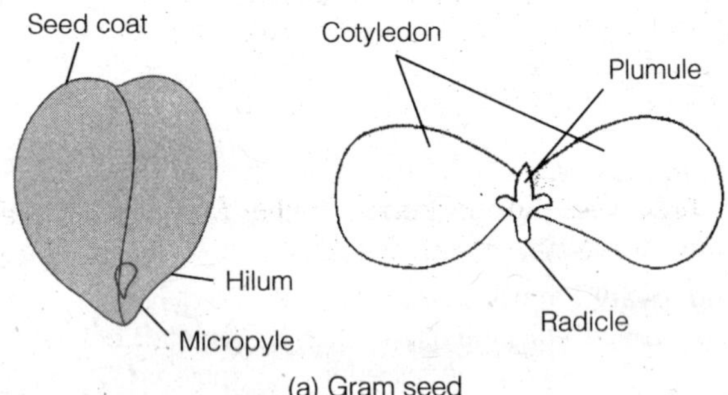

(a) Gram seed

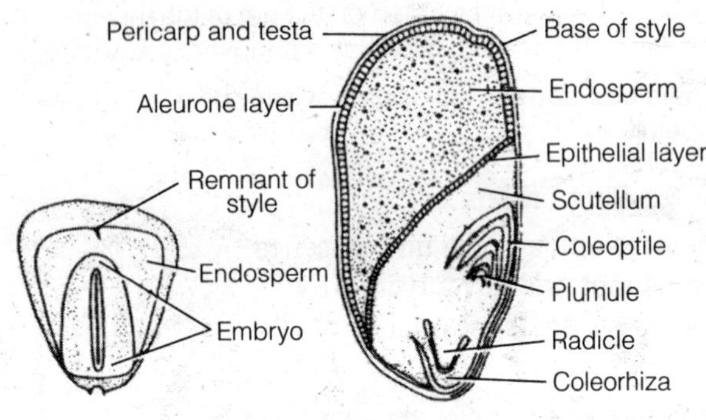

(b) V.S. of maize seed

Question 8. Describe modifications of stem with suitable examples.

Answer **Modifications of stem** Stems are modified to perform various functions. Stem modifications are as follows:

(a) **Stem tendril** They may be branched with scale leaves in the region of branching (i) Axillary, *e.g.*, *Passiflora*, (ii) Extra axillary, *e.g.*, *Luffa*, *Cucurbita*, (iii) Scorpioid stem tendrids, *e.g.*, *Vitis vinifera*, (iv) Floral bud, *e.g.*, *Antigonon*.

(b) **Stem thorns** These are stiff sharp structures which are formed for reducing transpiration and protection from animals. Thorns are generally axillary, *e.g.*, *Citrus, Pomegranate*, etc. In *Alhagi* the thorn bear flowers.

(c) **Phylloclades** They are green, photosynthetic, often succulent stems of indefinite growth. Function of leaves is performed by stem. Phylloclades are formed in an adaptation to dry habitats, *e.g., Euphorbia soyleana, Opuntia.*

(d) **Cladodes** (cladophylls) They are green photosynthetic stems of limited growth with leaves reduced to scales or modified into spines, *e.g., Ruscus, Asparagus.* Cladodes of *Ruscus* are leaf like, borne in the axils of scale leaves, having a floral bud and scale leaf in the middle.

Question 9. Take one flower each of the families Fabaceae and Solanaceae and write its floral formulae. Also draw their floral diagram after studying them.

Answer *Pisum sativum* (pea) flower of family–Fabaceae.

Floral Formula % ⚥ $K_{(5)}\ C_{1+2+(2)}\ A_{(9)+1}\ G_{\underline{1}}$

Solanum tuberosum (potato) flower of family–Solanaceae.

Floral Formula ⊕ ⚥ $K_{(5)}\ \overparen{C_{(5)}\ A_5}\ G_{(\underline{2})}$

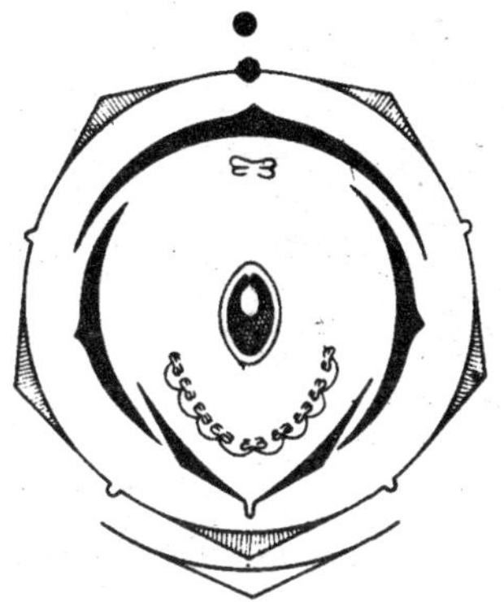

Floral formula of *Pisum*

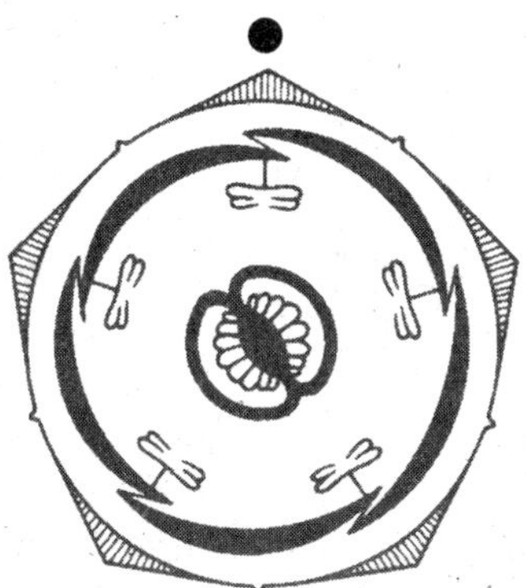

Floral formula of *Solanum*

Question 10. Describe the various types of placentations found in flowering plants.

Answer **Types of Placentations** The arrangement of ovules within the ovary is known as placentation. The placentations are of different types – marginal, axile, parietal, basal, central and free central.

Marginal placentation In this placentation, the placenta forms a ridge along the ventral suture of the ovary and the ovules are borne on this ridge forming two rows as in pea.

Axile placentation In this placentation, the placenta is axile and the ovules are attached to it in a multilocular ovary as in China rose, tomato, etc.

Parietal placentation In this placentation, the ovules develop on the inner wall of the ovary or on peripheral part. Ovary is one chambered but it becomes two chambered due to the formation of a false septum known as replam, *e.g.*, mustard.

Free central placentation In this type of placentation, the ovules are present on the central axis of ovary and septa are absent as in *Dianthus* and primrose.

Basal placentation In this placentation, the placenta develops at the base of ovary and a single ovule is attached to it, as in sunflower.

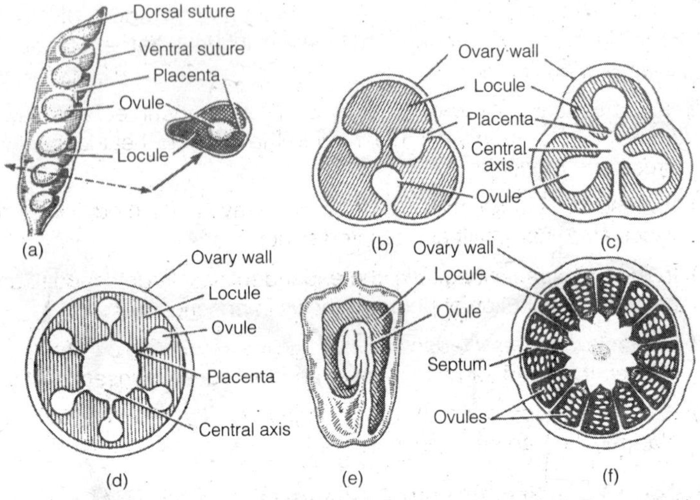

Types of placentation : (a) Marginal (b) Axile (c) Parietal (d) Free central (e) Basal (f) Superficial

Question 11. What is a flower? Describe the parts of a typical angiospermic flower.

Answer **Flower** It is a condensed modified reproductive shoot found in angiosperms. It often develops in the axile of a small leaf-like structure called **bract**. The stalk of the flower is called pedicel. The tip of the pedicel or the base of flower has a broad highly condensed multinodal region called **thalamus**.

A flower has four floral structures:

(i) **Calyx** It is made up of sepals. These are green in colour and help in photosynthesis.

(ii) **Corolla** It is the brightly coloured part containing petals.

(iii) **Androecium** It is the made up of reproductive part which consists of stamens. A stamen has a long filament and terminal anther. The anther produces the pollen grains.

(iv) **Gynoecium** It is the female reproductive part which consists of carpels. A carpel has three parts, *i.e.,* style, stigma and ovary. The ovary bears the ovules.

Question 12. How do the various leaf modifications help plants?

Answer Leaf modification in pants

(i) In some plant, the leaf and leaf parts get modified to form green, long, thin unbranched and sensitive thread-like structures called tendrils. The tendrils coil around the plant and provide support to the plant in climbing. Tendrils are present in pea, garden *Nasturtium, Clematis*, *Smilax*, etc.

(ii) In some plants, the leaves get modified to form curved stiff claw like hooks to help the plant in cleaning to the support. Leaf let hooks are present in *Bignonia*.

(iii) In case of *Acacia* and *Zizyphus*, the leaves get modified to form vasculated, hard, stiff and pointed structures.

(iv) In case of *Acacia longifolia*, the expanded petiole gets modified and perform the function of photosynthesis in absence of lamina.

(v) In plants such as *Nepenthes*, the lamina is modified to form large pitcher. It is used for storing water and for digesting insect protein.

(vi) In case of *Utricularia*, the leaf segments are modified into small bladders, to trap small animals.

Question 13. Define the term inflorescence. Explain the basis for the different types inflorescence in flowering plants.

Answer **Inflorescence** is the mode of arrangement of flowers in a group on a branch (peduncles). Depending upon whether the apex gets converted into a flower or continues to grow, the two major types of inflorescences are–racemose and cymose.

Racemose inflorescence In this type of inflorescences, the main axis continues to grow, the flowers are borne laterally in an acropetal succession. Racemose inflorescences are of various types such as raceme, corymb, umbel, spike, spikelet, strobile, catkin, spadix and capitulum inflorescence.

Cymose inflorescence It is also called definite or determinate inflore - scence because the growing point of the peduncle is used up in the formation of a flower. Cymose inflorescences are mainly of three types, *i.e.*, uniparous or monochasial cyme, biparous or dichasial cyme and multiparous or polychasial cyme.

Question 14. Write the floral formula of a actinomorphic, bisexual, hypogynous flower with five united sepals, five free petals, five free stamens and two united carpels with superior ovary and axile placentation.

Answer Floral formula ⊕, ⚥, $K_{(5)}$, C_5, A_5, $G_{(\underline{2})}$

Question 15. Describe the arrangement of floral members in relation to their insertion on thalamus.

Answer A flower is a condensed specialised reproductive shoot found in angiosperms. The stalk of the flower is known as pedicel. The tip of the pedicel or the base of the flower has a broad highly condensed multinodal region called thalamus. The floral parts of a flower are present on the thalamus. Starting from below, they are green sepals or calyx, coloured petals or corolla, stamens or androecium and carpels or gynoecium.

Selected NCERT Exemplar Problems

Very Short Answer Type Questions

Question 1. Roots obtain oxygen from air in the soil for respiration. In the absence or deficiency of O_2, root growth is restricted or completely absent. How do the plants growing in marsh lands or swamps obtain their O_2 required for respiration?

Answer In case of plants grown in swamps such as in *Rhizophora*, the roots come out of the ground and grow vertically upwards. Such roots called pneumatophores help to get oxygen for respiration. These roots are also known as respiratory roots.

Question 2. Write floral formula of a flower which is bisexual; actinomorphic; five sepals; twisted aestivation, five petals; valvate aestivation; six stamens; ovary tricarpellary; syncarpous; superior; trilocular with axile placentation.

Answer Floral formula of the flower

$$⊕, ⚥, K_{(5)}\ C_5\ A_6\ G_{(\underline{3})}$$

Question 3. In *Opuntia,* the stem is modified into a flattened green structure to perform the function of leaves (*i.e.*, photosynthesis). Cite some other examples of modifications of plant parts for the purpose of photosynthesis.

Answer *Euphorbia royleana, Euphorbia triacalli, Casuarina, Muhlebechbia*, etc. are examples of phylloclades which are modified for the purpose of photosynthesis. Similarly in cladodes found in *Asparagus*, the green stem branches are present which perform the function of photosynthesis in place of leaves.

Question 4. In swampy areas like the Sunderbans in West Bengal, plants bear special kind of roots called

Answer Pneumatophores.

Question 5. In aquatic plants like *Pistia* and *Eichhornia*, leaves and roots are found near.

Answer Water surface.

Question 6. Reticulate and parallel venation are characteristic of .... and .... respectively.

Answer Reticulate venation occurs in dicotyledonous plants and parallel venation occurs in monocotyledonous plants.

Question 7. Which parts in ginger and onion are edible?

Answer Both in ginger and onion, the edible parts are underground stem.

Question 8. In epigynous flower, ovary is situated below the

Answer Other floral parts on thalamus.

Question 9. Add the missing floral organs of the given floral formula of Fabaceae.

$$Br \; ⚥ \; K_5 \; ..... \; A_{(...)} \; \overline{G}_{(5)}$$

Answer $Br \ominus ⚥ \; K_{(5)} \; C_{1+2+2} \; A_{1+(9)} \; \overline{G}_{(5)}$

Question 10. Name the body part modified for food storage in the following

(a) Carrot ....
(b) *Colocasia* ....
(c) Sweet potato ....
(d) *Asparagus* ....
(e) Radish ....
(f) Potato ....
(g) Dahlia ....
(h) Turmeric ....
(i) Gladiolus ....
(j) Ginger ....
(k) *Portulaca* ....

Answer

(a) Carrot	Tap roots
(b) *Colocasia*	Stem
(c) Sweet potato	Roots
(d) *Asparagus*	Roots
(e) Radish	Roots
(f) Potato	Stem
(g) Dahlia	Adventitious roots
(h) Turmeric	Adventitious roots
(i) Gladiolus	Stem
(j) Ginger	Stem
(k) *Portulaca*	Adventitious roots.

Short Answer Type Questions

Question 1. Give one example of roots that develop from different parts of the plant other than radicle.

Answer In case of grass and banyan tree, the roots develop from different parts of the plant other than radicle. Such type of roots are known as adventitious roots. For example, **Prop** roots grow from horizontal branches of plant, *e.g., Ficus bengalensis.* Stilt roots develop from the basal node of the stem, *e.g.,* in *Zea mays* and *Sorghum officinarum*, etc.

Question 2. The essential functions of roots are anchorage and absorption of water and minerals in the terrestrial plant. What functions are associated with the roots of aquatic plants. How are roots of aquatic plants and terrestrial plants different?

Answer The roots of aquatic plants such as *Hydrilla, Ceratophyllum,* etc., function as a balancing and anchorage organ. In terrestrial plants, roots perform the function of water and mineral absorption. In case of aquatic plants, an elongated loose cap like covering called **root pockets** are present at the tips of roots, *e.g., Pistia* and *Lemna*. Root pockets function as balancers. In terrestrial plants, root cap is present.

Question 3. Draw diagrams of a typical monocot and dicot leaves to show their venation pattern.

Answer

(a) (b)

Venation in leaves : (a) reticulate venation (dicot leaf)
(b) Parallel venation (monocot leaf)

Question 4. Given below are a few floral formulae of some well known plants. Draw floral diagrams from these formulae.

(a) $\oplus ⚥\ K_{(5)}\ C_{(5)}\ A_{(5)}\ G_{(2)}$

(b) $\oplus ⚥\ K_{(5)}\ C_{1+2+(2)}\ A_{(9)+1}\ G_{\underline{1}}$

(c) $\oplus ⚥\ K_5\ C_5\ A_{5+5}\ G_{(5)}$

Answer

(a) It is the floral formula of Solanaceae family, *i.e., Solanum tuberosum* (patato).

(b) It is the floral formula of *Pisum sativum* (pea).

(c) It is the floral formula of *Hibiscus rosa-sinensis* (rose).

Note For floral formula of *Solanum* and *Pisum sativum* Refer to Ans. No. 9 in Exercises of this chapter.

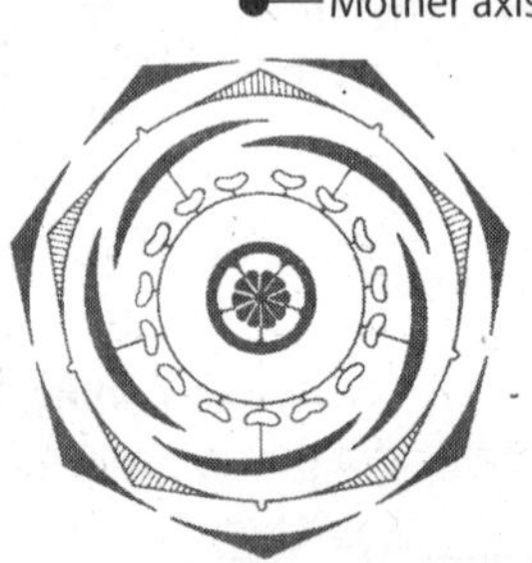

Floral digram of *Hibiscus rosa-sinensis*

Question 5. Reticulate venation is found in dicot leaves, while in monocot leaves venation is of parallel type. Biology being a 'Science of exceptions', find out any exception to this generalisation.

Answer Parallel venation is found in dicot *Calophyllum* and reticulate venation is found in monocot *Alocasia, Smilax*, etc. But in fact, reticulate venation is a characteristic feature of dicots and parallel venation that of monocots.

Question 6. You have heard of several insectivorous plants that feed on insects. *Nepenthes* or the pitcher plant is one such example, which usually grows in shallow water or in marsh lands. What part of the plant is modified into a 'pitcher'? How does this modification help the plant for food even though it can photosynthesise like any other green plant?

Answer In case of *Nepenthes* also known as pitcher plant, the lamina of the leaf is modified into a pitcher. It is an insectivorous plant. It grows in nitrogen deficit soil. Although this plant can photosynthesise its food, but this modification helps in engulfing the insect bodies. The plant utilises the protein and nitrogen content of the insect.

Question 7. How can you differentiate between free central and axile placentation?

Answer In case of free central type of placentation, the ovules are borne on central axis and septa are absent, as in *Dianthus* and Primrose. Whereas in case of axile placentation, the placenta is axile and the ovules are attached to it in a multilocular ovary. This type of placentation is seen in members of family–Malvaceae, *e.g.*, China rose, etc.

Question 8. Tendrils are found in the following plants. Identify whether they are stem tendrils or leaf tendrils.

(a) Cucumber (b) Peas
(c) Pumpkins (d) Grapevine
(e) Watermelons

Answer

Plant Type	Type of Tendrils they possess
(a) Cucumber	Stem tendrils
(b) Peas	Leaf tendrils
(c) Pumpkins	Stem tendrils
(d) Grapevine	Stem tendrils
(e) Watermelons	Stem tendrils

Question 9. Why is maize grain usually called as a fruit and not a seed?

Answer The maize grain is usually known as a fruit because it is in fact a ripened ovary which contains a ripened ovule, *e.g.*, a single seed. This fruit is known as caryopsis in which the pericarp is fused with the seed coat. The maize grain occurs attached to a thick cob or peduncle.

Question 10. Tendrils of grapevines are homologous to the tendrils of pumpkins but are analogous to that of pea. Justify the above statement.

Answer The tendrils of grapevine and tendrils of pumpkins are stem tendrils. These tendrils are fine, sensitive thread-like structures. Both these types of tendrils are homologous, as they resemble each other in their morphology and place of origin.

The tendrils of pea develop from the leaves. These are analogous to tendrils of grapevine and tendrils of pumpkins. Although these tendrils perform the similar function of providing support to the plant but they have different origin point and their morphology is different.

Question 11. Rhizome of ginger is like the roots of other plants that grows underground. Despite this fact ginger is a stem and not a root. Justify.

Answer Rhizome of ginger, *e.g.*, *Zingiber officinale* is a stem. Although, it grows underground similar to roots. But it is a stem, as it does not perform the function of anchorage and absorption similar to the roots. Instead, it is swollen and fleshy to store reserve food. It give rise to aerial shoots from terminal bud.

Question 12. Differentiate between

(a) Bract and Bracteole (b) Pulvinus and petiole
(c) Pedicel and peduncle (d) Spike and spadix
(e) Stamen and staminoid (f) Pollen and pollinium

Answer

(a) **Bract and Bracteolate** Bract is a leaf-like structure, in the axile of which flowers are borne. They can be small or scaly, green and coloured. Whereas bracteolate are bract-like structures borne on the stalk of a flower.

(b) **Pulvinus and petiole** Pulvinus is the leaf base, which is the proximal region with which a leaf is attached to the stem. Petiole is cylindrical or subcylindrical stalk which connects the leaf base with the lamina.

(c) **Pedicel and peduncle** The stalk of a flower is known as pedicle, whereas the stalk of whole of the inflorescence is known as peduncle.

(d) **Spike and spadix** In spike inflorescence, the flowers are sessile. They develop on an elongated peduncle in a acropetal succession, *e.g., Adhatoda*, etc. The spadix inflorescence is like spike but it is covered by one to a few large bracts called spathes, *e.g., Colocasia*, etc.

(e) **Stamen and staminoid** The male reproductive organs or microsporophylls of a flower is called stamen. A fully sterile stamen is called a staminoid, *e.g., Verbascum.*

(f) **Pollen and pollinium** Microspore of an angiospermic flower is known as pollen. It is haploid, whereas a group of pollen grains constitute the pollinium as in *Calotropis.*

Long Answer Type Questions

Question 1. Distinguish between families Fabaceae, Solanaceae, Liliaceae on the basis of gynoecium characteristics (with figures), Also write economic importance of any one of the above family.

Answer Gynoecium of Family–Fabaceae Ovary superior, non-carpellary, unilocular with many ovules, style single, *e.g., Pisum sativum.*

Gynoecium of family–Solanaceae Bicarpellary, syncarpous, ovary superior, bilocular, placenta swollen with many ovules.

Gynoecium of family–Liliaceae Tricarpellary, syncarpous, ovary superior, trilocular with many ovules, axile placentation.

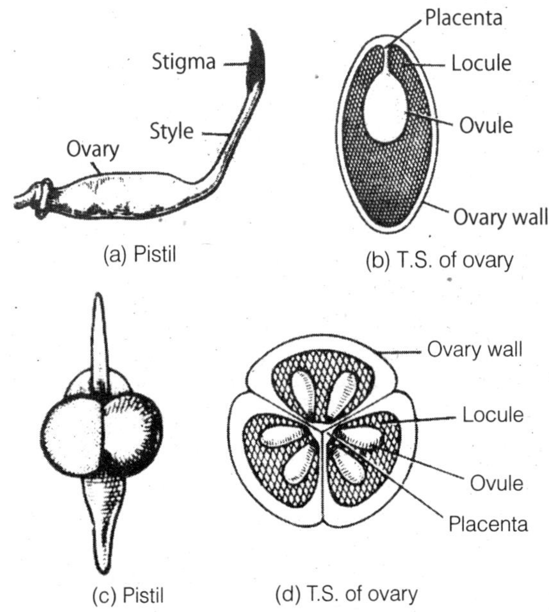

(a) Pistil (b) T.S. of ovary
(c) Pistil (d) T.S. of ovary

Economic Importance of Family–Fabaceae

(i) Many plants and belonging to the family are sources of pulses (gram, arhar, sem, moong and soyabean) edible oil (soyabean and groundnut), dye (*Indigofera*), fibres (sunnhemp), fodder (*Sesbania, Trifolium*), ornamentals (lupin, sweet pea); medicine (muliathi).

(ii) One of the best timber wood is obtained from *Dalbergia sissoo, Pterocarpus marsupium* and *Butea monospermum.*

(iii) Medicinally useful gum is obtained from *Butea monosperma* and *Astragalus gummifer.*

(iv) Roots of *Glycyrrhiza glabra* is an expectorant, they contain glycoside glycyrrhizin which is used in medicines.

Question 2. Stolon, offset and rhizome are different forms of stem modifications. How can these modified forms of stem be distinguished from each other?

Answer Stolons These are special above ground (*e.g.,* wild strawberry) or underground (*e.g., Colocasia*) horizontal branches which develop the base of a crown, grow obliquely can arch over small obstacles, root at intervals and form new crowns.

Offsets These are one internode long runners formed in rosette plants at ground or water level, *e.g.*, water lettuce, *Pistia*, water hyacinth (*Eichhornia*), *Agave*, etc. It is subaerial weak stem. It grow over the ground.

Rhizome It is an indefinitely growing perennial stem which occurs underground and give rise to annual aerial branches or leaves under favourable conditions.

Question 3. **The mode of arrangements of sepals or petals in a floral bud is known as aestivation. Draw the various types of aestivation possible for a typical pentamerous flower.**

Answer Aestivation is the mode of arrangement of sepals or petals in a floral bud. Aestivation can be open (margin sufficiently apart), valvate (no overlapping, margins just touching), twisted (regular overlapping of one margin) and imbricate (irregular and overlapping). It is of two types:

(i) Quincuncial

(ii) Vexillary

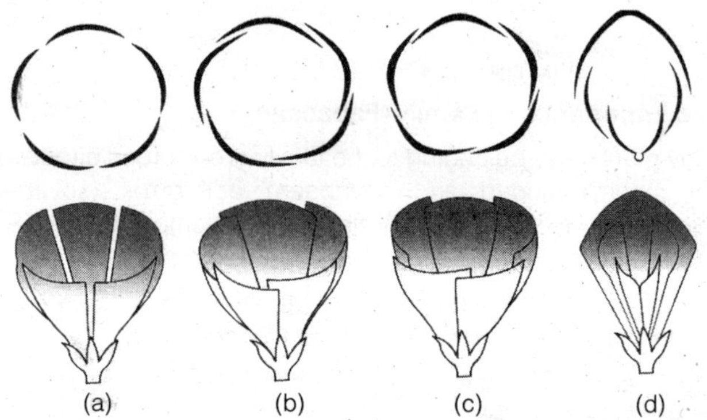

Types of aestivation in corolla (a) Valvate (b) Twisted (c) Imbricate (d) Vexillary

Question 4. **The arrangements of ovules within the ovary is known as placentation. What does the term placenta refer to? Name and draw various types of placentations in the flower as seen in T.S. or V.S..**

Answer The placenta is the central ridge within the ovary over which ovules are arranged. Different types of placentations are basal, marginal, axile, free central, parietal, etc.

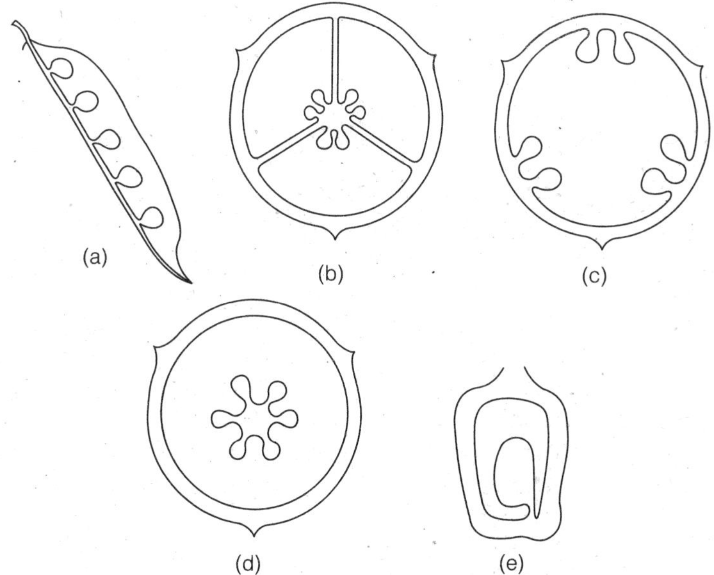

Types of placentations : (a) Marginal (b) Axile (c) Parietal (d) Free central (e) Basal

Question 5. Sunflower is not a flower. Explain.

Answer The inflorescence present in sunflower is capitulum or head. Sunflower is not a single flower but in turn it is an aggregate of many flowers. In it the main axis of the peduncle becomes flattened, termed as receptacle. It bears sessile bract, containing (bracteolate), centripetally arranged flowers or florets. A whorl of bracts called involucre also occurred at the base of the receptacle. The bracts are known as ray florets and disc florets.

Question 6. Seeds of some plants germinate immediately after shedding from plants, while in other plants they require a period of rest before germination. The later phenomenon is called as dormancy. Give the reasons for seed dormancy and some methods to break it.

Answer **Seed dormancy** It is the internal inhibition of germination of an otherwise viable seed even when it is placed in most favourable external conditions.

Reasons of Seed Dormancy

(i) Impermeability of the seed coats to water, *e.g., Chenopodium* or chemicals, *e.g., Xanthium.*

(ii) Tough seed coats, *e.g., Capsella, Lepidium.*

(iii) Inhibitors such as ABA, phenolic compounds, cyanogenic substanes, *e.g.,* ferubic acid inhibit, the germination of seeds, *e.g., Cucurbita*, etc.

(iv) Excess salts cause dormancy in seeds of *Atriplex.*

(v) The embryo is mature sometimes but the seed required a period for gaining the ability to germinate, *e.g.,* oat, barley, etc.

(vi) Immaturity of the embryo is also the one cause of seed dormancy.

Natural methods of breaking seed dormancy

(i) Certain small seeds regularly pass through the alimentary canal of animals when digestive enzymes make the seed soften and permeable.

(ii) Development and after ripening of embryo.

(iii) Development of growth hormones, *e.g.,* cytokinins, auxin, gibberellin.

(iv) Leaching of inhibitors and salts.

(v) Destruction of inhibitors by heat, cold, light and oxidation.

Artificial breaking of seed dormancy

(i) **Mechanical scarification** Rupturing of seed coats by filling, chipping or machine threshing.

(ii) **Chemical scarification** Weakening of seed coats by hot water, fat solvents, etc.

(iii) **Impaction** Vigorous shaking.

(iv) Chilling treatment, *e.g.,* peach, plum, cherry.

(v) Red light overcomes dormancy and induces seed germination in lettuce and tobacco.

Question 7. Take one flower of each of the families Fabaceae and Solanaceae and write down it's semi-technical description.

Answer

(i) **Fabaceae** *Pisum sativum* (pea) belongs to family–Fabaceae.

Vegetative characters Tree, shrubs, herbs, root with root nodules.

Stem Erect or climber.

Leaves Alternate, pinnately compound or simple, leaf base, pulvinate, stipulate and venation reticulate.

Floral characters

Inflorescence Racemose

Flower Bisexual zygomorphic

Calyx Five Sepals, gamosepalous, imbricate aestivation.

Corolla Five, Petals polypetalous, papilionaceous, consisting of a posterior standard, two lateral wings two anterior ones forming a keel (enclosing stamens and pistil), vexillary aestivation.

Androecium Ten, diadelphous and anther dithecous.

Gynoecium Ovary superior, monocarpellary, unilocular with many ovules and style single.

Fruit Legume; seed; one to many, non-endospermic.

Floral formula %, ⚥ $K_{(5)}\ C_{1+2+(2)}\ A_{(9)+1}\ G_{\underline{1}}$

(ii) **Family - Solanaceae**

Solanum tuberosum (potato) is an important member of this family.

Vegetative characters

Plants mostly herbs, shrubs and rarely small trees.

Stem Herbaceous rarely woody, aerial, erect, cylindrical, branched, solid or hollow, hairy and glabrous, underground stem in potato.

Leaves Alternate, simple, rarly pinnately compound, exstipulate, reticulate venation.

Floral characters

Inflorescence Solitary, axillary or cymose as in *Solanum*.

Flower Bisexual, actinomorphic.

Calyx Sepals five, united, persistent, valvate aestivation.

Corolla Petals five, united, valvate aestivation.

Androecium Stamens five, epipetalous.

Gynoecium Bicarpellary, syncarpous, ovary superior, bilocular placenta swollen with many ovules.

Fruit Berry or capsule

Seeds Many, endospermous

Floral formula ⊕, ⚥ $K_{(5)}\ \overset{\frown}{C_{(5)}\ A_5}\ G_{(\underline{2})}$.

6

Anatomy of Flowering Plants

Important Points

1. Anatomy includes the study of internal structure of plant.
2. Basic unit called cell is organised into tissues. Tissues are group of cells having common origin and usually perform a common function.
3. Most of the tissues occur as undifferentiated groups of apical cells, which shows continuous division. They later differentiate to form a permanent tissue. These are called **meristematic tissues**.
4. Growth in plants is restricted to specialised region of active division called **meristem**.
5. Meristem is divided into **apical, intercalary** and **lateral meristem.**
   (i) **Apical meristem** occurs at the tips of the roots or shoots. It is helpful in increasing length of the plant.
   (ii) **Intercalary meristem** are present on the axils of leaves and capable of forming a branch or a flower.
   (iii) **Lateral meristem** occurs in the mature region of roots and shoot. These are called **secondary meristem** and **cylindrical meristem**. They are responsible for increasing the thickness or girth of the plant.
6. Apical meristem and intercalary meristem are important to constitute primary plant body and appear early in life of a plant. Hence, known as **primary meristem**.

7. These primary and secondary meristem differentiate to give rise permanent mature cell. Which looses the ability to divide.
8. These permanent tissue give rise to epidermal ground and vascular tissues. **Permanent tissues** are of two types
   (i) Simple tissue (ii) Complex tissue
   (i) **Simple tissue** These are made up of same type of cell. This includes.
      (a) **Parenchyma** are thin-walled living cell made up of cellulosic cell wall. They form major component of organ. They may be spherical, oval, round, polygonal or elongated in shape. They may have intercellular spaces at young stage.

      Parenchyma could be specialised into chlorenchyma, palisade and spongy parenchyma. Their main role is photosynthesis.
      (b) **Collenchyma** is a mechanical tissue with living cells. It retains nucleus even at maturity.

      In dicotylodnous cell; these are present in below the epidermis. It is found as homogenous layer or in patches.
      - They may be oval, spherical or polygonal in shape. Cell wall is rich in pectin and hemicellulose.
      - Provides mechanical support to the plants.
      - Intercellular spaces is absent.
      (c) **Sclerenchyma** consist of long or short, narrow with thick-walled lignified cell walls having a few or numerous pits.
      - These are dead cells. These may be classified either as fibres and sclerids. They provide mechanical support.
      - **Fibres** are thick walled, elongated and pointed cells occurring in groups.
      - **Sclerids** are spherical, oval, cylindrical and highly thickened dead cells with narrow cavities.
   (ii) **Complex tissues** are made up of vascular tissues like **xylem** and **phloem**.
      (a) **Xylem** is a complex tissue composed of various components like trachieds, vessels, fibres and parenchymatous cells.
      - It is the chief conducting tissue for H_2O and minerals from root to stem and leaves. It also provide mechanical strength to the plant.

- **Tracheids** are elongated or tube-like cells with thick lignified walls and tapering ends. They are dead.
- **Vessels** are long cylindrical tube-like structure made up of many cells called **vessel members**.
- Vessels members are interconnected through perforations in their common walls. In gymnosperms, vessels are absent.
- Xylem fibres cell are thick-walled and have obliterated central lumen. These may be septate or aseptate.
- **Xylem parenchymatous cell** are thin and have cellulosic cell wall. Their main role is storage. It store food in form of fat, starch or tannins.
- On the basis of time of origin with respect to the growth of the plant body. Xylem is classified into **protoxylem** and **metaxylem**.
- **Protoxylem** develops first from the procambial strand.
- **Metaxylem** develops in the later stage and consist of bigger tracheid and vessel.
- Xylem is further classified depending upon protoxylem with respect to metaxylem.
  These are of four types :
  - **Exarch** Protoxylem lying outside the metaxylem.
  - **Mesarch** Protoxylem lying in middle of metaxylem.
  - **Endarch** Protoxylem lying inside the metaxylem.
  - **Centarch** Protoxylem lying the centre of metaxylem.

(b) **Phloem** is also a complex permanent tissue, which prencipally transport organic food. It is also of four types

- **Sieve elements** are slender elongated cells, which arrange one above the other to form sieve tubes. In gymnosperms, sieve plates are present. Nucleus is absent and large vacuole is present in nature sieve element.
- **Campanion cells** are thin-walled elongated phloem tissue associated with sieve tube. These are absent in gymnosperms and pteridophytes instead albuminous cells are present in them. Nucleus of companion cells regulate the activity of sieve tubes. These are living

and contain cytoplasmic content with conspicuous nucleus.

- **Phloem parenchyma** are living cell present in phloem tissue. Absent in dicots and pteridophytes cell wall is composed of cellulose and have pits throughout the plasmodesmatal connections.
- **Phloem fibres** are made up of scelerenchymatous cells. They differ from xylem fibres in having small, rounded or linear simple pits, which may be septate or non-septate.
- Phloem fibres of jute, flax and hemp are used for commercial purpose.
- **Protophloem** is first formed primary phloem and consist of narrow sieve tubes.
- **Metaphloem** is formed later and has bigger sieve tube.

9. On the basis of structure and location tissue system is three types.
   (i) **Epidermal tissue system** is derived from protoderm and forms outermost covering of whole plant body. It comprises of
      (a) **Epidermal cell**
      (b) **Stomata**
      (c) **Epidermal appendages**
      - **Eipdermis** is the outermost layer of cells covering the entire plant body it made up of closely arranged living cells forming a continuous layer.
      - It is composed of parenchymatous cell with large vacuole.
      - **Cuticle** is the continuous layer of fatty substance deposited in outer walls of eipdermal cells interupted with stomata. It prevents the loss of H_2O and absent in roots.
      - **Epidermal outgrowth** are the appendages which forms trichomes and emergence.
      - **Trichomes** are the epidermal hair present on stem.
      - Root hairs are the unicellular elongations of epidermal cells and help to absorb H_2O and mineral from soil.
      - Epidermis of green aerial parts possess minute apertures or openings called **stomata**. Composed of two bean-shaped cells known as **guard cells**, subsidiary cells or accessory cells. Surround the

overtop of the guard cell and constitutes stomatal apparatus.

- Stomatal cells are living, have chloroplast and performs the function of transpiration.
- The outer wall of guard cell (away from stomatal pore) is thin than the inner wall of guard cell. In grasses guard cells are dumb-bell-shaped.

(ii) **Ground tissue system** or **fundamental tissue system** constitutes main plant bulk body. It includes all tissues except epidermis and vascular bundles. It constitutes simple tissue such as **parenchyma, collenchyma** and **sclerenchyma**.

(iii) **Vascular tissue system** consist of complex tissues the **phloem** and the **xylem**.

- Xylem and phloem together forms vascular bundles. These are embedded in the ground tissue.
- Depending upon the relative position of xylem and phloem. Vascular bundles are classified as **radial** and **conjoint**.
- When xylem and phloem within a vascular bundle are arranged in a alternate manner on different radii, they arc known as **radial**, *e.g.*, in roots.

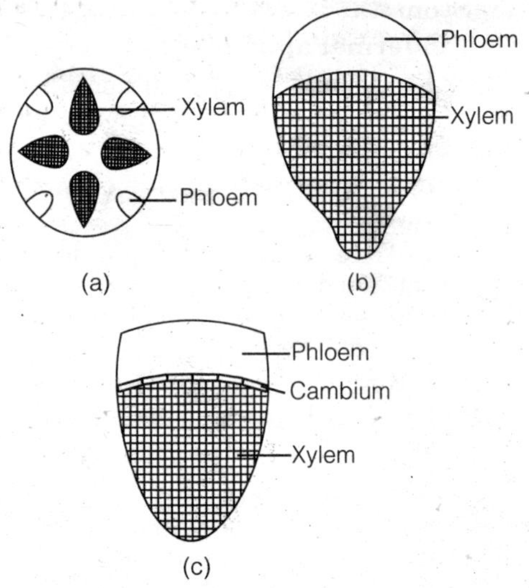

Various types of vascular bundles
(a) Radial (b) Conjoint closed (c) Conjoint open

- In **conjoint type,** vascular bundles are present at same radius of vascular bundles, *e.g.,* in stem and leaf.
- A lateral meristem called **cambium** is present in between xylem and phloem of vascular bundle also known as **vascular cambium**. They have ability to form secondary xylem and phloem and hence, known as **open vascular bundle**. It is present in dicotyledons.
- When cambium is absent in between xylem and phloem. Condition is called **closed vascular** bundle, which unable to form secondary xylem and phloem, *e.g.,* in monocots.

10. Anatomy of **dicotyledonous roots**
    (i) Outermost layer is epidermis.
    (ii) Epidermal cell protrude to form the unicellular root hair.
    (iii) Thin walled parenchyma cells form cortex with intercellular spaces.
    (iv) Innermost layer of cortex form endodermis.
    (v) An impermeable waxy material suberin is deposited on endodermal cell called **casparian strip**.
    (vi) Next to endodermis thick-walled parenchymatous cell form **pericycle**.
    (vii) Initiation of lateral root and vascular cambium during the secondary growth take place.
    (viii) Vascular bundles are radial and open.
    (ix) Vascular bundle, pith and pericycle forms stele.
11. In **moncots root** pith is large and well-developed and vascular bundle are closed. Number of vascular bundle is less.

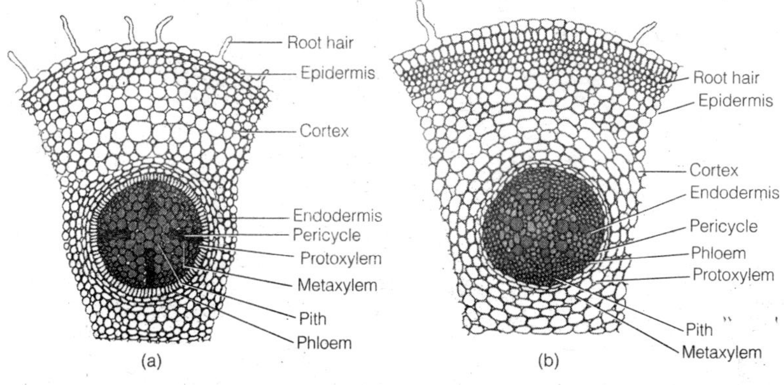

T.S. of root : (a) Dicot root (primary) (b) Monocot root

12. In **dicotyledonous stem** epidermis is the outermost protective layer of stem covered with thin layer of cuticle with trichome and few stomata. Sequential order of various cell is
    (i) Hypodermis (layer of collenchymatous cells).
    (ii) Cortical layer (with parenchymatous cell, with intracellular spaces).
    (iii) Endodermis is the innermost layer (rich in starch grain called starch sheath).
    (iv) Pericycle
    (v) Vascular bundles are conjoint open with endarch protoxylem.
    (vi) Pith is formed by parenchymatous cell.
13. In **monocot stem** vascular bundles are scattered surrounded by sclerenchymatous bundle sheath cell. Vascular bundles are conjoint and closed.

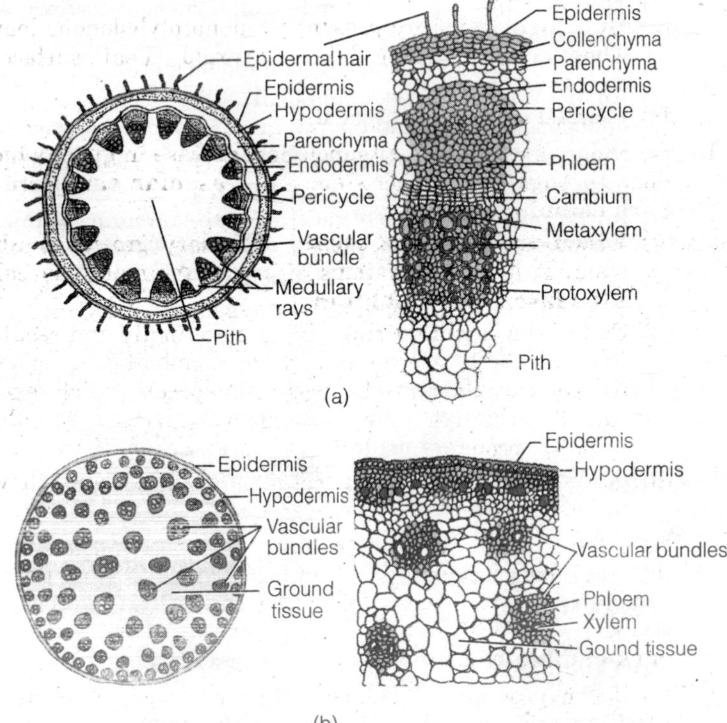

T.S. of stem : (a) Dicot (b) Monocot

14. **Dorsiventral** (dicotyledonous) **Leaf**
    (i) Epidermis covers both (adaxial epidermis) (upper surface) and lower surface (abaxial epidermis) (lower surface). More stomata are present on adaxial surface.
    (ii) Palisada parenchyma is present an adaxial surface made up of elongated cells arranged vertically and parallel to each other.
    (iii) Spongy parenchyma is situated below the palisade cells and extends to lower epidermis.
    (iv) Vascular system includes vascular bundles.
    (v) Reticulate venation occurs.
    (vi) Bundle sheath cells surround the vascular bundle.
    (vii) **Isobilateral** (monocotyledonous) **leaf** stomata are present on both the surfaces of epidermis and mesophyll cells are not differentiated into palisade or spongy parenchyma.
    (viii) **Bulliform cells** are present in monocotyledonous leaves. These absorb water become turgid. Leaf surface is exposed.
    (ix) Parallel venation is present.
15. Secondary growth of plants includes increase in girth, which is done through lateral meristem, *i.e.,* **vascular cambium** and **cork cambium**.
    (i) **Vascular cambium** causes secondary growth in dicot stem. It forms new strips of secondary meristem called **interfascicular cambium**.
    (ii) Cell of the cambium ring divide periclinally and result in new cells both outside and inside. Cambial cells adjacent to ray initials cut off parenchyma cell which extend radially through new secondary xylem and phloem forming secondary medullary rays.
    (iii) Secondary growth in monocot stem is absent since they do not possess vascular cambium.
16. Secondary growth in **dicot roots** take place in stelar region (by vascular cambium) and in extrastelar region (by cork cambium). Outer layers of pericycle become meristematic giving rise to thin-walled, rectangular cells which function as **cork-cambium** or **phellogen**.

    Phellogen produces secondary tissue outwardly the **cork** or **phellem** and **secondary cortex** or **phelloderm** towards the inner side.

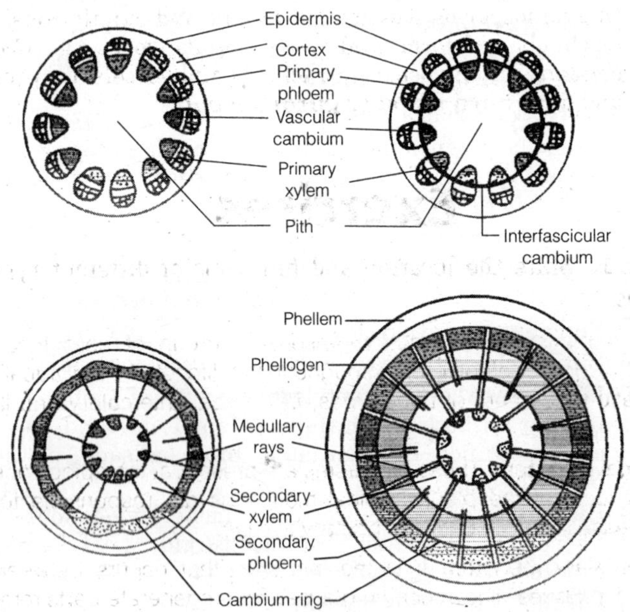

Different stages of the secondary growth in a typical dicot root

17. During spring season cambium is very active and produces plenty of xylem vessels. With wider cavities called **spring wood** or **early wood.**
    (i) In winter cambial activity slows down and give rise to narrower xylem elements. Wood thus, formed is called **autumn wood** or **late wood**.
    (ii) As the growth continues two types of wood produced year after year and appear together as a concentric ring in a transverse section. This ring is known a **annual ring** or **growth ring.**
    (iii) As a result of continued secondary growth older part of secondary xylem or wood becomes non-functional and looses the power of conduction.

    Cell of this wood filled up by resins and tannins and produced by functional cells. Due to these activities secondary xylem becomes hard and durable and blackish in colour called **heart wood** or **duramen**.
    (iv) When the function of secondary xylem (*i.e.,* H_2O and mineral conduction from roots) is performed by the outer younger rings of secondary xylem than wood is called **sapwood** or **alburum**.

(v) In gymnosperms, vessels are absent and chiefly consist of tracheids and form. Soft wood, porous wood, *e.g., Cedrus deodara.* In angiosperm, tracheids and vessels are present and form **hard wood** or **porous wood**.

Exercises

Question 1. State the location and functions of different types of meristems.

Answer A meristematic tissue represents a group of cells that have retained the power of division throughout the life of an individual. The meristematic tissues are of three types, *i.e.,* apical, intercalary and lateral meristem.

(i) **Apical meristem** These meristems are present at the apices of shoot and roots of the plants. Apical meristems are responsible for the increase in length of all the primary tissues.

(ii) **Intercalary meristem** It is the meristem that occurs between the mature tissues. They occur in grasses and regenerate parts removed by the grazing herbivores. It contributes to the formation of the primary plant body.

(iii) **Lateral meristem** It occurs in the mature regions of roots and shoots of many plants, particularly that produce woody axis. These meristems are responsible for producing the secondary tissues.

Question 2. Cork cambium forms tissues that form the cork. Do you agree with this statement? Explain.

Answer Yes, cork cambium forms tissues that form cork. As the stem continues to increase in girth another meristematic tissue called **cork cambium** or **phellogen** develops in cortex region of stem. The phellogen cuts off cells on both sides. The outer cells differentiate into **cork** or **phellem.** The inner cells differentiate into **secondary cortex** or **phelloderm**. Cork is impervious to water due to suberin and provides protection to underlying tissues.

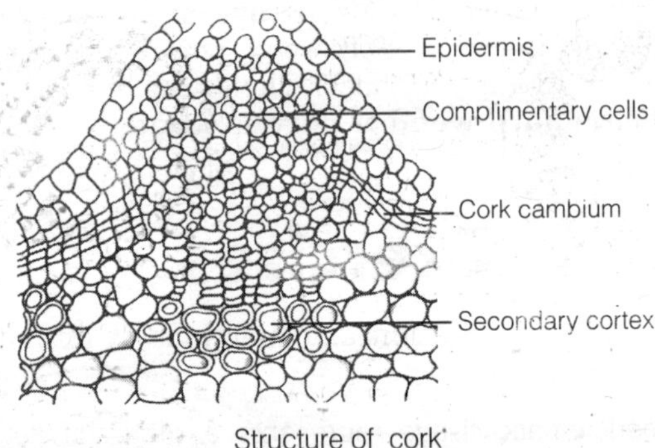

Structure of cork'

Question 3. Explain the process of secondary growth in the stems of woody angiosperms with the help of schematic diagrams. What is its significance?

Answer The increase in girth of stems of woody angiosperms is called **secondary growth**. The tissue involved in secondary growth are the two lateral meristems—vascular cambium and cork cambium.

(i) Vascular cambium is a vascular layer present between xylem and phloem (vascular tissues). It is responsible for the cutting off vascular tissues, later it forms a complete ring.

(ii) The cambial ring becomes active and begins to cut off new cells, both towards the inner and the outer sides.

(iii) The cells cut off towards pith, mature into secondary xylem and the cell cut of towards periphery, mature into secondary phloem.

(iv) The cambium is generally more active on the inner side than the outer. As a result, the amount of secondary xylem produced is more than the secondary phloem and soon forms a compact mass.

(v) The primary and secondary phloem get gradually crushed due to the continued formation and accumulation of secondary xylem.

(vi) The primary xylem however, remains more or less intact, in or around the centre.

(vii) At some places, the cambium forms a narrow band of parenchyma, which passes through the secondary xylem and the secondary phloem in the radial directions. These are the secondary medullary rays.

(viii) The stem continues to increase in girth due to the activity of vascular cambium.

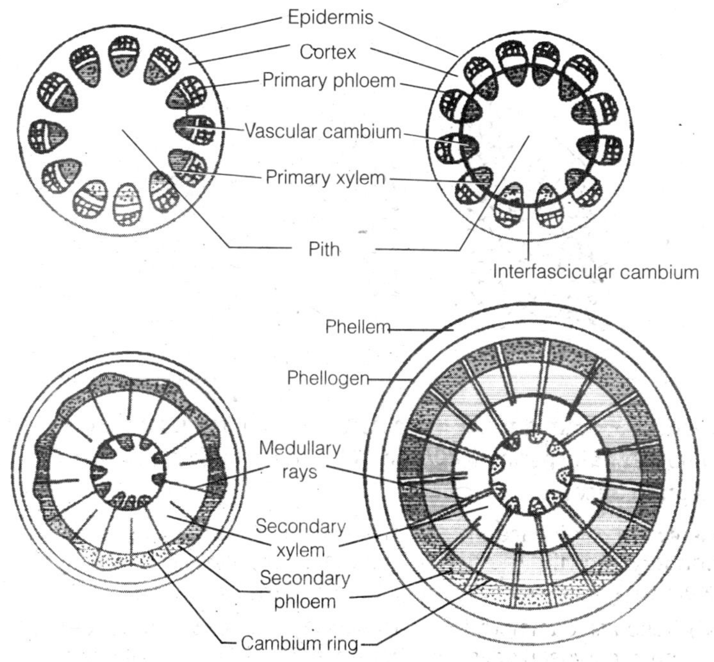

Secondary growth in a dicot stem (diagrammatic) stages in transverse views

Question 4. Draw illustrations to bring out the anatomical differences between

(a) Monocot root and dicot root

(b) Monocot stem and dicot stem

Answer (a) **Differences between Monocot and Dicot root**

S.N.	Monocot Root	Dicot Root
1.	Cortex is very wide.	Cortex is comparatively narrow.
2.	Outer cortex is usually differentiated into exodermis.	Outer cortex is usually not differentiated into exodermis.
3.	Endodermis contains prominant casparian strips only in young roots.	Endodermis contains prominant casparian strips.
4.	Xylem and phloem bundles are many in number 8 or more.	Xylem and phloem bundles vary in number from 2-6.
5.	Metaxylem vessels are oval or rounded.	Metaxylem vessels generally angular.
6.	No secondary growth.	Secondary growth takes place.
7.	Pith is large and well-developed.	Pith is small or absent.

S.N.	Monocot Root	Dicot Root

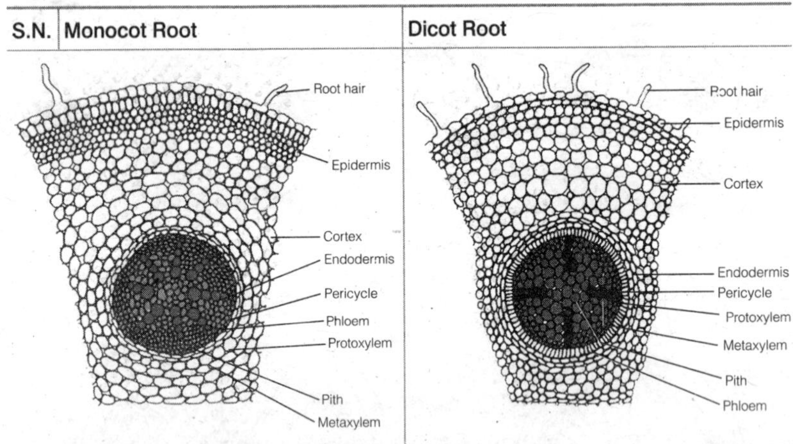

(b) **Differences between Monocot and Dicot stem**

S.N.	Monocot Stem	Dicot Stem
1.	Dumb bell-shaped guard cells in stomata occurring in epidermis.	Kidney-shaped guard cells present in stomata in epidermis.
2.	Ground tissue uniform and there is not any differentiation.	Ground tissue differentiated into cortex, endodermis, pericycle and pith.
3.	The vascular bundles are scattered in ground tissue many in number and vary in size.	The vascular bundles are arranged in a ring.
4.	Normally, no secondary growth occurs, few exceptions, *e.g.*, *Aloe*, etc.	Secondary growth takes place.
5.	The primary vascular tissues remains functional throughout the life of the plant.	The older vascular tissues cease functioning after sometimes are replaced by new ones.
6.	There is little increase in size.	The stem also increase in diameter with age due to secondary growth.

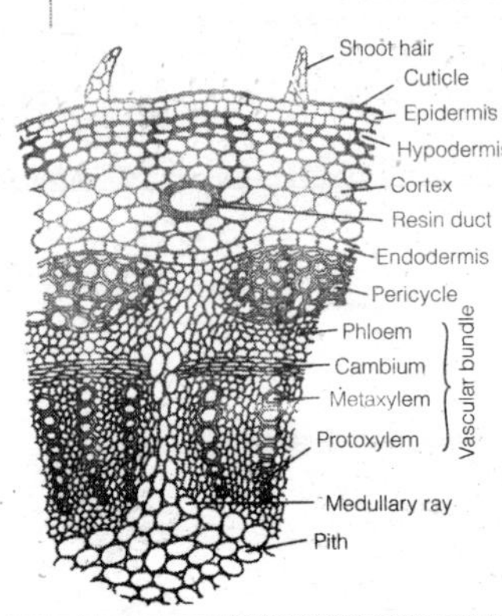

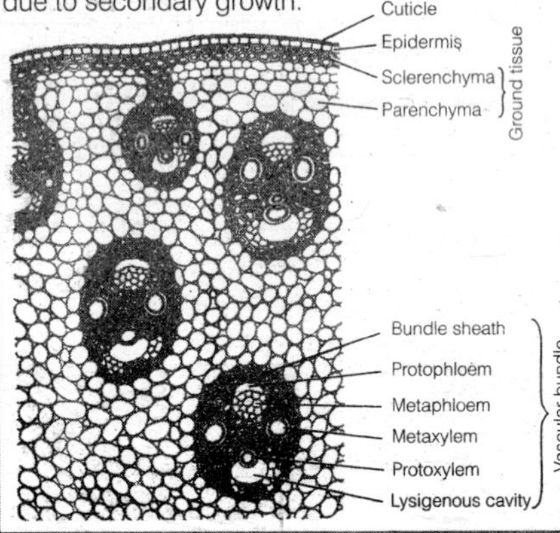

Question 5. Cut a transverse section of young stem of a plant from your school garden and observe it under the microscope. How would you ascertain whether it is a monocot stem or a dicot stem? Give reasons.

Answer **Transverse section of a monocot stem possess following characters**

(i) Dumbbell-shaped guard cells in stomata in epidermis.
(ii) Sclerenchymatous hypodermis.
(iii) No concentric arrangement of internal tissues.
(iv) Uniform ground tissue showing no tissue differentiation.
(v) More than 8 scattered vascular bundles.
(vi) Bundle sheath is present.
(vii) No secondary growth normally.
(viii) Xylem vessels arranged in Y-shaped manner.
(ix) Protoxylem cavity usually present in vascular tissues.

Transverse section of a dicot stem has following characters

(i) Kidney-shaped guard cells in stomata present in epidermis.
(ii) Collenchymatous hypodermis.
(iii) Concentric arrangement of internal tissues.
(iv) Differentiation of ground tissue into cortex, endodermis, pericycle and pith.
(v) The vascular bundles are arranged in a ring.
(vi) Conjoint collateral and open vascular bundles.
(vii) Without bundle sheath.
(viii) Secondary growth takes place.
(ix) Xylem vessels arranged in rows.

Question 6. The transverse section of a plant material shows the following anatomical features

(a) The vascular bundles are conjoint, scattered and surrounded by a sclerenchymatous bundle sheaths.
(b) Phloem parenchyma is absent. What will you identify it as?

Answer It is a transverse section of monocotyledons stem.

Question 7. Why are xylem and phloem called complex tissues?

Answer Xylem and phloem tissues are made up of more than one type of cells that is why they are known as complex tissues.

(i) **Xylem** is composed of four different kinds of elements, namely—tracheids, vessels, xylem fibres and xylem parenchyma. Tracheids are dead tube-like cells which are thick walled, vessels are made up of large number of tube cells placed end to end. Xylem fibres are thick walled cells that may be septate and aseptate. Xylem parenchyma is living and thin walled cells.

(ii) **Phloem** is composed of sieve tube elements, companion cells, phloem parenchyma and phloem fibres. Sieve tube elements are tube-like cells, whereas phloem parenchyma are living cells and phloem fibres are thick walled lignified cells.

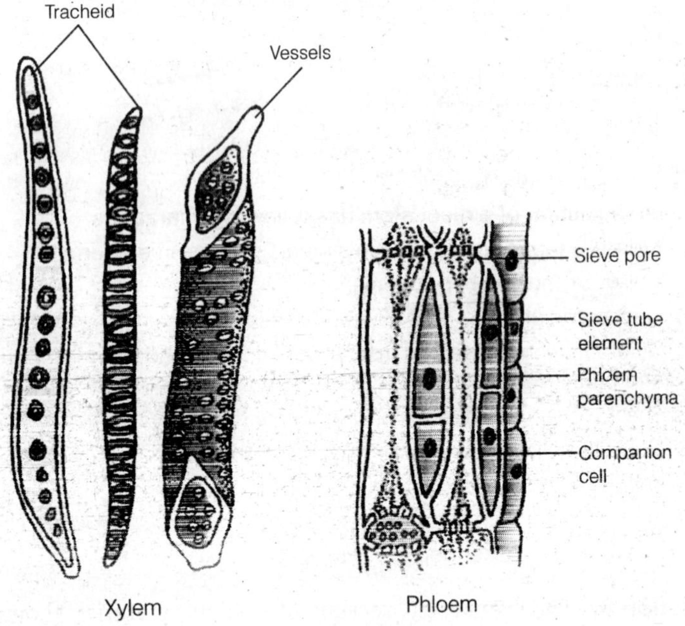

Question 8. What is stomatal apparatus? Explain the structure of stomata with a labelled diagram.

Answer The minute pores present in the epidermis are known as stomata. The stomata may be surrounded by either kidney-shaped (in dicots) or by dumb-bell-shaped (in monocots) guard cells. The guard cells in turn are surrounded by other epidermal cells, which are known as subsidiary or accessory cells. The stomatal aperture, guard cells, accessory cells constitute the stomatal apparatus.

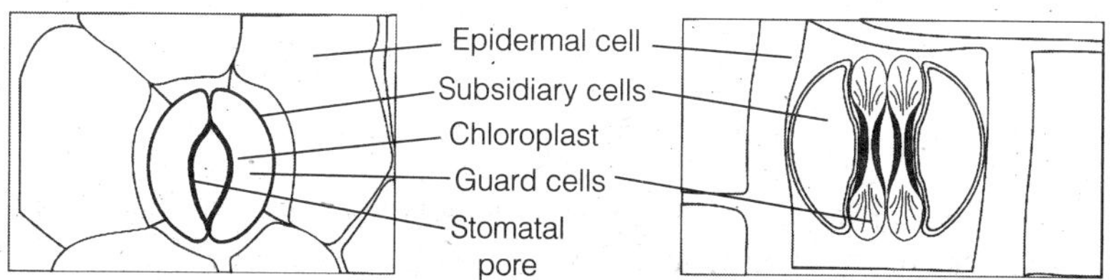

Diagrammatic representation of stomatal apparatus (a) stomata with bean-shaped guards cells (b) stomata with dumb-bell-shaped guard cells

Question 9. Name the three basic tissue systems in the flowering plants? Give the tissue names under each system.

Answer On the basis of structure and location the three basic tissue systems in the flowering plants are

(i) **Epidermal tissue system** It comprises tissues like epidermal cells, stomata and the epidermal appendages the trichome and hairs.

(ii) **Ground tissue system** It consists of simple tissues such as parenchyma, collenchyma and sclerenchyma.

(iii) **Vascular tissue system** It constitutes complex tissues like xylem and phloem.

Question 10. How is the study of plant anatomy useful to us?

Answer Plant anatomy is the study of internal structure of living organisms.

(i) It describes the tissues involved in assimilation of food and its storage, transportation of water, *i.e.,* xylem tissue, transportation of minerals, *i.e.,* phloem and those involved in providing mechanical support to the plant.

(ii) Study of internal structure of plants helps to understand their adaptations of diverse environments.

(iii) The study of plant anatomy also help in understanding the functional organisation of higher plants.

Question 11. What is periderm? How does periderm formations take place in the dicot stems.

Answer Phellogen, phellem and phelloderm are collectively called as periderm. Phellogan develops usually in the cortex region. Phellogen is a couple of layers thick. Phellogen cuts off cells on both sides. The outer cells differentiate into cork or phellem, while the inner cells differentiate into secondary cortex or phelloderm. All these together form periderm. All these together form perineum.

Question 12. Describe the internal structure of a dorsiventral leaf with the help of labelled diagrams?

Answer **Internal Structure of a Dorsiventral (dicotyledonous leaf)**

(i) It shows three main parts namely epidermis, mesophyll and vascular system.

(ii) The epidermis which covers both the upper surface (adaxial epidermis) and lower epidermis (abaxial surface) are covered with thick layer of cuticle.

(iii) The tissue between the upper and lower epidermis is known as mesophyll. This tissue possess chloroplasts and carryout photosynthesis, is made up of parenchyma.

(iv) The parenchyma has two types of cells, *i.e.*, palisade parenchyma and spongy parenchyma.

(v) There are large number of air cavities in between these cells.

(vi) In the midrib region and in veins vascular bundles made up of xylem and phloem are present.

(vii) The size of the vascular bundles are dependent on the size of veins. The veins vary in thickness in the reticulate venation of dicot leaves.

(viii) The vascular bundles are surrounded by bundle sheath cells.

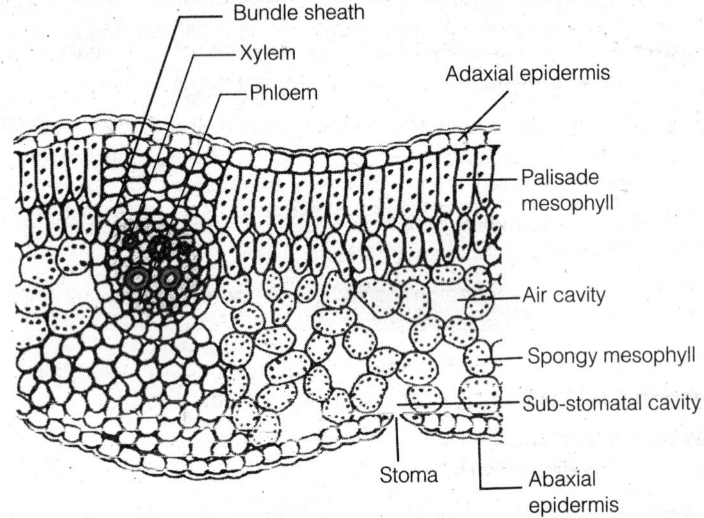

T.S of dicot leaf

Selected NCERT Exemplar Problems

Very Short Answer Type Questions

Question 1. Product of photosynthesis is transported from the leaves to various parts of the plants and stored in some cell before being utilised. What are the cells/tissues that store them?

Answer The product of photosynthesis is stored in modified epidermal cells. Lithocytes or crystal cells are specialised epidermal cells containing cystoliths, *e.g.,* in members of Apocynaceae, Moraceae, etc. The silica cells contain silica granules, whereas cork cells contain solid organic substances.

Question 2. Protoxylem is the first formed xylem. If the protoxylem lies next to phloem. What kind of arrangement of xylem would you call it?

Answer The xylem will exhibit endarch condition.

Question 3. What is the function of phloem parenchyma?

Answer **Function of Phloem Parenchyma** The phloem parenchyma cells store food material and other substances like resins, latex and mucilage phloem parenchyma is absent in most of the monocotyledons.

Question 4. What is present on the surface of the leaves which helps the plant prevent loss of water but is absent in roots?

Answer The leaves have on their surface special cells known as bulliform cells.

Question 5. What is the epidermal cell modification in plants which prevents water loss?

Answer In case of grasses or monocots, the epidermal cells get modified to form bulliform or motor cells which check water loss. The stomata also check loss of water.

Question 6. What part of the plant would show the following?

(a) Radial vascular bundle (b) Polyarch xylem
(c) Well-developed pith

Answer (a) Radial vascular bundles are present in roots.
(b) Monocotyledonous root.
(c) Stem has well-developed pith.

Question 7. What are the cells that make the leaves curl in plants during water stress?

Answer Bulliform or motor cells.

Question 8. What constitutes the cambial ring?

Answer The vascular tissues consist of xylem and phloem which are complex tissues. In case of open vascular bundles, a cambium layer or ring is present between xylem and phloem. The cambium ring helps in secondary growth.

Question 9. Give one basic functional difference between phellogen and phelloderm.

Answer Phellogen or cork cambium is made up of living permanent cells in the cortical region sometimes pericycle also. The cells of phellogen are meristematic. The cork cambium or phellogen cut off cells towards inside and add them to the cortex. These are called secondary cortex cells or phelloderm cells.

Question 10. Arrange the following in the sequence you would find them in a plant starting from the periphery–phellem, phellogen, phelloderm.

Answer Phellem or cork is the outermost layer, followed by phellogen which in turn is followed by phelloderm.

Question 11. If one debarks a tree, what parts of the plant is being removed?

Answer If one debarks a tree then all the tissues lying outside the xylem including phellem, phellogen, phelloderm, crushed primary cortex, secondary and primary phloem are removed. In fact all dead tissues are removed.

Question 12. What do hard wood and soft wood stand for?

Answer Gymnospermous wood that chiefly made up of tracheids and vessels are absent is known as soft wood, whereas a angiospermous wood, which is made up of both tracheids and vessels is known as hard wood.

Short Answer Type Questions

Question 1. While eating peach or pear it is usually seen that some stone-like structures get entangled in the teeth, what are these stone-like structures called?

Answer These stone-like structures are infact stone cells or sclerides, which are unbranched, short and isodiametric type of sclerides. These stone cells provide grit or stone-like structures that get entangled in the spaces between teeth.

Question 2. What is the commercial source of cork? How is it formed in the plant?

Answer The commercial cork is obtained from the cork tissue of *Quercus suber*, which yields bottle cork. Cork is formed by cork cambium or phellogen cells. Cork cambium cells divide periclinally, cutting cells towards the inside and outside. The cells cut off towards the outside become suberised and dead. These are compactly packed in radial rows without intercellullar spaces and form cork or phellem. Cork is impervious to water due to suberin and provides protection to the underlying tissues.

Question 3. Below is a list of plant fibres. From which part of the plant these are obtained
(a) coir (b) hemp (c) cotton (d) jute

Answer

(a) Coir is extracted from coconut seeds.
(b) Hemp is extracted from phloem tissue of stem.
(c) Cotton extracted from seeds.
(d) Jute extracted from phloem tissue of stem.

Question 4. What are the characteristic differences found in the vascular tissue of gymnosperms and angiosperms?

Answer Xylem and phloem are the vascular tissues of gymnosperms and angiosperms. Xylem is the chief water conducting tissue, whereas phloem is the food conducting tissue xylem consists of four elements, *e.g.*, xylem tracheids, vessels, xylem parenchyma and xylem fibres. Whereas phloem tissue consists of phloem parenchyma, sieve tube, companion cells and phloem fibres. In case of the gymnosperms, the vessels are absent whereas in angiosperms all the four xylem elements are present. In phloem tissue, the companion cells are absent in case of gymnosperms. The angiosperms have all the four phloem cells.

Question 5. Epidermal cells are often modified to perform specialised functions in plants. Name some of them and function they perform.

Answer Modified epidermal cells which perform special functions are

(i) **Bulliform cells** They are also known as motor cells, present in grasses. They loose water in dry conditions and cause rolling of leaves, thus reduce transpiration.

(ii) **Lithocytes or crystal cells** These are present in members of Apocynaceae and Moraceae. They contain crystals of calcium carbonate.

(iii) **Silica cells and cork cells** The silica cells contain granules of silica and the cork cells contain solid organic substances. These are present in graminaceous plants.

(iv) **Myrosin cells** These cells contain the enzyme myrosin and present in cruciferous plants.

Question 6. The lawn grass (*Cyanodon dactylon*) needs to be moved frequently to prevent its overgrowth. Which tissue is responsible for its rapid growth.

Answer Meristematic tissue. It is capable of rapid divisions.

Question 7. Plants require water for their survival. But when watered excessively, plants die. Discuss.

Answer Plants require water for their survival. But when watered excessively, it dies. This happens due to plugging of water conducting tissue, *i.e.*, xylem. The xylem tissue conducts water and solutes from the roots up to the top of the plant. The xylem tracheids and vessels are tube like elements, which help in conduction. The excess water cause their plugging.

Question 8. A transverse section of the trunk of a tree shows concentric rings which are known as growth rings. How are these rings formed? What is the significance of these rings?

Answer The cambium becomes more active during spring season and forms plenty of xylem vessels with wider cavities called as spring wood or early wood. In winter, however the cambial activity slows down and gives rise to narrower xylem elements. The wood thus formed in winter is called **autumn wood** or **late wood**. The growth rings help in determining the age of the plant. One year growth is indicated by one growth ring. These annual rings determine plant age.

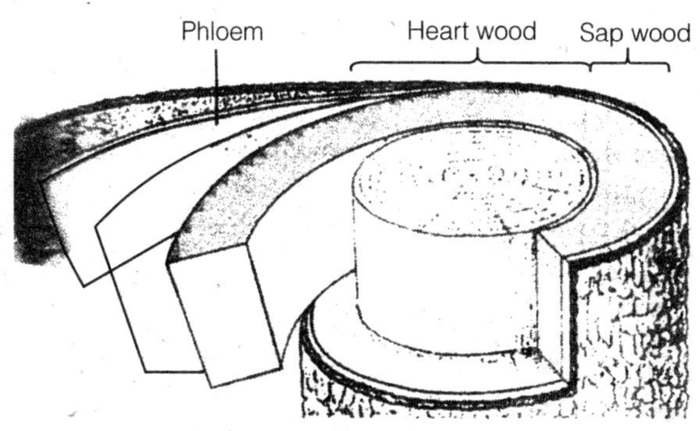

Structure showing growth rings

Question 9. Trunks of some of the aged tree species appear to be composed of several fused trunks. Is it a physiological or anatomical abnormality? Explain in detail.

Answer It is anatomical abnormality. It is an abnormal type of secondary growth, where a regular vascular cambium or cork cambium is not formed in its normal position. In case of old three trunks, anomalous secondary growth produces cortical and medullary vascular bundles. Thus, the additional or accessory vascular bundles give appearance of several fused trunks.

Question 10. What is the differences between lenticels and stomata?

Answer Lenticels are aerating pores present on the surface of bark. They represent a small portion of periderm. They help in exchange of gases. Stomata are minute apertures or openings present in the epidermis of all green aerial parts of plants. They are surrounded by guard cells, which may be dumb-bell-shaped or kidney-shaped.

Question 11. Write the precise function of

(a) Sieve tube
(b) Interfasicular cambium
(c) Collenchyma
(d) Aerenchyma

Answer

(a) **Sieve Tube** It is an elongated tube made up of sieve cells placed one after another in a row. The sieve tubes principally transports organic food in plants.

(b) **Interfascicular cambium** Interfascicular cambium is meristematic and it forms strips of cells by divisions, which join the strips of fascicular cambium and forms a complete cambial ring. The cambial ring helps in secondary growth. Thus, interfascicular cambium helps in secondary growth in plants.

(c) **Collenchyma** The collenchyma is a living mechanical tissue. It provides both mechanical strength and elasticity. It allows plant organs to grow in size. The cells of collenchyma may store food as well as manufacture it.

(d) **Aerenchyma** It is the parenchymatous tissue in aquatic plants, (*e.g., Hydrilla, Potamogeton*, etc.) and some land plants, (*e.g.*, petiole of banana, etc.). They make a network leaving wide air spaces for the gaseous exchange and make the aquatic plants light and buoyant so that they can easily afloat.

Question 12. The stomatal pore is guarded by two kidney-shaped guard cells. Name the epidermal cells surrounding the guard cells. How does a guard cell differ from an epidermal cell? Use a diagram to illustrate your answer?

Answer The epidermal cells which surround the guard cells are known as subsidiary cells or accessory cells. The guard cells are different from other epidermal cells, as these are living, bear chloroplasts, expand and contract in response to their turgidity and thus open or close the stomatal aperture. In case of dicot plants, the guard cells are kidney-shaped and in case of monocot plant are dumb-bell-shaped.

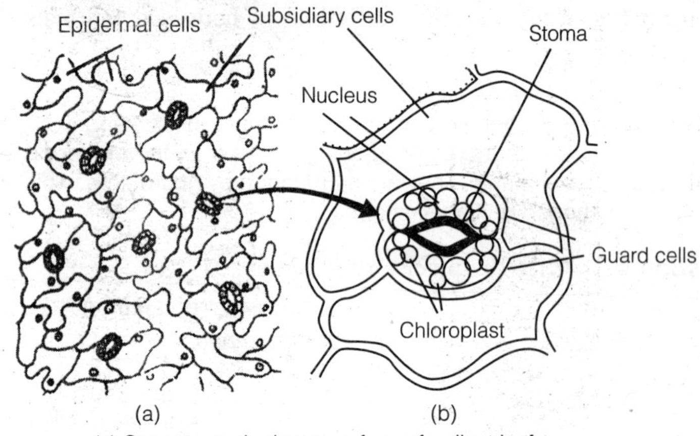

(a) Stomata on the lower surface of a dicot leaf

(b) Detailed structure

Question 13. Point out the differences in the anatomy of, leaf of peepal (*Ficus religiosa*) and maize (*Zea mays*). Draw the diagrams and label the differences.

Answer Peepal (*Ficus religiosa*) is a dicot and Maize (*Zea mays*) is a monocot.

Differences between *Ficus religiosa* leaf and *Zea mays* Leaf

S.N.	*Ficus religiosa* Leaf	*Zea mays* Leaf
1.	Stomata usually absent or less abundant in upper epidermis, while numerous in lower epidermis.	Stomata is almost equally distributed in upper and lower epidermis.
2.	Guard cells are kidney-shaped.	Guard cells are dumb-bell-shaped.
3.	Bulliform cells (motor cells) are absent.	Bulliform cells (motor cells) present.
4.	Mesophyll differentiated into palisade and spongy parenchyma.	Mesophyll is undifferentiated.
5.	Vascular bundles are arranged irregularly.	Vascular bundles are arranged in a row.
6.	Bundle sheath cells are colourless.	Bundle sheath are chlorophyllous.
7.	Bundle sheath extensions are parenchymatous.	Bundle sheath extensions are sclerenchymatous.
8.	Protoxylem almost indistinguishable. 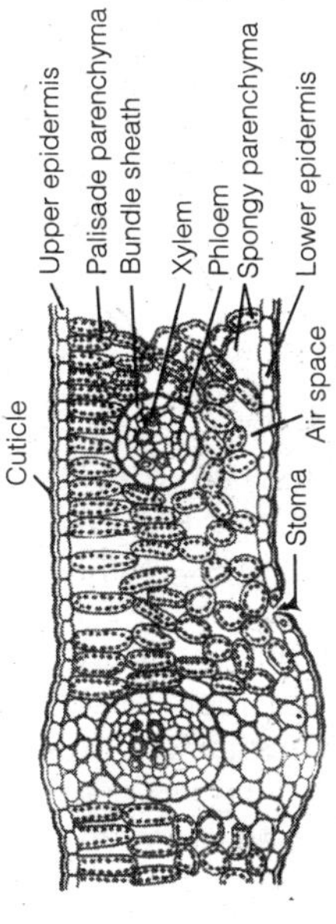	Protoxylem distinguishable. 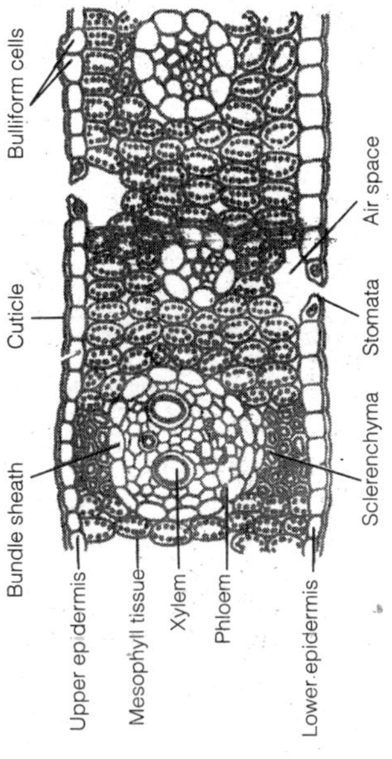

Question 14. Palm is a monocotyledonous plant, yet it increases in girth. Why and how?

Answer Secondary growth is usually absent in monocot stems as their vascular bundles are closed and they do not possess vascular cambium (fascicular cambium) like those of dicot stems. However, some arborescent monocots, *e.g.*, palms show prominant secondary growth and increase in their diameter.

In most of the palms and storage roots (rhizomes), the secondary growth is accomplished by primary thickening meristem, which originates below the region of attachment of the young leaf primordia. Primary thickening meristem produces anticlinal rows of cells by periclinal divisions, which at first and in the width of the plant but in later stages, it also brings about the increase in the height of the stem.

Long Answer Type Questions

Question 1. Deciduous plants shed their leaves during hot summer or in autumn. This process of shedding of leaves is called abscission. Apart from physiological changes, what anatomical mechanism is involved in the abscission of leaves.

Answer The process of shedding of leaves during hot summer or in autumn by deciduous plants is known as abcission. Anatomically, the cells of abcission zone are thin-walled and without deposition of lignin or suberin. At the time of abcission, the middle lamella may dissolve between the cells of two middle layers.

The middle lamella and primary walls of cells of middle layers and ultimately the whole cells of middle layer may dissolve and thus, there is separation of plant organ, *i.e.*, leaf.

Question 2. Is *Pinus* an evergreen tree. Explain.

Answer *Pinus* belongs to gymnosperms is an evergeen tree. The flowering plants under conditions of extreme cold shed their leaves and become dormant. But *Pinus* due to the presence of bark, which is thick, needle-like leaves having sunken stomata, reduce the rate of transpirations, the cold areas are both physiologically and physically dry due to scanty rainfall, precipitation as snow, decreased root absorption at low temperature and exposed habitats. But, *Pinus* is well adapted to such conditions. It continues to manufacture food during this period and grow to dominate other plants. This show that *Pinus* is an evergreen tree. It do not shed its leaves, *i.e.*, needles under any condition.

Question 3. Distinguish between the following

(a) Exarch and endarch condition of protoxylem

(b) Stele and vascular bundle

(c) Protoxylem and metaxylem

(d) Interfasicular cambium and intrafasicular cambium

(e) Open and closed vascular bundles

(f) Stem hair and root hair

Answer

(a) **Exarch and endarch condition of protoxylem** In exarch condition of protoxylem, it lies outside the metaxylem and in endarch condition the protoxylem lying inside the metaxylem.

(b) **Stele and vascular bundle** A ring of tissues that consist of epidermis, cortex, endodermis, pericycle along with xylem and phloem is known as stele, whereas vascular bundle is a ring of xylem and phloem vascular tissues.

(c) **Differences between Protoxylem and Metaxylem**

S.N.	Protoxylem	Metaxylem
1.	It is the first or earlier formed xylem.	It is the later formed xylem.
2.	Matures before the growth and differentiation of plant organs.	Matures after the growth and differentiation of plant organs.
3.	Protoxylem elements are smaller in diameter.	Metaxylem elements are broader and greater in diameter.
4.	Tyloses absent in protoxylem vessels.	Tyloses are generally present.
5.	Fibres are absent.	Fibres may be present.

(d) **Interfasicular cambium and intrafasicular cambium** In dicot stems, the cells of cambium present between primary xylem and primary phloem forms the intrafasicular cambium, whereas the cells of medullary rays. Adjoining these intrafasicular cambium become meristematic and forms the interfascicular cambium.

medullary rays. Adjoining these intrafasicular cambium become meristematic and forms the interfascicular cambium.

(e) **Differences between Open and Closed Vascular Bundles**

S.N.	Open Vascular Bundle	Closed Vascular bundle
1.	Intrafascicular combium between the phloem present.	Intrafascicular cambium absent.
2.	Occur in the stems of dicot and gymnosperms.	Occur in leaves and monocot stems.
3.	May be collateral or bicolateral.	May be collateral or concentric.
4.	Xylem and phloem not in direct contact with each other due to combial string.	Xylem and phloem are in direct contact due to back of cambial string.
5.	Intrafascicular cambium results in seconday growth.	No such activity found.
6.	Cambial activity produces secondary phloem and secondary xylem that push primary phloem and primary xylem away from each other.	No such activity found.

(f) **Differences between stem hair and root hair** The root hairs are elongated structure from the epidermal cells and help absorb water and minerals from the soil. On the stem, the epidermal hairs are known as trichomes. The trichomes in the shoot are usually multicellular. The trichomes help is preventing water loss due to transpiration.

7

Structural Organisation in Animals

Important Points

1. In animals multicellular organisms group of cells are specified to perform a particular function. Such an organization is called **tissue**.
2. There are four basic type tissues
   (i) Epithelial
   (ii) Connective
   (iii) Muscular
   (iv) Neural
   (i) **Epithelial tissue** provides a covering or lining for some organs/parts of the body.
      (a) There are two types of epithelial tissue—**simple epithelium** and **compound epithelium**.
         - **Simple epithelium** is made up of single layer of cells and functions as lining for body cavities, ducts and tubes. These cells are divided into four types
            - **Squamous epithelium** is present on absorptive and secretory surfaces. Made up of single thin layer of flattened cells with irregular boundaries found on wall of lungs.

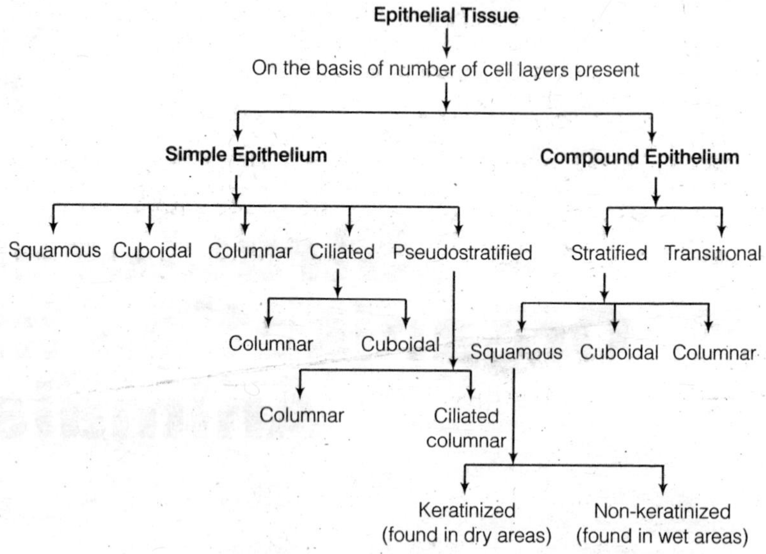

- **Cuboidal epithelium** consist of cuboidal cells with equal height and width. These are commonly found in ducts of glands and tubular parts of nephron in the kidney as microvilli. If microvilli are present at their surface than they are known as brush borbered.
- **Columnar epithelium** consist of tall prismatic cells placed side by side in form of columns. Nuclei is located at their base. These are found in the lining of stomach and intestine and help in secretions and absorption. These are seen with mucus secreting goblet cells.
- **Ciliated columnar epithelium** If columnar or cuboidal epithelium bear cilia on their surface these are known as **ciliated epithelium** cells. These are of two types
  (a) Ciliated columnar epithelium
  (b) Ciliated cuboidal epithelium
  Glandular epithelium consist of specialised columnar or cuboidal cell specialized for secretion. These may be unicellular, *e.g.*, glandular cell/goblet cells of alimentary canal and cluster of many cell, *e.g.*, in salivary gland.

- ➢ Glands may be exocrine glands or endocrine glands. Exocrine glands release, product through duct or a tube, while endocrine glands are known as ductless gland. They secrete the product directly into main stream.

- **Compound epithelium** is many cells thick. Its lowest cell rest on the basement membrane. All the cells arises from cell division by the lowest cell. There main role is to provide protection against chemical and mechanical stress. These are divided as
  - ➢ **Stratified squamous epithelium** Cells of uppermost layer are flat or scale like or squamous These are keratinized and non-keratinized.
  - ➢ **Stratified cuboidal epithelium** Cupper most layer is of cuboidal cells and basal layer of columnar cells.

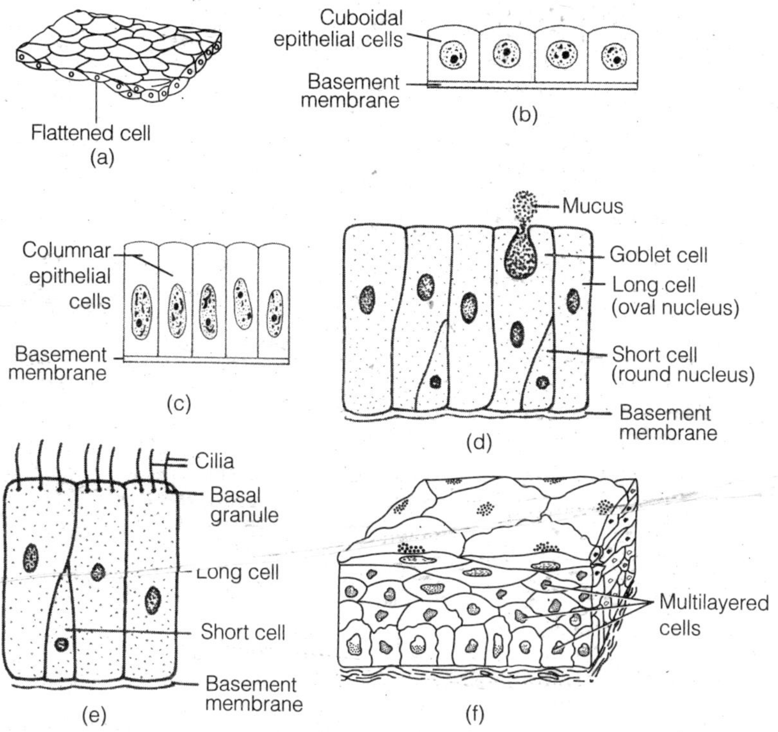

Type of tissues : (a) Squamous epithelium (b) Cuboidal epithelium (c) Columnar epithelium (d) Columnar pseudostratified epithelium (e) Columnar ciliated pseudostratified epithelium (f) Compound epithelium

- **Stratified columnar epithelium** Cupper most and basal layer both consist of columnar cells.
- **Transitional epithelium** appears stratified with five or more layer of pear-shaped cells during relaxed condition.
- There are three cell junctions found in epithelium and other tissues. These are known as **tight adhering** and gap **junctions**. Tight junctions seals the tissue. **Adhering junctions** perform cementing. Gap junctions facilitate the cells to communicate with each other by connecting the cytoplasm.

(ii) **Connective tissue** is the major supporting tissue of body which provides structural framework and support different tissues and help in body defence, tissue repair and fat storage.

These are classified as three basic type of tissues

(a) **Loose connective** tissues have fewer fibres and large amount of matrix. These are of two types

- **Areolar tissues** It contains transparent jelly like sticky matrix containing numerous fibres and cells. It contain fibroblast. Present beneath the skin.

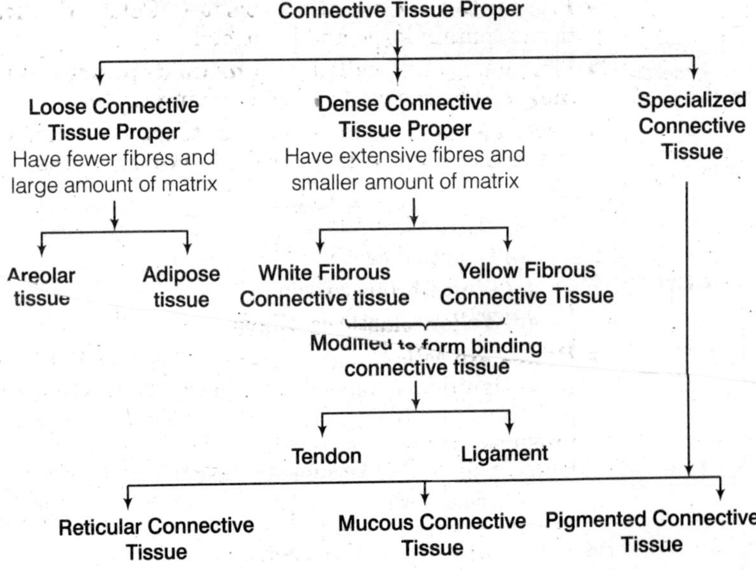

- **Adipose tissues** These are modified form of areolar tissue and is meant for fat storage. Its main cells is adipocytes. It is present beneath the skin, in the dermis region, around the kidney heart and eyeballs.

(b) **Dense connective tissue** Contains compactly packed fibres and fibroblasts. If fibres are arranged in a particular pattern they are known as dense regular tissue. If they are present in irregular pattern than known as dense irregular tissue.

- **Tendons** are the dense regular tissue, which attach skeletal muscles to bones. A type of white fibrous tissue.
- **Ligaments** are the irregular dense tissue, which attach one bone to another. A type of yellow fibrous tissue.

(c) Specialized connective tissue consist of

- **Reticular connective tissue** Cells are primitive and shows stellate appearance due to the presence of reticulin network. It forms reticulo endothelial system.
- **Mucous connective tissue** Present in embryo with Wharton's jelly as ground substance.
- **Pigmented connective tissue** Cells of these tissue contain large and branched.
- Pigment cells called **chromatophores** or **melanophores** containing melanin pigment.
- Cartilage is a solid semirigid tough and flexible connective tissue cells are called **chondrocytes**.

  e.g.,

  (a) Hyaline cartilage
  (b) Calcified cartilage
  (c) White fibrous cartilage
  (d) Yellow elastic cartilage.

- **Bones** are called osseous tissue. It is very hard and have significant deposits of inorganice calcium salt and collagen fibres. It is the main tissue which provides farmework to the body. It protects and support the softer tissues and organs. Bone cells are known as osteocytes, which are present in spaces called **lucunae**. Bone marrow in some bones is the site of production of new blood cells.

- Blood is the red coloured fluid connective tissue. It is the chief transport system of the body and play an important role in defense against diseases.

(iii) **Muscular tissue** Muscle is made up of many long cylindrical muscle fibres. Muscle cells are called myocytes or sarcocytes cytoplasm of muscle cells is known as **sarcoplasm**. Muscle fibres are composed of numerous fine fibrils called myofibril. Muscles plays an important role in all the movement of the body. Those are divided into

(a) **Smooth muscle** are involuntary muscles made up of spindle shaped cells and do not show-striations. It contains single nucleus surrounded by sarcoplasm. Myofibrils are arranged longitudinally. There is no sarcolemma. These are present in alimentary canal, urinary bladder, gall bladder, spleen, trachea, eyes, etc.

(b) **Striated or skeletal muscle** fibres are voluntary multinucleate, cylindrical structure. These are attached with bones and tendons responsible for the movement of skeleton. These have a clear display of longitudinal and cross striations.

(c) **Cardiac muscles** are found only in heart and forms myocardium. Its function is to pump blood through the circulatory system by contracting. These show striations. Myofibril are multinucleated, has numerous mitochondria and sarcomere. These cells are connected to each other by special *zig-zag* function called **intercalated disc**.

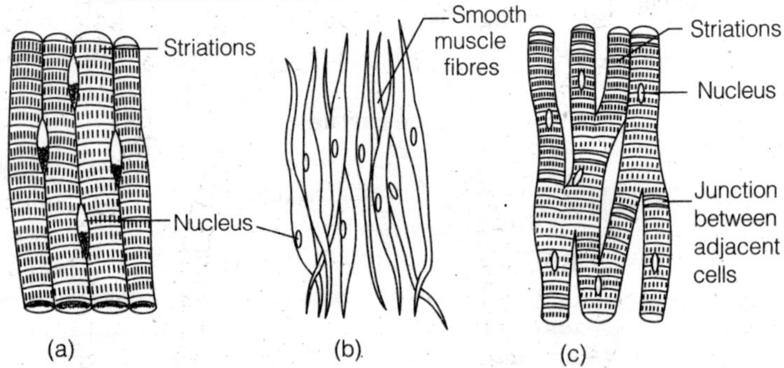

Muscle tissue : (a) Skeletal (striated) muscle tissue (b) Smooth muscle tissue (c) Cardiac muscle tissue

(iv) **Nervous tissue** or **Neural tissue** considered as specialized tissue with the property of excitability and conductivity. These are found in brain spinal cord and nerves.

(a) **Neurons** are basic unit of neural system. These are considered as the longest cells of the body. It has main cell body (also called cyton) and cytoplasmic processes arising from it called neurites/dendrites.

(b) All the four basic type of tissues constitutes organ system is multicellular organism morphology refers to the external appearance of the organ or part of the body.

3. *Pheretima posthuma* is a terrestrial earthworm living is burrows made in moist (soil) Earth.

(i) Earthworm has elongated cylindrical body, which is bilaterally symmetrical

(ii) Body is dark brown due to presence of porphyrin pigment and consist of 100-120 small ring like segments called somites or metameres shows true segmentation.

(iii) First body segment is peristomium or buccal segment which bears mouth.

(iv) A segment 14 to 16 prominant circular band of glandular tissue called **citellum** is present. Body is divided into preclitellar, clitellar and post-clitellar region.

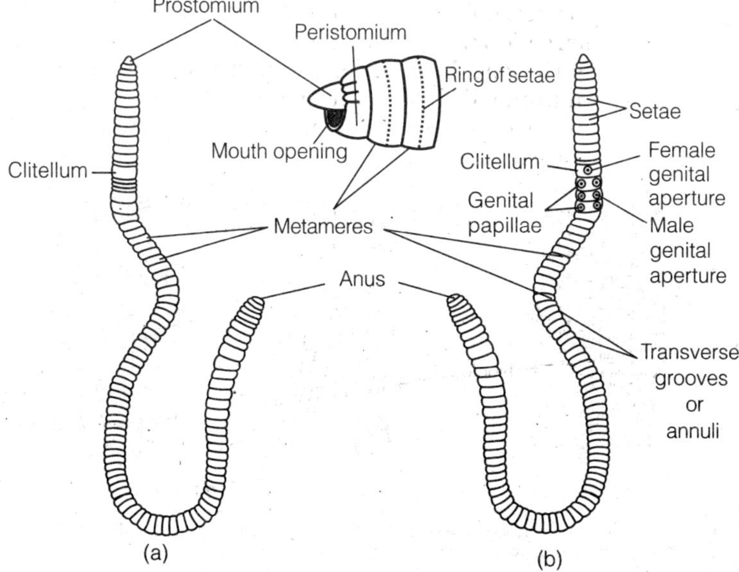

Body of earthworm : (a) Dorsal view (b) Ventral view
(c) Lateral view showing mouth opening

(v) Four pairs of spermathecal aperture is situated on ventro-lateral side of intersegmental groove 5-9th segment.

(vi) A pair of male genital pore are present on the ventro-lateral side of 18th segment.

(vii) **Nephridiopores** are the minute pores present on the body surface.

(viii) Setae or chaetae are the S-shaped, rod-like structure present in the middle of all the segments of body except first, last and clitellum. It helps is locomotion.

4. Anatomy is used to study the structure of internal organs in the animals

(i) Body wall of earthworm is covered by thin cuticle followed by epidermis well-developed musculature and coelomic epithelium.

(ii) Alimentary canal of *Pheretima* is complete runs between first and last segment of body mouth opens into buccal cavity (1-3 segments) leads to muscular pharynx. oesophagus starts from 3 to 9th segment when **gizzard** is present main grinding organ.

Stomach is tubular extending upto 14th segment longest and widest part of alimentary canal is intestine situated from 15th segment till the last segment of body large villi like internal fold is visible called **typhlosole**. Digestion is extracellular.

(iii) Closed type of circulatory system is present blood glands are present on the 4th, 5th and 6th segments produces blood cells and haemoglobin.

(iv) Respiratory exchange occurs, through moist body surface into their blood stream.

(v) Excretory system is made up of nephridia. According to their location these are classified as pharyngeal nephridia, integumentary nephridia and septal nephridia.

Pharyngeal nephridia open into alimentary canal and covers 4th, 5th and 6th segment. In tegumentary epithelium are seen from 7th segment 14th segment. The largest nephridia of earthworm are called **septal nephridia** as these are arranged sidewise the intersegmental septum.

(vi) It does not have eyes but have light and touch sensitive organs. Central nervous system consist of ventral nerve cord and a nerve ring. Worms have specialized chemoreceptors or (taste receptors). Which react to chemical stimuli.

(vii) Reproductive system of *Pheretima* is complicated with hermaphrodite condition.

(viii) Male reproductive organ include two pair of testes and two pair of testes sac. Situated at 10th and 11th segment.

(ix) Female reproductive organs includes ovaries one pair situated in the 13th segment being attached to the intersegmental septum of 12/13th segment 4 pairs of spermathecae or seminal receptacles are situated in 6th, 7th, 8th and 9th segments. Mutual exchanges of sperms occurs between two worms during mating cross fertilization occurs inspite of hermaphrodite condition. Process of fertilization occurs within the cocoon outside the body.

5. *Periplaneta americana* is a common cockroach, which is nocturnal omnivorous and cusorial in habitat.

(i) Morphology cockroach is divisible into three parts head, thorax and abdomen.

(ii) Body is covered by a hard chitinous exoskeleton. Exoskeleton has hardened plates called scleritis joined to each other by thin and flexible articular membrane (anthrodial membrane).

(iv) Head is triangular or pear-shaped and lies perpendicular to the longitudinal body axis. It is attached to thorax through the flexible neck or ceruicum. Head bears one pair of large and image forming compound eye and one pair of fenestra or ocellar spot compound eye consist of about 2000 **ommatidia**.

Mouth part consisting of labrum (upper lip). A pair of mandibles pair of maxillae and a labium (lower lip).

(v) Thorax is divided into prothorax (for wings arises from here) mesothorax and metathorax (second pair of wings arises) wind wings are used in flight.

(vi) Abdomen contain 10 segments, while in embryonic condition these are 11th segmented. In male genital aperture is situated in between 9th and 10th sterna.

(vii) Genital opening is placed on 8th sternum surrounded by gonophyses. Anus lies below 10th tergum between four pedical plates.

6. (i) Anatomically body wall of animal composed of cuticle, hypodermis and basement membrane cuticle is thick brown.

(ii) Alimentary canal of animal is complete and wall differentiated into midgut, hindgut and foregut.

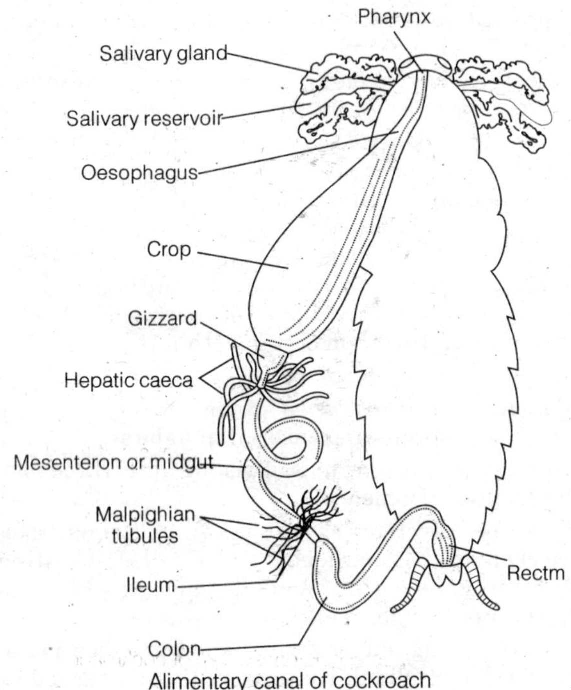

Alimentary canal of cockroach

(iii) Foregut includes mouth, pharynx, oesophagus, crop, gizzard. Mouth opens into a short tubular pharynx leading to narrow tubular passage called oesophagus. It enters into the prothorax and dialates into a pear shaped sac called **crop.** Crop serve as a reservoir for strong food.

(iv) **Gizzard** helps in grinding the food. A ring of 6-8 blind tubules called **hepatic** or **gastric caecae** present at the junction of forgut and midgut, which secretes digestive juice.

(v) At the junction of midgut and hindgut another ring of 100-150 yellow coloured.

(vi) Thin filamentous **Malpighian tubules** are present. Hindgut contains ileum colon and rectum.

(vii) Blood vascular system of cockroach is an open type with blood flowing in blood spaces or lacunae. It contains haemolymph. Heart of cockroach is pulsatile 13-chambered structure lying along mid dorsal line of thorax and abdomen blood from sinuses enter the heart through ostia and pumped anterior to sinuses again.

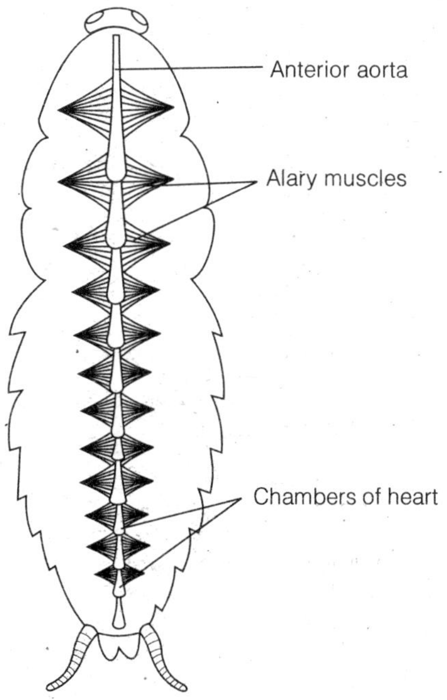

Open circulatory system of cockroach

(viii) Respiratory system of air tubes or trachea is present for gaseous exchange, which open at surface through spiracles or stigmata. In total 10 pairs of spiracles are present trachea ends up into large terminal cell containing few intracellular finer tubes called **tracheoles** or tracheal capillaries.

(ix) Cockroaches are uricotelic and excretion occurs through Malpighian tubule, fat body, cuticle and uricose gland.

(x) Nervous system of animal is well developed and differentiated into following three types

Central Nervous System (CNS).

Peripheral Nervous System (PNS).

Autonomic Nervous System (ANS).

(xi) It consist of series of fused segmentally arranged ganglia three ganglia is present in the thorax and six in abdomen.

Supra-oesophageal ganglia acts a brain.

(xii) In cockroach sense organ are antinnae eyes maxillary palps, labial palps, anal cerci, etc.

The compound eyes are located at the dorsal surface of head. It shows mosaic vision, receives several images of an object. Eyes consists 2000 hexagonal ommatidia.

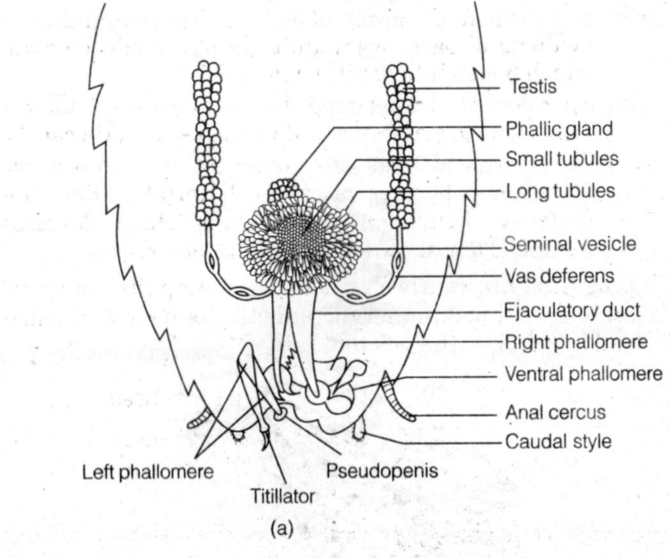

(a)

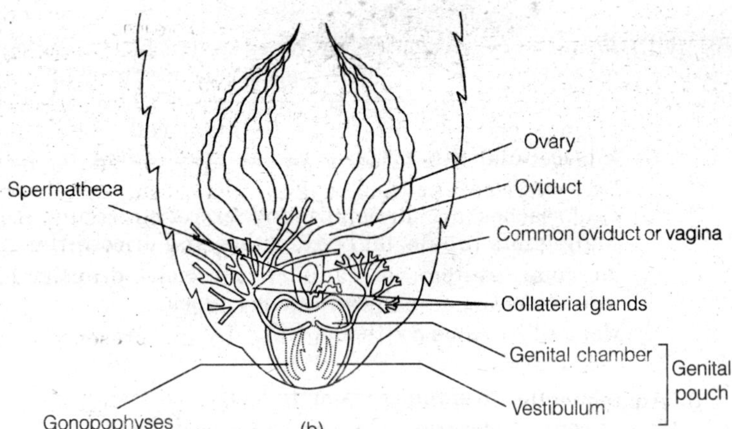

(b)

Reproductive system of cockroach : (a) Male (b) Female

(xiii) Cockroaches are dioecious and both sexes have well-developed reproductive organs. Male reproductive organ (testes) is situated from 4th to 6th abdominal segment from each testes there arises a thin vas deferens, which opens into a ejaculatory duct through seminal vesicle.

Ejaculatory duct open into male gonophore situated ventral to anus. Sperms are stored in seminal vesicle.

Female reproductive system consist of two large ovaries lying in 2-6th abdominal segment.

(xiv) It is formed of a group of eight ovarian tubules or ovarioles, oviducts of each ovary unite into a single median oviduct which opens into genital chamber.

(xv) Sperms are transferred through spermatophores. Their fertilized eggs are enclosed in a capsule oothecae.

(xvi) The fertilized eggs are arranged in 2 rowrs of 8 each surrounded by secretions of collaterial glands. Holoblastic cleavage occurs and a hatching stage develops called nymph. They show adult like characteristics.

7. Frog *(Rana tigrina)* belongs to class–Amphibia of vertebrate. A cold-blooded poikilothermic animal. Its body is consist of head and a trunck with neck and tail.

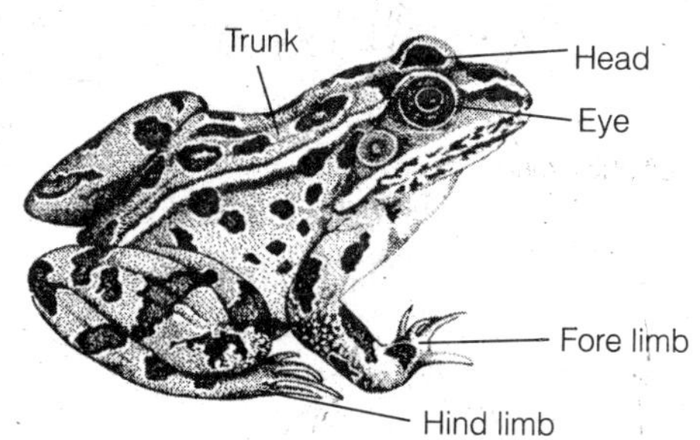

External features of frog

(i) A large mouth is situated at the anterior end of head. A thin transparent fold called nictitating membrane is produced by the lower eyelid. A pair of nostrils is present at the anterior region. Tympanum present on either side of the eyes receives the sound. Hind limbs end in five digits, while fore limb end in the four digits.

(ii) Male frogs can be distinguished by the presence of vocal sacs.

8. Anatomically frog have smooth, moist and scaleless skin. Colour of the skin is greenish yellow with dark spots on the dorsal surface. On ventral surface skin shows pale yellow colour.

(i) Digestive system consist of an alimentary canal. It consist of buccal cavity pharynx, oesophagus stomach, intestine and rectum, which opens into cloaca through anus.

(ii) Buccopharyngeal cavity is bounded by upper and lower jaws. The upper jaw bear a small uniform teeth. The lower jaw lacks teeth.

(iii) Tongue is sticky due to presence of mucous food is taken up by it and passed through oesophagus.

(iv) Oesophagous opens into stomach where food is digested by HCl and gastric juice.

(v) Gall bladder secretes bile juicy into duodenum and pancreatic juice from pancreas. It emulsifies fat and carbohydrates. Digested food is absorbed by numerous finger-like folds.

(vi) Respiration is cutaneous and occurs through skin outside the water. Respiration is pulmonary. During the process of breathing through buccopharyngeal cavity. The floor of buccal cavity shows oscillatory movements.

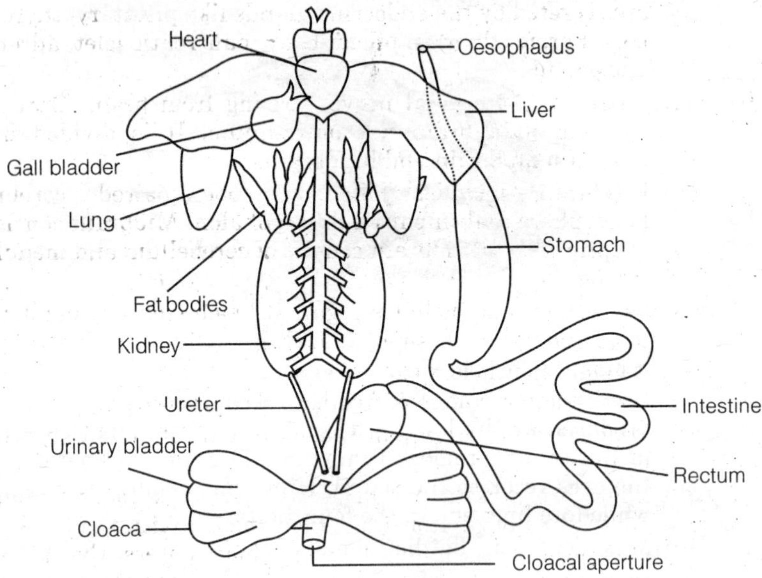

Diagrammatic representation of internal organs of frog showing complete digestive system

(vii) Circulatory system of frog consist of blood vascular system or lymphatic system. Heart of the frog is situated in the thoracic region within pericardial cavity and is three-chambered (two auricles and one ventricle).

(viii) Frog has highly developed nervous system consisting of a brain, a spinal cord and nerves. It has 10 pairs of cranial nerves and 10 pairs of spinal nerves.

(ix) Frog shows monocular vision. Harderian gland is present at the inner angle of the eye which produces oily secretion.

(x) Excretory system consist of a pair of kidneys, a pair of ureters, the urinary bladder and cloaca.

(xi) In adults kidney is **mesonephric** and in tadpoles it is pronephric. It is differentiated into cortex and medulla, it contain nephron along with transverse and longitudinal collecting ducts. Two ureters emerge from the kidneys in the male frogs. In females ureter and oviduct open separately in the cloaca.

(xii) Frog is **ureotelic** animal, *i.e.*, it excretes-urea.

(xiii) Neural and endocrine system is well-developed hormones are secreted by the endocrine glands like pituitary, thyroid, parathyroid, thymus, pineal body, pancreatic islet, adrenal and gonad.

(xiv) There are 10 cranial nerves arising from brain. Brain is enclosed in a brain box or cranium. It is divided into forebrain midbrain and hindbrain.

(xv) Forebrain includes olfactory lobe paired cerebral hemisphere and unpaired diencephalon. Midbrain consists of optic lobes. Hindbrain consist of cerebellum and medulla oblongata.

(xvi) Sensory organs includes organ of touch (sensory papillae), taste (taste buds), smell (nasal epithelium), vision (eyes), tympanum for hearing.

(xvii) Reproductive system of frog is well characterized.

(xviii) Male reproductive organ consist of pair of yellowish ovoid testes.

(xix) These are present on the upper part of kidneys through double fold of peritoneum called **mesorchium** 10-12 vasa efferentia arises from testes, which enters the kidney through bidder canal. It communicates with urogenital tract and opens into cloaca.

(xx) Female reproductive organs includes a pair of ovaries, which are not connected with kidneys. Pair of oviduct arises from ovary and opens into cloaca. On an average a mature female lays 2500 to 3000 ova at a time.

(xxi) Fertilization is external and require water development involves larval stage called tadpole, which metamorphosize to form an adult.

Exercises

Question 1. Answer in one word or one line.

(a) Give the common name of *Periplanata americana*.
(b) How many spermathecae are found in earthworm?
(c) What is the position of ovaries in cockroach?
(d) How many segments are present in the abdomen of cockroach?
(e) Where do you find Malpighian tubules?

Answer

(a) Cockroach
(b) Four pairs of spermathecae are present 6-9th segments.
(c) Ovaries present in 4th, 5th and 6th abdominal segments.
(d) 3-7 segments are present in the abdomen of cockroach.
(e) At the junction of midgut and hindgut of cockroach.

Question 2. Answer the following

(a) What is the function of nephridia?
(b) How many types of nephridia are found in earthworm based on their location?

Answer

(a) **The function of nephridia** The nephridia regulate the volume and composition of the body fluids. The nephridium starts out as a funnel that collects excess fluid from coelomic chamber. The funnel connects with a tubular parts of the nephridium, which delivers the wastes through a pore to the surface in the body wall in the digestive tube.

(b) Based on their location, there are three types of nephridia in earthworm.
- Septal nephridia.
- Pharyngeal nephridia.
- Integumentary nephridia.

Question 3. Draw a labelled diagram of the reproductive organs of an earthworm.

Answer

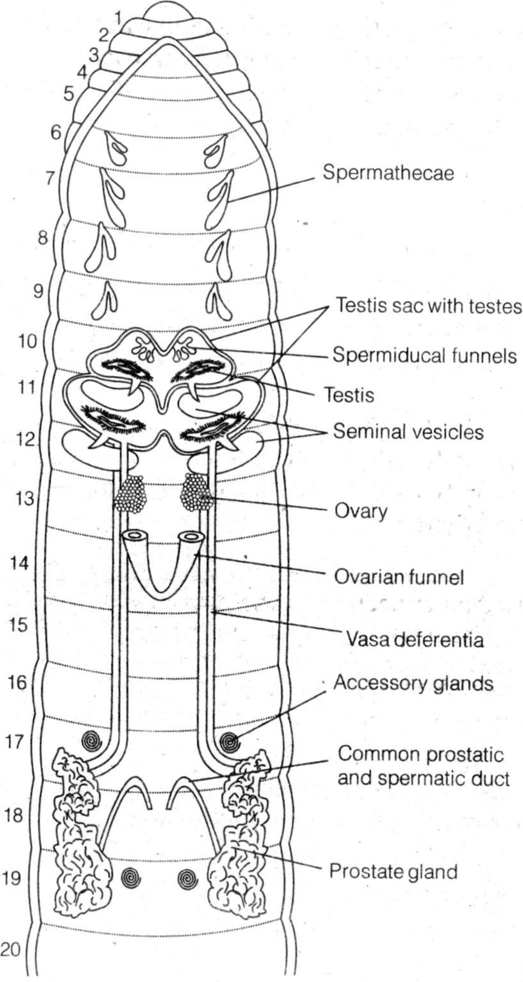

Reproductive system of earthworm

Question 4. Draw a labelled diagram of alimentary canal of a cockroach.

Answer

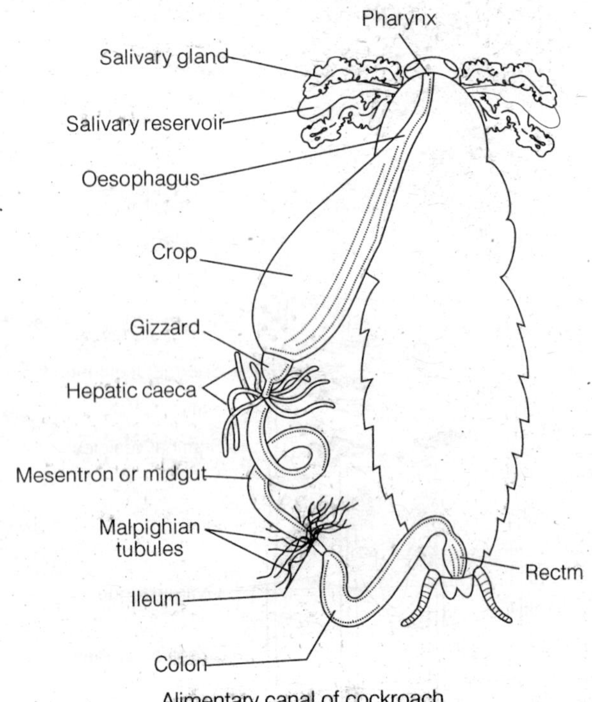

Alimentary canal of cockroach

Question 5. Distinguish between the followings

(a) Prostomium and peristomium.

(b) Septal nephridium and pharyngeal nephridium.

Answer

(a) **Prostomium and peristomium** The first segment of earthworm with a ventral mouth is known as **peristomium**. Prostomium is a dorsal lobe which is present on the ventral mouth.

(b) **Septal nephridia and pharyngeal nephridia** Septal nephridia are present on both the sides of intersegmental septa of segment 15 to the last that open into intestine.

The pharyngeal nephridia are closed (no nephrostome) nephridia present as three paired groups (of about 100) in 4th, 5th and 6th segments.

Question 6. What are the cellular components of blood?

Answer Blood is a fluid connective tissue containing plasma, red blood cells (RBC), white blood cells (WBC) and platelets. It is the main circulating fluid that helps in the transport of various substances.

Question 7. What are the following and where do you find them in animal body (a) Chondrocytes (b) Axons (c) Ciliated epithelium.

Answer

(a) **Chondrocytes** These are the matrix secreting cells of the cartilage. These are found in the cartilage of connecting tissue.

(b) **Axon** It is a long fibre, the distal end of which is branched. Each branch terminates as a bulb like structure called synaptic knob. The axon transmit nerve impulses away from the cell body.

(c) **Cilliated epithelium** If the columnar or cuboidal cells of columnar and cuboidal epithelium bear cillia on their free surface they are called cilliated epithelium.

Question 8. Describe various types of epithelial tissues with the help of labelled diagrams?

Answer **Epithelial tissues** Epithelial tissues provide covering to the inner and outer lining of various organs. There are two types of epithelial tissues:

(a) **Simple epithelium** Simple epithelium is composed of a single layer of cells. If functions as a lining for body cavities, ducts and tubes.

(b) **Compound epithelium** The compound epithelium consists of two or more cell layers. It has protective function as it does in our skin. It covers the dry surface of the skin, the moist surface of buccal cavity, pharynx, inner lining of ducts of salivary glands and of pancreatic ducts.

On the basis of structural modifications of the cells, simple epithelium is further divided into three types. These are:

(a) **Squamous epithelium** The squamous epithelium is made of a single thin layer of flattened cells with irregular boundaries. They are found in the walls of blood vessels and air sacs of lungs and are involved in a functions like forming a diffusion boundary.

(b) **Cuboidal epithelium** The cuboidal epithelium is composed of a single layer of cube-like cells. This is commonly found in the ducts of glands and tubular parts of nephrons in kidneys. Its main functions are secretion and absorption.

(c) **Columnar epithelium** The columnar epithelium is composed of a single layer of tall and slender cells. They are found in the lining of stomach and intestine and help in absorption and secretion.

(i) When the columnar or cuboidal cells bear cilia on their free surface they are called **ciliated epithelium**. Their function is to move particles or mucus in a specific direction over the epithelium organs like bronchioles and fallopian tubules.

(ii) Some of the columnar or cuboidal cells get specialized for secretion are caled **glandular eptheilium**. They are unicellular and multicellular.

Question 9. Distinguish between

(i) Simple epithelium and compound epithelium.
(ii) Cardiac muscle and striated muscle.
(iii) Dense regular and dense irregular connective tissues.
(iv) Adipose and blood tissue.
(v) Simple gland and compound gland.

Answer

(i) **Differences between Simple Epithelium and Compound Epithelium**

S.N.	Simple Epithelium	Compound Epithelium
1.	It is composed of a single layer of cells.	It consists of two or more cell layers.
2.	It functions as a lining for body cavities, ducts and tubes.	It is protective in function like our skin.

(ii) **Differences between Cardiac and Striated Muscle**

S.N.	Cardiac Muscle	Striated Muscle
1.	It occurs only in the wall of heart.	It occurs in the body wall, limb, tongue, pharynx, etc.
2.	They are short and cylindrical with truncate ends.	They are long and cylindrical with blunt ends.
3.	They have nerve supply from brain and autonomous nerve system.	They have nerve supply from central nervous system.

(iii) **Differences between Dense Regular and Dense Irregular Connective Tissues**

Dense Regular	Dense Irregular
Collagen fibres are present in rows between many parallel bundle of fibres. **Example** Tendons	Fibroblasts and many fibre are present that are oriented differently. **Example** Cartilage, bones and blood.

(iv) **Differences between Adipose Tissue and Blood**

S.N.	Adipose Tissue	Blood
1.	It is located mainly beneath the skin.	It flows within the blood vessels and contains RBCs, WBCs and platelet.
2.	It stores fat and excess nutrients.	It help in transport of various substance.

(v) **Differences between Simple and Compound Gland**

S.N.	Simple Gland	Compund Gland
1.	These glands have single, unbranched duct.	These glands have branched system to ducts.
2.	These may be simple tubular glants simple coiled tubular glands and simple alveolar glands.	These may be compound tubular glands, compound alveolar glands and compound tubloalveolar glands.

Question 10. Mark the odd one in each series

(a) Areolar tissue, blood, neuron, tendon
(b) RBC, WBC, Platelets, Cartilage
(c) Exocrine, endocrine, salivary gland; ligament
(d) Maxilla, mandible, labrum, antennae
(e) Protonema, mesothorax, metathorax, coxa

Answer (a) Neuron (b) Cartilage (c) Ligament
(d) Antennae (e) Coxa

Question 11. Match the terms in column I with those in column II.

Column I	Column II
A. Compound epithelium	1. Alimentary canal
B. Compound eye	2. Cockroach
C. Septal nephridia	3. Skin
D. Open circulatory system	4. Mosaic vision
E. Typhlosole	5. Earthworm
F. Osteocytes	6. Phallomere
G. Genitalia	7. Bone

Answer

Column I	Column II
A. Compound epithelium	3. Skin
B. Compound eye	4. Mosaic vision
C. Septal nephridia	5. Earthworm
D. Open circulatory system	2. Cockroach
E. Typhlosole	1. Alimentary canal
F. Osteocytes	7. Bone
G. Genitalia	6. Phallomere

Question 12. Mention briefly about the circulatory system of earthworm.

Answer **Circulatory system of earthworm** It is of closed type with different arrangement of blood vessels in the first thirteen segments as compared to the rest of the body. The circulatory system consists of blood vessels, capillaries and heart. Due to closed circulatory system, blood is confined to the heart and blood vessels. Smaller blood vessels supply the gut, nerve cord and the body wall. Blood glands are present on the 4th, 5th and 6th segments. They produce blood cells and haemoglobin which is dissolved in blood plasma. Blood cells are phagocytic in nature.

Question 13. Draw a neat diagram of digestive system of frog.

Answer

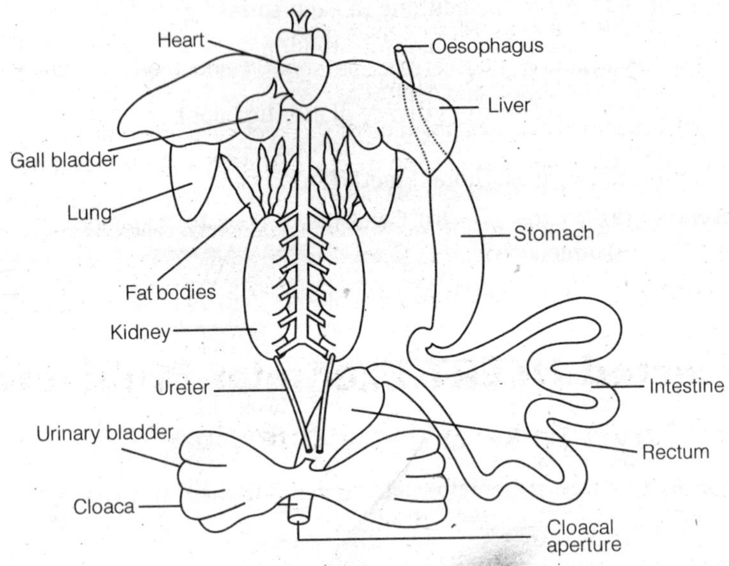

Diagrammatic representation of internal organs of frog showing complete digestive system

Question 14. Mention the function of the following

(a) Ureters in frog
(b) Malpighian tubules
(c) Body wall in earthworm

Answer

(a) **Functions of ureters in frog** In male frog, two ureters emerge from the kidneys. The ureters act as urinogenital duct which opens into the cloaca. Thus, the ureters carry both sperms and excretory wastes to the cloaca. In female frog, the ureters and oviduct open separately in the cloaca. The ureters in frog, thus acts as carrier of sperms and ova.

(b) **Functions of Malpighian tubules of cockroach** Excretion is carried out by Malpighian tubules. Each tubule is lined by glandular cells. They absorb excretory waste products and converts them into uric acid which is excreted out through the hindgut.

(c) **Functions of body wall of earthworm** The body wall of earthworm has five layers-cuticle, epidermis, circular muscle layer, longitudinal muscle layer, peritoneum.

  (i) Cuticle is a non-cellular elastic layer.

  (ii) The columnar cells of provide support and therefore, are also known as supporting cells.

  (iii) Epidermis also has gland cells, receptor cells and basal cells.

  (iv) The glandular cell secrete mucus and thus, keep the skin moist, this help in cutaneous respiration.

  (v) The last layer of the body wall is the outer membrane of the coelom called coelomic epithelium. The various muscle layers of the body wall provide strength and rigidity.

Selected NCERT Exemplar Problems

Very Short Answer Type Questions

Question 1. State the number of segments in earthworm which are covered by a prominent dark clitellum.

Answer Segments 14-16 are covered by clitellum.

Question 2. Where are sclerites present in cockroach?

Answer Sclerites are present in the exoskeleton in each segment of cockroach.

Question 3. How many times do nymphs moult to reach the adult form of cockroach?

Answer The nymphs of cockroach moult about 13 times to reach the adult stage.

Question 4. Identify the sex of a frog in which sound producing vocal sacs are present.

Answer Male frog.

Question 5. Name the process by which a tadepole develops into an adult frog.

Answer Metamorphosis.

Question 6. What is the scientific term given to earthworm's body segments?

Answer Metameres.

Question 7. A muscle fibre tapers at both the ends and does not show striations. Name the muscle fibre.

Answer Smooth muscle fibre.

Question 8. Name the different cell junctions found in tissues?

Answer The different cell junctions found in tissues are

(i) Tight junctions
(ii) Gap junctions
(iii) Adhering junctions

Question 9. Give two identifying features of an adult male frog.

Answer (a) Vocal sacs (b) Thumb pads/copulatory pad in thumb.

Question 10. Which mouth part of cockroach is comparable to our tongue?

Answer Hypopharynx.

Question 11. The digestive system of frog is made of the following parts. Arrange them in an order beginning from mouth.
Mouth, oesophagous, buccal cavity, stomach, intestine, cloaca, rectum, clacal aperture.

Answer Mouth – Buccal cavity – Oesophagous – Stomach – Intestine – Rectum – Cloaca – Clocal aperture.

Question 12. What is the difference between cutaneous and pulmonary respiration?

Answer In frog, two types of respiration take place. When respiration takes place through moist skin, then it is known as cutaneous respiration and when respiration takes place through lungs then it is known as pulmonary respiration.

Question 13. Special venous connection between liver and in-testine and between kidney and intestine is found in frog, what are they called?

Answer Special venous connection between liver and intestine of frog is known as **hepatic portal system** and venous connection between kidney and intestine is known as **renal portal system.**

Short Anwer Type Questions

Question 1. Give the location of hepatic caecae in cockroach. What is their function?

Answer In cockroach, the hepatic caecae are present at the junction of foregut and midgut. The hepatic caecae function similar to vertebrate liver. They secrete digestive juices and thus, help in the digestion.

Question 2. Frogs are beneficial for mankind, justify the statement.

Answer Frogs are beneficial for mankind because they eat insects and protect our crops. They eat mosquito larvae and help in preventing malaria. Frogs maintain ecological balance because they serve as important link of food chain and food web in the ecosystem. In some countries, the muscular legs of frogs are used as food by man.

Question 3. The body of sponges does not possess tissue level of organisation though it is made of thousand of cells. Comment.

Answer The level of organisation in sponges is cellular. The cells do not organise to form tissues, although they have thousand of cells. They may be solitary or colonial. The cells function more or less independently.

Question 4. Structural organisation in amimals attain different levels as cell, organ, organ system. What is missing in this chain? Mention the significance of such an organisation.

Answer Tissue is missing cells aggregate to form tissues, which in turn form organs and ultimately an organism. Such an organisation is essential for more efficient and better coordinated activities. The organs arrange into organ systems, which exhibits the division of labour and contribute to the survival of the body as a whole.

Question 5. Stratified epithelial cells have limited role in secretion. Justify their role in our skin.

Answer Stratified epithelium consists of two or more cell layers stacked one on top of the other. They regenerate from below when the basal cells divide and push apically to replace older cells. They have limited role in secretion and absorption. Their main function is to provide protection against chemical and mechanical stresses. They cover the dry surface of the skin, the moist surface of buccal cavity, pharynx, the inner lining of ducts of salivary glands and of pancreatic ducts.

Question 6. How does a gap junction facilitate intercellular communication?

Answer Gap junctions facilitate intercellular communication by allowing small signaling molecules to pass from cell to cell. In fact, gap junctions are fine hydrophilic channels between two adjacent animal cells that are formed with the help of two special protein cylinders called connexus. Each connexon consists of six protein subunits that surround a hydrophilic channel. Gap junctions connect small and large molecules.

Question 7. Why are blood, bone and cartilage called connective tissue?

Answer Blood is a fluid connective tissue, which contain cells like RBCs, WBCs and platelets.

Bone is the hardest tissue in the body which consists of numerous collagen fibres and osteocytes within the matrix. Cartilage is a tough but flexible connective tissue which consists of collagen and elastin fibres along with the chondrioblast cells in the matrix.

Question 8. Why are neurons called excitable cells? Mention special feature of the membrane of a neuron?

Answer Neurons, the unit of neural system are excitable cells. When a neuron is suitably stimulated, an electric disturbance is generated, which swiftly travels along its plasma membrane. Arrival of the disturbance at the neuron's ending or output zone, triggers events that may cause stimulation or inhibition of adjacent neurons and other cells. These are excitable cells due to differential concentration gradient of ions across the membrane.

Question 9. Why earthworm is called the friend of a farmer?

Answer Earthworms are known as 'friends of farmers' because they make burrows in the soil and make it porous. It helps in respiration and penetration of developing plant roots. The process of increasing fertility of soil by the earthworms is called vermicomposting. They are also used as bait in game fishing.

Question 10. How do you distinguish between dorsal and ventral surface of the body of earthworm.

Answer Earthworm have long cylindrical body animals. It dorsal surface of the body is marked by a dark medium mid dorsal line (dorsal blood vessel) along the longitudinal axis of the body. The ventral surface is distinguished by the presence of genital openings known as genital pores.

Question 11. Correct the wrong statements of the following

(a) In earthworm, a single male genital pore is present.
(b) Setae help in locomotion of earthworm.
(c) Muscular layer in the body wall of earthworm is made up of only circular muscles.
(d) Typhlosole is the part of intestine of earthworm.

Answer

(a) Wrong statement, a pair of male genital pores is present on the ventro-lateral side of the 18th segment.
(b) The statement is correct.
(c) Muscular layer in the body wall of earthworm is made up of circular and longitudinal muscles.
(d) The statement is correct.

Question 12. What is special about tissue present in the heart?

Answer The tissue present in the heart is known as cardiac muscle tissue. It is a highly contractile tissue, cells junctions fuse the plasma membranes of cardiac muscle cells and make them stick together. Communication junction at some fusion points allows the cells to contract as a unit.

Question 13. Why nephridia in earthworm that are basically similar in structure classified into three types? Mention the names of each.

Answer Nephridia are the excretory organs of earthworm. These are coiled structures. There are three types. These are basically similar in structure but are given different names depending upon the body segments in which they are present.

(i) **Septal nephridia**. These are present on both sides of intersegmental septa of segment 15 to the last that open into intestine.

(ii) **Integumentary nephridia** These are attached to lining of the body wall of segment 3 to the last that open on the body surface.

(iii) **Pharyngeal nephridia** These are present as three paired tufts in the 4th, 5th and 6th segments.

Question 14. Common names of some animals are given in column A, write their scientific name in column B.

Column A	Column B
(a) Tiger	(i) ....
(b) Peacock	(ii) ....
(c) Housefly	(iii) ....

Answer

Column A	Column B
(a) Tiger	(i) *Panthera tigris*
(b) Peacock	(ii) *Pavo cristatus*
(c) Housefly	(iii) *Musca domestica*

Question 15. Complete the following statement.

(a) In cockroach grinding of food particle is performed by ....
(b) Malpighian tubules help in the removal of ....
(c) Hind gut of cockroach is differentiated into ....
(d) In cockroach blood vessel open into spaces called ....

Answer

(a) Mandibles.
(b) Uric acid.
(c) Hind gut is differentiated into ileum, colon and rectum.
(d) Haemocoel.

Question 16. Mention special features of eye in cockroach.

Answer Cockroach have compound eyes for photoreception. Each eye consists of about 2000-2500 units called 'Ommatidium'. Compound eye contains from top to bottom a lens, two corneagen cells, a crystalline cone and surrounding four cone cells and seven retinular cells. Retinular cells after resting on basement membrane gives off nerve fibres, which unite to form an optic nerve. The lens is seen as a hexagonal facet of cuticle, which is bioconvex in appearance. All such facets of an eye together called cornea. Along with compound eyes for sight at the base of each antenna, a fenestra is present representing the simple eye.

Question 17. Frog is poikilotherm, exhibits camouflage and undergoes aestivation and hibernation. How are all these beneficial to it?

Answer Frog is a poikilothermal or ectothermal animal (*i.e.*, cold-blood). In this animal, temperature of the body varies according to that of surrounding. This enables to live them suitably both in freshwater and moist soil.

Frog can change the colour of its skin (metachrosis) to match its surroundings. This helps the animal in protecting itself from enemies and obtaining its prey easily.

Question 18. Write the function in brief in column B, appropriate to the structures given in column A.

Column A	Column B
A. Nictitating membrane	(i) ....
B. Tympanum	(ii) ....
C. Copulatory pad	(iii) ....

Answer

Column A	Column B
A. Nictitating membrane	(i) Protect eyes of frog
B. Tympanum	(ii) Hearing and balancing
C. Copulatory pad	(iii) Helps in copulation for holding the female

Question 19. Write the appropriate type of tissues in column B according to the functions mention in column A.

Column A	Column B
A. Secretion and absorption	(i) ....
B. Protective covering	(ii) ....
C. Linking and supporting framework	(iii) ....

Answer

Column A	Column B
A. Secretion and absorption	(i) Glandular epithelium
B. Protective covering	(ii) Compound epithelium
C. Linking and supporting framework	(iii) Connective tissue

Long Answer Type Questions

Question 1. Write down the common features of the connective tissue. On the basis of structure and function, differentiate between bones and cartilages.

Answer

Common Features of Connective Tissue

(i) Connective tissue develops from embryonic mesoderm. In the head region, it is mainly formed of neural crest.

(ii) It is made of two strucutres, living cells and extracellular matrix.

(iii) There are two or more types of living cells.

(iv) Living cells generally lie scattered. At times, they form small loose groups.

(v) Extracellular matrix is abundant.

(vi) Ground substance may be liquid, gel or solid.

(vii) The extracellular matrix has amorphous ground substance that is made of proteoglycans.

(viii) The tissue has good amount of regenerative ability.

(ix) It connects and provides support to various structures of animal body.

Differences between Bones and Cartilages

S.N.	Bone	Cartilage
1.	It has hard and non-pliable ground substance, which is rich in salts and collagen fibres	It is solid and pliable can resist compression.
2.	It is the main tissue that provides Structural frame work to the body.	It is present in tip of nose, outer ear joints, between adjacent bones of the vertebral column, limbs and hands in adults.

Question 2. Comment upon the gametic exchange in earthworm during mating.

Answer **Gametic exchange in cockroach** A mutual exchange of sperm occurs between two worms during mating. They mate juxtaposing opposite gonadal openings exchanging packets of sperms called spermatophores. Mature sperm and egg cells and nutritive fluid are deposited in cocoons produced by the gland cells of clitellum. Fertilization and development occur within these cocoons which are deposited in soil. The eggs are fertilized by the sperms within the cocoons which then slips off the worm and is deposited in or on the soil.

Question 3. Explain the digestive system of cockroach, with the help of a labelled sketch.

Answer The digestive system of cockroach The alimentary canal of cockroach is complete, *i.e.*, it opens by mouth and opens out through the anus. The alimentary canal is divided into three parts, *e.g.*, foregut, midgut and hindgut. The different parts of digestive system are as follows:

(i) The buccal chamber have mouth on one side of it and pharynx on the outer side.

(ii) The oesophagus enters into prothorax and gradually dilates into a pear-shaped sac called crop. Crop is thin walled and pear-shaped extending up to the 3rd and 4th abdominal segment.

(iii) Midgut is the portion between Malpighian tubule and hepatic caeca.

(iv) The hindgut contains ileum, colon and rectum. Colon is the longest part of hindgut.

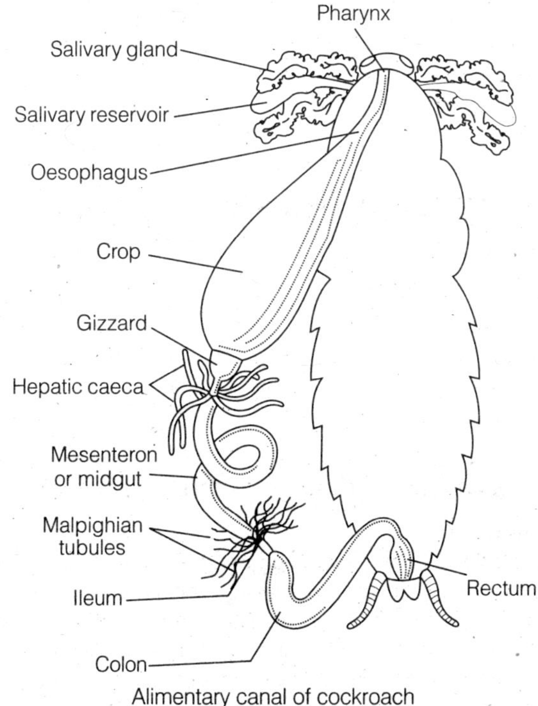

Alimentary canal of cockroach

Question 4. Draw a neat and well-labelled diagram of male reproductive system of frog.

Answer

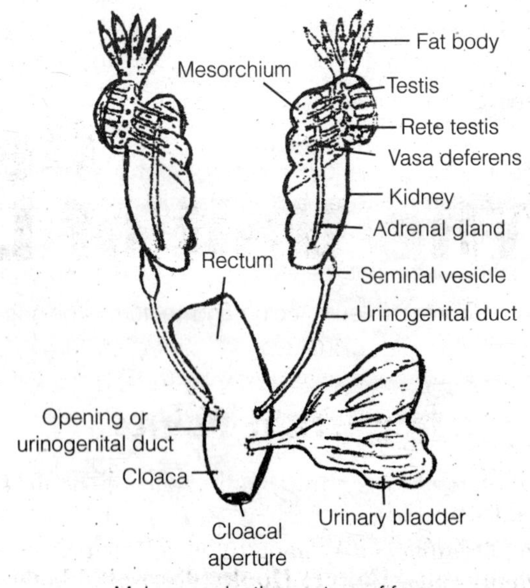

Male reproductive system of frog

8

Cell : The Unit of Life

Important Points

1. **Cell** is the basic functional and structural unit of **organisation**.
2. All living organisms are made up of cell, which may be single cell or many cells. **Robert Hooke** discovered honey comb-like structure in tissues.
3. **Antony von Leeuwenhoek** firstly saw living cell.
4. **Schleiden** and **Schwann** gave cell theory in (1838), which says.
   (i) All living beings are made up of cells and products formed by cells.
   (ii) Cells are the structural and functional unit of life.
5. **Virchow** expanded it further by his concept '*Omnis cellula e cellula* (all cells arising from pre-existing cells).
6. **Robert Brown** discovered the nucleus.
7. Living cells are classified into two types of cells **prokaryotic** and **eukaryotic cell**.
8. The basis of difference between the two types of cells is presence of distinct membrane bound nucleus.
9. Apart from presence and absence of nucleus. There are many difference in between prokaryotic and eukaryotic cell.

Comparison between Prokaryotic and Eukaryotic Cell

Feature	Prokaryotic Cell	Eukaryotic Cell
Organisms	Bacteria	Protista, fungi, plants and animals.
Cell size	Average diameter 0.5-10 μm.	10-100-μm diameter common; commonly 1000-10000 times volume of prokaryotic cells.
Form	Mainly unicellular	Mainly multicellular (except Protista, many of which are unicellular)
Cell division	Mostly binary fission, no spindle.	Mitosis, meiosis or both; spindle formed.
Genetic material	DNA is circular and lies free in the cytoplasm (no true nucleus) DNA is naked (not associated with proteins or RNA to form chromosomes).	DNA is linear and contained in a nucleus. DNA is associated with proteins ans RNA to form chromosomes.
Protein synthesis	70 S ribosomes (smaller). No endoplasmic reticulum present.	80 S ribosomes (larger). Ribosomes may be attached to endoplasmic reticulum.
Organelles	Few organelles. None are surrounded by an envelope (two membranes). Internal membranes scarce; if present usually associated with respiration or photosynthesis (mesosomes).	Many organelles. Envelope bounded organelles present, *e.g.*, nucleus, mitochondria and chloroplasts. Organelles bounded by single membrane, *e.g.*, Golgi apparatus, lysosomes, vacuoles, microbodies and endoplasmic reticulum.
Cell wall	Rigid and contain polysaccharides with amino acids; murein is main strengthening compound.	Cell wall of green plants and fungi rigid and contain polysaccharides, cellulose is main strengthening compound of plant walls, chitin of fungal walls (none in animal cells).
Respiration	Mesosomes in bacteria, except cytoplasmic membranes in blue-green bacteria.	Mitochondria for aerobic respiration.

10. Cells varies in size, shape and activities smallest cell is only 0.3 μm in length, while human blood cells are 7.0 μm in diameter. Longest cell is nerve cell.
   (i) Cells also vary in shape, *e.g.*,
      (a) **Red blood cells** round and biconcave.
      (b) **White blood cells** amoeboid.
      (c) **Columnar epithelial cells** long and narrow.
      (d) **Nerve cells** branched and long.

- (e) **Tracheids** elongated.
- (f) **Mesophyll cells** round and oval.

(ii) Bacteria also shows variable shapes like.
- (a) **Bacillus** rod-like.
- (b) **Coccus** spherical.
- (c) **Vibrio** comma-shaped.
- (d) **Spirillum** spiral.

11. The chief components of cells are
    - (i) **Cell envelope** (in case of bacteria)/ **Cell wall** (in case of plants).
    - (ii) **Cell membrane**
    - (iii) **Cytoplasm**
    - (iv) **Nucleus**
    - (v) **Cell organelles** (endoplasmic reticulum, lysosomes, vacuoles, ribosomes, cytoskeleton network, Golgi apparatus, mitochondria and chloroplast).
12. Bacteria cell possess cell envelope. Cell envelope consists of
    - (i) glycocalyx
    - (ii) cell wall
    - (iii) plasma membrane.
        - (a) On the basis of structure of cell envelope. Bacterial cells are divided into two classess
            - Gram positive bacteria
            - Gram negative bacteria
        - (b) Cell wall of bacterial cell is made up of peptidoglycan (polymer of N-acetyl glucose amine and N-acetyl muramic acid). Gram negative bacteria do have loss peptidoglycan layer.
        - (c) Glycocalyx may be present as loose sheath called slime layer, while others may have tough and thick layer forming a **capsule**.
        - (d) On the cell surface bacteria shows **flagellum, pili** or **fimbriae**.
            - **Flagellum** is composed of three parts–filament, hook and basal body.
            - **Pili** are elongated tubular structures made up of special protein.
            - **Fimbriae** are small bristle-like fibres.
13. Plant cells are covered by cell wall, which plays an important role in protection, help in cell-cell interaction and provides a barrier to undesirable macromolecules.

(i) In plant cells, it is made up of cellulose, hemicellulose, pectin and lignin.

(ii) The cell wall of young plant is known as **primary cell wall**. At maturity, secondary cell wall is laid down on the inner side of primary cell wall.

(iii) Between the two adjacent cells a cementing layer is present called **middle lamella**. It is made up of **calcium pectate**.

14. Components of the cells are enclosed in a membrane called **plasma membrane.** It is composed of lipids and proteinaceous protein which are amphipathic nature. It is **selectively permeable**, *i.e.*, it allows only certain component to go in and out.

(i) Lipids are arranged in bilayers and proteins are embedded in it. Lipids are arranged within the membrane with polar head towards the outer side. While hydrophobic tails towards the innerside. In case of RBC, 52% protein and 40% lipids are present. Composition of lipid and protein varies from cell to cell.

(ii) Two type of proteins are present, *i.e.*, **peripheral protein** and **integral protein**. Peripheral protein lies at the surface of the protein, while integral proteins are present inside the lipid bilayer.

(iii) In 1972, **Singer** and **Nicholson** has given widely accepted model of membrane are called **fluid mosaic model.** According to this model membrane consist of continuous bilayer of phospholipid molecule in which globular proteins are embedded. This arrangement corresponds to the icebergs floating in a sea of phospholipids.

Lipids can show lateral movement within the membrane. Ability to move within the membrane is called fluidity.

(iv) The transport of metabolities across the biomembrane occurs through

(a) **Passive transport** Transport of molecules across are membrane along concentration gradient.

This could occurs through simple diffusion or through facilitated diffusion (with the aid of some carriers or channels).

(b) **Active transport** Movement of molecules against the concentration gradient with the help of energy (ATP).

(c) In case of bacteria, plasma membrane forms extensions to form special membranous structure called **mesosome**. It plays an important role in respiration. In some prokaryotes like cyanobacteria membrane extensions form. **Chromatophores** which contain pigments.

15. In cytoplasm non-membranous RNA-protein complexes are present known as **ribosomes.** These are the site of protein synthesis. There are two basic types of ribosomes **70 S** and **80 S.**
16. In prokaryotes, 70 S ribosomes are present, which have two sub-units 50 S and 30 S, while in eurkayotes 80 S ribosomes are present, which have two sub-units 40 S and 60 S.
17. Membranous organelles forms distinct structures called **endomembrane system**.
18. **Endoplasmic reticulum, Golgi complex, lysosomes** and **vacuoles** forms endomembrane system.
19. Its primary role is synthesis and transport of proteins.
20. Endoplasmic reticulum is the network or reticulum of tiny tubular structure, which are the extensions of nuclear membrane. It has two distinct compartments
    (i) Luminal (inside ER)
    (ii) Extra luminal (cytoplasmic compartment).
    There are two types of endoplasmic reticulum.

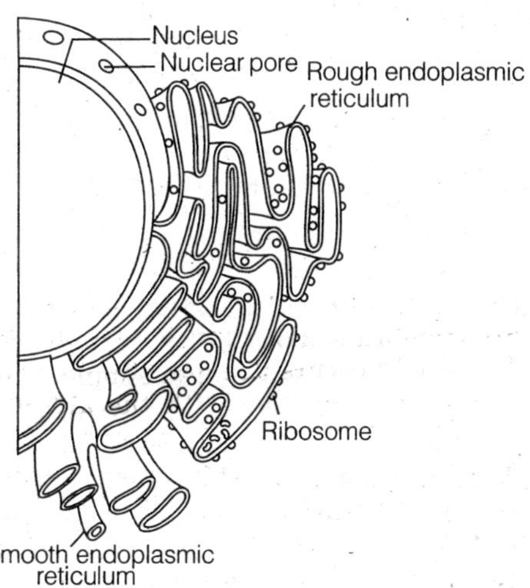

Endoplasmic reticulum

(a) **Rough Endoplasmic Reticulum** (RER) appears rough due to the presence of 80 S ribosomes. These are the sites of proteins synthesis.

(b) **Smooth Endoplasmic Reticulum** (SER) is the site of lipid biosynthesis and glycogen metabolism. It also detoxifies xenobiotic compounds.

21. **Golgi apparatus** is the group of cisternae first time observed by Camillo Golgi (1898). These consist of many flat, disc-shaped sacs or cisternae of 0.5-1.0 μm diameter.

(i) In plant cells, it is also known as dictyosome. Cisternae at convex end of dictyosome comprise proximal or *cis*-face and at concave form distal, maturing or *trans* face.

Vesicles may be secretory, clathrin coated.

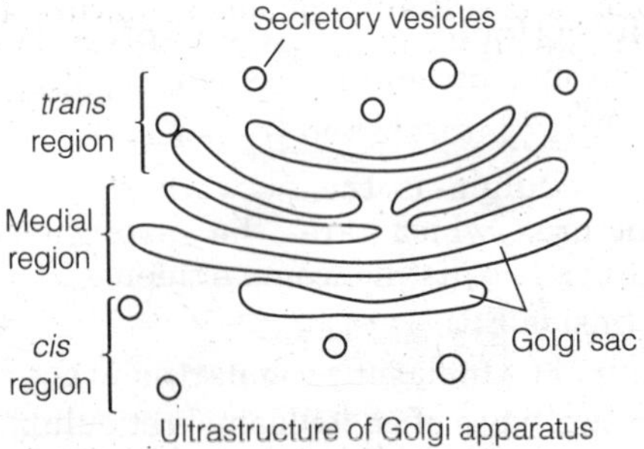

Ultrastructure of Golgi apparatus

(ii) Golgi apparatus is primarily involved in protein trafficking, it packages materials and deliver it to various cell targets. It is also involved in the glycosylation of proteins and lipids.

22. **Lysosomes** are single membrane bound structures, which contain hydrolytic enzymes. Due to presence of hydrolytic enzymes these are also known as **suicidal bags of cell**.

Various hydrolytic enzymes are lipases, proteases carbohydrases, which works at optimum acidic pH.

23. **Vacuoles** are the membrane bound space found in cytoplasm. It consist of H_2O, sap excretory product. In plants single large vacuole is present and enclosed *via* membrane called **tonoplast**. It facilitates the transport of number of ions and other materials against the concentration.

In *Amoeba* contractile vacuole is present, which helps in excretion, while in protist food vacuoles are present.

24. **Mitochondria** are granular structure, which was first observed by Kolliker in 1850. **Benda** gave the name mitochondria in 1897.

(i) Mitochondria is known as the **power house of cell**. Since, it is associated with cellular respiration and energy generation of the cell.

(ii) Structurally it is made up of two membrane, *i.e.,* the outer and the inner membrane and separated through intermembrane space.

(iii) Outer membrane is smooth, while the inner membrane forms series of folds called **cristae**. Inner chamber is called matrix.

(iv) Krebs' cycle occurs inside the matrix, while oxidative phosphorylation occurs on the cristae.

(v) Mitochondria is also involved in lipid biosynthesis and elongation of fatty acids.

(vi) Mitochondria is self-autonomous in nature as it contain its own DNA and 70 S ribosome.

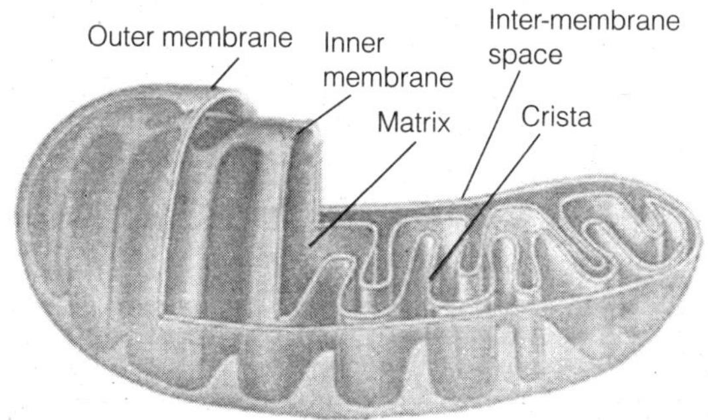

Structure of mitochondria

25. **Plastids** are exclusively found in plant cell and in euglenoids. They have specific type of pigments and impart specific colour to the plant.

(i) These are characterised into **chromoplast** and **leucoplasts. Chromoplasts** are used for trapping electromagnetic radiation. These can be **chloroplast, phaeoplast, rhodoplast** or **blue-green chromoplast**.

(ii) Leucoplasts are used for storage purposes and include

(a) **Elaioplast** (store oils).

(b) **Amyloplast** (store starch).

(c) **Proteinoplast** (store proteins).

(iii) Phaeoplast and rhodoplast are rich in carotenoids.

(iv) Chloroplast are involved in photosynthesis. It contain chlorophyll and carotenoids, which trap light energy for photosynthesis.

(v) Chloroplast is two membranous structure. It is bounded by an outer and an inner membrane with an intermembrane space.

(vi) The matrix inside chloroplast is known as **stroma**. Stroma contains disc-shaped membranous sac-like structure called **thylakoids**. The group of thylakoids forms grana, which are attached by granal lamellae. Two grana are attached with each other through stromal lamellae.

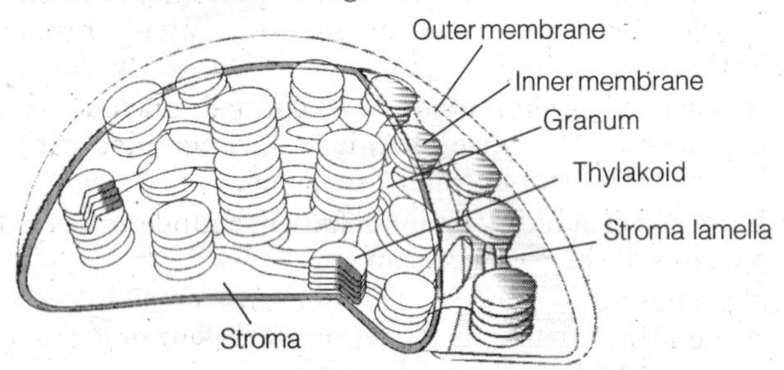

Sectional view of chloroplast

26. Maintenance, mechanical support and motility in the cell is maintained by **cytoskeleton**. It includes actin filaments microtubules and intermediate filament.

27. Some cell inclusion bodies are also present like **starch grains, glycogen granules, fat droplets, alurone grains and cystals.**

28. **Centrosome** and **centrioles** are the cylindrical structures, which are involved in the spindle formation during cell division.

    (i) Centrosome is formed by two cylindrical structures called **centrioles** central microtubule. In centrioles lies

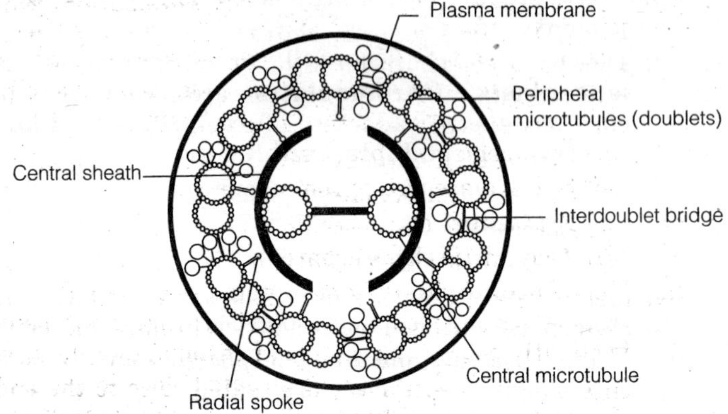

Diagrammatic representation of internal structure of centrioles

perpendicular to each other and organised in a cart wheel fashion 8 evenly spaced, triplet peripheral fibrils are formed by tubulin protein. These triplet fibrils are attached to each other. The central region of centrioles is attached to each other by Hub, while tubules of peripheral triplets are attached by radial spokes made up of protein.

29. **Nucleus** was first time identified by **Robert Brown** in 1831. Due to the presence of basic histone proteins, it is stained by the basic dyes and was given the name chromatin by **Flemming**.
   (i) In case of prokaryotes, well defined nucleus is absent, genetic material (*i.e.,* DNA) is loosely bounded with histone like proteins and known as nucleoid.
   (ii) In case of eukaryotes, DNA is bounded with histone proteins to form chromatin.
   (iii) Nucleus is enclosed by nuclear envelope/membrane, chromatin, nuclear matrix (nucleoplasm) and one or more spherical bodies called **Nucleoli**.
   (iv) Nuclear envelope consist of two parallel membrane. Outer membrane is continuous with the endoplasmic reticulum and bears ribosome on it. The space in between the two membranes is known as **perinuclear space**.
   (v) For the movement of proteins and RNA nuclear envelope is interrupted by minute pores called **nuclear pores**.
   (vi) Nucleolus is the site of ribosomal RNA synthesis. In interphase nucleus contain loose and indistinct network of nucleoprotein fibres called **chromatin**.
   (vii) During specific stages of cell division chromatin condenses and form chromosomes.
   (viii) Chromosome contains two sister chromatids, which are joined together at **centromere**. These forms a disc-like structure called **kinetochore,** where mitotic spindles attach during cell division during on the basis of position. Chromosomes are classified into four types
      (a) Metacentric chromosome
      (b) Sub-metacentric chromosome
      (c) Acrocentric chromosome
      (d) Telocentric chromosome
   (ix) Metacentric chromosome has two equal arms of chromosome. In sub-metacentric chromosome centromere is slightly away from middle of chromosome. In acrocentric chromosome, centromere is situated close to the end, while the telocentric chromosome has terminal centromere.

(x) **Kinetochore** is known as **primary constriction**. In some cases, chromosome contains non-staining secondary constriction called **satellite.**

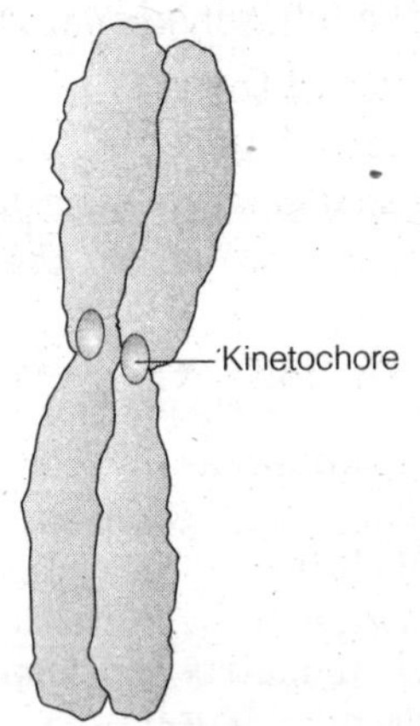

Chromosome with kinetochore

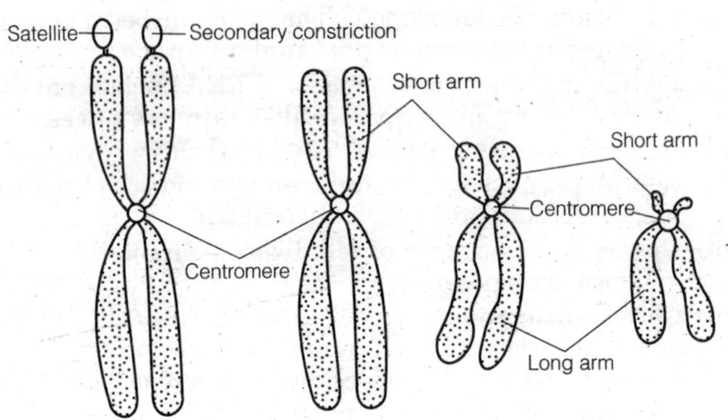

Types of chromosomes based on the position of centromere

Exercises

Question 1. Which of the following is not correct?

(a) Robert Brown discovered the cell
(b) Schleiden and Schwann formulated the cell theory
(c) Virchow explained that cells are formed from pre-existing cells
(d) A unicellular organism carries out its life activities within a single cell.

Answer (a) Robert Brown discovered the cell.

Question 2. New cells generate from

(a) bacterial fermentation
(b) regeneration of old cells
(c) pre-existing cells
(d) abiotic materials

Answer (c) New cell generate from pre-existing cells.

Question 3. Match the following columns.

Column I	Column II
A. Cristae	1. Fat membranous sacs in stroma.
B. Cisternae	2. Infoldings in mitochondria.
C. Thylakoids	3. Disc-shaped sacs in Golgi apparatus.

Answer

Column I	Column II
A. Cristae	2. Infoldings in mitochondria.
B. Cisternae	3. Disc-shaped sacs in Golgi apparatus.
C. Thylakoids	1. Fat membranous sacs in stroma.

Question 4. Which of the follownig is correct?

(a) Cells of all living organism have a nucleus
(b) Both animal and plant cells have a well defined cell wall
(c) In prokaryotes, there are no membrane bound organelles
(d) Cells are formed *de novo* from abiotic materials

Answer (a) Cell of all living organisms have a nucleus.

Question 5. What is a mesosome in a prokaryotic cell? Mention the functions that it performs.

Answer Mesosome is a special membrane structure, which is formed by the extension of the plasma membrane into the cell in a prokaryotic cell. It helps in cell wall formation, DNA replication and distribution to daughter cells. It also helps in respiration, secretion possesses, to increase the surface area of the plasma membrane and enzymatic content.

Question 6. How do neutral solutes move across the plasma membrane? Can the polar molecules also move across it in the same way? If not, then how are these transported across the membrane?

Answer Neutral solutes may move across the membrane by the process of simple diffusion along the concentration gradient. The polar molecules cannot pass through the non-polar lipid bilayer, they require a carrier protein to facilitate their transport across the membrane. A few ions or molecules are transported across the membrane against their concentration gradient, *i.e.,from lower to the higher concentration. Such a transport is an energy dependent process, in which ATP is utilised and is called active transport, e.g.,* Na^+ /K^+ pump.

Question 7. Name two cell organelles that are double membrane bound. What are the characteristics of these two organelles. State their functions and draw labelled diagrams of both.

Answer Chloroplasts and mitochondria are double membrane bound organelles.

Characteristics of Mitochondria

(i) The mitochondria are sausage-shaped or cylindrical having a diameter of 0.2-1.0 μm and average 0.5 μm and length 1.0-4.1 μm.

(ii) Each mitochondrion is a double membrane bound structure.

(iii) The inner compartment is called the matrix. The outer membrane of mitochondria forms the continuous limiting boundary of the organelle.

(iv) The inner membrane forms a number of infoldings called the cristae (single crista) towards the matrix. The cristae increase the surface area.

(v) The two membranes have their own specific enzymes associated with the mitochondrial function. The matrix of mitochonrdria also possess single circular DNA molecule, a few RNA molecules, ribosomes (70 S) and the components required for the synthesis of proteins.

Functions of Mitochondria Mitochondria are the sites of aerobic respiration. They produce cellular energy in the form of ATP, hence they are known as, 'power house of the cell.'

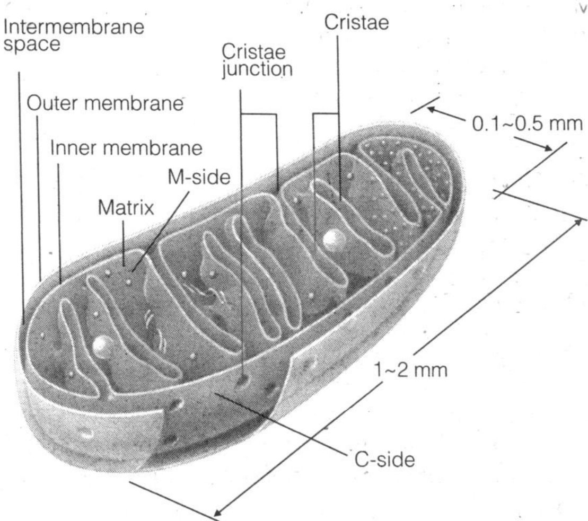

Structure of mitochondria

Characteristics of Chloroplasts

(i) The chloroplasts are also double membrane bound organelles.

(ii) The space limited by the inner membrane of the chloroplast is called the stroma.

(iii) A number of organised flattened membranous sacs called the thylakoids are present in the stroma.

(iv) Thylakoids are arranged in stacks-like the piles of coins called grana.

(v) In addition, there are flat membranous tubules called the stroma lamellae connecting the thylakoids of the different grana.

(vi) The stroma of the thylakoids enclose a space called a lumen.

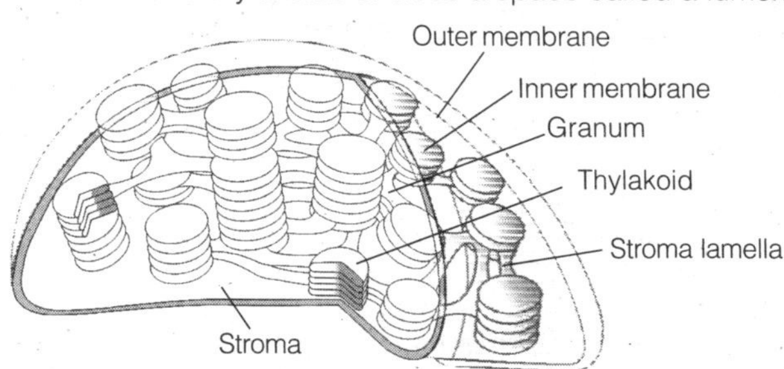

Sectional view of chloroplast

Question 8. What are the characteristics of prokaryotic cells?

Answer Characteristics of prokaryotic cells

(i) A prokaryotic cell, *i.e.*, of bacteria is surrounded by a cell membrane. The cell wall in turn is surrounded by a slimy layer.

(ii) Absence of well organised chloroplast, mitochondria and nucleus.

(iii) The true nucleus with nuclear membrane, nucleolus is absent. It is known as nucleoid. The DNA of a prokaryotic cell is circular and not associated with basic proteins.

(iv) The cytoplasm is filled with dense granules. Most of these granules are ribosomes.

(v) In chloroplast, the scattered thylakoids are present. They are not organised in the form of stacks.

Question 9. Multicellular organisms have division of labour. Explain.

Answer The body of a multicellular organism has cell as a basic structural unit. The cells organised to form tissues such as blood, bone, etc. The tissues organised to form organs such as heart, kidney, etc. The organs then organised to form organ systems such as digestive system, reproductive system and respiratory system, etc. The various organ systems of organism get arranged to form a complete individual.

Question 10. Cell is the basic unit of life. Discuss in brief.

Answer All organisms begin their life in a single cell. Certain organisms complete their life cycle as a single cell. They are called unicellular or acellular organisms, *e.g.*, *Amoeba, Chlamydomonas* bacteria and yeast. In other organisms, the single cell undergoes divisions to form multicellular ma ... of human being, is made up of trillion of cells. All the cells of an ... carry the same genetic material, develop from same pre-existing ... possess several organelles to perform various life activities. The ... therefore, basic unit of life and structural unit of an organism.

...ion 11. What are nuclear pores? State their function.

Answer Nuclear pores are small apertures present in the nuclear membrane.

Functions of Nuclear Pores Nuclear pores are highly selective in their permeation. They allow outward passage of newly formed ribosome units but prevent the entry of active ribosomes. Proteins synthesised in the cytoplasm enter the nuclear through nuclear pores but ions like K^+, Na^+ or Cl^- may not be able to gain entrance.

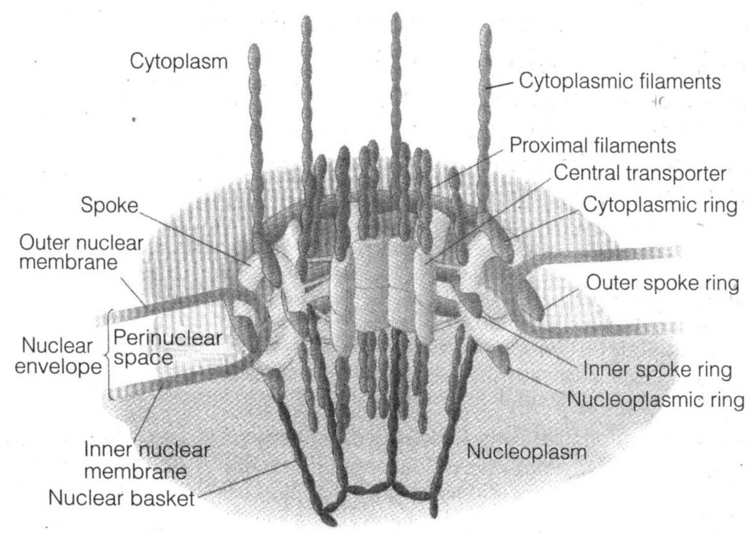

Nuclear pore complex

Question 12. Both lysosomes and vacuoles are endomembrane structures, yet they differ in terms of their functions. Comment.

Answer Both lysosomes and vacuoles are covered by a single membrane. Both of them perform different types of functions. Lysosomes contain hydrolysing enzymes and can hydrolyse all types of organic substances, except cellulose. They perform phagocytic function. Therefore, they are known as suicidal bags.

The vacuoles are non-cytoplasmic sacs which are also covered by a membrane. The sap vacuoles store sap or water with dissolved organic and inorganic substances. They maintain osmotic pressure or turgidity. Some freshwater invertebrates such as *Amoeba, Paramecium* occur contractile vacuoles, which perform osmoregulation and excretion. There is another type of vacuoles such as food vacuole which store food and gas vacuoles which store metabolic gases and take part in buoyancy regulation.

Thus, both lysosomes and vacuoles differ from each other in the type of functions they perform.

Question 13. Describe the structure of the following with the help of labelled diagrams.

(i) Nucleus (ii) Centrosome

Answer

(i) **Nucleus** It is a double membrane bounded protoplasmic body that carries hereditary information. Chemically it contains DNA, basic proteins, non-basic proteins, RNA, lipids and minerals, etc.

Nucleus has main parts, nucleoplasm, chromatin and nucleolus.

(a) **Nuclear envelope** It is made up of two nuclear membranes separated by 10-70 nm perinuclear space. The outer membrane is rough due to the presence of ribosomes. Nuclear envelope has many pores with diameter 200-800 Å.

(b) **Nucleoplasm or nuclear matrix** It is a colloidal complex that fills the nucleus. Nucleoplasm contains raw material for synthesis of DNA and RNA.

(c) **Chromatin** It is a fibrous hereditary material formed by DNA-histone complex. Some non-histone proteins and also RNA. A single human cell has about 2 metre long thread of DNA distributed among its 46 chromosomes.

(d) **Nucleolus** It was originally discovered by Fontana (1781) and given the present name by Bowman (1840). It is naked roughly rounded darkly stained structure that is attached to chromatin at specific spot called Nucleolar Organiser Region (NOR). Nucleolus is the site for elaboration of *r*RNA and synthesis of ribosomes. It is therefore, known as **ribosomal factory.**

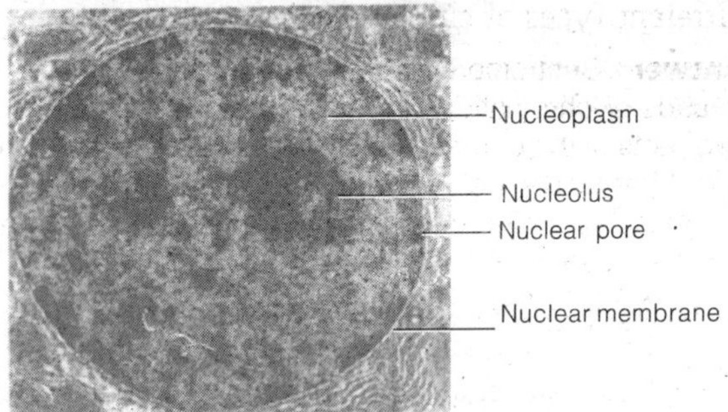

Structure of nucleus

(ii) **Centrosome** It is an organelle usually containing two cylindrical structure called **centrioles**. They are surrounded by amorphous pericentriolar materials. Both the centrioles in a centrosome lie perpendicular to each other in which each has an orgnisation like the cartwheel. They are made up of nine evenly spaced peripheral fibrils of tubulin protein the central past of the proximal region of centriole is called **hub**, which is connected with tubules of the peripheral triple by radial **spokes** made of protein. The centriole form the basal bodies of cilia or flagella and spindle fibres that give rise to spindle apparatus during cell division in animal life.

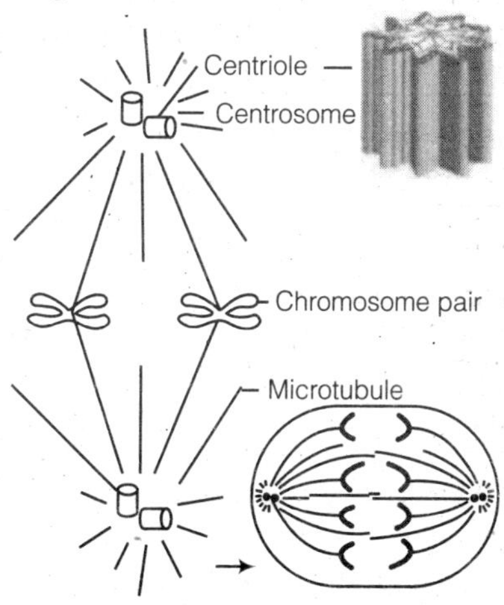

Structure of centrosome

Question 14. What is a centromere? How does the position of the centromere form the basis of classification of chromosomes. Support your answer with a diagram showing the position of centromere on different types of chromosomes.

Answer Centromere is a narrow non-stainable area, which join two similar threads or chromatids of a late prophase or metaphase chromosome. The two parts of the chromosome on either side of the centromere are known as arm. They may be isobranchial (equal) or heterobranchial (unequal in length). Depending upon the position of the centromere, the chromosomes are classified as follows

(i) **Acrocentric chromosome** Centromere sub-terminal, anaphasic stage J-shaped.

(ii) **Sub-metacentric chromosome** The centromere is sub-median and the anaphasic chromosome appear L-shaped.

(iii) **Metacentric chromosomes** The centromere is in the middle and the chromosome appears V-shaped.

(iv) **Telocentric chromosome** Centromere is terminal, anaphasic stage is I-shaped.

Depending upon the number of centromeres a chromosome possess, it may be monocentric, dicentric (two centromeres), polycentric (many centromeres), acentric chromosome (having no centromere).

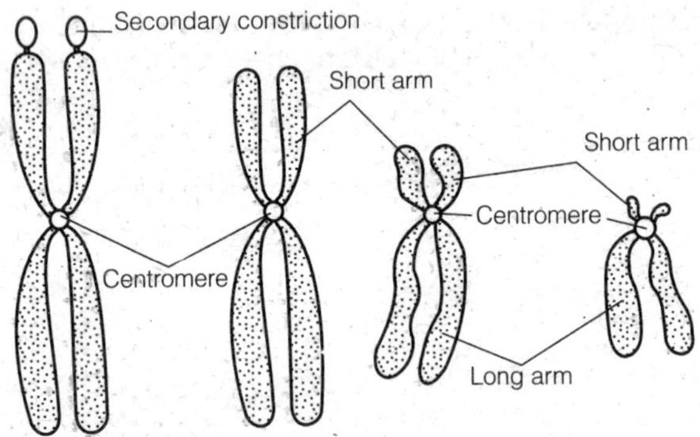

Types of chromosomes based on the position of centromere

Selected NCERT Exemplar Problems

Very Short Answer Type Questions

Question 1. What is the significance of vacuole in a plant cell?

Answer The vacuole in a plant cell helps to maintain osmotic pressure for turgidity and osmosis. It also stores useful as well as waste substances.

Question 2. What does 'S' refers in a 70 S and on 80 S ribosome?

Answer The 'S' refers to Svedberg units of sedimentation coefficient. The sedimentation coefficient is a measure of the speed of the sedimentation for a particular cell organelle in ultracentrifuge.

Question 3. Mention a single membrane bound organellel which is rich in hydrolytic enzymes.

Answer Lysosome.

Question 4. What are gas vacuoles? State their functions.

Answer **Gas Vacuoles** Occur in some prokaryotes. Each gas vacuole is made up of a large number of sub-microscopic hexagonal gas vesicles. A gas vacuole is surrounded by a thin protein membrane. Gas vacuoles store metabolic gases and take part in buoyancy regulation.

Question 5. What is the function of a polysome.

Answer A string of ribosomes on *m*RNA molecule is known as polysome. In a polysome all the small and large sub-units of ribosomes are united to form a chain of ribosomes. The protein synthesis take place on the chain.

Question 6. What is the features of metacentric chromosome?

Answer The metaphasic chromosome have centromere present in the middle and thus, the chromosome appears V-shaped.

Question 7. What is referred to as satellite chromosome?

Answer Sometimes a few chromosomes have non-staining secondary constrictions at a constant location. This gives the appearance of a small fragment called the **satellite**. The chromosome having satellite are known as satellite chromosomes.

Short Answer Type Questions

Question 1. Discuss briefly the role of nucleolus in the cells actively involved in protein synthesis.

Answer **Function of Nucleolus** Nucleolus is a ribosome factory. It combines *r*RNAs with proteins to produce ribosome sub-units. After their formation, the ribosome sub-units pass out and get established in the cytoplasm. It also receive and store ribosomal proteins formed in the cytoplasm.

Question 2. Briefly describe the cell theory?

Answer **The Cell Theory** In 1838, Matthias Schleiden examined a large number of plants and observed that all plants are made up of different kind of cells which in turn form the tissues of the plant. At about the same time, Theodore Schwann (1839), a British zoologist, studied different types of animal cells and reported that cells had a thin outer layer which is today known as 'plasma membrane. On the basis of this, Schwann proposed the hypothesis that the bodies of plants and animals are composed of cells and products of cells. **Schleiden** and **Schwann** together formulated the cell theory as follows.

Cell theory as understood today is as follows :

(i) All living organisms are composed of cells and products of cells.

(ii) All cells arise from pre-existing cells.

Question 3. Differentiate between Rough Endoplasmic Reticulum (RER) and Smooth Endoplasmic Reticulum (SER).

Answer Rough Endoplasmic Reticulum (RER) also known as granular ER bears ribosomes and involved in active protein synthesis, whereas Smooth Endoplasmic Reticulum (SER) also known as agranular ER bear no ribosomes. SER synthesise non-proteinaceous substanes, *e.g.*, phospholipids, glycolipids, steroid hormones, etc.

Question 4. Give the biochemical composition of plasma membrane. How are lipid molecules arranged in the membrane?

Answer Chemically the plasma membrane consists of proteins (20-70%), lipids (20-79%), carbohydrates (1-5%) and water (20%). Nucleic acids (DNA, RNA) are absent in the plasma membrane. The lipids present in the plasma membrane are phospholipids, glycolipids (sugar lipids) and sterols.

Arrangement of Lipids in the Plasma Membrane Each lipid molecule consists of a three carbon glycerol pole (head) which is hydrophilic

(water loving) in nature and two long tails of fatty acids which are hydrophobic (water-fearing) in nature. The hydrophilic glycerol poles of lipid are located towards the outside of the lipid bilayer, whereas the hydrophobic fatty acid tails are repelled by water and face towards the inner side of the membrane. The hydrophilic and hydrophobic forces in lipid molecules cause the membrane to become a bilayer.

Question 5. What are plasmids? Describe their role in bacteria.

Answer A plasmid is usually a circular (sometimes linear) piece of double-stranded DNA found in bacteria that is different from bacterium's chromosome. It carries non-essential genes that can augment a bacterium's ability to survive in certain circumstances. For example, some plasmids carry genes that enable a bacterium to metabolise a certain type of nutrient it otherwise cannot. Other plasmids carry genes that enable bacterium to conjugate, and still other plasmids carry genes that confer antibiotic resistance. Plasmids are used for a vast variety of experiments from expressing human genes in bacterial cells to DNA sequencing.

Question 6. What are histones? What are their functions?

Answer Histones are basic proteins, which are soluble in water or dilute acids but insoluble in dilute NH_3. The are rich in basic amino acids like histidine and arginine. Histones are readily hydrolysed by trypsin and pepsin and are considered as 'gene repressors'. The histone proteins are not coagulated by heat. The histone proteins are found to be associated with DNA of nucleus and forms the chromatin material.

Long Answer Type Questions

Question 1. What structural and functional attributes must a cell have to be called a living cell?

Answer The cell of living organism such as human being is surrounded by a double membrane. Inside each cell is a dense membrane bound structure called nucleus. The nucleus contains the chromosomes which in turn carry the genetic information. Proteins are produced by ribosomes which are present on ER membrane or nuclear membrane surface. The other cytoplasmic organelles present in a human cell or Golgi apparatus, lysosomes (containing hydrolytic enzymes), microbodies, vacuoles, mitochondria (power house of the cell due to ATP production.

All these structural and functional attributes keep a cell in living stock.

Question 2. Briefly give the contributions of the following scientists in formulating the cell theory

(a) Rudolf Virchow
(b) Schleiden and Schwann

Answer

(a) Rudolf Virchow (1855) first explained that the cells divide and new cells are formed from the pre-existing cells *(omnis cellula e cellula).*

(b) Schleiden and Schwann both observed the cells, cell membranes for the first time. They proposed that the animal and plant cells are composed of cells and products of cells.

Question 3. Is extra genomic DNA is present in prokaryotes and eukaryotes? If yes, locate their position in both types of organisms.

Answer Yes, extra genomic DNA is present in both prokaryotes and eukaryotes. In case of eukaryotes, extra genomic DNA is present in two organelles, *e.g.,* plastids and mitochondria. Both these organelles with the help of their own DNA synthesise some of their proteins. Thus, these organelles are known as semi-autonomous organelles.

In case of prokaryotic cells, the extragenomic DNA is present in the form of plasmids. The plasmids are circular DNA molecules which confer certain unique phenotypic characters to such bacteria. One such character is resistance to bacteria. This plasmid DNA is also used to monitor bacteria transformation with foreign DNA.

Question 4. Structure and functions are correlatable in living organism can you justify this by taking plasma membrane as an example?

Answer In plasma membrane, the structure and its function are correlated. A cell membrane consists of protein, lipids and carbohydrates. The protein component of present in the membranes act as solute channels. They allow flow of minerals, hormones and information from one organelles to another or from one cell to another. In case of plants, where minerals are absorbed actively from the soil, the plasma membrane possess proteinaceous carriers.

The oligosaccharides attached to membranes serve as recognition centres and recognise foreign entities before allowing their entry.

The lipid component of plasma membrane are arranged with their hydrophilic polar head directed outwards and non-polar hydrophobic tails directed inwards. This type of arrangement of lipid molecules give the membrane fluidity property. Glycocalyx present in cell membrane helps in cell attachment.

Question 5. Eukaryotic cells have organelles which may

(a) not bounded by a membrane.
(b) bounded by a single membrane.
(c) bounded by a double membrane.

Group the various sub-cellular organelles into these categories.

Answer

(a) Ribosomes are membraneless organelle..
(b) Lysosomes are single membrane bounded organelle. Sphaerosomes and microbodies are also have single membranes.
(c) Mitochondria and plastids are double membrane bounded organelles.

Question 6. The genomic content of the nucleus is constant for a given species, whereas the extrachromosomal DNA is found to be variable among the members of a population. Explain.

Answer The DNA content of the nucleus is constant for a given species. The haploid organisms have half the content of DNA than that of their diploid parents. The amount of DNA remains constant in all the members of a given species. On the other hand, the extrachomosomal DNA which occur either in the mitochondria or in chloroplast is found to be variable among the members of a population. In case of highly active organisms, the DNA (extrachromosomal) is found to be more as compared to less active ones.

Question 7. Justify the statement, 'Mitochondria are power house of the cell.'

Answer Mitochondria are known as power house of the cell because they generate ATP, the energy currency of the cell. Terminal oxidation takes place through oxidative phosphorylation. This produces ATP. Even the reduced coenzymes produced in cytosol through glycolysis, transfer their reducing power to mitochondria for ATP synthesis. ATP synthesised inside mitochondria provides energy for all cellular activities including over coming tendency for entropy. Therefore, mitochondria are known as power house of the cell.

Question 8. Is there a species or region specific type of plastids? How does one distinguish one from the other?

Answer Plastids are both region or species specific. These are as follows

(i) **Proplastids** These are colourless, rounded but amoeboid plastid precursors found in meristematic and newly formed cells of plants. It has a double membrane envelope that surrounds a colourless matrix. The matrix contains DNA, ribosomes and reserve food. A few vesicles and lamellae also occur in the matrix.

(ii) **Leucoplasts** These are colourless plastids occur in non-green plant cells commonly near the nucleus. They are as follows.

(a) **Amyloplasts** These leucoplasts store starch, *e.g.*, tuber of potato, grain of rice, grain of wheat.

(b) **Elaioplasts** These store fats, *e.g.*, rose.

(c) **Aleuroplasts** They are protein storing plastids, *e.g.*, castor endosperm.

(d) **Chromoplasts** These are non-photosynthetic coloured plastids which synthesise and store carotenoid pigments. They appear, orange, red or yellow. These mostly occur in ripe fruits (tomato, and chillies) carrot roots, etc.

Chloroplasts These are photosynthetic plastids, which are green in colour and found in the leaves of all green plants. They have lamellae organised in the form of grana.

Question 9. Write the functions of the following

(a) Centromere (b) Cell wall (c) Smooth ER
(d) Golgi apparatus (e) Centrioles

Answer

(a) **Functions of Centromere** It is a narrow non-stainable area which join chromatids together to form a chromosome. The centromere thus, keep the two chromatids of a chromosome in an intact stage. This is an essential step for chromosomes of a cell during cell division whether it may be mitosis or meiosis.

(b) **Functions of Cell Wall**

(i) It gives a definite shape and provides protection to the protoplast.

(ii) The pits of cell wall help in maintaining protoplasmic connections between the cells.

(iii) The plasmodesmata of the cell wall help in transport of materials from cell to cell.

(iv) It regulates the movement of substances across the cells.

(c) **Functions of Smooth Endoplasmic Reticulum**

(i) It provides mechanical support to colloidal complex of cytoplasmic matrix.

(ii) It holds various cell organelles in position.

(iii) It conducts information from outside to inside of cell.

(iv) It provides membrane to Golgi apparatus for the production of vesicles and Golgian vacuoles.

(v) It helps in detoxification of substances.

(vi) During telophase, part of the nuclear envelope is formed by the endoplasmic reticulum.

(d) **Functions of Golgi Apparatus**

(i) In plants, Golgi apparatus, synthesise carbohydrates of cell wall matrix.

(ii) It is also involved in the secretion and transport of materials out of the cell.

(iii) The vesicles released from Golgi apparatus also form lysosomes.

(iv) Vesicles of Golgi apparatus help in increasing the surface area during growth,

(v) In helps in the formation of cell plate in dividing cells.

(e) **Functions of Centrioles**

(i) Formation of new centrioles from pre-existing one during cell division.

(ii) They form basal bodies, which in turn form cilia and flagella.

(iii) Formation of sperm tail.

(iv) Centrioles form asters which function as spindle pole.

(v) They acts as nucleating centres for the formation of microtubules.

Question 10. **Are the different types of plastids interchangable? If yes, give examples where they are getting converted from one type of another.**

Answer The different types of plastids are leucoplasts (colourless), chromoplasts (coloured), chloroplasts (green coloured). The different types of plastids are interchangable. The transformation from chloroplasts is observed during ripening of fruits (*e.g.*, tomato, chilli) when they change their colour from green to reddish orange. It takes place through loss of chlorophylls and degeneration of lamellae. The most common carotenoid of the fruit is lycopene. Petals of *Calendula* develop orange yellow colour due to the formation of chromoplasts from proplastids.

Carrot root develops its characteristic colour because of the conversion of leucoplasts into chromoplasts. It is rich in carotene.

9

Biomolecules

Important Points

1. All the carbon compounds that we get from living tissues can be called **biomolecules**.
2. Living tissues also contain inorganic elements and compounds. How can we conclude this?
   (i) One weighs a small amount of a living tissue and dry it.
   (ii) All the water evaporates. The remaining material gives dry weight.
   (iii) If tissue is fully burnt. All the carbon compounds are oxidised to gaseous form CO_2, water vapour and are removed.
   (iv) The remaining ash contains inorganic elements (like calcium, magnesium, etc).
3. Therefore, elemental analysis gives elemental composition of living tissues in the form of hydrogen, oxygen, chlorine, carbon, etc.
4. **Amino Acids**
   (i) Organic compounds containing an amino group and an acidic group as substituents on the same carbon, *i.e.*, the α-carbon. Hence, they are called α-amino acids.
   (ii) They are substituted methanes.
   (iii) There are four substituents groups occupying the four valency positions → hydrogen, carboxyl group amino group and a variable group designated as *R* group. Based on the nature of *R* group, there are many amino acids. However, 20 amino acids occur in protein.

(iv) *R* group can be :
   (a) Hydrogen (glycine)
   (b) Methyl group (alanine)
   (c) Hydroxy methyl (serine)

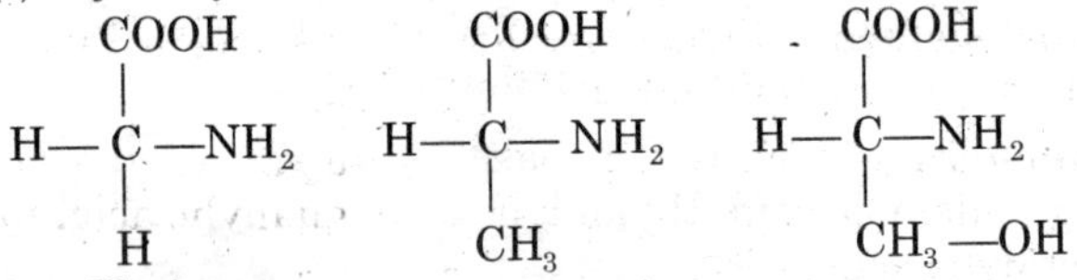

$$\underset{\text{Glycine}}{\mathrm{H{-}\overset{\overset{\displaystyle COOH}{|}}{\underset{\underset{\displaystyle H}{|}}{C}}{-}NH_2}} \qquad \underset{\text{Alanine}}{\mathrm{H{-}\overset{\overset{\displaystyle COOH}{|}}{\underset{\underset{\displaystyle CH_3}{|}}{C}}{-}NH_2}} \qquad \underset{\text{Serine}}{\mathrm{H{-}\overset{\overset{\displaystyle COOH}{|}}{\underset{\underset{\displaystyle CH_3{-}OH}{|}}{C}}{-}NH_2}}$$

(v) Chemical and physical properties:
   (a) Based on number of amino and carboxyl groups there are
      - Acidic (glutamic acid)
      - Basic (lysine)
      - Neutral (valine).
   (b) Aromatic amino acid (tyrosine, phenylalanine and tryptophan).
   (c) A particular property-ionizable nature of $—NH_2$ and $—COOH$ groups.

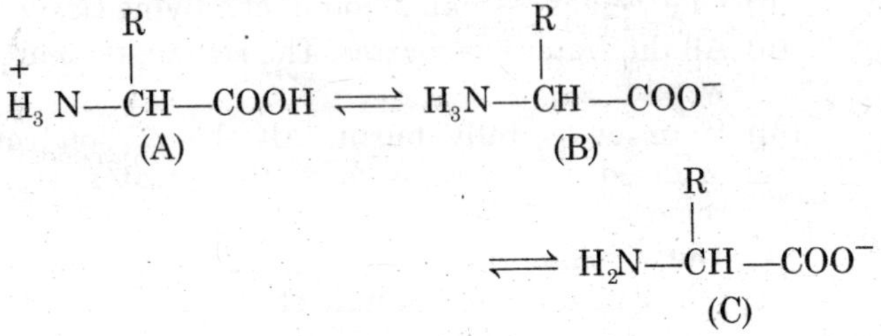

$$\underset{(A)}{\mathrm{\overset{+}{H_3}N{-}\overset{\overset{\displaystyle R}{|}}{C}H{-}COOH}} \rightleftharpoons \underset{(B)}{\mathrm{H_3N{-}\overset{\overset{\displaystyle R}{|}}{C}H{-}COO^-}} \rightleftharpoons \underset{(C)}{\mathrm{H_2N{-}\overset{\overset{\displaystyle R}{|}}{C}H{-}COO^-}}$$

B is called Zwitter ionic form.

5. **Lipids** Generally, water insoluble; simple fatty acid.

A fatty acid has a carboxyl group attached to an *R* group.

(i) The *R* group could be methyl ($—CH_3$) or ethyl (C_2H_5) or higher number of $—CH_2$ group (1 carbon to 19 carbons).
(ii) Fatty acids — Saturated (without double bond) and Unsaturated (with one or more C=C double bonds), *e.g.*, Trihydroxy propane (glycerol).
(iii) Many lipids have both glycerol and fatty acids. Here, fatty acids are found esterified with glycerol.
(iv) They can be monoglycerides, diglycerides and triglyceride. It also called **fats** —high melting point.

Oils low melting points (*e.g.*, Gingily oil) remain as oil in winters.

(v) It also called phospholipids → Phosphorus and a phosphorylated organic compound in them.
They are found in cell membranes, *e.g.*, lecithin.

6. **Nucleosides** Nitrogen base + sugar, *e.g.*, adenosine, guanosine, thymidine, uridine, cytidine.
7. **Nucleotides** Nitrogen base + sugar + phosphate group, *e.g.*, adenylic acid, thymidylic acid, guanylic acid, uridylic acid, cytidylic acid.

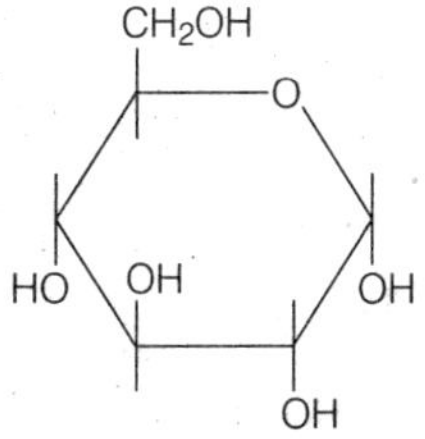
CH2OH
O
HO
OH
OH
OH
$C_6H_{12}O_6$ (glucose)

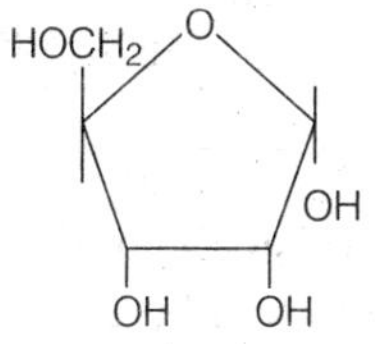
HOCH2
O
OH
OH
OH
$C_5H_{10}O_5$ (ribose)

$CH_3—(CH_2)_{14}—COOH$
Fatty acid
(palmitic acid)

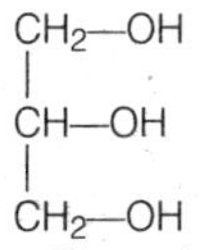
CH2—OH
CH—OH
CH2—OH
Glycerol

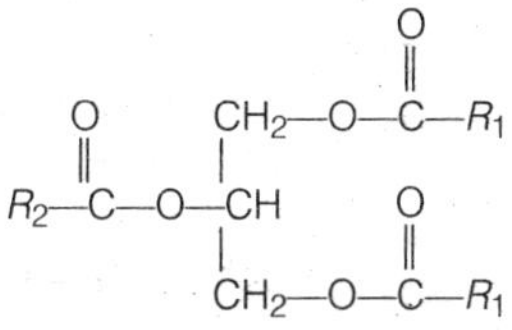
O
CH2—O—C—R1
O
R2—C—O—CH
O
CH2—O—C—R1
Triglycerides (R_1, R_2 and R_3 are fatty acids)

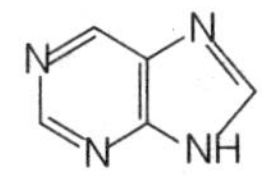
N
N
N
NH
Adenine (purine)

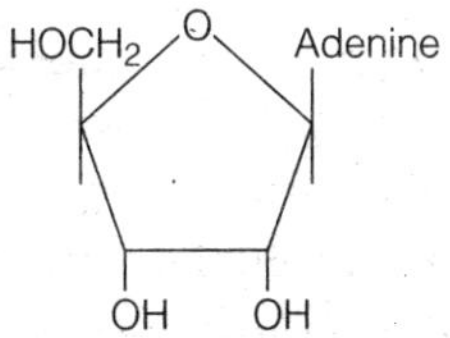
HOCH2
O
Adenine
OH
OH
Adenosine

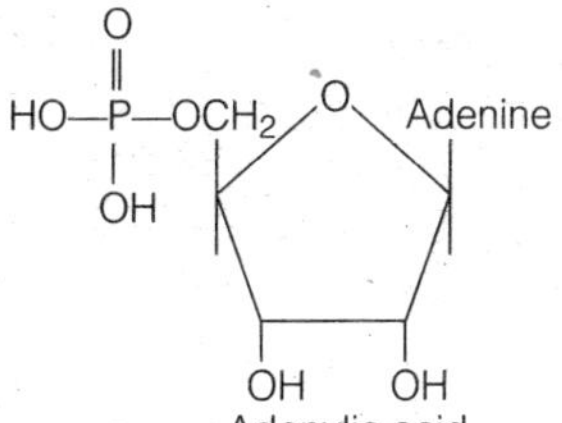
O
HO—P—OCH2
O
Adenine
OH
OH
OH
Adenylic acid

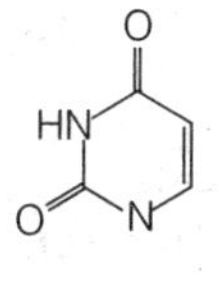
O
HN
O
N

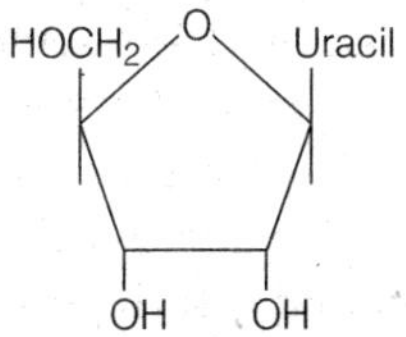
HOCH2
O
Uracil
OH
OH

Uracil (pyrimidine) Uridine
Nitrogen bases Nucleosides

Nucleotides

8. **Primary Metabolites** These are the organic compounds such as amino acids, sugars, etc.
9. **Secondary Metabolites** It found in plant, fungal and microbial cells. These are thousands of compounds other than primary metabolites, *e.g.,* Alkaloids, flavonoids, rubber, essential oils, antibiotics, coloured pigments, scents, gums, spices, etc.
10. **Biomacromolecules** It found in the acid insoluble fraction (molecular weights more than one thousand). Include proteins, nucleic acids, polysaccharides and lipids.
11. **Proteins**

    Polypeptides They are linear chains of amino acids linked by peptide bonds.

    Some Proteins and their Functions

Proteins	Functions
Collagen	Intercellular ground substance
Trypsin	Enzyme
Insulin	Hormone
Antibody	Fights infections against
Receptors	Sensory reception (smell, taste, hormone, etc.)
GLUT-4	Enables glucose transport into cells

12. **Polysaccharides**
    (i) They are long chains of sugars.
    (ii) They are threads containing different monosaccharides as building blocks.

    e.g., cellulose = Polymeric polysaccharide consisting of only one type of monosaccharides, i.e., glucose.

    Starch = Presents as a store house of energy in plant tissues.

    Glycogen = Present in animals

    Insulin = Polymer of fructose.

    (iii) In a polysaccharide chain, right end, reducing end, left end and non-reducing end.

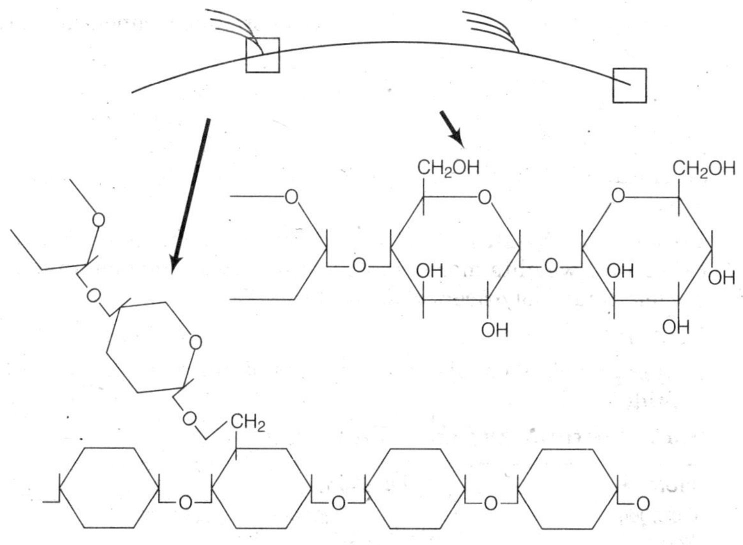

Diagrammatic representation of a portion of glycogen

13. **Nucleic Acid**
    (i) Polynucleotides
    (ii) Nucleotide is the building block
    (iii) Components of nucleic acid.
        (a) Heterocyclic compounds–Nitrogenous bases

Purines	Pyrimidines
Adenine	Uracil
Guanine	Cytosine
	Thymine

        (b) A monosaccharide–Either ribose or deoxyribose
        Ribose in RNA (ribonucleic acid)
        Deoxyribose in DNA (deoxyribonucleic acid)
        (c) A phosphoric acid or phosphate

14. **Structure of Proteins**
    (i) **Primary structure** The sequence of amino acids, *i.e.*, the positional information in a protein, which is the first amino acids, which is second and so on is called the primary structure.
        (a) Protein is imagined as a line left end represented by the first amino acid also called as N-terminal amino acid.
        Right end represented by last amino acid also called as **C-terminal amino acid.**

(b) A protein thread does not exist throughout as an extended rigid rod.

(c) The thread is folded in the form of a helix.

(d) Some portions are folded as helix.

(ii) **Secondary structure** Region of proteins other than helix folds into other forms and are called secondary structure.

(iii) **Tertiary structure** Long protein chain is folded upon itself like a hollow a woolen ball, giving rise to tertiary structure. This gives us a B-dimensional view of a protein. This structure is necessary for the many biological activities of proteins.

(iv) **Quaternary structure** Some proteins are an assembly of more than one polypeptide or sub-units. The manner in which these individual folded polypeptides or sub-units are arranged with respect to each other is the architecture of protein otherwise called quaternary structure of a protein.

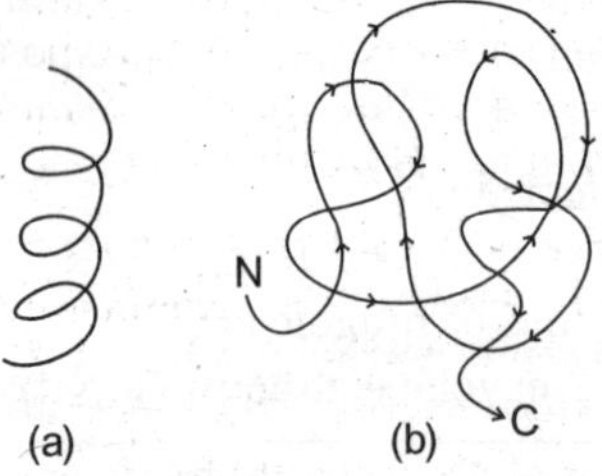

Cartoon showing : (a) A secondary structure and (b) A tertiary structure of proteins

15. **Peptide Bond** In proteins or polypeptide, amino acids are linked by peptide bond which is formed when carboxyl (—COOH) group of one amino acid reacts with amino (—NH_2) group of next amino acid with the elimination of a water moiety (the process is called dehydration).

16. **Glycosidic Bond** Individual monosaccharides are linked by glycosidic bond in a polysaccharides.

    This bond is also formed by dehydration. This bond is formed between two carbon atoms of two adjacent monosaccharides.

17. **Phosphodiester Bond** The bond between the phosphate and hydroxyl group of sugar is an ester bond. As there is one such ester bond on either side, it is called **phosphodiester**.

18. **Structure of DNA**

    Watson-Crick Model Features

    (i) DNA exists as a double helix.
    (ii) Two strands of polynucleotides are antiparallel, *i.e.*, run in the opposite direction.
    (iii) Backbone is formed by the sugar-phosphate-sugar chain.
    (iv) A and G of one strand base pairs with T and C, respectively on the other strand.
    (v) There are two hyrogen bonds between A and T and three hydrogen bonds between G and C.
    (vi) Each strands appears like a helical staircase.

19. **Turnover and Metabolism** All biomolecules have a turnover. This means that they are constantly being changed into some other biomolecules and also made from some other biomolecules.

    The making and breaking is through chemical reactions constantly occurring in living organism. Together all these chemical reactions are called metabolism, *e.g.*, removal of CO_2 from amino acid forms amine. Removal of amino group in a nucleotide base. Hydrolysis of a glycosidic bond in a disaccharide.

20. **Features of Metabolic Reactions** Flow of metabolites through metabolic pathways has a definite rate and direction like automobile traffic. This metabolite flow is called the dynamic state of body constituents.

21. Metabolic reactions are catalysed reactions.

    (i) **Enzymes** The catalysts which hastens the rate of a given metabolic conversion are also proteins. These proteins with catalytic power are named enzymes.
    (ii) **Anabolic pathway** Formation of complex structure from a simpler structure, *e.g.*, acetic acid becomes cholesterol.
    (iii) **Catabolic pathway** Degradation of a complex structure to form a simpler structure, *e.g.*, glucose becomes lactic acid in our skeletal muscles.

22. **ATP** (Adenosine Triphosphate) most important form of energy currency in living systems is the bond energy in ATP.

23. **Features of Enzymes**

    (i) Mostly proteins.
    (ii) Nucleic acids that behaves like enzymes are called **riboenzymes**.

(iii) Enzymes have active sites, it is a crevice or pocket into which the substrate fits.

(iv) Enzymes through active sites catalyse reactions at a high rate.

(v) **Difference between organic and inorganic catalysts** Inorganic catalysts work efficiently at high temperature and high pressure.

Enzymes gets damaged at high temperature (say above 40°C).

24. **Chemical Reactions** When bonds are broken and new bonds are formed during transformation, this is called **chemical reactions** :

Example Inorganic chemical reaction

$$Ba(OH)_2 + H_2SO_4 \longrightarrow BaSO_4 + 2H_2O$$

Organic chemical reaction Hydrolysis of starch into glucose.

Rate of a physical or chemical process = Amount of product formed per unit time.

$$\text{Rate} = \frac{\delta P}{\delta t}$$

25. **General Rule of Thumb** Rate doubles or decreases by half for every 10°C change in either direction.

26. Catalysed reactions proceed at rates vastly higher than that of uncatalysed ones.

e.g., $\underset{\text{Carbon dioxide}}{CO_2} + \underset{\text{Water}}{H_2O} \xrightarrow{\text{Carbonic anhydrase}} \underset{\text{Carbonic acid}}{H_2CO_3}$

In absence of enzyme, reaction slow-200 molecules of H_2CO_3 formed in an hour.

In presence of enzyme, reaction fast-600000 molecules formed every second.

27. **Working of Enzymes**

(i) **Substrate** (S) Chemical which is converted into a product.

(ii) **Enzyme** Proteins with three dimensional structures including an active site convert a substrate (S) into a product (P).

$$S \rightarrow P$$

(iii) The substrate has to diffuse towards the 'active site'. There is thus, an obligatory formation of an 'ES' complex. This complex formation is a transient phenomenon.

(iv) During this state, a new structure of the substrate called **transition state structure** is formed.

(v) After bond making/breaking is completed, the product is released from the active site.

(vi) There could be many more 'altered structural states' between the stable substrate and the product.

28. **Concept of Activation Energy**

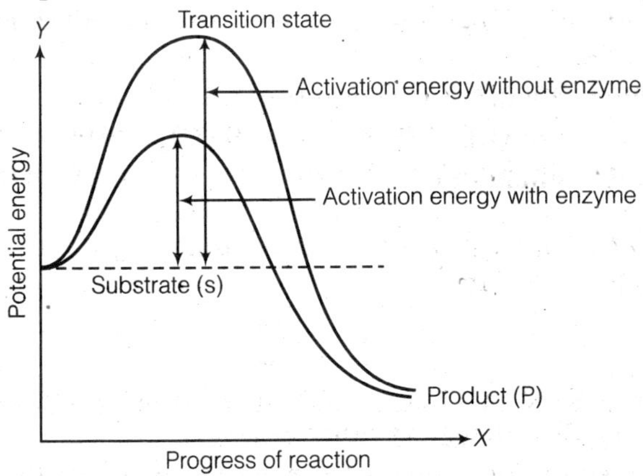

Y-axis = Potential energy

X-axis = Progression of the structural transformation or states through transition state.

Two features to notice

(a) If 'P' is at a lower level than 'S', the reaction is an exothermic reaction (no supply of energy is needed to form the product).

(b) **Activation energy** The difference in average energy content of 'S' from that of the transition state is called **activation energy**'.

29. **Nature of Enzyme Action**

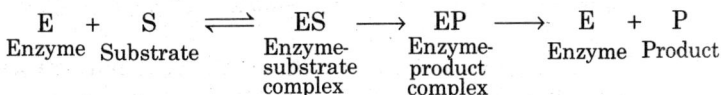

E	+	S	$\rightleftharpoons$	ES	$\longrightarrow$	EP	$\longrightarrow$	E	+	P
Enzyme		Substrate		Enzyme-substrate complex		Enzyme-product complex		Enzyme		Product

Steps (catalytic cycle)

(i) Substrate binds to the active sites of the enzyme.

(ii) Binding induces enzyme to alter its shape fitting more tightly around the substrate.

(iii) Active site of enzyme breaks the chemical bonds of the substrate and the new enzyme-product complex is formed.

(iv) Enzyme releases products of the reaction and the free enzyme is ready to bind to another molecule of the substrate and run through the catalytic cycle once again.

30. **Factors Affecting Enzyme Activity**

(i) Temperature and pH.

(a) Each enzyme shows its highest activity a particular temperature and pH called the optimum temperature and optimum pH.

(b) Activity declines both below and above the optimum value.

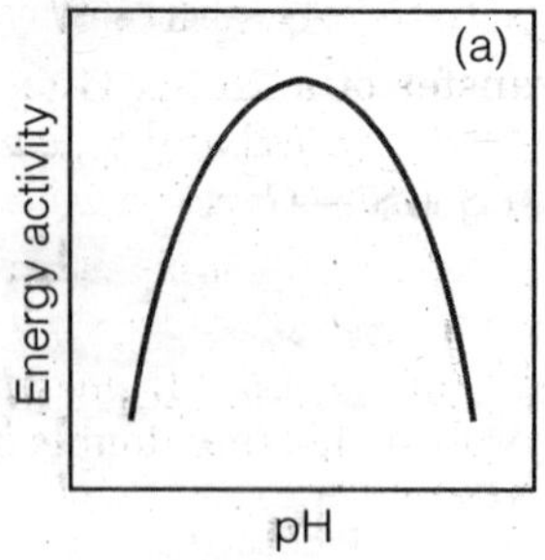

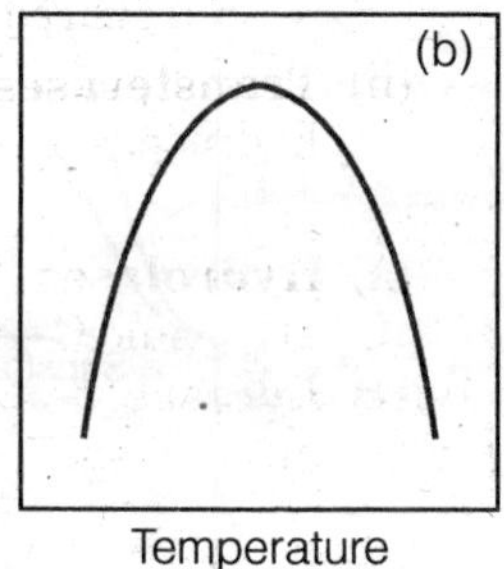

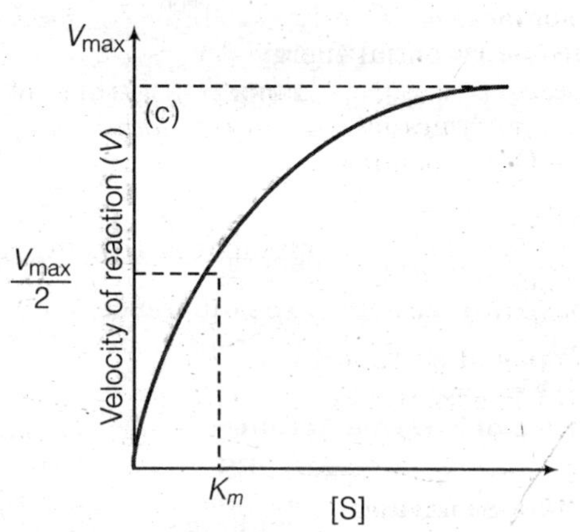

Effect of change in
(a) pH
(b) temperature
(c) concentration of substrate on enzyme.

(ii) Concentration of substrate :

(a) With the increase in substrate concentration, the velocity of the enzymatic reaction. The reaction ultimately reaches a maximum velocity (V_{max}) which is not exceeded by any further rise in concentration of substrate.

(b) When the binding of the chemical shuts off enzyme activity, the process is called inhibition and the chemical is called an inhibitor.

31. **Classification and Nomenclature of Enzymes**

(i) **Oxidoreductases/dehydrogenases** Catalyse oxidoreduction between two substrates S and S', *e.g.*,

$$S \text{ (reduced)} + S' \text{ (oxidised)} \rightarrow S \text{ (oxidised)} + S' \text{ (reduced)}$$

(ii) **Transferases** Catalyse transfer of a group. G (other than hydrogen) between a pair of substrate S and S', *e.g.*,

$$S - G + S' \rightarrow S + S' - G$$

(iii) **Hydrolases** Catalyse hydrolysis of ester, ether peptide glycosidic C—C, C—halide or P—N.

(iv) **Lyrases** Catalyse removal of groups from substrates mechanisms other than hydrolysis leaving double bonds.

$$\begin{matrix} X & Y \\ | & | \\ C & — C \end{matrix} \longrightarrow X - Y + C{=}C$$

(v) **Isomerases** Catalyse inter-conversion of optical, geometric or positional isomers.

(vi) **Ligases** Catalyse linking together of two compounds, *e.g., enzymes which catalyse joining of C—O, C—S, C—N,* P—O, *etc, bonds.*

32. **Co-factors**

(i) In some cases, non-protein constituents called co-factors are bound to the enzyme to make enzyme catalytically active.

(ii) Protein portion is called apoenzyme.

Types of co-factors

(a) **Prosthetic group** Organic compound,
e.g., peroxidase and catalase and haem is the prosthetic group.

(b) **Co-enzymes** Organic compound, but their association with the apoenzyme is only transient usually occurring during the course of catalysis.
e.g., Nicotinamide Adenine Dinucleotide (NAD and NADP).

(c) Metal ions, *e.g.,* zinc is a co-factor for the proteolytic enzyme carboxypeptidase.

Exercises

Question 1. What are macromolecules? Give examples.

Answer Chemical compounds, which are found in the acid insoluble fraction are called macromolecules or biomacromolecules. For example, proteins, lipids and carbohydrate, etc.

Question 2. Illustrate a glycosidic, peptide and a phosphodiester bond.

Answer **Glycosidic Bond** A glycosidic bond is a type of functional group that joins a carbohydrate (sugar) molecule to another group, which may or may not be another carbohydrate.

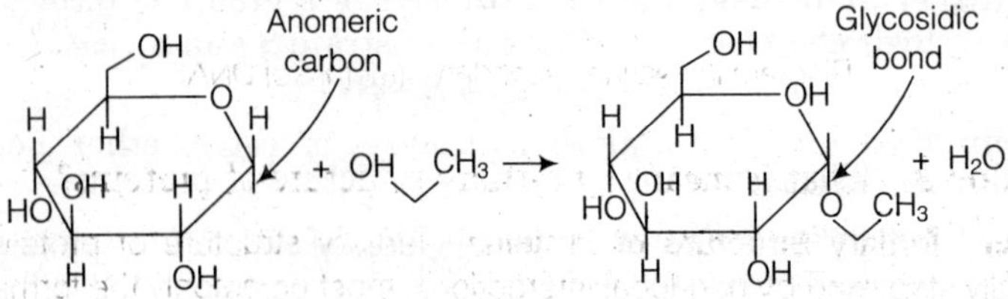

Peptide Bond A peptide bond (amide bond) is a chemical bond formed between two molecules when the carboxyl group of one molecule reacts with the amine group of the other molecule, thereby releasing a molecule of water (H_2O).

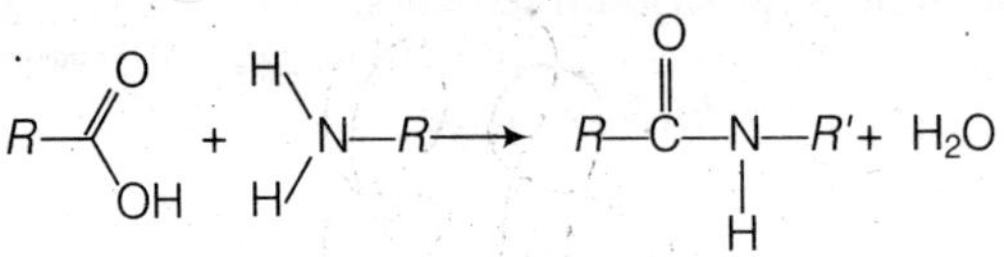

$$R{-}COOH + H_2N{-}R' \longrightarrow R{-}\overset{O}{\overset{\|}{C}}{-}\underset{H}{\underset{|}{N}}{-}R' + H_2O$$

Phosphodiester Bond A phosphodiester bond is a group of strong covalent bonds between a phosphate group and two other molecules over two ester bonds. In DNA and RNA, the phosphodiester bond is the linkage between the 3′ carbon atom of one sugar molecule and the 5′ carbon of another, deoxyribose in DNA and ribose in RNA.

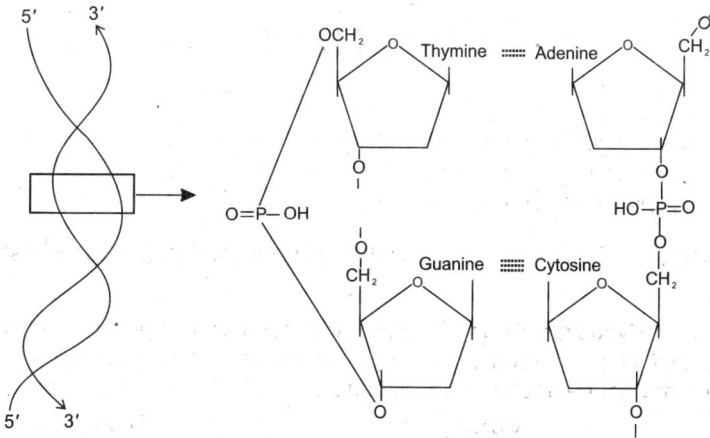

Diagram indicating secondary structure of DNA

Question 3. What is meant by tertiary structure of proteins?

Answer **Tertiary Structure of Proteins** Tertiary structure of proteins is generally stabilised by non-local interactions, most commonly the formation of a hydrophobic core, but also through salt bridges, hydrogen bonds, disulphide bonds and even post-translational modifications. The term 'tertiary structure' is often used as synonymous with the term fold. The tertiary structure is what controls the basic function of the protein.

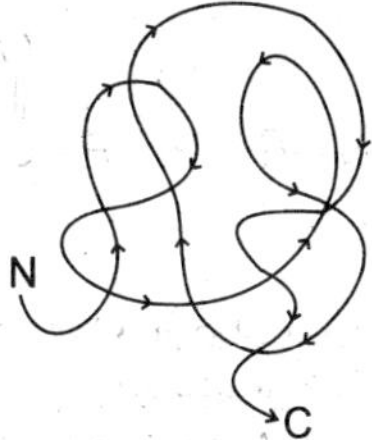

A tertiary structure of proteins

Question 4. Find and write down structures of 10 interesting small molecular weight biomolecules. Find if there is any industry which manufactures the compounds by isolation. Find out who are the buyers.

Answer

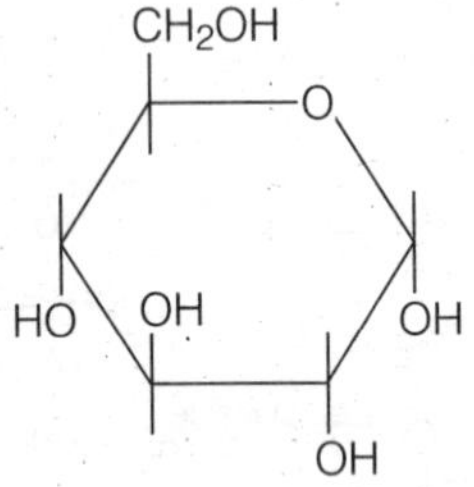

CH_2OH

HO OH OH OH

$C_5H_{12}O_5$ (Glucose)

$HOCH_2$ O OH OH OH

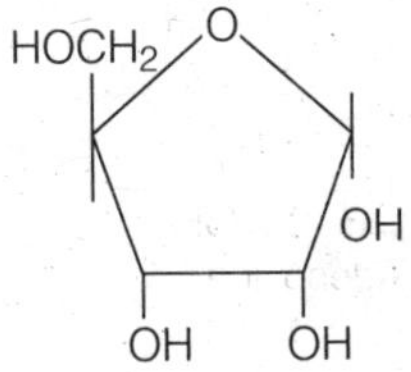

$C_5H_{10}O_5$ (Ribose)

Sugars (carbohydrates)

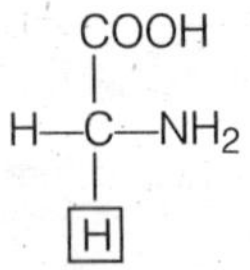

COOH | H—C—NH_2 | H

Glycine

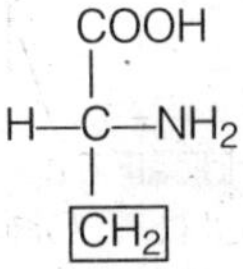

COOH | H—C—NH_2 | CH_2

Alanine

COOH | H—C—NH_2 | CH_2—OH

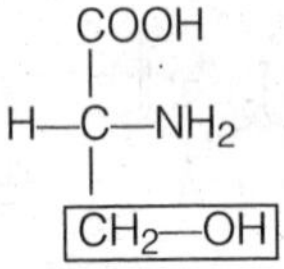

Serine

Amino acids

CH_3—$(CH_2)_{14}$—COOH

Fatty acid
(Palmitic acid)

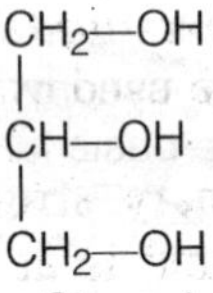

CH_2—OH | CH—OH | CH_2—OH

Glycerol

CH_2—O—C(=O)—R_1 | R_2—C(=O)—O—CH | CH_2—O—C(=O)—R_3

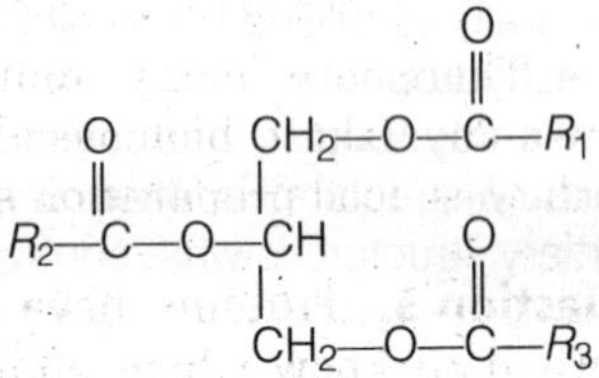

Triglyceride (R_1, R_2 and R_3 are fatty acids)

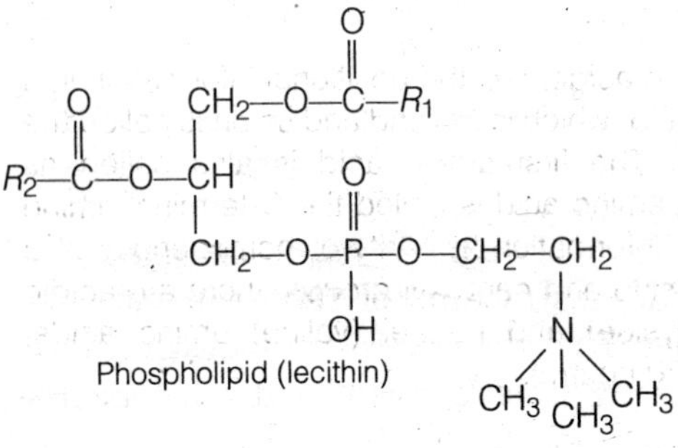

CH_2—O—C(=O)—R_1 | R_2—C(=O)—O—CH | CH_2—O—P(=O)(OH)—O—CH_2—CH_2—N(CH_3)$_3$

Phospholipid (lecithin)

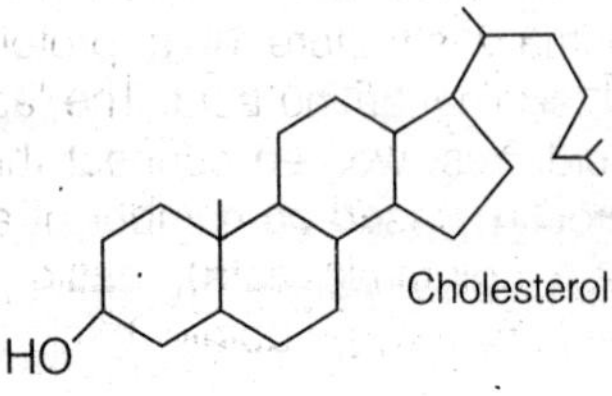

HO

Cholesterol

Fats and oils (lipids)

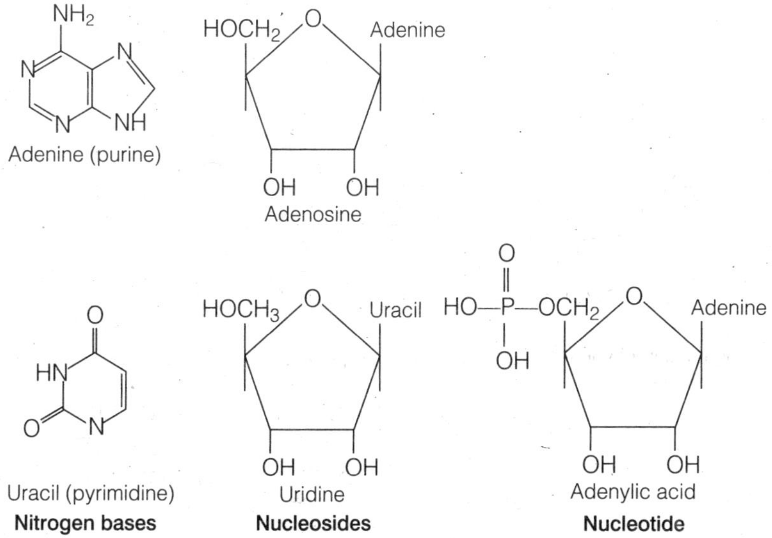

Adenine (purine)

Adenosine

Uracil (pyrimidine)

Uridine

Adenylic acid

Nitrogen bases **Nucleosides** **Nucleotide**

Diagrammatic representation of small molecular weight

There are many industries who make these biomolecules now-a-days these biomolecules are used in many drugs, injections, medicines, food preparation so are used by several people.

Question 5. Proteins have primary structure. If you are given a method to know which amino acid is at either of the two termini (ends) of a protein, can you connect this information to purity or homogeneity of a protein?

Answer The sequence of amino acids, *i.e.*, the positional information in a protein which is the first amino acid, which is second and so on is called the primary structure of a protein. The first amino acid is also called as N-terminal amino acid. The last amino acid is called the C-terminal amino acid. Yes, we can connect this information to purity or homogeneity of a protein. Based on number of amino and carboxyl groups, there are acidic (*e.g.*, glutamic acid), basic (lysine) and neutral (valine) amino acids, proteins may be acidic, basic and neutral.

Question 6. Find out and make a list of proteins used as therapeutic agents. Find other applications of proteins (*e.g.*, cosmetics, etc.)

Answer **Some Proteins and their Functions**

Protein	Functions
Collagen	Intercellular ground substance
Trypsin	Enzyme
Insulin	Hormone
Antibody	Fights infectious agents
Receptor	Sensory reception (smell, taste, hormone, etc.)
GLUT-4	Enables glucose transport into cells

Question 7. Explain the composition of triglyceride.

Answer Triglycerides are composed of two types of molecules, *i.e.*, glycerol (3 carbon molecules) and fatty acids which attach to the glycerol at the alcohol unit. The following is a structural representation of a triglyceride at the molecular level

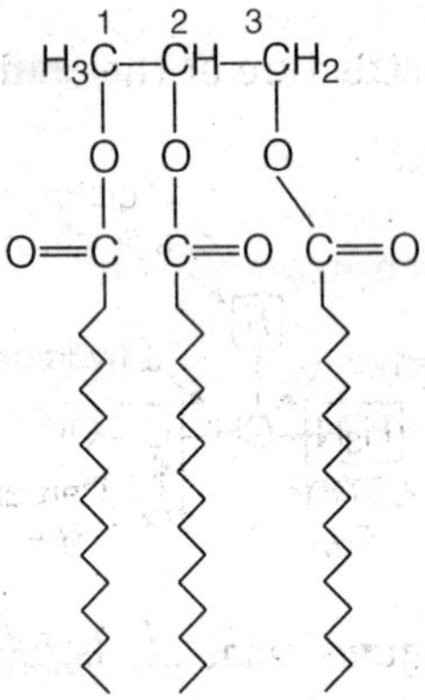

Fatty acids are chains of hydrocarbons 4-22 (or more) carbons a long with a carboxyl group at one end. If each carbon has two hydrogen atoms, the fatty acid is saturated. If two carbon atoms are double-bonded, so that there is less hydrogen in the fatty acid, it is unsaturated (monounsaturated). If more than two carbon atoms are unsaturated, the fatty acid is polyunsaturated.

Question 8. Can you describe what happens when milk is converted into curd or yoghurt, from your understanding of proteins.

Answer Milk contains a protein called casein. This protein gives milk its characteristic white colour. It is of high nutritional value because it contains all the essential amino acids required by man's body. The curd forms because of the chemical reaction between lactic acid bacteria and casein. When curd is added to milk, the lactic acid bacteria present in it cause coagulation of casein and thus, convert it into curd.

Question 9. Can you attempt building models of biomolecules using commercially available atomic models (Ball and stick models).

Answer Yes, we can make models of biomolecules using commercially available atomic models.

Question 10. Attempt titrating an amino acid against a weak base and discover the number of dissociating (ionisable) functional groups in the amino acid.

Answer When an amino acid is titrated against a weak base, it dissociates and gives two functional groups:

(i) — COOH group (carboxylic group)

(ii) Amino group (NH_2).

Question 11. Draw the structure of the amino acid and alanine.

Answer

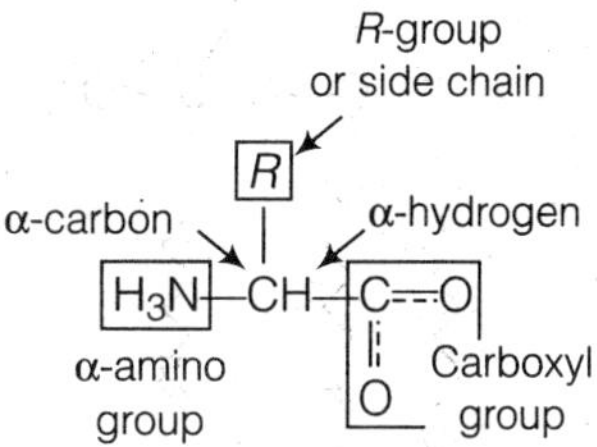

Question 12. What are gums made of? Is fevicol different?

Answer Gums are made of carbohydrates, *i.e.*, L-rhamnose, D-galactose and D-galacturonic acid, etc. Fevicol is different from natural gums. It is a synthetic product.

Question 13. Find out a qualitative test for proteins, fats and oils and starch amino acids and test any fruit juice, saliva, sweat and urine for them.

Answer A qualitative test for proteins.

(i) Xanthoproteic Test

Experimental Material	Observation	Inference
(a) Urine (b) Water	Yellow precipitate No precipitate	Formation of yellow precipitate indicates the presence of protein in the food material.

(ii) A qualitative test for fats.

Emulsification Test

Experimental Material	Observation	Inference
(a) Sweat (b) Water	Oil droplets No oil droplet	Formation of oil droplets, *i.e.*, emulsification indicates the presence of fats in the given food material.

(iii) A qualitative test for oils.

Paper Test

Experimental Material	Observation	Inference
(a) Food material (sample) (b) Water	Paper becomes translucent	Opaque paper becomes translucent which indicates the presence of fats in the food material.

(iv) A qualitative test for starch.

Iodine Test

Experimental Material	Observation	Inference
(a) Fruit juices (b) Water	Blue black colour	Formation of blue black colour indicates the presence of starch in the given food material.

Question 14. **Find out how much cellulose is made by all the plants in the biosphere and compare it with how much of paper is manufactured by man and hence, what is the consumption of plant material by man annually. What a loss of vegetation?**

Answer Most paper is formed from wood pulp. The main component of wood pulp is cellulose, a polymer made of many glucose molecules linked together. The cellulose molecules and their bonding to each other give paper its properties. About 33% of all plant matter is cellulose. The cellulose content of cotton is 90% and that of wood is 40-50%. For industrial use, cellulose is mainly obtained from wood pulp and cotton. It is mainly used to produce paperboard and paper; to a smaller extent. It is converted into a wide variety of derivative products such as cellophane and rayon.

Question 15. Describe the important properties of enzymes.

Answer

(i) Enzymes are proteins which catalyse biochemical reactions in the cells.

(ii) They are denatured at high temperatures.

(iii) Enzymes generally function in a narrow range of temperature and pH. Each enzyme shows its highest activity at a particular temperature and pH called the optimum temperature and optimum pH.

(iv) With the increase in substrate concentration, the velocity of the enzymatic reaction rises at first. The reaction ultimately reaches a maximum velocity (v_{max}) which is not exceeded by any further rise in concentration of the substrate.

(v) The activity of an enzyme is also sensitive to the presence of specific chemicals that bind to the enzyme.

(vi) Enzymes are substrate specific in their action.

Selected NCERT Exemplar Problems

Very Short Answer Type Questions

Question 1. Medicines are either man made (*i.e.*, synthetic) or obtained from living organisms like plants, bacteria, animals, etc., and hence, the latter are called natural products. Sometimes, natural products are chemically altered by man to reduce toxicity or side effects. Write against each of the following whether they were initially obtained as a natural product or as a synthetic chemical.

(i) Penicillin .... synthetic chemical.
(ii) Sulphonamide .... synthetic chemical.
(iii) Vitamin-C .... natural product ....
(iv) Growth hormone .... natural product ....

Answer (i) Penicillin — Natural product
(ii) Sulphonamide — Synthetic chemical
(iii) Vitamin-C — Natural product
(iv) Growth hormone — Natural product

Question 2. Select an appropriate chemical bond among ester bond, glycosidic bond, peptide bond and hydrogen bond and write against each of the following.

(i) Polysaccharide .... (ii) Protein ....
(iii) Fat .... (iv) Water ....

Answer (i) Polysaccharide — Glycosidic bond
(ii) Protein — Peptide bond
(iiii) Fat — Ester bond
(iv) Water — Hydrogen bond.

Question 3. Write the name of any one amino acid, sugar, nucleotide and fatty acid.

Answer Alanine is an amino acid, purine is a nucleotide and linolenic acid is a fatty acid.

Question 4. Reaction given below is catalysed by oxidoreductase between two substrates A and A′, complete the reaction.

A reduced + A′ oxidised ⟶

Answer A reduced + A′ oxidised ⟶ A oxidised + A′ reduced

Question 5. How are prosthetic groups different from co-factors?

Answer Differences between prosthetic groups and co-factors

Prosthetic Groups Prosthetic groups are organic compounds and are distinguished from other co-factors in that they are tightly bound to the apoenzyme.

Co-factors Enzymes are composed of one or several polypeptide chains. However, there are a number of cases in which non-protein constituents called co-factors are bound to the enzyme to make the enzyme catalytically active.

Question 6. Glycine and alanine are different with respect to one substituent on the α-carbon. What are the other common substituent groups?

Answer There are four substituent groups occupying the four valency positions in an amino acid. These are hydrogen, carboxyl group, amino group and a variable group designated as *R* group. The *R* group in amino acid glycine is a hydrogen and a methyl group in case of amino acid alanine, etc.

Question 7. Starch, cellulose, glycogen, chitin are polysaccharides found among the following. Choose the one appropriate and write against each.

Cotton fibre ....
Exoskeleton of cockroach ....
Liver ....
Peeled potato ....

Answer Cotton fibre — Cellulose
Exoskeleton of cockroach — Chitin
Liver — Glycogen
Peeled potato — Starch

Short Answer Type Questions

Question 1. Enzymes are proteins. Proteins are long chains of amino acids linked to each other by peptide bonds. Amino acids have many functional groups in their structure. These functional groups are many of them at least, ionisable. As they are weak acids and bases in chemical nature, this ionisation is influenced by pH of the solution. For many enzymes, activity is influenced by surrounding pH. This is depicted in the curve below, explain briefly.

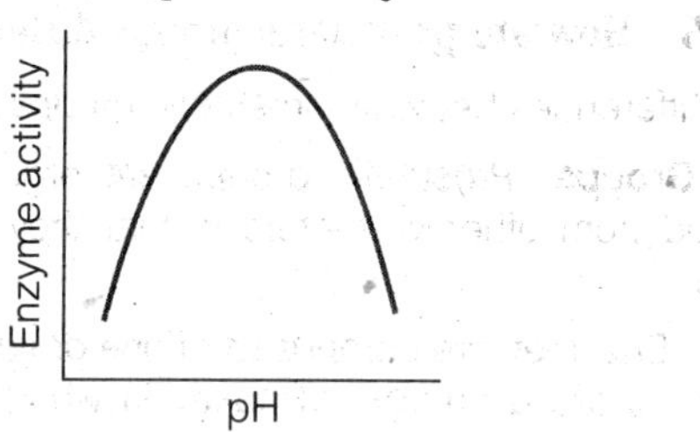

Answer Enzymes, generally function in a narrow range of pH. Each enzyme shows its highest activity at a particular the optimum pH. Activity declines both below and above the optimum value. The graph shows maximum enzyme activity at optimum pH. The rate of enzyme activity decreases above and below that of optimum pH.

Question 2. Is rubber a primary metabolite or a secondary metabolite? Write four sentences about rubber.

Answer

(i) Yes, It natural rubber (*cis*-1, 4-polyisoprene) is a secondary metabolite. It is extracted from the rubber tree (*Hevea brasiliensis*).

(ii) In the rubber tree, latex is produced in the highly specialised cells, called laticifers in phloem.

(iii) Rubber is a terpenoid and due to its high tensile strength, elasticity and plasticity properties it is widely used in industries.

(iv) It is a polymeric substance.

Question 3. Schematically represent primary, secondary and tertiary structures of a hypothetical polymer say for example a protein.

Answer **Structure of Proteins**

Primary Structure The sequence of amino acids, *i.e.*, the positional information in a protein, which is the first amino acid, which is second and so on is called the primary structure of a protein. The first amino acid is also called as N-terminal amino acid. The last amino acid is called the C-terminal amino acid.

Secondary Structure Regularly repeating local structures stabilised by hydrogen bonds. The most common examples are the alpha helix, beta sheet and turns. Because secondary structures are local, many regions of different secondary structure can be present in the same protein molecule.

Tertiary Structure Tertiary structure is generally stabilised by non-local interactions, most commonly the formation of a hydrophobic core, but also through salt bridges, hydrogen bonds, disulphide bonds and even post-translational modifications. The term 'tertiary structure' is often used as synonymous with the term fold. The tertiary structure is what controls the basic function of the protein.

Primary structure   Secondary structure   Tertiary structure

Question 4. Nucleic acids exhibit secondary structure, justify with example.

Answer For nucleic acids, the building block is a nucleotide. A nucleotide has three chemically distinct components. One is a heterocyclic compound, the second is a monosaccharide and the third a phosphoric acid or phosphate.

The heterocyclic compounds in nucleic acids are the nitrogenous bases named adenine, guanine, uracil, cytosine and thymine. Adenine and guanine are substituted purines while the rest are substituted pyrimidines.

The skeletal heterocyclic ring is called as purine and pyrimidine respectively. The sugar found in polynucleotides is either ribose (a monosaccharide pentose) or 2′ deoxyribose. A nucleic acid containing deoxyribose is called deoxyribonucleic acid (DNA) while that which contains ribose is called ribonucleic acid (RNA).

Question 5. Comment on the statement 'living state is a non-equilibrium steady state to be able to perform work'.

Answer The most important fact of biological systems is that all living organisms exist in a steady-state characterised by the concentrations of each of these biomolecules. These biomolecules are in a metabolic flux. Any chemical or physical process moves spontaneously to equilibrium. The steady state is a non-equilibrium state.

As living organisms work continuously, they cannot afford to reach equilibrium. Hence, the living state is a non-equilibrium steady-state to be able to perform work. This is achieved by energy input. Metabolism provides a mechanism for the production of energy. Hence, the living state and metabolism are synonymous. Without metabolism, there cannot be a living state.

Long Answer Type Questions

Question 1. Formation of Enzyme-Substrate complex (ES) is the first step in catalysed reactions. Describe the other steps till the formation of product.

Answer

Mechanisms of Enzymatic Action The catalytic cycle of an enzyme action can be described in the following steps

(i) First, the substrate binds to the active site of the enzyme, fitting into the active site.

(ii) The binding of the substrate induces the enzyme to alter its shape, fitting more tightly around the substrate.

The formation of the ES complex is essential for catalysis.

$$E + S \quad ES \longrightarrow EP \longrightarrow E + P$$

(iii) The active site of the enzyme, now in close proximity of the substrate breaks the chemical bonds of the substrate and the new enzyme product complex is formed.

(iv) The enzyme releases the products of the reaction and the free enzyme is ready to bind to another molecule of the substrate and run through the catalytic cycle once again.

Question 2. What are different classes of enzymes? Explain any two with the type of reaction they catalyse.

Answer Classification and nomenclature of enzymes

Enzymes are divided into six classes each with 4-13 sub-classes and named accordingly by a four-digit number.

Oxidoreductases/dehydrogenases Enzymes which catalyse oxidoreduction between two substrates S and S′, *e.g.*,

$$\text{S reduced} + \text{S}'\text{ oxidised} \longrightarrow \text{S oxidised} + \text{S}'\text{ reduced}$$

Transferases Enzymes catalysing a transfer of a group, G (other than hydrogen) between a pair of substrate S and S′, *e.g.*,

$$\text{S-G} + \text{S}' \longrightarrow \text{S} + \text{S}'\text{-G}$$

Hydrolases Enzymes catalysing hydrolysis of ester, ether, peptide, glycosidic, C—C, C—halide or P—N bonds.

Lyases Enzymes that catalyse removal of groups from substrates by mechanisms other than hydrolysis leaving double bonds.

Isomerases Includes all enzymes catalysing interconversion of optical, geometric or positional isomers.

Ligases Enzymes catalysing the linking together of two compounds, *e.g.*, enzymes which catalyse joining of C—O, C—S, C—N, P—O, etc., bonds.

Question 3. Nucleic acids exhibit secondary structure. Describe through Watson-Crick model.

Answer Watson and Crick model of DNA Structure

James Watson and Francis Crick proposed a structure for the DNA molecule that suggested the basic mechanism of DNA replication. According to them

(i) DNA is composed of two strands of DNA running anti-parallel (remember the 5′ and 3′-ends) to each other.

(ii) The hydrophilic sugar (ribose) and phosphate groups of the nucleotides are face the outside of the molecule and the relatively hydrophobic nitrogenous bases are on the inside of the molecule, hidden from water.

(iii) The nucleotides within each strand are held together by the phosphodiester bonds between the 5′ carbon of one nucleotide and the 3′ carbon of the adjacent nucleotide.

(iv) These strong covalent bonds form the glue that holds the sugar/phosphate backbone together and thus act to keep each strand together.

(v) The two strands of DNA are held together by weak **hydrogen bonds** between the nitrogenous bases.

(vi) These hydrogen bonds are base specific. That is A (adenine) can only form hydrogen bonds with T (thymine) and C (cytosine) can only form bonds with G (guanine).

(vii) The strands in such a molecule are said to be **complementary**.

(viii) The two strands wrap around each other to form a **double helix** structure.

(ix) **Watson** and Crick explained 'Chargraff's Rule' of DNA in which the amount of A in any DNA sample always equal to the amount of T and that the amount of G always equal to the amount of C.

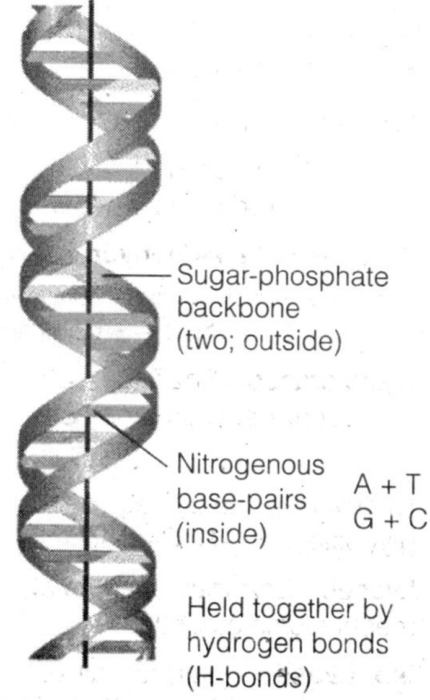

Structure of DNA

Question 4. What is the differences between a nucleotide and nucleoside? Give two examples of each with their structure.

Answer Nucleotides are building blocks of nucleic acids (DNA and RNA).

Differences between Nucleotide and Nucleoside

Nucleotide	Nucleoside
A nucleotide consists of a nitrogenous base, a sugar (ribose or deoxyribose) and one to three phosphate groups (*i.e.*, sugar + base + phosphate).	A nucleoside consists of a nitrogenous base covalently attached to a sugar (ribose or deoxyribose) but without the phosphate group (*i.e.*, sugar + base).
Examples adenine, guanine, cytosine, uracil and thymine.	**Examples** cytidine, uridine, adenosine, guanosine, thymidine and inosine.
O ‖ HO—P—OCH$_2$ (O) Adenine, OH; OH OH **Adenylic acid**	HOCH$_2$ (O) Adenine; OH OH **Adenosine**

10

Cell Cycle and Cell Division

Important Points

1. **Cell Cycle** The sequence of events by which a cell duplicates its genome, synthesises the other constituents of the cell and eventually divides into two daughter cells is called cell cycle.
2. **Phases of Cell Cycle** Cell cycle is divided into two basic phases
   (i) **Interphase** It is divided into
      (a) **G_1-phase** (Gap 1) Corresponds to the interval between mitosis and initiation of DNA replication.
      Cell is metabolically active and continuously grows but does not replicate its DNA.
      (b) **S-phase** (synthesis phase) Marks the period during which DNA synthesis or replication takes place.
      - Amount of DNA per cell doubles.
      - No increase in chromosome number.

      (c) **G_2-phase** (Gap 2) Proteins are sythesised in preparation for mitosis, while cell growth continues.

   (ii) **M-phase** (mitosis phase) Represent the phase when actual cell division or mitosis occurs.
      (a) Last only for one hour. Interphase lasts more than 95%.
      (b) Starts with nuclear division, corresponding to the separation of daughter chromosomes (karyokinesis) and usually ends with division of cytoplasm (cytokinesis).

3. **Quiescent Stage** (G_0) Some cells in the adult animals do not appear to exhibit (*e.g.*, heart cells) and many other cells divide only occassionally as needed to replace cells that have been lost because of injury or cell death.

   These cells that do not divide further exit G_1-phase to enter an inactive stage called quiescent stage (G_0).

4. **M-Phase**
   (i) Involves a major reorganisation of virtually all components of the cell.
   (ii) Since, the number of chromosomes in the parent and progeny cells is the same, it is also called equational division.

5. Mitosis is divided into four stages
   (i) Prophase
   (ii) Metaphase
   (iii) Anaphase
   (iv) Telophase

   (i) **Prophase**
      (a) Follows the S and G_2-phases of interphase.
      (b) Marked by initiation of condensation of chromosomal material.
      (c) Chromosomal material becomes untangled during chromatin condensation.
      (d) Centriole begins to move towards opposite poles of cell.
      (e) Completion can be marked by
         - Chromosomal material condenses to form compact mitotic chromosomes. Chromosomes are seen to be composed of two chromatids attached together at the centromere.
         - Initiation of the assembly of mitotic spindle, the microtubules, the proteinaceous components of the cell cytoplasm help in the process.

   (ii) **Metaphase**
      (a) Starts with complete disintegration of the nuclear envelope.
      (b) Chromosomes spread throughout the cytoplasm.
      (c) Morphology of chromosomes is most easily studied.
      (d) Metaphase chromosome made of two sister chromatids. Which are held together by the centromere.

(e) **Kinetochores** Small disc-shaped structures at the surface of the centromeres. They serve as the sites of attachement of spindle fibres to the chromosomes that are moved into position at the centre of the cell.

(f) All chromosomes lie at the equator with one chromatid of each chromosome connected by its kinetochore to spindle fibres from one pole and its sister chromatid connected by its kinetochore to spindle fibres from the opposite poles.

(g) The plane of alignment of the chromosomes at metaphase is referred to as the metaphase plate.

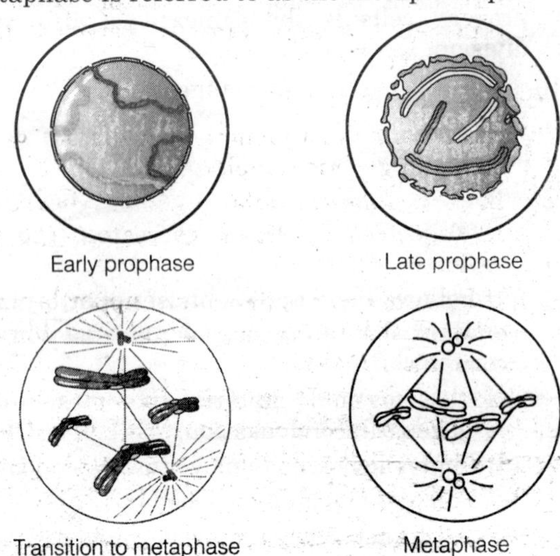

(iii) **Anaphase**

(a) Each chromosome arranged at the metaphase plate is split simultaneously and the two daughter chromatids now referred to as chromosomes of future daughter nuclei, begin their migration towards the two opposite poles.

(b) It is characterised by

- Centromeres split and chromatids separate.
- Chromatids moves to opposite poles.

(iv) **Telophase**

(a) Chromosomes cluster at opposite spindle poles and their identily is lost as discrete elements.

(b) Nuclear envelope assembles around the chromosomes clusters.

(c) Nucleolus, Golgi complex and ER reform.

6. **Cytokinesis**
   (i) Division of cell into two daughter cells by cytokinesis.
   (ii) In an animal cell, cytokinesis by the appearance of a furrow in the plasma membrane.
   (iii) Furrow gradually deepens and ultimately joins in the centre dividing the cell cytoplasm into two.
   (iv) In plant cell, wall formation starts in the centre of the cell and grows outward to meet the existing lateral walls.
   (v) The formation of the new cell wall begins with the formation of simple precursor called cell plate that represents middle lamella between the walls of two adjacent cells.
7. **Significance of Mitosis**
   (i) Results in the production of diploid daughter cells with identical genetic complement.
   (ii) Growth of multicellular organisms is due to mitosis.
   (iii) It helps cell to divide to restore the nucleocytoplasmic ratio.
   (iv) It leads to cell repair cells of upper layer of the epidermis, cells of the lining of the gut and blood cells are being constantly replaced.
   (v) Mitotic divisions in the meristematic tissues–the apical and the lateral cambium, result in a continuous growth of plants.

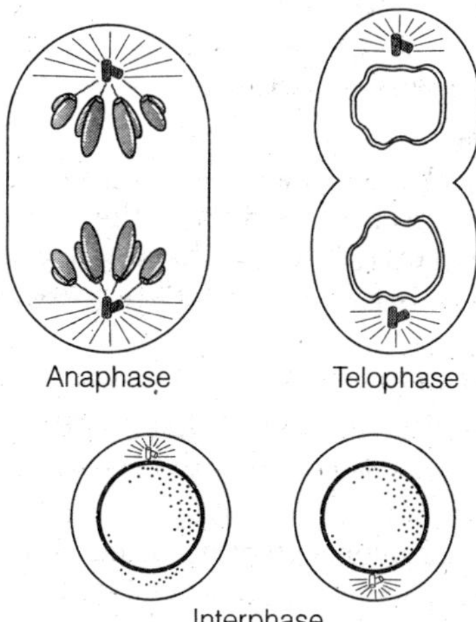

8. **Meiosis** The specialised kind of cell division that reduces the chromosome number by half results in the production of haploid daughter cells. This kind of division is called **meiosis**.

Key Features

(i) Involves two sequential cycles of nuclear and cell division called **meiosis**-I and meiosis-II but only a single cycle of DNA replication.

(ii) Meiosis-I is initiated after the parental chromosomes have replicated to produce identical sister chromatids at the S-phase.

(iii) Involves pairing of chromosome and recombination between them.

(iv) Four haploid cells are formed at the end of meiosis-II.

Meiosis-I	Meiosis-II
Prophase-I	Prophase-II
Metaphase-I	Metaphase-II
Anaphase-I	Anaphase-II
Telophase-I	Telophase-II

9. **Prophase-I**

Sub-divided into five phases based on chromosome behaviour.

(i) **Leptotene** Chromosome gradually become visible under microscope.

Compaction of chromosome continues through leptotene.

(ii) **Zygotene** Chromosome starts pairing together (process is called synapsis).

(a) Paired chromosomes are called homologous chromosomes.

(b) Chromosome synapsis is accompanied by formation of complex structure called **synaptonemal complex**.

(c) Complex formed by a pair of synapsed homologous chromosome is called a bivalent or a tetrad.

(iii) **Pachytene** Bivalent chromosomes clearly appear as tetrads.

(a) Recombination nodules appear at the sites at which crossing over occurs between non-sister chromatids of the homologous chromosomes.

(b) **Crossing Over** It is the exchange of genetic material between two homologous chromosomes.

(c) It is an enzyme mediated process, enzyme is called recombinase.

(d) It leads to recombination of genetic material on the two chromosomes.

(iv) **Diplotene**

(a) Synaptonemal complex dissolve.

(b) Recombined homologous chromosomes of the bivalents separate except at the sites of crossovers.

(c) These X-shaped structures are called chiasmata.

(v) **Diakinesis** Chiasmata terminalise

(a) Chromosomes are fully condensed and meiotic spindle is assembled to prepare the homologous chromosomes for separation.

(b) At the end-nucleolus disappears and nuclear envelope also breaks down.

10. **Metaphase-I**

(i) Bivalent chromosomes align on the equatorial plate.

(ii) Microtubules from the opposite poles of the spindle attach to the pair of homologous chromosomes.

11. **Anaphase-I** Homologous chromosomes separate, while sister chromatids remain associated at their centromeres.

12. **Telophase-I**

(i) Nuclear membrane and nucleolus reappear.

(ii) Cytokinesis occurs.

13. **Interkinesis** The stage between the two meiotic divisions is called **interkinesis**. Generally short lived.

14. **Prophase-II**

(i) Resembles to normal mitosis.

(ii) Nuclear membrane disappears by the end of prophase-II.

15. **Metaphase-II**

Chromosomes align at equator and microtubules from opposite poles of the spindle get attached to the kinetochores of sister chromatids.

16. **Anaphase-II**

Begins with simultaneous splitting of the centromere of each chromosome (which was holding the sister chromatids together) allowing them to move toward opposite poles of the cell.

17. **Telophase-II**
    (i) Two groups of chromosomes once again get enclosed by a nuclear envelope.
    (ii) Cytokinesis follows resulting in the formation of tetrad of cells, *i.e.*, four haploid daughter cells.

18. **Significance of Meiosis**
    (i) Mechanism by which conservation of specific chromosome number of each species is achieved across generations in sexually reproducing organisms.
    (ii) Increases genetic variability in the population of organisms from one generation to the next.

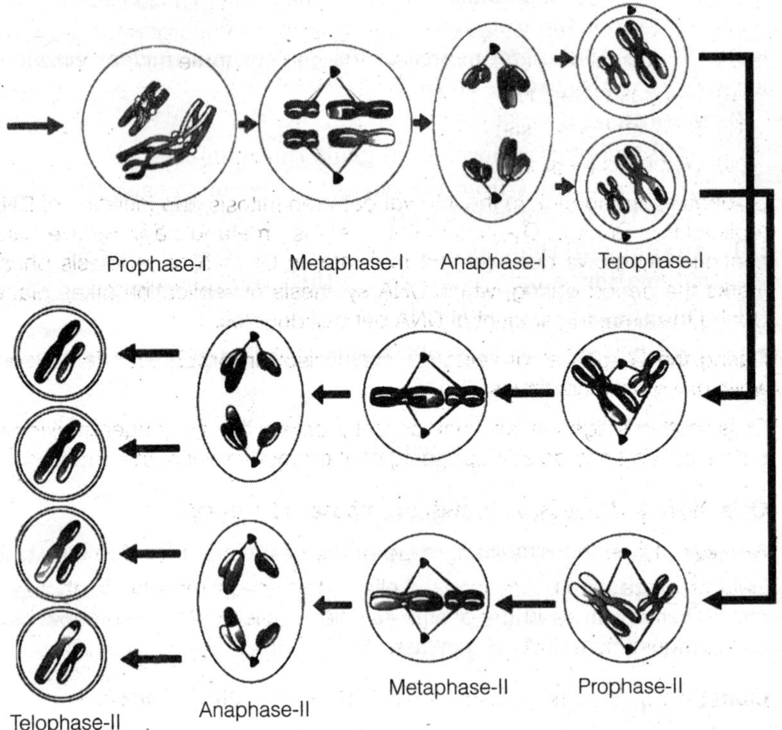

Stages of meiosis

Exercises

Question 1. What is the average cell cycle span for a mammalian cell?

Answer The average cell cycle span for a mammalian cell is 24 hours.

Question 2. Distinguish cytokinesis from karyokinesis.

Answer Cytokinesis is the division of cytoplasm, whereas karyokinesis is the division of nucleus of the cell.

Question 3. Describe the events taking place during interphase.

Answer The interphase, though called the resting phase, is the time during which the cell is preparing for division by undergoing cell growth and DNA replication. The interphase is divided into three further phases:

(i) G_1-phase (Gap 1)
(ii) S-phase (Synthesis)
(iii) G_2-phase (Gap 2)

G_1-phase corresponds to the interval between mitosis and initiation of DNA replication. During G_1-phase the cell is metabolically active and continuously grows but does not replicate its DNA. S or synthesis phase marks the period during, which DNA synthesis or replication takes place. During this time, the amount of DNA per cell doubles.

During the G_2-phase, proteins are synthesised in preparation for mitosis, while cell growth continues.

Cells in this stage remain metabolically active but no longer proliferate unless called on to do so depending on the requirement of the organism.

Question 4. What is G_0 (quiescent phase) of cell cycle?

Answer G_0 is the quiescent stage of the cell cycle. It is also known as inactive stage of the cell cycle. Cells in this stage remain metabolically remain active, but no longer proliferate unless called on to do so depending on the requirement of the organisms.

Question 5. Why is mitosis called equational cell division?

Answer Mitosis is the kind of cell division in which daughter cells have the same number and kind of chromosomes as that of parent cell. Mitosis is therefore, also known as equational cell division.

Question 6. Name the stage of cell cycle at which one of the following events occur?

(i) Chromosomes are moved to spindle equator.
(ii) Centromere splits and chromatids separate.
(iii) Pairing between homologous chromosomes take place.
(iv) Crossing over between homologous chromosomes takes place.

Answer (i) Prophase (ii) Anaphase
(iii) Zygotene stage of meiosis-I (iv) Pachytene stage

Question 7. Describe the following words.

(i) Synapsis (ii) Bivalent (iii) Chiasmata

Draw a diagram to illustrate your answer.

Answer

(i) **Synapsis** During meiosis-I, the process of pairing of chromosomes is known as synapsis. It is so exact that pairing is not merely between corresponding chromosomes but between corresponding individual units.

(ii) **Bivalent** The complex formed by a pair of synapsed homologous chromosomes is called a bivalent or a tetrad. It consists of four chromosomes.

(iii) **Chiasmata** The chiarma formation is the indication of completion of crossing over and beginning of separation of chromosomes. The chiasma is formed when the chromosomal parts begin to repel each other except in the region where these are in contact. Chiasmata formation is necessary for the separation of homologous chromosomes.

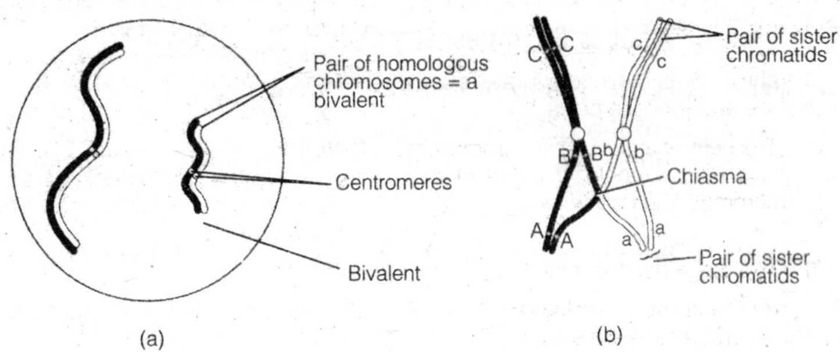

Chiasmata Formation

Question 8. How does cytokinesis in plant cells differ from that in animal cells?

Answer **Cytokinesis in an animal cell** It occurs by a process called cleavage. A cleavage furrow appears and at the site of the cleavage furrow, the cytoplasm has a ring of microfilaments made of actin associated with molecules of the protein myosin. This ring of proteins will contract causing the furrow to deepen, which will then in turn pinch the cell into two separate cells.

Cytokinesis in plant cell, In a plant, cell, vesicles containing cell wall material collect at the middle of the parent cell. They will fuse and form a membranous cell plate. This plate will grow outward and it accumulates more cell wall material. Eventually, the plate will fuse with the plasma membrane and the cell plate contents will join the parental cell wall. This results in two different daughter cells.

Question 9. Find examples where the four daughter cells from meiosis are equal in size and where they are found unequal in size.

Answer The four daughter haploid cells may or may not be equal in size at the end of meiosis-II with telophase-II.

Question 10. Distinguish anaphase of mitosis from anaphase-I of meiosis.

Answer Differences between anaphase of mitosis and anaphase-I of meiosis

S.N.	Anaphase of Mitosis	Anaphase-I of Meiosis
1.	Each chromosome arranged at the metaphase plate is split simultaneously and the two daughter chromatids, begin to migrate towards the two opposite poles.	The spindle fibres contract and pull the centromeres of homologous chromosomes towards the opposite poles.
2.	The centromere of each chromosome is towards the pole with arms of chromosome trailing behind.	The centromere is not divided, so half of the chromosomes of parent nucleus go to one pole and the remaining half in the opposite pole.
3.	This stage has following key events (a) Centromeres split and chromatids separate. (b) Chromatids move to opposite poles.	In this stage (a) Homologous chromosomes separate. (b) Sister chromatids remain associated at their centromere.

Question 11. List the main differences between mitosis and meiosis.

Answer **The Main Differences between Mitosis and Meiosis**

S.N.	Mitosis	Meiosis
1.	The division occurs in somatic cells.	It occurs in reproductive cells.
2.	It is a single division.	It is a double division.
3.	The daughter cells resemble each other as well as their mother cell.	The daughter cells neither resemble one another nor their mother cell.
4.	Replication of chromosomes occurs before every mitotic division.	Replication of chromosomes occurs only once though meiosis is a double division.
5.	Mitosis does not introduce variations.	Meiosis introduces variations.
6.	Mitosis is required for growth, repair and healing.	Meiosis is involved in sexual reproduction.

Question 12. What is the significance of meiosis?

Answer Meiosis is the mechanism by which conservation of specific chromosome number of each species is achieved across generations in sexually reproducing organisms.

It also increases the genetic variability in the population of organisms from one generation to the next. Variations are very important for the process of evolution.

Question 13. Discuss with your teacher about

(i) Haploid insects and lower plants where cell division occurs.

(ii) Some haploid cells in higher plants where cell division does not occur.

Answer

(i) In case of lower plants such as *Chlamydomonas*, *Spirogyra*, etc. The mitotic cell divisions occurs during the formation of gametophyte from haploid spores and meiotic divisions occur in the zygote during the formation of haploid spores. The honey bees, wasps and ants are examples of some of the haploid insects where cell divisions occur.

(ii) In case of angiosperms, the synergids and antipodal cells of the embryo sac are haploid in which no cell division occurs and they get degenerated.

Question 14. Can there be mitosis without DNA replication in S-phase?

Answer No, DNA replication is required for doubling the chromosome number.

Question 15. Can there be DNA replication without cell division?

Answer In animal cells, during the S-phase, as DNA replication beings in the nucleus,the centrioles, initiate replication in the cytoplasm.

Question 16. Analyse the events during every stage of cell cycle and notice how the following two parameters change?

(i) Number of chromosomes (n) per cell

(ii) Amount of DNA content (C) per cell.

Answer

(i) The number of chromosomes (n) is double in the prophase, metaphase and anaphase stage of an organism. In the telophase stage, during daughter cell formation, the number of chromosomes get reduced to half.

(ii) Amount of DNA content (C) per cell also changes during different phases of cell division. It is double in the prophase, metaphase and anaphase stage of an organism. In the telophase stage, during daughter cell formation, the number of chromosomes get reduced to half than that of their parents.

Selected NCERT Exemplar Problems

Very short Answer Questions

Question 1. Between prokaryote and eukaryote, which cell has a shorter cell division time?

Answer Prokaryotic cells being less active have shorter cell division time.

Question 2. Which of the phases of cell cycle is of longest duration?

Answer Interphase.

Question 3. Name a stain commonly used to stain chromosomes?

Answer Giemsa stain is also used to visualise chromosomes.

Question 4. Which tissue of animals and plants exhibits meiosis?

Answer Reproductive tissue.

Question 5. Given that average duplication time of *E. coli* is 20 minutes. How much time will two *E. coli* cells take to become 32 cells?

Answer 2 hours.

Question 6. Which part of the human body should one use to demonstrate stages in mitosis?

Answer All somatic cells of the body except reproductive cells.

Question 7. What attributes does a chromatid require to be classified as a chromosome.

Answer In telophase-I of meiosis-I, halving of chromosome number occurs but chromosomes are still composed of two chromatids. If crossing over occurred, these chromatids are not genetically identical. They divide in 2nd meiotic division. Hence, crossing over is an attribute, which classify chromatids as chromosome.

Question 8. The diagram shows a bivalent at prophase-I of meiosis. Which of the four chromatids can cross over?

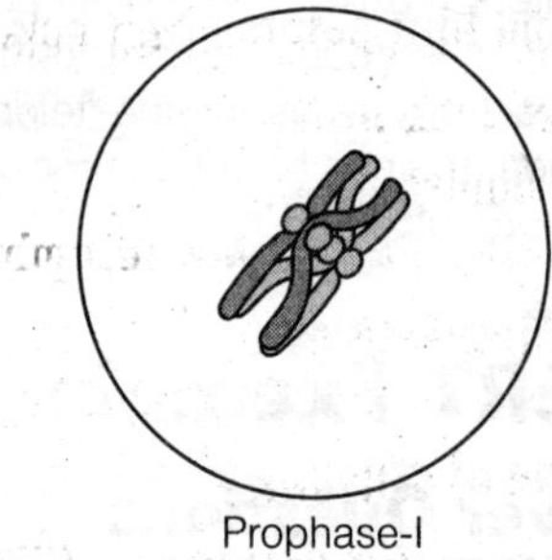

Prophase-I

Answer The sister chromatids, *i.e.*, chromatids of the same chromosome can cross.

Question 9. If a tissue has a given time 1024 cells, how many cycles of mitosis had the original parental single cell undergone?

Answer Eleven divisions.

Question 10. An anther has 1200 pollen grains. How many pollen mother cells must have been there to produce them?

Answer Three hundred pollen mother cells are required to produce 1200 pollen grains.

Question 11. At what stage of cell cycle does DNA synthesis take palce?

Answer S-phase or synthetic phase.

Question 12. It is said that one cell cycle of cell division in human cells (eukaryotic cells) takes 24 h. Which phase of the cycle, do you think occupies the maximum part of the cell cycle.

Answer Interphase.

Question 13. It is observed that heart cells do not exhibit cell division. Such cells do not divide further and exit ....phase to enter an inactive stage called ....of cell cycle. Fill in the blanks.

Answer It is observed that heart cells do not exhibit cell division. Such cells do not divide further and exit .....G_1..................phase to enter an inactive stage called ....quiescent stage (G_0) ....of cell cycle.

Question 14. In which phase of meiosis are the following formed? Choose the answers from hint points given below.

(i) Synaptonemal complex ....

(ii) Recombination nodules ....

(iii) Appearance/activation of enzyme recombinase ....

(iv) Termination of chiasmata ....

(v) Interkinesis ....

(vi) Formation of dyad of cells...... .

[**Hints** (i) Zygotene, (ii) Pachytene, (iii) Pachytene, (iv) Diakinesis (v) After telophase-I/ before Meiosis-II, (vi) Telophase-I/After, Meiosis-I.]

Answer

(i) Synaptonemal complex ..... zygotene .....

(ii) Recombination nodules ..... pachytene .....

(iii) Appearance/activation of enzyme recombinase ..... telophase-I / After, meiosis-I .....

(iv) Termination of chiasmata ..... diakinesis .....

(v) Interkinesis- After telophase -I/before meiosis-II .....

(vi) Formation of dyad of cells ..... pachytene ....

Short Answer Type Questions

Question 1. State the role of centrioles other than spindle formation.

Answer Centrioles play an important role in cell division. They play an important role in the formation of spindle, cilia and flagella, which are locomotory organelles. They generate the cell's cytoskeleton and help form the mitotic spindles. In organisms with flagella and cilia, the position of these organelles is determined by the mother centriole, which becomes the basal body. They organise the mitotic spindle and thus, help in the completion of cytokinesis.

Question 2. Mitochondria and plastids have their own DNA (genetic material). What is known about their fate during nuclear division like mitosis?

Answer Mitochondria and plastids have their own DNA (genetic material). The DNA of these organelles multiply independent of genomic DNA.

Question 3. Label the diagram and also determine the stage at which this structure is visible.

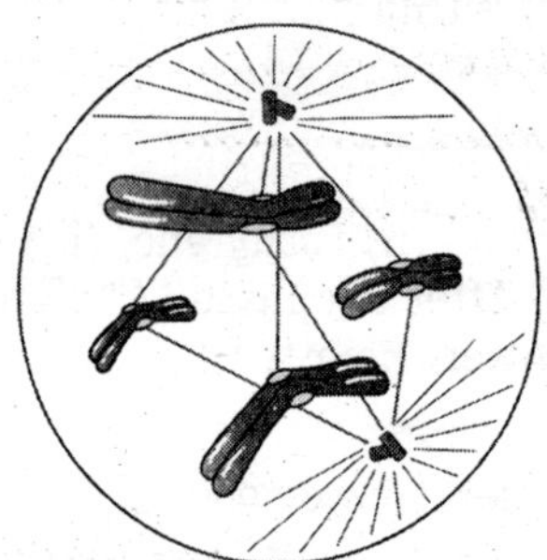

Answer Transition stage between prophase and metaphase of mitosis.

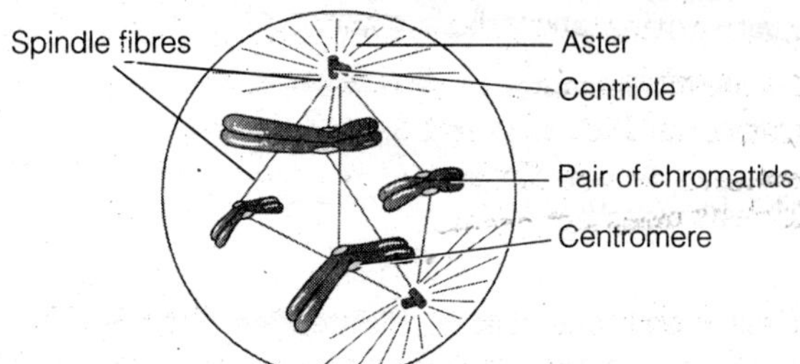

Question 4. A cell has 32 chromosomes. It undergoes mitotic divisions. What will be the chromosome number (n) during metaphase? What would be the DNA content (C) during anaphase?

Answer The number of chromosome during metaphase will be 32. The DNA content during anaphase will be same as in the parent cell.

Question 5. While examining the mitotic stage in a tissue. One finds some cells with 16 chromosomes and some with 32 chromosomes. What possible reasons could you assign to this difference in chromosome number. Do you think that cells with 16 chromosomes number could have arisen from cells with 32 chromosomes or *vice-versa*?

Answer The cells with 16 chromosomes show that they had undergone mitotic divisions, whereas cells with 32 chromosomes do not undergo divisions.

Question 6. The following events occur during the various phases of the cell cycle. Name the phase against each of the events;

(i) Disintegration of nuclear membrane ....

(ii) Appearance of nucleolus ....

(iii) Division of centromere ....

(iv) Replication of DNA ....

Answer (a) Prophase

(b) Telophase

(c) Anaphase

(d) S-phase

Question 7. Mitosis results in producing two cells which are similar to each other. What would be the consequence if each of the following irregularities occur during mitosis?

(a) Nuclear membrane fails to disintegrate

(b) Duplication of DNA does not occur?

(c) Centromeres do not divide.

(d) Cytokinesis does not occur.

Answer

(i) If nuclear membrane fails to disintegrate, then spindle is formed within the nucleus and it is called intranuclear mitosis or pre-mitosis. Intranuclear spindle may be acentric.

(ii) If duplication of DNA does not occur, no formation of chromosomes take place.

(iii) If centromeres do not divide, then the number of chromosome sets or genomes increases. The phenomenon is known as endopolyploidy. In human beings, it occurs in the liver cells.

(iv) If cytokinesis does not occur, then multinucleate condition called coenocyte, syncytium is produced, as in *Rhizopus* and *Vaucheria*, etc.

Question 8. Both unicellular and multicellular organisms undergo mitosis. What are the differences. If any, observed in the process between the two.

Answer Cell division is the first stage of growth in living organisms whereby cells divide to form new cells.

(i) In unicellular organisms, cell division is a process of asexual reproduction. It leads to an increase in the total number of individuals.

(ii) In multicellular organisms, the division of all cells, other than the reproductive cells, is known as mitosis. In them, mitosis is a cell division related to growth and is accompanied by The cellular enlargement and differentiation.

Question 9. Name the pathological condition when uncontrolled cell division occurs.

Answer Cancer.

Question 10. Two key events take place during S-phase in animal cells. DNA replication and duplication of centriole. In which parts of the cell do events occur?

Answer DNA replication take place, nucleus and duplication of centriole occur in the cytoplasm.

Question 11. Comment on the statement-meiosis enables the conservation of specific chromosome number of each species even though the process per results in the reduction of chromosome number.

Answer Meiosis is the mechanism by which conservation of specific chromosome number of each species is achieved across generations in sexually reproducing organisms, even though the process, results in reduction of chromosome number by half.

Meiosis also increases the genetic variability in the population of organisms from one generation to the next. Variations are very important for the process of evolution.

Question 12. Name a cell that is found arrested in diplotene stage for months and years. Comment in 2-3 lines how it completes cell cycle?

Answer The cells found arrested in diplotene stage for months and years are oocyte cells of vertebrates such as tailed and tailless amphibians, birds and insects.

The chromosomes of these cells transform into the Lampbrush form during the diplotene stage of meiotic prophase due to an active transcription of many genes. These chromosomes are producing large amounts of RNA for the oocyte and most of the genes present in the DNA loops are being actively expressed.

Long Answer Type Questions

Question 1. Comment on the statement-Telophase is reverse of prophase.

Answer In prophase, the chromatin network begins to coil and appears as long thread like structures called chromosomes. Each chromosome consists of two chromatids disappears from early prophase to late prophase. The nuclear membrane also starts disappearing in late prophase. In telophase opposite poles of the choromosomes lose their identity and nuclear membranes is formed around the daughter nuclei. Nucleolus also reappers. So, it is reverse of prophase.

Question 2. What are the various stages of meiotic prophase-I? Enumertate the chromosome events during each stage?

Answer **Prophase-I**

(i) It occurs over a long duration and involves several complicated changes. It has following sub stages:

Leptotene

(i) The chromatin network opens out and threads become clear.

(ii) The chromosomes are thin, slender and long.

(iii) Chromosome number is diploid.

Zygotene

(i) Corresponding chromosome become intimately associated.

(ii) The process of pairing is known as synapsis. It is so exact that pairing is not merely between corresponding chromosomes but between corresponding individual units.

(iii) The chromosomes become shorter and thicker.

Pachytene or Pachynema

(i) The synaptic chromosomes become very intimately associated.

(ii) The pair of chromosomes becomes short and thick.

(iii) Crossing over occurs at this stage. Chiasmata are clearly seen.

Diplotene

(i) Homologous chromosomes start separating from one another.

(ii) Chiasmata tend to slip out of the chromosomes. This is known as terminalisation of chiasmata.

(ii) Chromosomes start separating out but the separation is not complete.

(iv) Nuclear membrane and nucleolus start degenerating.

Diakinesis

(i) The bivalents condense further and get randomly distributed in the cytoplasm.

(ii) The separation of paired chromosomes is almost complete.

(iii) Terminalisation of chiasmata is almost complete.

(iv) Nuclear membrane and nucleolus disappear.

Question 3. Write brief note on the following

(i) Synaptonemal complex (ii) Metaphase plate

Answer

(i) **Synaptonemal complex** Corresponding chromosome become intimately associated. The process of pairing is known as synapsis. It is so, exact that pairing is not merely between corresponding chromosomes but between corresponding individual units.

(ii) **Metaphase plate** The bivalents come to lie in the equatorial plane in such a way that one member faces one pole of the spindle apparatus, and the other member the other pole. Thus, two members of the pair lie on the opposite side of the equator. Centromeres of the chromosomes are attached to the spindle fibres and face towards their respective poles. Chromosomes are aligned on equatorial plate.

Question 4. Write briefly the significance of mitosis and meiosis in muticellular organisms?

Answer **Significance of Mitosis**

The formation of new cells is necessary for the following reasons:

(i) Multicellular plants and animals start life as single cells. The process of mitosis gives rise to many cells which differentiate to form tissues, organs and organ-systems of the organism.

(ii) It results in increase in size and growth of an organ.

(iii) Cell reproduction is used to form new cells to renew certain tissues and to replace worn out cells.

(iv) Mitosis is also used as a form of asexual reproduction in some organisms like in unicellular. *Amoeba* and multicellular *Hydra* as well as vegetative reproduction in plants.

Significance of Meiosis

(i) Meiosis is the mechanism by which conservation of specific chromosome number of each species is achieved across generations in sexually reproducing organisms.

(ii) Meiosis also increases the genetic variability in the population of organisms from one generation to the next.

(iii) Variations are very important for the process of evolution.

11

Transport in Plants

Important Points

1. **Translocation** Transport over longer distances proceeds through the vascular system (the xylem and phloem).
2. **Diffusion**
   (i) Movement of substance from regions of higher concentration to regions of lower concentration.
   (ii) Means of gaseous movement within plant body.
   (iii) Passive movement.
   (iv) Affected by gradient of concentration, permeability of membrane separating them and temperature and pressure.
3. **Facilitated Diffusion**
   (i) Substance that have hydrophilic moiety find it difficult to pass through the membrane; their movement has to be facilitated.
   (ii) Membrane proteins provide sites at which such molecules cross membranes.
   (iii) Concentration gradient must already be present for molecules to diffuse even if facilitated by proteins.
   This process is called facilitated diffusion.

   Features
   (i) Special proteins help move substances across membranes without expenditures of ATP energy.

(ii) Cannot cause net transport of molecules.

(iii) Very specific allows cell to select substance for uptake.

(iv) Proteins form channels in membrane for molecules to pass through. Some channels are always open others can be controlled.

4. **Proteins**

(i) **Porins** From huge pores in the outer membranes of plastids, mitochondria and some bacteria allowing molecules upto size of small proteins to pass through.

(ii) **Symport** Allow diffusion only when two types of molecules cross the membrane in the same direction.

(iii) **Antiport** When the two types of molecules move in opposite direction.

(iv) **Uniport** When a molecules moves across a membrane independent of other molecules.

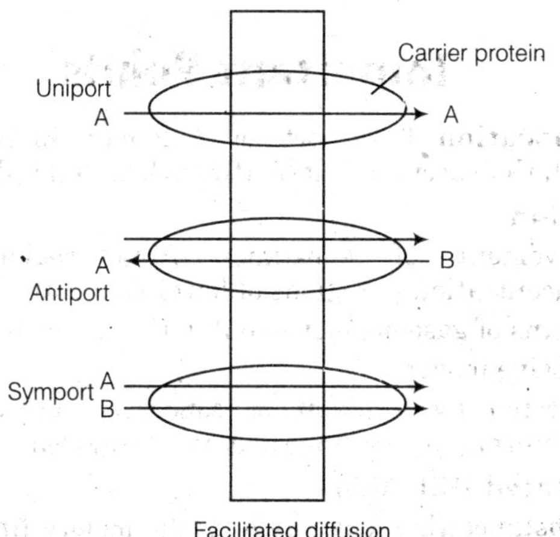

Facilitated diffusion

5. **Active Transport**

(i) Use energy to pump molecules against a concentration gradient.

(ii) Carried out by membrane-protein.

(iii) **Pumps** Proteins that use energy to carry substances across cell membrane. They can carry substances from a low concentration to a high concentration.

(iv) Carrier proteins are very specific, sensitive to inhibitors.

6. **Water Potential (Ψ_w)**

It is a concept fundamental to understanding water movement.

Factors determining water potential

(i) **Solute potential (Ψ_s)**

(a) All solutions have a lower water potential than pure water. The magnitude of this lowering due to dissolution of a solute is called solute potential or Ψ_s.

(b) It is always negative.

(c) The more the solute molecules, the lower (more negative is Ψ_s.

(ii) **Water potential (Ψ_w)**

(a) If two systems containing water in contact random movement of water will occur from higher water potential to lower water potential.

(b) Denoted by Greek symbol psi or Ψ

(c) Unit-Pascals (Pa).

(d) Pure water at standard temperature is taken to be zero.

7. Pressure can build up in a plant system when water enters a plant cell due to diffusion causing a pressure built up against the cell wall. It makes the cell turgid. This increase pressure potential.

(i) It is usually positive.

(ii) Denoted as Ψ_p

(iii) $\Psi_w = \Psi_s + \Psi_p$

Water potential is affected by both solute and pressure potential.

8. **Osmosis**

(i) Refers to diffusion of water across a differentially or semi-permeable membrane.

(ii) It occurs spontaneously in response to a during force.

(iii) Net direction and rate of osmosis depend on pressure gradient and concentration gradient.

(iv) Water will move from its region of higher chemical potential to its region of lower chemical potential until equilibrium is reached.

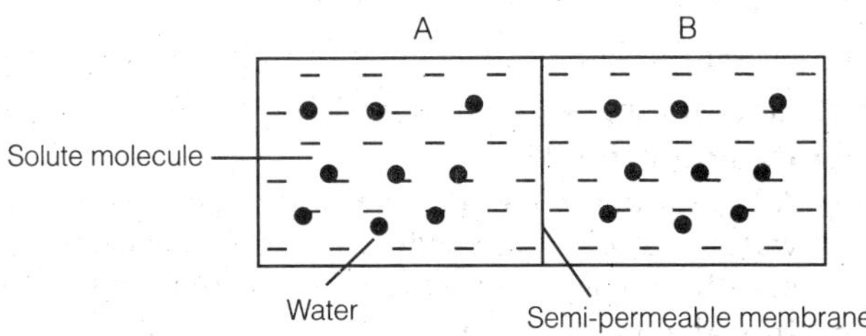

9. **Plasmolysis**

Isotonic	Hypotonic	Hypertonic
The external solution balances the osmotic pressure of cytoplasm	The external solution is more dilute than the cytoplasm. Cell swells	The external solution is more concentrated than cytoplasm. Cell shrinks

(i) Plasmolysis occur when water moves out of the cell and the cell membrane of a plant cell shrinks away from its cell wall.

(ii) Occurs in hypertonic solution.

(iii) Water moves out, first from, cytoplasm and then vacuole → this causes → shrinkage of protoplast from wall.

(iv) When water flows into the cell and out of the cell and are in equilibrium the cells are said to flaccid.

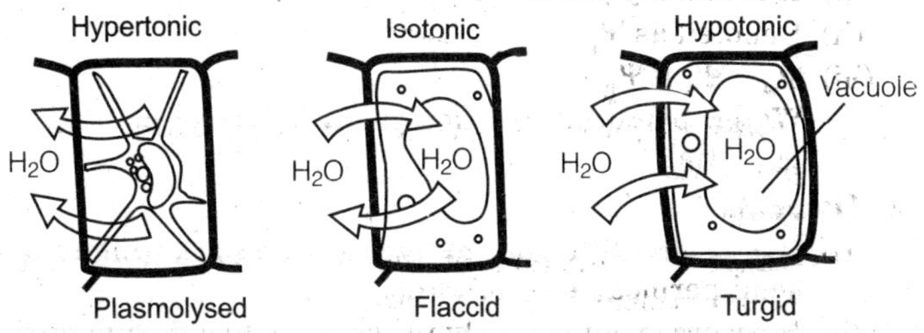

10. **Turgor Pressure**

(i) When the cells are placed in a hypotonic solution (higher water potential or dilute solution as compared to the cytoplasm). Water diffuses into the cell causing the cytoplasm to build up a pressure against the wall that is called turgor pressure.

(ii) Pressure exerted by the protoplasts due to entry of water against the rigid walls is called pressure potential.

(iii) Responsible for enlargement and extension growth of cells.

11. **Imbibition** It is a special type of diffusion when water.

12. **Water Movement up a Plant**
    (i) **Root pressure** As various ion from the soil are actively transported into the vascular tissues of the roots, water follows and increases the pressure inside roots. This positive pressure is called **root pressure**.

    Responsible for pushing up water to small heights in the stem.

    Effect of root pressure-guttation Observable at night and early morning, when evaporation is low, excess water collects in the form of droplets around special openings of veins near the tip of grass blades and leaves of many herbaceous parts.

    (ii) **Transpiration pull** Most researches agree that water is mainly 'pulled' through the plant and that the during force for this process is transpiration from leaves.

    This is referred to as the cohesion-tension-transpiration pull model of water transport is absorbed by solids-colloids causing them to enormously increase in volume, *e.g.*, absorption of water by seeds and dry woods.

13. **Translocation** Bulk movement of substances through the conducting or vascular tissues of plants is called translocation.

General pathway of water absorption

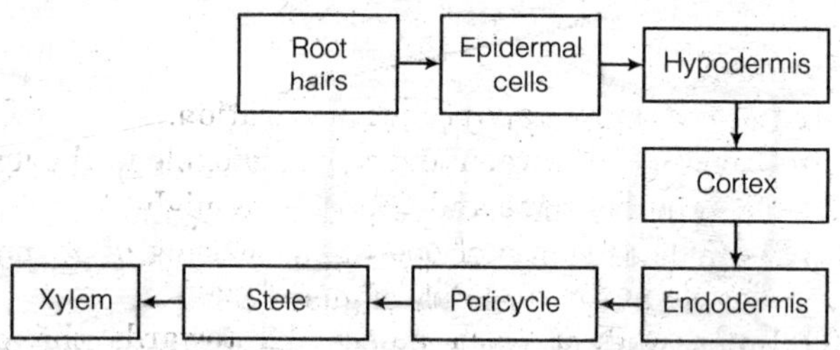

Once entering root hairs water follows two pathways

(i) **Apoplast pathway** Apoplast is the system of adjacent cell walls that is continuous throughout the plant except at casparian strips of the endodermis in the roots.

Occurs exclusively through intercellular spaces and the walls of the cells.

Apoplast does not provide any barrier to water movement.

(ii) **Symplast pathway** It is the system of interconnected protoplasts.

Neighbouring cells are connected through cytoplasmic strands that extends through plasmodesmata.

14. Most water flow occurs through apoplast however, the inner boundary of cortex the endodermis is impervious to water because of a band of suberised matrix called the casparian strip water molecules are unable to penetrate the layer, so they are directed to wall regions that are not suberised into the cells proper through the membranes water then move through symplast.

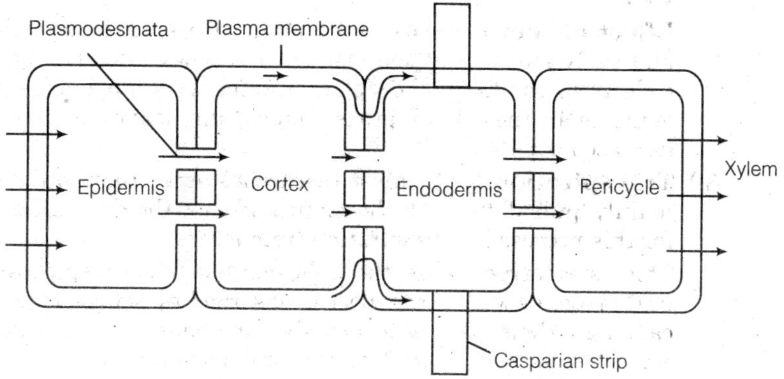

Pathway of water movement

15. **Transpiration** Transpiration is the evaporative loss of water by plants. Occurs mainly through stomata in the leaves.

(i) **Stomata**

(a) Loss of water vapour in transpiration.

(b) Exchange of oxygen and carbon dioxide in the leaf.

(c) Open in day time and close during night.

(d) Immediate cause of opening or closing of stomata is a change in the turgidity of guard cells.

(e) Inner wall of each guard cell towards the pore or stomatal aperture is thick and elastic.

(f) When turgidity increases within the two guard cells

↓

Thin outer walls bulge out

↓

Force inner walls into crescent shape

↓

Stomata opens

(g) Guard cells loose turgor (due to water loss)

↓

Elastic inner walls regain original shape

↓

Guard cells become flaccid

↓

Stoma closes

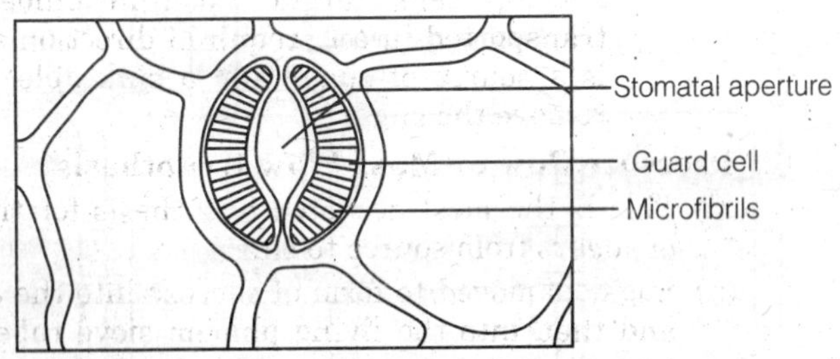

A stomatal operture with guard cells

(ii) Transpiration is affected by

External factors

(a) Temperature
(b) Light
(c) Humidity
(d) Wind speed

Plant factors

(a) Number of stomata
(b) Distribution of stomata
(c) Per cent of open stomata
(d) Water status of plant
(e) Canopy structure

(iii) Transpiration driven ascent of xylem sap depends mainly on the following physical properties of water.

(a) **Cohesion** Mutual attraction between water molecules.

(b) **Adhesion** Attraction of water molecules to polar surfaces.

(c) **Surface tension** Water molecules are attracted to each other in the liquid phase more than to water in the gas phase.

(iv) These properties gives water.

(a) **High tensile strength** Ability to resist a pulling force.

(b) **High capillarity** Ability to rise in thin tubes.

(v) Advantages of transpiration

(a) Creates transpiration pull for absorption and transport of plants.

(b) Supplies water for photosynthesis.

(c) Transports minerals from the soil to all parts of the plant.

(d) Cools leaf surfaces, sometimes 10 to 15 degrees, by evaporative cooling.

(e) Maintains the shape and structure of the plants by keeping cells turgid. Food in phloem sap can be transported in any required direction so long as there is a source of sugar and a sink able to use, store or remove the sugar.

16. **Pressure flow or Mass Flow Hypothesis**

(i) This is the most accepted hypothesis for the translocation of sugars from source to sink.

(ii) Sugar is moved to form of sucrose into the companion cells and then into the living phloem sieve tube cells by active transport.

(iii) This process of loading at the source produces a hypertonic condition in the phloem.

(iv) Movement of sugars begins at source, where sugars are loaded (actively transported) into a sieve tube. Loading of the phloem sets up a water potential gradient that facilitates the mass movement in the phloem.

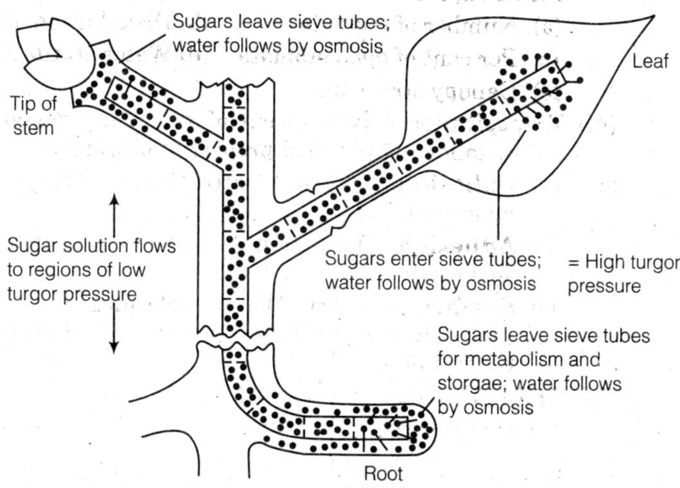

Mechanism of translocation

17. **Minerals cannot be passively absorbed by roots because**

(i) minerals are present in soil as charged particles (ions) which cannot move across cell membranes.

(ii) concentration of minerals in the soil is usually lower than the concentration of minerals in roots.
   (a) Therefore, most minerals enter the root by active absorption into cytoplasm of epidermal cells.
   (b) This needs energy in form of ATP.
   (c) Ions are absorbed from soil by both passive and active transport.
   (d) Specific proteins in root hair cells actively pump ions from soil into the cytoplasms of epidermal cells.
   (e) Minerals are translocated with the help of xylem.

18. **Phloem Transport**

From source Part of plant which synthesise the food (leaf).

Sink Part that needs or stores the food.

Since the source Sink relationship is variable, the direction of movement in the phloem can be upwards or downward, *i.e.*, bidirectional.

Exercises

Question 1. What are the factors affecting the rate of diffusion?

Answer Factors affecting the rate of diffusion

(i) Gradient of concentration (ii) Permeability of membrane
(iii) Temperature (iv) Pressure

Question 2. What are porins? What role do they play in diffusion?

Answer The porins are proteins that form huge pores in the outer membranes of the plastids, mitochondria and some bacteria allowing molecules up to the size of small proteins to pass through. Porins facilitate diffusion.

Question 3. Describe the role played by protein pumps during active transport in plants.

Answer Proteins pumps use energy to carry substances across the cell membrane. These pumps can transport substances from a low concentration to a high concentration ('uphill' transport). Transport rate reaches a maximum when all the protein transporters are being used or are saturated. Like enzymes, the carrier protein is very specific in what it carries across the membrane. These proteins are sensitive to inhibitors that react with protein side chains.

Question 4. Explain why pure water has the maximum water potential.

Answer Water molecules possess kinetic energy. In liquid and gaseous form, they are in random motion that is both rapid and constant. The greater the concentration of water in a system, the greater is its kinetic energy or 'water potential'. Hence, pure water will have the greatest water potential. Water potential is denoted by the Greek symbol psi or ψ and is expressed in pressure units such as pascals (Pa).

Question 5. Differentiate between the following

(a) Diffusion and osmosis
(b) Transpiration and evaporation
(c) Osmotic pressure and osmotic potential
(d) Imbibition and diffusion
(e) Apoplast and symplast pathways of movement of water in plants
(f) Guttation and transpiration

Answer (a) **Differences between Diffusion and Osmosis**

S.N.	Diffusion	Osmosis
1.	It is a movement of molecules from high concentration to low concentration.	It is a movement of molecules from high concentration to low concentration through semiperme able membrane.
2.	It does not require any driving force.	It occurs in response to a driving force.

(b) **Differences between Transpiration and Evaporation**

S.N.	Transpiration	Evaporation
1.	It is the loss of water through the aerial parts of plants.	It is loss of water from free surface of water.
2.	It occurs in living tissues.	It occurs in non-living surfaces.
3.	It is both physical and physiological process.	It is only a physical process. controlled by environmental factors.

(c) **Differences between Osmotic Pressure and Osmotic Potential**

S.N.	Osmotic Pressure	Osmotic Potential
1.	It is the pressure required to stop the movement of water molecules through a semipermeable membrane.	It is the amount by which water potential is reduced by the presence of solute.
2.	Osmotic pressure is the positive pressure.	Osmotic potential is nigative.

(d) **Differences between Imbibition and Diffusion**

Imbibition	Diffusion
It is a special type of diffusion, where water is absorbed by solids-colloids causing them to increase in volume. For example, absorption of water by dry seeds and dry wood.	In diffusion, molecules move in a random fashion. It is not depedent on a living system.

(e) **Differences between Apoplast and Symplast Pathway of Movement of Water**

S.N.	Apoplast	Symplast
1.	It is the system of adjacent cell walls that is continous throughout the plant except casparian strips of the endodermis of the roots.	It is the system of interconnected protoplast.
2.	Water moves through the intercellular spaces and the walls of cells.	Water travels through the cytoplasm of cells and intercellular movement is through plasmodesmata.
3.	Movement does not involve crossing the cell membrane.	Water has to move in cells through the cell membrane.

(f) **Differences between Guttation and Transpiration**

S.N.	Guttation	Transpiration
1.	It occurs through hydathodes, present at the vein ends.	It occurs through general surface, stomata and lenticles.
2.	It occurs in leaves only.	It can occur through all aerial parts.
3.	It does not occur in deficient water conditions and never leads to wilting.	It can occur in water deficient conditions, leading to wilting.
4.	It is regulated by humidity, temperature and presence of water in soil.	It is regulated by a number of external and internal factors such as relative humidity, temperature opening and closing of stomata, etc.

Question 6. Briefly describe water potential. What are the factors affecting it?

Answer Water potential is the potential energy of water relative to pure free water (*e.g.*, deionised water). It quantifies the tendency of water to move from one area to another due to osmosis, gravity, mechanical pressure or matrix effects including surface tension. Water potential is measured in units of pressure and is commonly represented by the Greek letter ψ (psi). This concept has proved especially useful in understanding water movement within plants, animals and soil.

Water potential of a cell is affected by both solute and pressure potential. The relationship between them is as follows

$$\psi_w = \psi_s + \psi_p$$

Question 7. What happens when a pressure greater than the atmospheric pressure is applied to pure water or a solution?

Answer If a pressure greater than atmospheric pressure is applied to pure water or a solution its water potential increases. It is equivalent to pumping water from one place to another. Pressure can be build up in a plant system when water enters a plant cell due to diffusion causing a pressure build up against the cell wall. It makes the cell turgid, this increases the pressure potential. Pressure potential is usually positive. It is devoted by ψ_s.

Question 8. (a) With the help of well-labelled diagrams, describe the process of plasmolysis in plants, giving appropriate examples.

(b) Explain what will happen to a plant cell if it is kept in a solution having higher water potential.

Answer

(a) Plasmolysis occurs when water moves out of the cell and the cell membrane of a plant cell shrinks away from its cell wall. This occurs when the cell is kept in a solution that is hypertonic (has more solutes) to the protoplasm. Water moves out from the cell through diffusion causes the protoplasm to shrink away from the walls. In such situation, cell becomes plasmolysed.

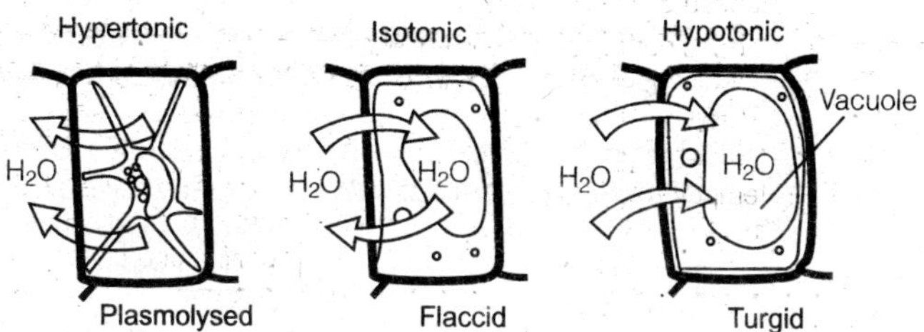

When the cell is placed in an isotonic solution. There is not flow of water towards the inside or outside. If the external solution balances the osmotic pressure of the cytoplasm, it is said to be isotonic. When the water flow into the cell and out of the cells are in equilibrium the cell is called flaccid.

(b) When the plant cell is kept in a solution having high water potential (hypotonic solution or diluite solution as compared to cytoplasm), water diffuses into the cell causing the cytoplasm to build up a pressure against the wall, called turgor pressure. The pressure exerted by the protoplasts due to entry of water against the rigid walls is called pressure potential Ψ_p. Because of the rigidity of the cell wall, the cell does not rupture. This turgor pressure is ultimately responsible for enlargement of cells.

Question 9. **How is the mycorrhizal association helpful in absorption of water and minerals in plants?**

Answer A mycorrhiza is a symbiotic association of a fungus with a root system. The fungal filaments form a network around the young root or they penetrate the root cells. The hyphae have a very large surface area that absorb mineral ions and water from the soil from a much larger volume of soil that perhaps a root cannot do. The fungus provides minerals and water to the roots, in turn the roots provide sugars and N-containing compounds to the mycorrhizae.

Question 10. **What role does root pressure play in water movement in plants?**

Answer This positive pressure is called root pressure and can be responsible for pushing up water to small heights in the stem. The greatest contribution of root pressure may be to re-establish the continuous chains of water molecules in the xylem which often break under the enormous tensions created by transpiration. Root pressure does not account for the majority of water transport, most plants meet their need by transpiratory pull.

Question 11. **Describe transpiration pull model of water transport in plants. What are the factors influencing transpiration? How is it useful to plants?**

Answer Transpiration mainly through the stomata in the leaves. As water evaporates through the stomata, since the thin film of water over the cells is continuous, it results in pulling of water, molecule by molecule, into the leaf from the xylem. Also, because of lower concentration of water vapour in the atmosphere as compared to the substomatal cavity and intercellular spaces, water diffuses into the surrounding air. This creates a transpiration 'pull'.

Factors Affecting Transpiration Temperature, light, humidity and wind speed.

Importance of Transpiration Transport of liquids and minerals is facilitated because of transpiration.

Question 12. Discuss the factors responsible for ascent of xylem sap in plants.

Answer The transpiration driven ascent of xylem sap depends mainly on the following physical properties of water

(i) **Cohesion** Mutual attraction between water molecules.

(ii) **Adhesion** Attraction of water molecules to polar surfaces (such as the surface of tracheary elements).

(iii) **Surface Tension** Water molecules are attracted to each other in the liquid phase more than to water in the gas phase.

These properties give water high tensile strength, *i.e.*, an ability to resist a pulling force and high capillarity, *i.e.*, the ability to rise in thin tubes. In plants, capillarity is aided by the small diameter of the tracheary elements, the tracheids and vessel elements.

Question 13. What essential role does the root endodermis play during mineral absorption in plants?

Answer The endodermis of roots have many transport proteins embedded in their plasma membrane. They let some solutes cross the membrane but not all. Transport proteins in endodermis cells enable plant cells to adjust the quantity and types of solutes to be absorbed from the soil. It regulators the quantity and type of minerals and ions. That reach the xylem tissue of plants.

Question 14. Explain why xylem transport is unidirectional and phloem transport bi-directional?

Answer The source sink (food making tissue-tissue which stores food) relationship is variable in plants so, the direction of movement in the phloem can be upwards downwards, *i.e.*, bi-directional. It is opposite to xylem, where the movement is always unidirectional. Hence, unlike one-way flow of water in transpiration, food in phloem sap can be transported in any required direction so long there is a source of sugar and a sink is able to use, store or remove the sugar. Here, in case of unidirectional flow in xylem tissue, it is important to note that root endodermis because of the layer of suberin has the ability to actively transport ions in one diretion only.

Question 15. Explain pressure flow hypothesis of translocation of sugars in plants.

Answer **The Pressure Flow or Mass Flow Hypothesis** The accepted mechanism used for the translocation of sugars from source to sink is called the **pressure flow hypothesis**. As glucose is prepared at the source (by photosynthesis) it is converted to sucrose (a dissacharide). The sugar is then moved in the form of sucrose into the companion cells and then into the living phloem sieve tube cells by active transport.

As osmotic pressure builds up, the phloem sap will move to areas of lower pressure. At the sink, osmotic pressure must be reduced. Again active transport is necessary to move the sucrose out of the phloem sap and into the cells which will use the sugar converting it into energy, starch or cellulose. As sugars are removed, the osmotic pressure decreases and water moves out of the phloem.

Hydrostatic pressure in the phloem sieve tube increases, pressure flow begins and the sap moves through the phloem. Meanwhile, at the sink, incoming sugars are actively transported out of the phloem and removed as complex carbohydrates. The loss of solute produces a high water potential in the phloem and water passes out, returning eventually to xylem.

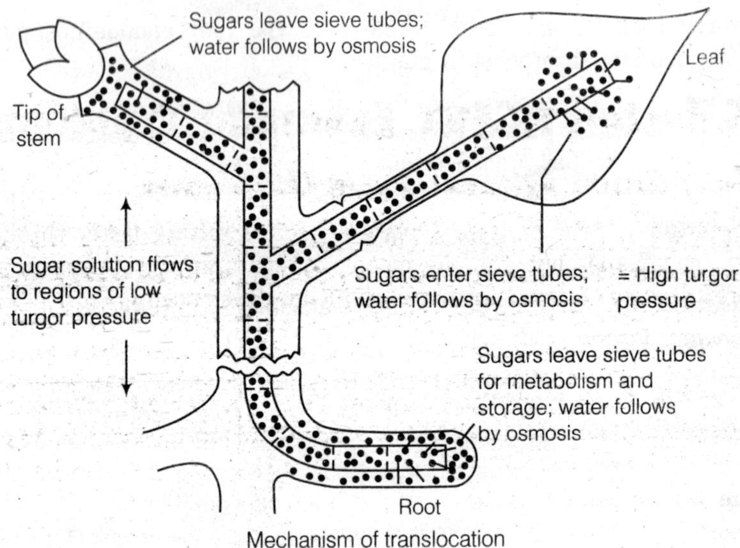

Mechanism of translocation

Question 16. What causes the opening and closing of guard cells of stomata during transpiration?

Answer The immediate cause of the opening or closing of the stomata is a change in the turgidity of the guard cells. The inner wall of each guard cell, towards the pore or stomatal aperture, is thick and elastic. When turgidity increases within the two guard cells flanking each stomatal aperture or pore, the thin outer walls bulge out and force the inner walls into a crescent shape. The opening of the stoma is also aided due to the orientation of the microfibrils in the cell walls of the guard cells. Cellulose microfibrils are oriented radially rather than longitudinally making it easier for the stoma to open. When the guard cells lose turgor, due to water loss (or water stress) the elastic inner walls regain their original shape, the guard cells become flaccid and the stoma closes.

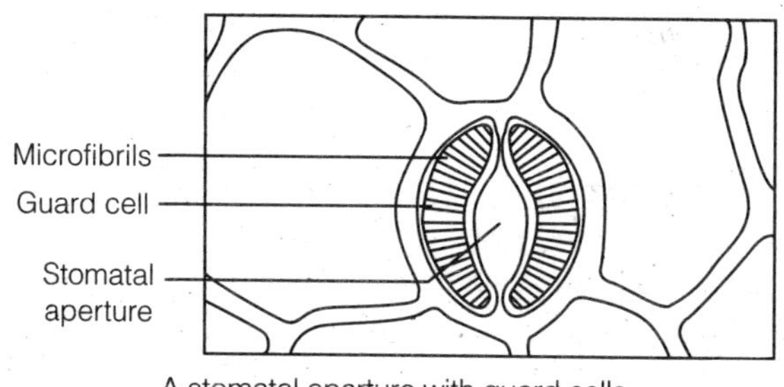

A stomatal aperture with guard cells

Selected NCERT Exemplar Problems

Very Short Answer Type Questions

Question 1. Smaller, lipid soluble molecules diffuse faster through cell membrane, but the movement of hydrophilic substances are facilitated by certain transporters which are chemically

Answer Protein

Question 2. In a passive transport across a membrane, when two protein molecule move in opposite direction and independent of each other, it is called as

Answer Antiport transport

Question 3. Osmosis is a special kind of diffusion, in which water diffuses across the cell membrane. The rate and direction of osmosis depends upon both

Answer Pressure and concentration gradient.

Question 4. A flowering plant is planted in an earthen pot and irrigated. Urea is added to make the plant grow faster, but after some time the plant dies. This may be due to

Answer Exosmosis

Question 5. Absorption of water from soil by dry seeds increases the ...., thus helping seedlings to come out of soil.

Answer Pressure

Question 6. Water moves up against gravity and even for a tree of 20 m height, the tip receives water within two hours. The most important physiological phenomenon which is responsible for the upward movement of water is

Answer Transpiration pull

Question 7. The plant cell cytoplasm is surrounded by both cell wall and cell membrane. The specificity of transport of substances are mostly across the cell membrane, because

Answer The cell wall is freely permeable to water and substances in solutions but membrane is selectively permeable.

Question 8. The C_4-plants are twice as efficient as C_3-plants in terms of fixing CO_2 but lose only .... as much water as C_3-plants for the same amount of CO_2 fixed.

Answer The C_4-plants are twice as efficient as C_3-plants in terms of fixing CO_2 but lose only half as much water as C_3-plants for the same amount of CO_2 fixed.

Question 9. Movement of substances in xylem is unidirectional while in phloem it is bidirectional. Explain.

Answer The water is present in the soil and it moves from soil through the root hairs into various parts of the plant by xylem tissue. But no movement of water from top of plant in the downward direction through xylem take place. But regarding food transport, the source-sink relationship is available and it may be variable, the direction of movement in the phloem can be upwards or downwards, *i.e.*, bidirectional. Food in phloem sap can be transported in any required direction so long as there is a source of sugar and a sink able to use, store or remove the sugar.

Question 10. Identify the process occurring in I, II and III.

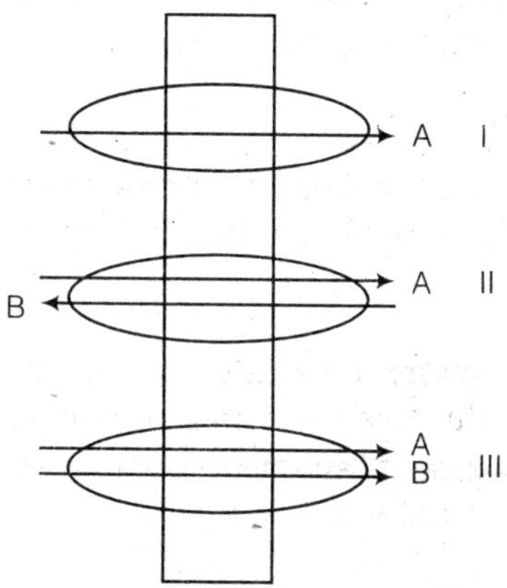

Answer I. Uniport II. Antiport III. Symport

Question 11. Given below in the table. Fill in the gaps

Property	Simple Diffusion	Facilitated Diffusion	Active Transport
Highly selective		Yes	
Uphill transport			Yes
Requires ATP			

Answer

Property	Simple Diffusion	Facilitated Diffusion	Active Transport
Highly selective		Yes	
Uphill transport	Yes		Yes
Requires ATP			Yes

Question 12. Define water potential and solute potential.

Answer Water potential ψ (psi) is the potential energy of water relative to pure free water (*e.g.*, deionised water) in reference conditions. It quantifies the tendency of water to move from one area to another due to osmosis, gravity, mechanical pressure or matrix effects including surface tension.

Solute Potential

If some solute is dissolved in pure water, the solution has fewer free water and the concentration of water decreases, reducing its water potential. Hence, all solutions have a lower water potential than pure water; the magnitude of this lowering due to dissolution of a solute is called solute potential or ψ_s. ψ_s is always negative. The more the solute molecules, the lower (more negative) is the ψ_s. For a solution at atmospheric pressure

Water potential ψ_w = Solute potential (ψ_s)

Question 13. Why is solute potential always negative? Explain $\Psi_w = \Psi_s + \Psi_p$.

Answer Hence, all solutions have a lower water potential than pure water; the magnitude of this lowering due to dissolution of a solute is called solute potential or ψ_s. ψ_s is always negative. The more the solute molecules, the lower (more negative) is the ψ_s. For a solution at atmospheric pressure

(water potential) ψ_w = (solute potential) ψ_s

Question 14. An onion peel was taken and

(i) placed in salt solution for five minutes.

(ii) after that it was placed in distilled water.

When seen under the microscope what would be observed in 1 and 2?

Answer (i) Plasmolysis indicated by shrinkage of cell contents

(ii) Deplasmolysis

Question 15. How does most of the water moves within the root?

Answer By transpiration pull, cohesion and adhesion property of water molecules.

Question 16. Give the location of casparian strip and explain its role in the water movement.

Answer Casparian strips are located in the endodermis. The endodermal cells have many transport proteins embedded in their plasma membrane help in water movement. It is important to note that the root endodermis because of the layer of suberin has the ability to actively transport water.

Question 17. Transpiration is a necessary evil in plants. Explain.

Answer Transpiration controls the rate of water absorption, helps in the absorption of minerals and water and regulate the temperature. At the same time, it has disadvantages such as water deficiency in the plants thus, impairment in the processes of photosynthesis and growth, etc., it is truly called 'transpiration is a necessary evil'.

Question 18. Describe briefly the three physical properties of water which helps in ascent of water in xylem.

Answer The transpiration driven ascent of xylem sap depends mainly on the following physical properties of water

(i) **Cohesion** Mutual attraction between water molecules.

(ii) **Adhesion** Attraction of water molecules to polar surfaces (such as the surface of tracheary elements).

(iii) **Surface Tension** Water molecules are attracted to each other in the liquid phase more than to water in the gas phase.

These properties give water high tensile strength, *i.e.*, an ability to resist a pulling force and high capillarity, *i.e.*, the ability to rise in thin tubes.

Question 19. A gardener forgot to water a potted plant for a day during summer, what will happen to the plant? Do you think it is reversible? If yes, how?

Answer It gets wilt due to excessive loss of water.

Question 20. Identify a type of molecular movement which is highly selective and requires special membrane proteins, but does not require energy.

Answer Passive antiport transport.

Question 21. Correct the statements

(i) Cells shrink in hypotonic solutions and swell in hypertonic solutions.

(ii) Imbibition is a special type of diffusion when water is absorbed by living cells.

(iii) Most of the water flow in the roots occurs *via* the symplast.

Answer

(i) Cells shrink in hypertonic solutions and swell in hypotonic solutions.

(ii) Imbibition is a special type of diffusion when water is absorbed by non-living cells .

(iii) Most of the water flow in the roots occurs *via* the apoplast.

Short Answer Type Questions

Question 1. If one wants to find minerals and in the form they are mobilised in the plant, how will an analysis of the exudate help?

Answer An analysis of the xylem exudates shows that though some of the nitrogen travels as inorganic ions, much of it is carried in the organic form as amino acids and related compounds. Similarly, small amount of P and S are carried as organic compounds. In addition, small amount of exchange of materials does take place between xylem and phloem.

Question 2. From your knowledge of physiology can you think of some method of increasing the life of cut plants in a vase?

Answer The life of cut plants in a vase can be increased by placing them in water.

Question 3. Cut pieces of beet root do not leave colour in cold water but do so in hotwater. Explain.

Answer Cut pieces of beet root do not leave colour in cold water but do so in hot water because they dissolve and diffuse readily in hot water.

Question 4. In a girdled plant, when water is supplied to the leaves above the girdle, leaves may remain green for sometime then wilt and ultimately die. What does it indicate?

Answer In a girdled plant, when water is supplied to the leaves above the girdle, leaves may remain green for sometime because leaves can synthesise their own carbohydrate food through photosynthesis , then wilt due to non-availability of water and ultimately die as there is no photosynthesis in absence of water.

Question 5. Various types of transport mechanisms are needed to fulfil the mineral requirements of a plant. Why are they not fulfilled by diffusion alone?

Answer The organic solutes in plants have to be move various directions. For example, the food substances synthesised in the leaves are translocated downwardly towards in the stem and roots. Similarly, the upward movement of solutes from the leaves to the developing buds, flowers and fruits take place. The food materials or minerals are also translocated radially from the cells of pith to those of cortex and epidermis. Thus, the various processes such as active diffusion, electrochemical potential and mass flow, etc., are needed in addition for the transport of minerals and organic solutes.

Question 6. How can plants be grown under limited water supply without compromising on metabolic activities?

Answer Under conditions of limited water supply plants manage to carry on metabolic activities such as photosynthesis, growth and movements, etc., by reducing the rate of transpiration by closing the stomata.

Question 7. Will the ascent of sap be possible without the cohesion and adhesion of the water molecules? Explain.

Answer The cohesion and adhesion of the water molecules alone are found to be 350 atm, which alone are responsible for conducting water to great heights in tall tress without breaking the water column. On the other hand, all forces such as imbibition pressure, root pressure have been found to be only 50 atm.

Question 8. Keep some freshly cut flowers in a solution of food colour. Wait for sometime for the dye to rise in the flower, when the stem of the flower is held up in light, coloured strands can be seen inside. Can this experiment demonstrate which tissue is conducting water up the stem?

Answer Yes, it shows that xylem tissue conducts and water.

Question 9. When a freshly collected *Spirogyra* filament is kept in a 10% potassium nitrate solution, it is observed that the protoplasm shrinks in size

(i) What is this phenomenon called?

(ii) What will happen if the filament is replaced in distilled water?

Answer

(i) This phenomenon is known as plasmolysis.

(ii) If filaments are replaced in water, the protoplasm starts swelling. It comes in contact with cell wall and cell regains its original size. The swelling of plasmolysed protoplast under the influence of a weak solution or water is called deplasmolysis.

Question 10. Sugar crystals do not dissolve easily in ice cold water. Explain.

Answer Because in ice cold water, there is rapid dissociation of hydrogen bonds of water which are necessary for fluidity and dissociation properties of water.

Question 11. Salt is applied to tennis lawns to kill weeds. How does salting tennis lawns help in killing of weeds without affecting the grass?

Answer Due to plasmolysis.

Question 12. What is the chemical composition of xylem and phloem sap?

Answer The xylem sap consists of mainly water and some solutes and the phloem sap is mainly water and sucrose, but other sugars, hormones and amino acids.

Question 13. If you are provided with two tubes (A and B), where one is narrow and the other is relatively wider and if both are immersed in a beaker containing water as shown in the figure given below.

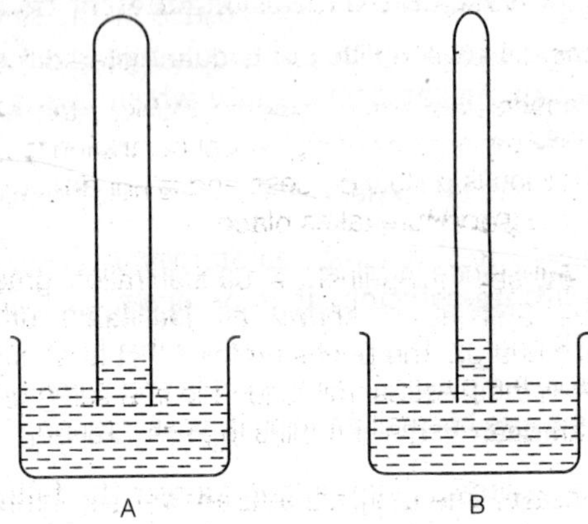

Why does B show higher water rise than A?

Answer B shows higher water rise than A because in tube B, which is narrow the water potential is high and has large surface area as compared to that in tube A.

Question 14. ABA (abscisic acid) is called a stress hormone. (i) How does this hormone overcome stress conditions? (ii) From where does this hormone get released in leaves?

Answer

(i) ABA, abscisic acid stimulates the closure of stomata in the epidermis and increases the tolerance of plants to various kinds of stresses. In this way, overcome the stress conditions.

(ii) ABA is transported from stem apices to leaves.

Question 15. We know that plants are harmed by excess water. But plants survive under flooded condition. How are they able to manage excess water?

Answer The plants survive under flooded condition by losing the excess water through transpiration (increased transpiration rate).

Question 16. Differentiate between diffusion and translocation in plants.

Answer In diffusion, molecules move in a random fashion, the net result being substances moving from regions of higher concentration to regions of lower concentration. Diffusion is a slow process and is not dependent on a 'living system'. No energy expenditure takes place.

Whereas, the transport of substance over long distances through the vascular system (the xylem and the phloem) is known as translocation.

Question 17. How is facilitated diffusion different from diffusion?

Answer Differences between diffusion and facilitated diffusion

In **diffusion**, molecules move in a random fashion, the net result being substances moving from regions of higher concentration to regions of lower concentration. Diffusion is a slow process and is not dependent on a 'living system'. No energy expenditure takes place.

The diffusion of substance against a concentration gradient, which is facilitated by the proteins is known as **facilitated diffusion** without expenditure of ATP energy. The porins proteins that form huge pores in the outer membranes of the plastids, mitochondria and some bacteria allowing molecules up to the size of small proteins to pass through.

Question 18. Observe the diagram and answer the following

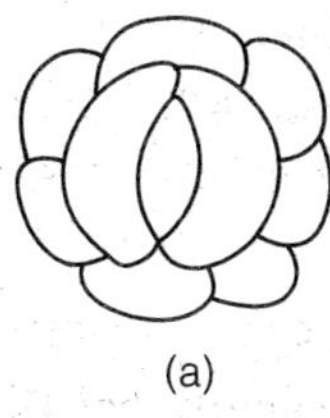

(a)

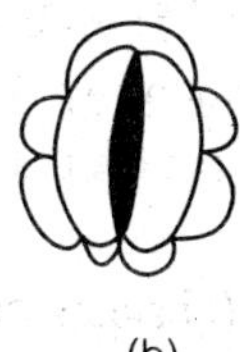

(b)

(i) Are these types of guard cells found in monocots or dicots?
(ii) Which of these shows a higher water content (a) or (b)?
(iii) Which element plays an important role in the opening and closing of stomata?

Answer

(i) These types of guard cells are found in dicots.

(ii) (a) shows higher water content .

(iii) K^+ element plays an important role in the opening and closing of stomata.

Question 19. Define uniport, symport and antiport. Do they require energy?

Answer **Uniport, symport and antiport** Some carrier or transport proteins allow diffusion only if two types of molecules move together.

(i) When a molecule moves across a membrane independent of other molecules, the process is called uniport. They do not require energy.

(ii) In a symport, both molecules cross the membrane in the same direction;

(iii) In an antiport, they move in opposite directions.

Long Answer Type Questions

Question 1. Minerals are present in the soil in sufficient amount.

(i) Do plants need to adjust the types of solutes that reach the xylem?

(ii) Which molecules help to adjust this?

Answer

(i) An analysis of the xylem exudates shows that though some of the nitrogen travels as inorganic ions, much of it is carried in the organic form as amino acids and related compounds. Similarly, small amount of P and S are carried as organic compounds. In addition, small amount of exchange of materials does take place between xylem and phloem.

(ii) Mineral ions are frequently remobilised, particularly from older, senescing parts. Older dying leaves export much of their mineral content to younger leaves. Similarly, before leaf fall in decidous plants, minerals are removed to other parts. Elements most readily mobilised are phosphorus, sulphur, nitrogen and potassium. Some elements that are structural components like calcium are not remobilised.

Question 2. Plants show temporary and permanent wilting. Differentiate between the two. Do any of them indicate the water status of the soil?

Answer **Differences between Temporary Wilting and Permanent Wilting** Hebaceous plants which wilt during hot summer, regain their freshness (turgor) during the night then this is known as temporary or transient wilting. The temporary wilting occurs in plants, when the rate of transpiration (water loss) exceeds the rate of water absorption. In **permanent wilting**, even after absorption of water from any source the plants do not regain their turgidity. Yes, permanent wilting indicate the water deficiency of the soil.

Question 3. Which of these is a semipermeable membrane and which is selectively permeable (SL)?

(i) Animal bladder
(ii) Plasmalemma
(iii) Tonoplast
(iv) Parchment membrane
(v) Egg membrane

Answer **Semipermeable membrane** Animal bladder, parchment paper and egg membrane. **Selectively permeable** (SL) Plasmalemma and tonoplast.

Question 4. The radio labelled carbon in carbon dioxide supplied to potato plants in an experiment was seen in the tuber eventually. Trace the movement of the labelled carbon dioxide.

Answer If a leaf of potato plant is illuminated in presence of radioactive 14 CO_2, it forms radioactive products of photosynthesis. These products with radioactivity are then transported to the stem. It was detected by autoradiography that these substances are translocated through phloem and particularly through the sieve tubes.

Question 5. Comment on the experimental set-up

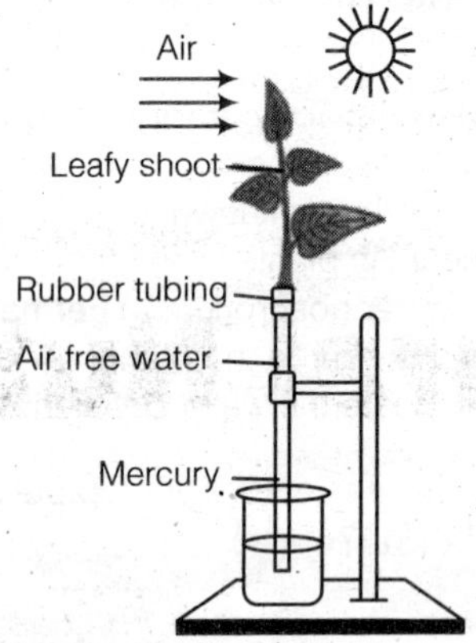

(i) What does the set-up demonstrate?

(ii) What will happen to the level of water if a blower is placed close to set-up.

(iii) Will the mercury level fluctuate (go up/down) if phenyl mercuric acetate is sprayed on leaves?

Answer

(i) This set-up demonstrates transpiration pull.

(ii) Water will rise up

(iii) The mercury level goes down, if phenyl mercuric acetate is sprayed on the leaves.

12

Mineral Nutrition

Important Points

1. **Methods to Study the Mineral Requirements of Plants**
   (i) **Julius** von **Sachs** in 1860 demonstrated for the first time that plants could be grown to maturity in a defined nutrient solution in complete absence of soil. This technique of growing plants in a nutrient solution is known as **hydroponics**.
   (ii) Methods involves culture of plants in a soil free defined mineral solution.
   (iii) Require purified water and mineral nutrient salts.

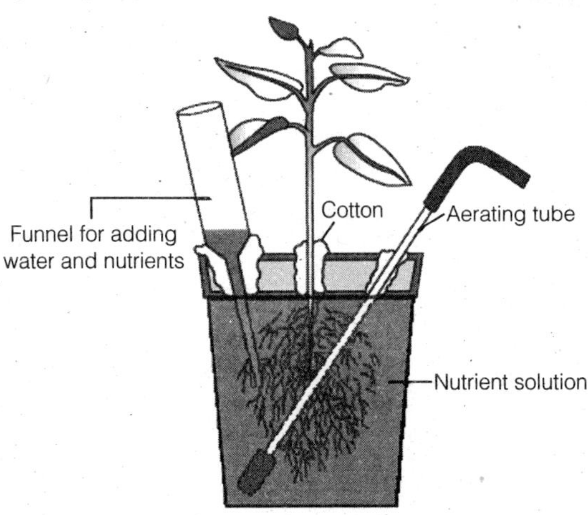

Diagram of a typical set-up for nutrient solution culture

(iv) Hydroponics have been successfully employed technique for commercial production of vegetables such as tomato, seedless cucumber and lettuce.

2. **Criteria for Essentiality of Mineral Elements**
   (i) Element must be absolutely necessary for supported normal growth and reproduction.
   (ii) Requirement of element must be specific and not replaceable by another element.
   (iii) The element must be directly involved in the metabolism of the plant.

3. **Elements are Divided into two Categories**
   (i) **Macronutrients**
      (a) Generally present in plant tissues in large amounts (in excess of 10 m mole kg^{-1} of dry matter).
      (b) Include carbon, hydrogen, oxygen, nitrogen, phosphorus, sulphur, potassium, calcium and magnesium.
      (c) Carbon, hydrogen and oxygen are obtained from CO_2 and H_2O, while others are absorbed from soil as mineral nutrition.
   (ii) **Micronutrients**
      (a) Trace elements, needed in small amount (less than 10 m mole kg^{-1} of dry matter).
      (b) Include Iron, manganese copper; molybdenum zinc, boron, chlorine and nickel.

4. **Elements are Grouped into Four Broad Categories**
   (i) Components of biomolecules/structural elements of cells (*e.g.*, carbon, hydrogen, oxygen and nitrogen).
   (ii) Components of energy related chemical compounds in plants (*e.g.*, magnesium in chlorophyll and phosphorus in ATP).
   (iii) Essential elements that activate or inhibit enzymes, *e.g.*, Mg^{+2} is an activator for both ribulose bisphosphate carboxylase-oxygenase and phosphoenol pyruvate carboxylase.
   (iv) Some essential elements can alter osmotic potential of a cell, *e.g.*, potassium plays an important role in opening and closing of stomata.

5. Role of Macro and Micronutrients

Mineral Element	Obtained As	Functions	Deficiency Symptoms
Nitrogen	NO_3^-, NO_2^-, NH_4^{2-}	Constituent of proteins nucleic acids, vitamins and hormones.	Chlorosis, stunted growth, inhibition of cell division.
Phosphorus	$H_2PO_4^-$	Constituent of cell membranes, proteins, nucleic acids and nucleotides. Required for all phosphorylation reactions.	Delay in seed germination. Leaves becomes darker. Poor growth.
Magnesium	Mg^{+2}	Activates enzymes of respiration and photosynthesis. Involved in synthesis of DNA and RNA. Constituent of the ring structure of chlorophyll. Maintain ribosome structure.	Interveinal chlorosis. Purple spots on older leaves. Premature leaf fall.
Calcium	Ca^{2+}	During cell division used in synthesis of cell wall. Formation of mitotic spindle Normal functioning of cell membranes. Regulate metabolic activates.	Necrosis of young meristematic regions. Stunted growth.
Potassium	K^+	Maintains ionic balance, involved in stomatal movement, involved in protein synthesis, opening and closing of stomata maintain turgidity of cell	Scorched leaf tips. Shorter internodes. Yellow edges of leaves, bushy habit.
Sulphur	SO_4^{2-} (Sulphate)	Present in two amino acid cysteine and methionine. Main constituent of coenzymes, vitamins and ferredoxin	Chlorosis, stunted growth, anthocyanin accumulation.
Iron	Fe^{3+} (ferricions)	Constituent of proteins involved in transfer of electrons like ferredoxin and cytochromes. Activates catalase enzyme. Formation of chlorophyll.	Chlorosis

Mineral Element	Obtained As	Functions	Deficiency Symptoms
Manganese	Mn^{2+} (manganous-ions)	Activates enzyme involved in photosynthesis, respiration and nitrogen metabolism Spitting of water to liberate oxygen during photosynthesis	Chlorosis, grey spots on leaves
Zinc	Zn^{2+}	Activates various enzymes-carboxylases Synthesis of auxin	Interveinal chlorosis stunted growth causes mottle leaf
Copper	Cu^{2+} (cupric ions)	Overall metabolism Associated with certain enzymes involved in redox reactions.	Necrosis of tips of leaves Dieback of shoots
Boron	BO_3^{3-}, $B_4O_7^{2-}$	Uptake and utilisation of Ca^{2+} Membrane functioning Pollen germination Cell elongation Carbohydrate metabolism.	Death of shoot and roots tips leaf abscission stunted growth.
Molybdenum	MoO_2^{2-} (Molybdate ions)	Component of several enzymes including nitrogenase and nitrate reductase.	Slower nitrogen metabolism, Interveinal chlorosis
Chlorine	Cl^- (Chloride anion)	Helps in determining the solute concentration Maintain ionic balance Essential for water splitting reaction in photosynthesis.	Stunted growth wilting of leaves and reduced fruiting

6. Toxicity of Micronutrients

Requirement of micronutrients is always in low amount, their moderate decrease causes deficiency symptoms and moderate increase causes toxicity.

7. Mechanism of Absorption of Elements

S.N.	Apoplast	Simplest
1.	Initial rapid uptake of ions into the 'free space' or 'outer space' of cells.	Ions are taken in slowly into the 'inner space' of cells.
2.	Occurs through ion channels, trans membrane proteins that function as selective pores.	Entry or exit of ions to and from symplast requires the expenditure of metabolic energy.
3.	It is a passive process.	It is an active process.

(i) The movement of ions is usually called flux, the inward movement into the cells is influx and the outward movement is efflux.

(ii) Minerals are translocated through xylem along with the ascending stream of water, which is pulled up through the plant by transpirational pull.

8. **Metabolism of Nitrogen and Nitrogen Cycle**

(i) Nitrogen exists as two nitrogen atoms joined by a very strong triple covalent ($N \equiv N$).

(ii) The process of conversion of nitrogen (N_2) to ammonia is termed as nitrogen fixation.

(iii) Decomposition of organic nitrogen of dead plants and animals into ammonia is called ammonification.

(iv) Some of this ammonia volatilises and re-enters the atmosphere but most of it is converted into nitrate by soil bacteria in following steps

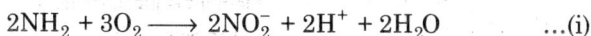

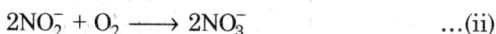

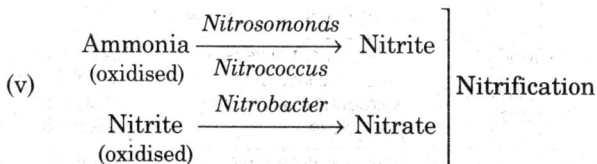

$$2NH_2 + 3O_2 \longrightarrow 2NO_2^- + 2H^+ + 2H_2O \quad \text{...(i)}$$

$$2NO_2^- + O_2 \longrightarrow 2NO_3^- \quad \text{...(ii)}$$

(v) Ammonia (oxidised) $\xrightarrow[\textit{Nitrococcus}]{\textit{Nitrosomonas}}$ Nitrite

Nitrite (oxidised) $\xrightarrow{\textit{Nitrobacter}}$ Nitrate

} **Nitrification**

(vi) Nitrifying bacteria are chemoautotrophs.

(vii) Nitrate → absorbed by plants → transported to leaves → reduced to form ammonia → finally form amine group of amino acids.

(viii) Denitrification Nitrate present in the soil is also reduced to nitrogen by denitrification. It is carried by bacteria *Pseudomonas* and *Thiobacillus*.

9. **Biological Nitrogen Fixation** Reduction of nitrogen to ammonia by living organisms is called **biological nitrogen fixation**.

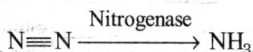

$$N \equiv N \xrightarrow{\text{Nitrogenase}} NH_3$$

Nitrogen fixing microbes

(i) Free living nitrogen fixers are

Aerobic *Azotobacter* and *Beijernickia*

Anaerobic *Rhodospirillum*

(ii) Cyanobacteria—*Anabaena* and *Nostoc*.

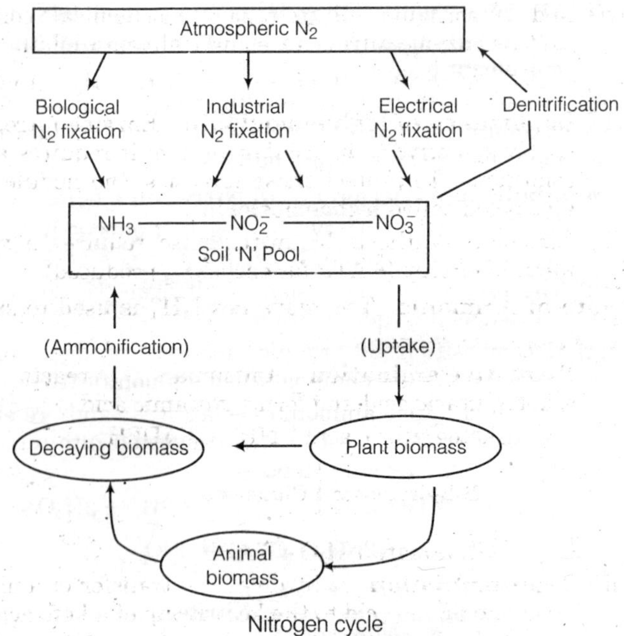

Nitrogen cycle

10. **Symbiotic Biological Nitrogen Fixation**
    (i) Most prominent symbiotic biological nitrogen fixing associations is the legume bacteria relationship.
    (ii) Species of rod-shaped *Rhizobium* has such relationship with the roots of several legumes such as alfalfa sweet clover, sweet pea, lentils, garden pea, broad beans, clover, beans, etc.
    (iii) Most common association is nodules-small outgrowth on the roots.
11. **Nodule Formation**
    (i) Rhizobia multiply and colonise the surroundings of roots and get attached to epidermal and root hair cells.
    (ii) Root hairs curl and the bacteria invade the root hair.
    (iii) Infection thread is produced carrying the bacteria into the cortex of the root. They initiate the nodule formation in cortex of root.
    (iv) Bacteria are released from the thread into cells → differentiation of specialised nitrogen fixing cells.
    (v) Nodule establishes a direct vascular connection with the host for exchange of nutrients.

(vi) Nodule contains all necessary biochemical components such as enzyme nitrogenase and leghaemoglobin.

$$N_2 + 8e^- + 8H^+ + 16ATP \longrightarrow 2NH_3 + H_2 + 16ADP + 16Pi$$

(vii) **Importance of leghaemoglobin** Enzyme nitrogenase is highly sensitive to molecular oxygen; it requires anaerobic conditions. To protect these enzymes, the nodule contains an oxygen called leghaemoglobin.

(viii) Ammonia synthesis by nitrogenase requires a very high input of energy (8 ATP for each NH_3 produced).

12. **Fate of Ammonia** Two ways law NH_4^+ is used to synthesise amino acids in plants

(i) **Reductive amination** Ammonia reacts with α-ketoglutaric acid and forms glutamic acid

$$\alpha\text{-ketoglutaric acid} + NH_4^+ + NADPH \xrightarrow{\text{Glutamate Dehydrogenase}} \text{Glutamate} + H_2O + NADP$$

(ii) **Transamination** It involves the transfer of amino group from one amino acid to the keto group of a keto acid.

(a) Glutamic acid is the main amino acid from which the transfer of NH_2, the amino group takes place and other amino acids are formed through transamination.

(b) Enzyme transaminase catalyses all such reactions.

$$\underset{\text{Amino donor}}{R_1-\overset{\displaystyle H}{\underset{\displaystyle NH_3^+}{C}}-COO^-} + \underset{\text{Amino acceptor}}{R_2-\underset{\displaystyle \| \atop O}{C}-COO^-} \rightleftharpoons R_1-\underset{\displaystyle \| \atop O}{C}-COO^- + R_2-\overset{\displaystyle H}{\underset{\displaystyle NH_3^+}{C}}-COO^-$$

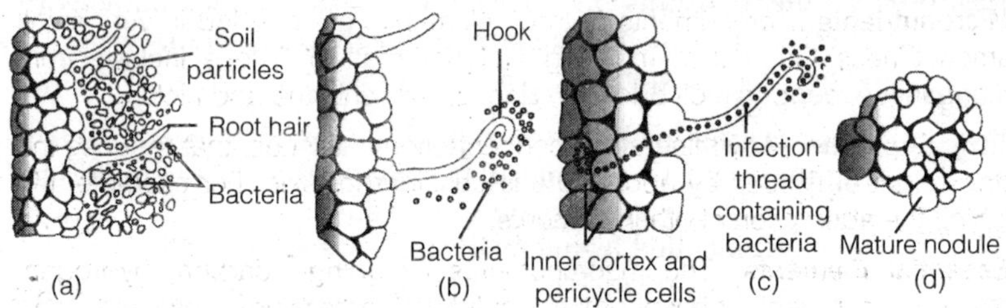

Development of root nodules in soyabean

(a) *Rhizobium* bacteria contact a susceptible root hair.
(b) Successful infection of the root hair causes it to curl.
(c) Infected thread carries the bacteria to inner cortex.
(d) A mature nodule is complete with vascular tissues continuous with those of the root.

Exercises

Question 1. 'All elements that are present in a plant need not be essential to its survival'. Comment.

Answer All elements that are present in a plant need not be essential to its survival because they do not directly involved in the composition of their body. However, if the concentration of micronutrients such as Fe, Mn, Cu, Zn, Cl, etc., rise above their critical values, they appear to be toxic for the plant.

Question 2. Why is purification of water and nutrient salts so important in studies involving mineral nutrition using hydroponics.

Answer It is to know the essentiality of a mineral element in the life cycle of a plant. Further, it helps in improving the deficiency symptoms of the plants. The nutrient solution must be adequetly aerated to obtain the optimal growth.

Question 3. Explain with examples macronutrients, micronutrients, beneficial nutrients, toxic elements and essential elements.

Answer **Macronutrients** Macronutrients are generally present in plant tissues in large amount (in excess of 10 m mole kg^{-1} of dry matter). The macronutrients include carbon, hydrogen, oxygen, nitrogen, phosphorus, sulphur, potassium, calcium and magnesium.

Micronutrients Micronutrients or trace elements, are needed in very small amount (less than 10 m mole kg^{-1} of dry matter). These include iron, manganese, copper, molybdenum, zinc, boron, chlorine and nickel.

Toxic Elements Any mineral ion concentration in tissues, that reduces the dry weight of tissues by about 10% is considered toxic. For example, Mn inhibit the absorption of other elements.

Essential Elements The macronutrients including carbon, hydrogen, oxygen, nitrogen, phosphorous, sulphur, potassium, calcium and magnesium, which are require directly for the growth and metabolism of the plants and whose deficiency produces certain symptoms in the plants are known as essential elements.

Question 4. Name at least five different deficiency symptoms in plants. Describe them and correlate with the concerned mineral deficiency.

Answer The kind of deficiency symptoms shown in plants include chlorosis, necrosis, stunted plant growth, premature fall of leaves and buds, and inhibition of cell division.

(i) Chlorosis is the loss of chlorophyll leading to yellowing in leaves. This symptom is caused by the deficiency of elements N, K, Mg, S, Fe, Mn, Zn and Mo.

(ii) Necrosis or death of tissue, particularly leaf tissue, is due to the deficiency of Ca, Mg, Cu, K.

(iii) Lack or low level of N, K, S, Mo causes an inhibition of cell division.

(iv) Some elements like N, S, Mo delay flowering if their concentration in plants is low.

Question 5. If a plant shows a symptom which could develop due to deficiency of more than one nutrient, how would you find out experimentally, the real deficient mineral element?

Answer Every element shows certain characteristic deficiency symptoms in the plants. The deficiency of any one element cannot be met by supplying some other element. So, by absorbing the type of deficiency symptom, we can determine the real deficient mineral element.

Question 6. Why is that in certain plants deficiency symptoms appear first in younger parts of the plant, while in others they do so in mature organs?

Answer For elements that are actively mobilised within the plants and exported to young developing tissues, the deficiency symptoms tend to appear first in the older tissues. For example, the deficiency symptoms of nitrogen, potassium and magnesium are visible first in the senescent leaves. In the older leaves, biomolecules containing these elements are broken down, making these elements available for mobilising to younger leaves.

The deficiency symptoms tend to appear first in the young tissues, whenever the elements are relatively immobile and are not transported out of the mature organs. For example, elements like sulphur and calcium are a part of the structural component of the cell and hence are not easily released.

Question 7. How are the minerals absorbed by the plants?

Answer Mechanism of Absorption of Minerals

The process of absorption can occur into two main phases.

(i) In the first phase, an initial rapid uptake of ions into the 'free space' or 'outer space' of cells the apoplast, is passive.

(ii) In the second phase of uptake, the ions are taken in slowly into the 'inner space' **the symplast of the cells**. The passive movement of ions into the apoplast usually occurs through ion-channels, the *trans*-membrane proteins that function as selective pores. On the other hand, the entry or exit of ions to and from the symplast requires the expenditure of metabolic energys. The movement of ions is usually called the inward movement into the cells is **influx** and the outward movement, **efflux**.

Question 8. What are the conditions necessary for fixation of atmospheric nitrogen by *Rhizobium*. What is their role in Nitrogen-fixation?

Answer The first essential condition for nitrogen fixation is lagume-bacteria relationship. *Rhizobium* bacteria cause nodule formation for this association. The enzyme nitrogenase is highly sensitive to the molecular oxygen. The nodules protect these enzymes by an oxygen scavenger called leghaemoglobin.

Rhizobium bacteria are free living in soil. They are symbionts, which can fix atmospheric nitrogen for plants.

Question 9. What are the steps involved in formation of a root nodule?

Answer Steps in Nodule Formation

Nodule formation involves a sequence of multiple interactions between *Rhizobium* and roots of the host plant. Principal stages in the nodule formation are:

(i) Rhizobia multiply and colonise the surroundings of roots and get attached to epidermal and root hair cells.

(ii) The root-hairs curl and the bacteria invade the root-hair.

(iii) An infection thread is produced carrying the bacteria into the cortex of the root, where they initiate the nodule formation in the cortex of the root. Then the bacteria are released from the thread into the cells which leads to the differentiation of specialised nitrogen fixing cells.

(iv) The nodule thus formed, establishes a direct vascular connection with the host for exchange of nutrients.

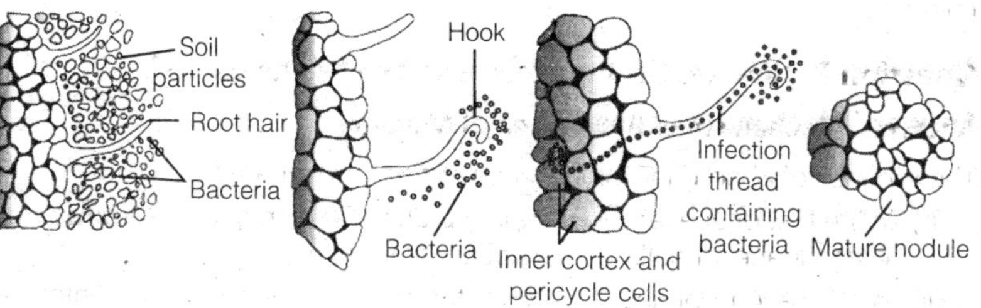

Root nodules

Question 10. Which of the following statements are true? If false, correct them

(i) Boron deficiency leads to stout axis.

(ii) Every mineral element that is present in a cell is needed by the cell.

(iii) Nitrogen as a nutrient element, is highly immobile in the plants.

(iv) It is very easy to establish the essentiality of micronutrients because they are required only in trace quantities.

Answer

(i) Boron deficiency leads to stout axis.

(iv) It is very easy to establish the essentiality of micronutrients because they are required only in trace quantities.

Selected NCERT Exemplar Problems

Very Short Answer Type Questions

Question 1. Name a plant, which accumulate silicon.

Answer *Equisetum*, a pteridophyte.

Question 2. Mycorrhiza is a mutualistic association. How do the organisms involved in this association gain from each other?

Answer Mycorrhiza is a symbiotic association between roots of higher plants, *i.e.*, conifers and fungi. Fungi being heterotrophic in their mode of nutrition depend upon higher plants for food requirements, whereas in turn provide water and mineral nutrients to the algae.

Question 3. Nitrogen fixation is shown by prokaryotes and not eukaryotes. Comment?

Answer Nitrogen fixation is show by prokaryotes and not by eukaryotes, because the enzyme nitrogenase, which is capable of nitrogen reduction is present exclusively in prokaryotes. Such microbes are called N_2 fixers.

Question 4. Carnivorous plants like *Nepenthes* and *Venus* fly trap have nutritional adaptations. Which nutrient do they especially obtain and from where?

Answer *Nepenthes* and Venus fly trap grow in water logged and swampy soils deficient in nitrogenous compounds. They have to depend on captered insects for their nitrogen requirement.

Question 5. Think of a plant which lacks chlorophyll. From where will it obtain nutrition? Give an example of such a type of plant.

Answer *Cuscuta* , the total stem parasite is an example of such plant. It is long filamentous non-chlorophyllous, pale yellow colour with small scale leaves. It obtains organic food, water and mineral nutrients from the host with the help of absorbing organs, *i.e.*, haustoria.

Question 6. Name an insectivorous angiosperm.

Answer *Nepenthes* (the pitcher plant).

Question 7. A farmer adds *Azotobacter* culture to soil before sowing maize. Which mineral element is being replenished?

Answer Nitrogen mineral element.

Question 8. What type of conditions are created by leghaemoglobin in the root nodule of a legume?

Answer The pigment leghaemoglobin is a product of host tissue. This pigment has the ability to combine very readily with O_2 and thus acts as a very efficient O_2 scavanger. It helps to maintain steady supply of O_2 at lower concentrations and thus provides favourable conditions for the activity of enzyme system nitrogenase (as the enzyme is active in anaerobic conditions).

Question 9. What is common to *Nepenthes, Utricularia* and *Drosera* with regard to mode of nutrition?

Answer *Nepenthes, Utricularia* and *Drosera*, all three are carnivorous or insectivorous plants. These plants grow in water logged and swampy soils deficient in nitrogenous compounds. These plants possess poorly developed roots , thus they have to depend on captered insects for their nitrogen requirement.

Question 10. Plants with zinc deficiency show reduced biosynthesis of

Answer Auxin hormone.

Question 11. Yellowish edges appear in leaves deficient in

Answer Magnesium.

Question 12. Name the macronutrient which is a component of all organic compounds but is not obtained from soil.

Answer Nitrogen.

Question 13. Name one non-symbiotic nitrogen fixing prokaryote.

Answer Cyanobacteria, *i.e.*, *Nostoc* and *Anabaena*, etc.

Question 14. Rice fields produce an important greenhouse gas. Name it.

Answer Methane gas.

Question 15. Complete the equation for reductive amination

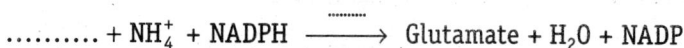

$$\ldots\ldots\ldots + NH_4^+ + NADPH \xrightarrow{\ldots\ldots} Glutamate + H_2O + NADP$$

Answer

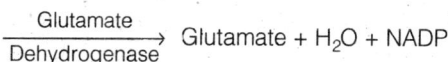

$$\alpha\text{-ketoglutaric acid} + NH_4^+ + NADPH \xrightarrow[\text{Dehydrogenase}]{\text{Glutamate}} \text{Glutamate} + H_2O + NADP$$

Question 16. Excess of Mn in soil leads to deficiency of Ca, Mg and Fe. Justify.

Answer Manganese competes with iron and magnesium for uptake and with magnesium for binding with enzymes. Manganese also inhibit calcium translocation in shoot apex. Therefore, excess of manganese may, in fact, induce deficiency of iron, magnesium and calcium.

Short Answer Type Questions

Question 1. How is sulphur important for plants? Name the amino acids in which it is present.

Answer Plants obtain sulphur in the form of sulphate (SO_4^{2-}) and is the main constituent of several coenzymes, vitamins (thiamine, biotin, coenzyme-A) and ferredoxin. It plays role in the synthesis of chlorophyll. It is essential for nodulation in legumes. It determines the structure of protein. Sulphur is present in two amino acids-cysteine and methionine.

Question 2. How are organisms like *Pseudomonas* and *Thiobacillus* of great significance in nitrogen cycle?

Answer The organisms like *Pseudomonas* and *Thiobacillus* are of great significance in nitrogen cycle, because these bacteria convert the nitrates and ammonia are converted to nitrous oxide and finally to nitrogen gas.

$$6KNO_3 + 5S + 2H_2O \longrightarrow K_2SO_4 + KHSO_4 + 3N_2 + \text{Energy}$$

The nitrogen gas; released from denitrification, is lost to atmosphere and completes the complex nitrogen cycle.

Question 3. Carefully observe the following figure?

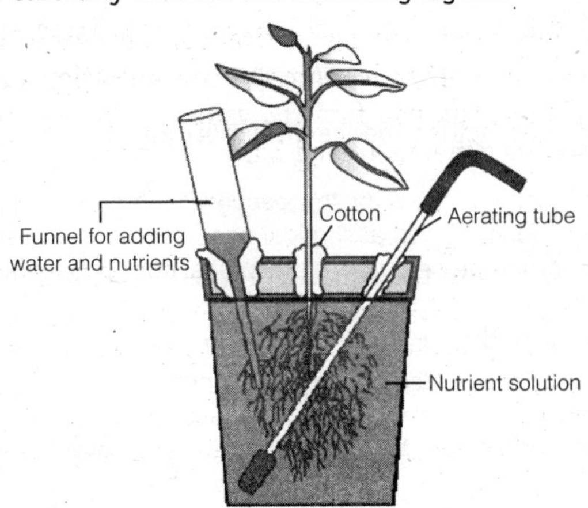

(i) Name the technique shown in the figure and the scientist who demonstrated this technique for the first time.

(ii) Name atleast three plants for which this technique can be employed for their commercial production.

(iii) What is the significance of aerating tube and feeding funnel in this setup?

Answer

(i) The technique shown in the figure is known as hydroponics and the scientist who demonstrated this technique for the first time was **Julius Von Sachs**.

(ii) This technique can be employed for their commercial production of tomato, seedless cucumber and lettuce.

(iii) The aerating tube is used for aeration of the solution, for forcing the air through the solution and feeding funnel in this setup is used for puring mineral nutrients.

Question 4. Name the most crucial enzyme found in root nodules for N_2 fixation? Does it require a special pink coloured pigment for its functioning? Elaborate.

Answer Nitrogenase enzyme is found in root nodules for N_2 fixation. Enzymes responsible for nitrogenase action are very susceptible to destruction by oxygen (in fact, many bacteria cease production of the enzyme in the presence of oxygen). This enzyme requires a special pink coloured pigment for its functioning. Many nitrogen-fixing organisms exist only in anaerobic conditions, respiring to draw down oxygen levels or binding the oxygen with a protein such as leghaemoglobin.

Question 5. How are the terms 'critical concentration' and 'deficient' different from each other in terms of concentration of an essential element in plants? Can you find the values of 'critical concentration' and 'deficient' for minerals Fe and Zn.

Answer The concentration of the essential element below which plant growth is retarded is termed as 'critical concentration'. The element is said to be deficient when present below the critical concentration.

Yes, we can you find the values of 'critical concentration' and 'deficient' for minerals Fe and Zn by absorbing the morphological changes. If the concentrations of these elements are present below 'critical values', then it may eventually lead to the death of the plant. Morphological changes are indicative of certain element deficiencies and are called deficiency symptoms.

Question 6. Carnivorous plants exhibit nutritional adaptation. Citing an example explain this fact.

Answer *Nepenthes* and Venus fly trap plants are carnivorous or insectivorous, which grow in water logged and swampy soils deficient in nitrogenous compounds. These plants possess poorly developed roots, thus they have to depend on captered insects for their nitrogen requirement. These plants are partially heterotrophic as these can manufacture their organic food with the help of chlorophyll present in the leaves and stems. These plants obtain nitrogen mineral from insect bodies.

Question 7. A farmer adds/supplies Na, Ca, Mg and Fe regularly to his field and yet he observes that the plants show deficiency of Ca, Mg and Fe. Give a valid reason and suggest a way to help the farmer improve the growth of plants.

Answer It is important to know that manganese competes with iron and magnesium for uptake and with magnesium for binding with enzymes. Manganese also inhibit calcium translocation in shoot apex. Therefore, excess of manganese may, in fact, induce deficienciy of iron, magnesium and calcium. Thus, what appears as symptoms of manganese toxicity may actually be the deficiency symptoms of iron, magnesium and calcium.

The farmer should not excess manganese in the soil to prevent manganese toxicity.

Long Answer Questions

Question 1. It is observed that deficiency of a particular element showed its symptoms initially in older leaves and then in younger leaves.

(i) Does it indicate that the element is actively mobilised or relatively immobile?

(ii) Name two elements which are highly mobile and two which are relatively immobile.

(iii) How is the aspect of mobility of elements important to horticulture and agriculture?

Answer

(i) Yes, it indicate that the element is actively mobilised or relatively immobile. The parts of the plants that show the deficiency symptoms also depend on the mobility of the element in the plant. For elements that are actively mobilised within the plants and exported to young developing tissues, the deficiency symptoms tend to appear first in the older tissues.

(ii) Two elements which are highly mobile are phosphorus and sulphur and two which are relatively immobile are Mo and boron.

(iii) The aspect of mobility of elements is important to horticulture and agriculture. The deficiency symptoms tend to appear first in the young tissues where the elements are relatively immobile and are not transported out of the mature organs. For example, elements like sulphur and calcium are a part of the structural component of the cell and hence are not easily released.

Question 2. We find that *Rhizobium* forms nodules on the roots of leguminous plants. Also *Frankia* another microbe forms nitrogen fixing nodules on the roots of non-leguminous plant *Alnus*.

(i) Can we artificially induce the property of nitrogen fixation in a plant, leguminous or non-leguminous?

(ii) What kind of relationship is observed between mycorrhiza and pine trees?

(iii) Is it necessary for a microbe to be in close association with a plant to provide mineral nutrition? Explain with the help of one example.

Answer

(i) Yes, we can artificially induce the property of nitrogen fixation in a plant, leguminous or non-leguminous by genetically engineering. It involves the introduction of *nif* genes that cause the synthesis of nitrogenase enzyme by some vector in the plant in which we have to induce symbiosis.

(ii) Symbiotic association.

(iii) Yes, it is necessary for a microbe to be in close association with a plant to provide mineral nutrition. For example, plants that contribute to nitrogen fixation include the legume family–Fabaceae, with taxa such as clover, soyabeans, alfalfa, lupines and peanuts. They contain symbiotic bacteria called Rhizobia within nodules in their root systems, producing nitrogen compounds that help the plant to grow and compete with other plants.

Question 3. What are essential elements for plants? Give the criteria of essentiality? How are minerals classifieds depending upon the amount in which they are needed by the plants?

Answer **Essential Elements** The macronutrients including carbon, hydrogen, oxygen, nitrogen, phosphorus, sulphur, potassium, calcium and magnesium, which are require directly for the growth and metabolism of the plants and whose deficiency produces certain symptoms in the plants are known as essential elements.

Criteria for Essentiality

(i) The element must be absolutely necessary for supporting normal growth and reproduction. Micronutrients or trace elements are needed in very small amount (less than 10 m mole kg^{-1} of dry matter). These include iron, manganese, copper, molybdnum, zinc, boron, chlorine and nickel.

(ii) The requirement of the element must be specific and not replaceable by another element.

(iii) The element must be directly involved in the metabolism of the plant. Based upon the above criteria only a few elements have been found to be absolutely essential for plant growth and metabolism. These elements are further divided into two broad categories based on their quantitative requirements.

(a) Macronutrients

(b) Micronutrients

Question 4. **With the help of examples describe the classification of essential elements based on the function they perform.**

Answer Essential elements can be grouped into four broad categories on the basis of their diverse functions. These categories are:

(i) Elements as components of biomolecules and hence structural elements of cells (*e.g.*, carbon, hydrogen, oxygen and nitrogen).

(ii) Elements that are components of energy-related chemical compounds in plants (*e.g.*, magnesium in chlorophyll and phosphorus in ATP).

(iii) Elements that activate or inhibit enzymes. For example, Mg^{2+} is an activator for both ribulose bisphosphate carboxylaseoxygenase and phosphoenol pyruvate carboxylase, both of which are critical enzymes in photosynthetic carbon fixation; Zn^{2+} is an activator of alcohol dehydrogenase and Mo of nitrogenase during nitrogen metabolism.

(iv) Some essential elements can alter the osmotic potential of a cell. Potassium plays an important role in the opening and closing of stomata.

Question 5. **We know that plants require nutrients. If we supply these in excess, will it be beneficial to the plants? If yes, how/ If no, why?**

Answer Excess minerals are not beneficial for the plants. Any mineral ion concentration in tissues that reduces the dry weight of tissues by about

10% is considered toxic. Toxicity levels for any element also vary for different plants. Many a times, excess of an element may inhibit the uptake of another element. For example, the prominent symptom of manganese toxicity is the appearance of brown spots surrounded by chlorotic veins. It is important to know that manganese competes with iron and magnesium for uptake and with magnesium for binding with enzymes. Manganese also inhibit calcium translocation in shoot apex. Therefore, excess of manganese may, in fact, induces deficiency of iron, magnesium and calcium.

Question 6. Give the biochemical events occurring in the root nodule of a pulse plant. What is the end products? What is its fate?

Answer

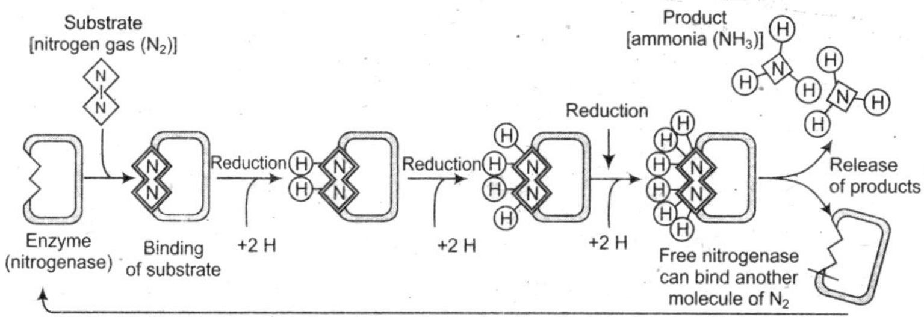

The reaction is as follows

$$N_2 + 8e^- + 8H^+ + 16ATP \longrightarrow 2NH_3 + H_2 + 16ADP + 16Pi$$

Ammonia is the end product.

Fate of Ammonia At physiological pH, the ammonia is protonated to form NH_4^+ (ammonium) ion. The NH_4^+ is used to synthesise amino acids in plants. There are two main ways in which this can take place

(i) **Reductive** In these processes, ammonia reacts with α-ketoglutaric acid and forms glutamic acid as indicated in the equation given below

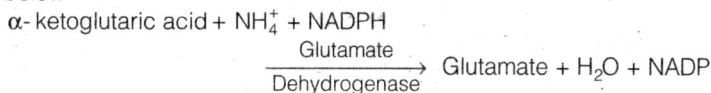

$$\alpha\text{-ketoglutaric acid} + NH_4^+ + NADPH \xrightarrow[\text{Dehydrogenase}]{\text{Glutamate}} \text{Glutamate} + H_2O + NADP$$

(ii) **Transamination** It involves the transfer of amino group from one amino acid to the keto-group of a keto acid. Glutamic acid is the main amino acid from which the transfer of NH_2, the amino group takes place and other amino acids are formed through transamination. The enzyme transaminase catalyses all such reactions.

For example,

$$R_1-\underset{NH_3^+}{\overset{H}{\underset{|}{\overset{|}{C}}}}-COO^- + R_2-\underset{O}{\underset{||}{C}}-COO^- \rightleftharpoons R_1-\underset{O}{\underset{||}{C}}-COO^- + R_2-\underset{NH_3^+}{\overset{H}{\underset{|}{\overset{|}{C}}}}-COO^-$$

Amino-donor Amino-accptor

Question 7. Hydroponics have been shown to be a successful technique for growing of plants. Yet most of the crops are still grown on land. Why?

Answer The technique of growing plants in a nutrient solution is known as hydroponics. This method requires purified water and mineral nutrient salts. After a series of experiments, in which the roots of the plants were immersed in nutrient solutions and wherein an element was added / removed or given in varied concentration, a mineral solution suitable for the plant growth was obtained. By this method, essential elements were identified and their deficiency symptoms discovered. Hydroponics has been successfully employed as a technique for the commercial production of vegetables such as tomato, seedless cucumber and lettuce.

Yet, most of the crops are still grown on land because the nutrient solutions must be adequately aerated to obtain the optimum growth. Moreover, the minerals must be continuously added in the solution. No, such activity is required in the soil.

13

Photosynthesis in Higher Plants

Important Points

1. Green plants carry out 'photosynthesis' a physico-chemical process by which they use light energy to drive the synthesis of organic campounds.
2. Photosynthesis in plants requires chlorophyll, light and CO_2 .
3. **Joseph priestley** (1733-1804) in 1770, performed experiments to find out the role of oxygen in growth of green plants.
4. **Jan Ingenhousz** (1730-1799) showed that sunlight is essential to the plants.
5. **Julius Von Sachs** (1854) showed that the chlorophyll is located in chloroplasts in plants cells.
6. **Cornelius Van Niel** (1897-1985) demonstrated that photosynthesis is essentially a light dependent reaction.
7. Photosynthesis reaction can be expressed as:

$$6CO_2 + 12H_2O \xrightarrow[\text{Chlorophyll}]{\text{Light}} \underset{\text{Glucose}}{C_6H_{12}O_6} + 6H_2O + 6O_2$$

8. The mesophyll cells of leaves contain a large number of chloroplasts.
9. The chloroplast contains grana, the stroma lamella and the fluid stroma.
10. The membrane system of chloroplast traps light energy and synthesises ATP and NADPH.

11. In stroma, enzymatic reactions incorporate CO_2 into the plant leading to the synthesis of sugar which in turn forms starch. These reactions are light driven, so are called **light reactions.**
12. The latter reactions in photosynthesis are not directly driven, but are dependent on the products of light reactions (ATP and NADPH). So, they are called **dark reactions**.
13. Pigments are substances that have an ability to absorb light, at specific wavelengths.
14. The chromatographic separation of the leaf pigments shows that the colour of the leaf is due to four pigments chlorophyll-*a, b* and carotenoids.
15. The wavelength at which there is maximum absorption of chlorophyll-*a*, *i.e.*, in the blue and red regions, also show higher rate of photosynthesis this shows that chlorophyll-*a* is the chief pigment associated with photosynthesis.
16. The other accessory pigments (thylakoid pigments) like chlorophyll-*b* xanthophylls and carotenoids also absorb light and transfer it to chlorophyll-*a* and also protect it from photo oxidation.
17. **Light reaction** or the **Photochemical** phase include light absorption, water splitting, oxygen release and the formation of high energy intermediates, ATP and NADPH.
18. In light reaction, pigments are associated into two discrete photochemical Light Harvesting Complexes (LHC) within the Photosystem I (PS-I) and Photosystem II (PS-II).
19. Each photosystem has all the pigments (except one molecule of chlorophyll-*a*) forming a light harvesting system also called antennae.
20. The single chlorophyll-*a* molecule forms the reaction centre.
21. In PS-I, the reaction centre chlorophyll-*a* has an absorption peak at 700 nm, hence is called P_{700}, while in PS-II, it has absorption maxima at 680 nm and called P_{680}.
22. In PS-II, the chlorophyll-*a* absorbs 680 nm wavelength of red light causing electrons to become excited and jump into an orbit.
23. These electrons are picked up by an electron acceptor, which passes them to an electrons transport system consisting of cytochromes.
24. These electrons are not used up but are passed on to the pigments of PS-I.

25. The electrons in the reaction centre PS-I are also excited when they receive red light of wavelength 700 nm and are transferred to another acceptor molecule.
26. These electrons move downhill to a molecule of energy rich $NADP^+$. The addition of these electrons reduces $NADP^+$ to $NADPH + H^+$.
27. This whole scheme of transfer of electrons, starting from PS-II, uphill to the acceptor and finally down hill to $NADP^+$ causing it to reduced to $NADPH + H^+$ is called **Z-scheme**, due to its characteristic shape.

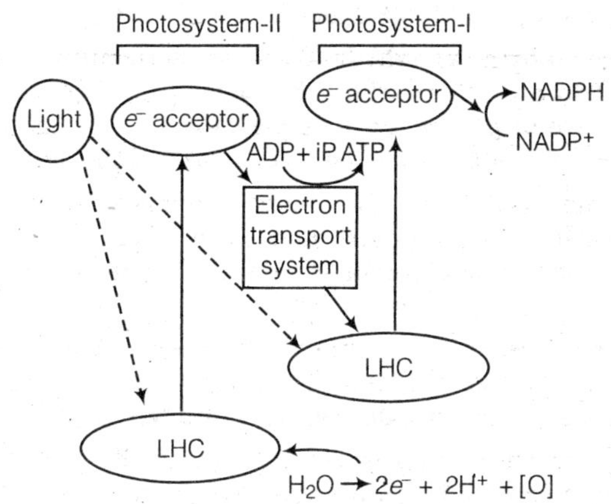

Cyclic photophosphorylation

28. PS-II supplies electrons continuously by splitting of water. Water is split into H^+, [O] and electrons. This creates oxygen the net products of photosynthesis.

$$2H_2O \longrightarrow 4H^+ + O_2 + 4e^-$$

29. The process by which ATP is synthesised by cells (in mitochondria and chloroplasts) is called **phosphorylation**.
30. Photophosphorylation is the synthesis of ATP from ADP and inorganic phosphate in the presence of light. It can be of two types:
    (i) **Non-cyclic photophosphorylation** occurs when two photosystems work in a series, first PS-II and then PS-I.
    (ii) **Cyclic photophosphorylation** occurs when only PS-I is functional. The electron is circulated within the photosystem and cyclic flow of electrons occur. It occurs in stroma, lamelle and when wavelength of beyond 680 nm is available.

31. The cyclic flow results only in synthesis of ATP but of NADPH + H^+.
32. Chemiosmotic hypothesis explains the mechanism of ATP synthesis in chloroplast. ATP synthesis is related to development of a proton gradient across a membrane.
33. The steps that cause a proton gradient to develop are:
    (i) The proton or hydrogen ions that are produced by splitting of water, accumulate within the lumen of thylakoids.
    (ii) As electrons move through the photosystems, protons are transported across the membrane. This is because the primary acceptor of electron, which is located towards the outer side of membrane transfers its electrons not to an electron carrier but to H carrier. Hence, this molecule removes a proton from the stroma, while transporting an electron. The proton is then released into the inner side of the membrane.
    (iii) The NADP reductase enzyme is located on the stroma side of membrane. The protons are necessary for the reduction of $NADP^+$ to NADPH + H^+. These protons are also removed from the stroma.
34. A proton gradient develops when within the chloroplast protons in the stroma decrease in number, while in the lumen there is accumulation of protons.
35. The proton gradient is necessary as the breakdown of gradient releases energy.
36. The breakdown of gradient provides enough energy to cause a change in F_1 particle of the ATPase, which makes the enzyme synthesise several molecules of energy packed ATP. ATPase enzyme catalyses the formation of ATP.
37. The ATP is used immediately in biosynthetic reaction taking place in stroma, responsible for fixing CO_2 and synthesis of sugar.
38. Biosynthetic phase or dark reaction does not directly depend on the presence of light but is dependent on the products of light reaction, *i.e.*, ATP and NADPH, besides CO_2 and H_2O.
39. CO_2 assimilation during photosynthesis follow two routes:
    (i) C_3-**pathway**, in which first product of CO_2 fixation is a C_3 acid (PGA-3 phosphoglyceric acid).
    (ii) C_4-**pathway**, in which the first product was a C_4 acid (Oxaloacetic acid-OAA).

40. **Calvin cycle** occurs in all photosynthetic plants, whether they have C_3 or C_4-pathways.
41. There stages of Calvin cycle are (i) Carboxylation (ii) Reduction (iii) Regeneration.
42. Carboxylation is the step in which CO_2 is utilised for the carboxylation of RuBP (Ribulose bisphosphate). RuBP is a acceptor molecule of CO_2, a 5-carbon ketose sugar. Carboxylation is catalysed by RuBP carboxylose oxygenase (RuBisCO), which results in formation of 3-PGA.
43. **Reduction** involves two molecules of ATP for phosphorylation and two of NADPH for reduction per CO_2 molecule fixed.
44. **Regeneration** of CO_2 acceptor molecule RuBP require one ATP for phosphorylation to form RuBP.

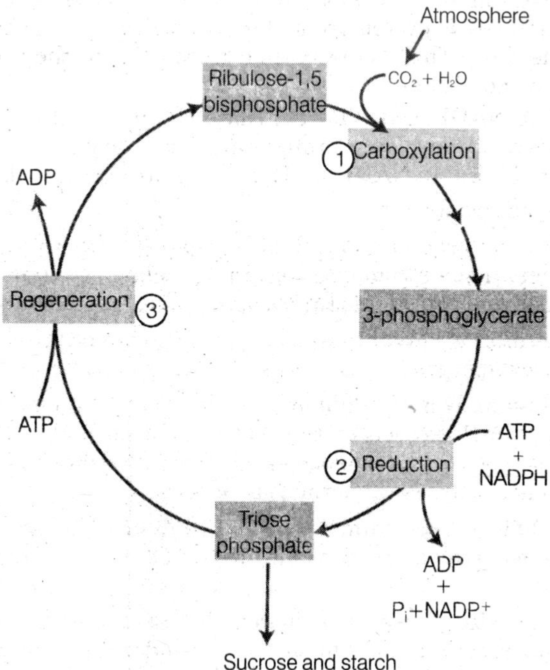

The Calvin cycle proceeds in three stage: (1) carboxylation during which CO_2 combines with ribulose-1, 5-bisphosphate: (2) reduction, during which carbohydrate is formed at the expenses of the photochemically made ATP and NADPH: and (3) regeneration during which the CO_2 accepter ribulose-1, 5-bisphosphate is formed again, so that the cycle continues.

45. For every CO_2 molecule entering the Calvin cycle, 3 molecules of ATP and two of NADPH are required. To make one molecule of glucose 6 turns of cycle are required.
46. C_4-pathway is present is plants that are adapted to live in dry tropical regions.
47. These plants (C_4-plants) have the C_4 oxaloacetic acid as the first CO_2 fixation product, they use the C_3-pathway or the Calvin cycle as the main biosynthetic pathway.
48. Characteristics of C_4-plants:
    (i) They have a special type of leaf anatomy.
    (ii) They can tolerate high temperatures.
    (iii) They show a highlight intensities.
    (iv) They lack a process called photorespiration and have greater productivity of biomass.
49. C_4-plants have bundle sheath cells in their leaves called as 'Kranz anatomy'.
50. In Kranz anatomy, bundle sheath cells form several layers around the vascular bundles, having a large number of chloroplasts, thick walls impervious to gas exchange and no intercellular spaces.
51. C_4-plants follow Hatch and Slack pathway. In this, the primary acceptor is a 3 carbon molecule Phosphoenol Pyruvate (PEP) and is present in mesophyll cells. The enzyme used is PEP carboxylase.
52. The mesophyll cells lack RuBisCO enzyme. The C_4-acid OAA is formed in the mesophyll cells.
53. OAA then forms other 4-carbon compounds like malic acid or aspartic acid in the mesophyll cells itself.
54. The 3-carbon molecule released is transported back to mesophyll cells where it is converted to PEP again, thus completing the cycle.
55. The CO_2 released in bundle sheath cells now enters the C_3 or the Calvin pathway (common to all plants). Calvin cycle does not take place in mesophyll cells in C_4-plants but occurs only in bundle sheath cells.
56. Photorespiration is also a process, which creates an important difference between C_3 and C_4-plants.

57. In C_3-plants, photorespiration occurs.
    (i) O_2 bind to the RuBisCO, so CO_2 fixation is decreased.
    (ii) Here, RuBP binds with O_2 to form one molecule of phosphoglycerate and phosphoglycolate in the pathway called **photorespiration**.
    (ii) In this pathway, there is neither synthesis of sugars nor of ATP. Rather, it results in release of CO_2 with the utilisation of ATP. So, photorespiration is a wasteful process here.
58. In C_4-plants, photorespiration does not occur, this is because they have the mechanism that increases the concentration of CO_2 at the enzyme site.
    (i) This takes place C_4-acid from mesophyll cells is broken down in the bundle sheath cells to release CO_2, this results in increasing the intracellular concentration of CO_2.
    (ii) In turn, this ensures that the RuBisCO functions as a carboxylase minimising the oxygenase activity.
    (iii) The C_4-plants lack photorespiration, that is why the productivity and fields are better in these plants.
59. Photosynthesis is under the influence of both internal (plant) and external factors.
    (i) Internal factors are the number, size, age and orientation of leaves, mesophyll cells and chloroplasts, internal CO_2 concentration and the amount of chlorophyll.
    (ii) External factors are availability of sunlight temperature, CO_2 concentration and water.
60. Black man's law of limiting factors state that 'if a chemical process is attached by more than one factor, then its rate will be determined by the factor, which is nearest to its minimal value. It is the factor, which directly affects the process, if its quantity is changed.
61. Light as a limiting factor:
    (i) At higher intensities, gradually the rate does not show further increase as other factors become limiting.
    (ii) Light saturation occurs at 10% of the full sunlight.
    (iii) Increase in incident light beyond a point causes the breakdown of chlorophyll and a decrease in photosynthesis.
62. Carbon dioxide as a limiting factor:
    (i) The C_3 and C_4-plants respond differently to CO_2 concentrations.

(ii) At high light intensities, both C_3 and C_4-plants show increase in the rates of photosynthesis. Hence, C_4-plants show saturation at about $360/\mu lL^{-1}$, while C_3 responds to increased CO_2 concentration acting as a limiting factor.

(iii) This is the reason C_3 plants like tomatoes and bell pepper are allowed to grow in CO_2 enriched atmosphere that leads to high yield.

63. Temperature as a limiting factor:

(i) The C_4-plants respond to higher temperatures and show higher rate of photosynthesis, while C_3-plants have a much lower optimum temperature.

64. Water stress causes stomata to close hence, reducing the CO_2 availability.

Exercises

Question 1. By looking at a plant externally can you tell whether a plant is C_3 or C_4? Why and how?

Answer Usually plants growing in dry conditions use C_4-pathways. It cannot be said conclusively, if the plant is a C_4 or C_4 buy looking at external appearance.

Question 2. By looking at which internal structure of a plant can you tell whether a plant is C_3 or C_4? Explain.

Answer The particularly large cells around the vascular bundles of the C_4-pathway plants are called bundle sheath cells and the leaves, which have such anatomy are said to have 'Kranz' anatomy. 'Kranz' means 'wreath' and is a reflection of the arrangement of cells. The bundle sheath cells may form several layers around the vascular bundles; they are characterised by having a large number of chloroplasts, thick walls impervious to gaseous exchange and no intercellular spaces.

Question 3. Even though a very few cells in a C_4-plant carry out the biosynthetic-Calvin pathway, yet they are highly productive. Can you discuss why?

Answer C_4-plants chemically fix carbon dioxide in the cells of the mesophyll by adding it to the three-carbon molecule phosphoenolpyruvate (PEP), a reaction catalysed by an enzyme called PEP carboxylase. It creates the four-carbon organic acid, oxaloacetic acid. Oxaloacetic acid or malate synthesised by this process is then translocated to specialised bundle sheath cells where the enzyme, RuBisCO and other Calvin cycle enzymes are located and where CO_2 released by decarboxylation of the four-carbon acids is then fixed by RuBisCO activity to the three-carbon sugar 3-phosphoglyceric acids.

The physical separation of RuBisCO from the oxygen-generating light reactions reduces photorespiration and increases CO_2 fixation and thus photosynthetic capacity of the leaf.

Question 4. **RuBisCO is an enzyme that acts both as a carboxylase and oxygenase. Why do you think RuBisCO carries out more carboxylation in C_4-plants?**

Answer RuBisCO has a much greater affinity for CO_2 than for O_2. It is the relative concentration of O_2 and CO_2 that determines which of the two will bind to the enzyme.

In C_4-plants some O_2 does bind to RuBisCO and hence, CO_2 fixation is decreased. Here the RuBP instead of being converted to two molecules of PGA binds with O_2 to form one molecule and phosphoglycolate in a pathway called photorespiration. In the photorespiratory pathway, there is neither synthesis of sugars, nor of ATP. Rather it results in the release of CO_2 with the utilisation of ATP. In the photorespiratory pathway. There is no synthesis of ATP or NADPH. Therefore, photorespiration is a wasteful process.

In C_4-plants, photorespiration does not occur. This is because they have a mechanism that increases the concentration of CO_2 at the enzyme site. This takes place when the C_4 acid from the mesophyll is broken down in the bundle cells to release CO_2-this results in increasing the intracellular concentration of CO_2. In turn, this ensures that the RuBisCO functions as a carboxylase minimising the oxygenase activity.

Question 5. **Suppose there were plants that had a high concentration of chlorophyll-*b*, but lacked chlorophyll-*a*, would it carry out photosynthesis? Then why do plants have chlorophyll-*b* and other accessory pigments?**

Answer Though chlorophyll is the major pigment responsible for trapping light, other thylakoid pigments like chlorophyll-*b*, xanthophylls and carotenoids, which are called accessory pigments, also absorb light and transfer the energy to chlorophyll-*a*. Indeed, they not only enable a wider range of wavelength of incoming light to be utilised for photosynthesis but also protect chlorophyll-*a* from photo oxidation.

Question 6. Why is the colour of a leaf kept in the dark frequently yellow or pale green? Which pigment do you think is more stable?

Answer This is due to the interconversion of pigments, *i.e.*, change of green chlorophyll pigment into yellow coloured carotenoids. The carotene pigment is more stable.

Question 7. Look at leaves of the same plant on the shady side and compare it with the leaves on the sunny side. Or, compare the potted plants kept in the sunlight with those in the shade. Which of them has leaves that are darker green? Why?

Answer The leaves of the same plant on the sunny side are dark green as compare it with the leaves on the sunny side.

Question 8. The following figure shows the effect of light on the rate of photosynthesis. Based on the graph, answer the following questions

(i) At which point/s (*A*, *B* or *C*) in the curve is light a limiting factor?
(ii) What could be the limiting factor/s in region *A*?
(iii) What do *C* and *D* represent on the curve?

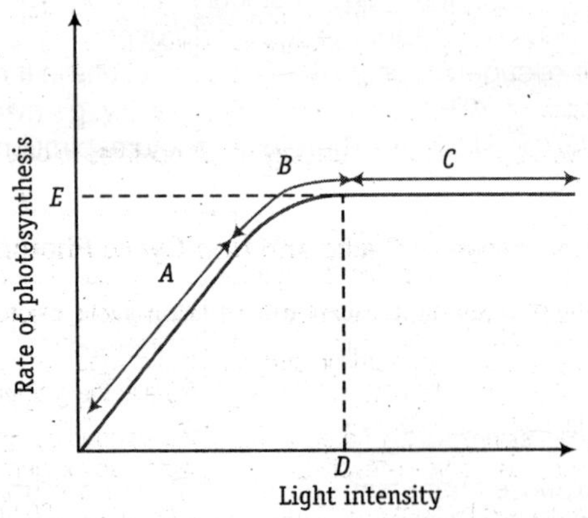

Graph of light intensity on the rate of photosynthesis

Answer

(i) Points *B*-*C* of the curve, the rate did not increase with an increase in its concentration, because light becomes a limiting factor under these conditions.

(ii) In *A* region, the rate of photosynthesis shows proportionate increase up to a certain CO_2 concentration, beyond, which the rate again becomes constant.

(iii) Points *C* and *D* represent that if the light intensity is doubled, CO_2 concentration again becomes limiting factor beyond this concentration.

Question 9. Give comparison between the following

(i) C_3 and C_4-pathways

(ii) Cyclic and non-cyclic photophosphorylation

(iii) Anatomy of leaf in C_3 and C_4-plants

Answer (i) **Comparison between C_3 and C_4-Pathways**

S.N.	C_3-Pathway	C_4-Pathway
1.	The primary acceptor of CO_2 is RuBP, a 5 carbon compound.	The primary acceptor of CO_2 is PEP, a 3 carbon compound.
2.	It operated under low concentration of CO_2 in mesophyll cells.	It can operate under very low CO_2concentration in mesophyll cells.
3.	CO_2 once fixed is not released back.	CO_2 once fixed is released back in bundle sheath cells.
4.	Fixation of one molecule of CO_2 needs 3ATP and 2 $NADPH_2$ molecules. It requires 18 ATP for the synthesis of one molecule of glucose.	C_4-pathway requires 30 ATP for the synthesis of one molecules of glucose.
5.	C_3-cycle operates in all category of plants.	It operates in only C_4-plants.

(ii) **Comparison between Cyclic and Non-Cyclic Photophosphorylation**

S.N.	Cyclic Photophosphorylation	Non-cyclic photophosphorylation
1.	It occurs in photosystem I in stromal or intergranal thylakoids	It is carried out by both PS-I and PS-II in the granal thylakoids.
2.	It is not connected to photolysis of water so no oxygen is evolved.	It is connected with photolysis of water, so oxygen is evolved in it.
3.	It is activated by light of 700 nm wavelength.	It occurs in 680 nm as well as 700 nm wavelength.
4.	It generates ATP only there is no formation of $NADPH_2$.	It produces both ATP as well as $NADPH_2$.
5.	Chlorophyll does not receive any electrons from donor.	The source of electrons is photolysis of water.
6.	The system does not take part in photosynthesis expect in bacteria.	This system is connected with CO_2 fixation and is dominant in green plants.

(iii) **Comparison between Anatomy of Leaf in C_3 and C_4-Plants**

S.N.	C_3 Leaf Anatomy	C_4 Leaf Anatomy
1.	Only one type of chloroplast is present.	Kranz anatony, *i.e.*, two types of cell, each with its own type of chloroplast is present.
2.	Less efficient in photosynthesis than C_4 leavens.	More efficient in photosynthesis than C_3 leaves.
3.	Only mesophyll cells carryout photosynthesis.	Both mesophyll cells and bundle sheath cells carryout photosynthesis.

Selected NCERT Exemplar Problems

Very Short Answer Type Questions

Question 1. Examine the figure

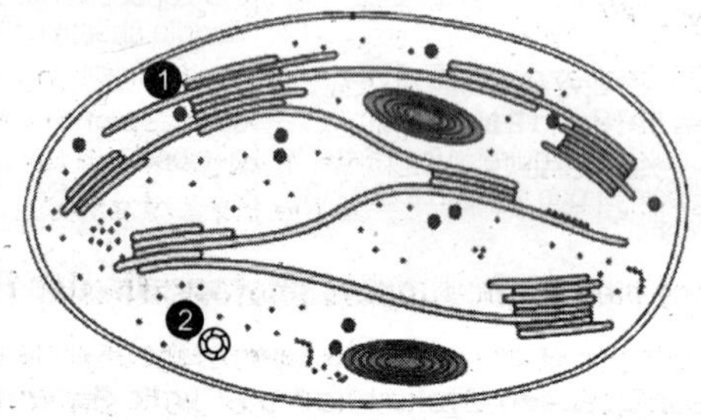

(i) Is this structure present in animal cell or plant cell.
(ii) Can these be passed on to the progeny? How?
(iii) Name the metabolic processes taking place in the places marked (1) and (2).

Answer

(i) Plant cell
(ii) Yes, through female gametes
(iii) In part (1) Photophosphorylation, in part (2) Calvin cycle

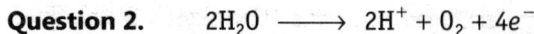

Question 2. $2H_2O \longrightarrow 2H^+ + O_2 + 4e^-$

Based on the above equation, answer the following questions
(i) Where does this reaction take place in plants?
(ii) What is the significance of this reaction?

Answer

(i) Lumen of the thylakoids.

(ii) O_2 is evolved during this reaction, moreover electrons are made available to PS-II continuously.

Question 3. Cyanobacteria and some other photosynthetic bacteria don't have chloroplasts. How do they conduct photosynthesis?

Answer Cyanobacteria and some other photosynthetic bacteria have thylakoids suspended freely in the cytoplasm (*i.e.*, they are not enclosed in membrane) and they have bacteriochlorophyll.

Question 4. (i) NADP reductase enzyme is located on ....

(ii) Breakdown of proton gradient leads to release of ....

Answer (i) Grana-lamellae, (ii) Energy

Question 5. Can girdling experiments be done in monocots? If yes, How? If no, why not?

Answer Yes, girdling experiments can be performed in monocots. They also have phloem tissue through which food prepared in the leaves is transported to various parts of the plants. It involves the removal of a ring of bark up to the depth of phloem layer on the trunk of a tree.

Question 6. Does moonlight support photosynthesis? Find out.

Answer The intensity of moonlight is several thousands times less than that of direct sunlight, insufficient for the light-dependent phase of photosynthesis.

Question 7. Where is NADP reductase enzyme located in the chloroplast? What is the role of this enzyme in proton gradient development?

Answer NADP reductase enzyme located in the grana-lamellae of the chloroplast. This enzyme causes breakdown of proton gradient to release energy.

Question 8. ATPase enzyme consists of two parts. What are those parts? How are they arranged in the thylakoid membrane? Conformational change occur in which part of the enzyme?

Answer ATPase enzyme consists of two parts, *i.e.*, a stalk and a headpiece. These two parts are located completely across the inner mitochondrial membrane. The conformational changes occur in the headpiece of this enzyme.

Question 9. Which products formed during the light reaction of photosynthesis are used to drive the dark reaction?

Answer ATP and NADP formed during the light reaction of photosynthesis are used to drive the dark reaction.

Question 10. What is the basis for designating C_3 and C_4-pathways of photosynthesis?

Answer **C_3 pathway** or Calvin cycle represents phase-II, *i.e.,* dark reaction of photosynthesis. In Calvin cycle, a 5-C pentose sugar, Ribulose diphosphate (RuDP) acts as a first acceptor of CO_2. **C_4 pathway** this is also called Hatch-slack pathway. In this pathway, the first CO_2 acceptor is 3-C phosphoenol pyruvate (PEP).

Short Answer Type Questions

Question 1. Succulents are known to keep their stomata closed during the day to check transpiration. How do they meet their photosynthetic CO_2 requirements?

Answer Succulents (water storing) plants such as cacti, fix CO_2 into organic compound using PEP carboxylase at night, when the stomata are open.

Question 2. Do reactions of photosynthesis called, as 'dark reaction' need light? Explain.

Answer A dark reaction is done in the Calvin cycle. Light is not needed at the time of the dark reaction but it also doesn't hinder the reaction if there is light at that time.

Question 3. How are photosynthesis and respiration related to each other?

Answer **Relation between Photosynthesis and Respiration** In both ways, cells gain energy. In photosynthesis, cells use solar energy to produce glucose and oxygen from carbon dioxide and water. In cellular respiration, cells make ATP (which is used as energy by the cells) and consume oxygen during the conversion of glucose to carbon dioxide and water.

Question 4. If a green plant is kept in dark with proper ventilation, can this plant carry out photosynthesis? Can anything be given as supplement to maintain its growth or survival?

Answer It would die because plants need sun light for photosynthesis. The sun is the only thing that will help plants make their own food. If there is a small opening in the room that let in sunlight however, the plant would grow towards the opening or the light to get it's food.

Question 5. Photosynthetic organisms occur at different depths in the ocean. Do they receive qualitatively and quantitatively the same light? How do they adapt to carry out photosynthesis under these conditions?

Answer Photosynthetic organisms at different depths in the ocean do not receive qualitatively and quantitatively the same light. The plants, which require wholesome light remain in the shallow waters of the banks. Algae which can tolerate more dilutions of light penetrate deeper inside water. Green algae remain in the shore line, brown algae descend to intermediate depths, while red algae form the limit below where no other autotrophic plants can grow.

Question 6. In tropical rain forests, the canopy is thick and shorter plants growing below it, receive filtered light. How are they able to carry out photosynthesis?

Answer The light filtering through the canopy of broad leaved trees is richer in red waves and poorer in blue-violet radiations. Red rays induce maximum growth and development in leaves and stems. Blue-violet radiations keep the growth under check but the plant organs are otherwise normal .

Question 7. What conditions enable RuBisCO to function as an oxygenase? Explain the ensuring process.

Answer Carboxylation is the most crucial step of the Calvin cycle, where CO_2 is utilised for the carboxylation of RuBP. This reaction is catalysed by the enzyme RuBP carboxylase which results in the formation of two molecules of 3-PGA. Since, this enzyme also has an oxygenation activity, it would be more correct to call it RuBP carboxylase-oxygenase or RuBisCO.

Question 8. Explain how during light reaction of photosynthesis, ATP synthesis is a chemiosmotic phenomenon.

Answer Chemiosmosis requires a membrane, a proton pump, a proton gradient and ATPase. Energy is used to pump protons across a membrane, to create a gradient or a high concentration of protons within the thylakoid lumen. ATPase enzyme catalyses the formation of ATP. Along with the NADPH produced by the movement of electrons, the ATP will be used immediately in the biosynthetic reaction taking place in the stroma, responsible for fixing CO_2 and synthesis of sugars.

Question 9. Find out how Melvin Calvin worked out the complete biosynthetic pathway for the synthesis of sugar.

Answer Calvin discovered the 'Calvin cycle' by choosing a suitable organism to work with a single-celled alga called *Chlorella*, devising a claver piece of apparatus and by applying two carefully-chosen techniques.

(i) The first technique he used was to track the path of carbon during photosynthesis by using a radioactive isotope, ^{14}C.

(ii) The second technique was two-dimensional paper chromatography. By this technique, the separated the substances, which the had extracted from the cells.

At the end, he was able to describe the sequence of compounds through which the carbon passed as it was converted from carbon dioxide to carbohydrate. He discovered that it was in fact a cycle of reactions, hence the name 'Calvin cycle'.

Question 10. Six turns of Calvin cycle are required to generate one mole of glucose. Explain.

Answer Calvin cycle is a series of reactions that lead to the formation of glucose. The steps involve utilisation of 2 molecules of ATP for phosphorylation and two of NADPH for reduction per CO_2 molecule fixed. The fixation of six molecules of CO_2 and six turns of the cycle are required for the removal of one molecule of glucose from the pathway.

Hence, for every CO_2 molecule entering the Calvin cycle, 3 molecules of ATP and 2 of NADPH are required. It is probably to meet this difference in number of ATP and NADPH used in the dark reaction that the cyclic phosphorylation takes place. To make one molecule of glucose six turns of the cycle are required.

Question 11. Complete the flow chart for cyclic photophosphorylation of the photosystem-I.

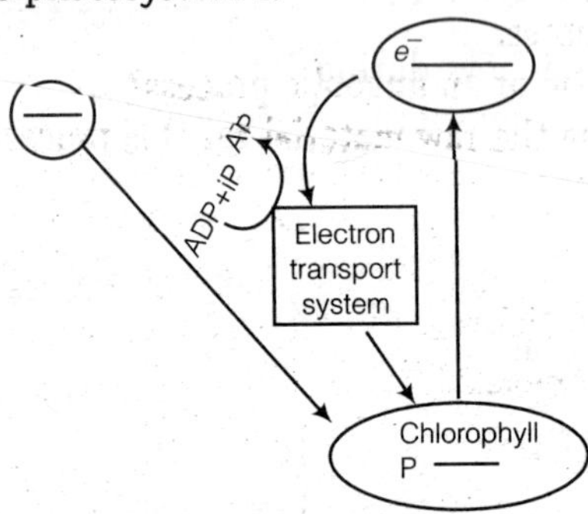

Answer

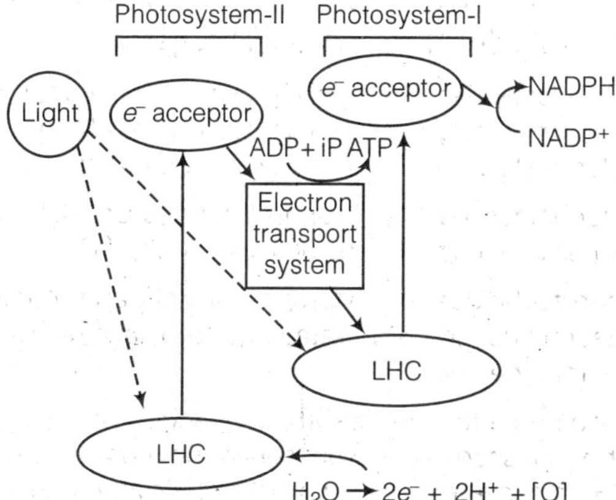

Question 12. In what kind of plants do you come across 'Kranz' anatomy? To which conditions are those plants better adapted? How are these plants better adapted than the plants, which lack this anatomy?

Answer C_4-plants have Kranz anatomy. These plants are better adapted to dry tropical regions. These plants are better adapted than plants which lack this anatomy (Kranz anatomy) because

(i) They can tolerate high temperatures.

(ii) They show a response to highlight intensities.

(iii) They lack a process called photophosphorylation and have greater productivity of biomass.

Question 13. A process is occurring throughout the day, in 'X' organism. Cells are participating in this process. During this process, ATP, CO_2 and water are evolved. It is not a light dependent process.

(i) Name the process.

(ii) Is it a catabolic or an anabolic process?

(iii) What could be the raw material for this process?

Answer

(i) Respiration

(ii) It is a catabolic process

(iii) Glucose, fat or protein.

Question 14. Tomatoes, carrots and chillies are red in colour due to the presence of one pigment. Name the pigment. Is it a photosynthetic pigment?

Answer Lycopene pigment, which is a chromoplast. It is a non-photosynthetic pigment.

Question 15. Why do we believe chloroplast and mitochondria to be semi-autonomous organelle?

Answer Chloroplast and mitochondria are known to be semi-autonomous organelle because they have their own DNA, RNA and enzymes. Thus, they can synthesis their own protein.

Question 16. Observe the diagram and answer the following

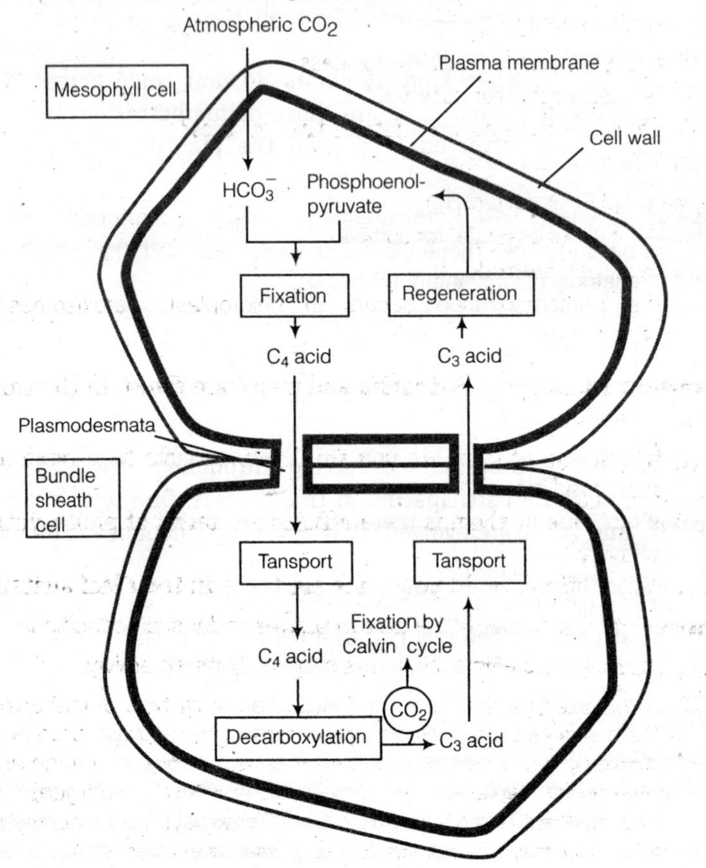

(i) Which group of plants exibits these two types of cells?
(ii) What is the first product of C_4-cycle?
(ii) Which enzyme is there in bundle sheath cells and mesophyll cells?

Answer

(i) C_4-plants, *i.e.*, sugarcane, maize, etc.
(ii) Oxaloacetic acid (OAA).
(iii) The enzyme present in bundle sheath cells is malic enzyme and that present in mesophyll cells is phosphoenol pyruvate carboxylase kinase.

Question 17. A cyclic process is occurring in C_3-plant, which is light dependent and needs O_2. This process doesn't produce energy rather it consumes energy.

(i) Can you name the given process?
(ii) Is it essential for survival?
(iii) What are the end products of this process?
(iv) Where does it occur?

Answer (i) Photorespiration.
(ii) No, it is not essential for survival.
(iii) Hydrogen peroxide
(iv) The photorespiration occurs in chloroplast, peroxisomes and mitochondria.

Question 18. Suppose *Euphorbia* and maize are grown in the tropical area.

(i) Which one of them do you think will be able to survive under such conditions?
(ii) Which one of them is more efficient in terms of photosynthetic activity?
(iii) What difference do you think are there in their leaf anatomy?

Answer (i) *Euphorbia* will be able to survive under such conditions.
(ii) Maize is more efficient in terms of photosynthetic activiy.
(iii) The maize is a C_4-plants have Kranz anatomy type of leaf anatomy. The bundle sheath cells are characterised by having a large number of chloroplasts, thick walls impervious to gaseous exchange and no intercellular spaces. In *Euphorbia*, which undergoes CAM (Crassulacean Acid Metabolism) both pathways occur in mesophyll cells only they do not have Kranz anatomy. Their stomata remain closed during the day.

Long Answer Type Questions

Question 1. Is it correct to say that photosynthesis occurs only in leaves of a plant? Besides leaves, what are the other parts that may be capable of carrying out photosynthesis? Justify.

Answer Although all cells in the green parts of a plant have chloroplasts, most of the energy is captured in the leaves. The cells in the interior tissues of a leaf, called the mesophyll, can contain between 450000 and 800000 chloroplasts for every square millimeter of leaf. The surface of the leaf is uniformly coated with a water-resistant waxy cuticle that protects the leaf from excessive evaporation of water and decreases the absorption of ultraviolet or blue light to reduce heating. The transparent epidermis layer allows light to pass through to the palisade mesophyll cells, where most of the photosynthesis takes place. The green stems are also capable of performing photosynthesis.

Question 2. The entire process of photosynthesis consists of a number of reactions. Where in the cell do each of these take place?

(a) Synthesis of ATP and NADPH ....
(b) Photolysis of water ....
(c) Fixation of CO_2 ....
(d) Synthesis of sugar molecule ....
(e) Synthesis of starch ....

Answer

(a) Synthesis of ATP and NADPH in **thylakoids**.
(b) Photolysis of water occurs in **inner side of thylakoid membrane**.
(c) Fixation of CO_2 occurs in **stroma of chloroplast**.
(d) Synthesis of sugar molecule occurs in **chloroplast**.
(e) Synthesis of starch occurs in **cytoplasm**.

Question 3. Under what conditions are C_4-plants superior to C_3?

Answer C_4-plants can produce more sugar than C_4-plants in conditions of high light and temperature. Many important crop plants are C_4-plants including maize, sorghum, sugarcane and millet. C_4-plants are superior to C_3 as

(i) They have a special type of leaf anatomy.
(ii) They tolerate higher temperatures.
(iii) They show response to highlight intensities.
(iv) They lack a process called photorespiration.
(v) They have greater productivity of biomass.

Question 4. In the figure given below, the black line (upper) indicates action spectrum for photosynthesis and the lighter line (lower) indicates the absorption spectrum of chlorophyll-*a*, answer the followings

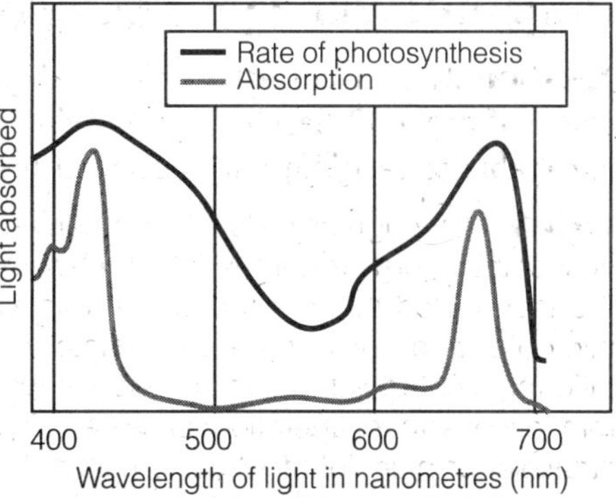

(i) What does the action spectrum indicate? How can we plot an action spectrum? Explain with an example.

(ii) How can we derive an absorption spectrum for any substance?

(iii) If chlorophyll-*a* is responsible for light reaction of photosynthesis, why do the action spectrum and absorption spectrum not overlap?

Answer

(i) The effectiveness of different wavelengths of light on photosynthesis is measured and plotted the amount of action. This is called the action spectrum of photosynthesis.

(ii) Absorption of different wavelengths of light by a particular pigment is plotted and is called the absorption spectra of that pigment.

(iii) Chlorophyll-*a* is responsible for light reaction of photosynthesis, but the action spectrum and absorption spectrum do not overlap because though chlorophyll is the main pigments responsible for absorption of light, other thylakoid pigments like chlorophyll-*b*, xanthophylls and carotenoids, which are called accessory pigments also absorb and transfer the energy to chlorophyll-*a*. Indeed they not only enable a wider range of wavelength of incoming light to be utilised for photosynthesis but also protect chlorophyll-*a* from photo-oxidation.

Question 5. What are the important events and end products of the light reaction?

Light reaction or the photochemical phase include light absorption. Water splitting, oxygen release and the formation of high-energy chemical intermediaries, *i.e.*, ATP and NADPH. The pigments are organised in photosystem I (PS-I) and photosystem-II (PS-II). The pigments help to make photosynthesis more efficient by absorbing different wavelengths of light. Products of light reaction (cyclic and non-cyclic) are ATP, $NADPH_2$ and O_2.

The oxygen is liberated from the green plants. ATP and $NADPH_2$ are used in dark reaction for the reduction of CO_2 to form carbohydrates. Hence, the ATP and $NADPH_2$-the products of light reaction are called assimilatory power.

Question 6. In the diagram shown below label *A, B, C*. What type of phosphorylation is possible in this?

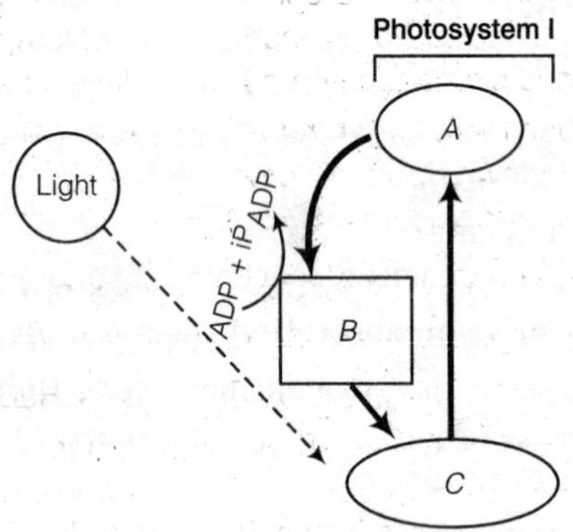

Answer It is the process called cyclic photophosphorylation. Here, '*A*' is *e*-acceptor, '*B*' is electron transport system and '*C*' is chlorophyll P_{700}. In cyclic photophosporylation, only PS-I is functional. The electron is circulated within the photosystem and the phosphorylation occurs due to cyclic flow of electrons.

Question 7. Why is the RuBisCO enzyme more appropriately called RUBP carboxylase-oxygenase and what important role does it play in photosynthesis?

Answer The RuBisCO enzyme more appropriately called RuBP.

This is due to the fact that its active site can bind to both CO_2 and O_2^- hence, the name RuBisCO. It has a much greater affinity for CO_2 than for O_2. This binding is competitive. It is the relative concentration of O_2 and CO_2 that determines, which of the two will bind to the enzyme.

Importance In C_3-plants, some O_2 does bind to RuBisCO, hence CO_2 fixation is decreased. Here the RuBP instead of being converted to 2 molecules of PGA binds with O_2 to form one molecule and phosphoglycolate in a pathway called photorespiration. In C_4 plants, photorespiration does not occur. This is because they have a mechanism that increases the concentration of CO_2 at the enzyme site. They release more CO_2. This results in increasing the intracellular concentration of CO_2. In turn, the RuBisCO functions as a carboxylase minimising the oxygenase activity.

Question 8. What special anatomical features are displayed by leaves of C_4-plants? How do they provide advantage over the structure of C_3-plants?

Answer The particularly large cells around the vascular bundles of the C_4-pathway plants are called bundle sheath cells and the leaves which have such anatomy are said to have 'Kranz' anatomy. 'Kranz' means 'wreath' and is a reflection of the arrangement of cells. The bundle sheath cells may form several layers around the vascular bundles; they are characterised by having a large number of chloroplasts, thick walls impervious to gaseous exchange and no intercellular spaces.

C_4-plants can produce more sugar than C_3-plants in conditions of high light and temperature. Many important crop plants are C_4-plants including maize, sorghum, sugarcane, and millet.

Question 9. Name the two important enzymes of C_3 and C_4-pathway, respectively? What important role do they play in fixing CO_2?

Answer The important enzymes of C_3-cycle is RuBisCO and that of C_4-pathway is PEP carboxylase. They help in the fixation of CO_2. In C_3-cycle the CO_2 acceptor is ribulose-1, 5 diphosphate (RuDP) and the first stable product is phophoglyceric acid (PGA). In C_4-cycle, the CO_2 acceptor is PEP carboxylase and the first stable product is phosphoglyceric acid (PGA).

Question 10. Why is RuBisCO enzyme the most abundant enzyme in the world?

Answer The enzyme ribulose-1, 5-bisphosphate carboxylase/oxygenase, most commonly known by the shorter name RuBisCO is used in the Calvin cycle to catalyse the first major step of carbon fixation. RuBisCO is thought to be the most abundant protein in the world since it is present in every plant that undergoes photosynthesis and molecular synthesis through the Calvin cycle. It makes about 20-25% of the soluble protein in leaves and is made on the Earth at the rate of about 1000 kg/s. It is estimated that every person on Earth is supported by about 44 kg of RuBisCO.

Question 11. Why does not photorespiration take place in C_4-plants?

Answer In C_4-plants, photorespiration does not occur. This is because they have a mechanism that increases the concentration of CO_2 at the enzyme site. This takes place when the C_4-acid from the mesophyll is broken down in the bundle sheath cells to release CO_2. This results in increasing the intracellular concentration of CO_2. In turn, this ensures that the RuBisCO functions as a carboxylase minimising the oxygenase activity.

14

Respiration in Plants

Important Points

1. **Cellular Respiration** Mechanism of breakdown of food materials within the cell to release energy.
2. **Respiration** Breaking of the C—C bonds of complex compounds through oxidation within the cells, leading to release of considerable amount of energy is called respiration.
3. **Respiratory Substrates** The compounds that are oxidised during this process are known as respiratory substrates.
4. During oxidation within a cell, all energy contained in respiratory substrates are released in small stepswise reactions controlled by enzymes and it is trapped as chemical energy in the form of ATP.
5. ATP acts as the energy currency of the cell. This energy trapped in ATP is utilised in various energy requiring processes of the organisms and the carbon skeleton produced during respiration is used as precursors for biosynthesis of other molecules in the cell.
6. **Reaction**

$$\underset{\text{Carbohydrate}}{C_6H_{12}O_6} + \underset{\text{Oxygen}}{6O_2} \longrightarrow \underset{\text{Carbon dioxide}}{6CO_2} + \underset{\text{Water}}{6H_2O} + \text{Energy}$$

7. **Basic Scheme of Respiration**

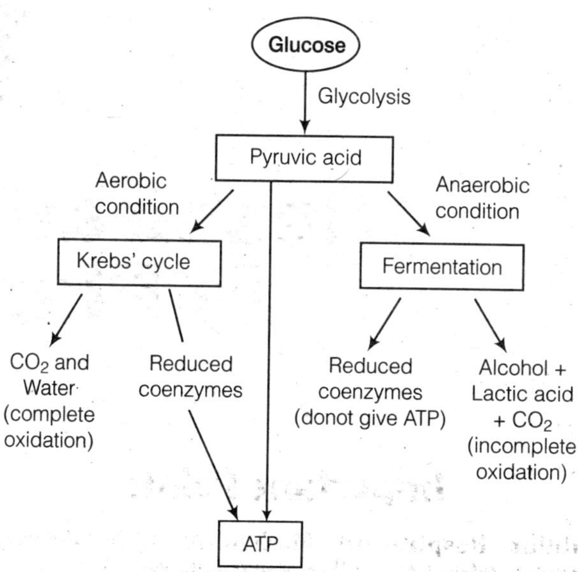

8. **Glycolysis**
   (i) Originated from Greek words '*glycos*' for sugar *lysis* for splitting.
   (ii) Scheme was given by **Gustav Embden**, **Otto Meyerhof** and **J Parnas** and is often referred to as EMP pathway.
   (iii) Occur in cytoplasm of the cell in all living organisms.
   (iv) Glucose undergoes partial oxidation to form two molecules of pyruvic acid.

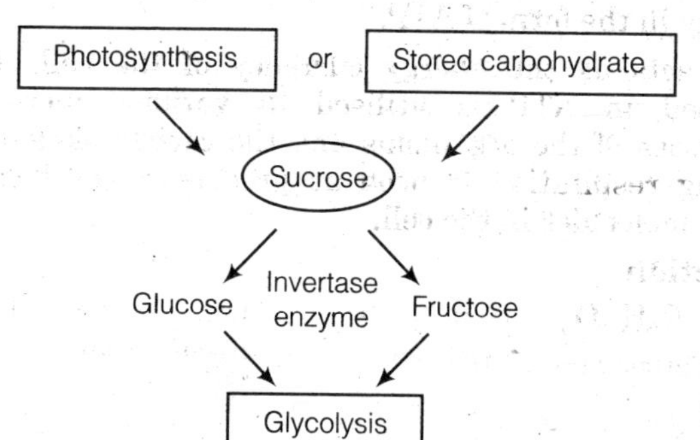

(v) Steps

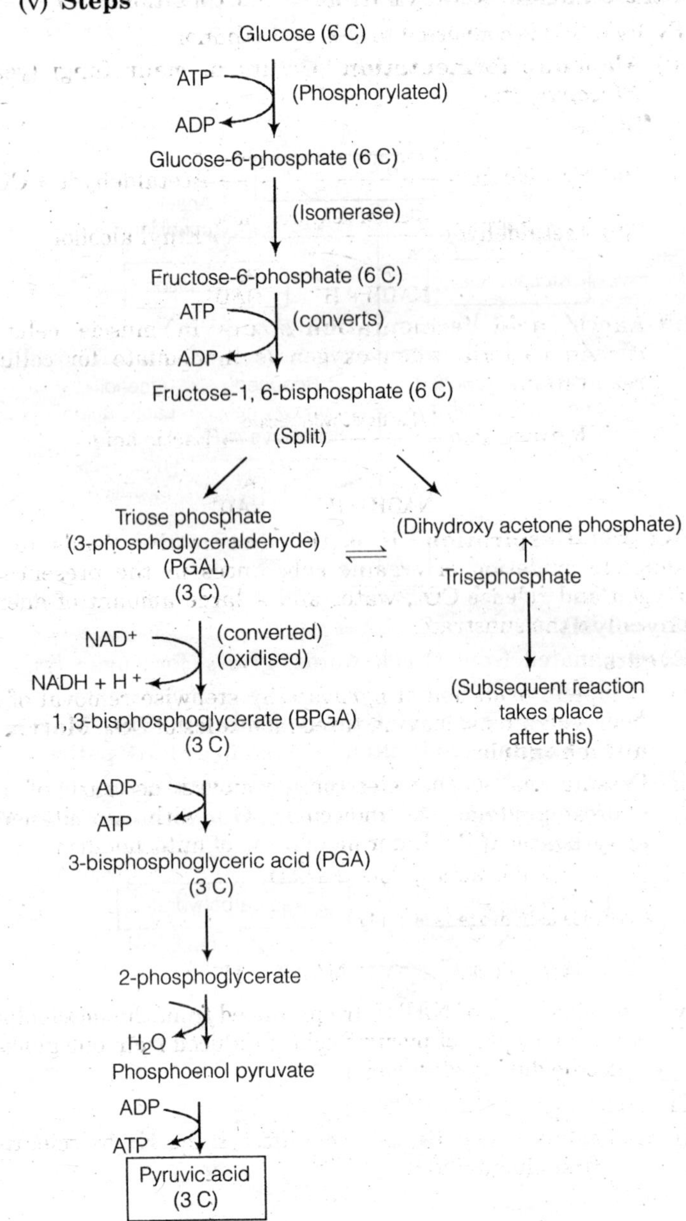
Glucose (6 C)
ATP
(Phosphorylated)
ADP
Glucose-6-phosphate (6 C)
(Isomerase)
Fructose-6-phosphate (6 C)
ATP
(converts)
ADP
Fructose-1, 6-bisphosphate (6 C)
(Split)
Triose phosphate
(3-phosphoglyceraldehyde)
(PGAL)
(3 C)
(Dihydroxy acetone phosphate)
Trisephosphate
(Subsequent reaction
takes place
after this)
NAD^+
(converted)
(oxidised)
$NADH + H^+$
1, 3-bisphosphoglycerate (BPGA)
(3 C)
ADP
ATP
3-bisphosphoglyceric acid (PGA)
(3 C)
2-phosphoglycerate
H_2O
Phosphoenol pyruvate
ADP
ATP
Pyruvic acid
(3 C)

9. **Fermentation** occurs under anaerobic conditions.
   Pyruvic acid is converted to CO_2 and ethanol.
   (i) **Alcoholic fermentation** Occurs in many fungi (yeast, *Rhizopus,* etc).
   Steps

   $$\text{(a) Pyruvic Acid} \xrightarrow{\text{Pyruvate decarboxylase}} \text{Acetaldehyde} + CO_2$$

   $$\text{(b) Acetaldehyde} \xrightarrow{\text{Alcohol dehydrogenase}} \text{Ethyl alcohol}$$

   $$\text{NADH} + H^+ \curvearrowright \text{NAD}^+$$

   (ii) **Lactic acid fermentation** occurs in muscle cells or certain bacteria when oxygen is inadequate for cellular respiration.

   $$\text{Pyruvic acid} \xrightarrow{\text{Lactic dehydrogenase}} \text{Lactic acid}$$

   $$\text{NADH} + H^+ \curvearrowright \text{NAD}^+$$

10. **Aerobic Respiration** It is the process that leads to a complete oxidation of organic substances in the presence of oxygen and release CO_2, water and a large amount of energy present in the substrate.
   Events
   (i) Complete oxidation of pyruvate by stepwise removal of all hydrogen atoms, leaving three molecules of CO_2. **Matrix of mitochondria**.
   (ii) Passing on of the electrons removed as part of the hydrogen atoms to molecular O_2 with simultaneous synthesis of ATP – Inner membrane of mitochondria.
   (iii)

   $$\text{Pyruvic acid} + \text{Co-A} + \text{NAD}^+ \xrightarrow[\text{Mg}^{2+}]{\text{Pyruvate dehydrogenase}} \text{Acetyl Co-A} + CO_2 + \text{NADH} + H^+.$$

   (iv) Two molecules of NADH are produced from the metabolism of two molecules of pyruvic acid (produced from one glucose molecule during glycolysis).
11. **Tricarboxylic Acid Cycle**
   (i) Commonly called Krebs' cycle after Hans Krebs scientist, who first elucidated it.

Steps

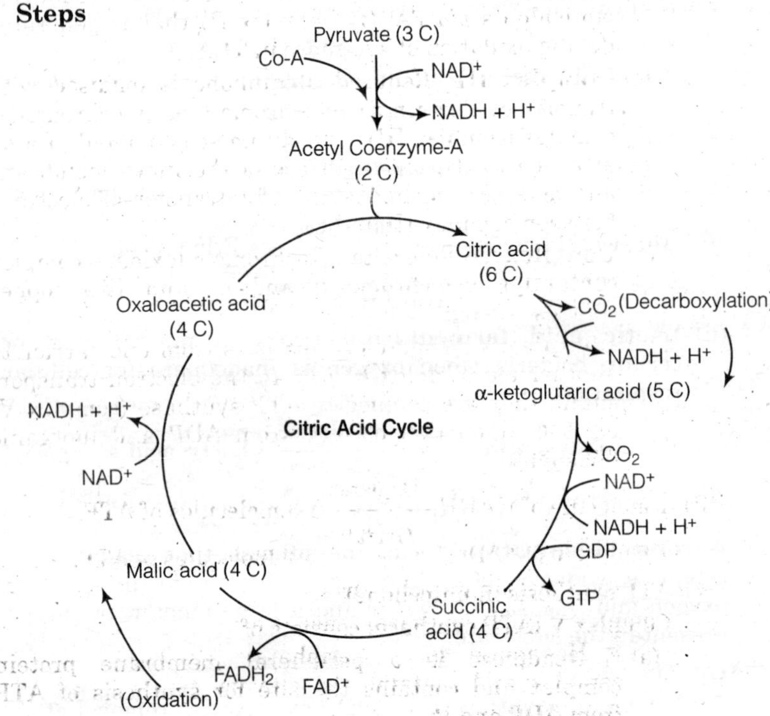

(ii) **Reaction**

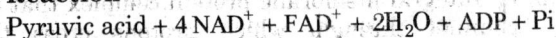

$$\text{Pyruvic acid} + 4\,NAD^+ + FAD^+ + 2H_2O + ADP + Pi \xrightarrow{\text{Mitochondrial matrix}} 3CO_2 + 4NADH + 4H^+ + FADH_2 + ATP$$

12. **Electron Transport System (ETS) and Oxidative Phosphorylation**

(i) Process occurs to release and utilise energy stored in $NADH + H^+$ and $FADH_2$.

(ii) The metabolic pathway through which the electron passes from one carrier to another is called Electron Transport System (ETS).

Steps

(a) **Complex I** Electrons from NADH produced in the mitochondrial matrix during citric acid cycle are oxidised by an NADH dehydrogenase. Electrons are then transferred to ubiquinone.

(b) **Complex II** Ubiquinone receives reducing equivalents *via* $FADH_2$ (complex II) that is generated during oxidation of succinate in TCA.

(c) **Complex III** Reduced ubiquinone is oxidised with transfer of electron to cytochrome (*via* cytochrome-bc_1 complex (complex III). Cytochrome-*c* is a small protein attached to the outer surface of the inner membrane and acts as a mobile carrier for transfer of electrons between complex III and IV.

(d) **Complex IV** Refers to cytochrome-*c* (oxidase complex containing cytochromes-*a* and a_3 and two copper centres.

(e) **Complex V** When electrons pass from one carrier to another *via* complex I to IV in the electron transport chain, they are coupled to ATP synthase (complex V) for the production of ATP from ADP and inorganic phosphate.

(iii) 1 molecule of NADH $\xrightarrow{\text{Oxidation}}$ 3 molecules of ATP.

1 molecule of $FADH_2$ $\xrightarrow{\text{Oxidation}}$ 2 molecules of ATP.

(iv) ATP synthesis in mitochondria :

Complex V (ATP synthase) consists of

(a) F_1 Headpiece is a peripheral membrane protein complex and contains the site for synthesis of ATP from ADP and Pi.

(b) F_0 Integral membrane protein complex that forms the channel through, which protons cross the inner membrane.

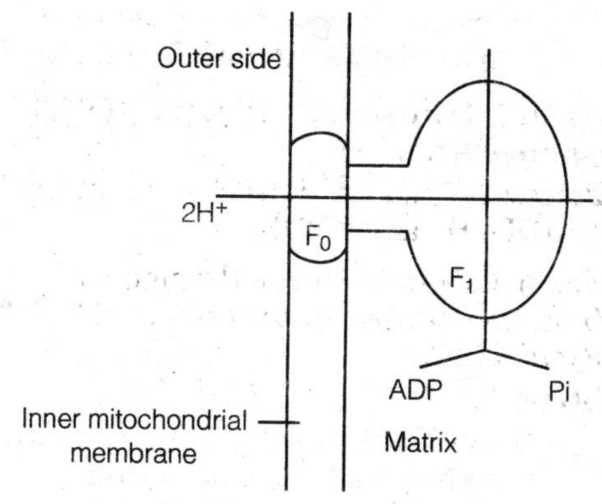

ATP synthesis in mitochondria

(c) Passage of protons through the channel is coupled to the catalytic site of the F_1 component for the production of ATP.

(d) For each ATP produced $2H^+$ passes through F_0 from the intermembrane space to the matrix down the electrochemical proton gradient.

13.

S.N.	Fermentation	Aerobic Respiration
1.	Accounts only a partial breakdown of glucose.	Complete degradation to CO_2 and H_2O.
2.	Net gain of only two molecules of ATP for each molecule of glucose degraded to pyruvic acid.	Many more ATP generated.
3.	NADH is oxidised to NAD^+ rather slowly in fermentation.	Reaction is very vigorous

14. **Amphibolic Pathway** Since, respiratory pathway is involved in both anabolism and catabolism, it is considered as amphibolic pathway.

(i) At each point in respiratory pathway different substrates would enter if they were to be respired and used to derive energy. These compounds would we withdrawn from the respiratory pathway for the synthesis of the said substrates.

(ii) Respiratory pathway comes into picture both during breakdown and synthesis of fatty acid.

(iii) During breakdown and synthesis of protein too respiratory intermediates form the link.

15. **Respiratory Quotient** The ratio of volume of CO_2 evolved to the volume of O_2 consumed in respiration is called **Respiratory Quotient** (RQ)

$$RQ = \frac{\text{Volume of } CO_2 \text{ evolved}}{\text{Volume of } O_2 \text{ evolved}}$$

Substrate	RQ
Carbohydrates	1 (complete oxidation)
Fats	Less than 1
Proteins	0.9

Exercises

Question 1. Differentiate between
(a) Respiration and Combustion
(b) Glycolysis and Krebs' cycle
(c) Aerobic respiration and Fermentation

Answer (a) **Differences between Respiration and Combustion**

S.N.	Respiration	Combustion
1.	It is the breakdown of complex compounds through oxidation within the cells, leading to release of considerable amount of energy.	Combustion is the complete burning of glucose, which produces CO_2 and H_2O and yield energy which is given out as heat.
2.	It is a controlled biochemical process.	It is an uncontrolled physico chemical process.
3.	Many chemical bonds break simultaneously by releasing large amount of energy	Chemical bonds break one after another to release energy.
4.	Enzymes are involved.	Enzymes are not involved.

(b) **Differences between Glycolysis and Krebs' Cycle**

S.N.	Glycolysis	Krebs' Cycle
1.	It is also called as Embden Meyerhof-Parnas (EMP) pathway.	It is also known as citric acid cycle or tricarboxylic acid cycle.
2.	It occurs in the cytosol of prokaryotes as well as eukaryotes.	In eukaryotes, is occurs in matrix of mitochondria and in prokaryotes, it occurs in cytoplasm .
3.	It starts with the oxidation of glucose.	It starts with the oxidation of pyruvic acid.
4.	It is an enzyme-controlled 10 steps process by which glucose, fructose or sucrose is reduced to form pyruvic acid with the production of ATP and $NADH_2$.	It involves 8 steps to oxidise two molecules of acetyl Co-A.

(c) **Differences between Aerobic Respiration and Fermentation**

S.N.	Aerobic Respiration	Fermentation
1.	The presence of O_2 is required for complete oxidation of organic substances.	In complete oxidation of glucose occurs in the absence of oxygen.
2.	It releases CO_2 water and a large amount of energy present in the substrate.	Pyruvic acid is converted to CO_2 and ethanol and less amount of energy is released.
3.	Only to molecules of ATP are produced.	Many molecules of ATP are produced.
4.	NADH is oxidised to NAD^+ slowly.	This reaction is very vigorous under aerobic respiration.

Question 2. What are respiratory substrates? Name the most common respiratory substrate.

Answer The organic substances, which are catabolised in the living cells to release energy are called as respiratory substrates. Though any food stuff-carbohydrate, fat or protein may act as a respiratory substrate, the common respiratory substrate is glucose.

Question 3. Give the schematic representation of glycolysis?

Answer Glycolysis

(i) In this process, glucose undergoes partial oxidation to form two molecules of pyruvic acid.

(ii) In plants, this glucose is derived from sucrose which converted into glucose and fructose by the enzyme, invertase and these two monosaccharides readily enter the glycolytic pathway.

(iii) Glucose and fructose are phosphorylated to give rise to glucose-6-phosphate by the activity of the enzyme hexokinase.

(iv) This phosphorylated form of glucose then isomerises to produce fructose-6-phosphate.

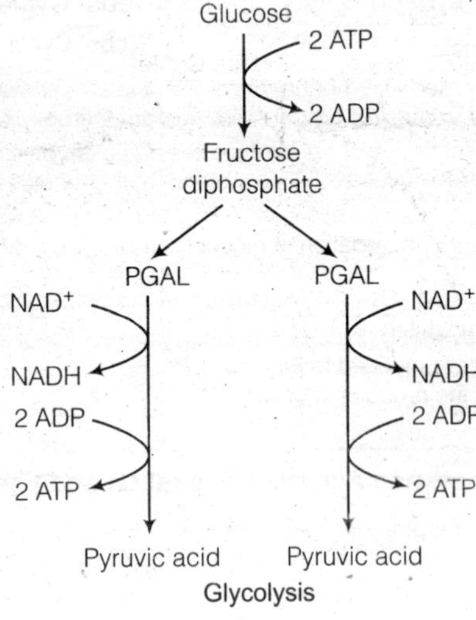

Glycolysis

(v) A chain of ten reactions, under the control of different enzymes, takes place to produce pyruvate from glucose.

(vi) **Utilisation of ATP during glycolysis**

(a) During the conversion of glucose into glucose-6-phosphate.

(b) During the conversion of fructose-6-phosphate to fructose-1, 6-diphosphate.

Question 4. What are the main steps in aerobic respiration? Where does it take place?

Answer The main steps in aerobic respiration are as follows

(i) Glycolytic breakdown of glucose in to pyruvic acid.

(ii) Oxidative decarboxylation of pyruvic acid to acetyl Co-A (acetyl coenzyme-A).

(iii) Kerbs' cycle.

(iv) Terminal oxidation and phosphorylation in respiratory chain. It occurs inside the mitochondrial matrix.

Question 5. Give the schematic representation of an overall view of Krebs' cycle.

Answer **Tricarboxylic Acid Cycle**

(i) The TCA cycle starts with the condensation of acetyl group with oxaloacetic acid (OAA) and water to yield citric acid.

(ii) The reaction is catalysed by the enzyme citrate synthase and a molecule of Co-A is released.

(iii) Citrate is then isomerised to isocitrate.

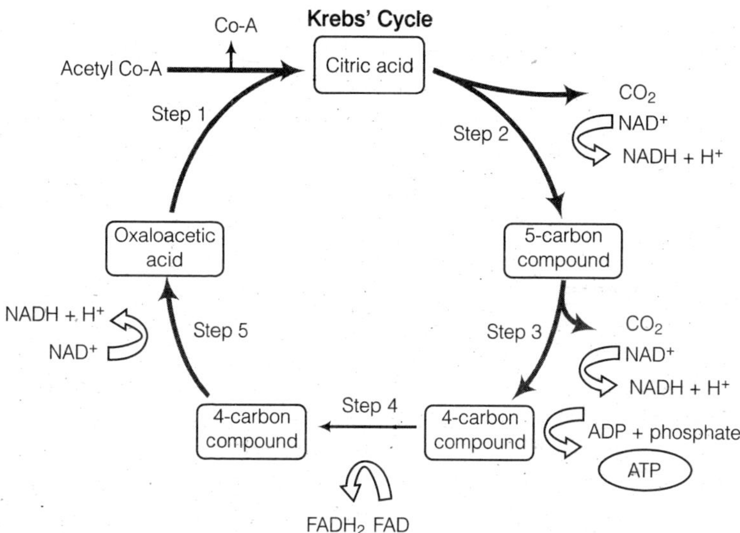

(iv) It is followed by two successive steps of decarboxylation, leading to the formation of → α-ketoglutaric acid and then succinyl Co-A.

(v) During the conversion of succinyl Co-A to succinic acid, a molecule of GTP is synthesised. This is a substrate level phosphorylation.

(vi) In a coupled reaction, GTP is converted to GDP with the simultaneous synthesis of ATP from ADP.

(vii) NAD^+ is reduced to $NADH+H^+$ + and FAD^+ is reduced to $FADH_2$.

The continued oxidation of acetic acid *via* the TCA cycle requires the continued replenishment of oxaloacetic acid, the first member of the cycle. In addition, it also requires regeneration of NAD^+ and FAD^+ from $NADH_2$ and $FADH_2$ respectively.

Question 6. Explain ETS.

Answer Electron Transport System (ETS) The metabolic pathway through which the electron passes from one carrier to another, is called the Electron Transport System (ETS).

(i) It occurs in the inner mitochondrial membrane.

(ii) Electrons from NADH produced in the mitochondrial matrix during citric acid cycle are oxidised by an NADH dehydrogenase (complex-I).

(iii) They are then transferred to ubiquinone located within the inner membrane.

(iv) Ubiquinone also receives reducing equivalents *via* $FADH_2$ (complex-II) that is generated during oxidation of succinate in the citric acid cycle.

(v) The reduced ubiquinone (ubiquinol) is then oxidised with the transfer of electrons to cytochrome-*c* *via* cytochrome-bc_1 complex (complex-III).

(vi) Cytochrome-*c* is a small protein attached to the outer surface of the inner membrane.

(vii) When the electrons pass from one carrier to another *via* complex-I to IV in the electron transport chain, they are coupled to ATP synthase (complex-V) for the production of ATP from ADP and inorganic phosphate.

(viii) The number of ATP molecules synthesised depends on the nature of the electron donor.

(ix) Oxidation of one molecule of NADH gives rise to 3 molecules of ATP, while that of one molecule of $FADH_2$ produces 2 molecules of ATP.

(x) Although, the aerobic process of respiration takes place only in the presence of oxygen, the role of oxygen is limited to the terminal stage of the process. Yet, the presence of oxygen is vital, since, it drives the whole process by removing hydrogen from the system.

(xi) Oxygen acts as the final hydrogen acceptor.

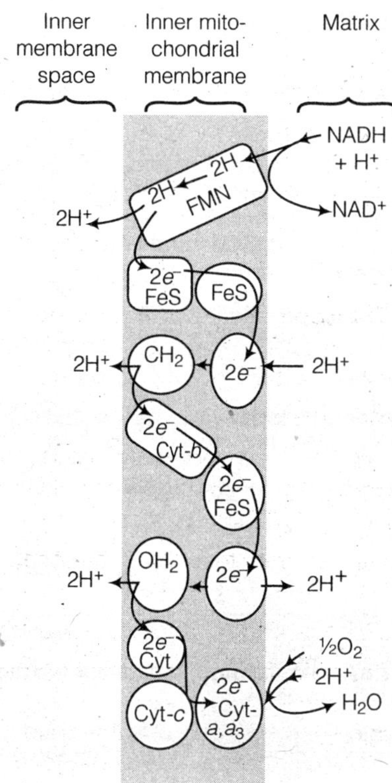

Electron Transport System (ETS)

Question 7. Distinguish between the following

(a) Aerobic respiration and anaerobic respiration
(b) Glycolysis and fermentation
(c) Glycolysis and citric acid cycle

Answer

(a) **Differences between Aerobic and Anaerobic Respiration**

S.N.	Aerobic Respiration	Anaerobic Respiration
1.	Presence of oxygen is essential.	Occurs without oxygen.
2.	Complete oxidation of substrates occurs into CO_2 and H_2O.	Incomplete degradations of substrates.
3.	End products are non-toxic.	End products are toxic when accumulated in large amount.

S.N.	Aerobic Respiration	Anaerobic Respiration
4.	Involves glycolysis, Krebs' cycle and terminal oxidation.	Involves only glycolysis followed by incomplete breakdown of pyruvic acid.
5.	36 ATP molecules are produced from each glucose molecule.	Only two molecules of ATP are produced from each glucose molecule.

(b) **Differences between Glycolysis and Fermentation**

S.N.	Glycolysis	Fermentation
1.	It occurs in cytoplasm of the cell and in all living things.	It occurs in yeast and muscle cells in animals when oxygen is not sufficient for cellular respiration.
2.	Glucose undergoes partial oxidation to form two molecules of pyruvic acid.	The enzyme like pyruvic acid decarboxylase and alcohol dehydrogenase catalyse these reactions.
3.	The end products are CO_2, H_2O and energy.	The end products are CO_2 and ethanol and in animal cells lactic acid is released.

(c) Refer to Ans. 1 (b) in this chapter.

Question 8. What are the assumptions made during the calculation of net gain of ATP?

Answer The calculations of net gain of ATP can be made only on certain assumptions

(i) There is a sequential, orderly pathway functioning, with one substrate forming the next and with glycolysis, TCA cycle and ETS pathway following one after another.

(ii) The NADH synthesised in glycolysis is transferred into the mitochondria and undergoes oxidative phosphorylation.

(iii) None of the intermediates in the pathway are utilised to synthesise any other compound.

(iv) Only glucose is being respired-no other alternative substrates are entering in the pathway at any of the intermediary stages.

But this kind of assumptions are not really valid in a living system. All pathways work simultaneously and do not take place one after another. Substrates enter the pathways and are withdrawn from it as and when necessary; ATP is utilised as and when needed; enzymatic rates are controlled by multiple means. In over all steps, there is a net gain of 36 ATP molecules during aerobic respiration of one molecule of glucose.

Question 9. Discuss 'the respiratory pathway is an amphibolic pathway.'

Answer **Amphibolic Pathway** Glucose is the favoured substrate for respiration. All carbohydrates are usually first converted into glucose before they are used for respiration. Other substrates can also be respired but then they do not enter the respiratory pathway at the first step.

Since, respiration involves breakdown as well as synthesis of substrates, the respiratory process involves both catabolism and anabolism. That is why respiratory pathway is considered to be an amphibolic pathway rather than as a catabolic one.

Question 10. Define RQ. What is its value for fats?

Answer **Respiratory Quotient** The ratio of the volume of CO_2 evolved to the volume of O_2 consumed in respiration is called the respiratory quotient (RQ) or respiratory ratio.

$$RQ = \frac{\text{Volume of } CO_2 \text{ evolved}}{\text{Volume of } O_2 \text{ consumed}}$$

The respiratory quotient depends upon the type of respiratory substrate used during respiration.

For fats, its value is less than 1. For example, RQ for a fatty acid, tripalmitin, if used as a substrate is shown as

$$\underset{\text{Tripalmitin}}{2(C_{51}H_{96}O_6)} + 145\,O_2 \longrightarrow 102CO_2 + 98\,H_2O + \text{energy}$$

$$RQ = \frac{102\,CO_2}{145\,O_2} = 0.7$$

$$RQ = 0.7$$

Question 11. What is oxidative phosphorylation?

Answer The final step of aerobic respiration is the oxidation of 10 molecules of NADH+ H^+ and 2 molecules of $FADH_2$ generated from a molecules of a glucose. These are oxidised in the presence of oxygen through respiration chain. In this step, oxygen from the atmosphere is used for the oxidation of reduced co-enzymes and it is called **terminal oxidation**. This is also associated with ATP synthesis, so also called as oxidative phosphorylation.

Thus, the production of ATP with the help of energy liberated during oxidation of reduced co-enzymes and terminal oxidation is called oxidative phosphorylation. Oxidative phosphorylation is an endothermic process that occurs on the inner membrane including the cristae of mitochondria (eukaryotes) and inner side to cell membrane or mesosomes (prokaryotes).

Question 12. What is the significance of step-wise release of energy in respiration?

Answer During oxidation within a cell, all the energy contained in respiratory substrates is not released free in a single step. It is released in a series of slow step wise reactions controlled by enzymes and it is trapped as chemical energy in the form of ATP. The significance of this step-wise release of energy is that some energy is used to synthesise ATP. This ATP is stored for the later utilisation wherever required. Hence, ATP acts as the energy currency of cell. The energy stored in ATP can be utilized following:

(i) In various energy requiring processes of organisms.

(ii) The carbon skeleton produced during respiration is used as precursors for the synthesis of other molecules.

Selected NCERT Exemplar Problems

Very Short Answer Type Questions

Question 1. Explain the term 'energy currency'. Which substance acts as energy currency in plants and animals?

Answer Energy currency of the cell is used for the compounds which act as reservoir of energy storage and its discharge. ATP (adenosine triphosphate) acts as energy currency in plants and animals.

Question 2. Different substrates get oxidised during respiration. How does respiratory quotient (RQ) indicate which type of substrate, *i.e.*, carbohydrate, fat or protein is getting oxidised?

RQ = A/B

What do A and B stand for?

What type of substrates have RQ of 1, < 1 or > 1?

Answer A stands for volume of carbon dioxide released and B stands for volume of oxygen released.

The respiratory quotient of carbohydrates is 1, that of proteins and fats is less 1 and succulents have RQ more than one.

Question 3. F_0-F_1 particles participate in the synthesis of ....

Answer ATP(Adenosine Triphosphate) the energy currency of the cell.

Question 4. When does anaerobic respiration occur in man and yeast?

Answer Anaerobic respiration occurs in man in the situation of deficiency of oxygen during cellular respiration. In such situation, pyruvic acid is reduced to lactic acid by the lactate dehydrogenase. In yeast also, anaerobic respiration occurs in the condition of absence of oxygen.

Question 5. The product of aerobic glycolysis in skeletal muscle and anaerobic fermentation in yeast are respectively .... and ....

Answer Lactic acid and ethyl alcohol.

Short Answer Type Questions

Question 1. If a person is feeling dizzy, glucose or fruit juice is given immediately but not a cheese sandwich, which might have more energy. Explain.

Answer A person is feeling dizzy, glucose or fruit juice is given immediately because it is readily oxidised and oxidation of 1 gm of glucose yield more energy than a cheese sandwich which is a fat oxidation of 1 gm of fat yield less energy.

Question 2. What is meant by the statement 'aerobic respiration is more efficient'?

Answer The aerobic respiration is a high energy yielding process. During the process of aerobic respiration as many as 36 molecules of ATP are produced for every molecule of glucose that is utilised.

This shows that aerobic produced much more energy than anaerobic respiration, which produces only 2 ATP molecules.

Question 3. The energy yield in terms of ATP is higher in aerobic respiration than during anaerobic respiration. Why is there anaerobic respiration even in organisms that live in aerobic condition like human beings and angiosperms?

Answer The anaerobic respiration occur even in organisms that live in aerobic condition like human beings and angiosperms under conditions of oxygen scarcity that happens in the muscle tissue. Under intense use, muscles demand too much energy (ATP) and consume much more oxygen to produce that energy. This high consumption leads to oxygen scarcity and the muscle cells begin to make lactic acid by anaerobic respiration trying to fulfill their energetic needs. Similarly, yeast cells under deficient conditions carry out anaerobic respiration .

Question 4. Oxygen is an essential requirement for aerobic respiration but it enters the respiratory process at the end? Discuss.

Answer Oxygen enters the respiratory process at the end because an element of strong electronegativity to pull the electrons down the chain is needed. It ensures that protons are pumped into the outer lumen of the mitochondria, where they can come down their concentration gradient through ATP synthase making ATP. The oxygen picks up electrons and protons, thus forming water.

Question 5. Respiration is an energy releasing and enzymatically controlled catabolic process which involves a step-wise oxidative breakdown of organic substances inside living cells. In this statement about respiration explain the meaning of I step-wise oxidative breakdown II organic substances (used as substrates).

Answer

I. **Step wise oxidative breakdown** The series of reactions transfers the energy of glucose to ATP.
II. **Organic substances** (used as substrates) The organic substances, which are catabolised in the living cells to release energy are called as respiratory substrates. Though any food stuff-carbohydrate, fat or protein may act as a respiratory substrate, the common respiratory substrate is glucose because it can be oxidised easily and is present abundantly.

Question 6. Comment on the statement. Respiration is an energy producing process but ATP is being used in some steps of the process.

Answer Respiration is a complex oxidative process implying the formation of several intermediate molecules until finally, water is produced and ATP is released. Although ATP molecules are consumed in the glycolysis and Kerbs' cycle, there is also production of more molecules of ATP, thus a positive balance of ATP molecules is obtained.

Question 7. The figure given below shows the steps in glycolysis. Fill in the missing steps *A, B, C, D* and also indicate whether ATP is being used up or released at step *E*?

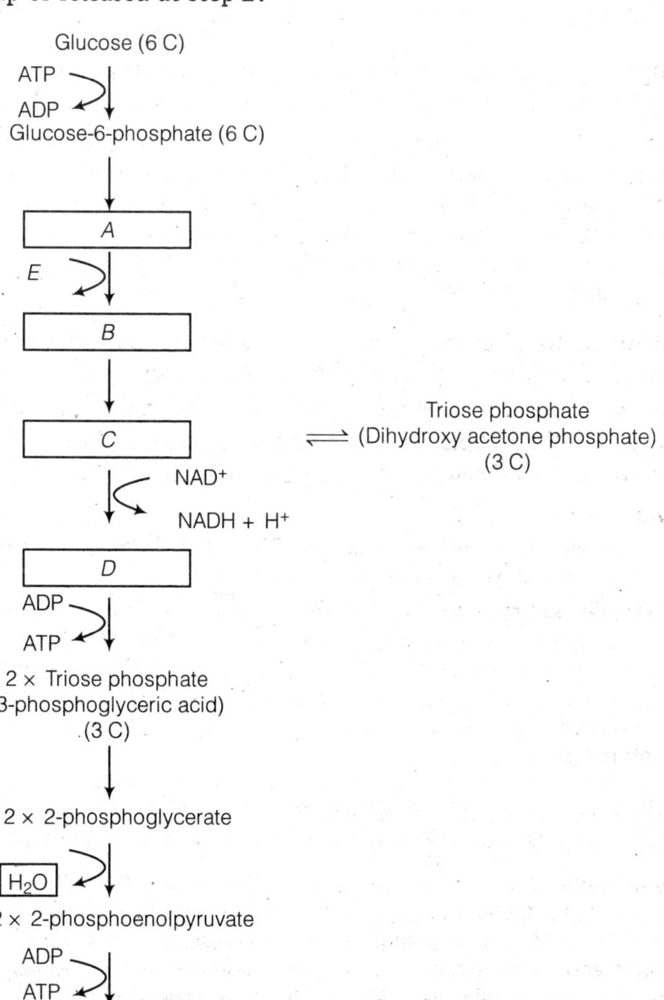

Answer

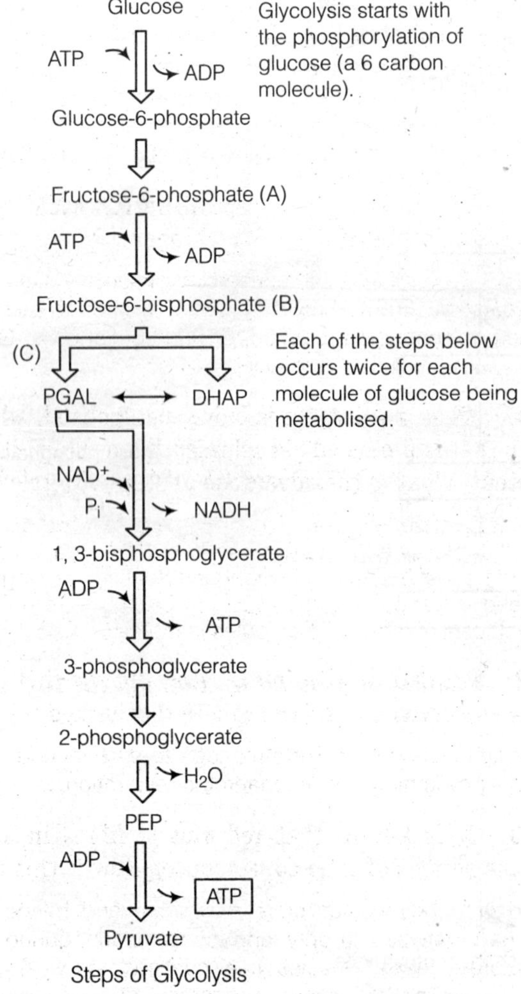

Steps of Glycolysis

Question 8 We commonly call ATP as the energy currency of the cell. Can you think of some other energy carriers present in a cell? Name any two.

Answer ATP is known as the energy currency of the cell because it acts as reservoir of energy storage and its discharge. The other energy carriers present in a cell are ADP and AMP.

Question 9. ATP produced during glycolysis is a result of substrate level phosphorylation. Explain.

Answer Substrate-level phosphorylation is a type of metabolism that results in the formation and creation of adenosine triphosphate (ATP) or guanosine triphosphate (GTP) by the direct transfer and donation of a phosphoryl (PO_3) group to adenosine diphosphate (ADP) or guanosine diphosphate (GDP) from a phosphorylated reactive intermediate.

Question 10. Do you know any step in the TCA cycle, where there is substrate level phosphorylation. Which one?

Answer In TCA cycle, during the conversion of succinyl Co-A to succinic acid a molecule of GTP is synthesised. This is a substrate level phosphorylation. In a coupled reaction, GTP is converted to GDP with the simultaneous synthesis of ATP from ADP.

Question 11. When a substrate is being metabolised, why does not all the energy that is produced get released in one step? It is released in multiple steps. What is the advantage of step-wise release?

Answer The step-wise release of energy have advantage to the cell. Because if all the energy from the glucose would be released at once then most of it would be lost in the form of light and heat. This energy is trapped in ATP is utilised in various energy requiring processes of the organisms and for the synthesis of other biomolecules in the cell.

Question 12. Respiration requires O_2. How did the first cells on the Earth manage to survive in an atmosphere that lacked O_2?

Answer The first cells on the Earth manage to survive in an atmosphere that lacked O_2 by switching over to anaerobic respiration.

Question 13. It is known that red muscle fibres in animals can work for longer periods of time continuously. How is this possible?

Answer Red or dark muscles store myoglobin and hence oxygen for meeting the gap between supply and consumption during continuous activity. Therefore, these muscles can continuously work and respire aerobically for long periods. High proportion of these muscles allow athletes to participate in long duration events like cycleing, swimming and distance running.

Question 14. The energy yield in terms of ATP is higher in aerobic respiration than during anaerobic respiration. Explain.

Answer The aerobic respiration is a high energy yielding process. During the process of aerobic respiration as many as 36 molecules of ATP, whereas in anerobic respiration only 2 ATP molecules are produced.

Question 15. RuBP carboxylase, PEPcase, pyruvate dehydrogenase, ATPase, cytochrome oxidase, hexokinase, lactate dehydrogenase. Select/choose enzymes from the list above which are involved in

(i) photosynthesis
(ii) respiration
(iii) photosynthesis and respiration

Answer

(i) **Photosynthesis** RuBP carboxylase, hexokinase and cytochrome oxidase.
(ii) **Respiration** Pyruvate dehydrogenase, ATPase, lactate dehydrogenase and cytochrome oxidase.
(iii) Both in photosynthesis and respiration.

Question 16. How does a tree trunk exchange gases with the environment although it lacks stomata?

Answer In stems, also have openings called lenticels. The cells in the interior are dead and provide only mechanical support. Thus, most cells of a plant have atleast a part of their surface in contact with air. This is also facilitated by the loose packing of parenchyma cells in leaves, stems and roots, which provide an interconnected network of air spaces.

Question 17. Write two energy yielding reactions of glycolysis.

Answer The conversion of DPGA to 3-phosphoglyceric acid (PGA), is also an energy yielding process; this energy is trapped by the formation of an ATP. Another ATP is synthesised during the conversion of PEP to pyruvic acid.

Question 18. Name the site (s) of pyruvate synthesis. Also, write the chemical reaction, where in pyruvic acid dehydrogenase acts as a catalyst.

Answer Pyruvate synthesis takes place in cytoplasm.

The chemical reaction, where in pyruvic acid dehydrogenase acts as a catalyst is as follows:

The reactions catalysed by pyruvic dehydrogenase require the participation of several coenzymes, including NAD^+ and coenzyme-A.

$$\text{Pyruvic acid} + \text{Co-A} + NAD^+ \xrightarrow[\text{Pyurvate dehydrogenase}]{Mg^{2+}} \text{Acetyl Co-A} + NADH + H^+$$

Question 19. Mention the important series of events of aerobic respiration that occur in the matrix of the mitochondrion as well as one that take place in inner membrane of the mitochondrion.

Answer **Aerobic Respiration** For aerobic respiration to take place within the mitochondria, the final product of glycolysis, pyruvate is transported from the cytoplasm into the mitochondria. The crucial events in aerobic respiration are

(i) The complete oxidation of pyruvate by the step-wise removal of all the hydrogen atoms, leaving three molecules of CO_2. It occurs in the matrix of the mitochondria.

(ii) The passing on of the electrons removed as part of the hydrogen atoms to molecular O_2 with simultaneous synthesis of ATP. This step occurs on the inner membrane of the mitochondria.

Long Answer Type Questions

Question 1. Glucose...... (a) ...... 3-phosphoglyceric acid ...... (b) ...... pyruvic acid ...... C + CO_2.

Answer Glucose (a) **Glyceraldehyde-3-phosphate** 3-phosphoglyceric acid

(b) **Phosphoenol pyruvic acid** pyruvic acid (c) Ethanol + CO_2

Question 2. Oxygen is critical for aerobic respiration. Explain its role with respect to ETS.

Answer Oxygen is an essential requirement for aerobic respiration because an element of strong electronegativity to pull the electrons down the chain is needed. It ensures that protons are pumped into the outer lumen of the mitochondria, where they can come down their concentration gradient through ATP-synthase making ATP. The oxygen picks up electrons and protons, thus forming water. As the electrons in the ETS are used to do work, the electrons lose energy and reach a point at the end of the ETS, where they have to be gotten rid of. The scheme the cell uses to do this is to combine the electrons with hydrogen ions and oxygen to produce water.

15

Plant Growth and Development

Important Points

1. The most important fundamental and the conspicuous characteristic of living beings is **growth**.
2. It is the irreversible permanent increase in size of an organ or its parts or an individual cell. It involves both catabolic and anabolic processes at the expense of energy.
3. Plants are capable of indeterminate growth due to the presence of meristem at various positions. It shows capacity to divide and make up the plant body.
4. Growth could be measured by the variety of parameters like
   (i) Dry weight (ii) Fresh weight (iii) Length
   (iv) Area (v) Volume (vi) Cell number.

   e.g., increase in cell number occurs during meristematic cell division. Pollen tube is measured in terms of length, growth in dorsiventral leaf is denoted by increase in surface area.
5. Growth phase is divided into three phases
   (i) Meristematic (ii) Elongation (iii) Maturation
   (i) **Meristematic phase** includes the rapidly dividing cells at root and shoot apical meristem.
   (ii) **Elongation phase** includes the cells, which lies just beneath the meristematic tissue and shows characteristics of cell enlargement, deposition of new cell wall.
   (iii) **Maturation phase** the cells which lies for away from meristematic tissue attains maturity.

6. Growth could be measured by a growth curve. Size and weight of an organism could be plotted against time. Usually sigmoid growth curve is seen. Sigmoid curve shows three phases
   (i) Lag phase or slow phase
   (ii) Log phase or exponential phase
   (iii) Senesence phase or steady phase

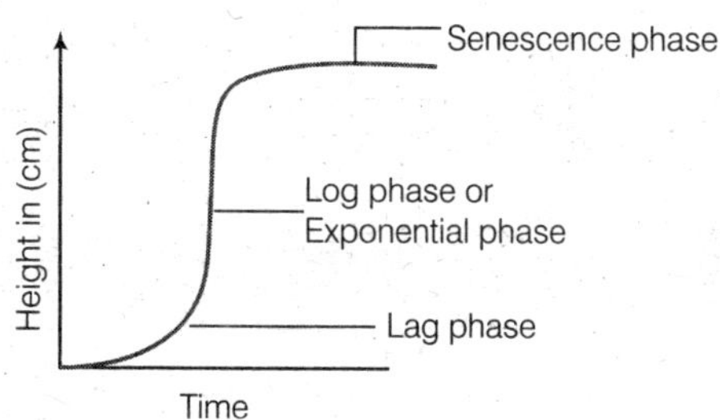

   (a) During lag phase cell prepare itself for cell division and growth is slow.
   (b) During exponential or log phase cells rapidly divides and shows exponential growth rate.
   (c) As the time progresses growth becomes stationary due to the presence of secondary metabolites and depletion of nutrients.
   (d) The exponential growth can be expressed as

$$W_1 = W_0 e^{rt}$$

W_1 = Final size (weight, height, number, etc)
W_0 = Initial size at the beginning of the period
r = Growth rate
t = Time of growth
e = Base of natural logarithms

   (e) r is also known as efficiency index as it measures the ability of the plant to produce new plant material.
   (f) Growth rate shows the increase in cell number or biomass through **arithmetic cell division** or **geometric cell division**.
   (g) In case of arithmetic cell division one daughter cell continues to divide, while the others differentiate.
   Mathematically is expressed as length of organ against time

$$L_t = L_0 + rt$$

L_t = Length of time 't'.
L_0 = Length at time 'zero'.
r = Growth rate/elongation per unit time.

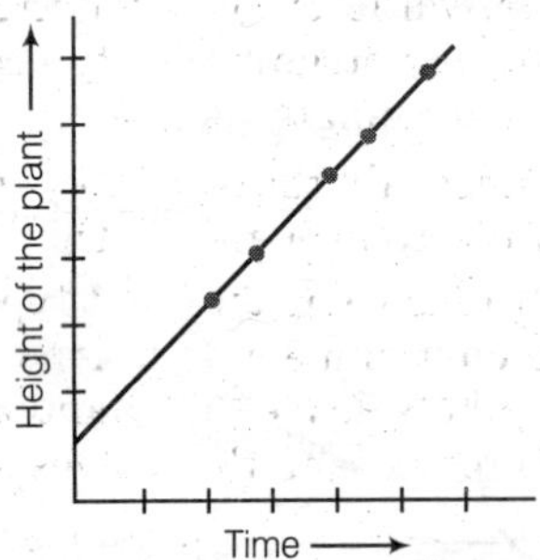

Constant linear growth a plot of length L against time t.

7. Geometric cell division follow exponential growth rate.
   (i) Growth rate is of two types. Absolute growth rate and relative growth rate.
   When measurement in growth is done as the total growth per unit time than it is called absolute growth rate. In relative growth rate growth is expressed per unit initial parameter.
   (ii) Essential elements of growth are water oxygen and nutrients.
   (iii) Water is essential for plants growth since, it provides medium for enzymatic activities needed for growth. It maintains the turigidity of cells. Micro and macronutrients are required by plants for the synthesis of protoplasm.
8. Plant cells shows a very special property of differentiation, dedifferentiation and redifferentiation.
   (i) Differentiation is the process through, which plant cell undergoes maturation. Plant cell loosses protoplasm and develops lignocellulosic secondary cell wall, which enables the cell to carry water to long distances even under extreme stress conditions.
   (ii) Under certain conditions living differentiated cell which have lost the ability to divide regains ability of cell division. This process is called dedifferentiation.
   (iii) The dedifferentiated cells divide to give rise to new cells, which differentiate to perform specific function and attains maturation. They looses the capacity to divide further. Such process is known as **redifferentiation**.

9. Growth in plants is of two types **indeterminate** or **determinate** type. Since, plant shows the property of dedifferentiation and redifferentiation the growth is open or indeterminate type, while by determining the location of the cell one can predict the structure of the cell at maturity such growth pattern is determinate type.
10. Development includes all the changes, which occurs during different stages of life cycle of an orgaism.
    (i) Ability of plant to develop different type of plant structures in response to environment signals is known as plasticity, *e.g.,* in some plants leaves of plant at younger (juvenile phase) is different from the leaves of plant at mature phase.
    (ii) This is known as heterophylly, *e.g.,* heterophylly in cotton, larkspur and corainder.
    (iii) Growth of an organism depends upon both intrinsic and extrinsic factors.

    Internal (intrinsic) factors includes genetic factors, growth regulators, etc, while external factors include regulators like light, temperature, water, oxygen, nutrition, etc.
11. Physiological activities in plant is regulated by the action and interaction of some chemical substance known as plant growth regulators. These may be
    (i) Indole compounds (indole-3-acetic acid IAA).
    (ii) Adenine compounds (N-furfural amino purine, kinetin).
    (iii) Terpenes (gibberellic acid, GA_3).
    (iv) Gases (ethylene, C_2H_4).
12. Various growth regulators are auxin cytokinine, gibberellin ABA, ethylene.
13. **Charles Darwin** and **Francis Darwin** first time observed that the cleoptiles of canary grass bends towards unilateral illumination later they concluded that coleoptile contains a transmittable substance, which helped coleoptile to bend towards the light source.

    Later FW Went isolated auxin from the tips of coleoptile of at seedling. Auxin was the transmittable substance.
    (i) **Auxins** were isolated from human urine natural auxins are indole-3-acetic acid (IAA) and indole butyric acid IBA. NAA (Naphthalene Acetic Acid) and 2, 4-D (2, 4-dichlorophenoxy acetic acid) are synthetic auxin.

(ii) Auxin plays an important role in

(a) Growth of apical bud and inhibition of axillary buds. Such phenomenon is called apical dominance.

(b) Promotes flowering.

(c) It prevents leaf absicission and early fruit drop.

(d) Induces parthenocarpy (development of fruit/plant without fertilisation) *e.g.*, in tomatoes.

(e) Act as weedicides (*e.g.*, 2, 4-D). It kills dicotyledonous weeds.

(f) It controls xylem differentiation.

14. E Kurosawa identified the 'Bakane' (foolish seedling) disease of rice seedlings. The active substance, which was responsible for this disease was identified as **gibberellic acid**. There are more than 100 gibberellins reported till now.

15. These are denoted as $\mathbf{GA_1}$, $\mathbf{GA_2}$, $\mathbf{GA_3}$ and so on. First identified gibberellic acid was $\mathbf{GA_1}$, $\mathbf{GA_2}$, $\mathbf{GA_3}$ and so on.

Main role of gibberellic acids are

(i) It helps in increasing the internodal length, phenomenon is known as **bolting**.

(ii) It delays senescence.

(iii) It is used to speed up the malting process in brewing industry.

(iv) GAs hastens the maturity period and leads to early seed production.

(v) It breaks dormancy of seed.

16. Cytokinin is another naturally occurring growth hormone in plants. F Skoog and his co-workers identified and crystallise the cytokinesis promoting substance kinetin. It was present in extracts of coconut milk and isolated from autoclaved herring sperm DNA. These are synthesised in meristematic tissues like root apices, developing shoot buds young fruits, etc.

Zeatin is a natural **cytokinin** present in coconut milk. These are derivatives of purines. Chief role of cytokinin are

(i) Cell division in apical meristem.

(ii) It plays an important role in the formation of leaves chloroplast in leaves.

(iii) It help the plant to overcome apical dominance. It promotes lateral shoot growth and adventitious shoot formation.

(iv) It promotes nutrient mobilisation.

(v) It delays leaf senescence (falling of leaves).

17. The gaseous plant growth regulator ethylene was identified by Cousins. He confirmed the presence of volatile substance from ripened oranges that promotes the ripening of unripened bananas.
    (i) It promotes senescence and abscission of plant organ.
    (ii) Promotes fruit ripening.
    (iii) It breaks seed and bud dormancy.
    (iv) It is also known as **climactric hormone** since, it increases the respiration rate during ripening of fruits and increase in temperature occurs.
    (v) It promotes femaleness (promotes female flowering).
    (vi) It is used to initiate flowering and causes fruit set in pineapples.
    (vii) It also promotes internode and petiole elongation in deep H_2O rice plants.
18. Ethepton is cheif source of ethylene. It accelerates the formation of abscission layer in fruits and flower.
19. ABA (abscisic acid) plays an important role in regulating abscission and dormancy. It usually acts as a plant growth inhibitor and also known as stress hormone.
    (i) It inhibits seed germination.
    (ii) Stimulates the closure of stomata in epidermis and imparts stress tolerance.
    (iii) Accumulates during unfavourable conditions and help seed to withstand desiccation.
    (iv) It acts antagonastically or opposite to gibberellic acid.
20. Response of plants to periodic exposure of light an induction of flowering is known as **photoperiodism**.
    (i) Some plants are required for the exposure of light for a period exceeding a well defined critical duration, while some plants are to be exposed to light for a periodic less than this critical period.
    (ii) Long day plants are exposed to light exceeding their critical period. Short day plants are exposed to light below/less than their critical period.
    If day period is interrupted in long day plants than flowering does not occur, while if night/dark period is interrupted in short day plants flowering does not occur. Hence, day/light period is critical for long-day plants, while night/dark period is critical for short day plants.
    (iii) There is no correlation in between duration of light exposure and flowering in case of day neutral plants.

(iv) Prior to flowering shoot apices modifies themselves into flowering apices.

(v) These cannot receive leaves are site of perception of light, which induces the synthesis of hypothetical flowering hormone florigen.

(vi) It migrates to shoot and leaves apices.

21. Induction of early flowering in plant by giving chilling or low temperature treatment to seed is known as **vernalisation**. Vegetative period of the plant is cut short and initiation of reproductive phase occurs by early flowering. Stimulus of low temperature is perceived by active embryo tip, shoot tip and meristematic region.

Exercises

Question 1. Define growth, differentiation, development, dedifferentiation, redifferentiation, determinate growth, meristem and growth rate.

Answer Growth It is an irreversible permanent increase in size of an organ or its parts or even of an individual cell.

Development It is the process of whole series of changes which an organism goes through during its life cycle.

Meristems The cells of which the capacity to divide and self-perpetuate.

Growth Rates The increased growth per unit time is termed as growth rate. Thus, rate of growth can be expressed mathematically. An organism, or a part of the organism can produce more cells in a variety of ways. The growth rate shows an increase that may be arithmetic or geometrical.

Differentiation The cells derived from root apical and shoot-apical meristems and cambium differentiate and mature to perform specific functions. This act leading to maturation is termed as differentiation.

Dedifferentiation The living differentiated cells, that by now have lost the capacity to divide can regain the capacity of division under certain conditions. This phenomenon is termed as dedifferentiation. For example, formation of meristems; interfascicular cambium and cork cambium from fully differentiated parenchyma cells.

Redifferentiation While undergoing dedifferentiation plant cells once again lose their capacity to divide and become mature. This process is called redifferentiation.

Question 2. Why is not any one parameter good enough to demonstrate growth throughout the life of a flowering plant?

Answer Any one parameter is not good enough to demonstrate growth throughout the life of a flowering plant because the plants exhibit different types of growths during different stages of their life cycle.

In the seedling stage, they are in state of active cell division (*i.e.*, mitotic divisions), then they undergo active cell enlargement stage during growing stage. In the reproductive or flowering stage of their life cycle, they exhibit reductional divisions. Finally, after the formation of various organs, they undergo cell differentiation or get matured.

Question 3. Describe briefly

(a) Arithmetic growth
(b) Geometric growth
(c) Sigmoid growth curve
(d) Absolute and relative growth rates

Answer

(a) **Arithmetic growth** In arithmetic growth, following mitotic cell division, only one daughter cell continues to divide while the other differentiates and matures. Example is a root elongating at a constant rate.

(b) **Geometric growth** In geometrical growth, in most systems, the initial growth is slow (lag phase), and it increases rapidly thereafter at an exponential rate (log or exponential phase). Here, both the progeny cells following mitotic cell division retain the ability to divide and continue to do so.

(c) **Sigmoid growth curve** If we plot the parameter of growth against time, we get a typical sigmoid or S-curve. A sigmoid curve is a characteristic of living organism growing in a natural environment. It is typical for all cells, tissues and organs of a plant.

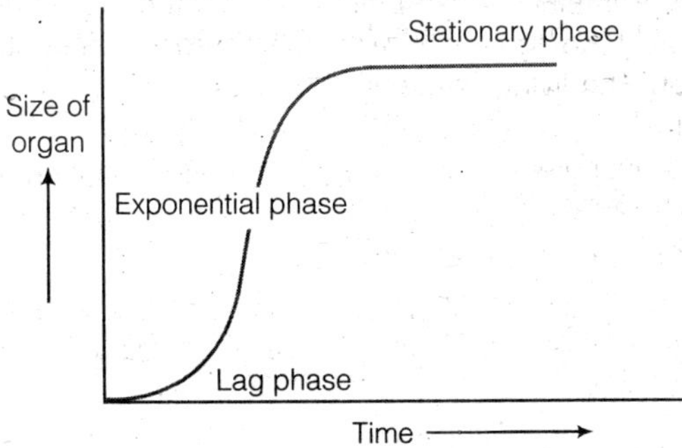

(d) **Absolute and relative growth rates** The measurement and the comparison of total growth per unit time is called the absolute growth rate. And the growth of the given system per unit time expressed on a common basis, *e.g.*, per unit initial parameter is called the relative growth rate.

Question 4. List five main groups of natural plant growth regulators. Write a note on discovery, physiological functions and agricultural/horticultural applications of any one of them.

Answer Five main groups of natural plant growth regulators are auxins, gibberellins, ethylene, cytokinins and ABA.

Auxins

(i) **Discovery** Auxins was first isolated from human urine. They are generally produced by the growing apices of the stems and roots. Auxins like IAA and indole butyric acid (IBA) have been isolated from plants. NAA (naphthalene acetic acid) and 2, 4-D (2, 4-dichlorophenoxyacetic) are synthetic auxins.

(ii) **Physiological function** They help to initiate rooting in stem cuttings, an application widely used for plant propagation. Auxins promote flowering, *i.e.*, in pineapples. They help to prevent fruit and leaf drop at early stages but promote the abscission of older mature leaves and fruits.

(iii) **Agricultural horticultural applications** Auxins also induce parthenocarpy, *e.g.*, in tomatoes. They are widely used as herbicides 2, 4-D, widely used to kill dicotyledonous seeds, does not affect mature monocotyledonous plants. It is used to prepare seed-free lawns by gardeners. Auxin also controls xylem differentiation and helps in cell division.

Question 5. What do you understand by photoperiodism and vernalisation? Describe their significance.

Answer **Photoperiodism** The response of plants to periods of day/night is termed as photoperiodism. The site of perception of light/dark duration are the leaves.

Significance The significance of photoperiodism is in regulating flowering in plants. Flowering is an important step towards seed formation and seeds are responsible for continuing the generation of a plant.

Vernalisation There are plants in which flowering is either quantitatively or qualitatively dependent on exposure to low temperature. This phenomenon is termed as vernalisation. Vernalisation refers specially to the promotion of flowering by a period of low temperature.

Significance Vernalisation prevents precocious reproductive development late in the growing season. This enables the plant to have sufficient time to reach maturity.

Question 6. Why is abscisic acid also known as stress hormone?

Answer Abscisic acid acts as a general plant growth inhibitor and an inhibitor of plant metabolism. ABA inhibits seed germination. ABA stimulates the closure of stomata in the epidermis and increases the tolerance of plants to various kinds of stresses. Therefore, it is also called the stress hormone.

Question 7. 'Both growth and differentiation in higher plants are open'. Comment.

Answer Plant growth is unique because plants retain the capacity for unlimited growth throughout their life. This ability of the plants is due to the presence of meristems at certain locations in their body. The cells of such meristems have the capacity to divide and self-perpetuate. The product, however, soon loses the capacity to divide and such cells make up the plant body. This form of growth wherein new cells are always being added to the plant body by the activity of the meristem is called the open form of growth.

Question 8. 'Both a short day plant and a long day plant can produce can flower simultaneously in a given place'. Explain.

Answer Petkus winter rye (*Secale cerele*) gives responses of low temperatue at very young seedlings or even at seed stage. If winter rye is shown in the spring, the seeds germinate and produce vegetative plants in the following summer. In this case, the period of vegetative growth is extended and flowering occurs only in the next summer when the cold requirements is fulfilled during winters. The same variety, if grown in early autumn, produces flowers in the following summer.

Question 9. Which one of the plant growth regulators would you use if you are asked to

(a) induce rooting in a twig
(b) quickly ripen a fruit
(c) delay leaf senescence
(d) induce growth in axillary buds
(e) 'bolt' a rosette plant
(f) induce immediate stomatal closure in leaves.

Answer (a) Cytokinin (b) Ethylene
(c) Cytokinins (d) Auxin
(e) Gibberellins (f) Abscisic acid.

Question 10. Would a defoliated plant respond to photoperiodic cycle? Why?

Answer No, a defoliated plant do not respond to photoperiodic cycle. Because leaves of a plant are the sites of light perception for the induction of flowering.

Question 11. What would be expected to happen if

(a) GA_3 is applied to rice seedlings.
(b) dividing cells stop differentiating.
(c) a rotten fruit gets mixed with unripe fruits.
(d) you forget to add cytokinin to the culture medium.

Answer

(a) The rice seedlings show extraordinary elongation of stem and leaf sheaths.
(b) Tissue and organ differentiation will not take place.
(c) Unripe fruits will also get rotten due to ethylene hormone secreted by rotten fruit.
(d) No root and shoot formation will take place.

Selected NCERT Exemplar Questions

Very Short Answer Type Questions

Question 1. Fill in the places with appropriate word/words.

(i) A phase of growth which is maximum and fastest is ....
(ii) Apical dominance as expressed in dicotyledonous plants is due to the presence of more .... in the apical bud than in the lateral ones.
(iii) In addition to auxin, a .... must be supplied to culture medium to obtain a good callus in plant tissue culture.
(iv) .... of a vegetative plants are the sites of photoperiodic perception.

Answer

(i) log phase
(ii) auxin hormone
(iii) cytokinin
(iv) Leaves.

Question 2. Plant Growth Substances (PGS) have innumerable practical applications. Name the PGS you should use to

(i) Increase yield of sugar cane.
(ii) Promote lateral shoot growth.
(iii) Cause sprouting of potato tuber.
(iv) Inhibit seed germination.

Answer (i) Gibberellins (ii) Auxins

(iii) Cytokinin (iv) Abscisic acid.

Question 3. Gibberellins were first discovered in Japan when rice plants were suffering from bakane (the foolish seedling disease) caused by a fungus *Gibberella fujikuroi*.

(i) Give two functions of this phytohormone.
(ii) Which property of gibberellin caused foolish seedling disease in rice?

Answer

(i) **Two functions of gibberellin** (a) It causes an increase in length of axis, *e.g.*, to increase the length of grape stalks. Gibberellins, cause fruits like apple to elongate and improve its shape.

(b) It also delays senescence.

(ii) Gibberellin causes foolish seedling disease in rice because it is capable of causing active cell division and cell elongation.

Question 4. Gibberellins promote the formation of ...... flowers on genetically ..... plants in *Cannabis* whereas ethylene promotes formation of .... flowers on genetically ...... plants.

Answer Male; female; female; male.

Question 5. Classify the following plants into long-day plants (LDP), short day plants (SDP) and day neutral plants (DNP) *Xanthium*, henbane (*Hyoscyamus niger*), spinach, rice, strawberry, *Bryophyllum*, sunflower, tomato, maize.

Answer **Long-day plants** (LDP)—Henbane (*Hyoscyamus niger*), rice, spinach.

Short day plants (SDP)— *Xanthium*, strawberry and sunflower

Day neutral plants (DNP)— Maize and tomato

Long-short day plants— *Bryophyllum*.

Question 6. A farmer grows cucumber plants in his field. He wants to increase the number of female flowers in them. Which plant growth regulator can be applied to achieve this?

Answer Ethylene hormone

Question 7. Where are the following hormones synthesised in plants

(i) IAA (ii) Gibberellins
(iii) Cytokinins

Answer (i) IAA is synthesised in tip of coleoptile.

(ii) Gibberellins are synthesised in side the plastids of immature seeds, young leaves or even roots.

(iii) Cytokinins are synthesised in meristematic regions such as in root tips of plants.

Question 8. In botanical gardens and tea gardens, gardeners trim the plants regularly so that they remain bushy. Does this practice have any scientific explanation?

Answer The phenomenon behind this practice is apical dominance. It is the phenomenon of suppresses of growth of lateral buds by the terminal bud. Removal of apical bud causes the sprouting of lateral buds. However, a paste of auxin can stimulate the effect of apical bud.

Question 9. Light plays an important role in the life of all organisms. Name any three physiological processes in plants which are affected by light.

Answer The three physiological processes in plants which are affected by light are phototrophism, photosynthesis and photomorphogenesis.

Question 10. Growth is one of the characteristic of all living organism? Do unicellular organism also grow? If so, what are the parameters?

Answer Yes, unicellular also grow. The cell size increases up to a certain fixed size only.

Question 11. The rice seedlings infected with fungus *Gibberella fujikuroi* is called foolish seedlings? What was the reason behind it?

Answer The rice seedlings infected with fungus *Gibberella fujikuroi* is called foolish because seedlings grew foolishly so tall that they ultimately resulted into death of plants.

Short Answer Type Questions

Question 1. *Nicotiana tabacum*, a short day plant, when exposed to more than critical period of light fails to flower. Explain.

Answer *Nicotiana tabacum*, a short day plant has a critical day length of 12 h for photoperiodic induction . This means that if the plant get 12 h, light and 12 h, dark then it flowers. In this plant, 12 h. darkness is very important. If this period becomes less, no flowering occurs. This made it clear that short day plants require continuous and uninterrupted critical dark period for flowering.

Question 2. What are the structural characteristics of

(i) meristematic cells near root tip?
(ii) the cells in the elongation zone of the root?

Answer

(i) Meristematic cells near root tip are in the process of active divisions, *i.e.*, mitosis divisions. Each chromosome is split lengthwise into two homologous chromatids, which pass equally into daughter cells taken place.

(ii) The cells in the elongation zone of the root have enlarge size due to vacuolation, *i.e.*, by absorption of water. In these a large central vacuole is present, which push the cytoplasm to a thin boundary layer against the cell wall. The daughter cells formed after divisions have half the size of the parent cell.

Question 3. Does the growth pattern in plants differ from that in animals? Do all the parts of plant grow indefinitely? If not, name the regions of plant, which can grow indefinitely.

Answer Yes, the growth pattern in plants differ from that in animals. The trees continue to increase in height or girth over a period of time. However, the leaves, flowers and fruits of the same tree not only have limited dimensions but also appear and fall periodically and some time repeatedly. All the parts of plant do not grow indefinitely. The shoot tips and the root tips of the plants can grow indefinitely.

Question 4. Auxins are growth hormones capable of promoting cell elongation. They have been used in horticulture to promote growth, flowering and rooting. Write a line to explain the meaning of the following terms related to auxins.

(i) Auxin precursors (ii) anti-auxins
(iii) Synthetic auxins

Answer

(i) **Auxin precursors** These are the substances, which synthesise auxins. *e.g.*, IAA is synthesised from tryptophan hormone.

(ii) **Anti-auxins** The substances which inhibit the polar movement of auxins, are known as anti-auxins, *e.g.*, 2, 3, 5-trichlorobenzoic acid (TIBA) and naphthalamic acid (NPA).

(iii) **Synthetic auxins** These are the auxins synthesised in the laboratories that cause various physiological responses similar to IAA. *e.g.*, indole-3-butyric acid (IBA), naphthalene acetic acid (NAA), etc.

Question 5. The role of ethylene and abscisic acid is both positive and negative. Justify the statement.

Answer The role of ethylene and abscisic acid is both positive and negative. Ethylene is a simple gaseous PGR. As a **negative effect**, it is synthesised in large amount by tissues undergoing senescence and ripening. It also promotes senescence and abscission of plant organs especially of leaves and flowers.

As a **positive effect**, ethylene breaks seed and bud dormancy, initiates germination in peanut seeds, sprouting of potato tubers. It promotes internode/petiole elongation in deep water rice plants. It helps leaves/ upper parts of the shoot to remain above water.

Question 6. While experimentation, why do you think it is difficult to assign any affect seen to any single hormone?

Answer All the hormones are synergistic to each other in their functions. During experimentation, we can not judge whether a particular effect is produced by a single hormone or many. For example

(i) Auxins help to initiate rooting in stem cuttings, an application widely used for plant propagation. Cytokinins also show the similar function of root formation. Auxins promote flowering, *e.g.*, in pineapples. They also induce parthenocarpy, *e.g.*, in tomatoes.

(ii) Both gibberellins and ethylene are synergistic to auxin in initiating flowering and for synchronising fruit set in pineapples.

(iii) Cytokinins and gibberellins help overcome the apical dominance and delay the process of leaf senescence.

(iv) On the other hand, ethylene promotes senescence and abscission of plant organs especially of leaves and flowers.

This shows that all hormones are synergistic to each other in their mode of action in plants.

Question 7. What is the mechanism underlying the phenomenon by which the terminal/apical bud suppresses the growth of lateral buds? Suggest measures to overcome this phenomenon.

Answer This phenomenon is known as apical dominance. It is the phenomenon of suppresses of growth of lateral buds by the terminal bud. Removal of apical bud causes the sprouting of lateral buds. However, a paste of auxin can stimulate the effect of apical bud.

Question 8. In animals, there are special glands secreting hormones, whereas there are no glands in plants. Where are the plant hormones formed? How are the hormones translocated to the site of activity?

Answer The plant hormones are mostly formed in the meristematic regions of the plants such as root tips and shoot tips.

Auxins exhibit polar transport, *i.e.*, the movement of auxin occurs from stem apex downwards to the base, (*i.e.*, besipetal) and from root upwards to the shoot (*i.e.*, acropetal). Unlike auxins, gibberellin exhibits non-polar movement. It moves from one part to the another in the phloem, similar to the transport of carbohydrates and other organic substance. GA is translocated in the xylem also. Cytokinins are translocated upwards probably through xylem. Abscisic acid is translocated to stem apices through the phloem tissues.

Question 9. Many discoveries in science have been accidental. This is true for plant hormones also. Can you justify this statement by giving an example? Also what term is used for such accidental findings?

Answer The discovery of each of the five major groups of PGRs have been accidental. Charles Darwin and his son Francis Darwin when observing the coleoptiles of canary grass reported that it respond to unilateral illumination by growing towards the light source (phototropism). After a series of experiments, it was concluded that the tip of coleoptile was the site of transmittable influence that caused the bending of the entire coleoptile next figure. Auxin was isolated by FW Went from tips of coleoptiles of oat seedlings.

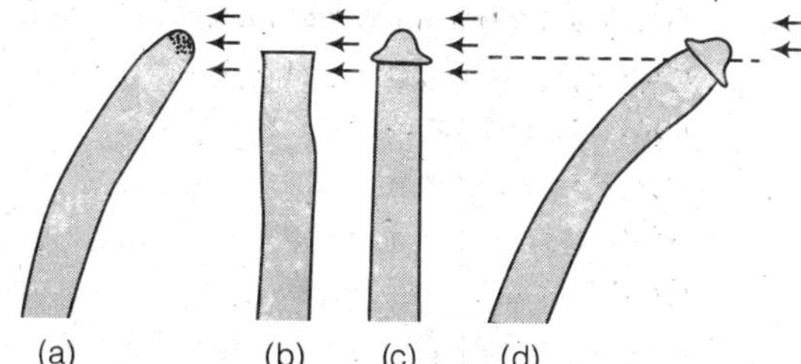

Experiment used to demonstrate that tip of the coleoptile is the source of auxin. Arrows indicate direction of light.

Question 10. To get a carpet-like grass lawns are mowed regularly. Is there any scientific explanation for this?

Answer Mowing of grass results in removal of apical buds, stimulation of growth of axillary buds and intercalary meristems.

Question 11. In a slide showing different types of cells, can you identify which type of the cell may be meristematic and the one which is incapable of dividing and how?

Answer Meristematic cells are actively dividing cells which show mitotic divisions, *i.e.*, each chromosome is split lengthwise into two homologous chromatids, which pass equally into daughter cells. Mature cells are incapable of divisions because in these cells differentiation has taken place.

Question 12. Label the diagram

(i) This is which part of a dicotyledonous plant?
(ii) If we remove part 1 from the plant, what will happen?

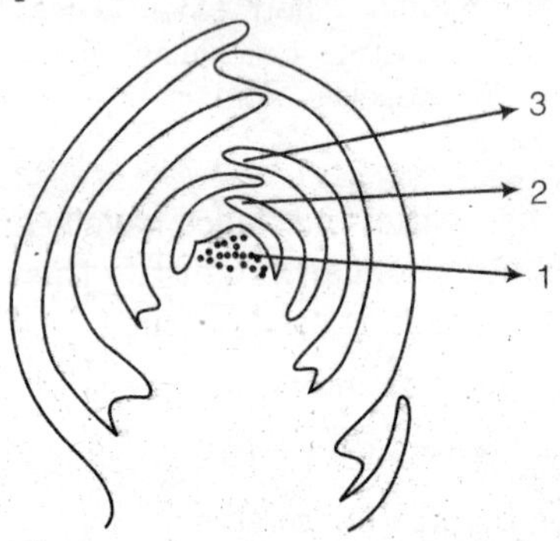

Answer 1. Apical meristem, 2. Axillary bud, 3. Leaf primordium

(i) Tip of the shoot.
(ii) Removal of part, 1 *i.e.*, apical bud causes the lateral buds to sprout. It suppresses the effect of apical bud on lateral buds.

Question 13. Both animals and plants grow. Why do we say that growth and differentiation in plants is open and not so in animals? Does this statement hold true for sponges also?

Answer Plant growth is unique because plants retain the capacity for unlimited growth throughout their life. This ability of the plants is due to the presence of meristems at certain locations in their body. The cells of such meristems have the capacity to divide and self-perpetuate. The product, however, soon loses the capacity to divide and such cells make up the plant body. This form of growth wherein new cells are always being added to the plant body by the activity of the meristem is called the open form of growth. Yes, this statement holds true for sponges also.

Question 14. Define parthenocarpy. Name the plant hormone used to induce parthenocarpy.

Answer **Parthenocarpy** It is the phenomenon of formation of seedless fruits without fertilisation, *i.e.*, tomato, apples and cucumbers, etc., auxins and gibberellins induce parthenocarpy.

Question 15. While eating watermelons, all of us wish it was seedless. As a plant physiologist, can you suggest any method by which this can be achieved.

Answer Gibberellins and auxin hormones can be used to produce seedless watermelons as they induce parthenocarpy.

Question 16. A gardener finds some broad-leaved dicot weeds growing in his lawns. What can be done to get rid of the weeds efficiently?

Answer In order to get rid off broad-leaved dicot weeds growing in the lawns, gardner has to use synthetic growth inhibitors such as morphactins, malic hydrazide and chlorocholine chloride, etc.

Question 17. On germination, a seed first produces shoots with leaves and flowers appear later.

(i) Why do you think this happens?

(ii) How is this advantageous to the plant?

Answer

(i) On germination, a seed first produces shoots with leaves, flowers appear later, because the flower hormone florigen is synthesised in the leaves and is transmitted to the growing points, where flowering occurs.

(ii) Photosynthesis provides energy and substrate which are used during dark period.

Question 18. Fill in the blanks

(i) Maximum growth is observed in .... phase.

(ii) Apical dominance is due to ....

(iii) .... initiate rooting.

(iv) Pigment involved in photoperception in flowering plants is ....

Answer (i) log phase
(ii) auxin hormone
(iii) Cytokinins
(iv) phytochrome

Long Answer Type Questions

Question 1. It is known that some varieties of wheat are sown in autumn but are harvested around next mid summer.

(i) What could be the probable reason for this?
(ii) What term is used for this promotion of flowering under low temperature?
(iii) Which plant hormone can replace the cold treatment?

Answer

(i) If wheat is shown in the spring, the seeds germinate and produce vegetative plants in the following summer. In this case, the period of vegetative growth is extended and flowering occurs only in the next summer when the cold requirements is fulfilled during winters. The same variety, if grown in early autumn, produces flowers in the following summer.
(ii) Vernalisation
(iii) Gibberellin hormone.

Question 2. Name a hormone, which

(i) is gaseous in nature
(ii) is responsible for phototropism
(iii) induces femaleness in flowers of cucumber
(iv) is used for killing weeds (dicots)
(v) induces flowering in long day plants

Answer

(i) Ethylene
(ii) Auxin hormone
(iii) Ethylene hormone
(iv) Abscisic acid (growth inihibtors)
(v) Gibberellin hormone.

16

Digestion and Absorption

Important Points

1. The basic requirement of all living beings is food. The major components of food are carbohydrates, fats, proteins, vitamins and minerals. These are essential for growth and repair of tissues. All these are complex biomacromolecules and have to be broken down into simpler substances in digestive system by the process called **digestion.**
2. The human digestive system includes alimentary canal and various digestive glands.
3. Alimentary canal is a tube-like structure and lumen at the centre called enteric cavity. It begins with the anterior opening called mouth and end with the posterior opening anus.
4. Mouth is the opening on the ventral side and opens into buccal cavity. Mouth is guarded by two movable lips, *i.e.,* upper and lower lip.
5. In buccal cavity, tooth is embedded in socket of jaw bone called **thecodont** condition. Buccal cavity also contain tongue and palate it forms the roof of the buccal cavity.

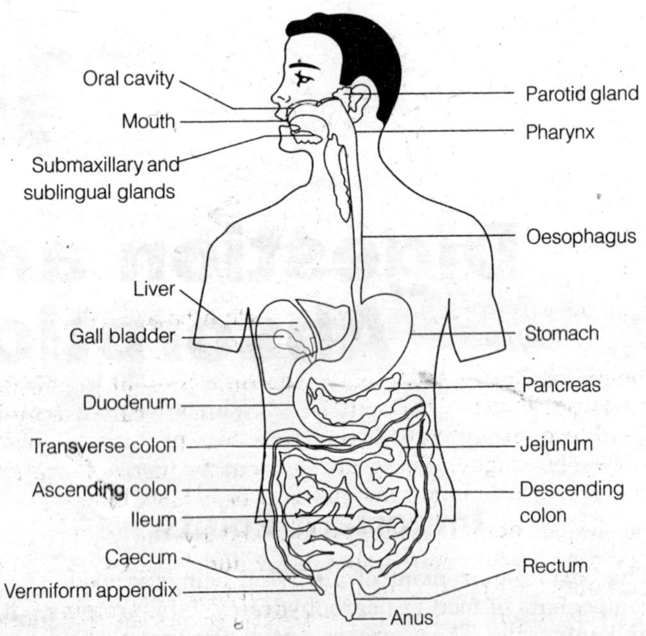

The human digestive system

6. Usually mammals like human being forms two sets of teeth during their life time. One set is of temporary or deciduous teeth and another a set of permanent or adult teeth. Such type of appearance of teeth in life time is known as diphyodont condition.
7. In monophyodont condition teeth appear only once in life time. Some lower most vertebrates also show polyphyodont condition.
8. **Diphyodont teeth** is the characteristic of mammals.
9. In adult humans, heterodont (different types) dentition is present namely incisors (I), canine (C), premolars (Pm) and molars (M). There are 32 permanent teeth with the dental formula $\frac{2123}{2123}$. It shows the arrangement of teeths in each half of the upper and lower jaw. Teeths are made up of enamel, which helps in chewing of food.

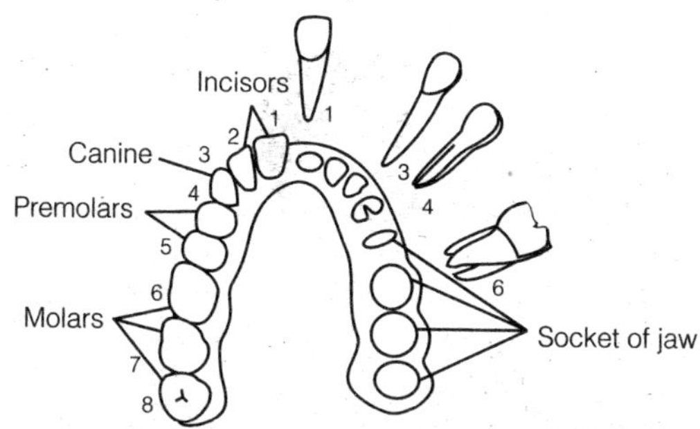

Arrangement of different types of teeth in the jaws on one side and the sockets on the other side

10. Tongue is the muscular movable organ present at the floor of the buccal cavity through an attachment called **frenulum.** Small projections called **papillae** are present all over the surface of tongue. Those are present to increase the surface area of mucous membrane and may bear taste buds.

11. The buccal or oral cavity is followed by the pharynx, which serves as a common passage of air and food. Oesophagus is a muscular long tube, which opens into pharynx. Trachea (wind pipe) also opens into pharynx. Glottis covers the wind pipe and epiglottis prevents the entry of food into glottis. It passes posteriorly through neck, thorax and diaphragm and opens into stomach through gastro-oesophageal spinchter.

12. Stomach is a **J-shaped muscular bag-like** structure, located in the upper left portion of abdominal cavity. Stomach has three major portions
    - (i) Cardiac portion
    - (ii) Fundic region
    - (iii) Pyloric region

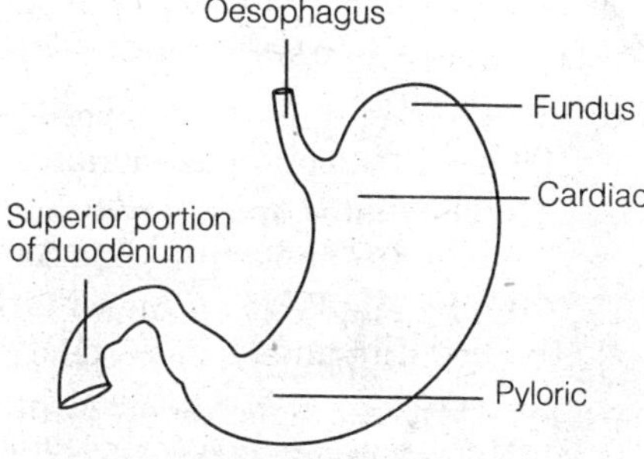

Anatomical regions of human stomach

13. Pyloric portion of the stomach opens into part of small intestine through pyloric sphincter.

14. Small intestine, the longest part of digestive tract is divided in duodenum, jejunum and ileum.
    - (i) **Duodenum** is connected to two major digestive glands liver and pancreas.

(ii) **Jejunum** is the long coiled middle portion whose chief role is secretion.

(iii) **Ileum** is the highly coiled portion and its chief role is of absorption. It opens into large intestine.

15. Large intestine consist of **caecum, colon** and **rectum.**

(i) **Caecum** in the beginning of the large intestine. Some symbiotic microorganisms are present in it.

(ii) from caecum a finger-like projection arises called vermiform appendix.

(iii) Caecum opens into colon. Colon is divided into three parts an ascending, descending and transverse part.

(iv) Rectum is the terminal part of large intestine as well as the digestive tract and opens through the anus.

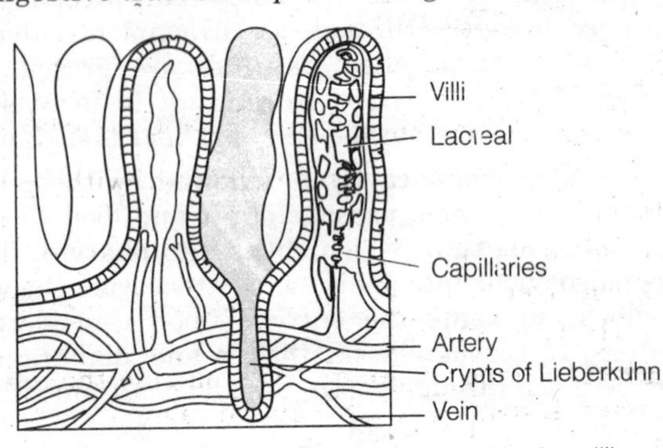

A section of small intestinal mucosa showing villi

16. Alimentary canal is composed of four layers, these are serosa, muscularis, sub-mucosa and mucosa.

(i) The outer most layer called serosa is made up of thin mesothelium with some connective tissues.

(ii) The middle layer muscularis is composed of smooth muscle cells arranged in a inner circular and outer longitudinal layer.

(iii) Submucosa layer is composed of loose connective tissue containing nerves, blood lymph and vessels.

(iv) Mucosa is the innermost layer of alimentary canal.

(v) In small intestine small finger-like projections are present called villi. These contain brush/bordered epithelium. These projections increases the surface area and are helpful in absorption.

(vi) These are supplied with network of capillaries and lymph called the **lacteal.**

(vii) Mucosal epithelium is present in linings of goblet cells. Which secretes mucus for secretion.

(viii) Mucosa is present on the lining of glands in stomach and on the base of villi in intestine known as **crypts of Lieberkuhn.**

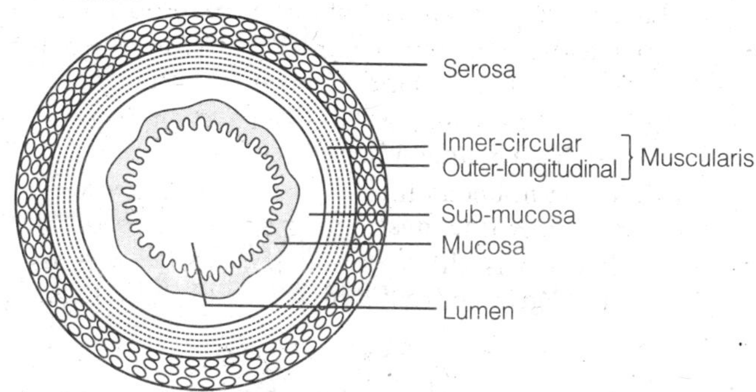

Diagrammatic representation of transverse section of gut

17. Alimentary canal is also associated with various digestive glands like.
    (i) Salivary gland
    (ii) The liver
    (iii) The pancreas
18. Salivary gland is situated just outside the buccal cavity and secretes salivary juice into buccal cavity.

    There are three pairs of salivary gland
    (i) Parotid gland (present near cheek)
    (ii) Sub-maxillary/ sub-mandibular gland (lower jaw)
    (iii) Sub-lingual gland (below the tongue).
19. Liver is the largest gland of vertebrate body. Situated in the anterior part of the body and divided into two lobes, *i.e.,* right lobe and left lobe. In humans, it weighs 1.2-1.5 kg.
    (i) Hepatic lobules are the functional unit of liver containing hepatic cells arranged in the form of cords.
    (ii) Lobules are covered by a thin sheath called **Glissons capsule.**
    (iii) Hepatic cells secretes bile juice from hepatic cells through hepatic duct.
    (iv) The secreted bile juice is stored and concentrated in sac like structure called gall bladder.

20. **Gall bladder** is a sac-like structure located on the inner surface of the liver. Bile secreted from liver is stored in gall bladder.

    The bile duct (cystic duct) along with hepatic duct forms the common bile duct.

21. **Pancreas** is elonged irregularly branched compound (exocrine and endocrine) digestive gland situated between the limbs of U-shaped duodenum.
    (i) It secretes pancreatic juice, which contain various proteolytic enzymes.
    (ii) Endocrine portion of the pancreas secretes various hormones like insulin and glucagon.
    (iii) Pancreatic duct along with bile duct opens into common hepatopancreatic duct in duodenum. It is guarded by sphincter of oddii.

22. Various mechanical and chemical processes are involved in the process of digestion.
    (i) Mastication of the food take place in mouth with the help of teeths and saliva. Mucus in saliva helps in lubrication and adhers the masticated food as bolus.
    (ii) Bolus is swallowed (deglutition) into pharynx and later into oesophagus through successive muscular contractions called **peristalis.**
    (iii) Gastro-oesophageal spincter controls the passage of food into stomach.
    (iv) Carbohydrate are hydrolysed by the action of salivary amylase enzyme and lysozyme 30% of starch is hydrolysed into a disaccharide maltose

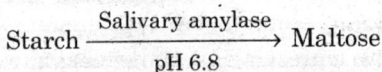

$$\text{Starch} \xrightarrow[\text{pH 6.8}]{\text{Salivary amylase}} \text{Maltose}$$

    (v) In stomach, gastric glands are present, which have three specific type of cells
        (a) Mucus neck cells, which secrete mucus.
        (b) Peptic or chief cells, it secretes pepsinogen.
        (c) Parietal and oxyntic cells secretes HCl and intrinsic factor vitamin-B_{12}.
    (vi) The food mixes thoroughly with the acidic gastric juice of the stomach by the churning movement of its muscular wall and known as **chyme**. Acidic pH converts proenzyme pepsinogen into active enzyme pepsin.

(vii) Pepsin is a proteolytic enzymes and converts proteins into protease and peptone (peptides).

(viii) Mucosal epithelium is protected by the mucus and bicarbonate ion present in gastric juice.

(xi) In infants, rennin is produced, which helps in the digestion of milk proteins. Small amount of lipases is also secreted by gastric glands.

(x) In small intestine bile, pancreatic and intestinal juice are secreted. Pancreatic juice contain inactive enzymes trypsinogen, chymotrypsinogen, procarboxypeptidases, amylases, lipases and nucleases.

(xi) Trypsinogen is activated by an enzyme enterokinase, which is secreted by the intestinal mucosa into active trypsin.

(xii) **Bile juice** is secreted from duodenum. It contains bile pigments (bilirubin, bili verdin, bile salts, cholesterol and phospholipids). It emulsifies fats into small micelle. It also activates lipases.

(xiii) Intestinal juice contain variety of enzymes like maltases, lipases, nucleosidases, etc.

(xiv) It is formed by the secretion of the brush border cell of mucosa alongwith the secretion of goblet cells. Mucus and bicarbonates from pancreas protects the intestinal mucosa from acidic pH and also provide alkaline medium for various enzymatic activities.

(xv) In pancreatic juice

(a) $\left.\begin{array}{l}\text{Proteins}\\ \text{Peptones}\\ \text{Proteoses}\end{array}\right\} \xrightarrow[\text{Hydrolysed}]{\text{Trypsin/Chymotrypsin}} \text{Dipeptides}$

(b) Carbohydrates (starch) $\xrightarrow[\text{Hydrolysed}]{\text{Amylase}}$ Diasaccharides

(c) Fats $\xrightarrow[\text{Hydrolysed}]{\text{Lipases}}$ Diglycerides $\longrightarrow$ Monoglycerides

(d) Nucleic acid $\xrightarrow[\text{Hydrolysed}]{\text{Nucleases}}$ Nucleotides $\longrightarrow$ Nucleosides

(xvi) Breakdown of biomacromolecule occurs in the duodenum region of the small intestine.

(xvii) In large intestine simple substance are absorbed in jejunum and ileum regions of small intestine.

23. Absorption of simple food products occurs when the end products passes through the intestinal mucosa into blood and lymph.
   (i) Some simpler compounds like glucose, amino acid and some electrolytes like chloride ion are absorbed by simple diffusion.
   (ii) Fructose and amino acids are absorbed with the help of carrier ions like Na^+ and through facilitated transport.
   (iii) Fatty acid and glycerol are insoluble and forms small droplets called **micelle**, they move to intestinal mucosa. These reform into very small protein globule called **chylomicrons**.
   (iv) Chylomicrons are transported into lymph vessels (lacteals) in villi for absorption.
   (v) Absorption of the substances in tissues is known as assimilation.
24. The undigested unabsorbed substances called **faeces** enters into the caecum of large intestine. Through ileo-caecal valve. It is temporarily stored for defaecation in rectum.
25. The activity of gastro-intestinal tract is under the neural and hormonal control.
26. Various disorders are associated with the digestive system. Due to viral and bacterial infections inflammation of the intestinal tract occurs.

   Various diseases associated with these are
   (i) **Jaundice** Liver is affected, skin and eyes turn yellow.
   (ii) **Vomiting** Ejection of stomach contents through mouth.
   (iii) **Diarrhoea** Abnormal frequence of bowel movement and liquidity in faecal discharge.
   (iv) **Constipation** Faeces are retained within rectum.
   (v) **Indigestion** It is due to inadequate enzyme secretion, anxiety, food poisoing, over eating and spicy food.

Exercises

Question 1. Choose the correct answer among the following

(i) Gastric juice contains

(a) pepsin, lipase and rennin
(b) trypsin, lipase and rennin
(c) trypsin, pepsin and lipase
(d) trypsin, pepsin and rennin

(ii) Succus entericus is the name given to

(a) a junction between ileum and large intestine
(b) intestinal juice
(c) swelling in the gut
(d) appendix

Answer (i) (a) Pepsin, lipase and rennin

(ii) (b) Intestinal juice.

Question 2. Match the column I with column II.

Column I		Column II	
A.	Bilirubin and biliverdin	1.	Parotid
B.	Hydrolysis of starch	2.	Bile
C.	Digestion of fat	3.	Lipase
D.	Salivary gland	4.	Amylase

Answer

Column I		Column II	
A.	Bilirubin and biliverdin	2.	Bile
B.	Hydrolysis of starch	4.	Amylase
C.	Digestion of fat	3.	Lipase
D.	Salivary gland	1.	Parotid

Question 3. Answer briefly

(a) Why are villi present in the intestine and not in the stomach?
(b) How does pepsinogen change into its active form?
(c) What are the basic layers of the wall of alimentary canal?
(d) How does bile help in the digestion of fats?

Answer

(a) The mucosa layer of alimentary canal forms small finger-like foldings called villi in the small intestine. The cells lining the villi produce numerous microscopic projections called microvilli giving a brush border appearance. These modifications increase the surface area enormously. Villi are supplied with the network of capillaries and large lymph vessel called the lacteal mucosal.

(b) The inactive form of enzyme pepsinogen is activated by HCl.

(c) The wall of alimentary canal from oesophagus to rectum possesses four layers namely serosa, muscularis, sub-mucosa and mucosa. Serosa is the outermost layer, followed by muscularis, sub-mucosa and mucose.

(d) Bile salts help in emulsification of lipids and activate the lipases.

Question 4. State the role of pancreatic juice in digestion of proteins.

Answer The pancreatic juice contains inactive enzymes trypsinogen, chymotrypsinogen, procarboxypeptidases, amylases, lipases and nucleases. Trypsinogen is activated by an enzyme, enterokinase, secreted by the intestinal mucosa into active trypsin, which in turn activates the other enzymes in the pancreatic juice. Proteins, proteoses and peptones (partially hydrolysed proteins) in the chyme reaching the intestine are acted upon by the proteolytic enzymes of pancreatic juice as given below

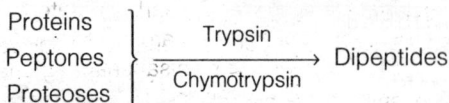

$$\left.\begin{matrix}\text{Proteins}\\ \text{Peptones}\\ \text{Proteoses}\end{matrix}\right\} \xrightarrow[\text{Chymotrypsin}]{\text{Trypsin}} \text{Dipeptides}$$

Question 5. Describe the process of digestion of protein in stomach.

Answer The process of digestion of protein in stomach. The food mixes thoroughly with the acidic gastric juice of the stomach by the churning movements of its muscular wall and is called the chyme. The pepsinogen, on exposure to hydrochloric acid gets converted into the active enzyme pepsin, the proteolytic enzyme of the stomach. Pepsin converts proteins into proteoses and peptones (peptides).

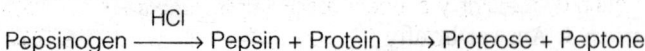

$$\text{Pepsinogen} \xrightarrow{\text{HCl}} \text{Pepsin} + \text{Protein} \longrightarrow \text{Proteose} + \text{Peptone}$$

HCl provides the acidic pH (pH 1.8) optimal for pepsins. Rennin is a proteolytic enzyme found in gastric juice of infants which helps in the digestion of milk proteins.

Question 6. Give the dental formula of human beings.

Answer The dental formula of human beings is $\frac{2123}{2123}$.

Question 7. Bile juice contains no digestive enzymes, yet it is important for digestion. Why?

Answer Bile is yellowish green alkaline solution with 89-98% water, having no digestive enzymes. The bile released into the duodenum contains bile pigments (bilirubin and biliverdin), bile salts, cholesterol and phospholipids but no enzymes. Bile helps in emulsification of fats, *i.e.*, breaking down of the fats into very small micelles. Bile also activates lipases.

Question 8. Describe the digestive role of chymotrypsin. Which two other digestive enzymes of the same category are secreted by its source gland?

Answer Chymotrypsin is the active form of chymotrypsinogen. It is activated by trypsin. It curdles milk. Nucleases like DNAase and RNAase and pancreatic lipase are other enzymes secreted by the pancreas.

Question 9. How are polysaccharides and disaccharides digested?

Answer The chemical process of digestion of carbohydrates is initiated in the oral cavity by the hydrolytic action of the carbohydrate splitting enzyme, the salivary amylase. About 30 per cent of starch is hydrolysed here by this enzyme (optimum pH 6.8) into a disaccharide-maltose. Further, carbohydrates in the chyme are hydrolysed by pancreatic amylase into disaccharides.

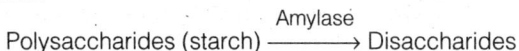

$$\text{Polysaccharides (starch)} \xrightarrow{\text{Amylase}} \text{Disaccharides}$$

Question 10. What would happen if HCl were not secreted in the stomach?

Answer The mucus and bicarbonates present in the gastric juice play an important role in lubrication and protection of the mucosal epithelium from excoriation by the highly concentrated hydrochloric acid.

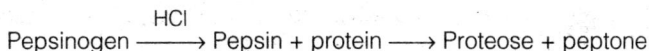

$$\text{Pepsinogen} \xrightarrow{\text{HCl}} \text{Pepsin + protein} \longrightarrow \text{Proteose + peptone}$$

HCl provides the acidic pH (pH 1.8) optimal for pepsins. Rennin is a proteolytic enzyme found in gastric juice of infants which helps in the digestion of milk proteins. Small amount of lipases are also secreted by gastric glands.

Question 11. How does butter in your food get digested and absorbed in the body?

Answer Bile helps in emulsification of fats, *i.e.*, breaking down of the fats into very small micelles. Bile also activates lipases.

Question 12. Discuss the main steps in the digestion of proteins as the food passes through different parts of the alimentary canal.

Answer **Digestion of protein in stomach** The proenzyme pepsinogen, on exposure to HCl, gets converted into **active enzyme** pepsin.

$$\text{Protein} \xrightarrow{\text{Pepsin}} \text{Proteoses} + \text{Peptones}$$

Pepsin always outs in acidic medium (pH 1.8). In infants, mail proteins are digested by rennin.

Digestion of protein in small intestine Pancreatic juice contains proenzyme trypsinogen. It is activated by enterokinase, secreted by intestinal mucosa, into active trypsin. Trypsin acts in alkaline medium.

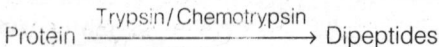

$$\text{Protein} \xrightarrow{\text{Trypsin/Chemotrypsin}} \text{Dipeptides}$$

The dipeptides are changed into amino acids by the enzyme succus enterics (intestinal juiice).

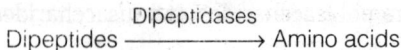

$$\text{Dipeptides} \xrightarrow{\text{Dipeptidases}} \text{Amino acids}$$

Question 13. Explain the term 'thecodont' and 'diphyodont'.

Answer Each tooth is embedded in a socket of jaw bone. This type of attachment is called thecodont.

Majority of mammals including human being forms two sets of teeth during their life, a set of temporary milk or deciduous teeth replaced by a set of permanent or adult teeth. This type of dentition is called diphyodont.

Question 14. Name different types of teeth and their number in an adult human.

Answer An adult human has 32 permanent teeth which are of four different types (heterodont dentition)-incisors (I), canine (C), premolars (Pm) and molars (M).

Question 15. What are the functions of liver?

Answer **Functions of Liver**

(i) Bile secreted by the liver helps in emulsification of fats, *i.e.*, breaking down of the fats into very small micelles.

(ii) Bile also activates lipases.

(iii) Liver producers RBCs in embryo.

(iv) It produces heparin to prevent clotting of blood inside blood vessels.

(v) It generates about 12% of total body heat.

Selected NCERT Exemplar Problems

Very Short Answer Type Questions

Question 1. The food mixes thoroughly with the acidic gastric juice of the stomach by the churning movements of its muscular wall. What do we call the food then?

Answer Chyme.

Question 2. Trypsinogen is an inactive enzyme of pancreatic juice. An enzyme, enterokinase, activates it. Which tissue/ cells secrete this enzyme?/ How is it activated?

Answer The cells of duodenum secrete enzyme entrokinase. It is activated by food in the duodenum.

Question 3. In which part of alimentary canal does absorption of water, simple sugars and alcohol takes place?

Answer Stomach.

Question 4. Name the enzymes involved in the breakdown of nucleotides into sugars and bases?

Answer Nucleosidases.

Question 5. Define digestion in one sentence.

Answer This process of conversion of complex food substances to simple absorbable forms is called digestion.

Question 6. What do we call the types of teeth attachment to jaw bones in which each tooth is embedded in a socket of jaws bones?

Answer Thecodont dentition

Question 7. Stomach is located in upper left portion of the abdominal cavity and has three major parts. Name these three parts.

Answer The stomach, as three major parts

(i) A cardiac portion into which the oesophagus opens.

(ii) A fundic region.

(iii) A pyloric portion which opens into the first part of small intestine.

Question 8. Does gall bladder make bile?

Answer No, liver makes bile and gall bladder stores it.

Question 9. Correct the following statements by deleting one of entries (given in bold).

(a) Goblet cells are located in the intestinal mucosal epithelium and secrete chymotrypsin/mucus.
(b) Fats are broken down into di and monoglycerides with the help of amylase/lipases.
(c) Gastric glands of stomach mucosa have oxyntic cell/chief cells which secrete HCl.
(d) Saliva contains enzymes that digest starch/protein.

Answer

(a) Goblet cells are located in the intestinal mucosal epithelium and secrete mucus.
(b) Fats are broken down into di and monoglycerides with the help of lipases.
(c) Gastric glands of stomach mucosa have oxyntic cell which secrete HCl.
(d) Saliva contains enzymes that digest starch.

Short Answer Type Questions

Question 1. What is pancreas? Mention the major secretions of pancreas that are helpful in digestion.

Answer The pancreas is a gland (both exocrine and endocrine) situated between the duodenum. The exocrine portion of pancreas secretes an alkaline pancreatic juice containing enzymes and the endocrine portion secretes hormones, insulin and glucagen.

Question 2. Name the part of the alimentary canal, where major absorption of digested food takes place. What are the absorbed forms of different kinds of food materials?

Answer The maximum absorption of digested food occurs in the small intestine of alimentary canal. The absorbed form of different food materials are

Food Materials	Absorbed form
Carbohydrate	Glucose
Protein	Amino acids
Fat	Fatty acids

Question 3. List the organs of human alimentary canal and name the major digestive glands with their location.

Answer Organs of human alimentary canal are mouth, oesophagus, stomach, small intestine, large intestine and anus. The major digestive glands and their location are

Digestive Gland	Location
Salivary glands	Mouth cavity
Liver	In abdominal cavity, just below the diaphragm.
Pancreas	Between the limbs of U-shaped duodenum

Question 4. What is the role of gall bladder? What may happen if it stops functioning or is removed?

Answer The gall bladder is a thin muscular sac that stores and concentrates, bile secreted by the liver. If it stops functioning or is removed, then no digestion of fats take place.

Question 5. Correct the statement given below by the right option shown in the bracket against them

(a) Absorption of amino acids and glycerol takes place in the (small intestine/large intestine).
(b) The faeces in the rectum initiate a reflex causing an urge for its removal. (neural/hormonal).
(c) Skin and eyes turn yellow in infection. (liver/stomach).
(d) Rennin is a proteolytic enzyme found in gastric juice in (infants/adults).
(e) Pancreatic juice and bile are released through. (intestine pancreatic/hepato-pancreatic duct).
(f) Dipeptides, disaccharides and glycerides are broken down into simple substances in region of small intestine. (jejunum/duodenum).

Answer

(a) Absorption of amino acids and glycerol takes place in the small intestine.
(b) The faeces in the rectum initiate a reflex causing an urge for its removal neural.
(c) Skin and eyes turn yellow in infection of liver.
(d) Rennin is a proteolytic enzyme found in gastric juice in infants.
(e) Pancreatic juice and bile are released through hepato-pancreatic duct.

(f) Dipeptides, disaccharides and glycerides are broken down into simple substances in region of small intestine (duodenum).

Question 6. What are three major types of cells found in the gastric glands? Name their secretions.

Answer The mucosa of stomach has gastric glands. Gastric glands have three major types of cells namely

(i) Mucus neck cells which secrete mucus.

(ii) Peptic or chief cells which secrete the proenzyme pepsinogen.

(iii) Parietal or oxyntic cells which secrete HCl and intrinsic factor (factor essential for absorption of vitamin-B_{12}).

Question 7. How is the intestinal mucosa protected from the acidic food entering from stomach?

Answer The mucus secreted by the goblet cells along with the bicarbonates from the pancreas, protects the intestinal mucosa from acid as well as provide an alkaline medium (pH 7.8) for enzymatic activities. Sub-mucosal glands (Brunners' glands) also help in this.

Question 8. How are the activities of gastro-intestinal tract regulated?

Answer The activities of the gastro-intestinal tract are under neural and hormonal control for proper coordination of different parts.

(i) The sight, smell and/or the presence of food in the oral cavity can stimulate the secretion of saliva.

(ii) Gastric and intestinal secretions are also similarly stimulated by neural signals.

(iii) The muscular activities of different parts of the alimentary canal can also be moderated by neural mechanisms, both local and through CNS.

(iv) Hormonal control of the secretion of digestive juices is carried out by the local hormones produced by the gastric and intestinal mucosa.

Question 9. Distinguish between constipation and indigestion. Mention their major causes.

Answer Constipation In constipation, the faeces are retained within the rectum as the bowel movements occur irregularly. The causes of constipation are water deficiency, lack of raughage in diet, etc.

Indigestion In this condition, the food is not properly digested leading to a feeling of fullness. The causes of indigestion are inadequate enzyme secretion, anxiety, food poisoning, over eating and spicy food.

Question 10. Describe the enzymatic action on fats in the duodenum.

Answer Fats are broken down by lipases with the help of bile into di and monoglycerides in the duodenum of small intestine as follows

$$\text{Fats} \xrightarrow{\text{Lypase}} \text{Diglycerides} \longrightarrow \text{Monoglycerides}$$

Long Answer Type Questions

Question 1. A person had roti and dal for his lunch. Trace the changes in those during its passage through the alimentary canal.

Answer Changes in food (roti and dal in the passage of alimentary canal.

(i) These food substances are first masticated by the teeth in the mouth, where carbohydrate part of the food is digested by the action of salivary amylase enzyme secreted by the salivary glands.

(ii) This partially digested food reached the stomach, where it receive acidic HCl and mainly the protein part of the food is digested by the action of proteolytic enzymes.

(iii) The lipid part of the food is digested by the bile secreted by the gall bladder.

(iv) In the small intestine, particularly in the duodenum this semidigested food is finally digested by the digestive enzymes present in the intestinal and pancreatic juices.

(v) After digestion, the broken down products of food, *i.e.* amino acids, glycerol, starch, etc., are observed mainly in the small intestine.

(vi) The undigested remains of food finally pass through the anus.

Question 2. What are the various enzymatic types of glandular secretions in our gut helping digestion of food? What is the nature of end products obtained after complete digestion of food?

Answer The bile, pancreatic juice and the intestinal juice are the secretions released into the small intestine. Pancreatic juice and bile are released through the hepato-pancreatic duct. The pancreatic juice contains inactive enzymes; trypsinogen, chymotrypsinogen, procarboxypeptidases, amylases, lipases and nucleases. Trypsinogen is activated by an enzyme, enterokinase, secreted by the intestinal mucosa into active trypsin, which in turn activates the other enzymes in the pancreatic juice. The bile released into the duodenum contains bile pigments (bilirubin and biliverdin), bile salts, cholesterol and phospholipids but no enzymes. Bile helps in emulsification of fats, *i.e.*, breaking down of the fats into very small micelles. Bile also activates lipases.

The secretions of the brush border cells of the mucosa along with the secretions of the goblet cells constitute the intestinal juice or succus entericus. This juice contains a variety of enzymes like disaccharidases (*e.g.*, maltase), dipeptidases, lipases, nucleosidases, etc. The mucus along with the bicarbonates from the pancreas protects the intestinal mucosa from acid as well as provide an alkaline medium (pH 7.8) for enzymatic activities. Sub-mucosal glands (Brunner's glands) also help in this.

Nature (i)

$$\left.\begin{array}{l}\text{Proteins}\\\text{Peptones}\\\text{Proteoses}\end{array}\right\} \xrightarrow[\text{Carboxypeptidase}]{\text{Trypsin/Chymotrypsin}} \text{Dipeptides}$$

$$\text{Dipeptides} \xrightarrow{\text{Dipeptidases}} \text{Amino acids}$$

(ii) $\text{Carbohydrates} \xrightarrow{\text{Amylase}} \text{Disaccharides}$

$$\text{Maltose} \xrightarrow{\text{Maltase}} \text{Glucose + Glucose}$$

$$\text{Lactose} \xrightarrow{\text{Lactase}} \text{Glucose + Galactose}$$

$$\text{Sucrose} \xrightarrow{\text{Sucrase}} \text{Glucose + Fructose}$$

(iii) $\text{Fats} \xrightarrow[\text{Hydrolysed}]{\text{Lipases}} \text{Diglycerides} \longrightarrow \text{Monoglycerides}$

$$\text{Di and Monoglycerides} \xrightarrow{\text{Lipases}} \text{Fatty acids + Glycerol}$$

(iv) $\text{Nucleic acids} \xrightarrow{\text{nucleases}} \text{Nucleotides} \longrightarrow \text{Nucleosides}$

$$\text{Nucleotides} \xrightarrow{\text{Lipases}} \text{Nucleosides} \xrightarrow{\text{Nucleosidases}} \text{Sugars + Bases}$$

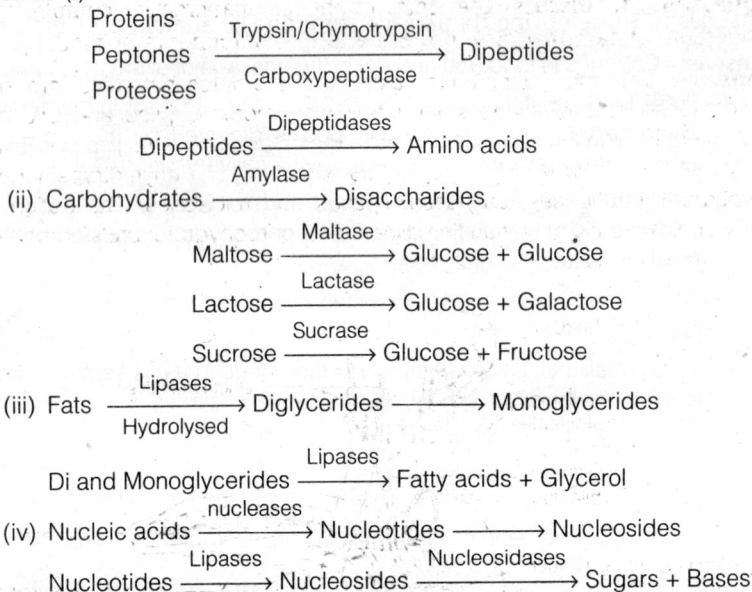

Question 3. Discuss the mechanisms of absorption.

Answer Absorption The simple substances formed after digestion are absorbed in the jejunum and ileum regions of the small intestine. The undigested and unabsorbed substances are passed on to the large intestine.

During absorption of nutrients, active transport occurs against the concentration gradient and hence, requires energy. Various nutrients like amino acids, monosaccharides like glucose, electrolytes like Na^+ are absorbed into the blood by this mechanism.

Fatty acids and glycerol being insoluble, cannot be absorbed into the blood. They are first incorporated into small droplets called micelles which move into the intestinal mucosa. They are re-formed into very small protein coated fat globules called the chylomicrons which are transported into the lymph vessels (lacteals) in the villi. These lymph vessels ultimately release the absorbed substances into the blood stream.

Absorption of substances takes place in different parts of the alimentary canal, like mouth, stomach, small intestine and large intestine. However, maximum absorption occurs in the small intestine.

Question 4. **Discuss the role of hepato-pancreatic complex in digestion of carbohydrate, protein and fat components of food.**

Answer The bile, pancreatic juice and the intestinal juice are the secretions released in the small intestine. Pancreatic juice and bile are released through the hepato-pancreatic duct. The pancreatic juice contains inactive enzymes — trypsinogen, chymotrypsinogen, procarboxypeptidases, amylases, lipases and nucleases. The action of hepato-pancreatic secretions on digestion of carbohydrate; protein and fats is summarised below:

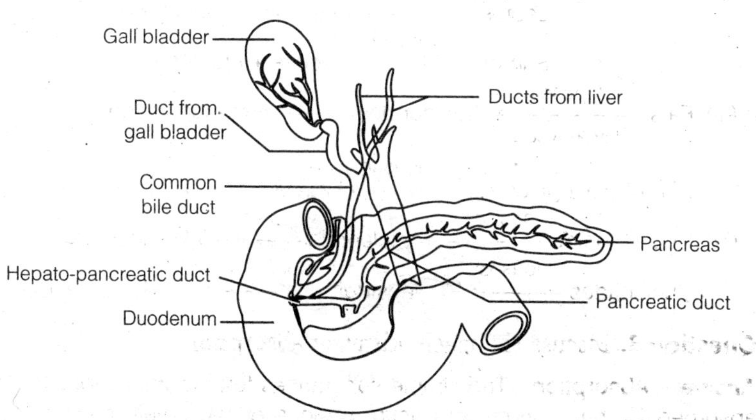

The duct systems of liver, gall bladder and pancreas

(i) Carbohydrates in the chyme are hydrolysed by pancreatic amylase into disaccharides.

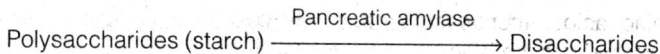

$$\text{Polysaccharides (starch)} \xrightarrow{\text{Pancreatic amylase}} \text{Disaccharides}$$

(ii) Fats are broken down by lipases with the help of bile into di and monoglycerides.

$$\text{Fats} \xrightarrow[\text{bile}]{\text{Lipases}} \text{Diglycerides} \longrightarrow \text{Monoglycerides}$$

(iii) Proteins in the chyme reaching the intestine are acted upon by the proteolytic enzymes of pancreatic juice.

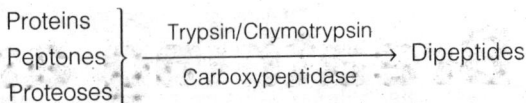

$$\left.\begin{array}{l}\text{Proteins}\\ \text{Peptones}\\ \text{Proteoses}\end{array}\right\} \xrightarrow[\text{Carboxypeptidase}]{\text{Trypsin/Chymotrypsin}} \text{Dipeptides}$$

Question 5. Explain the process of digestion in the buccal cavity with a note on the arrangement of teeth.

Answer Digestion in buccal cavity The buccal cavity performs two major functions—mastication of food and facilitation of swallowing.

(i) The teeth and the tongue with the help of saliva masticate and mix up the food throughly.

(ii) Mucus in saliva helps in lubricating and adhering the masticated food particles into bolous.

(iii) The bolous in then passes into the pharynx and then into oesophagus for further digestion.

Arrangement of teeth

The human have two sets of teeth a temporary and a permanent. This type of denotation in called diphyodont.

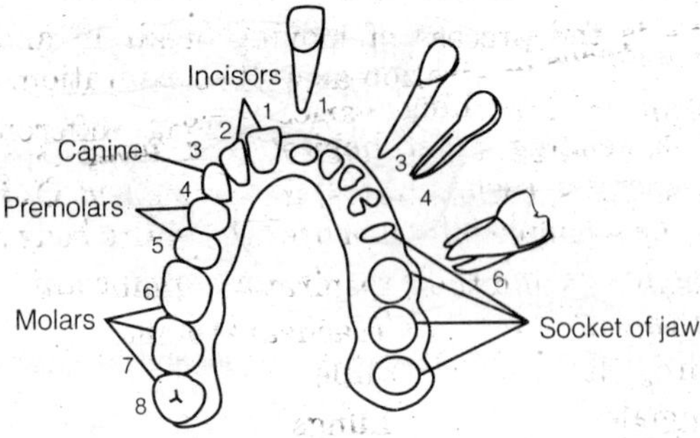

Arrangement of different types of teeth in the jaws on one side and the sockets on the other side

17

Breathing and Exchange of Gases

Important Points

1. Respiration is the process of exchange O_2 with CO_2 along with its transport in includes mainly two processess
   (i) Breathing
   (ii) Gaseous exchange along with its transport.
2. Breathing is the process of moving of air in and out of the lungs. It includes inspiration as well as expiration.
3. Mechanism of breathing varies among different group of animals depending upon habitat and level of organisation, *e.g.*, like sponges, coelenterates, flatworms, etc. O_2 is exchanged with CO_2 by a simple diffusion over the entire body surface.

   Some organisms and their respiratory organs are
   (i) Earthworm – Tracheal system
   (ii) Arthropods – Gills
   (iii) Mammals – Lungs
   (iv) Amphibians – Moist skin
4. Human respiratory system is well-developed and divided into nostrils, nasal passage, pharynx, larynx, trachea, bronchi and lungs.
   (i) Nostrils are the openings above the upper lips, it leads to nasal chamber through the nasal passage.

(ii) Nasal chamber opens into nasopharynx a portion of pharynx. It is the common passage for food and air.

(iii) Nasopharynx extends/opens through the glottis of larynx region into trachea.

(iv) Sound box is cartilaginous larynx, which helps in sound production.

(v) Epiglottis is a cartilaginous flap used to prevent the entry of food into larynx.

(vi) Trachae (wind pipe) extends to the mid thoracic cavity and divide at the level of 5th thoracic vertebra into right and left primary bronchi. The primary bronchi divides into many primary bronchioles. These bronchioles further divided into 2 to 11 alveolar ducts.

(vii) alveoli are the bag-like structure. It is the basic unit of gas exchange in lungs.

(viii) The whole network of bronchi, bronchioles and alveoli is comprised of lungs. Lungs are covered by double layered **pleura** with pleural fluid between them.

(ix) Lungs are present or situated in a thoracic chamber, which is anatomically an air tight chamber.

Thoracic chamber is consist of

(a) vertebral column at dorsal side

(b) ventrally by sternum

(c) ribs at the lateral side

(d) at the lower side, a dome-shaped diaphragm

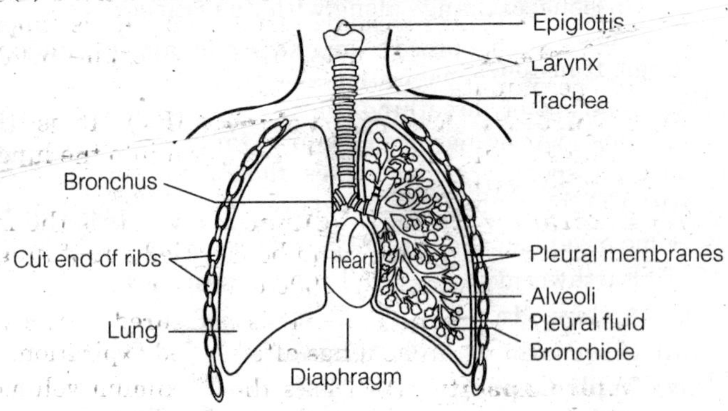

Diagrammatic view of human respiratory system (sectional view of the left lung is also shown)

5. The first stage breathing involve two process. Also known as **pulmonary ventilation**, process of moving air into and out of lungs.
   (i) **Breathing**

   - Inspiration (Air is drowen inside)
   - Expiration (Alveolar air is released out)

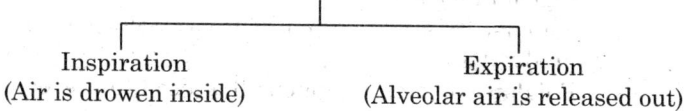

   (ii) Intercoastal muscles, which are present between the ribs plays an important role in the process of breathing.
   (iii) Inspiration is carried out by the movement of diaphragm. The external intercostal muscle contract. Ribs move in upward and outward direction. Due to such type of movement diameter of thoracic cavity increases. Negative pressure develops in lungs and air rushes inside the lungs.
   (iv) Expiration or exhalation involves relaxation of external intercoastal muscles. Ribcage moves downwards and inwards reducing the volume of thoracic cavity. The reduced volume causes positive pressure, which leads to exhalation.
   (v) On an average a healthy human breathes 12/16 times per minutes. Volume of air involved in breathing movements is estimated by using a spirometer.
6. Respiratory volumes and capacities are expressed in different ways
   (i) **Tidal Volume** (TV) It is the amount of air inspired or expired during normal respiration. It is approximate (500 mL). A healthy man inspire are expire 6000 to 8000 mL per minute.
   (ii) **Inspiratory Reserve Volume** (IRV) It is the extra volume of air, which could be inhaled into the lungs during maximal inspiration.
   (iii) **Expiratory Reserve Volume** (ERV) It is the maximum amount of air, which could be expelled out of lungs during forcible expiration. It is 1000 to 1100 mL.
   (iv) **Residual Volume** (RV) It is measured as the volume of air remaining in the lungs after forced expiration.
   (v) **Vital Capacity** (VC) It is the maximum volume of air, which can be moved in and out of the lungs.

   $$VC = \text{Tidal volume} + IRV + ERV$$

   (vi) **Inspiratory Capacity** (IC) Volume of air a person can inspire after normal expiration. It is $\rightarrow$ (IRV+ TV).

(vii) **Expiratory Capacity** (EC) Volume of air a person can expire after normal inspiration. It is (TV+ ERV).

(viii) **Functional Residual Capacity** (FRC) It is the volume of air that will remain in lungs after a normal expiration. It includes (ERV+RV).

(ix) **Total lung capacity** is the volume of air accomodated in lungs at the end of forced inspiration. It is (vital capacity + residual volume).

7. Primary sites for the exchange of gases is alveoli. Exchange of gases occurs between O_2 and CO_2 by simple diffusion.
   (i) Oxygen is transported throughout the body in combined form with haemoglobin.
   (ii) Release of O_2 into tissues is done on the basis of partial pressure, which is the pressure contributed by individual gas partial pressure of O_2 is more in alveoli than in tissues due to this gradient O_2 is transported to the tissues. Tissues, where pO_2 is low. Blood becomes deoxygenated.
   (iii) In tissues pCO_2 (partial pressure of CO_2 is more) is high. Blood take up CO_2 from tissues and releases CO_2 in alveoli, where pCO_2 is low.
   (iv) Diffusion layer of alveoli is made up of three major layers namely
      (a) thin squamous epithelium
      (b) endothelium
      (c) basement membrane.

8. Blood is the main medium for the transport of O_2 and CO_2
   (i) O_2 is mainly (97%) transported by RBC in the blood. 3% of O_2 is carried in dissolved state.
   (ii) CO_2 is chiefly transported in dissolved state through the plasma.
      70% is carried as bicarbonate form.
      7% is carried in dissolved state.
      20-25% is transported by RBC.

9. Oxygen is transported in bound form with haemoglobin, which is a red coloured iron containing pigment. O_2 binds with Hb to for oxyhaemoglobin.
   (i) One molecule of haemoglobin binds with O_2 molecule, Binding of haemoglobin with O_2 depends upon
      (a) partial pressure of O_2 (b) partial pressure of CO_2.
      (c) H^+ ion concentration (d) temperature.

(ii) When the percentage saturation of haemoglobin is plotted against the pO_2 than curve is called **oxygen dissociation curve.**

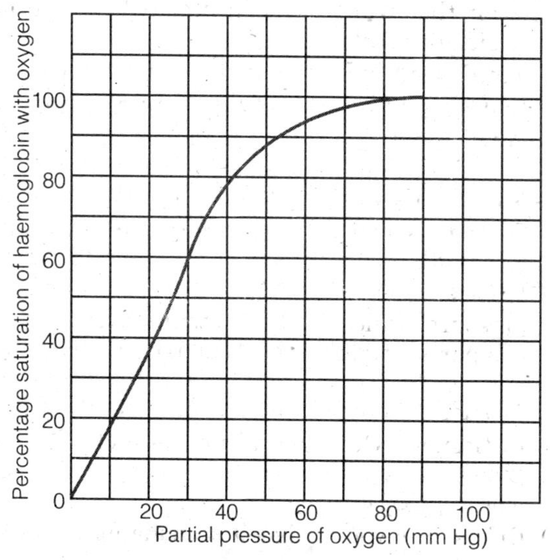

Oxygen dissociation curve

(iii) In low temperature, high pO_2, low pCO_2, less H^+ ion concentration (acidic pH). Shifts the curve toward right indicating formation of oxyhaemoglobin, whereas in low pO_2, high CO_2, basic pH, high temperature curve shifts towards left, which indicates the dissociation of O_2 with haemoglobin.

10. CO_2 transport is carried out in form of carbamino-haemoglobin (*i.e.*, about 20-25%).

(i) More binding of CO_2 occurs during high pCO_2 and low pO_2.

(ii) From high concentration (high pCO_2). CO_2 diffuses into blood and forms $HOCO_3^-$ and H^+ ions. Under the action of enzyme carbonic anhydrase.

$$CO_2 + H_2O \underset{}{\overset{\text{carbonic anhydrase}}{\rightleftharpoons}} H_2CO_3 \overset{\text{carbonic anhydrase}}{\rightleftharpoons} HCO_3^- + H^+$$

Reaction is proceeded in opposite direction, where pCO_2 is low.

11. Respiration is under the control of our neural system
    (i) Respiratory rhythm centre is present in the medulla region in the brain responsible for regulation of respiration.
    (ii) **Pneumotoxic centre** is also present in the pons region of the brain.
    (iii) A chemosensitive area present adjacent to this rhythmic centre is highly sensitive to CO_2 and H^+ ion concentration.

12. Various disorder is associated with respiratory system
    (i) **Asthma** Inflammation of bronchi and bronchioles occur, which causes difficulty in breathing and cause wheezing.
    (ii) **Emphysema** It is a chronic disorder respiratory surface is decreased due to damage in alveolar walls.
    (iii) **Fibrosis** It is occupational respiratory disorder. Long term exposure to dust causes inflammation in lungs. It is usually seen in workers involved in grinding or stone breaking.

Exercises

Question 1. Define vital capacity. What is its significance?

Answer **Vital Capacity** (VC) The maximum volume of air a person can breathe in after a forced expiration is called vital capacity. Vital capacity is higher in atheletes and singers. Vital capacity shows the strength of our inspiration and expiration.

Question 2. State the volume of air remaining in the lungs after a normal breathing.

Answer The volume of air remaining in the lungs even after a forcible expiration averages 1100 mL to 1200 mL.

Question 3. Diffusion of gases occurs in the alveolar region only and not in the other parts of respiratory system. Why?

Answer Alveoli are the primary sites of gas exchange in the respiratory system. Exchange of gases occur between blood and these tissues. O_2 and CO_2 are exchanged in these sites by simple diffusion mainly based on pressure/concentration gradient. The diffusion membrane for gas exchange is made up of three major layers. These layers are

(i) Squamous epithelium of alveoli.

(ii) Endothelium of alveolar capillaries.

(iii) Basement substance in between them. Its total thickness in much less than a millimeter. Therefore, all the factors in our body are favourable for diffusion of O_2 from alveoli to tissues and that of CO_2 from tissues to alveoli.

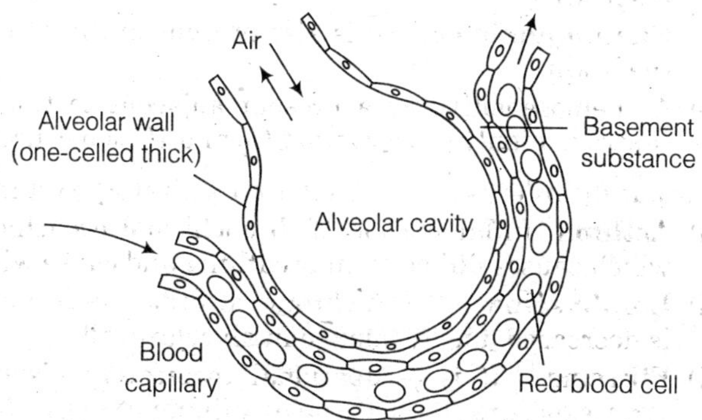

A diagram of a section of an alveolus with a pulmonary capillary

Question 4. What are the major transport mechanisms for CO_2? Explain.

Answer **Transport of carbon dioxide** CO_2 is carried by haemoglobin as carbamino-haemoglobin (about 20-25%). This binding is related to the partial pressure of CO_2, pO_2 is a major factor, which could affect this binding. When pCO_2 is high and pO_2 is low as in the tissues, more binding of carbon dioxide occurs whereas, when the pCO_2 is low and pO_2 is high as in the alveoli, dissociation of CO_2 from carbamino-haemoglobin takes place, *i.e.*, CO_2 which is bound to haemoglobin from the tissues is delivered at the alveoli. RBCs contain a very high concentration of the enzyme, carbonic anhydrase and minute quantities of the same is present in the plasma too. This enzyme facilitates the following reaction in both directions.

$$CO_2 + H_2O \underset{}{\overset{\text{carbonic anhydrase}}{\rightleftharpoons}} H_2CO_3 \underset{}{\overset{\text{carbonic anhydrase}}{\rightleftharpoons}} HCO_3^- + H^+$$

At the tissue site, where partial pressure of CO_2 is high due to catabolism, CO_2 diffuses into blood (RBCs and plasma) and forms HCO_3^- and H^+. At the alveolar site, where pCO_2 is low, the reaction proceeds in the opposite direction leading to the formation of CO_2 and H_2O Thus, CO_2 trapped as bicarbonate at the tissue level and transported to the alveoli is released out as CO_2. Every 100 mL of deoxygenated blood delivers approximately 4 mL of CO_2 to the alveoli.

Question 5. What will be the pO_2 and pCO_2 in the atmospheric air compared to those in the alveolar air?

(i) pO_2 lesser and pCO_2 higher (ii) pO_2 higher and pCO_2 lesser
(iii) pO_2 higher and pCO_2 higher (iv) pO_2 lesser and pCO_2 lesser

Answer

(i) In the alveolar tissues, where low pO_2, high pCO_2, high H^+ concentration, these conditions are favourable for dissociation of oxygen from the oxyhaemoglobin.

(ii) When there is high pO_2, low pCO_2, less H^+ concentration and lesser temperature, the factors are all favourable for formation of oxyhaemoglobin.

(iii) When pO_2 is high in the alveoli and pCO_2 is high in the tissues then the oxygen diffuses into the blood and combines with oxygen forming oxyhaemoglobin and CO_2 diffuses out.

(iv) When pO_2 is low in the alveoli and pCO_2 is low in the tissues then these conditions are favourable for dissociation of oxygen from the oxyhaemoglobin.

Question 6. Explain the process of inspiration under normal conditions.

Answer Inspiration is the process during which atmospheric air is drawn in. Inspiration is initiated by the contraction of diaphragm, which increases the volume of thoracic chamber in the antero-posterior axis. The contraction of external intercostal muscles lifts up the ribs and the sternum causing an increase in the volume of the thoracic chamber in the dorso-ventral axis.

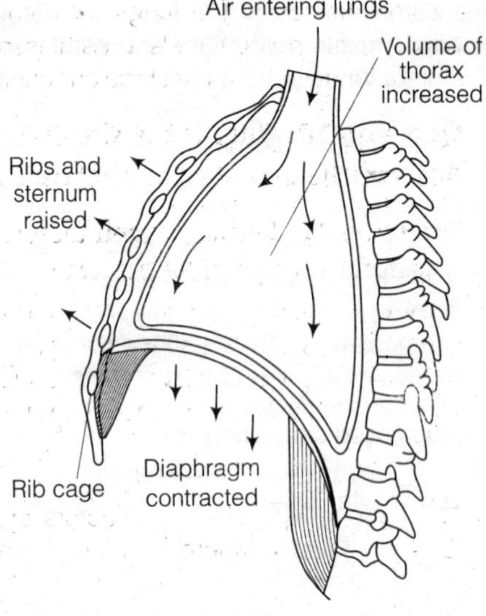

Process of inspiration

The overall increase in the thoracic volume causes a similar increase in pulmonary volume. An increase in pulmonary volume decreases the intrapulmonary pressure to less than the atmospheric pressure, which forces the air from outside to move into the lungs, *i.e.*, inspiration. On an average, a healthy human breathes 12-16 times/minute.

Question 7. How is respiration regulated?

Answer **Regulation of Respiration** A specialised centre present in the medulla region of the brain called respiratory rhythm centre is primarily responsible for the regulation of respiration. Another centre present in the pons region of the brain called pneumotaxic centre can moderate the functions of the respiratory rhythm centre. Neural signal from this centre can reduce the duration of inspiration and thereby alter the respiratory rate.

Question 8. What is the effect of pCO_2 on oxygen transport?

Answer Partial pressure of CO_2 (pCO_2) can interfere the binding of oxygen with haemoglobin, *i.e.*, to form oxyhaemoglobin.

(i) In the alveoli, where there is high pO_2 and low pCO_2, less H^+ concentration and low temperature, more formation of oxyhaemoglobin occur.

(ii) In the tissues, where low pO_2, high pCO_2, high H^+ concentration and high temperature exist, the conditions are responsible for dissociation of oxygen from the oxyhaemoglobin.

Question 9. What happens to the respiratory process in a man going up a hill?

Answer At hills, the pressure of air falls and the person cannot get enough oxygen in the lungs for diffusion in blood. Due to deficiency of oxygen, the person feels breathlessness headache, dizziness, nausea, mental fatigue and a bluish colour on the skin, nails and lips.

Question 10. What is the site of gaseous exchange in an insect?

Answer Trachea are the site of gaseous exchange in an insect.

Question 11. Define oxygen dissociation curve. Can you suggest any reason for its sigmoidal pattern?

Answer A sigmoid curve is obtained when percentage saturation of haemoglobin with O_2 is plotted against the pO_2. This curve is called the oxygen dissociation curve and is highly useful in studying the effect of factors like pCO_2, H^+ concentration, etc., on binding of O_2 with haemoglobin.

In the alveoli, where there is high pO_2, low pCO_2, lesser H^+ concentration and lower temperature, the factors are all favourable for the formation of oxyhaemoglobin, whereas in the tissues, where low pO_2, high pCO_2, high H^+ concentration and higher temperature exist, the conditions are favourable for dissociation of oxygen from the oxyhaemoglobin. This clearly indicates that O_2 gets bound to haemoglobin in the lung surface and gets dissociated at the tissues. Every 100 mL of oxygenated blood can deliver around 5 mL of O_2 to the tissues under normal physiological conditions.

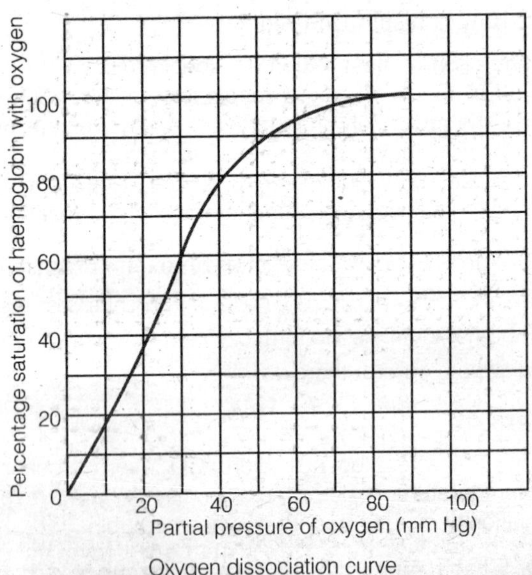

Oxygen dissociation curve

Question 12. Have you heard about hypoxia? Try to gather information about it, and discuss with your friends.

Answer Hypoxia is the shortage of oxygen supply to the blood due to

(a) Normal shortage in air

(b) Oxygen dificiency on high mountains (mountain sickness), anaemia and histotoxicity or poisoning of electron transport system.

Question 13. Distinguish between

(a) IRV and ERV

(b) Inspiratory capacity and Expiratory capacity

(c) Vital capacity and total lung capacity

Answer

(a) **IRV and ERV**

Inspiratory Reserve Volume (IRV) Additional volume of air, a person can inspire by a forcible inspiration. This is about 2500-3000 mL.

Expiratory Reserve Volume (ERV) Additional volume of air, a person can expire by a forcible expiration. This is about 1000-1100 mL.

(b) **Inspiratory capacity and Expiratory capacity**

Inspiratory Capacity (IC) Total volume of air a person can inspire after a normal expiration. This includes tidal volume and inspiratory reserve volume (TV+IRV).

Expiratory Capacity (EC) Total volume of air a person can expire after a normal inspiration. This includes tidal volume and expiratory reserve volume (TV+ERV).

(c) **Vital capacity and Total lung capacity**

Vital Capacity (VC) The maximum volume of air, a person can breathe in after a forced expiration. This includes ERV, TV and IRV or the maximum volume of air a person can breathe out after a forced inspiration.

Total Lung Capacity Total volume of air accommodated in the lungs at the end of a forced inspiration. This includes RV, ERV, TV and IRV or vital capacity + residual volume.

Question 14. What is Tidal volume? Find out the Tidal volume (approximate value) for a healthy human in an hour.

Answer **Tidal Volume (TV)** Volume of air inspired or expired during a normal respiration is called tidal volume. It is about 500 mL., *i.e.*, a healthy man can inspire or expire approximately 6000 to 8000 mL of air per minute.

Selected NCERT Exemplar Problems

Very Short Answer Type Questions

Question 1. A fluid-filled double membranous layer surrounds the lungs. Name it and mention its important function.

Answer The membrane is called pleura. It reduces friction on the lungs.

Question 2. Name the primary site of exchange of gases in our body?

Answer Alveoli.

Question 3. Cigarette smoking causes emphysema. Give reason.

Answer Cigarette smoking causes damage of the alveolar walls leading to decreased respiratory surfaces for the exchange of gases.

Question 4. A major percentage (97%) of O_2 is transported by RBCs in the blood. How does the remaining percentage (3%) of O_2 transported?

Answer Through plasma.

Question 5. Arrange the following terms based on their volumes in an ascending order

(a) Tidal Volume (TV)
(b) Residual Volume (RV)
(c) Inspiratory Reserve Volume (IRV)
(d) Expiratory Capacity (EC)

Answer

(a) **Expiratory Capacity (EC)** Approximate volume of blood is 1000 mL.
(b) **Residual Volume (RV)** Approximate volume of blood is 1200 mL.
(c) **Inspiratory Reserve Volume (IRV)** Approximate volume of blood is 2500 to 3000 mL.
(d) **Tidal Volume (TV)** Approximate volume of blood is 6000 to 8000 mL.

Question 6. Complete the missing terms.

(a) Inspiratory Capacity (IC) = ...+IRV
(b) .... = TV + ERV
(c) Functional Residual Capacity (FRC) = ERV + ...

Answer (a) TV
(b) Expiratory Capacity(EC)
(c) RV.

Question 7. Name the organs of respiration in the following organisms

(a) Flatworm ......
(b) Birds ......
(c) Frog ......
(d) Cockroach ......

Answer (a) Body surface
(b) Lungs
(c) Skin and Lungs
(d) Trachea

Question 8. Name the important parts involved in creating a pressure gradient between lungs and the atmosphere during normal respiration.

Answer The diaphragm and a specialised set of muscles external and internal intercostals between the ribs, help in generation of such gradients.

Short Answer Type Questions

Question 1. Compared to O_2, diffusion rate of CO_2 through the diffusion membrane per unit difference in partial pressure is much higher. Explain.

Answer As the solubility of CO_2 is 20-25 times higher than that of O_2, the amount of CO_2 that can diffuse through the diffusion membrane per unit difference in partial pressure is much higher compared to that of O_2. Thus, the main reason for this is higher solubility of CO_2 across the membranes. The diffusion membrane is made up of three major layers namely, the thin squamous epithelium of alveoli, the endothelium of alveolar capillaries and the basement substance in between them. However, its total thickness is much less than a millimetre.

Question 2. For completion of respiration process, write the given steps in sequential manner

(a) Diffusion of gases (O_2 and CO_2) across alveolar membrane.

(b) Transport of gases by blood.

(c) Utilisation of O_2 by the cells for catabolic reactions and resultant release of CO_2.

(d) Pulmonary ventilation by which atmospheric air is drawn in and CO_2 rich alveolar air is released out.

(e) Diffusion of O_2 and CO_2 between blood and tissues.

Answer

(a) Pulmonary ventilation by which atmospheric air is drawn in and CO_2 rich alveolar air is released out.

(b) Diffusion of gases (O_2 and CO_2) across alveolar membrane.

(c) Transport of gases by blood.

(d) Diffusion of O_2 and CO_2 between blood and tissues.

(e) Utilisation of O_2 by the cells for catabolic reactions and resultant release of CO_2.

Question 3. Differentiate between

(a) Inspiratory and expiratory reserve volume.

(b) Vital capacity and total lung capacity Vital Capacity (VC).

(c) Emphysema and occupational respiratory disorder.

Answer

(a) **Inspiratory and Expiratory Reserve Volume**

Inspiratory Reserve Volume (IRV) Additional volume of air, a person can inspire by a forcible inspiration. This averages 2500 mL to 3000 mL.

Expiratory Reserve Volume (ERV) Additional volume of air, a person can expire by a forcible expiration. This averages 1000 mL to 1100 mL.

(b) **Vital Capacity and Total Lung Capacity Vital Capacity (VC)** Vital Capacity The maximum volume of air a person can breathe in after a forced expiration. This includes ERV, TV and IRV or the maximum volume of air a person can breathe out after a forced inspiration.

Total Lung Capacity Total volume of air accommodated in the lungs at the end of a forced inspiration. This includes RV, ERV, TV and IRV or vital capacity + residual volume.

(c) **Emphysema and Occupational Respiratory Disorder**

Emphysema is a chronic disorder in which alveolar walls are damaged due to which respiratory surface is decreased. One of the major causes of this is cigarette smoking.

Occupational Respiratory Disorders In industries, especially those involving grinding or stone-breaking, so much dust is produced that the defense mechanism of the body cannot fully cope with the situation. Long exposure to these pollutants can give rise to inflammation, leading to fibrosis (proliferation of fibrous tissues) and thus, causing serious lung damage.

Long Answer Type Questions

Question 1. Explain the transport of O_2 and CO_2 between alveoli and tissue with diagram

Answer **Exchange of Gases**

(i) Pressure contributed by an individual gas in a mixture of gases is called partial pressure and is represented as pO_2 for oxygen and *pCO_2 for carbon dioxide.*

(ii) As the solubility of CO_2 is 20-25 times higher than that of O_2, the amount of CO_2 that can diffuse through the diffusion membrane per unit difference in partial pressure is much higher compared to that of O_2.

(iii) The diffusion membrane is made up of three major layers namely, the thin squamous epithelium of alveoli, the endothelium of alveolar capillaries and the basement substance in between them.

(iv) However, its total thickness is much less than a millimetre.

(v) Therefore, all the factors in our body are favourable for diffusion of O_2 from alveoli to tissues and that of CO_2 from tissues to alveoli.

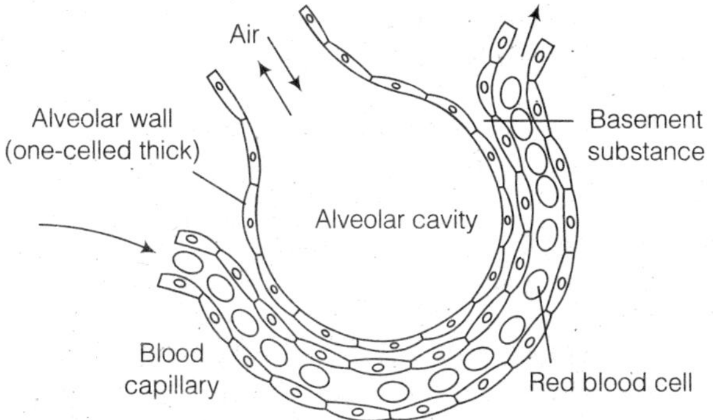

A diagram of a section of an alveolus with a pulmonary capillary

Question 2. Explain the mechanism of breathing with neat labelled sketches.

Answer **Mechanism of breathing involves two stages** *i.e.,* inspiration and expiration. Inspiration during, which atmospheric air is drawn in and expiration by the alveolar air is released out.

Inspiration It is initiated by the contraction of diaphragm, which increases the volume of thoracic chamber in the antero-posterior axis. The contraction of external inter-costal muscles lifts up the ribs and the sternum causing an increase in the volume of the thoracic chamber in the dorso-ventral axis.

The overall increase in the thoracic volume causes a similar increase in pulmonary volume. An increase in pulmonary volume decreases the intra-pulmonary pressure to less than the atmospheric pressure, which forces the air from outside to move into the lungs, *i.e.,* inspiration.

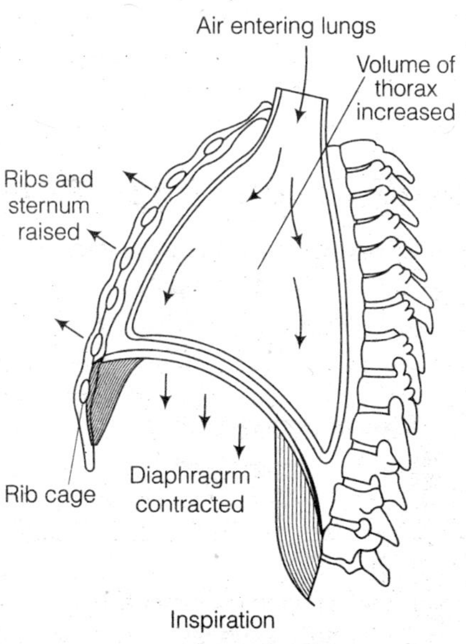

Inspiration

Expiration Relaxation of the diaphragm and the inter-costal muscles returns the diaphragm and sternum to their normal positions and reduce the thoracic volume and thereby the pulmonary volume. This leads to an increase in intra-pulmonary pressure to slightly above the atmospheric pressure causing the expulsion of air from the lungs, *i.e.*, expiration.

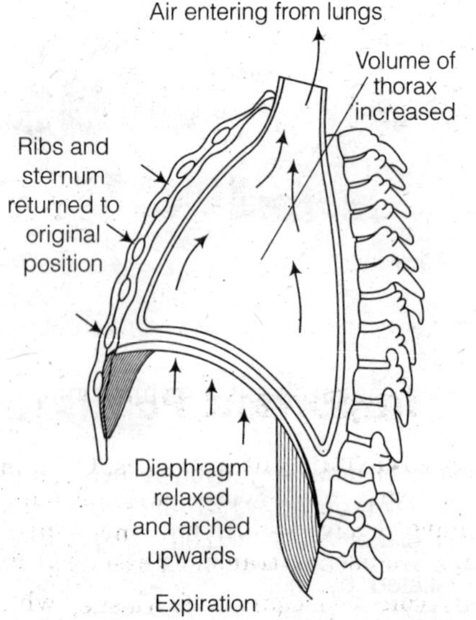

Expiration

Question 3. Explain the role of neural system in regulation of respiration.

Answer Respiration is regulated by the neural system.

(i) A specialised centre present in the medulla region of the brain called respiratory rhythm centre is primarily responsible for this regulation. Another centre present in the pons region of the brain called pneumotaxic centre, can moderate the functions of the respiratory rhythm centre. Neural signal from this centre, can reduce the duration of inspiration and thereby alter the respiratory rate.

(ii) A chemosensitive area is situated adjacent to the rhythm centre which is highly sensitive to CO_2 and hydrogen ions. Increase in these substances can activate this centre, which in turn can signal the rhythm centre to make necessary adjustments in the respiratory process by which these substances can be eliminated.

(iii) Receptors associated with aortic arch and carotid artery also can recognise changes in CO_2 and H^+ concentration and send necessary signals to the rhythm centre for remedial actions.

18

Body Fluids and Circulation

Important Points

1. In order to provide different nutrients, O_2 and other essential substance to each and every part of our body, different organism have evolved different mechanism of transport. Special fluids are used to transport essential substance.
2. Blood is red coloured connective tissue, which is commonly used body fluid by most of the higher organism including human lymph also helps in transport of certain substance. It consists of fluid matrix, plasma and formed elements.
   (i) Blood is composed of **fluid element** (blood plasma) and cellular elements (blood cells).
   Blood plasma is cystallo colloidal mixture and forms 55-60% of the blood.
   It contain 90-92% of water. It is straw coloured, viscous fluid and constitute about 5% of body weight. It chiefly contains inorganic salts (0.9%). Proteins (albumins), immunoglobulin (Ab), Anticoagulants (fibrinogen). Fibrinogen is needed for clotting or coagulation of blood. Various factors involved in blood clotting is present in blood.
   (ii) **Plasma** without clotting factors is called **serum** (Serum = plasma-fibrinogen).
   (iii) **Formed elements** (45%) in blood constitutes erythrocytes leucocytes and platelets.

(iv) Red blood cells are the most abundant cells in blood, *i.e.*, 5 million to 5.5 million of RBC mm^{-3}. At maturity it is devoid of nucleus and biconcave in shape. In camels nucleated RBC is present which is an exception. RBC has red colour due to presence of iron containing protein haemoglobin. Average life span of RBC is 120 days after which they are destroyed in spleen (graveyard of RBC).

(v) Leucocyte are known as WBCs (White Blood Cells). These are colourless due to lack of haemoglobin. These are nucleated are less in number, *i.e.*, 6000-8000 mm^{-3} of blood. WBC constitutes granulocyte and agranulocytes.

(vi) Neutrophil, eosinophils and basophils are granulocytes due to the presence of dense granules in their cytoplasm. Neutrophils are most abundant and basophils are least among the total WBC.

(vii) In inflammatory response basophils secrete histamine, serotonin, heparin, etc., which is stored in their granules. Neutrophils and monocytes are phagocytic cells, which destroys foreign organism entering the body. Eosinophils are also associated with allergic reactions.

(viii) Lymphocytes are most important cells responsible for immune response in body. These are of two types B-cells and T-lymphocytes.

(ix) Thrombocytes are also produced from megakaryocytes (special cells in bone marrow). These play chief role in blood coagulation. Blood contains 150000-350000 platelets mm^3. Reduction in their number can lead to clotting or disorders ultimately leading to excessive loss of blood from the body.

3. On the basis of surface antigens present on the surface of blood cells. Blood cells are grouped according to two grouping system ABO and Rh grouping system.

(i) ABO blood grouping is based on the presence or absence of anitgen A, B or both (antigen A^+ and antigen B). Antigen of donor and recipient need to be checked matched before blood transfusion.

(ii) Immune system does not form any antibody against its self antigen. When blood with different antigen is transfused to the recipient with other antigen. Agglutination of blood cell occur. Since, immune system recognized the antigen as foreign antigen and makes antibodies against it.

(iii) Organisms with blood group O does not contain any antigen. Hence, does not elicit immune response to produce antibody. The persons with blood group O are known as universal donors. On the other hand person with blood group AB does not produce antibody against antigen-A and B. They can accept blood from persons with AB as well as other blood groups. They are universal recipients

(iv) Another antigen Rh antigen is present similar to one present in Rhesus monkeys (hence, Rh). Such individuals are called Rh positive, while in the persons where, Rh factor is absent such individuals are known as Rh negative individual.

(v) Rh factor needs to be checked before blood transfusion. When Rh^- person is exposed to Rh^+ person it form specific antibodies against Rh antigens.

(vi) A special case of Rh incompatibility is observed in Rh^- blood of pregnant mother with Rh^+ foetus. In first pregnancy Rh^+ foetus is not exposed to Rh^- mother. Since, the two bloods are separated through placenta during delivery mother blood is exposed to Rh^- blood of boby. During subsequent pregnancies. Rh antibodies from Rh^- mother passes to Rh^+ foetus and destroys foetal RBC. This causes severe anaemia and jaundice in the body. This condition is known as erythroblastosis foetalis.

4. Blood clotting refers the coagulation of blood in order to prevent excessive loss of blood from the body.
   (i) Clot or coagulum is formed mainly of a network of fibrins in which dead and damaged formed elements of blood are trapped.
   (ii) When the vessels are damaged or ruptured they stimulate the platelets in blood to release certain factors. Which forms prothrombin activator complex.
   (iii) These activators catalyze the conversion of prothrombin to thrombin.
   (iv) Thrombin acts as an enzyme and converts fibrinogen into fibrin.
   (v) Fibrin forms a mesh like structure in which formed elements are trapped.
5. Lymph is a interstitial connective tissue composed of blood plasma and white blood corpuscles (mostly lymphocytes). It has same mineral distribution as in plasma. When the blood flow in capillaries some water with small water soluble substances move out into the spaces between the cells forming lymph. It contain B and T-lymphocytes, which plays an important role in cell defense system.

6. The system which plays a key role in the circulation of body fluids constitutes circulatory system. It consist of
   (a) Heart (b) Capillaries
   (c) Arteries (d) Veins
7. Circulatory system is of two types open or **closed**.
8. In open type of blood circulation blood is pumped through heart through large vessels and open into body cavities called sinuses like in arthropods and molluscs.
9. Annelids and chordates show closed circulatory system in which blood is pumped with heart and circulated in a close blood vessels.
10. The human circulatory system constitute.
    (i) Blood vessels (ii) Heart
11. Blood vessels are the tubular structure in which blood flows. There are of three types arteries, capillaries and veins.
    (i) Arteries transport the blood away from the heart.
    Artery is thick-walled in which blood flows under high pressure. The largest artery in the body is **aorta**. Arteries always contain oxygenated blood or pure blood except pulmonary artery which carries impure blood from right ventricles to lungs.
    (ii) Veins always contain deoxygenated blood or impure blood except pulmonary vein which carries pure blood from lungs to left auricle the lumen of veins is larger than that of arterioles. Veins contain tissue folds into their lumen that serve as valves.
    (iii) Arteries and veins are further divided into smaller and smaller vessels called **capillaries**. Cell wall is only one cell thick.
12. Heart is a hollow muscular organ, which acts as a pumping machine and beats non-stop throughout the life of an individual. Its pumping action drives the blood into arteries, which carry it to the organs. Veins carry deoxygenated blood back to the heart.
    (i) Human, birds and mammals have a four-chambered heart, fishes have two chambered heart, while reptiles and amphibians have three-chambered heart with two atria and one ventricle. In amphibians and reptiles left artrium receives oxygenated blood from the gill, lungs, skin and right artrium gets the deoxygenated blood from other body part but both blood mixed up in a single ventricle which pumps out the mixed blood. This is known as double circulation.

(ii) In humans double circulation occurs oxygenated and deoxygenated bloods do not get mixed up.

(iii) Heart is mesodermal in origin and situated in the thoracic cavity in between two lungs slightly tilted to left.

(iv) It is protected by double membrane called pericardium. Fluid inside them is called pericardial fluid.

(v) Heart consist of four-chambers two artria and two lower chamber called ventricles.

(vi) Right auricle receives venous (impure) blood from the body. Left auricle has opening of pulmonary veins and receives oxygenated blood from lungs. The right auricle opens into the right ventricle and the auriculo-ventricular aperture is guarded by a tricuspid valve.

The opening of left auricle into left ventricle is guarded by a bicuspid valve. These valves permit the flow of blood from atrium (auricle) to ventricle and not in reverse order. From the right ventricle originates the pulmonary aorta which goes to lungs and carries deoxygenated blood.

Left ventricle is continues into aorta, which supplies oxygenated blood to the body.

(vii) The heart is made up largely of cardiac muscles. Heart beat is due to rhythmic contraction and relaxation of heart muscles. When muscles of all four-chambers of the heart are relaxed, blood from large veins (vena cava), is poured into right atrium. This blood comes from the tissues, which have used up all the oxygen so, a very little amount of oxygen is found in it. Pulmonary vein from lungs, pours oxygenated blood into the left atrium then the atria contract.

(viii) During arterial contraction deoxygenated blood from right atrium enters the right ventricle and oxygenated blood from left atrium is poured into the left ventricle. Subsequently, the ventricles contract and from the left ventricle oxygenated blood is distributed to all the parts of the body through the largest artery, called **aorta**. From the right ventricle deoxygenated blood flows to the lungs through pulmonary artery. In this way deoxygenated blood comes to the heart, it is oxygenate in the lungs and comes back to the heart.

(ix) Sinoatrial node (SAN) is present on the right corner of the right atrium.

(x) Another mass of tissue is present in the lower left corner of right artrium close to the atrio ventricular septum called Atrioventicular node (AVN). A bundle of nodal fibres continues from AVN to atrioventricular septa and give rise to minute fibres throughout the ventricular musculature. The fibres along the right and left bundles are known as bundle of **His**. These fibres have ability to generate action potential without any external stimuli is auto excitable. It helps in maintaining the rhythmic contractile activity of the heart and known as pacemaker.

(xi) Normally heart beats 70-75 time per minutes.

13. The sequence of events that occur during single heart beat is called **cardiac cycle**. The portion of the cycle in which contraction occurs is known as **systole** the period of relaxation is diastole.

 (i) When heart rate is 72 beats/min a cardiac cycle lasts 0.8 sec.

 (ii) During a cardiac cycle ventricle pumps out 70 mL of blood and known as stroke volume.

 (iii) Cardiac output is

 stroke volume × heart rate (no. of beats per min.) or it can be explained as volume of blood pumped out by each ventricle per minute for a healthy individual this volume is 5 L.

 (iv) During each cardiac cycle two characteristic sounds are produced. The first heart sound lub occur when tricuspid valve and bicuspid valve closes. The second heart sound dub is associated with the closure of semilunar valves.

14. Electrical activity of heart during a cardiac cycle is graphically represented by ECG (Electrocardiogram).

 (i) To obtain ECG patient is connected to the machine with three electrical leads (cone to each wrist and to left ankle). It continuously monitors the heart activity.

 (ii) Each peak of ECG is characterized by P wave. It represents electrical excitation or depolarisation of the artria leading to the contraction of both the artria.

 (iii) Depolarization of ventricles is represented by QRS complex. It initiates ventricular contraction. Q marks the beginning of systole.

 (iv) T represents repolarization, the return of ventricles from excited to normal state.

 (v) By determing the number of QRS complexes occurring in a given time period heart beat of a individual could be determined.

15. The two types of circulation occurs in humans
    (i) **Systemic circulation** includes the pulmonary circulation. Blood is pumped into right ventricle enters the pulmonary artery, whereas the left ventricle pumps blood into aorta. It provides nutrients O_2 and other essential substances to the tissues.
    (ii) **Hepatic portal** system includes vascular connection between the digestive tract and liver.

    Before delivering to systemic circulation hepatic portal vein carries blood from intestine to liver. Cardiac activity is regulated by specialized muscles (nodal tissues) and this regulation is called myogenic. Cardiac function is also controlled by autonomic nervous system special neural centre is present in medulla oblongata. It is under the control of sympathetic nervous system, which increases the heart beat cardiac output.

    Parasympathetic nervous system decreases the rate of heart beat speed of conduction of action potential and cardiac output.
16. Various disorders are associated with circulatory system
    (i) High blood pressure (hypertension) state of body in which blood pressure is higher than normal (120/80). 120 mm Hg is systolic, while 80 mm Hg is diastolic pressure. In high pretension blood pressure is 140/90.
    (ii) Coronary Heart Diseases (CAD) These are referred as antherosclerosis. It is caused by deposits of calcium, fat cholesterol and fibrous tissues.
    (iii) Angina also known as angina pectoris when sufficient O_2 is not reached to the heart muscle characterized by acute chest pain.
    (iv) Heart failure It is the state of heart when it is not pumping the blood effectively to meet the needs of the body. In heart attack muscles are suddenly damaged by an inadequate blood supply.

Exercises

Question 1. Name the components of the formed elements in the blood and mention one major function of each of them.

Answer The formed elements of the blood are erythrocytes, leucocytes and platelets and they constitute nearly 45% of the blood.

Major Functions

(i) **Erythrocytes** The erythrocytes or red blood cells play a significant role in transport of respiratory gases (O_2 and CO_2).

(ii) **Leucocytes** The leucocytes or white blood cells play an important role to fight against infections.

(iii) **Platelets** Platelets or thrombocytes, are involve in the coagulation or clotting of blood. A reduction in their number can lead to clotting disorders, which will lead to excessive loss of blood from the body.

Question 2. What is the importance of plasma proteins?

Answer Fibrinogen, globulins and albumins are the major plasma proteins. Fibrinogens are needed for clotting or coagulation of blood. Globulins primarily are involved in defense mechanisms of the body and the albumins help in osmotic balance.

Question 3. Match column I with column II.

	Column I		Column II
A.	Eosinophils	1.	Resist Infections
B.	RBC	2.	Gas transport
C.	AB Group	3.	Universal recipient
D.	Platelets	4.	Coagulation
E.	Systole	5.	Contraction of heart

Answer A-3, B-5, C-2, D-1, E-4

Question 4. Why do we consider blood as a connective tissue?

Answer Blood is a mobile connective tissue derived from mesoderm which consists of fibre free fluid matrix, plasma and other cells. It regularly circulates in the body, takes part in transport of materials.

Question 5. What is the differences between blood and lymph?

Answer **Differences between Blood and Lymph**

S.N.	Blood	Lymph
1.	It is reddish in colour.	It is colourless.
2.	Blood is opaque.	It is almost transparent.
3.	Water content is nearly 55%.	Water content is nearly 94%.
4.	Blood is quite viscous. Viscosity is about 4.7.	It is less viscous. Viscosity is less than 2.0.
5.	It contains erythrocytes.	It has no erythrocytes.
6.	Blood possess a lot of platelets.	It has no platelets.
7.	Leucocyte content is high 5000-8000 mn^3.	Leucocyte content is low 5000 mn^3.
8.	Fibrinogen percentage is 0.3.	Fibrinogen percentage is negligible.
9.	Calcium and phosphate conent is high.	Calcium and phosphate conent is low.
10.	Blood flow is rapid.	Lymph flow is very slow.
11.	Blood circulates throughout the body.	It passes from tissues to brachiocephatic veins.

Question 6. What is meant by double circulation? What is its significance?

Answer **Double circulation** In double circulation, the blood passes twice through the heart during one complete cycle. Double circulation is carried out by two ways

(i) Pulmonary circulation

(ii) Systemic circulation

Significance

Double Circulation In birds and mammals, oxygenated and deoxygenated blood received by the left and right atria respectively passes on to the ventricles of the same sides. The ventricles pump it out without mixing up, *i.e.*, two separate circulatory pathways are present in these organisms. This is the importance of double circulation.

Question 7. Write the differences between

(a) Blood and lymph

(b) Open and closed system of circulation

(c) Systole and diastole

(d) P-wave and T-wave

Answer (a) **Differences between Blood and Lymph.** Refer to Ans. 5 of This chapter (see above).

(b) **Differences between Open and Closed Circulatory System**

S.N.	Open Circulatory System	Closed Circulatory System
1.	It is present in arthropods and molluscs.	It is present in annelids and chordates.
2.	Blood pumped by heart passes through large vessels into open spaces or body cavities called sinuses.	Blood pumped by the heart is circulated through a loosed network of blood vessels.
3.	Flow of blood is not regulated precisely.	It is more advantageous as the blood flow is more precisely regulated.

(c) **Differences between Systole and Diastole**

S.N.	Systole	Diastole
1.	The contraction of the musclesof auricles and ventricles is called systole.	It is the relaxation of atria and ventricle muscle.
2.	It increase the ventricular pressure causing the closure of tricuspid and bicuspid valves due to attempted back flow of blood into atria.	The ventricular pressure falls causing the closure of semilunar values which prevent back flow of blood into the ventricle.
3.	Systolic pressure is higher and occurs during ventricular contraction.	Diastolic pressure is lower and occurs during ventricular expansion.

(d) **Differences between P-wave and T-wave**

P-wave	T-wave
The P-wave represents the electrical excitation (or depolarisation) of the atria, which leads to the contraction of both the atria.	The T-wave represents the return of the ventricles from excited to normal state (repolarisation). The end of the T-wave marks the end of systole.

Question 8. Describe the evolutionary change in the pattern of heart among the vertebrates.

Answer The heart among the vertebrates show different patterns of evolution. Different groups of animals have evolved different methods for this transport. All vertebrates possess a muscular chambered heart.

(i) Fishes have a 2-chambered heart with an atrium and a ventricle.

(ii) Amphibians and the reptiles (except crocodiles) have a 3-chambered heart with two atria and a single ventricle,

(iii) In crocodiles, birds and mammals possess a 4-chambered heart with two atria and two ventricles.

(iv) In fishes the heart pumps out deoxygenated blood which is oxygenated by the gills and supplied to the body parts from where deoxygenated blood is returned to the heart.

(v) In amphibians and reptiles, the left atrium receives oxygenated blood from the gills/lungs/skin and the right atrium gets the deoxygenated blood from other body parts. However, they get mixed up in the single ventricle which pumps out mixed blood.

(vi) In birds and mammals, oxygenated and deoxygenated blood received by the left and right atria respectively passes on to the ventricles of the same sides. The ventricles pump it out without any mixing up, *i.e.*, two separate circulatory pathways are present in these organisms, hence, these animals have double circulation.

Question 9. Why do we call our heart myogenic?

Answer The normal activities of the heart are regulated intrinsically. It means the heart is autoregulated by specialised muscle (nodal tissue), hence, it is called myogenic.

Question 10. Sino-atrial node is called the pacemaker of our heart. Why?

Answer Sino-atrial node of heart is responsible for initiating and maintaining its rhythmic activity, therefore it is known as pacemaker of the heart.

Question 11. What is the significance of atrio-ventricular node and atrio-ventricular bundle in the functioning of heart?

Answer **Atrioventricular Node (AVN)** It is the mass of tissue present in the lower left corner of the right atrium close to the atrioventricular septum. It is stimulated by the impulses that sweep over the atrial myocardium. It is too capable of initiating impulses that cause contraction but at slower rate than SA node.

Atrioventricular bundle (AV bundle) It is a bundle of nodal fibres, which continues from AVN and passes through the atriaventricular septa to emerge on the top of interventricular septum. The AV bundle, bundle branches and Purkinje fibres convey impulses of contraction from the AV node to the apex of the myocardium. Here the wave of ventricular contraction begins, then sweeps upwards and outwards, pumping blood into the pulmonary artery and the aorta.

This nodal musculature has the ability to generate action potentials without any external stimuli.

Question 12. Define a cardiac cycle and the cardiac output.

Answer **Cardiac cycle** The sequential event in the heart which is cyclically repeated is called the cardiac cycle. It consists of systole and diastole of both the atria and ventricles.

Cardiac output It is the volume of blood pumped out by each ventricle per minute and averages 5000 mL or 5 L in a healthy individual. The body has the ability to alter the stroke volume as well as the heart rate and thereby the cardiac output. For example, the cardiac output of an athlete will be much higher than that of an ordinary man.

Question 13. Explain heart sounds.

Answer During each cardiac cycle, two prominent sounds are produced which can be easily heard through a stethoscope. The first heart sound (lub) is associated with the closure of the tricuspid and bicuspid valves, whereas the second heart sound (dup) is associated with the closure of the semilunar valves. These sounds are of clinical diagnostic significance.

Question 14. Draw a standard ECG and explain the different segments in it.

Answer **Electrocardiograph** (ECG) ECG is a graphical representation of the electrical activity of the heart during a cardiac cycle. A patient is connected to the machine with three electrical leads (one to each wrist and to the left ankle) that continuously monitor the heart activity. For a detailed evaluation of the heart's function, multiple leads are attached to the chest region.

Each peak in the ECG is identified with a letter from P to T that corresponds to a specific electrical activity of the heart. The **P-wave** represents the electrical excitation (or depolarisation) of the atria, which leads to the contraction of both the atria. The **QRS complex** represents the depolarisation of the ventricles, which initiates the ventricular contraction. The contraction starts shortly after Q and marks the beginning of the systole.

The **T-wave** represents the return of the ventricles from excited to normal state (repolarisation). The end of the T-wave marks the end of systole. Obviously, by counting the number of QRS complexes that occur in a given time period, one can determine the heart beat rate of an individual. Since the ECGs obtained from different individuals have roughly the same shape for a given lead configuration, any deviation from this shape indicates a possible abnormality or disease. Hence, it is of a great clinical significance.

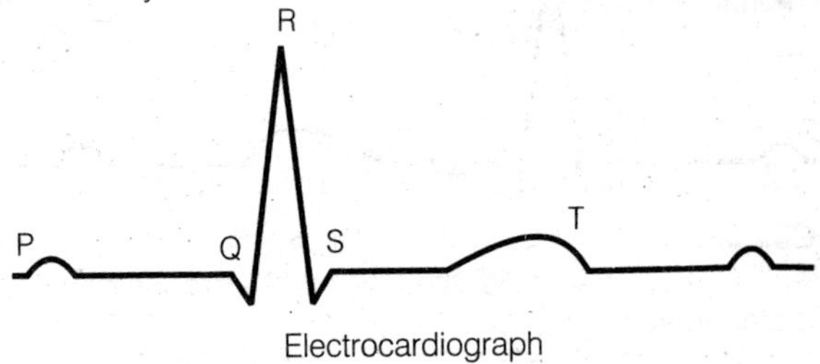

Electrocardiograph

Selected NCERT Exemplar Problems

Very Short Answer Type Questions

Question 1. Name the blood component which is viscous and straw coloured fluid.

Answer Plasma

Question 2. Complete the missing word in the statement given below.

(a) Plasma without .... factors is called serum.

(b) .... and monocytes are phagocytic cells.

(c) Eosinophils are associated with .... reactions.

(d) .... ions play a significant role in clotting.

(e) One can determine the heart beat rate by counting the number of .... in an ECG.

Answer

(a) Clotting (b) Neutrophils

(c) Allergic (d) Calcium

(e) QRS complex

Question 3. Given below is the diagrammatic representation of a standard ECG. Label its different peaks.

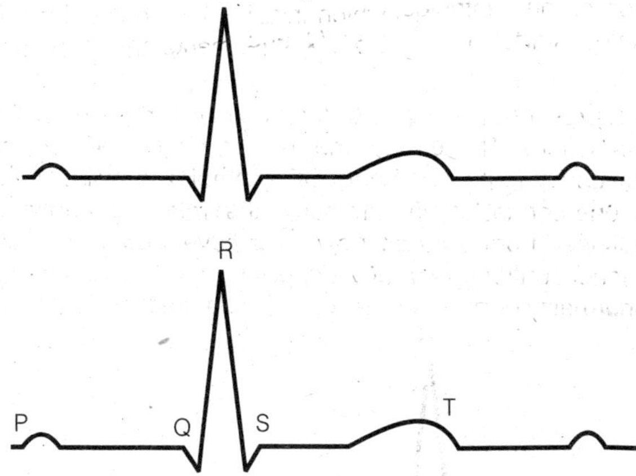

Question 4. Name the vascular connection that exists between the digestive tract and liver.

Answer Hepatic portal system.

Question 5. Given below are the abnormal conditions related to blood circulation. Name the disorders.

(a) Acute chest pain due to failure of O_2 supply to heart muscles.
(b) Increased systolic pressure.

Answer (a) Angina (b) High blood pressure

Question 6. Which coronary artery diseases is caused due to narrowing of the lumen of arteries?

Answer Atherosclerosis, affects the vessels that supply blood to the heart muscle. It is caused by the deposits of calcium, fat, cholesterol and fibrous tissues, which makes the lumen of arteries narrower.

Question 7. Define the following terms and give their location?

(a) Purkinje fibre (b) Bundle of His

Answer **Purkinje Fibres** A bundle of nodal fibres (AV bundle) give rise to minute fibres throughout the ventricular musculature of the respective called as Purkinje fibres.

Bundle of His These are fibres along with right and left bundles are known as bundle of His. Both of these are located on ventricular musculature.

Question 8. State the functions of the following in blood

(a) Fibrinogen (b) Globulin
(c) Neutrophils (d) Lymphocytes

Answer Functions of the followings

(a) Fibrinogens are needed for clotting or coagulation of blood.
(b) Globulins primarly are involved in immunity, *i.e.*, defense mechanisms of the body.
(c) Neutrophils and monocytes are phagocytic cells which destroy foreign organisms entering the body.
(d) Lymphocytes provide immunity to the body.

Question 9. What physiological circumstances lead to erythroblastosis foetalis?

Answer **Rh incompatibility** Rh antigens of the foetus do not get exposed to the Rh^- blood of the mother in the first pregnancy. However, during the delivery of the first child, there is a possibility of exposure of the maternal blood to small amounts of the Rh^+ blood from the foetus. In such cases, the mother starts preparing antibodies against Rh antigen in her blood. In case of her subsequent pregnancies, the Rh antibodies from the mother (Rh^-) can leak into the blood of the foetus (Rh^+). The could cause severe anaemia and jaundice to the baby. This condition is called erythroblastosis foetalis.

Question 10. Explain the consequences of a situation in which blood does not coagulate.

Answer It blood is lacking the coagulating factors like platelets, there will be excessive loss of blood from the body.

Question 11. What is the significance of time gap in the passage of action potential from sino-atrial node to the ventricle?

Answer The time gap in the passage of action potential from sino-atrial node to the ventricles allows ventricles to relax. The ventricular pressure falls, causing the closing of semilunar valves, which prevent the backflow of blood into ventricles.

Short Answer Type Questions

Question 1. The walls of ventricles are much thicker than atria. Explain.

Answer The contraction of atria completes filling of the ventricles. The ventricles have thicker walls because they contract much more strongly than the atria, especially the left ventricle, which must pump blood to all body organs through the systemic circuit.

Question 2. Differentiate between

(a) Blood and lymph (b) Basophils and eosinophils

(c) Tricuspid and bicuspid valve

Answer (a) **Differences between Blood and Lymph**

Refer to Ans. 5 in Exercises of this chapter.

(b) **Differences between Basophils and Eosinophils**

S.N.	Basophils	Eosinophils
1.	Their amount is 0.5-1% only.	These have 2-3% in blood.
2.	They secrete histamine, serotonin, heparin, etc.	These resist infection,
3.	These are involved in inflammatory reaction.	These are associated with allergic reactions.

(c) **Difference Between Tricuspid and Bicuspid Valve**

Tricuspid	Bicuspid valve
This valve is present between the opening of right atrium and the right ventricle.	It guards the opening between left atrium and the left ventricle.

Question 3. Briefly describe the followings

(a) Anaemia
(b) Angina pectoris
(c) Atherosclerosis
(d) Hypertension
(e) Heart failure
(f) Erythroblastosis foetalis

Answer

(a) **Anaemia** It is a condition arises due to very few erythrocytes in blood or erythrocytes do not contain sufficient haemoglobin in blood. It often causes loss of blood leading to weakness

(b) **Angina pectoris** A symptom of acute chest pain appears when no enough oxygen is reaching the heart muscle. Angina can occur in men and women of any age but it is more common among the middle-aged and elderly. It occurs due to conditions that affect the blood flow.

(c) **Atherosclerosis** Atherosclerosis, affects the vessels that supply blood to the heart muscle. It is caused by the deposits of calcium, fat, cholesterol and fibrous tissues, which makes the lumen of arteries narrower.

(d) **Hypertension** Hypertension is the term used for blood pressure that is higher than normal (120/80). In this measurement, 120 mm Hg (millimeters of mercury pressure) is the systolic or pumping, pressure and 80 mm Hg is the diastolic or resting, pressure. If repeated checks of blood pressure of an individual is 140/90 (140 over 90) or higher, it shows hypertension. It leads to heart diseases and also affects vital organs like brain and kidney.

(e) **Heart failure** Heart failure means when it is not pumping blood effectively enough to meet the needs of the body. Heart failure is not the same as cardiac arrest (when the heart stops beating) or a heart attack (when the heart muscle is suddenly damaged by an inadequate blood supply).

(f) **Erythroblastosis foetalis** It is a condition of Rh incompatibility (mismatching of Rh^- blood of a pregnant mother with Rh^+ blood of foetus. In this condition.The mother starts preparing antibodies against Rh factor in her blood. In case of her subsequent pregnancies, the Rh antibodies from the mother R' can leak into the blood or the foetus R^+ and destroy the foetal RBCs. This could be fatal to the foetus or could cause severe anaemia and jaundice to the boby.

Question 4. Explain the advantage of the complete partition of ventricle among birds and mammals and hence leading to double circulation.

Answer Advantage of Double Circulation In birds and mammals, oxygenated and deoxygenated blood received by the left and right atria respectively passes on to the ventricles of the same sides. The ventricles pump it out without any mixing up, *i.e.*, two separate circulatory pathways are present in these organisms, hence, these animals have double circulation.

Question 5. What is the significance of hepatic portal system in the circulatory system?

Answer Hepatic Portal Circulation A unique vascular connection exists between the digestive tract and liver called hepatic portal system. The hepatic portal vein carries blood from intestine to the liver before it is delivered to the systemic circulation. This ensures that the liver, which has the metabolic versatility to interconvert various organic molecules has first access to nutrients after a food is digested.

Question 6. Explain the functional significance of lymphatic system?

Answer As the blood passes through the capillaries much of it move out into the spaces between the cells. This fluid released out is called the interstitial fluid or tissue fluid. It has the same mineral distribution as that in plasma. Exchange of nutrients, gases, etc., between the blood and the cells always occur through this fluid. An elaborate network of vessels called the lymphatic system collects this fluid and drains it back to the major veins. The fluid present in the lymphatic system is called the lymph. It is responsible for the immune responses of the body an important carrier for nutrients, hormones, etc. Fats are absorbed through lymph in the lacteals present in the intestinal villi.

Question 7. Write the features that distinguish between the two

(a) Plasma and serum
(b) Open and closed circulatory system
(c) Sinoatrial node and atrio-ventricular node

Answer (a) **Difference between Plasma and Serum**

Plasma	Serum
Plasma contains fibrinogen needed for clotting of blood.	It is a plasma from, which the fibrin and clotting factors are removed by centrifugation.

(b) **Differences between Open Circulatory System and Closed Circulatory System.** Refer to Ans. 7 (b) in Exercises of this chapter.

(c) **Differences between SA Node and AV Node**

S.N	SA Node	AV Node
1.	It is the small mass of specialized muscle cells in the wall of right atrium near the opening of vena cava.	It is situated in the fibrous ring between the right atrium and ventricle of the heart.
2.	It initiates and maintains the heart beat.	It is the pathway through, which electrical impulses can pass.

Question 8. Answer the following

(a) Name the major site where RBCs are formed.

(b) Which part of heart is responsible for initiating and maintaining its rhythmic activity?

(c) What is specific in the heart of crocodiles among reptilians?

Answer

(a) Bone marrow

(b) Sino-atrial node (SA node)

(c) Reptiles have 3-chambered heart except crocodile, which has 4-chambered heart.

Long Answer Type Questions

Question 1. Explain Rh incompatibility in humans.

Answer Rh Incompatibility Rh antigen is observed on the surface of RBCs of majority (nearly 80%) of humans. Such individuals are called **Rh positive** (Rh^+) and those in whom this antigen is absent are called **Rh negative** (Rh^-). An Rh^- person, if exposed to Rh^- blood, will form specific antibodies against the Rh antigens. Therefore, Rh group should also be matched before transfusion.

A special case of Rh incompatibility (mismatching) has been observed between the Rh^- blood of a pregnant mother with Rh^+ blood of the foetus. Rh antigens of the foetus do not get exposed to the Rh^- blood of the mother in the first pregnancy as the two bloods are well separated by the placenta.

In case of her subsequent pregnancies, the Rh antibodies from the mother (Rh^-) can leak into the blood of the foetus (Rh^+) and destroy the foetal RBCs. This could be fatal to the foetus or could cause severe anaemia and jaundice to the baby. This condition is called erythroblastosis foetalis. This can be avoided by administering anti-Rh antibodies to the mother immediately after the delivery of the first child.

Question 2. Describe the events in cardiac cycle. Explain 'double circulation'.

Answer **Cardiac Cycle** Initially, all the four chambers of heart are in a relaxed state, *i.e.*, they are in joint diastole.

(i) As the tricuspid and bicuspid valves are open, blood from the pulmonary veins and vena cava flows into the left and the right ventricle respectively through the left and right atria.

(ii) The semilunar valves are closed at this stage. The SAN now generates an action potential which stimulates both the atria to undergo a simultaneous contraction — the atrial systole. This increases the flow of blood into the ventricles by about 30%.

(iii) The action potential is conducted to the ventricular side by the AVN and AV bundle from, where the bundle of His transmits it through the entire ventricular musculature. This causes the ventricular muscles to contract, (ventricular systole), the atria undergoes relaxation (diastole), coinciding with the ventricular systole.

(iv) Ventricular systole increases the ventricular pressure causing the closure of tricuspid and bicuspid valves due to attempted backflow of blood into the atria.

(v) As the ventricular pressure increases further, the semilunar valves guarding the pulmonary artery (right side) and the aorta (left side) are forced open, allowing the blood in the ventricles to flow through these vessels into the circulatory pathways.

(vi) The ventricles now relax (ventricular diastole) and the ventricular pressure falls causing the closure of semilunar valves which prevents the backflow of blood into the ventricles.

(vii) As the ventricular pressure declines further, the tricuspid and bicuspid valves are pushed open by the pressure in the atria exerted by the blood which was being emptied into them by the veins.

(viii) The blood now once again moves freely to the ventricles. The ventricles and atria are now again in a relaxed (joint diastole) state, as earlier.

(ix) Soon the SAN generates a new action potential and the events described above are repeated in that sequence and the process continues.

(x) This sequential event in the heart which is cyclically repeated is called the cardiac cycle and it consists of systole and diastole of both the atria and ventricles.

Double Circulation Refer to Ans. No. 6 of this chapter (Exercises).

Question 3. Explain different types of blood groups and donor compatibility making a table.

Answer **Blood groups** Two such groupings the ABO and Rh^- are widely used all over the world. ABO grouping is based on the presence or absence of two surface antigens (chemicals that can induce immune response) on the RBCs namely A and B. Similarly, the plasma of different individuals contain two natural antibodies (proteins produced in response to antigens).

Blood Groups and Donor Compatibility

Blood Group	Antigen on RBCs	Antibody in Plasma	Donor's Group
A	A	Anti-b	A, O
B	B	Anti-a	B, O
AB	A, B	NIL	AB, A, B, O
O	NIL	Anti a, b	O

From the above mentioned table it is evident that group 'O' blood can be donated to persons with any other blood group and hence 'O' group individuals are called 'universal donors'. Persons with 'AB' group can accept blood from persons with AB as well as the other groups of blood. Therefore, such persons are called 'universal recipients'.

Question 4. Write short notes on the following

(a) Hypertension
(b) Coronary artery disease.

Answer

(a) **High blood pressure** (hypertension) Hypertension is the term for blood pressure that is higher than normal (120/80). In this measurement, 120 mm Hg (millimeters of mercury pressure) is the systolic or pumping pressure and 80 mm Hg is the diastolic or resting pressure. If repeated, checks of blood pressure of an individual is 140/90 (140 over 90) or higher, it shows hypertension. High blood pressure leads to heart diseases and also affects vital organs like brain and kidney.

(b) **Coronary artery disease** Formation of a clot (thrombus) in a narrow coronary artery stops blood supply to the part of the heart muscle beyond the clot. The muscle cells of this part die due to lack of oxygen nd glucose. This condition is called 'heart attack' (coronary thrombosis or myocardial infraction) or MI. It may prove fatal, if the area affected is large condition of electrical impulses through cardiac muscles is interrupted and heart stop breathing. The heart attack is characterised by severe pain in the chest, breathlessness, restlessness, nausea and vomiting.

A thrombus that causes a heart attack may form in the coronary artery itself or elsewhere in the blood vessels and reach the heart *via* blood steam and get lodged in an artery too narrow for it to to pass.

Question 5. In the diagrammatic representation of the heart given below, mark and label, SAN, AVN, AV bundles, bundle of His and Purkinje fibres.

Answer

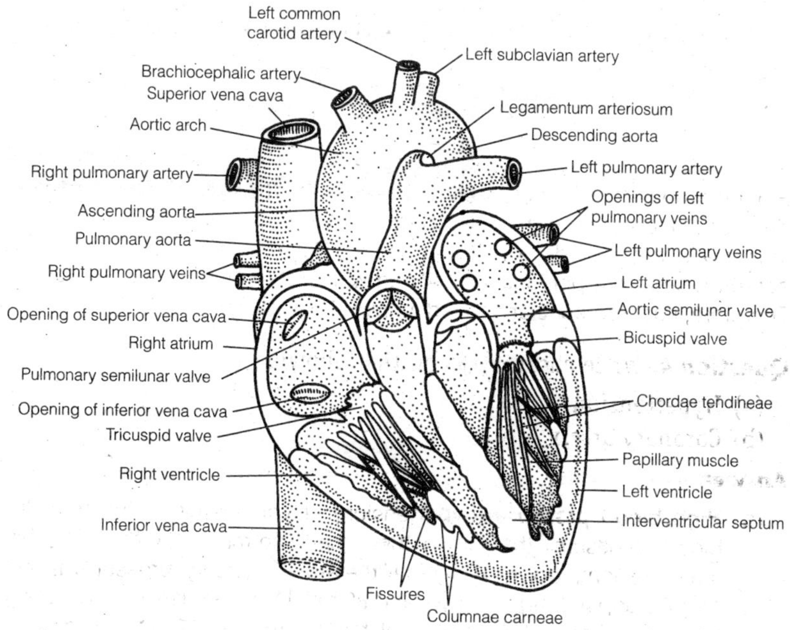

Section of a human heart

19

Excretory Products and their Elimination

Important Points

1. **Excretion** is the removal or elimination of waste products of metabolism from the body either is solid, liquid or in gaseous state.
2. **Osmoregulation** means balancing the osmotic pressure between the extracellular fluid (blood) and intracellular fluid, *i.e.,* maintenance of salt-water balance.

   The organs involved in the process of excretion are called **excretory organs,** which show a great variety in different organisms.

Excretory Organs of Some Organisms

Organism	Excretory Organ
Amoeba	General body surface, contractile vacuole for osmoregulation
Coelenterates	General body surface, mouth (solid wastes)
Flatworms	Flame cells
Earthworms	Nephridia
Cockroaches	Malpighian tubules
Prawns	Green glands

3. Human excretory system consists of following structures.
   (i) Kidneys (one pair) (ii) Ureters (one pair)
   (iii) Urinary bladder (single) (iv) Urethra (single)
4. Kidneys are reddish brown, bean-shaped structures situated between the last thoracic and third lumbar vertebra. It measures 10-12 cm in length, 5-7 cm in width and 2-3 cm in thickness, with an average weight of 120-170 grams.
5. A small notch called **hilum** is present towards the center of inner concave surface. Ureter, blood vessels and nerves enter through hilum. A broad funnel-shaped space is present called renal pelvis, some projections arises from it called calyces.
6. Outer layer of kidney is covered by **capsule**.
7. There are two zones in kidney the outer cortex and inner medulla. Medulla forms medullary pyramids projecting into **calyces**.
8. Cortex extends between the medullary pyramids to form columns of **Bertini**.

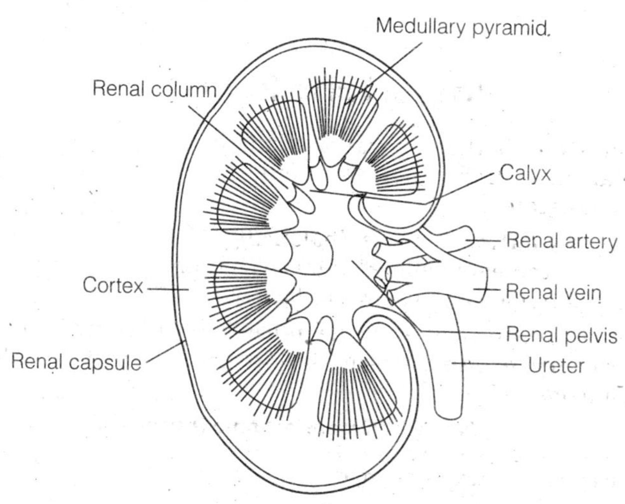

Longitudinal section (diagrammatic) of kidney

9. Basic functional unit of kidney is nephron. It is complex tubular structure consists of two parts.
   (i) glomerulus
   (ii) renal tububle

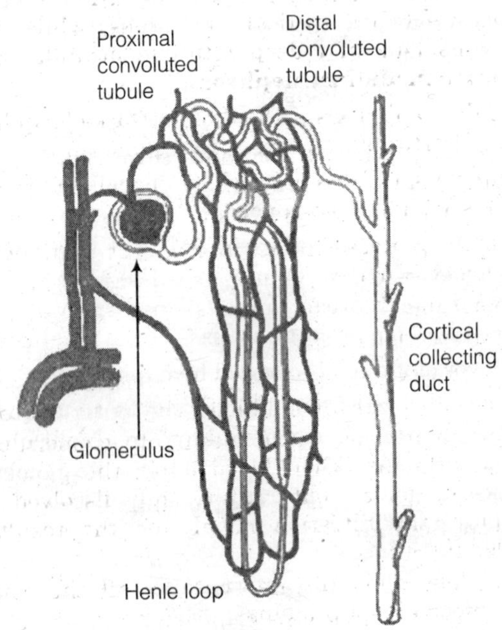

A diagrammatic representation of a nephron showing blood vessels duct and tubule

10. **Glomerulus** is the network of capillaries formed afferent and efferent arteriole. Afferent arteriole is fine branch of renal artery. Efferent arteriole take away blood from glomerulus.
11. **Renal tubules** begins with a double walled cup-like structure called Bowman's capsule. It encloses glomerulus. Glomerulus and Bowman's capsule together known as Malpighian body as renal corpuscle.
12. The Bowman's capsule continues further to form
    (i) Proximal Convoluted Tubule (PCT)
    (ii) Distal Convoluted Tubule (DCT)

    In between them a hair pin-shaped Henle's loop is present.

    Henle's loop has ascending and descending limb. Ascending limb continues to form DCT.
13. DCT opens into collecting duct it converges into renal pelvis through medullary pyramids in clayces.
14. **Loop of Henle** is present in medulla, while Malpighian corpuscle, PCT and DCT of the nephron is present in the cortical region.

15. When loop of Henle is short and dips little into medulla, such nephron are called cortical nephrons, while when loop of Henle runs long and deep into the medulla, nephrons are called **juxta medullary nephron.**
16. Peritubular capillaries is the fine network of capillaries formed by efferent arteriole emerging from glomerulus.
17. A minute vessel of this network run parallel to the Henle's loop and forms V-shaped **vasa recta**.
18. Three main processes occur in different parts of the nephron during urine formation namely
    (i) Glomerular filtration
    (ii) Ultrafiltration
    (iii) Reabsorption
    (i) Glomerular filtration is the first step in urine formation. Efferent arteriole bring blood into glomerulus with high blood pressure when blood enter the glomerulus. Blood pressure forces out water and dissolved components through the filtration membrane the resulting fluid is called filtration.
        (a) Glomerulus filtrate contains all the constituents of blood except proteins.
        (b) The three layers through, which filtration occurs in
            - the endothelium of glomerular blood vessels
            - the epithelium of Bowman's capsule
            - basement membrane between the two layers.
        (c) Podocytes are epithelial cells of Bowman's capsule, which are arranged in a intricate manner to form small filtration slits or slit pores.
        (d) The amount of filtrate formed by kidney per minute is called glomerular filtration rate.
    (ii) Blood is filtrated finely through slit pores into Bowman's capsule through three layers. This process is called ultrafiltration. From the Bowman's capsule, filtrate enters the PCT 65% of the glomerular filtrate is reabsorbed by PCT before reaching to the loop of Henle.
    (iii) **Reabsorption** of substance is done through active or passive transport', *e.g.*, in glucose, amino acids, Na^+, etc.
    (ix) In urine formation, tubular cells secreate substances like H^+, K^+ and ammonia into filtrate. It helps in maintenance of ionic and acidic balance of body fluids.

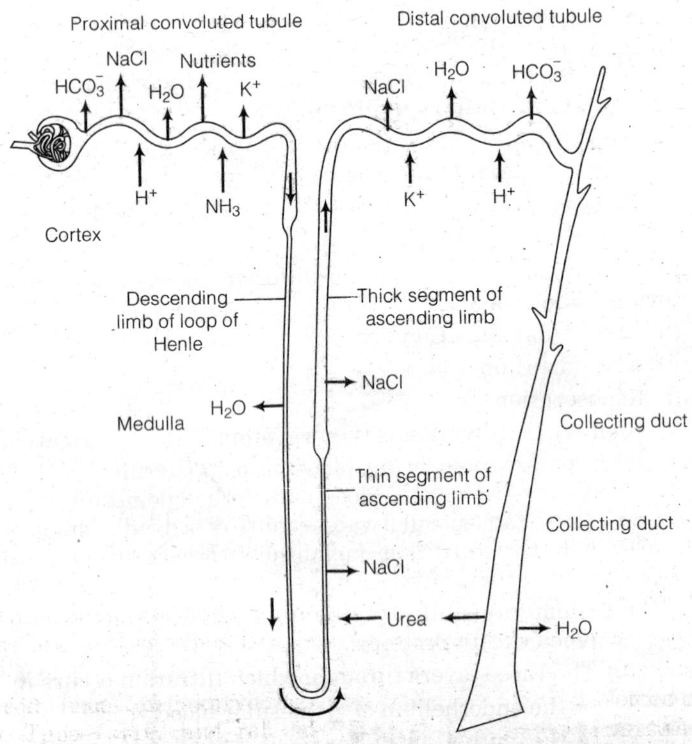

Reabsorption and secretion of major substances at different parts of the nephron (arrows indicate direction of movement of materials)

19. 70-80% of electrolytes and H_2O is reabsorbed by Proximal Convoluted Tubule (PCT). It is lined by simple cuboidal brush border epithelium. It increases the surface area for reabsorption, H^+ ion, ammonia, K^+ ion are secreted.
   (i) Na^+ and K^+ ions are reabsorbed through active transport (with the help of energy).
   (ii) Glucose and amino acids are reabsorbed passively.
   (iii) Reabsorption of water take place through osmosis.
   (iv) Cl^-, urea and other solutes are reabsorbed through osmosis.
   (v) In decending limb of loop of Henle urine gets concentrate as it is permeable to water but impermeable to electrolytes, while in the ascending limb of loop of Henle urine is diluted, it is impermeable to water but permeable to many electrolytes.

20. Sodium potassium balance in blood is maintained by DCT (Distal Convoluted Tubule). Reabsorption of Na^+, HCO^-_3 and water take place in this segment. Selective secretion of potassium and hydrogen ion take place to maintain pH.
21. Collecting duct extends from cortex of kidney to the inner parts of the medulla to produce concentrated urine large amount of water is reabsorbed. In collecting duct selective secretion of H^+ and K^+ ions occurs to maintain osmolarity and pH.
22. Counter current flow of ions occurs in two limbs of Henle's loop in which filtrate mouse in opposite direction.
    (i) The glomerular filtrate enters in to descending limb of Henle's loop in an isotonic state. Due to secretion of Na^+ ions from surrounding interstial fluid. It makes the filtrate hypertonic.

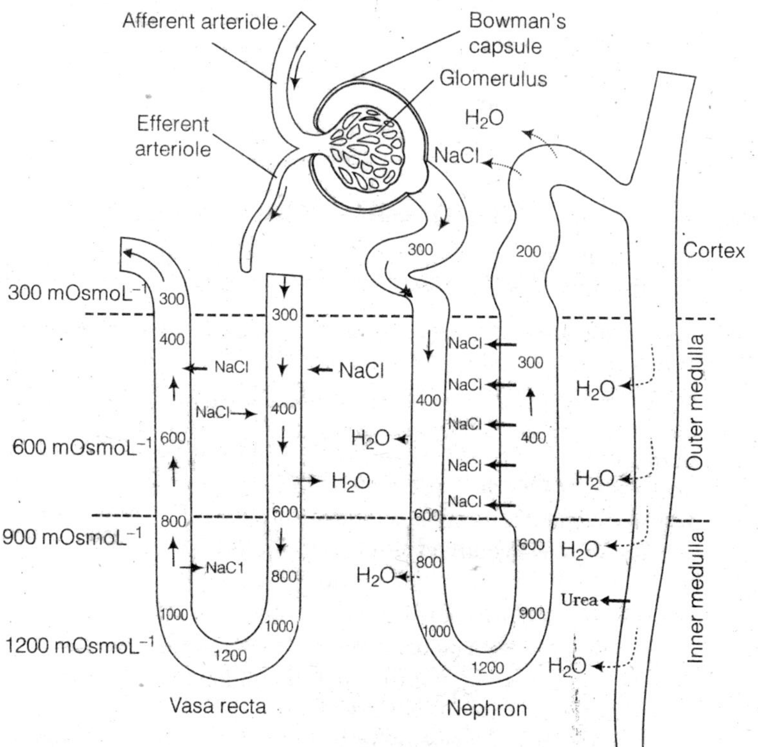

Diagrammatic representation of a nephron and vasa recta showing counter current mechanisms

(ii) When this filtrate mouse to the ascending limbe filtrate becomes hypotonic due to selective reabsorption of Na^+ ions

(iii) This hypotonic filtrate becomes isotonic in DCT (Distal Convoluted Tubule) due to action of ADH (Anti Diuretic Hormone).

(iv) This isotonic filtrate becomes hypertonic in the collecting tubule due to ionic and water exchange between the tubular fluid and medullary tissue fluid (hypertonic). This hypertonic fluid is urine, which passes through ureter.

23. Kidney function is regulated by two feed back mechanism.

(i) Control by Juxta Glomerular Apparatus (JGA).

(ii) Control by Antidiuretic Hormone.

(a) When glomerular blood flow/glomerular blood pressure/GFR falls. Juxtaglomerular cells are activated and release renin. Renin convert angiotensinogen in blood to angiotensin I and to angiotensin II.

(b) Angiotensin II increases the glomerular blood pressure by vasoconstriction. It also activate antidiuretic hormone (ADH) or aldosterone. It causes selective reabsorption from distal parts of tubule. This leads to the increase in blood pressure and GFR. This complex system is known as Renin-Angiotensin **mechanism**.

(c) Increase in blood flow to atria causes the release of ANF (Atrial Natriuretic Factor). It causes vasodilation *(i.e.,* dilation of blood vessels) and decrease the blood pressure. It acts as a check on renin angiotensin mechanism.

24. Micturition is the act of releasing the urine. The release of urine occurs by contraction of smooth muscle of urinary bladder wall and relaxation of muscle sphincter around the opening of bladder voluntary signals is given by **central nervous system.**

(i) On an average an adult excretes 1 to 1.5 L urine per day.

(ii) It is light yellow coloured watery fluid.

(iii) It is slightly acidic (pH 6.0) and has characteristic odour.

(iv) On an average 25-30 gm of urea is excreted out per day.

25. Apart from kidney, lungs, liver and skin helps in the elimination of excretory wastes.

(i) Lungs remove large amount of CO_2.

(ii) Liver secretes bile containing substance like bilirubin and biliverdin, which degrade steroid hormones. It ultimately passes out with the digestive waste.

(iii) Sebaceous glands also secrete certain amount of urea, lactic acid, sterols, hydrocarbons and waxes.

26. Various disorders associated with excretory system are

(i) **Uremia** accumulastion of urea in blood due to malfunctioning of kidneys patients suffering from uremia under goes haemodialysis. It may be defined as the separation of small molecules from large molecule in a solution by interpresing a semipermeable membrane between the solution and water. Haemodilyzer is a cellophane tube suspended in salt water solution of same composition as normal blood plasma blood of the patient is pumped from one of the arteries into cellophane tube cooling it to 0°C and mixing with the anticoagulant (heparin).

Pores of cellophane tubes allow urea. Uric acid, creatinine excess salt and excess H^+ to diffuse from blood into surrounding solution. The blood is purified and pumped into the vein of patient after blood is warmed to the body temperature and antiheparin treatment is given.

(ii) **Renal failure** Inability of kidney to carry out excretory and salt water regulatory functions called renal or kidney failure.

(iii) **Renal calculi/Renal stones** It is the insoluble mass of crystallised salts. (oxalates, etc).

(iv) **Glomerulonephritis** It is caused by injury to the kidney due to allergic reaction to toxins of bacteria such as *Streptococci.* Glomeruli become inflamed and engorged in with blood.

Exercises

Question 1. Define Glomerular Filtration Rate (GFR).

Answer **Glomerular Filtration Rate** (GFR) The amount of the filtrate formed by the kidneys per minute is called Glomerular Filtration Rate (GFR). GFR in a healthy individual is approximately 125 mL/minute, *i.e.*, 180 L per day.

Question 2. Explain the autoregulatory mechanism of GFR.

Answer **Regulation of GFR** The kidneys have builtin mechanisms for the regulation of glomerular filtration rate. One such efficient mechanism is carried out by juxtaglomerular apparatus (JGA). JGA is a special sensitive region formed by cellular modifications in the distal convoluted tubule and the afferent arteriole at the location of their contact. A fall in GFR can activate the JG cells to release renin which can stimulate the glomerular blood flow and thereby the GFR back to normal.

Question 3. Indicate whether the following statements are true or false

(a) Micturition is carried out by a reflex.
(b) ADH helps in water elimination, making the urine hypotonic.
(c) Protein-free fluid is filtered from blood plasma into the Bowman's capsule.
(d) Henle's loop plays an important role in concentrating the urine.
(e) Glucose is actively reabsorbed in the proximal convoluted tubule.

Answer (a) True (b) False (c) True
(d) True (e) False

Question 4. Give a brief account of the counter current mechanism.

Answer **Counter-Current Mechanism** (See Text)

(i) The counter current mechanism takes place in Henle's loop and vasa recta.
(ii) The flow of filtrate in the two limbs of Henle's loop is in opposite directions and thus, forms a counter-current.
(iii) The flow of blood through the two limbs of vasa recta is also in a counter current pattern.
(iv) NaCl is transported by the ascending limb of Henle's loop which is exchanged with the descending limb of vasa recta.

(v) NaCl is returned to the interstitium by the ascending portion of vasa recta.

(vi) Similarly, small amount of urea enter the thin segment of the ascending limb of Henle's loop, which is transported back to the interstitium by the collecting tubule.

(vii) This transport of substances facilitated by the special arrangement of Henle's loop and vasa recta is called the counter current mechanism.

(viii) It helps to maintain a concentration gradient in the medullary interstitium. Which facilitates an easy passage of water from the collecting tubule thereby concentrating the filtrate (urine).

Question 5. Describe the role of liver, lungs and skin in excretion.

Answer Role in Excretion

Lungs These remove large amount of CO_2 (18 L/day) and also significant quantities of water everyday.

Liver It secretes bile containing substances like bilirubin, biliverdin, cholesterol, degraded steroid hormones, vitamins and drugs. Most of these substances ultimately pass out along with digestive wastes.

Skin The sweat and sebaceous glands in the skin can eliminate certain substances through their secretions. Sweat produced by the sweat glands is a watery fluid containing NaCl, small amount of urea, lactic acid, etc. Sebaceous glands eliminate certain substances like sterols, hydrocarbons and waxes through sebum. This secretion provides a protective oily covering to the skin.

Question 6. Explain micturition.

Answer Micturition The process of release of urine is called micturition and the neural mechanisms causing it is called the micturition reflex. An adult human excretes, on an average, 1 to 1.5 L of urine per day. The urine formed is a light yellow coloured watery fluid which is slightly acidic (pH-6.0) and has a characteristic odour.

Question 7. Match the items of column I with those of column II

S.N.	Column I	Column II
A.	Ammonotelism	1. Birds
B.	Bowman's capsule	2. Water reabsorption
C.	Micturition	3. Bony fish
D.	Uricotelism	4. Urinary bladder
E.	ADH	5. Renal tubule

Answer

S.N.	Column I	Column II
A.	Micturition	3. Bony fish
B.	ADH	5. Renal tubule
C.	Uricotelism	4. Urinary bladder
D.	Ammonotelism	1. Birds
E.	Bowman's capsule	2. Water reabsorption

Question 8. What is meant by the term osmoregulation?

Answer It is the phenomena of regulation of change in the concentration of body fluids according to the concentration of external environment, *i.e.*, most marine invertebrates, some freshwater invertebrates, hagfish (a vertebrate).

Question 9. Terrestrial animals are generally either ureotelic or uricotelic, not ammonotelic, why?

Answer Terrestrial adaptation requires the production of lesser toxic nitrogenous wastes like urea and uric acid for the conservation of water. Mammals, many terrestrial amphibians and marine fishes mainly excrete urea and are called ureotelic animals. Ammonia produced by metabolism is converted into urea in the liver of these animals and released into the blood which is filtrated and excreted out by the kidneys.

Some amount of urea may be retained in the kidney matrix of some of these animals to maintain a desired osmolarity. Reptiles, birds, land snails and insects excrete nitrogenous wastes as uric acid in the form of pellet or paste with a minimum loss of water and are called uricotelic animals.

Question 10. What is the significance of juxtaglomerular apparatus (JGA) in kidney function?

Answer The juxtaglomerular apparatus (JGA) plays inportant role in monitoring and regulation of kidney functioning by hormonal feedback, mechanism, involving hypothalamus and to a certain extent, the heart.

Question 11. Name the following

(a) A chordate animal having flame cells as excretory structures.
(b) Cortical portions projecting between the medullary pyramids in the human kidney.
(c) A loop of capillary running parallel to the Henle's loop.

Answer (a) Flatworms (b) Columns of Bertini (c) Vasa recta

Question 12. Fill in the gaps

(a) Ascending limb of Henle's loop is ...... to water, whereas the descending limb is ...... to it.
(b) Reabsorption of water from distal parts of the tubules is facilitated by hormone ....
(c) Dialysis fluid contain all the constituents as in plasma except ....
(d) A healthy adult human excretes (on an average) ...... gm of urea/day.

Answer

(a) impermeable
(b) antidiuretic hormone (ADH)
(c) nitrogenous wastes
(d) 25-30.

Selected NCERT Exemplar Problems

Very Short Answer Type Questions

Question 1. Where does the selective reabsorption of glomerular filtrate take place?

Answer The selective reabsorption of glomerular filtrate take place in the DCT and collecting duct.

Question 2. What is the excretory product from kidneys of reptiles?

Answer Reptiles excrete nitrogenous wastes as uric acid in the form of pellet or paste with a minimum loss of water and are called uricotelic animals.

Question 3. What is the composition of sweat produced by sweat glands?

Answer **Composition of sweat** is a watery fluid containing NaCl, small amount of urea, lactic acid, etc.

Question 4. Identify the glands that perform the excretory function in prawns.

Answer Antennal glands or green glands.

Question 5. What is the excretory structure in *Amoeba?*

Answer Contractile vacuole.

Question 6. The following abbreviations are used in the context of excretory functions, what do they stand for?

(a) ANF
(b) ADH
(c) GFR
(d) DCT

Answer (a) ANF — Antinatriuretic Factor
(b) ADH — Antidiuretic Hormone
(c) GFR — Glomerular Filtration Rate
(d) DCT — Distal Convoluted Tubule.

Question 7. Differentiate glycosuria from ketonuria.

Answer Glycosuria is the presence of glucose in the urine, whereas ketonuria is the presence of ketone bodies in the urine.

Question 8. What is the role of sebaceous glands?

Answer **Role of sebaceous glands** Sebaceous glands eliminate certain substances like sterols, hydrocarbons and waxes through sebum. This secretion provides a protective oily covering for the skin.

Question 9. Name two actively transported substances in Glomerular filtrate.

Answer Glucose and amino acids.

Question 10. Mention any two metabolic disorders, which can be diagnosed by analysis of urine.

Answer Glycosuria and ketonuria.

Question 11. What are the main processes of urine formation?

Answer The main processes in urine formation are filtration, reabsorption, secretion and concentration /dilution.

Question 12. Sort the following into actively or passively transported substances during reabsorption of GFR.

Glucose, amino acids, nitrogenous wastes, Na^+, water

Answer Actively transported — Glucose, amino acids and Na^+

Passively transported —Nitrogenous wastes and water.

Question 13. Complete the following

(a) Urinary excretion = tubular reabsorption + tubular secretion
(b) Dialysis fluid = Plasma

Answer

(a) Urinary excretion = Filtration + tubular reabsorption + tubular secretion
(b) Dialysis fluid = Plasma – Nitrogenous wastes

Question 14. Mention the substances that exit from the tubules in order to maintain a concentration gradient in the medullary interstitium.

Answer Small amount of urea along with, H^+, K^+ and NH_3 are the substances that exit from the tubules in order to maintain a concentration gradient in the medullary interstitium.

Question 15. Fill in the blanks appropriately

Organ	Excretory wastes
(a) Kidneys	......
(b) Lungs	......
(c) Liver	......
(d) Skin	......

Answer

Organ	Excretory wastes
(a) Kidneys	Urine
(b) Lungs	CO_2
(c) Liver	Bile
(d) Skin	Salty watery fluid with some urea.

Short Answer Type Questions

Question 1. Show the structure of a renal corpuscle with the help of a diagram.

Answer

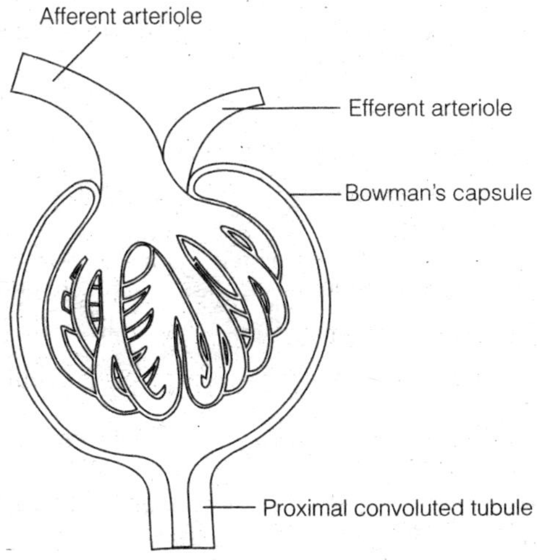

Structure of a renal corpuscle or Malpighian body

Question 2. What is the role played by renin-angiotensin in the regulation of kidney function?

Answer Role Played by Renin-angiotensin in the Regulation of Kidney function Renin is released from JGA on activation due to fall in the glomerular blood pressure/flow. Renin converts angiotensinogen in blood to angiotensin I and further to angiotensin II. Angiotensin II, being a powerful vasoconstrictor, increases the glomerular blood pressure and thereby GFR. Angiotensin II also activates the adrenal cortex to release aldosterone. Aldosterone causes reabsorption of Na^+ and water from the distal parts of the tubule. This also leads to an increase in blood pressure and GFR. This complex mechanism is generally known as the renin-angiotensin mechanism.

Question 3. Aquatic animals generally are ammonotelic in nature, whereas terrestrial forms are not. Comment.

Answer Many bony fishes, aquatic amphibians and aquatic insects are ammonotelic in nature. Ammonia, as it is readily soluble, is generally, excreted by diffusion across body surfaces or through gill surfaces (in fish) as ammonium ions.

Terrestrial animals produce lesser toxic nitrogenous wastes like urea and uric acid for conservation of water. Mammals, many terrestrial amphibians and marine fishes mainly excrete urea and are called ureotelic animals. Ammonia produced by metabolism is converted into urea in the liver of these animals and released into the blood which is filtrated and excreted out by the kidneys. Some amount of urea may be retained in the kidney matrix of some of these animals to maintain a desired osmolarity.

Question 4. The composition of glomerular filtrate and urine is not the same. Comment.

Answer The composition of glomerular filtrate and urine is not the same because the glomerular filtrate contains sodium, potassium and chloride ions, glucose, amino acids, along with urea, uric acid, creatine, ketone bodies and a large amount of water. The concentration of various materials in the glomerular filtrate is nearly equal to their respective concentrations in the plasma.

The glomerular filtrate therefore, also resembles the protein free and cell free plasma in their composition. The urine consists of water and inorganic substances. Water alone forms about 95% of it, other substances form only 5%. The nitrogenous organic compounds include urea, uric acid, creatine and hippuric acid.

Of these, urea is the principal component of human urine. The non-nitrogenous organic compounds include vitamin-C, oxalic acid and phenolic substances and a trace of glucose.

Sodium chloride is the principal mineral salt of the urine. Urine also contains some other substances, such as pigments and drugs and some epithelial cells and leucocytes.

Question 5. What is the procedure advices for the correction of extreme renal failure? Give a brief account of it.

Answer **Procedure for Extreme Renal Failure** Kidney transplantation is the ultimate method in the correction of acute renal failures (kidney failure). A functioning kidney is used in transplantation from a donor, preferably a close relative, to minimise its chances of rejection by the immune system of the host. Modern clinical procedures have increased the success rate of such a complicated technique.

Question 6. How the terrestrial organisms adapted themselves for conservation of water?

Answer Reptiles, birds, land snails and insects excrete nitrogenous wastes as uric acid in the form of pellet or paste with a minimum loss of water and are called uricotelic animals.

Question 7. Explain, why a haemodialysing unit called artificial kidney?

Answer The malfunctioning of kidneys can lead to accumulation of urea in blood. This condition is called uremia, which is highly harmful and may lead to kidney failure. In such cases urea can be removed from blood by a haemodialysis. The haemodialysis technique is a boon for thousands of uremic patients all over the world.

Long Answer Type Questions

Question 1. Explain the mechanism of formation of concentrated urine in mammals.

Answer The Henle's loop and vasa recta, play a significant role in the mechanism of formation of concentrated urine in mammals.

(i) The proximity between the Henle's loop and vasa recta, as well as the counter current in them help in maintaining an increasing osmolarity towards the inner medullary interstitium, *i.e.*, from 300 mOsmolL-1 in the cortex to about 1200 mOsmolL-1 in the inner medulla.

(ii) This gradient is mainly caused by NaCl and urea. NaCl is transported by the ascending limb of Henle's loop, which is exchanged with the descending limb of vasa recta.

(iii) NaCl is returned to the interstitium by the ascending portion of vasa recta.

(iv) Similarly, small amount of urea enter the thin segment of the ascending limb of Henle's loop which is transported back to the interstitium by the collecting tubule.

(v) This special arrangement of Henle's loop, and vasa recta is called the counter current mechanism.

(vi) This mechanism helps to maintain a concentration gradient in the medullary interstitium.

(vii) Presence of such interstitial gradient helps in an easy passage of water from the collecting tubule thereby concentrating the filtrate (urine).

(viii) Human kidneys can produce urine nearly four times concentrated than the initial filtrate formed.

Question 2. Draw a labelled diagram showing reabsorption and secretion of major substances at different parts of the nephron.

Answer

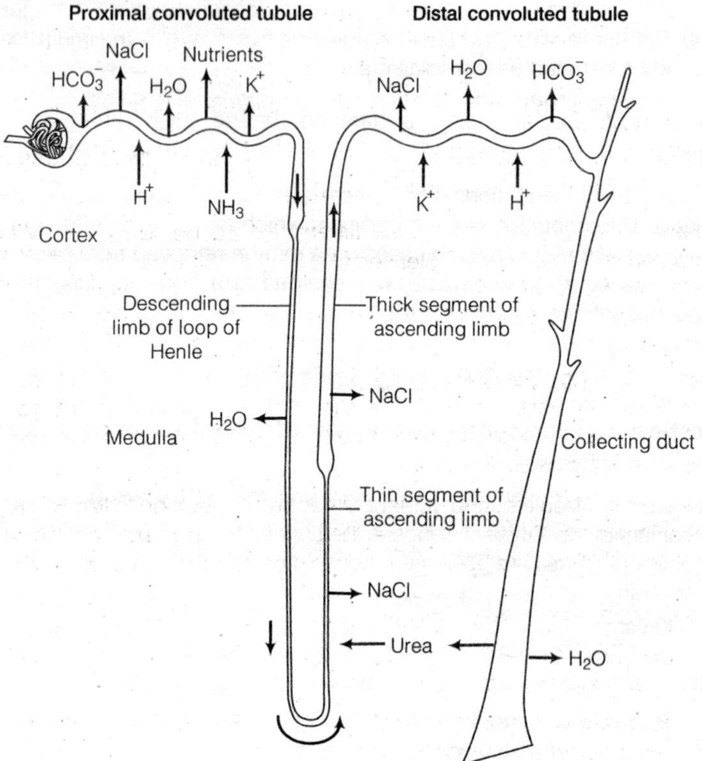

Reabsorpiton and secretion of major substances at different parts of the nephron (arrows indicate direction of movement of materials)

Question 3. Explain briefly, micturition and disorders of the excretory system.

Answer Micturition Urine formed by the nephrons is ultimately carried to the urinary bladder, where it is stored till a voluntary signal is given by the Central Nervous System (CNS). This signal is initiated by the stretching of the urinary bladder as it gets filled with urine. In response, the stretch receptors on the walls of the bladder send signals to the CNS. The CNS passes on motor messages to initiate the contraction of smooth muscles of the bladder and simultaneous relaxation of the urethral sphincter causing the release of urine. The process of release of urine is called micturition and the neural mechanisms causing it is called the micturition reflex.

Disorders of the Excretory System

(i) **Uremia** It is the malfunctioning of kidneys which lead to accumulation of urea in blood. This is highly harmful and may lead to kidney failure.

(ii) **Renal calculi** Stone or insoluble mass of crystallised salts (oxalates, etc.) formed within the kidney.

(iii) **Glomerulonephritis** Inflammation of glomeruli of kidney.

Question 4. How does tubular secretion help in maintaining ionic and acid-base balance in body-fluids?

Answer When the volume of the filtrate formed per day (180 L/day) is compared with that of urine released (1.5 L), it is seen that about 99% of the filtrate has to be absorbed by the renal tubules. This process is called reabsorption. The epithelial cells of the tubules in different segments of nephrons perform this by active or passive mechanisms. For example, substances like glucose, amino acids, Na^+, etc., in the filtrate are reabsorbed actively, whereas the nitrogenous wastes are absorbed by passive transport. Reabsorption of water also occurs passively in the initial segments of the nephron.

During urine formation, the tubular cells secrete substances like H^+, K^+ and ammonia into the filtrate. Therefore, tubular secretion is an important step in urine formation as it helps in the maintenance of ionic and acids balance of body fluids.

20

Locomotion and Movement

Important Points

1. Change in the body position is known as movement. Plants show phototropic geotrophic nastic and other movements Animal exhibit wide range of movements like movement of cilia, flagella and tentacles. Some movement result in the change of position or location. Such voluntary movement is known as locomotion. All locomotion are movements but all movements do not result in locomotion.
   (i) Walking, running, climbing, flying, swimming are locomotory movements.
   (ii) Locomotion is generally for the search of food, shelter, mate, suitable breeding grounds.
2. Various type of movements is exhibited by human like
   (i) **Amoeboid movement** (by *Amoeba*) pseudopodia is formed by the streaming of protoplasm.
   (ii) **Ciliary movement** It occurs in most of the internal tubular organ lined by ciliated epithelium coordinated movements of cilia in trachea help in removing dust particle. Passage of ova through the female reproductive tract is facilitated by the ciliary movement.
   (iii) **Muscular movement** It occurs due to contractile property of muscles like movement of limbs, jaws, tongue, etc. Locomotion requires a perfect coordinated activity of muscular, skeletal and neural system.

3. Muscle is a specialised tissue which is mesodermal origin. It shows special properties like excitability, contractility extensibility and elasticity. It constitute 40-50% of the total body weight. On the basis of location these are identified as
   (i) Skeletal muscle
      (a) These are striated voluntary muscles organised into strong compact bundles or bands.
      (b) These are known as skeletal muscles because they are attached to the skeletal elements and are responsible for the movement of trunk and appendages.
      (c) Skeletal muscles are multinucleated. Plasma membrane is called **sarcolemma** and cytoplasm is called **sarcoplasm**. They show abundance of glycogen and contain red pigment myoglobin.
      (d) Mitochondria is called sarcosome.
   (ii) **Visceral/non-striated** muscle/smooth muscle
      (a) These are unstriated involuntary muscles.
      (b) These are uninucleated long and tapering at ends.
      (c) These are located in the inner walls of hollow visceral organs of the body like alimentary canal, reproductive tract, etc.
   (iii) **Cardiac muscles** are the muscles of heart
      (a) They resemble like striated muscle but are uninucleated.
      (b) **Cardiac muscle** assemble in a branching pattern to form a cardiac muscles.
      (c) These are involuntary in nature and are under indirect control of control nervous system.
      (d) Cardiac fibre is a short cylindrical and uninucleate structure placed end-to-end in rows.
4. **Skeletal muscles** are organised into strong compact bundles or bands called **muscle bundles** of fascicles. There are held together by collagenous connective tissue layer called fascia.
   (i) Sarcolemma is a plasma membrane which encloses muscle fibre.
   (ii) Endoplasmic reticulum is the store house of calcium ions and known as sarcoplamic reticulum.
   (iii) Large number of parallely arranged filaments in sarcoplasm called myofilaments or myofibrils. These myofibrils are arranged in number of sections called **sarcomere**.

(iv) A dark anisotropic band (A-band) is present at the centre of sarcomere adjacent to this lies a light isotropic band (I-band). Alternate arrangement of dark and light bands gives the striated appearance to the skeletal muscle.

(v) Striated and light appearance is due to the presence of actin while dark appearance is due to the presence of myosin. So, A-band is consist of myosin filament while I-band is consist of actin filament.

(vi) These are also known as thin or thick filaments since actin filaments are thinner in comparison to myosin filaments Z-line is located at the centre of I-band.

(vii) At the centre of the actin filament a loss dark zone is present called H-zone is present. In the centre of the H-zone M-line is present.

(viii) Portion of the myofibril between two successive Z-line is known as sarcomere. It is the functional unit of contraction.

5. Thick myofibrils are composed of three different proteins
   (i) Actin
   (ii) Tropomyosin
   (iii) Troponin
   (i) **Actin** is globulin protein. It occurs in two forms G-actin globular form and polymeric F-actin. G-actins polymerises to form F-actin.
   (ii) **Tropomyosin** is double stranded and α-helical red and a fibrous molecules attaches to F-actin in the groove between its filaments.
   (iii) **Troponin** is complex of three polypeptides
      (a) Troponin-T
      (b) Troponin-I
      (c) Troponin-C (calcium binding) polypeptide. It mask the active binding site for myosin on the actin filament.

6. Thick myofilament constitutes myosin protein
   (i) It is mainly composed of myosin protein. The manometric sub-unit is called **meromyosin**.
   (ii) Myosin is composed of six polypeptide chains, two identical heavy chain and four light chain.
   (iii) Meromyosin has two important parts globular head with short arm called heavy meromyosin (HMM) and short tail called light meromyosin (LMM).
   (iv) Globular head is the active site for actin and ATPase activity.

7. Muscle contraction occurs in accordance with sliding filament theory contraction of muscle fibre take place by the sliding of the thin filaments over the thick filaments.
   (i) Muscle contraction is initiated by the signal sent by central nervous system *via* motor neuron.
   (ii) The junction between motor neuron and sarcoplasma of muscle fibre is called neuromuscular junction or motor end plate.
   (iii) Acetylcholine (neurotransmitter) is released from the neural junction and generates action potential in sarcolemma.
   (iv) This action potential causes the release of Ca^{2+} ions from sarcoplasmic reticulum.
   (v) Calcium ions binds to the sub-unit of myosin masked by troponin. Calcium ions remove the masking active site of myosin.
   (vi) Myosin head now binds to the exposed active site on actin to form a cross bridge after hydrolysis of ATP.
   (vii) Due to this attachment Z-line attached to these actin is also pulled inwards causing shortening of sarcomere.
   (viii) I bands are reduced, whereas A-bands retain the length. The myosin after releasing the ADP goes back to its relaxed state ATP is hydrolysed by myosin head.
   (ix) Repetitive activation leads to the accumulation of lactic acid due to anaerobic breakdown of glycogen.
   (x) In some muscle, myoglobin content is high which give reddish appearance. These are called red fibres. While fibres less quantity of myoglobin and therefore, appears pale or whitish. In red fibres, the number of sarcoplasmic reticulum is more.
8. Hard supportive or protective element of animal body form skeletal system or skeleton. It consist of frame work of bones and few cartilages
   (i) Bones and cartilages are specialised connective tissue.
   (ii) Bones are hard due to presence of calcium salts.
   (iii) Cartilage is slightly pliable matrix due to chandroitin salts
   (iv) Human skeletal system is composed of 206 bones and few cartilages.
   (v) Skeletal system is grouped into two skeleton system
      (a) Axial skeleton type
      (b) Appendicular skeleton

9. Axial skeleton system is present at the axis of body it includes 80 bones including
   (i) Skull
   (ii) Vertebral column
   (iii) Sternum
   (iv) Ribs
   (i) **Skull** Skeleton of head is called skull.
      (a) It is composed of 29 bones which constitutes two sets cranial and facial.
      (b) Cranial bones provide body protection to brain and these are 8 in number.
      (c) Facial region is made up of 14 skeletal elements forming the front part of the skull.
      (d) There are 6 ear ossicles found in the skull, *i.e.*, malleus incus and stapes.
   (ii) Vertebral column is 71 cm long and is curved lying in the mid dorsal line of neck and trunk.
      (a) It is made up of 26 vertebrae. Each vertebra has central hollow portion called neural canal through which spinal cord possess.
      (b) Vertebral column is differentiated into
         Cervical (7)
         Thoracic (12)
         Lumber (5)
         Sacral (1-fused)
         Coccyged (1-fused)
      (c) It is the point of attachment of or the ribs and musculature of the back.
   (iii) Sternum is a flat bone present just under the skin in middle of the front of the chest. It is about 15 cm long.
   (iv) There are 12 pairs of ribs which form lateral walls of the thoracic cage.
      (a) The first seven pairs are called true ribs. Since, their anterior end are attached to the sternum by means of hyaline cartilage.
      (b) The VIII, IX and X are called false ribs. They articulate by cartilage with coastal cartilage of the VII rib, these are attached indirectly to sternum.
      (c) Last two pairs of ribs is called floating ribs since, their anterior are not attached to either the sternum or the cartilage of another rib. Floating ribs protect the kidneys.

10. Appendicular skeleton consist of forelimbs, hindlimbs, pectoral girdle and pelvic girdle.
    (i) Each limb is made up of 30 bones.
    (ii) Bones of hand (forelimb) are
        (a) humerus
        (b) radius
        (c) ulna
        (d) carples (8 in number)
        (e) metacarpel (5 in number)
        (f) phalanges (14 in number).
    (iii) Bones of legs (hindlimb) are
        (a) femur (thigh bone longest bone)
        (b) tibia and fibula
        (c) tarsal (ankle bone-7 in number)
        (d) meta tarsals (5 in number)
        (e) phalanges (14 in number)
        (f) knee cap (A cup-shaped bone called patella which covers the knee ventrally).
11. Pectoral pelvic girdle help in the artriculation of upper and lower limbs respectively with axial skeleton.
    (i) Each girdle is made up of two halves.
    (ii) Each half of pectoral girdle consist of clavicle and a scapula.
    (iii) Scapula is large triangular flat bone situated in the dorsal part of the thorax between second and seventh rib.
    (iv) Posterior surface of each scapula is marked by the prominent ridge or spine which obliquely extends from the medial margin to the lateral margin of scapula project beyond the upper lateral angle as triangular acromian process.
    (v) Another process called coracoid process projects upward from the superior border of scapula near acromian process.
    (vi) Just below it a cup like glenoid cavity is present.
    (vii) Clavicle is a long slender bone with two curvatures. This bone is commonly called collar bone.
12. Pelvic girdle consist of 2 coxal bones. It is formed by the fusion of three bones
    (i) ilium
    (ii) ischium
    (iii) pubis
    (iv) **Acetabulum** is the point of fusion of two bones. Thigh bone articulated in this cavity.

13. Joints are the structural arrangement of tissues by which bones are joined together. These are classified into three
   (i) immovable
   (ii) slightly movable
   (iii) freely movable joints.
   (a) **Fibrous joints** These do not allow any movement, *e.g.*, in flat skull bones which fused end to end.
   (b) **Cartilagenous joints** It permits limited movement. These are joined together with the help of cartilages, *e.g.*, in joints between adjacent vertebrae in the vertebrae column.
   (c) Synovial joints are characterised by presence of synovial fluid between two bones various such type of joints are
   - ball and socket joint (between humerus two pectoral girdle).
   - hinge joint (knee joint)
   - pivot joint (between atlas and axis)
   - gliding joint (between the carpals)
   - saddle joint (between carpal and matacarpal of thumb).
14. Disorders associated with muscular and skeletal system
   (i) **Mysthamia gravis** An autoimmune disease affecting neuro-muscular junction causing fatigue, weakening and paralysis of skeletal muscle.
   (ii) **Muscular** dystrophy Progressive degeneration of skeletal muscle occurs due to genetic disorder.
   (iii) **Tetany** Due to low Ca^{2+} ion content in the body fluid wild contractions rapid spasms occur in muscles.
   (iv) **Arthritis** It is inflammation of syovial fluid joints.
   (v) **Osteoporosis** It is reduction in bone tissue causing weakening of skeletal strength. It results from excessive resorption of calcium and phosphorus from bone.
   (vi) **Government** It is inherited disorder of purine metabolism. Excess amount of uric acid and crystals of urate are deposited in the syovial joints leads to severe arthritis.

Exercises

Question 1. Draw the diagram of a sarcomere of skeletal muscle showing different regions.

Answer Structure of a sacromere of skeletal muscle

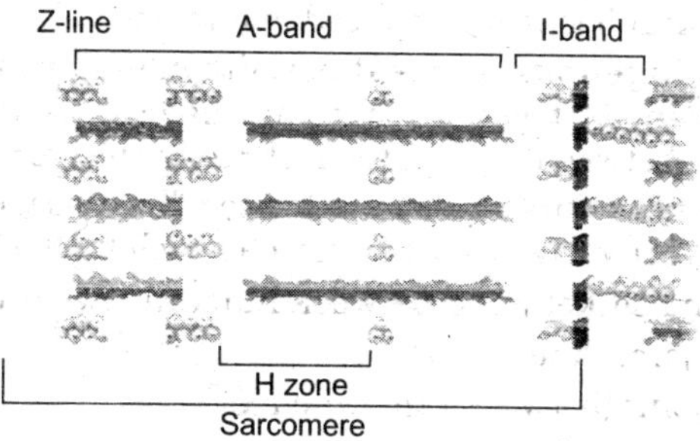

A Sarcomere

Question 2. Define sliding-filament theory of muscle contraction.

Answer **Sliding Filament Theory of Muscle Contraction**

The sliding-filament, theory states that the contraction of a muscle fibre takes place by the sliding of the thin filaments over the thick filaments.

Question 3. Describe the important steps in muscle contraction.

Answer

(i) A neural signal reaching the neuromuscular junction releases a neurotransmitter (acetyl choline) which generates an action potential in the sarcolemma.

(ii) This spreads through the muscle fibre and causes the release of calcium ions into the sarcoplasm.

(iii) Increase in Ca^{2+} level leads to the binding of calcium with a sub-unit of troponin on actin filaments and thereby remove the masking of active sites for myosin.

(iv) Utilising the energy from ATP hydrolysis, the myosin head now binds to the exposed active sites on actin to form a cross bridge.

(v) This pulls the attached actin filaments towards the centre of A-band.

(vi) The Z-line attached to these actins are also pulled inwards thereby causing a shortening of the sarcomere, *i.e.*, contraction.

(vii) During shortening of the muscle, *i.e.*, contraction, the I-bands get reduced, whereas, the A-bands retain the length.

(viii) The myosin, releasing the ADP and P1 goes back to its relaxed state. A new ATP binds and the cross-bridge is broken.

(ix) The ATP is again hydrolysed by the myosin head and the cycle of cross bridge formation and breakage is repeated causing further sliding.

(x) The process continues till the Ca^{2+} ions are pumped back to the sarcoplasmic cisternae resulting in the masking of actin filaments. This causes the return of Z-lines back to their original position, *i.e.*, relaxation.

Question 4. Write true or false. If false change the statement so that it is true.

(a) Actin is present in thin filament.
(b) H-zone of striated muscle fibre represents both thick and thin filaments.
(c) Human skeleton has 206 bones.
(d) There are 11 pairs of ribs in man.
(e) Sternum is present on the ventral side of the body.

Answer (a) True

(b) False, H-zone represents thick filaments.

(c) True

(d) False, there are 12 pairs of ribs in man.

(e) True

Question 5. Write the differences between

(a) Actin and myosin
(b) Red and white muscles
(c) Pectoral and pelvic girdle

Answer

(a) **Differences between Actin and Myosin**

S.N.	Action	Myosin
1.	These are thin filaments.	These are thick filaments.
2.	Actin has low molecular weight filamentous protein.	Myosin has high molecular weight small globular proteins.
3.	The thin filament also contain the contractile protein called tropomyosin.	Each myosin molecule also has two components, a tail and a head.
4.	It is a rod-shaped fibrous protein.	It is a globular protein.

(b) **Differences between Red and White Muscles**

S.N.	Red Muscles	White Muscles
1.	In some muscles, myoglobin content is high, which gives a reddish colour to them, such muscles are called red muscles.	Some muscles possess very less quantity of myoglobin, so they appear whitish called as white muscles.
2.	These contain plenty of mitochondria.	These have less number of mitochondria but amount of sarcoplasmic reticulum is high.
3.	These are called aerobic muscles.	They depend on anaerobic process of energy.

(c) **Differences between Pectoral and Pelvic Girdle**

S.N.	Pectoral Girdle	Pelvic Girdle
1.	It helps in the articulation of upper limbs.	It helps in the articulation of lower limbs.
2.	It is situated in the pectoral region of the body.	It is situated in the pelvic region of the body.
3.	Each help of pectoral girdle is formed of a clavicle and a scapula.	Pelvic girdle consists of two coxal bones.
4.	Scapula is a large triangular, flat bone and clavicle is a long slender bone.	Each coxal bone is formed of three bones, ischium and pubis.
5.	An expanded process, acromion from scapula forms a depression called glenoid cavity, which articulates with the head of humerus to form shoulder joint.	Ilium, ischium and pubis fuse at a point to form a cavity called acetabulum to which the thigh bone articulates.

Question 6. Match the column I with column II.

S.N.	Column I	Column II
A.	Smooth muscle	1. Myoglobin
B.	Tropomyosin	2. Thin filament
C.	Red muscle	3. Sutures
D.	Skull	4. Involuntary

Answer

S.N.	Column I	Column II
A.	Smooth muscle	4. Involuntary
B.	Tropomyosin	2. Thin filament
C.	Red muscle	1. Myoglobin
D.	Skull	3. Sutures

Question 7. What are the different types of movements exhibited by the cells of human body?

Answer Cells of the human body exhibit three main types of movements–amoeboid, ciliary and muscular.

Amoeboid Movement Some specialised cells in our body like macrophages and leucocytes in blood exhibit amoeboid movement. It is effected by pseudopodia formed by the streaming of protoplasm (as in *Amoeba*). Cytoskeletal elements like microfilaments are also involved in amoeboid movement.

Ciliary Movement Ciliary movement occurs in most of our internal tubular organs which are lined by ciliated epithelium. The coordinated movements of cilia in the trachea help us in removing dust particles and some of the foreign substances inhaled along with the atmospheric air. Passage of ova through the female reproductive tract is also facilitated by the ciliary movement.

Muscular Movement Movement of our limbs, jaws, tongue, etc., require muscular movement. Locomotion requires a perfect coordinated activity of muscular, skeletal and neural systems.

Question 8. How do you distinguish between a skeletal muscle and a cardiac muscle?

Answer **Differences between Skeletal Muscles and Cardiac Muscles**

S.N.	Skeletal Muscle	Cardiac Muscle
1.	These are associated with skeletal parts of the body.	These are present only in heart.
2.	They are voluntary in nature.	They are involuntary in nature.
3.	They are involved in locomotor. actions and changes in body postures.	They are related to heart activities

Question 9. Name the type of joint between the following

(a) Atlas/axis
(b) Carpal/metacarpal of thumb
(c) Between phalanges
(d) Femur/acetabulum
(e) Between cranial bones
(f) Between pubic bones in the pelvic girdle

Answer (a) Pivot joint (b) Saddle joint
(c) Gliding joint (d) Ball and socket joint
(e) Fibrous joint (f) Cartilagenous joint

Question 10. Fill in the blank spaces.

(a) All mammals (except a few) have ...... cervical vertebra.
(b) The number of phalanges in each limb of human is ......
(c) Thin filament of myofibril contains 2 'F' actins and two other proteins namely ...... and ....
(d) In a muscle fibre Ca^{2+} is stored in ......
(e) ...... and ...... pairs of ribs are called floating ribs.
(f) The human cranium is made of ...... bones.

Answer

(a) seven
(b) fourteen
(c) troponin and tropomyosin
(d) sarcoplasm
(e) 11 th; 12th
(f) eight.

Selected NCERT Exemplar Problems

Very Short Answer Type Questions

Question 1. Name the cells / tissues in human body which

(a) exhibit amoeboid movement
(b) exhibit ciliary movement

Answer (a) Macrophages and leucocytes
(b) Ciliated epithelium of nasal passage.

Question 2. Locomotion requires a perfect coordinated activity of muscular .... systems.

Answer Skeletal and neural.

Question 3. Sacrolemma, sacroplasm and sacroplasmic reticulum refer to particular type of cell in our body. Which is this cell and to what parts of that cell do these names refer to?

Answer The cell is a muscle fibre. Sacrolemma is the plasma membrane, sarcoplasm is the cytoplasm of the muscle fibre and sacroplasmic reticulum is the endoplasmic reticulum of a muscle fibre.

Question 4. Label the different components of actin filament in the diagram given below

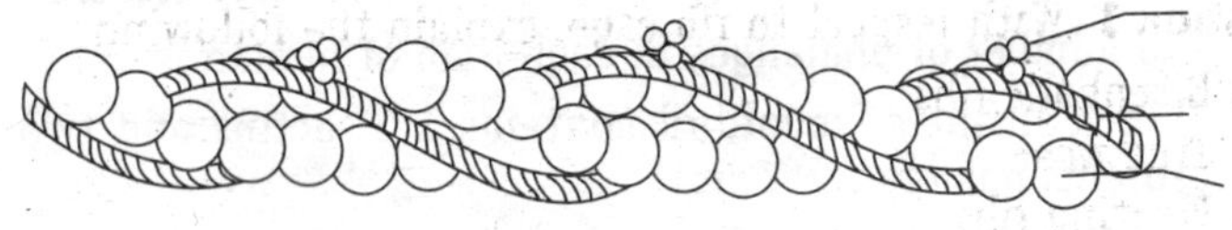

Answer

Troponin

Tropomyosin

F-actin

Question 5. The three tiny bones present in middle ear are called ear ossicles. Write them in correct sequence beginning from ear drum.

Answer Malleus, incus and stapes.

Question 6. Which tissue is afflicted by Myasthenia gravis ? What is the underlying cause.

Answer Myasthenia gravis is an autoimmune disorder affecting neuromuscular junction leading to fatigue, weakening and paralysis of skeletal muscle.

Question 7. How do our bone joints function without grinding noise and pain?

Answer Our bone joints function without grinding noise and pain due to the presence of synovial fluid.

Question 8. Give the location of a ball and socket joint in a human body

Answer Ball and socket joint in a human body is present between humerus and pectoral girdle.

Question 9. Our fore arm is made of three different bones. Comment.

Answer The fore arm is made of three different bones, *i.e.*, humerus, radius and ulna.

Short Answer Type Questions

Question 1. With respect to rib cage, explain the following

(a) Bicephalic ribs
(b) True ribs
(c) Floating ribs

Answer

(a) **Bicephalic ribs** Each rib has two articulation surfaces on its dorsal end and is hence called bicephalic.

(b) **True ribs** First seven pairs of ribs are called true ribs. Dorsally, they are attached to the thoracic vertebrae and ventrally connected to the sternum with the help of hyaline cartilage.

(c) **Floating ribs** Last two pairs (11th and 12th) of ribs are not connected ventrally and are therefore, called floating ribs.

Question 2. In old age, people often suffer from stiff and inflamed joints. What is this condition called? What are the possible reasons for these symptoms?

Answer This is osteoporosis. Age-related disorder characterised by decreased bone mass and increased chances of fractures. Decreased levels of oestrogen is a common cause.

Question 3.

(a) Exchange of calcium between bone and extracellular fluid take place under the influence of certain hormones. What will happen if more of Ca^{2+} is in extracellular fluid?

(b) What will happen if very less amount of Ca^{2+} is in the extracellular fluid?

Answer

(a) If concentration of Ca^{2+} is more in the extracellular fluid, this cause the release of calcium ions into the sarcoplasm from the extracellular fluid, where their concentration is high. Increase in Ca^{2+} level leads to the binding of calcium with a sub-unit of troponin on actin filaments and thereby remove the masking of active sites for myosin. Utilising the energy from ATP hydrolysis, the myosin head now pulls the attached actin filaments towards the centre of A-band. The Z-line attached to these actins are also pulled inwards thereby causing a shortening of the sarcomere, *i.e.*, contraction.

(b) If the amount of Ca^{2+} is very low in the extracellular fluid then the Ca^{2+} are pumped back from the sacroplasmic reticulum into the extracellular fluid, resulting in the masking of actin filaments. This causes the return of Z-lines back to their original position, *i.e.*, relaxation.

Question 4. Name at least two hormones which result in fluctuation of Ca^{2+} level.

Answer Parathormone and thyroxin result in fluctuation of Ca^{2+} level.

Question 5. Rahul excercises regularly by visiting a gymnasim. Of late he is gaining weight. Choose the correct answer and elaborate.

(a) Rahul has gained weight due to accumulation of fats in the body.
(b) Rahul has gained weight due to increased muscle and less of fat.
(c) Rahul has gained weight because his muscle shape has changed.
(d) Rahul has gained weight because he is accumulating water in the body.

Answer (b) Rahul has gained weight because his muscle shape has changed. Exercise develops the body muscles. The muscles enlarge due to increase in the amount of sacroplasm and increase in the number of myofilaments and mitochondria. There is also an increase in the number of muscle cells. Enlargement of muscle cells is called hypertrophy.

Question 6. Write a few lines about gout.

Answer When metabolic waste uric acid crystals are accumulated in bones, then it results into inflammation of bone and joints. The joints thereby cause pain. This disorder of skeletal system is called gout.

Question 7. What is the source of energy for muscle contraction?

Answer ATP (Adenosin Triphosphate).

Question 8. What are the points for articulation of pelvic and pectoral girdles?

Answer The components of pelvic girdle are ilium, ischium and pubis. It articulates with femur through a cavity called acetabulum.

The components of pectoral girdle are scapula and clavicle. It is the glenoid cavity of pectoral girdle in which head of humerus articulates.

Long Answer Type Questions

Question 1. Calcium ion concentration in blood affects muscle contraction. Does it lead to tetany in certain cases? How will you correlate fluctuation in blood calcium with tetany?

Answer Muscle tension is the phenomenon of sustained contraction of a muscle due to succession of nerve impulse /stimuli being received by it. Rigorous homeostatic control of the blood calcium level is criticle because calcium ions (Ca^{2+}) are essential to the normal functioning of all cells. If blood Ca^{2+} level falls substantially skeletal muscles begin to contract convulsively, a condition called tetany.

For the muscles fibre to contract, the binding site on thin filaments, must be uncovered. This occurs when Ca^{2+} bind to another set of regulatory proteins the troponin complex which controls the position of tropomyosin on the thin filament. The calcium binding rearranges the tropomyosin, troponin complex, exposing ther myosin-binding sites on the thin filament. When Ca^{2+} is present in the cytosol, the thin and thick filaments slide part each other and the muscles fibre contracts.

When the Ca^{2+} concentration falls, the binding sites are covered and contraction stops.

Question 2. An elderly woman slipped in the bathroom and had severe pain in her lower back. After X-ray examination doctors told her it is due to a slipped disc. What does that mean? How does that affect our health?

Answer It is the displacement of a vertebra from its normal position due to displacement or degeneration of a part of intervertebral disc, deposition of a hard tissue around it, mechanical injury and ossification ligaments holding the vertebrae. It is painful to keep body (neck and trunk) straight in this condition.

Question 3. How does a muscle shorten during its contraction and return to its original form during relaxation?

Answer A neurotransmitter (acetylcholine) causes the release of calcium ions into the sarcoplasm of a muscle fibre on receiving a signal. Increase in Ca^{2+} level leads to the binding of calcium with a sub-unit of troponin on actin filaments. Utilising the energy from ATP hydrolysis, the myosin head now binds to the exposed active sites on actin to form a cross bridge.

This pulls the attached actin filaments towards the centre of A-band. The Z-line attached to these actins are also pulled inwards thereby causing a shortening of the sarcomere, *i.e.*, contraction. During, contraction, the

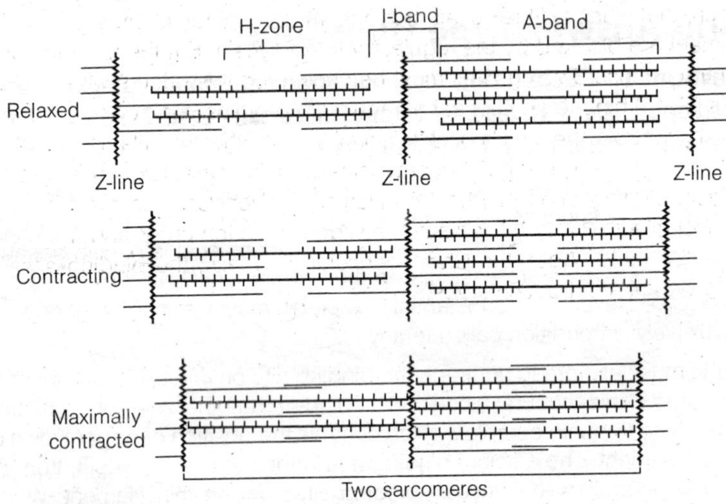

Sliding-filament theory of muscle contraction

I-bands get reduced, whereas the A-bands retain the length (figure). The myosin, releasing the ADP and P1 goes back to its relaxed state. A new ATP binds and the cross-bridge is broken. The ATP is again hydrolysed by the myosin head and the cycle of cross bridge formation and breakage is repeated causing further sliding. The process continues till the Ca^{2+} ions are pumped back to the sarcoplasmic cisternae resulting in the masking of actin filaments. This causes the return of Z-lines back to their original position, *i.e.*, relaxation.

Question 4. Discuss the role of Ca^{2+} ions in muscle contraction. Draw neat sketches to illustrate your answer.

Answer

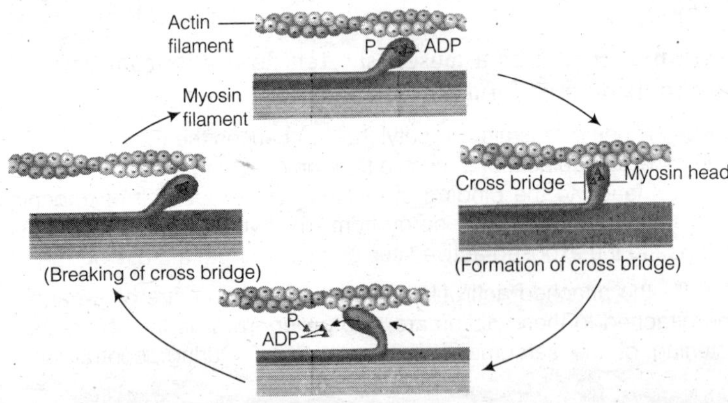

When the muscle fibre is at rest, the myosin binding sites on the thin filament are blocked by the regulatory tropomyosin. For the muscle fibre to contract, those binding sites must be uncovered this occurs when calcium ions (Ca^{2+}) bind to another set of regulatory proteins, the troponin complex, which controls the position of tropomyosin on the thin filament. Calcium binding rearranges the tropomyonin-troponin complex, exposing the myosin-binding sites on the thin filament. When Ca^{2+} is present in the cytosol, the thin and thick filaments slide past each other and the muscle fibre contracts. When the Ca^{2+} concentration falls, the binding sites are covered and contraction stops.

21

Neural Control and Coordination

Important Points

1. Nervous system provides the fastest means of communication within the body.
2. Coordination is the process through, which two or more organs interact and complement, the functions of one other. For quick coordination our neural system is organized into point to point connections.
3. Basic unit of neural organisation is neuron detect receive and transmits different kind of stimuli.
4. Human neural system is composed of
   (i) Central Nervous System (CNS) includes
      (a) Brain
      (b) Spinal cord
   (ii) Peripheral Nervous System (PNS) includes nerves of body associated with CNS (brain and spinal cord).
      The nerve fibre of PNS are of two types.
      (a) Afferent fibres carries impulse from tissue organ to the CNS.
      (b) Efferent fibres carries impulse from CNS to the target organ tissue.

(iii) Peripheral nervous system is divided into

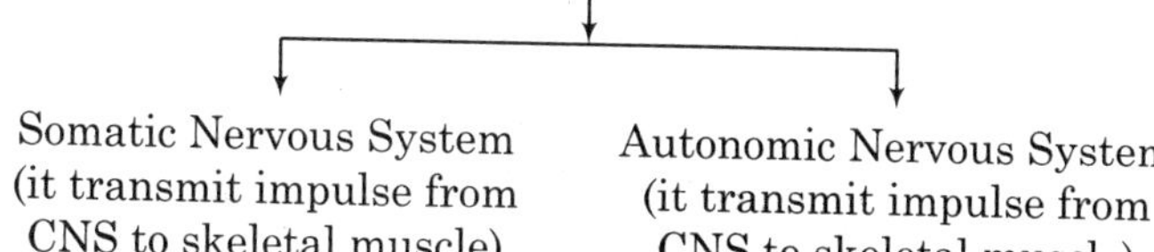

(iv) Autonomic Nervous System (ANS) is divided into

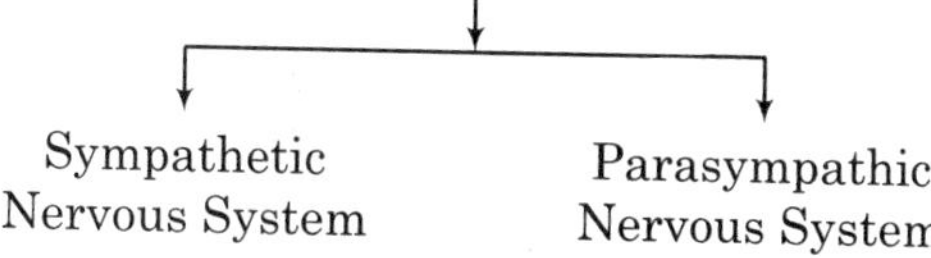

5. The basic structural and functional unit of nervous system is neuron.

   It consist of mainly three major parts namely cells body, dendrites axon.

   (i) **Cell Body** It contains cytoplasm, certain in granular bodies called **Nissl's granules.**

   (ii) **Dendrites** are the short fibre which branch repeatedly and projects out of the cell body. They also contain **Nissl' granules**.

   They transmit impure towards the cell body.

   (iii) Axon is a long fibre its distal end is branched. It terminates as the bulb like structure called **synaptic knob**

   (iv) Synaptic knob possess synaptic vesicles, which contain certain chemicals called neurotransmitters. Axons transmit the nerve impulse away from cell body to the neuromuscular junction.

   (v) **Neurons** are divided into three types on the basis of number of axon and dendrites.

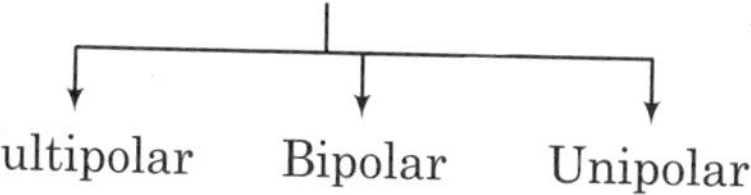

   (vi) Axons are mainly of two types, *i.e.,* **myelinated** and **non-myelinated nerve fibres**. Schwann cells form myelin sheath around the axon.

   (vii) The gaps between the two adjacent myelin sheath is known as **nodes of Ranvier**.

(viii) Unmyelinated nerve fibres are present in autonomous and somatic neural system myelinated nerve fibres are present in spinal and cranial nerves.

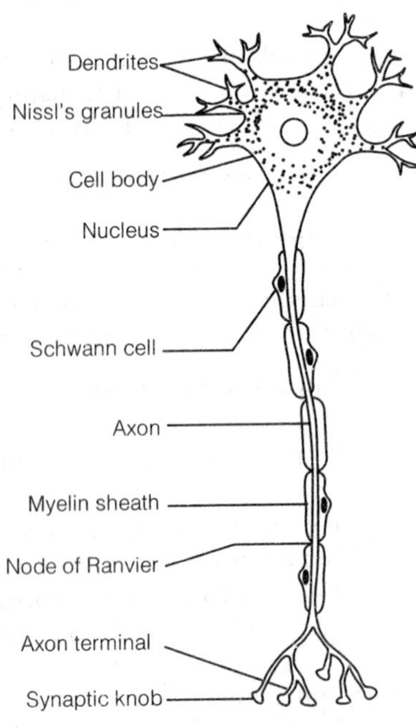

Structure of a neuron

6. Neural membrane possess different type ion channels.
   (i) In resting phase axonemal membrane is more permeable to K^+ ions and less for Na^+ ion.
   (ii) Concentration of K^+ is more inside the axonemal membrane than outside, where Na^+ ion concentration is more. Ionic gradient is maintained by Na^+/K^+ pump.

   3 Na^+ ions moves outwards, while $2K^+$ ions moves inwards.

   So, outer surface has five charge, while the inner one has negative charge. This stage is known as polarised phase. The electrical potential is known as resting potential.
   (iii) When the stimulus is given to the target neurons become depolarised as Na^+ ions moves insides the membrane and polarity of the membrane is reversed.
   (iv) The electrical potential difference across the plasma membrane is called **action potential** also known as **nerve impulse**. This sequence is repeated along the length of axon.

(v) The rise in the stimulus induced permeability to Na^+ is extremely short lived. It is quickly followed by the rise in premeability to K^+ ion, it moves outside the membrane and restores the resting potential of the membrane.

7. Synapse is a neuromuscular junction in which nerve impulse is transmitted from one neuron to another. It is formed by the membranes of a pre synaptic neuron and post synaptic neuron.
   (i) Synaptic cleft is the gap between presynaptic neuron and post synaptic neuron.
   (ii) Synapses is of two types
   (a) Chemical synapses (b) Electrical synapses
   (iii) In electrical synapse pre and post synaptic neurons are in close proximity. It flows directly from one neuron into another. It is faster than the chemical synapse.
   (iv) Chemical synapse is reported by **synaptic cleft**.
   (a) When an impulse (action potential arrives at the axon terminal). It stimulate the movement of the synaptic vesicle towards the membrane.
   (b) These synaptic vesicles contain neurotransmitter synaptic vesicles.
   (c) Fuses with the plasma membrane and releases neurotransmitter in the synaptic cleft.
   (d) Released **neurotransmitter** binds to the receptor present on post synaptic membrane. This binding helps in the opening of ion channels allowing the entry of ions, which generates a new potential in post synaptic neuron.

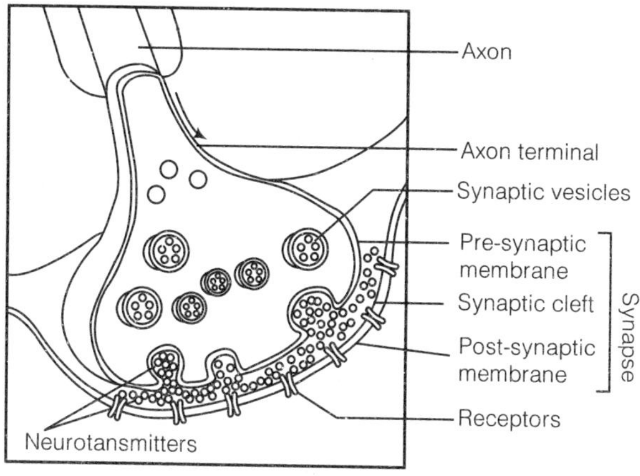

Diagram showing axon terminal and synapse

8. Central nervous system controls various voluntary and involuntary movement.
   (i) Brain is well protected by skull. It is covered by three membranes called cranial meninges. These are.
      (a) Duramater (outer layer)
      (b) Arachnoid (middle layer)
      (c) Piamater (inner layer).
   (ii) Brain is divided into three major parts
      (a) Forebrain (b) Midbrain (c) Hindbrain
      (a) Forebrain consist of three parts
         - **Cerebrum**
            - Cerebrum is the largest part of the brain.
            - Cerebrum is longitudinally divided into two cerebral hemisphere, which are connected by corpus callosum.
            - Cerebral hemisphere is covered by cerebral cortex (layer of cell) it folds to form prominant folds.
            - Cerebral cortex is also known as grey matter it contains motor area and sensory area.
            - Association area is responsible for functions like intersensory association, memory and communication this is also known as white matter due to the presence of myelinated sheath.

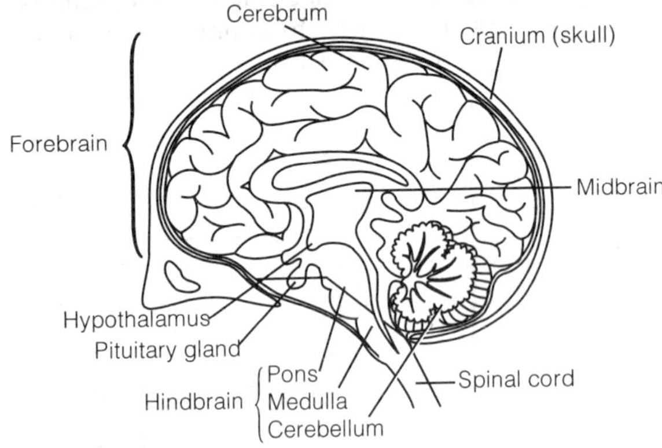

Diagram showing sagital section of the human brain

         - **Thalamus** Cerebrum wraps up thalamus it regulates sensory and mater signalling.

- **Hypothalamus** in present at the base of thalamus. It is the main centre which controls temperature, urge for eating and thirst also secretes hypothalamic hormones.

(b) **Midbrain** is located between thalamus and hypothalamus.

- Cerebral aqueduct passes through midbrain.
- Dorsal portion consist of four lobes called corpora quadrigemia. Midbrain and hindbrain form the brain stem.

(c) **Hindbrain** is consist of

- **Pons** has fibre tracts
- **Cerebellum** has convoluted surface to provide additional space for many neurons.
- **Medulla oblongata** Medulla is connected to the spinal cord. It controls, respiration, cardiovascular reflexes and dastric decretions.

9. **Reflex action** and **reflex Arc** is the process of response to the peripheral nervous system, which acts involuntary.
   (i) It comprises atleast one afferent neuron or receptor and one efferent neuron.
   (ii) The afferent neuron receive signal from sensory organ and transfer it to CNS. Efferent neuron carrier signal from CNS to the effector. This is known as reflex arc.

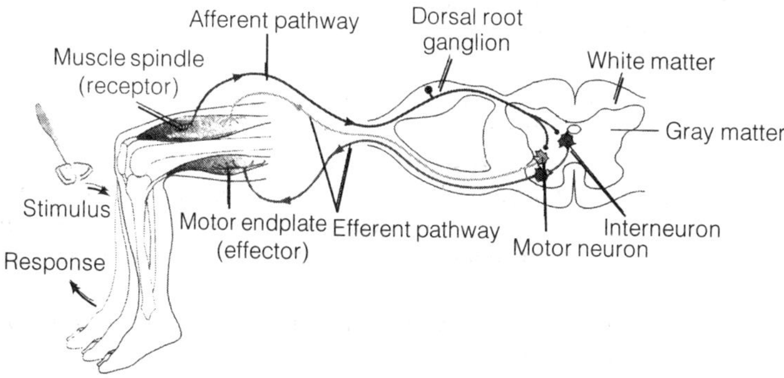

Diagrammatic presentation of reflex action (showing knee jerk reflex)

10. Human eye is one of the most valuable sensory organ, which enables us to see the wonderful world and colours around us.

    They carry specialized receptor cell, which are sensitive to light and are known as visual receptors.

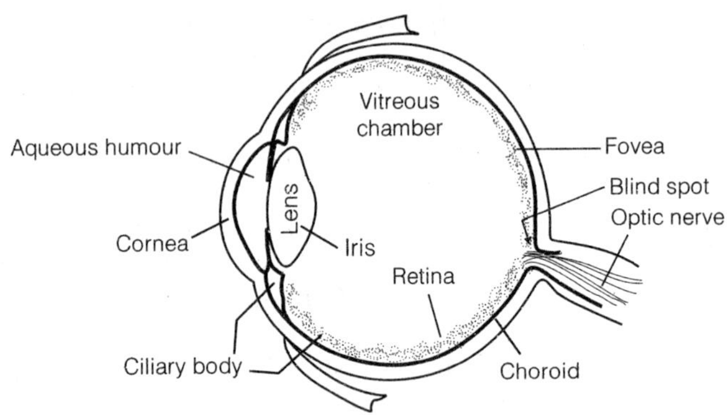

Diagram showing parts of an eye

(i) **Eye ball** constitutes three specialized structures sclera, choroid and retina.

(ii) Sclera maintains the shape of the eye and it is visible white portion of the eye.

(iii) Behind sclera choroid layer is present. It absorbs scattered light and ensure a clear image on retina.

(iv) Choroid changes into two structure the iris and the ciliary body.

(v) Iris is a dark muscular diaphragm, which controls the size of the pupil.

(vi) Pupil regulates the amount of light which reachior interne and the retina.

(vii) Ciliary body is connected to lens. It consist of smooth muscles and contraction of these muscles causes an alteration in shape of the lens.

(viii) Lens is the transparent and flexible structure made up of protein it forms an image on light sensitive screen called retina. Lens is filled with a watery fluid called aqueous humour. At back of the lens it is filled with vitreous humour.

(ix) Light enters the eye through a transparent thin membrane called cornea.

(x) Retina is the delicate third and innermost layer eye lens forms an inverted real image of the object on the retina.

(xi) The retina has light sensitive cells, *i.e.*, cones and rods.

(xii) Red cells contain rhodopsin and functions in dim light or night.

(xiii) **Cone cells** contain pigment called **visual voilet iodopsin**. They function in day light and gives colour vision.

(xiv) When person from light room enters the dark room, person is not able to see properly for some time. It is due to the regulation and amount of light entering the eye. In light pupil contracts and permits less light to enter the eye. When person enters the dark room pupil takes some time to expand and allow more light to enter the eye.

(xv) **Near point** of an eye is the minimum distance at which objects can be seen most distinctly, without strain also known as least distance of distinct vision. For an adult with normal vision near point of an eye is about 25 cm.

(xvi) **Farthest point** Point upto, which the eye can see objects clearly is called farthest point of eye for a normal eye it is infinity.

(xvii) **Cataract** At old age lens becomes opaque (it becomes milky and cloudy). This condition is called cataract and cause partial or complete loss of vision.

11. **Defects of vision**

(i) **Myopia** Also known as near sightedness in this case image of the distant object is formed in front of retina. It occurs due to

(a) excessive curvature of eye ball.

(b) elongation of the eye ball.

Myopic persons are cured by using concave lens.

(ii) **Hypermetropia** Also known as far sightedness person can see the farther objects but cannot see nearby object. In this case image of the nearby object is formed behind the retina. It occurs due to

(a) focal length of the eye is too long

(b) eyeball has become too small.

This defect is corrected by using conves lens.

(iii) **Presbyopia**

It occurs due to gradual weakening of ciliary muscles and dimishing flexibility of the eye lens.

12. **Ear** performs very important function of hearing and maintenance of the body.

(i) Ear is divided into three major sections

(a) outer ear (b) middle ear (c) inner ear

(ii) Outer ear is consist of

(a) pinna

(b) external auditory meatus called canola. These extents up further to tympanic membrane or ear drum.

(c) pinna collects the Vibration in air and collects sound. In pinna wax screating sebaceous glands are present.

(iii) **Middle ear** contains three ossicles.
 (a) malleus is attached to the tympanic membrane
 (b) stapes is attached to the oval window of cochlea.
 (c) incus

(iv) **Ossicle** increases the efficiency of transmission of sound waves to inner ear.

(v) Middle ear cavity is connected to pharynx through eusta-chian tube.

(vi) Pluid filled inner ear is called labyrinth. It consist of two parts the bony and membranous labyrinth.
 (a) Labyrinth is filled by fluid endolymph.
 (b) Coiled portion of labyrinth is cochlea.
 (c) Bony labyrinth is divided into upper scala vestibuli and lower scala tympani.

(vii) On the basilar membrane organ of Corti is present, which possess hair cell, which acts as a auditory receptor.

(viii) A large number of processes called stereo cilia are projected from the apical part.

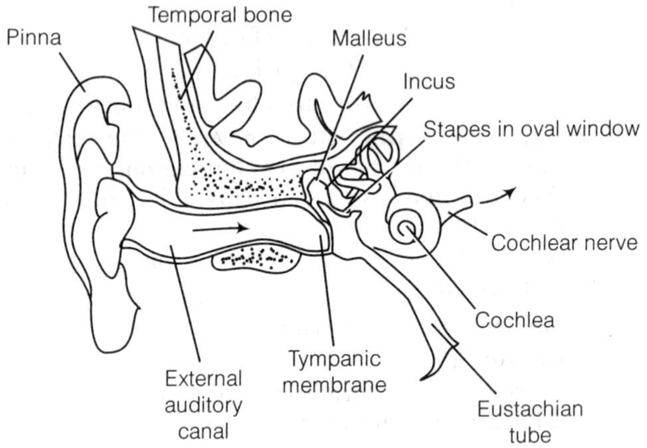

Diagrammatic view of ear

(ix) **Inner ear** contains a complex system called **vestibular** apparatus vestibular apparatus is composed of three semicircular canals and the otolith organ. It consist of sacculi and utricle.

(x) Base of the canals is swollen and known as ampulla. It contain a projecting ridge called crista ampullaris. Macula is the projecting ridge between saccule and utricle.

13. The external ear receives sound waves and directs them to ear drum, which vibrates in response to the sound waves.
    (i) These sound waves are transmitted through the ear ossicles (malleus, incus and stapes).
    (ii) Vibrations are passed through the oval window onto the fluid of cochlea where they generates waves in lymphs. It induces ripple in the basilar membrane.
    (iii) Basiliar membrane bend the hair cells pressing them against the tectorial membrane nerve impulse are generated in associated afferent neuron.

Exercises

Question 1. Briefly describe the structure of the following

(a) Brain (b) Eye (c) Ear

Answer

(a) **Structure of Brain** The human brain is well protected by the skull. The brain can be divided into three major parts forebrain, midbrain and hindbrain.

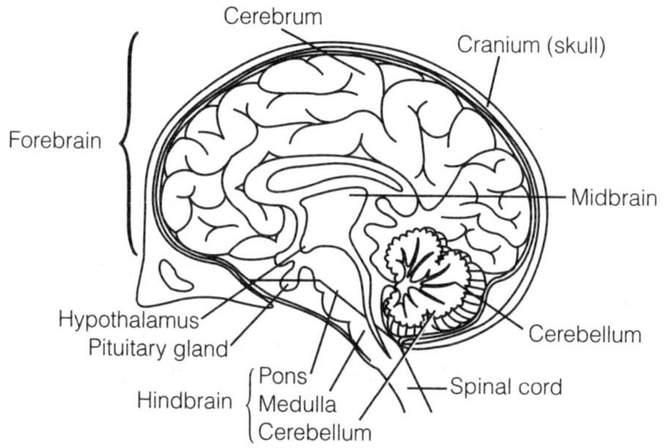

Sagital section of human brain

(i) **Forebrain** The various parts of forebrain are cerebrum, thalamus and hypothalamus. Cerebrum is responsible for complex functions like intersensory associations, memory and communication.

(ii) **Midbrain** The midbrain is located between the thalamus/hypothalamus of the forebrain and pons of the hindbrain.

(iii) **Hindbrain** The hindbrain comprises pons, cerebellum and medulla (also called the medulla oblongata). The medulla contains centres, which control respiration cardiovascular reflexes and gastric secretions.

(b) **Structure of Eye** The wall of the human eye ball is composed of three layers. The external layer is called the sclera. The anterior portion of this layer is called the **cornea**.The middle layer, choroid, contains many blood vessels and looks bluish in colour. The ciliary body itself continues forward to form a pigmented and opaque structure called the iris. The eye ball contains a transparent crystalline lens. In front of the lens, the aperture surrounded by the iris is called **the pupil.**

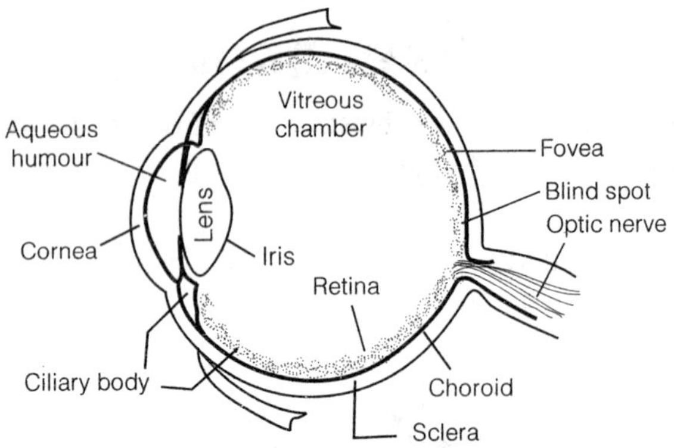

Diagram showing parts of an eye

There are two types of photoreceptor cells namely rods and cones. The optic nerves leave the eye and the retinal blood vessels enter it at a point medial to and slightly above the posterior pole of the eye ball. Photoreceptor cells are not present in that region and hence, it is called the blind spot.

(c) **Structure of Ear** Anatomically, the ear can be divided into three major sections called the **outer ear**, the **middle ear** and the **inner ear.**

(i) **Outer ear** The outer ear consists of the pinna and external auditory meatus (canal).

(ii) **Middle ear** The middle ear contains three ossicles called malleus, incus and stapes which are attached to one another like a chain. The malleus is attached to the tympanic membrane and the stapes is attached to the oval window of the cochlea. An eustachian tube connects the middle ear cavity with the pharynx.

(iii) **Inner ear** The fluid-filled inner ear called labyrinth consists of two parts, the bony and the membranous labyrinths.

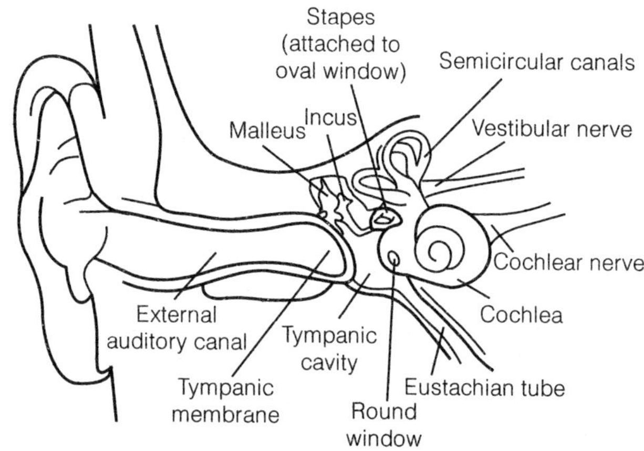

Diagrammatic view of ear

The organ of Corti is a structure located on the basilar membrane which contains hair cells that act as auditory receptors. The inner ear also contains a complex system called vestibular apparatus, located above the cochlea. The vestibular apparatus is composed of three semi-circular canals and the otolith organ.

Question 2. Compare the following

(a) Central Neural System (CNS) and Peripheral Neural System (PNS)
(b) Resting potential and action potential
(c) Choroid and retina

Answer

(a) **Comparison between Central Neural System (CNS) and Peripheral Neural System** (PNS) The CNS includes the brain and the spinal cord and is the site of information processing and control. The PNS comprises of all the nerves of the body associated with the CNS (brain and spinal cord). The nerve fibres of the PNS are of two types

(i) Afferent fibres (ii) Efferent fibres

(b) **Comparison between Resting Potential and Action Potential** The electrical potential difference across the resting plasma membrane A is called the resting potential. The electrical potential difference across the plasma membrane at the site A is called the action potential, which is in fact termed as a nerve impulse.

(c) **Comparison between Choroid and Retina** The middle layer of eye ball which contains many blood vessels and looks bluish in colour is known as **choroid**. The choroid layer is thin over the posterior two-thirds of the eye ball, but it becomes thick in the anterior part to form the ciliary body. The ciliary body itself continues forward to form a pigmented and opaque structure called the iris.

Retina is the inner layer of eye ball and it contains three layers of cells from inside to outside, *i.e.*, ganglion cells, bipolar cells and photoreceptor cells. There are two types of photoreceptor cells, namely, rods and cones. These cells contain the light-sensitive proteins called the photopigments.

Question 3. Explain the following processes

(a) Polarisation of the membrane of a nerve fibre
(b) Depolarisation of the membrane of a nerve fibre
(c) Conduction of a nerve impulse along a nerve fibre
(d) Transmission of a nerve impulse across a chemical synapse

Answer

(a) **Polarisation of the Membrane of a Nerve Fibre** In resting state, the neuron membrane is polarized with outer surface positively charged and inner surface negatively charged. The resting membrane potential is about – 40 mV to – 90 mV with an average of –70 mV.

(b) **Depolarisation of the Membrane of a Nerve Fibre** In a depolarized membrane, a stimulus causes the opening of voltage gated Na^+ channels. There is a rapid inflow of Na^+ ions which wipes out the local electrical potential difference. The threshold stimulus for opening of Na^+ channel is generally – 55 to – 60 mV (about 10 mV less than the resting potential.

(c) **Conduction of a Nerve Impulse along a Nerve Fibre** A nerve impulse is transmitted from one neuron to another through junctions called **synapses**. A synapse is formed by the membranes of a pre-synaptic neuron and a post-synaptic neuron, which may or may not be separated by a gap called **synaptic cleft**. There are two types of synapses namely, electrical synapses and chemical synapses. At electrical synapses, the membranes of pre-and post-synaptic neurons are in very close proximity. Electrical current can flow directly from one neuron into the other across these synapses.

At a chemical synapse, the membranes of the pre and post-synaptic neurons are separated by a fluid-filled space called synaptic cleft. Chemical called neurotransmitters are involved in the transmission of impulses of these synapes. When an impulse (action potential) arrives at the axon terminal, it stimulates the movement of the synaptic vesicles towards the membrane, where they fuse with the plasma membrane and release their neurotransmitters in the synaptic cleft. The released neurotransmitters bind to their specific receptors, present on the post-synaptic membrane. This binding opens ion channels allowing the entry of ions which can generate a new potential in the post-synaptic neuron.

(d) **Transmission of a Nerve Impulse Across a Chemical Synapse** A nerve impulse is transmitted from one neuron to another through junctions called synapses. A synapse is formed by the membranes of a pre-synaptic neuron and a post-synaptic neuron, which may or may not be separated by a gap called synaptic cleft. At a chemical synapse, the membranes of the pre- and post-synaptic neurons are separated by a fluid-filled space called synaptic cleft.

Chemicals called neurotransmitters are involved in the transmission of impulses at these synapses. The axon terminals contain vesicles filled with these neurotransmitters. When an impulse (action potential) arrives at the axon terminal, it stimulates the movement of the synaptic vesicles towards the membrane where they fuse with the plasma membrane and release their neurotransmitters in the synaptic cleft.

The released neurotransmitters bind to their specific receptors, present on the post-synaptic membrane. This binding opens ion channels allowing the entry of ions which can generate a new potential in the post-synaptic neuron. The new potential developed may be either excitatory or inhibitory.

Question 4. Draw labelled diagrams of the following

(a) Neuron (b) Brain (c) Eye (d) Ear

Answer (a) **Diagram of Neuron**

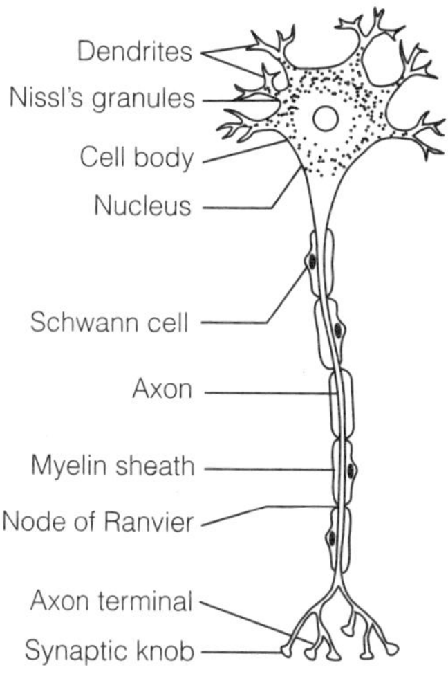

Structure of neuron

(b) **Diagram of Brain** Refer to Ans. 1 (a) of this chapter (Exercises).

(c) **Diagram of Ear** Refer to Ans. 1 (c) of this chapter (Exercises).

(d) **Diagram of Eye** Refer to Ans. 1 (b) of this chapter (Exercises).

Question 5. Write short notes on the following

(a) Neural coordination (b) Forebrain (c) Midbrain
(d) Hindbrain (e) Retina (f) Ear ossicles
(g) Cochlea (h) Organ of Corti (i) Synapse

Answer

(a) **Neural Coordination** The organised network of point-to-point connection for quick coordination provided by neural system is called neural coordination. The mechanism of neural coordination involves transmission of nerve impulse, impulse conduction across a synapse and the physiology of reflex action.

(b) **Forebrain** It forms, the major part of human brain. The various parts of forebrain are cerebrum, thalamus and hypothalamus. It forms the major part of the human brain. It consists of two cerebral hemispheres connected by a tract of nerve fibres called corpus callosum. The layer of cells which covers the cerebral hemisphere is called cerebral cortex. The cerebral cortex contains motor areas and sensory areas. These regions are responsible for complex functions like intersensory associations, memory and communication.

The cerebrum wraps around a structure called thalamus, which is a major coordinating centre for sensory and motor signaling. The **hypothalamus** lies at the base of the thalamus. The hypothalamus control body temperature, urge for eating and drinking.

(c) **Midbrain** The midbrain is located between the thalamus/hypothalamus of the forebrain and pons of the hindbrain. A canal called the cerebral aqueduct passess through the midbrain. The dorsal portion of the midbrain consists mainly of four round swellings (lobes) called corpora quadrigemina.

(d) **Hindbrain** The hindbrain comprises pons, cerebellum and medulla (also called the medulla oblongata). Pons consists of fibre tracts that interconnect different regions of the brain. Cerebellum has very convoluted surface and the medulla of the brain is connected to the spinal cord.

(e) **Retina** The inner layer of eye ball is the retina and it contains three layers of cells from inside to outside – ganglion cells, bipolar cells and photoreceptor cells. There are two types of photoreceptor cells namely, rods and cones. These cells contain the light-sensitive proteins called the photopigments.

(f) **Ear ossicles** The middle ear contains three ossicles called malleus, incus and stapes which are attached to one another in a chain-like fashion.The malleus is attached to the tympanic membrane and the stapes is attached to the oval window of the cochlea. The ear ossicles increase the efficiency of transmission of sound waves to the inner ear.

(g) **Cochlea** The membranous labyrinth of inner ear is filled with a fluid called endolymph. The coiled portion of the labyrinth is called cochlea. The membranes constituting cochlea, the reissner's and basilar, divide the surounding perilymph filled bony labyrinth into an upper scala vestibuli and a lower scala tympani. The space within cochlea called scala media is filled with endolymph. At the base of the cochlea, the scala vestibuli ends at the oval window, while the scala tympani terminates at the round window which opens to the middle ear.

(h) **Organ of Corti** The organ of Corti is a structure located on the basilar membrane of inner ear, which contains hair cells that act as auditory receptors. The hair cells are present in rows on the internal side of the organ of Corti. The basal end of the hair cell is in close contact with the afferent nerve fibres. A large number of processes called stereo cilia are projected from the apical part of each hair cell. Above the rows of the hair cells is a thin elastic membrane called tectorial membrane.

(i) **Synapse** It is junction between two neurons, where one neuron expands and comes in near contact with another neuron. A synapse is formed by the membranes of a pre-synaptic neuron, and a post-synaptic neuron, which may or may not be separated by a gap called synaptic cleft. There are two types of synapses– an electrical synapse and a chemical synapse. In electrical synapse, membranes of pre and post-synaptic neurons are is very close proximity field. In chemical synapse, there membranes are separated by a fluid filled space called **synaptic cleft**.

Question 6. Give a brief account of

(a) Mechanism of synaptic transmission
(b) Mechanism of vision
(c) Mechanism of hearing

Answer

(a) **Mechanism of Synaptic Transmission** There are two types of synapses namely– electrical synapses and chemical synapses. At electrical synapses, electric current can flow directly from one neuron into the other across these synapses. Transmission of an impulse across electrical synapses is very similar to impulse conduction along a single axon.

At a chemical synapse, the membranes of the pre- and post-synaptic neurons are separated by a fluid-filled space called synaptic cleft. The rise in the stimulus-induced permeability to Na^+ is extremely short lived. It is quickly followed by a rise in permeability to K^+. Within a fraction of a second, K^+ diffuses outside the membrane and restores the resting potential of the membrane at the site of excitation and the fibre becomes once more responsive to further stimulation.

(b) **Mechanism of Vision** The light rays in visible wavelength focusses on the retina through the cornea and lens generates potentials (impulses) in rods and cones.

Light induces dissociation of the retinal from opsin resulting in changes in the structure of the opsin. This causes membrane permeability changes. As a result, potential differences are generated in the photoreceptor cells. This produces a signal that generates action potentials in the ganglion cells through the bipolar cells. These action potentials (impulses) are transmitted by the optic nerves to the visual cortex area of the brain, where the nerve impulses are analysed and the image formed on the retina.

(c) **Mechanism of Hearing** The external ear receives sound waves and directs them to the ear drum. The ear drum vibrates in response to the sound waves and these vibrations are transmitted through the ear ossicles to the oval window. The vibrations are passed through the oval window on to the fluid of the cochlea, where they generate waves in the lymphs. The waves in the lymphs induce a ripple in the basilar membrane.

These movements of the basilar membrane bend the hair cells, pressing them against the tectorial membrane. As a result, nerve impulses are generated in the associated afferent neurons. These impulses are transmitted by the afferent fibres via auditory nerves to the auditory cortex of the brain, where the impulses are analysed and the sound is recognised.

Question 7. Answer briefly

(a) How do you perceive the colour of an object?

(b) Which part of our body helps us in maintaining the body balance?

(c) How does the eye regulate the amount of light that falls on the retina?

Answer

(a) The daylight (photopic) vision and colour vision are functions of cones. In the human eye, there are three types of cones which possess their own characteristic photopigments that respond to red, green and blue lights. The sensations of different colours are produced by various combinations of these cones and their photopigments. When these cones are stimulated equally, a sensation of white light is produced.

(b) The crista and macula are the specific receptors of the vestibular apparatus of inner ear which are responsible for the maintenance of balance of the body and posture.

(c) The diameter of the pupil is regulated by the muscle fibre of iris. Photoreceptors, rods and cones regulate the amount of light that falls on the retina.

Question 8. Explain the following

(a) Role of Na^+ in the generation of action potential.

(b) Mechanism of generation of light-induced impulse in the retina.

(c) Mechanism through which a sound produces a nerve impulse in the inner ear.

Answer

(a) **Role of Na^+ in the Generation of Action Potential**

When a stimulus is applied to a nerve, the membrane of the nerve becomes freely permeable to Na^+. This leads to a rapid influx of Na^+ followed by the reversal of the polarity at that site, *i.e.*, the outer surface of the membrane becomes negatively charged and the inner side becomes positively charged. The electrical potential difference across the plasma membrane at the membrane is called the action potential, which is in fact termed as a nerve impulse. Thus, this shows that Na^+ ions play an important role in the conduction of nerve impulse.

(b) **Mechanism of Generation of Light-Induced Impulse in the Retina** Light induces dissociation of the retinal from opsin resulting in changes in the structure of the opsin. This causes membrane permeability changes. As a result, potential differences are generated in the photoreceptor cells. This produces a signal that generates action potentials in the ganglion cells through the bipolar cells. These action potentials (impulses) are transmitted by the optic nerves to the visual cortex area of the brain, where the nerve impulses are analysed and the image formed on the retina is recognised.

(c) **Mechanism through which a Sound Produces a Nerve Impulse in the Inner Ear** In the inner ear, the vibrations are passed through the oval window on to the fluid of the cochlea, where they generate waves in the lymphs. The waves in the lymphs induce a ripple in the basilar membrane. These movements of the basilar membrane bend the hair cells, pressing them against the tectorial membrane. As a result, nerve impulses are generated in the associated afferent neurons. These impulses are transmitted by the afferent fibres *via* auditory nerves to the auditory cortex of the brain, where the impulses are analysed and the sound is recognised.

Question 9. Differentiate between

(a) Myelinated and non-myelinated axons
(b) Dendrites and axons
(c) Rods and cones
(d) Thalamus and hypothalamus
(e) Cerebrum and cerebellum

Answer

(a) **Differences between Myelinated and Non-myelinated Axons**

S.N.	Myelinated Axon	Non-myelinated Axon
1.	The myelinated nerve fibres are enveloped with Schwann cells, which form a myelin sheath around the axon.	Unmyelinated nerve fibre are enclosed by a Schwann cell that does not form a myelin sheath around the axon.
2.	Myelinated nerve fibres are found in spinal and cranial nerves.	There are commonly found in autonomous and the somatic nervous systems.

(b) **Differences between Dendrites and Axons**

S.N.	Dendrite	Axon
1.	These are short fibres which branch repeatedly and project out of the cell body also contain Nissl's granules.	The axon is a long branched fibre, Which terminates as a bulb-like structure called synaptic knob. It possess synaptic vesicles containing chemicals called neurotransmitters.
2.	These fibres transmit impulses towards the cell body.	The axons transmit nerve impulses away from the cell body to a synapse.

(c) **Differences between Rods and Cones**

S.N.	Rod	Cone
1.	The twilight vision is the function of rods.	The daylight vision and colour vision are functions of cones.
2.	The rods contain a purplish-red protein called the rhodopsin or visual purple, which contains a derivative of Vitamin-A.	In the human eye, there are three types of cones which possess their own characteristic photopigments that respond to red, green and blue lights.

(d) **Differences between Thalamus and Hypothalamus**

S.N.	Thalamus	Hypothalamus
1.	The cerebrum wraps around a structure called thalamus.	It lies at the base of the thalamus.
2.	All types of sensory input passes synapses in the thalamus.	It contains neurosecretory cells that secrete hypothalamus hormones.
3.	It controls emotional and memory functions.	It regulates, sexual behaviour expresion of emotional reactions and motivation.

(e) **Differences between Cerebrum and Cerebellum**

S.N.	Cerebrum	Cerebellum
1.	It is the most developed part in brain.	It is the second developed part of brain also called as little cerebrum
2.	A deep cleft divides cerebrum into two cerebral hemispheres.	Externally the whole surface contains gyri and sulci.
3.	Its functions are intelligence, learning, memory, speech, etc.	It contains centres for coordination and error checking during motor and cognition.

Question 10. Answer the following

(a) Which part of the ear determines the pitch of a sound?
(b) Which part of the human brain is the most developed?
(c) Which part of our central neural system acts as a master clock?

Answer (a) Inner ear (b) Cerebrum (c) Brain

Question 11. The region of the vertebrate eye, where the optic nerve passes out of the retina, is called the

(a) fovea (b) iris
(c) blind spot (d) optic chaisma

Answer Optic chaisma.

Question 12. Distinguish between

(a) afferent neurons and efferent neurons
(b) impulse conduction in a myelinated nerve fibre and unmyelinated nerve fibre
(c) aqueous humour and vitreous humour
(d) blind spot and yellow spot
(e) cranial nerves and spinal nerves

Answer

(a) **Differences between Afferent and Efferent Neurons**

S.N.	Afferent Neuron	Efferent Neuron
1.	The afferent nerve fibres transmit impulses from tissues/organs to the CNS.	The efferent fibres transmit regulatory impulses from the CNS to the concerned peripheral tissues/organs.

(b) **Differences between the Impulse Conduction in a Myelinated and Unmyelinated Nerve Fibre**

Refer to Ans. 9 (a) of this chapter.

(c) **Differences between Aqueous and Vitreous Humour**

S.N.	Aqueous Humour	Vitreous Humour
1.	It is the space between the cornea and the lens.	The space between the lens and the retina is called the vitreous chamber.
2.	It contains a thin watery fluid.	It is filled with a transparent gel.

(d) **Differences between Blind and Yellow Spot**

S.N.	Blind Spot	Yellow Spot
1.	Photoreceptor cells are not present in this region.	Yellow shot or macula lutea is located at the posterior pole of the eye lateral to the blind spot. It has a central pit called fovea.
2.	The light focuses on that part of the retina is not detected.	The fovea of yellow spot is a thinned-out portion of retina where only the cones are densely packed is the point where visual cavity is greatest.

(e) **Differences between Cranial and Spinal Nerves**

S.N.	Cranial Nerve	Spinal Nerve
1.	The cranial nerves originate in the brain and terminate mostly in organs head and upper body.	The spinal nerves originate in the spinal cord and extend to parts of the body bellow the head.
2.	There are 12 pairs of cranial nerves.	There are 31 pair of spinal nerves.
3.	Most of the cranial nerves contain axon and both sensory and motor neurons.	All of the spinal nerves contain axons of both sensory and motor neurons.

Selected NCERT Exemplar Problems

Very Short Answer Type Questions

Question 1. Rearrange the following in the correct order of involvement in electrical impulse movement–Synaptic knob–dendrites–cell body–axon terminal–axon

Answer Dendrites – cell body – axon – axon terminal – synaptic knob.

Question 2. Comment upon the role of ear in maintaining the balance of the body and posture.

Answer The crista and macula are the specific receptors of the vestibular apparatus responsible for the maintance of the body and posture.

Question 3. Which cells of the retina enable us to see coloured objects around us?

Answer Cone cells of the retina enable us to see coloured objects around us.

Question 4. Arrange the following in the order of reception and transmission of sound wave from the ear drum: Cochlear nerve-external auditory canal-ear drum-stapes-incus-malleus-cochlea.

Answer Ear drum-malleus-incus-stapes-cochlea-cochlear nerve.

Question 5. Name the structures involved in the protection of the brain.

Answer The human brain is well protected by the skull. Inside the skull, the brain is covered by cranial meninges consisting of an outer layer called duramater, a very thin middle layer called arachnoid and an inner layer (which is in contact with the brain tissue) called piamater.

Question 6. Our reaction like aggressive behaviour, use of abusive words, restlessness, etc., are regulated by brain, name the parts involved.

Answer Cerebrum, hypothalamus and cerebral hemispheres.

Question 7. What do grey and white matter in the brain represent?

Answer Gray matter is a part of the central nervous system which represent the cell bodies, dendrites and non-myelinated nerve fibres. White matter is a part of the central nervous system which represent the cell bodies, dendrites and myelinated nerve fibres also.

Question 8. Where is the hunger centre located in human brain?

Answer Hypothalamus.

Question 9. Which sensory organ is involved in vertigo (sensation of oneself or objects spinning around)?

Answer The vestibular system of inner ear is most often involved with vertigo. Movement at an angle is detected by the semicircular canals. These components work together to provide a sense of spatial orientation.

Question 10. While travelling at a higher altitude, a person complains of dizziness and vomiting sensation. Which part of the inner ear is disturbed during the journey?

Answer The labyrinth, is an important part of our vestibular (balance) system is disturbed during journey to higher altitude.

Question 11. Complete the statement by choosing appropriate match among the following

Answer

(a) Resting potential (i) chemicals involved in the transmission of impulses at synapses.
(b) Nerve impulse (ii) Gap between the pre-synaptic and post-synaptic neurons
(c) Synaptic cleft (iii) Electrical potential difference across the resting neural membrane
(d) Neurotransmitters (iv) An electrical wave like response of a neuron to a stimulation.

Answer

(a) Resting potential (iii) Electrical potential difference across the resting neural membrane.
(b) Nerve impulse (iii) An electrical wave like response of a neuron to a stimulation.
(c) Synaptic cleft (ii) Gap between the pre-synaptic and post-synaptic neurons.
(d) Neurotransmitters (i) Chemicals involved in the transmission of impulses at synapses.

Short Answer Type Questions

Question 1. The major parts of the human neural system is depicted below. Fill in the empty boxes with appropriate words.

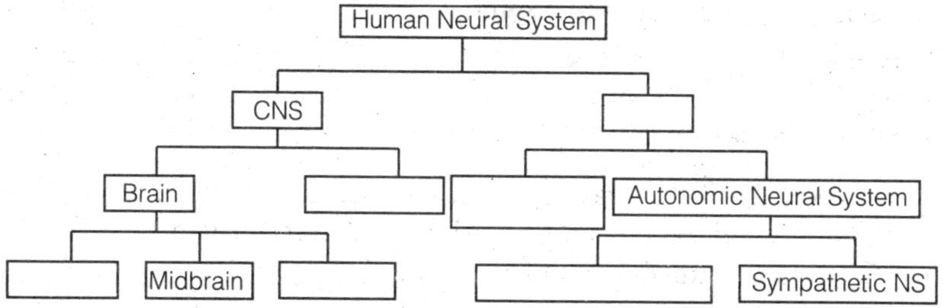

Answer

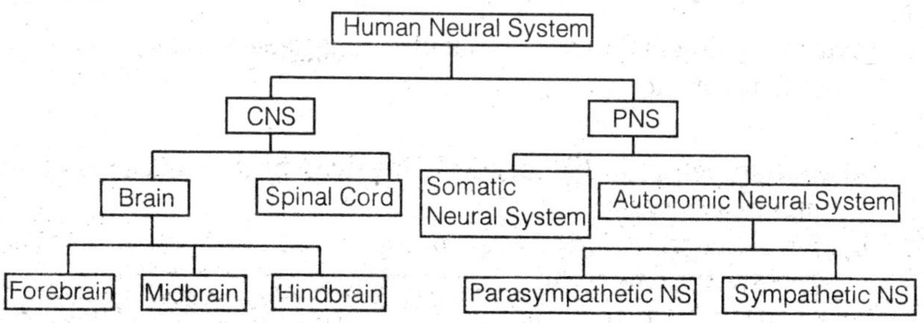

Question 2. What is the difference between electrical transmission and chemical transmission?

Answer **Differences between Electrical and Chemical Transmission**

S.N.	Electrical Transmission	Chemical Transmission
1.	It occurs by electric synapse	It occurs by chemical synapse.
2.	Synaptic cleft is may or may not present.	Synaptic cleft is present.
3.	At electrical synapses, electrical current can flow directly from one neuron into the other across these synapses.	The rise in the stimulus-induces permeability to Na^+ is extremely short lived. It is quickly followed by a rise in permeability to K^+. Within a fraction of a second, K^+ diffuses outside the membrane and restores the resting potential of the membrane at the site of excitation.
4.	Impulse transmission across an electrical transmission is always faster. Electrical synapses are rare in our system.	Chemical transmission is slower.

Question 3. Neural system and computers share certain common features. Comment in five lines. (Hint: CPU, input-output devices).

Answer The brain might be compared to a computer as its memory banks. The spinal cord to the conducting cable for the computer's input and output, and the nerves to a circuit supplying input information to the cable and transmitting the output to muscles and organs. The most important of these components is the Central Processing Unit (CPU) or microprocessor, which acts as the 'brain' of your computer.

Question 4. If someone receives a blow on the back of neck, what would be the effect on the person's CNS?

Answer If a person receives a blow on the back, it results in an impairment of cognitive abilities or physical functioning. It can also result in the disturbance of behavioural or emotional functioning. Cervical injuries often result in quadriplegia (tetraplegia).

Question 5. What is the function ascribed to Eustachian tube?

Answer An Eustachian tube connects the middle ear cavity with the pharynx. The Eustachian tube helps in equalising the pressures on either sides of the ear drum.

Question 6. Label the following parts in the given diagram using arrow.

(a) Aqueous chamber
(b) Cornea
(c) Lens
(d) Retina
(e) Vitreous chamber
(f) Blind spot

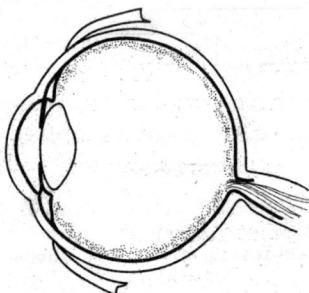

Answer

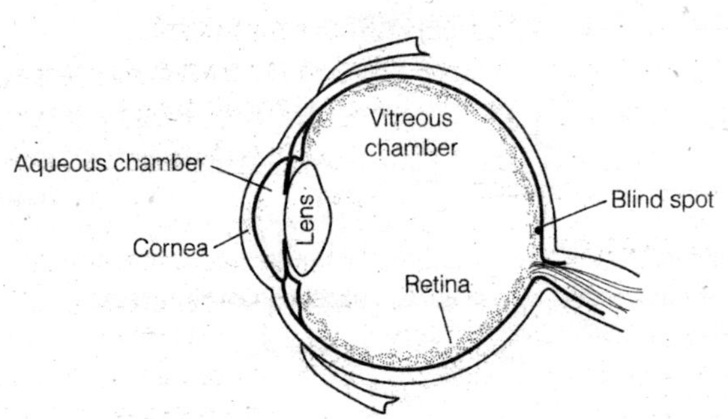

Long Answer Type Questions

Question 1. Explain the process of the transport and release of a neurotransmitter with the help of a labelled diagram showing a complete neuron, axon terminal and synapse.

Answer Transport and release of a neurotransmitter occurs within a synapse. At a chemical synapse, the membranes of the pre- and post-synaptic neurons are separated by a fluid-filled space called synaptic cleft. Chemicals called neurotransmitters are involved in the transmission of impulses at these synapses. The axon terminals contain vesicles filled with these neurotransmitters.

When an impulse (action potential) arrives at the axon terminal, it stimulates the movement of the synaptic vesicles towards the membrane, where they fuse with the plasma membrane and release their neurotransmitters in the synaptic cleft. The released neurotransmitters bind to their specific receptors, present on the post-synaptic membrane. This binding opens ion channels allowing the entry of ions which can generate a new potential in the post-synaptic neuron.

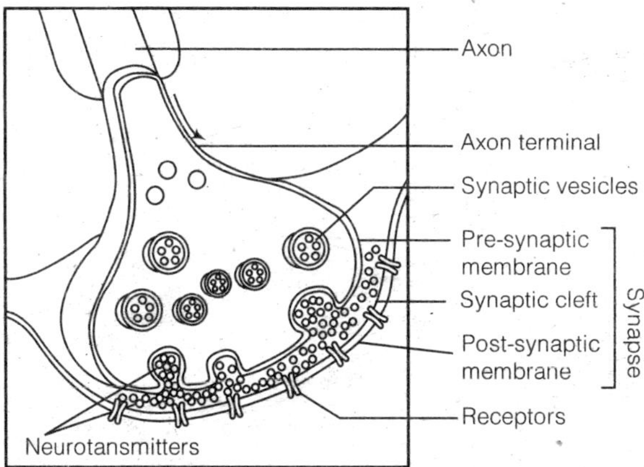

Question 2. Name the parts of human forebrain indicating their respective functions.

Answer The various parts of human forebrain are

(i) **Cerebrum** forms the major part of the human brain. It is responsible for complex functions like intersensory associations, memory and communication.

(ii) The cerebrum wraps around a structure called **thalamus**, which is a major coordinating centre for sensory and motor signaling.

(iii) **Hypothalamus** lies at the base of the **thalamus**. It contains a number of centres which control body temperature, urge for eating and drinking. It also contains several groups of neurosecretory cells, which secrete hormones called hypothalamic hormones.

Question 3. Explain the structure of middle and internal ear with the help of diagram.

Answer **Middle Ear** The middle ear contains three ossicles called malleus, incus and stapes which are attached to one another in a chain-like fashion.

The malleus is attached to the tympanic membrane and the stapes is attached to the oval window of the cochlea. The ear ossicles increase the efficiency of transmission of sound waves to the inner ear.

An Eustachian tube connects the middle ear cavity with the pharynx. The Eustachian tube helps in equalising the pressures on either sides of the ear drum.

Inner Ear The fluid-filled inner ear called labyrinth consists of two parts, the bony and the membranous labyrinths. The coiled portion of the labyrinth is called cochlea. The space within cochlea called scala media is filled with endolymph. At the base of the cochlea, the scala vestibuli ends at the oval window, while the scala tympani terminates at the round window which opens to the middle ear.

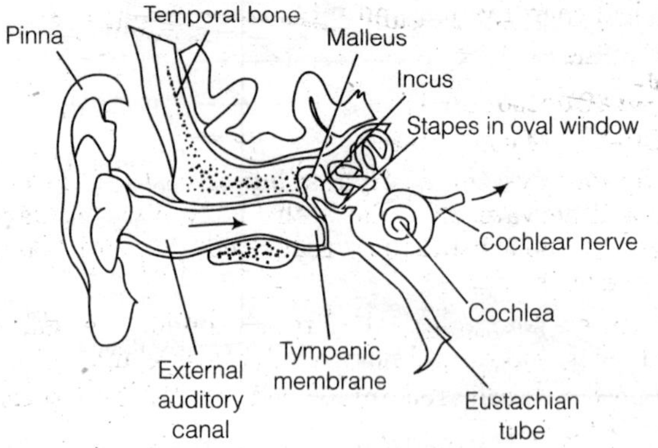

The organ of Corti is a structure located on the basilar membrane which contains hair cells that act as auditory receptors. The inner ear also contains a complex system called vestibular apparatus, located above the cochlea. The vestibular apparatus is composed of three semi-circular canals and the otolith organ consisting of the saccule and utricle. Each semi-circular canal lies in a different plane at right angles to each other. The saccule and utricle contain a projecting ridge called macula. The crista and macula are the specific receptors of the vestibular apparatus responsible for maintenance of balance of the body and posture.

22

Chemical Coordination and Integration

Important Points

1. Chemical coordination and integration in our body depends on two system.
   (i) **Nervous** coordination
   (ii) **Chemical** coordination
   Nervous system is very fast but short lived. Nerve fibres do not innervate all cells of the body and cellular functions need to be continuously regulated, which is carried out by hormones.
2. **Hormones** are released through endocrine glands. These gland lacks ducts and known as ductless gland.
   (i) These are released into blood stream and transported to target organ.
   (ii) Hormones are non-nutrient chemicals, which acts as intracellular messengers and produced in trace amount.
      (a) PRH — Prolactin Releasing Hormone
      (b) PRIH—Prolactin Releasing Inhibiting Hormone.
      (c) MSH-RH—Melanocyte Stimulating Hormone Releasing Hormone.
      (d) MSH-RIH—Melanocyte Stimulating Hormone Releasing Inhibiting Hormone.

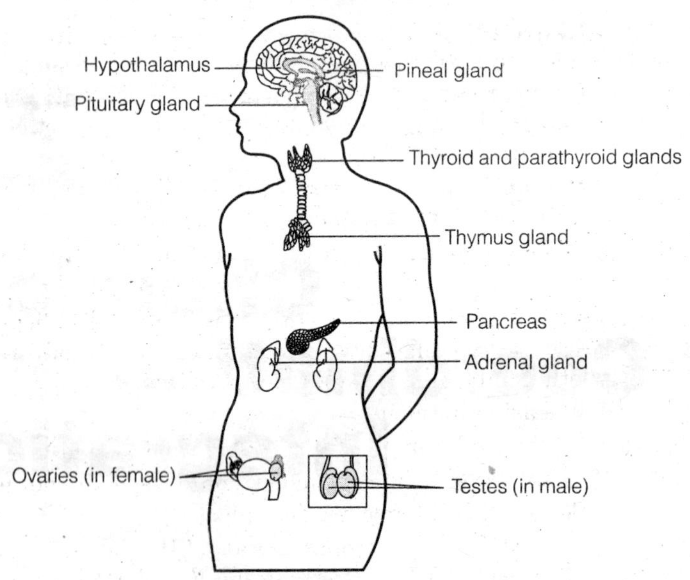

Location of endocrine glands

3. The pituitary or master hypothalamic gland. It is the most protected gland and lies in a body cavity as hypophysial fossa
   (i) Gland has dual origin. It contain two parts—adenohypophysis and neurohypophysis

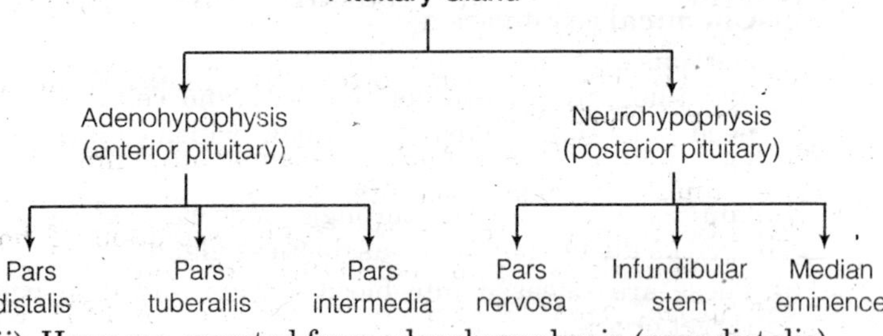

   (ii) Hormone secreted from adenohypophysis (pars distalis)
      (a) Growth Hormone (GH).
      (b) Prolactin (PRL).
      (c) Thyroid Stimulating Hormone (TSH).
      (d) Adenocorticotrophic Hormone (ACTH).
      (e) Luteinising Hormone (LH).
      (f) Follicle Stimulating Hormone (FSH)
      (pars intermedia) secretes.
      (g) Melanocyte Stimulating Hormone.

(iii) **Neurohypophysis** (known as posterior pituitary). Two released hormones are oxytocin and vasopressin

(iv) Over secretion of growth hormone stimulate abnormal body growth leading to gigantism its low secretion causes dwarfism.

(v) **Prolactin** promotes the growth of mammary glands and formation of milk in them.

4. Hormone producing glands are located in different parts of our body.

5. **Hypothalamus** In forebrain basal part of diencephalon represents hypothalamus. It regulates many body functions. Hypothalamus produce two types of hormones.

 (i) Releasing hormone

 (ii) Inhibiting hormone.

 These are also called gonadotrophin releasing hormone.

 Some hypothalamic hormones are

 (a) TRH — Thyrotropin Releasing Hormone

 (b) ARH — Adrenocorticotropin Releasing Hormone

 (c) LH-RH — Luteinising Hormone Releasing Hormone

 (d) FSH-RH — Follicle Stimulating Hormone Releasing Hormone

 (e) GH-RIH — Stomatostin.

 (f) GH-RH — Somatotrophin.

(vi) TSH stimulates the synthesis of thyroid hormones from thyroid gland.

(vii) ACTH acts on adrenal cortex and stimulates the secretion of glucocorticoids.

(viii) LH and FSH are known as gonadotrophins since, they stimulates gonadal activity.

(ix) LH stimulates the synthesis and secretion of hormones from testis called androgens (testosterone).

(x) Spermatogenesis in males is regulated by FSH, while LH induces ovulation of Graafian follicles and maintains corpus luteum.

(xi) MSH acts on melanin containing cells called melanocytes. It regulates pigmentation of the skin.

(xii) Oxytocin acts on smooth muscles of our body and stimulates their contraction (it induces labour pain) Contraction of uterus at the time of child birth and milk ejection from the mammary gland.

(xii) Vasopressin also known as antidiuretic hormone, which acts on kidney and stimulates reabsorption of H_2O and electrolytes by the distal tubules.

6. Pineal gland is located on the dorsal side of forebrain. It secretes melatonin: It plays a very important role in the regulation of a 24 hour rhythm or circardian rhythm of our body.
   (i) It maintains sleep wake cycle.
   (ii) It also maintains body temperature.
   (iii) It influences metabolism, pigmentation, the menstrual cycle as well as our defense capability.
7. Thyroid gland is situated in neck in front of trachea and larynx.
   (i) It is composed of two lobes one on either side of thyroid cartilage joined together by a connective tissue isthmus.
   (ii) Thyroid gland is composed of follicles and stromal tissues.
   (iii) Follicles of cuboidal epithelial cells is enclosed in a cavity.
   (iv) These follicles synthesise hormones as mono, di, tri and tetra iodothyxonin or thyroxine.
   (v) Main function of thyroid gland is energy production, oxygen uptake and BMR increase.
   (vi) It increases heart rate.
   (vii) Iodine is essential for the normal rate of hormone synthesis in the thyroid.
   (viii) Deficiency of iodine in our diet results into hypothyroidism causing enlargement of thyroid gland. known as **goitre**.
   (ix) Hypothyroidism causes menstrual cycle to become irregular. In pregnant ladies it may lead to defective development two maturation of body, mental retardation, low intelligence quotient, abnormal skin.
   (x) Hyperthyroidism is abnormal development of nodules of the thyroid gland. Rate of synthesis and secretion of thyroid hormones leads to abnormal level.
   (xi) It also secretes thyrocalcitonin, which maintain blood calcium levels.

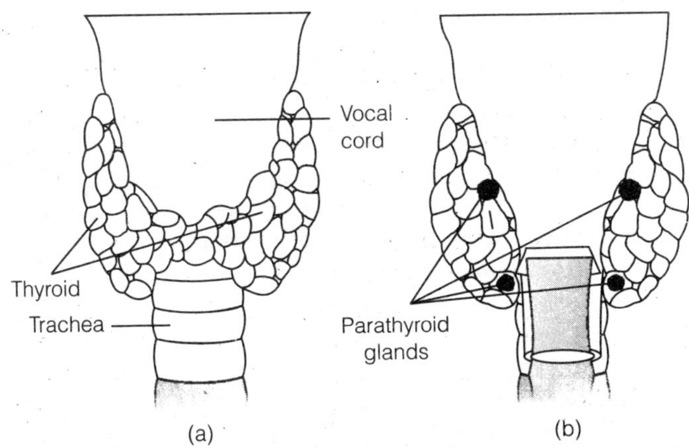

Diagrammatic view of the position of thyroid and parathyroid
(a) Ventral side (b) Dorsal side

8. Parathyroid gland is present as four small pouches. Present on the back side of thyroid gland. Two each embedded in the posterior surface of each lobe of thyroid gland.
   (i) It secretes peptide hormone called parathyroid hormone (PTH).
   (ii) It increases the Ca^{2+} levels in blood.
   (iii) It acts directly on bones to increase bone resorption and mebilises Ca^{2+} ion.
   (iv) It stimulates the reabsorption of Ca^{2+} ion by renal tubule and increase Ca^{2+} absorption from the digested food. It is known as hypercalcemic hormone.
9. Thymus gland in endodermal in origin and developed from epithelium of outer part of 3rd gill pouch or epithelium of gill cleft. It is a lobular structure present on dorsal side of heart and aorta.
   (i) It plays an important role in development of immune system. It provides cell mediated immunity and plays major role in differentiation of T-lymphocytes.
   (ii) As the age progresses, thymus is degenerated in old persons and resulting in a decreased production of thymosins.
10. There are two adrenal glands situated on the upper pole of each kidney enclosed within renal fascia. It is composed of two type of tissues, *i.e.*, adrenal medulla and adrenal cortex.

(i) **Adrenal medulla** is surrounded by cortex. It is stimulated by extensive sympathetic nervous system. It produces adrenaline or epinephrine and noradrenaline or non-epinephrine.

(ii) These hormones are also known as **catecholamine**s.

(iii) **Adrenaline** and **noradrenaline** are known as **emergency hormone**, or hormones of fight or flight. Since, these are secreted in response to stress condition.

(iv) The hormones

(a) increase alertness (b) dialates pupil

(c) causes pilo erection (d) causes sweating

(v) Noradrenaline causes general vasoconstriction.

(vi) Adrenal cortex is divided into three layers.

(a) **zona reticularis** (inner layer).

(b) **zona fasciculata** (middle layer)

(c) **zona glomerulosa** (outer layer)

(vii) Adrenal cortex secretes

(a) glucocorticoids (b) Mineral corticaids

(viii) Glucocorticoids stimulates

(a) gluconeogenesis (b) lipolysis and proteolysis

(c) RBC production

(ix) **Cortisol** is glucocorticoid, which regulates cardiovascular system and kidney functions. It produces anti-inflammatory response and suppress the immune system.

(x) Mineral corticoid **aldosterone** acts on the DCT and stimulates the reabsorption of Na^+ and H_2O. It helps in maintaining the electrolytic balance, body fluid volume osmotic pressure and blood pressure.

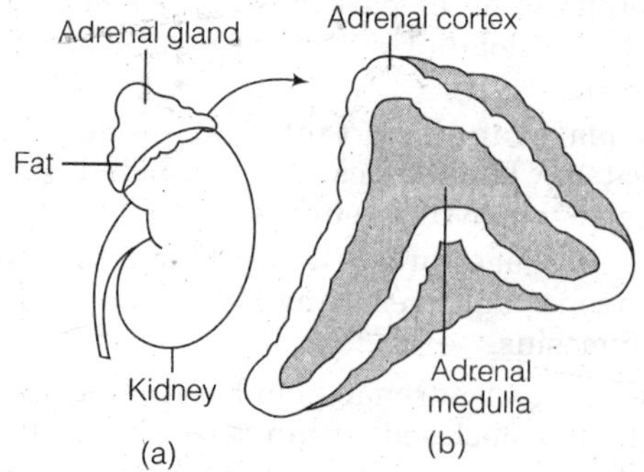

Diagrammatic representation of (a) Adrenal gland above kidney (b) section showing two parts of adrenal gland

11. **Pancreas** is a composite gland, which acts as both exocrine and endocrine gland. Its about 15cm in length. 2.5 cm width and 85 gms weight, which lies close to duodenum.
   (i) Exocrine part includes acini, which secretes pancreatic juice.
   (ii) Endocrine part consist of islet of Langerhans. The two main type of Langerhan cells are
      (a) α-cells (b) β-cells
   (iii) α-cells secrete 'glycagon' a peptide hormone, which plays an important role in maintaining blood glucose level.
      (a) It acts on hepatocytes (liver cells) and stimulates glycogenolysis, *i.e.,* breakdown of glucose.
      (b) It results in increased blood sugar level, *i.e.,* hyper glycemia.
      (c) Also known as hyperglycemic hormone and reduces the cellular glucose uptake.
   (iv) β-cells secrete **insulin** which acts on hepatocytes and adipocytes and enhances cellular glucose uptake
      (a) It converts glucose into glycogen known as glycogenesis.
      (b) Rapid movement of glucose from blood to hepatocytes results in hypoglycmic condition.
      (c) Increased concentration of glucose in blood leads to hyperglycemic condition called **diabetes mellitus**. It is associated with the loss of glucose through urine and formation of harmful ketone bodies.
12. In male individuals a pair of **testis** is present in the scrotal sac. It is primary sex organ and functions as endocrine gland also.
   (i) It is composed of seminiferous tubules, stromal/intestial tissue Leydig cells.
   (ii) Leydig cells are present in intertubular spaces and produce sex hormones called **androgens** mainly testosterone.
   (iii) Androgens mainly testosterone plays an important role in the process of spermatogenesis (*i.e.,* formation of spermatozoa.
   (iv) It regulates the development, maturation and functions of male accessory sex organs like epididymis, vas deferens, seminal vesicle, prostate gland, urethra, etc.
   (v) This hormone also stimulates secondary sex characteristics like muscular growth, growth of facial and axillary hair aggressiveness low pitch of veice, etc.

(vi) It acts on the central nervous system and influence male sexual behaviour (libido). These hormones also produce anabolic (synthetic) effects on protein and carbohydrate metabolism.

13. Ovary is the primary female sex organ located in the abdomen. It also act as exocrine gland by synthesising two groups of steroid hormone oestrogen and progesterone.
   (i) Each ovary produces one ovum during each menstrual cycle
   (ii) It is composed of ovarian follicles and stromal tissues.
   (iii) Growing ovarian follicle secretes oestrogen. It stimulates the growth of
      (a) female secondary sex organs
      (b) mammary gland development
      (c) it regulates female sexual behaviour.
      (d) it stimulates female secondary sex characters.
   (iv) Progesterone is secreted by corpus luteum, which is a ruptured follicle.
   (v) Progesterone supports pregnancy. It acts on the mammary gland and stimulates the formation of alveoli and milk secretion.

14. Hormones are also secreted by some tissues, which are not the endocrine glands.
   (i) Atrial wall of heart secretes a very important peptide hormone called. ANF (Atrial Natriuretic Factor). It decreases blood pressure by causing dilation of blood vessels.
   (ii) **Erythropoietin** is a peptide hormone secreted by the juxtaglomerular cells of kidney and stimulates erythropoiesis (*i.e.*, formation of RBC).
   (iii) Major peptide hormone are secreted by the gastrointestinal tract
      (a) gastrin
      (b) secretin
      (c) cholecystokinin (CCK)
      (d) gastric inhibitory peptide (GIP).
      (a) gastrin acts on the gastric gland and stimulates the secretion of HCl and pepsinogen.
      (b) secretin acts on pancreas and stimulates the secretion of water and bicarbonate ion.

(c) CCK (cholecystokinin acts on both pancreas and gall bladder. It stimulates the secretion of pancreatic enzyme and bile juice.

(d) Gastric Inhibitory Peptide (GIP) Inhibits the gastric secretion.

15. Hormone are transported through the blood stream and produces their effects on the target tissues.

(i) They bind to target tissue through hormone receptor located in the target tissue. These receptors may be

(a) intracellular receptor (b) nuclear receptor

(c) membrane bound receptor

(ii) When hormone binds to receptor they form hormone receptor complex.

(iii) Each hormone is specific for specific hormone.

(iv) Formation of hormone-receptor complex causes downstream biochemical changes and effects target tissue metabolism.

(v) On the basis of chemical nature, hormones are divided into groups

(a) peptide, polypeptide, protein hormone (insulin, glycogen, etc).

(b) Steroids (testosterone, cortisol, etc).

(c) Iodothyronins (thyroid hormone).

(d) Amino acid derivatives (*e.g.*, epinephrine).

Exercises

Question 1. Define the following

(a) Exocrine gland (b) Endocrine gland

(c) Hormone

Answer

(a) **Exocrine Gland** It is a gland that pours its secretion on the surface or into a particular region by means of ducts for performic a metabolic activity, *e.g.*, sebaceous glands, sweat glands, salivary glands, etc.

(b) **Endocrine Gland** It is a gland that pours its secretion into blood or lymph for reaching the target organ because the gland is not connected with the target organ by any duct. It is also known as ductless gland.

(c) **Hormone** Hormones are non-nutrient chemicals which act as intercellular messengers and are produced in trace amount.

Question 2. Diagrammatically indicate the location of the various endocrine glands in our body.

Answer

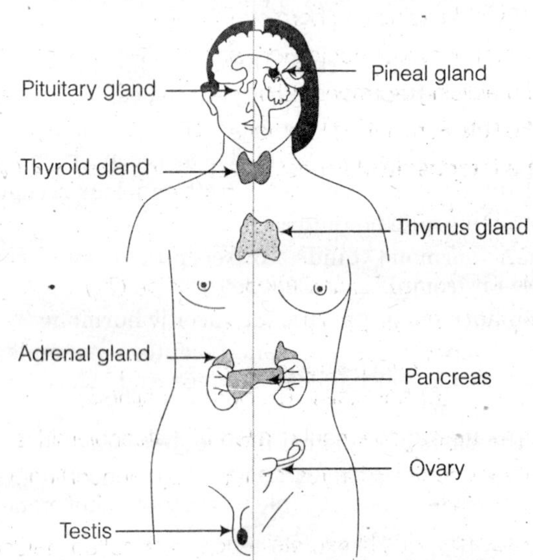

Endocrine glands in human body

Question 3. List the hormones secreted by the following

(a) Hypothalamus	(b) Pituitary	(c) Thyroid
(d) Parathyroid	(e) Adrenal	(f) Pancreas
(g) Testis	(h) Ovary	(i) Thymus
(j) Atrium	(k) Kidney	(l) GI Tract

Answer

(a) **Hypothalamus**

(i) Thyrotropin Releasing Hormone (TRH)

(ii) Adrenocorticotropin releasing hormone

(iii) Gonadotropin releasing hormone

(iv) Somatotropin releasing hormone

(v) Prolactin releasing hormone

(vi) Melanocyte stimulating hormone releasing hormone (MSH-RH).

(b) (i) **Pars distalis part of pituitary (anterior pituitary)**
- Growth hormone (GH)
- Prolactin (PRL)
- Thyroid stimulating hormone (TSH)
- Adrenocorticotrophic Hormone (ACTH)
- Luteinising Hormone (LH)
- Follicle Stimulating Hormone (FSH)

(ii) **Pars intermedia** Melanocyte stimulating hormone (MSH)

(iii) Pars nervosa

(a) Oxytocin (b) Vasopressin

(c) **Thyroid** Thyroxine (T_4) and triiodothyronine (T_3)

(d) **Parathyroid** Parathyroid hormone (PTH).

(e) **Adrenal** (i) Adrenal medulla secretes
(a) Adrenaline (b) Noradrenaline

These are two commonly called as catecholamines.

(ii) Adrenal cortex secretes corticoids (glucocorticoid and mineralo corticoid).

(f) **Pancreas** The α-cells secrete a hormone called glucagon, while the β-cells secrete insulin.

(g) **Testis** Androgens mainly testosterone.

(h) **Ovary** Oestrogen and progesterone.

(i) **Thymus** Thymosins.

(j) **Atrium** Atrial Natriuretic Factor (ANF).

(k) **Kidney** Erythropoietin

(l) **GI Tract** Gastrin, secretin, cholecystokinin (CCK) and Gastric Inhibitory Peptide (GIP).

Question 4. Fill in the blanks

Hormones	Target gland
(a) Hypothalamic hormones	....
(b) Thyrotrophin (TSH)	....
(c) Corticotrophin (ACTH)	....
(d) Gonadotrophins (LH, FSH)	....
(e) Melanotrophin (MSH)	....

Answer

Hormones		Target gland
(a) Hypothalamic hormones	–	Pituitary gland
(b) Thyrotrophin (TSH)	–	Thyroid gland
(c) Corticotrophin (ACTH)	–	Adrenal glands
(d) Gonadotrophins (LH, FSH)	–	Testis and ovary
(e) Melanotrophin (MSH)	–	Hypothalamus

Question 5. Write short notes on the functions of the following hormones

(a) Parathyroid hormone (PTH) (b) Thyroid hormones
(c) Thymosins (d) Androgens
(e) Oestrogen (f) Insulin and Glucagon

Answer Functions of the following hormones are as follows

(a) **Parathyroid Hormone** (PTH) The parathyroid glands secrete a peptide hormone called parathyroid hormone (PTH). PTH acts on bones and stimulates the process of bone resorption (dissolution/demineralisation). PTH also stimulates reabsorption of Ca^{2+} by the renal tubules and increases Ca^{2+} absorption from the digested food. It plays a significant role in calcium balance in the body.

(b) **Thyroid Hormones** Thyroid hormones play an important role in the regulation of the basal metabolic rate. These hormones also support the process of red blood cell formation. Thyroid hormones control the metabolism of carbohydrates, proteins and fats. The Maintenance of water and electrolyte balance is also influenced by thyroid hormones. Thyroid gland also secretes a protein hormone called thyrocalcitonin (TCT), which regulates the blood calcium levels.

(c) **Thymosins** This thymus gland secretes the peptide hormones called thymosins. Thymosins play a major role in the differentiation of T-lymphocytes, which provide cell-mediated immunity. In addition, thymosins also promote production of antibodies to provide humoral immunity.

(d) **Androgens** Androgens regulate the development, maturation and functions of the male accessory sex organs like epididymis, vas deferens, seminal vesicles, prostate gland, urethra, etc. These hormones stimulate muscular growth, growth of facial and axillary hair, aggressiveness, low pitch of voice, etc. Androgens play a major stimulatory role in the process of spermatogenesis (formation of spermatozoa), influence the male sexual behaviour (libido).

(e) **Oestrogens** Oestrogens produce wide ranging actions such as stimulation of growth and activities of female secondary sex organs, development of growing ovarian follicles, appearance of female secondary sex characters (*e.g.*, high pitch of voice, etc.), mammary gland development. Oestrogens also regulate female sexual behaviour.

(f) **Insulin and Glucagon** Glucagon acts mainly on the liver cells (hepatocytes) and stimulates glycogenolysis resulting in an increased blood sugar (hyperglycemia). In addition, this hormone stimulates the process of gluconeogenesis, which also contributes to hyperglycemia. Glucagon reduces the cellular glucose uptake and utilisation.

Insulin is a peptide hormone, which plays a major role in the regulation of glucose homeostasis. Insulin acts mainly on hepatocytes and adipocytes and enhances cellular glucose uptake and utilisation. Insulin also stimulates conversion of glucose to glycogen (glycogenesis) in the target cells. The glucose homeostasis in blood is thus maintained jointly by the two – insulin and glucagons.

Question 6. Give example(s) of

(a) Hyperglycemic hormone and hypoglycemic hormone
(b) Hypercalcemic hormone
(c) Gonadotrophic hormones
(d) Progestational hormone
(e) Blood pressure lowering hormone
(f) Androgens and oestrogens

Answer

(a) Glucagon and insulin respectively
(b) Parathyroid hormone
(c) Follicle stimulating hormone and luteinising hormones
(d) Progesterone
(e) Atrial Natriuretic Factor (ANF)
(f) Androgens are mainly testosterone and oestrogens include oestrogen

Question 7. Which hormonal deficiency is responsible for the following

(a) Diabetes mellitus (b) Goitre (c) Cretinism

Answer (a) Diabetes mellitus is due to deficiency of insulin.

(b) Goitre is due to deficiency of thyroxine (T_4) and triiodothyronine (T_3).

(c) Cretinism is due to deficiency of thyroxine hormone.

Question 8. Briefly mention the mechanism of action of FSH.

Answer Follicle Stimulating Hormone (FSH) In males, FSH and androgens regulate spermatogenesis. FSH stimulates growth and development of the ovarian follicles in females. It stimulate the secretion of estrogens in ovaries.

Question 9. Match the following columns.

Column I	Column II
A. T_4	1. Hypothalamus
B. PTH	2. Thyroid
C. GnRH	3. Pituitary
D. LH	4. Parathyroid

Answer

Column I	Column II
A. T_4	2. Thyroid
B. PTH	4. Parathyroid
C. GnRH	1. Hypothalamus
D. LH	3. Pituitary

Selected NCERT Exemplar Problems

Very Short Answer Type Questions

Question 1. There are many endocrine glands in human body. Name the glands which is absent in male and the one absent in female.

Answer The glands, which are absent in male are ovary and the which are absent in female are testis.

Question 2. Which of the two adrenocortical layers, zona glomerulosa and zona reticularis lies outside enveloping the other?

Answer Zona glomerulosa (outer layer) envelopes zona reticularis (inner layer) from the outside.

Question 3. What is erythropoiesis? Which hormone stimulates it?

Answer Erythropoiesis is the process of formation of RBCs. The juxtaglomerular cells of kidney produce a peptide hormone called erythropoietin which stimulates it.

Question 4. Name the only hormone secreted by pars intermedia of the pituitary gland.

Answer Melanocyte Stimulating Hormone (MSH).

Question 5. Name the endocrine gland that produces calcitonin and mention the role played by this hormone.

Answer Calcitonin (CT) or Thyrocalcitonin hormone is produced by thyroid glands. It is hypocalcemic and hypophosphatemic peptide hormone, which checks excess plasms Ca^{2+} and phosphate by decreasing mobilisation from bones. Deficiency of calcitonin results in osteoporosis or loss of bone density (due to dissolution of parathormone).

Question 6. Name the hormone that helps in cell-mediated immunity.

Answer Thymosin.

Question 7. What is the role of second messenger in the mechanism of protein hormone action?

Answer Hormones which do not the enter the target cells, but generate second messengers (*e.g.*, cAMP) on the inner side of the plasma membrane. The second messenger, in turn, carries out all the hormonal functions.

Question 8. State whether true or false

(a) Gastrointestinal tract, kidney and heart also produce hormones.
(b) Pars distalis produces six trophic hormones.
(c) B-lymphocytes provide cell-mediated immunity.
(d) Insulin resistance results in a disease called diabetes mellitus.

Answer (a)True (b) True (c) True (d) False

Question 9. A patient complains of constant thirst, excessive passing of urine and low blood pressure. When the doctor checked the patients' blood glucose and blood insulin level, the level were normal or slightly low. The doctor diagnosed the condition as diabetes insupidus. But he decided to measure one more hormone in patients' blood. Which hormone does the doctor intend to measure?

Answer Glucogen.

Question 10. Correct the following statements by replacing the term underlined.

(a) Insulin is a steroid hormone.
(b) TSH is secreted from the corpus luteum.
(c) Tetraiodothyronine is an emergency hormone.
(d) The pineal gland is located on the anterior part of the kidney.

Answer

(a) Insulin is a proteinaceous hormone.
(b) TSH is secreted from the thyroid glands.
(c) Adrenaline is an emergency hormone.
(d) The pineal gland is located on the dorsal side of the forebrain.

Question 11. Rearrange the following hormones in column I so as to match with their chemical nature in column II.

Column I	Column II
A. Oxytocin	1. Amino acid derivative
B. Epinephrine	2. Steroid
C. Progesterone	3. Protein
D. Growth hormone	4. Peptide

Answer

Column I	Column II
A. Oxytocin	1. Protein
B. Epinephrine	2. Steroid
C. Progesterone	3. Peptide
D. Growth hormone	4. Amino acid derivative

Short Answer Type Questions

Question 1. What is the role-played by luteinising hormones in males and females respectively?

Answer LH stimulates the synthesis and secretion of androgens called male hormones. In females, LH is essential for ovulation.

In females, LH induces ovulation of fully mature follicles (Graafian follicle) and maintains the corpus luteum formed from the remanants of the Graafian follicle after ovulation.

Question 2. What is the role of second messenger in hormone action?

Answer Hormones which do not the enter the target cells, interact with specific receptors located on the surface of the target cell membranes and generates second messengers (*e.g.*, *c*AMP) on the inner side of the plasma membrane. The second messenger, in turn, carries out all the hormonal functions.

Question 3. On an educational trip to Uttaranchal, Ketki and her friends observe that many local people were having swollen necks. Please help Ketki and her friends to find out the solutions to the following questions.

(a) Which probable disease are these people suffering from?
(b) How is it caused?
(c) What effect does this condition have on pregnancy?

Answer

(a) People with swollen necks are suffering from goitre.
(b) It is caused due to the deficiency of iodine in diet. Iodine is essential for the normal rate of hormone synthesis in the thyroid. Tetraiodothyronine or thyroxine (T_4) and tridothyronine (T_3).
(c) Hypothyroidism during pregnancy causes defective development an maturation of the growing baby leading to
   (i) stunted growth
   (ii) mental retardation
   (iii) low IQ
   (iv) abnormal skin
   (v) deafmutism.

Question 4. George comes on a vacation to India from US. The long journey disturbs his biological system and he suffers from jet lag. What is the cause of his discomfort?

Answer Jet lag is caused by the disruption of the body clock as it is out of synchronisation with the unfamiliar time zone of the destination. The body experiences different patterns of light and dark than it is normally used to, which disrupts the natural sleep-wake cycle.

Melatonin is a hormone that plays a key role in body rhythms and jet lag. After the sun sets, the eyes perceive darkness and alert the hypothalamus to begin releasing melatonin, which promotes sleep. Conversely, when the eyes perceive sunlight, they tell the hypothalamus to withhold melatonin production. However, the hypothalamus cannot readjust its schedule instantly; it takes several days.

Question 5. Inflammatory responses can be controlled by a certain steroid. Name the steroid, its source and also its other important functions.

Answer Inflammatory responses are controlled by steroid hormones called **glucocorticoids**. Glucocorticoids are secreted by adrenal cortex. Its other functions are to stimulate gluconeogenesis, lipolysis and proteolysis; and inhibit cellular uptake and utilisation of amino acids.

Question 6. Old people have weak immune system. What could be the reason?

Answer Thymus is degenerated in old individuals resulting in a decreased production of thymosins. As a result, the immune responses of old persons become weak.

Question 7. What are the effects of hypothyroidism (observed during pregnancy) on the development and maturation of a growing baby?

Answer Hypothyroidism during pregnancy causes defective development and maturation of the growing baby leading to stunted growth (cretinism), mental retardation, low intelligence quotient, abnormal skin, deafmutism, etc.

Question 8. Mention the difference between hypothyroidism and hyperthyroidism.

Answer **Hypothyroidism** It is a low secretion of thyroxine hormone.

Hyperthyrodism It is over secretion of thyroid hormones. It occurs due to cancer of the thyroid gland.

Long Answer Type Questions

Question 1. A milkman is very upset one morning as his cow refuses to give any milk. The milkman's wife gets the calf from the shed. On fondling by the calf, the cow gave sufficient milk. Describe the role of endocrine gland and pathway associated with this response?

Answer Sucking by the calf creats a neuroendocrine reflex which results in increase of oxytocin from the neurohypophysis. Oxytocin brings about contraction of smooth muscle of the udder resulting in milk flow. A direct intra-udder junction of oxytocin like hormone would do the same function.

It is summerised as follows:

Udder (suckling stimulus) → Brain (hypothalamus) → Neurohypophysis → Blood (oxytocin → Udder (smooth muscle) → Milk flow.

Question 2. A sample of urine was diagnosed to contain high content of glucose and ketone bodies. Based on this observation, answer the following

(a) Which endocrine gland and hormone is related to this condition?
(b) Name the cells on which this hormone acts.
(c) What is the condition called and how can it be rectified?

Answer

(a) Pancreas gland and insulin hormone is related to this condition.
(b) The B-cells of islets of Langerhans of pancreas.
(c) Prolonged hyperglycemia leads to a complex disorder called diabetes mellitus, which is associated with loss of glucose through urine and formation of harmful compounds known as ketone bodies. Diabetic patients are successfully treated with insulin therapy.

Question 3. Calcium plays a very important role in the formation of bones. Write on the role of endocrine glands and hormones responsible for maintaining calcium homeostasis.

Answer The secretion of parathyroid hormone (PTH) regulated the concentration of calcium ions.

Parathyroid hormone (PTH) increases the Ca^{2+} levels in the blood. PTH acts on bones and stimulates the process of bone resorption (dissolution/ demineralisation). PTH also stimulates reabsorption of Ca^{2+} by the renal tubules and increases Ca^{2+} absorption from the digested food. It is, thus, clear that PTH is a hypercalcemic hormone, *i.e.*, it increases the blood Ca^{2+} levels. Along with TCT, it plays a significant role in calcium balance in the body.

Question 4. Hypothalamus is a super master endocrine gland. Elaborate.

Answer **The Hypothalamus** regulates a wide spectrum of body functions. It contains several groups of neurosecretory cells called nuclei, which produce hormones. These hormones regulate the synthesis and secretion of pituitary hormones. However, the hormones produced by hypothalamus are of two types, the releasing hormones (which stimulate secretion of pituitary hormones) and the inhibiting hormones (which inhibit secretions of pituitary hormones).

The hormones reach the pituitary gland thrugh a portal circulatory system and regulate the functions of the anterior pituitary. The posterior pituitary is under the direct regulation of hypothalamus. The oxytocin and vasopressin two hormones synthesised by hypothalamus are transported to posterior pituitary.

Question 5. Illustrate the differences between the mechanism of action of a protein and a steroid hormone.

Answer Differences between mechanism of action of a protein and a steroid hormone

S.N.	Protein Hormone	Steroid Hormone
1.	Protein hormone interact with membrane bound receptors.	These interact with intracellular receptors.
2.	They generate second messengers (cyclic AMP, IP_3, Ca^{2+}, etc)	They regulate gene expression or chromosome function by the interaction of hormone-receptor complex with the genome.
3.	The second messengers regulate cellular metabolism.	Cumulative biochemical action of hormone - receptor complex result in physiological and developmented effects.

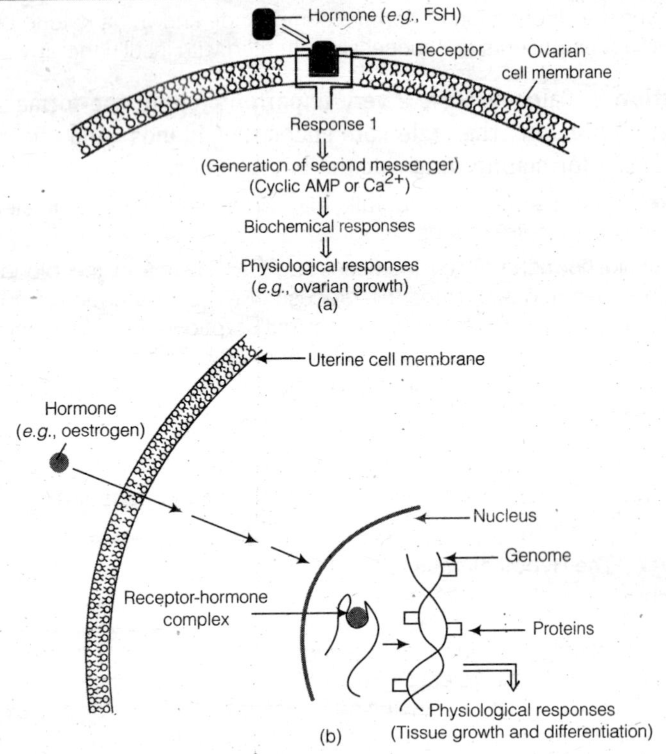

Diagrammatic representation of the mechanism of hormone action
(a) Protein hormone (b) Steroid hormone